Handbook of Computer Game Studies

Handbook of Computer Game Studies

edited by Joost Raessens and Jeffrey Goldstein

The MIT Press Cambridge, Massachusetts London, England

First MIT Press paperback edition, 2011

© 2005 Massachusetts Institute of Technology

This book was set in Janson and Rotis Semi-sans on 3B2 by Asco Typesetters, Hong Kong.

Library of Congress Cataloging-in-Publication Data
Handbook of computer game studies / Joost Raessens and Jeffrey Goldstein, [editors].
   p. cm.
 Includes bibliographical references and index.
 ISBN 0-262-18240-8 (hc. : alk. paper)—978-0-262-51658-7 (pb. : alk. paper)
 1. Computer games—Handbooks, manuals, etc. I. Raessens, Joost, 1960– II. Goldstein, Jeffrey H.
GV1469.15.H36 2005
794.8—dc22   2004053069

To Gerda Kuiper, my partner in the virtual game of life. To Brian Sutton-Smith, who taught me nearly everything I know about play, but not nearly everything he knows.

—J.G.

To my partner, Sandra. To Jos de Mul, sometimes teacher, always friend.

—J.R.

CONTENTS

Acknowledgments ix

Introduction xi

Part I: Computer Games

1 Slots of Fun, Slots of Trouble: An
   Archaeology of Arcade Gaming 3
   Erkki Huhtamo

2 The History of the Video Game 23
   Steven Malliet and Gust de Meyer

3 Future of Games: Mobile Gaming 47
   Justin Hall

Part II: Design

4 Game Design and Meaningful Play 59
   Katie Salen and Eric Zimmerman

5 Click Reading: Screenwriting and
   Screen-Reading Practices in Film
   and Multimedia Fictions 81
   Isabelle Raynauld

6 Computer Games and Learning:
   Digital Game-Based Learning 97
   Marc Prensky

Part III: Reception

7 Cognitive Effects of Video Games 125
   Sandra L. Calvert

8 Children's Social Behavior during
   Video Game Play 133
   Robyn M. Holmes and Anthony D.
   Pellegrini

9 Psychological Effects of Video
   Games 145
   Barrie Gunter

10 The Therapeutic Value of Video
   Games 161
   Mark Griffiths

Part IV: Games as an Aesthetic Phenomenon

11 Games, the New Lively Art 175
   Henry Jenkins
   Genres

12 Genre and the Video Game 193
   Mark J. P. Wolf

13 The Role of Artificial Intelligence
   in Computer Game Genres 205
   John E. Laird and Michael van Lent
   Storytelling

14 Games Telling Stories? 219
   Jesper Juul

15 Narrativity in Computer Games 227
   Britta Neitzel

Part V: Games as a Cultural Phenomenon
   Identity

16 The Game of Life: Narrative and
   Ludic Identity Formation in
   Computer Games 251
   Jos de Mul

17 Computer Games as Evocative
   Objects: From Projective Screens
   to Relational Artifacts 267
   Sherry Turkle
   Representation of Identity: Gender,
   Ethnicity, and History

18 Gaming with Grrls: Looking for
   Sheroes in Computer Games 283
   Birgit Richard and Jutta Zaremba

19 Gendered Gaming
   in Gendered Space 301
   Jo Bryce and Jason Rutter

20 Serious Play: Playing with Race in Contemporary Gaming Culture 311

Anna Everett

21 Simulation, History, and Computer Games 327

William Uricchio

Part VI: Games as a Social Phenomenon

22 Violent Video Games 341

Jeffrey Goldstein

23 Does Video Game Addiction Exist? 359

Mark Griffiths and Mark N. O. Davies

Participation

24 Computer Games as Participatory Media Culture 373

Joost Raessens

25 I Am What I Play: Participation and Reality as Content 389

Jan-Willem Huisman and Hanne Marckmann

26 Game Reconstruction Workshop: Demolishing and Evolving PC Games and Gamer Culture 405

Anne-Marie Schleiner

27 Renaissance Now! The Gamers' Perspective

Douglas Rushkoff 415

About the Contributors 423

Games Index 429

Name Index 435

Subject Index 447

Acknowledgments

The editors would like to thank Joep Damen and Anca Minescu for their contributions to this project. We benefited from discussions with Rosi Braidotti, Henry Jenkins, Chiel Kattenbelt, Jos de Mul, William Uricchio, and Gloria Wekker, who offered useful advice on computer games and gamers. Doug Sery at The MIT Press was enthusiastic about this project from the beginning, and we are grateful for his support.

Introduction

Why This Book at This Time?

We were both at the Massachusetts Institute of Technology for the first conference on the business and science of computer games, Computer and Video Games Come of Age (2000, web.mit.edu/cms/games)[1] and found ourselves at the MIT Press bookstore early the first morning, independently asking whether there were any books on computer games. Only one scholarly book, said the clerk, *From Barbie to Mortal Kombat: Gender and computer games* (MIT Press, 1998), co-edited by Justine Cassell and Henry Jenkins. As fine as that book is, we were searching for a broader view of computer games. We wanted a book suitable for the growing number of students interested in new media, a book with the history of computer games, studies of their design, reception, aesthetics, cultural meanings, and social effects and uses. We agreed to edit a book to fill these needs. The *Handbook of computer game studies* is the result.

The literature on computer games already contains some classic texts, such as J. C. Herz, *Joystick nation* (1997, Little, Brown), A. Le Diberder and F. Le Diberder, *L'Univers des jeux vidéo* (1998, La Découverte), G. and E. Loftus, *Mind at play: The psychology of video games* (1983, Basic Books), S. Poole, *Trigger happy* (2000, Fourth Estate), and E. Provenzo, *Video kids: Making sense of Nintendo* (1991, Harvard University Press), as well as recent overviews (G. King & T. Krzywinska, *Screen play*, 2002, Wallflower Press; J. Newman, *Videogames*, 2004, Routledge; M. J. P. Wolf, *The medium of the video game*, 2001, University of Texas Press; M. J. P. Wolf & B. Perron, *The video game theory reader*, 2003, Routledge). But there is no comparable scholarly book in English suitable for classroom use and as a guide to researchers. Existing books about computer games tend to focus on a single theme, such as history (Kent, *The ultimate history of video games*, 2001, Prima), gender (J. Cassell & H. Jenkins, 1998), children (D. Rushkoff, *Playing the future* 1996,

Harper Collins; S. Calvert, *Children's journeys through the information age*, 2000, McGraw-Hill; M. Kinder, *Playing with power*, 1991, University of California Press), violence (D. Grossman, *On killing*, 1995, Little Brown), interactive storytelling (J. Murray, *Hamlet on the holodeck*, 1997, Free Press), popular culture (A. A. Berger, *Video games. A popular culture phenomenon*, 2002, Transaction), or social identity (S. Turkle, *Life on the screen*, 1995, Simon & Schuster). The *Handbook of computer game studies* covers all these topics and many more.

The *Handbook* is unique in including the broadest range possible of perspectives on gaming—those from cognitive science and artificial intelligence, developmental, social and clinical psychology, history, film and theatre, cultural studies, and philosophy. There are also contributions from gamers, game artists, and developers. We have tried to cover all the bases, although given the rapid pace of game development there will inevitably be changes in the playing field and limitations to our vision of it.

The *Handbook of computer game studies* is intended to reflect the state of the art in the year 2004, and how we got here. It is designed to serve an audience that wishes access to the important scholarly literature on computer games, students and researchers in particular. Since 2003 there is an international association of researchers and practitioners whose work focuses on digital games, the Digital Games Research Association (www.digra.org). In November 2003, DiGRA and the University of Utrecht organized Level Up, the inaugural DiGRA conference. The structure of both the conference and the conference proceedings (*Level Up. Digital Games Research Conference 2003*, edited by Marinka Copier and Joost Raessens) was inspired by the different approaches from which computer games can be studied, as described in this handbook (www.gamesconference.org).

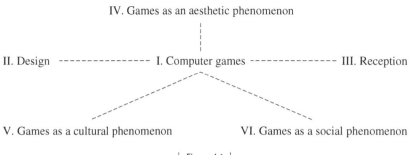

| Figure I.1 |
Approaches to computer games

The computer game industry rivals the film industry in revenues, reaching sales of $7 billion in the United States in the year 2003 and more than $6.5 billion in Europe. Worldwide turnover is estimated at around $20 billion. In 1994, fewer than three hundred computer games were published. In 2003, the number reached 1,217. According to statistics from the Entertainment Software Association (www.theesa.com), over 239 million computer games were sold in the United States in 2003, almost two games per household.

Over 90 percent of all games purchased are bought by adults over age eighteen. Playing computer games is no longer something only for the young, but cuts across age and gender lines. In 2003, 60 percent of all Americans over age six played interactive games on a regular basis. Forty percent of Americans who play computer games are age thirty-five or older, 13 percent are age fifty or over. Forty-three percent of computer game players are women, and their average age is twenty-nine years. Comparable statistics about online gaming are not readily available. However, according to figures from South Korea, the number one online gaming country relative to population size, 80 percent of all youngsters aged eight to twenty-four go online to play (www.game-research.com/statistics.asp). Many of the youngsters who grew up with Atari, Nintendo, and Sega video game systems continue to play into adulthood, broadening the base of game players.

Computer Games: Terminology
"Electronic games" and "digital games" are generic terms that include arcade games (stand-alone games played in public locations or arcades), video games played on a dedicated console connected to a TV set or other display, and computer games, those played with a personal computer either off-line or online. When authors use other definitions in their chapters, for example, using "computer games" to include video games, or using the two terms interchangeably, these are stated or are clear from the context.

Structure
In the *Handbook* we distinguish different points of view or approaches from which one can consider computer games. These approaches are ideal types; because they are abstracted from existing research, they are not to be found in pure form in the literature. In most chapters, one of these approaches is favored, although other perspectives are also implicated. We distinguish the six approaches outlined in figure I.1.

In the first part (Computer Games) we concentrate on computer games themselves, presenting the history of computer games in three phases: an analysis of electronic gaming as a prehistory of computer games (Huhtamo), the historical development of computer games themselves (Malliet & De Meyer), and an analysis of mobile gaming as one of the possible perspectives on the future of computer games (Hall).

Part II (Design) is concerned with the relationship between the designer and the game. Three chapters describe game development from the designer's point of view: a general introduction to the design of play elements in computer games (Salen & Zimmerman), an analysis of screenwriting practices in multimedia fictions in comparison with film (Raynauld), and an analysis of game design as applied to game-based learning (Prensky).

The third part (Reception) focuses on the individual player's relationship to the computer game. Four chapters review empirical research on the psychological effects of computer games. Calvert reviews the psychological literature on video games and child development. Holmes and Pellegrini explore nonverbal and verbal behavior during play. Gunter gives a broad overview of psychological research on video games. Griffiths considers the uses and applications of video games in educational, medical, and therapeutic settings.

The fourth part considers games as an aesthetic phenomenon. Five chapters focus on the similarities and differences between computer games and other media (namely, film and literature) in an effort to determine the unique qualities of computer games: Jenkins considers games as an art, whereas Wolf, and Laird and Van Lent describe video game genres. Juul and Neitzel tackle the question of whether computer games should be regarded as narratives.

Part V (Games as a Cultural Phenomenon) takes a cultural approach. How games are interpreted, their meaning and significance to the player, contribute to an understanding of oneself, of relationships with others, and of one's world. In six chapters we concentrate particularly on the manner in which computer games affect our discussions and understanding of identity (De Mul and Turkle), representation and construction of identity in terms of gender (Richard & Zaremba, and Bryce & Rutter), ethnicity (Everett), and history (Uricchio).

Part VI, Games as a Social Phenomenon, considers normative aspects of computer gaming and the effects of games on social behavior. Issues include the effects of computer games on unacceptable or undesirable behavior, such as aggression (Goldstein) and the potential of games to become addictive (Griffiths & Davies). The final four chapters concern different forms of participation in computer games (Raessens, Huisman, & Marckmann, Schleiner, and Rushkoff).

I. Computer Games

Looking backward to the nineteenth and early twentieth century, Erkki Huhtamo ("Slots of Fun, Slots of Trouble: An Archaeology of Arcade Gaming") demonstrates that electronic gaming is related to phenomena that preceded it and prepared the ground for its emergence. He sketches the cultural background and the social context (gender divisions, association with negative values, participation) of the emergence of "useless" automatic, and proto-interactive machines, not meant for productive purposes in factories and offices but intended for public amusement, such as gambling machines, strength testers, fortune-telling machines, and mechanical game machines, such as pinball. Although the interactive possibilities these machines offered were limited, at least by later digital standards, the ways in which they managed to create desire, pleasure, and intense involvement already anticipated the user relationships with computer games.

Steven Malliet and Gust de Meyer ("The History of the Video Game") summarize the history of the video game by dividing it into a number of crucial periods. After a prehistory (1958–1972), they continue with the birth of an industry (1973–1977), in which they focus on technical and economic aspects of the console and arcade market and the foundations for a number of genres. Considering when a first crisis awakened the industry (1978–1982), they cover the first crisis of the computer game industry and its "golden years." When a second crisis guided the industry into the Nintendo era (1983–1989), Nintendo became the absolute leader. The period of the war of the bits (1990–1999) was a chaotic acceleration, both technically and economically. Finally, Malliet and de Meyer speculate on the promises of the latest generation consoles in the years to come: online gaming, the breakthrough of virtual reality, and an increased integration of different forms of entertainment.

According to Justin Hall ("Future of Games: Mobile Gaming"), the advent of mobile communications devices with the power to play merge gaming and communication into a constant state of mediated social exchange. These mobile communication machines can transform every environment into a gaming environment. The first generation of wireless games (mobile phone games such as *Snake*) were not the object of focused attention, they were played in passing moments. Despite the fact that mobile communication devices do not seem as fit for fun as a GameBoy, Hall shows their potential through an analysis of remarkable wireless games, such as *Sorcery* (2001). A major development took place with *BotFighters*, the first entertaining use of "location based" technology. In this form of pervasive gaming, you don't play *on* but *with* a mobile device; your mobile phone is not just a screen on which you play a game, but the device's location-based technology becomes part of the game.

II. Design

Game designers and scholars Katie Salen and Eric Zimmerman ("Game Design and Meaningful Play") focus on the play element in computer games. They consider games as systems with different types of interactivity, including cognitive, functional, and explicit interactivity. Participation can extend beyond the designed system, as illustrated by fan culture in which participants construct communal realities. Relying on play theories from Huizinga and Sutton-Smith, they define the elements that make play meaningful, namely the relationship between player action and system action. Salen and Zimmerman closely examine key gaming concepts—play, design, participation, and choice, among others

—and illustrate how game designers translate these into ludic experiences.

Departing from the fact that terms such as interactivity, virtual worlds and agency are here to stay, Isabelle Raynauld ("Click Reading: Screenwriting and Screen-Reading Practices in Film and Multimedia Fictions") examines their importance and their impact on the practices of screenwriting and screenreading. As with film, the introduction of multimedia fictions has been greeted by two reactions: a triumph of the new over the old and a danger best avoided. Raynauld illuminates these opposite ends of the spectrum while concentrating on their differences and on their medium specificities. Taking into account both the new competencies of scriptwriters as well as of readers-users-navigators, Raynauld analyzes two main genres of fictional CD-ROMs: those that explicitly promise a story (the *Myst* trilogy) and those that offer a fictional universe or environment (*Liquidation*).

Marc Prensky ("Computer Games and Learning: Digital Game-Based Learning") argues that today's students differ from the predigital generation in ways so fundamental as to require new means of learning and teaching. Game-based learning is fun, involving, has clear goals, is interactive, provides continuous feedback and outcomes, is creative, rewarding, and enriching, many of the things that traditional forms of teaching are not. Game-based learning has been used to teach reading and vocabulary to elementary school pupils, health care, science, and electoral politics to high school students, and financial trading to stockbrokers; game simulations have taught navigation to sailors and pilots, and trained executives in how to run a department store or an oil refinery. Prensky offers advice on how to select or develop games for specific teaching purposes.

III. Reception

Sandra L. Calvert ("Cognitive Effects of Video Games") summarizes psychological research on electronic games and child development. She uses an information theory perspective, relying particularly on Piaget and Bruner, to describe how children's perception, visual attention, representation, and memory may be affected by video games. Calvert describes the development of multitasking, the ability to perform multiple tasks simultaneously. Children with attention difficulties, such as attention deficit hyperactivity disorder, may benefit from video games that reward them for producing faster brain waves (beta waves). Sex differences in perceptual and cognitive skills are examined in relation to

video game experience, which may help reduce the gender gap on visual-spatial relations tasks.

Different game formats, whether playing simultaneously, face-to-face, or computer-mediated, limit the types of social interaction possible. Likewise, the play setting—home, video arcade, Internet café—affect social behavior during and following play. Robyn M. Holmes and Anthony D. Pellegrini ("Children's Social Behavior during Video Game Play") summarize their research on the nonverbal behavior of young players. They recorded verbal and nonverbal behavior of boys and girls who were playing violent or nonviolent video games. Regardless of the games' contents, children displayed neutral and positive expressions and behavior, indicative of concentration and enjoyment, respectively. Conversation while playing violent video games was positive, referring mainly to the game itself. There was no evidence that playing violent video games resulted in more aggressive behavior during play.

Whereas the chapters by Calvert, and Holmes and Pellegrini focus on children, the broad overview of psychological research on video games by Barrie Gunter ("Psychological Effects of Video Games") includes studies of adolescents and adults. Gunter first describes the demographics of gamers before reviewing studies of cognitive and social effects of games, including the effects of violent video games on aggressive behavior. He concludes that computer games can have negative as well as positive effects on health. For example, Gunter reviews studies of "Nintendinitis" and epileptic seizures induced during play. He also describes the use of video games in treating cognitive and perceptual-motor disorders, and their uses in educational settings and public service information campaigns.

Mark Griffiths ("The Therapeutic Value of Video Games") describes the uses and applications of video games in clinical practice. Games offer many advantages in diagnostic, therapeutic, and research situations: they are a reliable measurement tool, can be altered for experimental research, can assist in setting goals and maintaining records, can assess individual differences, are self-motivating, challenging, lightweight, and portable. Griffiths describes case studies of the applications of computer games in physiotherapy, occupational therapy, and pain management. Video games have been used as treatment modality in psychotherapy, cognitive rehabilitation, and speech therapy. They can enhance communication and social skills, help in the control of impulsivity and attention deficit disorders, and have proven useful in enhancing the physical and social lives of the elderly.

IV. Games as an Aesthetic Phenomenon

Henry Jenkins ("Games, the New Lively Art") traces the development of the video game as a cultural phenomenon, and its relation to what Gilbert Seldes called "the lively arts," popular entertainments of mass appeal, including film, jazz, and comic strips. A late stage in the development of lively arts is their growing respectability as subjects worthy of academic study, a phase already entered by video games. Jenkins describes the "memorable moments" of gaming, peak experiences that make games so compelling. He concludes that as a contemporary art form games, like earlier popular arts, require constant experimentation and innovation; that's what makes the lively arts lively.

Mark J. P. Wolf ("Genre and the Video Game") focuses on the categorization of video games by genre. Departing from the idea of genre in the study of literature and film, the author argues that genre study differs from one medium to another. Whereas literary or film genre studies often focus on subject matter and iconography, and neglect the role of the audience, according to Wolf video game genre study should focus on player participation as arguably the central determinant in describing and classifying video games. By beginning with the various forms of interaction required by the game's primary objective, the author divides the wide variety of video games into a series of interactive genres. Wolf's summary of genres takes into consideration the dominant characteristics of the interactive experience, the game's goals and objectives, and the nature of the game's player-character and player controls.

Artificial intelligence is the ability of a computer to mimic human thought or intelligent behavior. John E. Laird and Michael van Lent ("The Role of Artificial Intelligence in Computer Game Genres") describe the reciprocal relationship between AI and technological developments in creating new game genres. The computer has greatly expanded the types of games we can play, and advances in natural language understanding and speech generation could lead to new sorts of games played via cellphone. Laird and van Lent's classification of game genres is based on the roles that AI can create, such as racing opponents, enemies and partners, and support characters. This results in seven genres: action, role playing, adventure, strategy, simulation, sports, and racing. For each genre, they offer considerations for game developers.

Jesper Juul ("Games Telling Stories?") offers three possible answers to the question: Do games tell stories? He begins by examining three common arguments *for* games as narrative: we use narratives for everything, most games feature narrative introductions and backstories, and games share some traits with narratives. Juul then considers three important reasons for describing games as being non-narrative: games are not part of the narrative media ecology formed by movies, novels, and theatre; time in games works differently than in narratives; and the relation between the reader/viewer and the story world is different than the relation between the player and the game world. Being aware that the first two answers presuppose fairly traditional definitions of stories and narratives, as a final point Juul considers whether various experimental narratives of the twentieth century can in some way reconcile games and narratives.

Britta Neitzel ("Narrativity in Computer Games") argues that any position that simply treats the computer game as narrative, or one that negates any relation between narratives and games, is too narrow in scope. In the former case, there is a danger of overlooking differences between games and narratives; computer games are more than "interactive narratives." The second position, on the other hand, risks disregarding similarities between computer games and narratives just because not every game has the same structure, and computer games are structured differently than, for example, ball games. According to Neitzel, the fact that computer games are games by no means excludes them from having narrative qualities. Therefore she takes a third viewpoint based on the assumption that there are commonalities and overlapping elements in computer games and narratives, as well as a transitional zone between non-narrative and narrative computer games.

V. Games as a Cultural Phenomenon

According to Jos de Mul ("The Game of Life: Narrative and Ludic Identity Formation in Computer Games"), human identity is socially constructed with the aid of various media and stories. Narratives not only mediate between individuals and the world (referentiality), and between individuals themselves (communicability), but also between an individual and her/himself (self-understanding). Changes in media reflect changes in the relationship between individuals and their environment, in social relationships, and in self-identity. In recent decades the domain of expression has been extended by computer games and, as a result, an important new tool for identity construction has been developed. Critically elaborating on Ricoeur's theory of narrative identity, the author examines the impact of computer games (as compared to older media, such as novels and films) on the cognitive, volitional, and emotional dimensions of human identity, and discusses some pedagogical implications.

Sherry Turkle ("Computer Games as Evocative Objects: From Projective Screens to Relational Artifacts") argues that engaging with a variety of computational objects (game-interfaces, MUDs, interactive toys, and simulation games) provides material for reconsidering categories of knowing, of identity, and of what is alive. Refering to the way children play *SimLife*, the author argues in the first place that by exploring the superficial world of interfaces, they learn to take things at "interface" value. Secondly, she argues that the key element of MUDs lies in the creation and projection of a "persona" into a virtual space. Referring to the development of the windows metaphor for computer interfaces, she argues that windows have become a potent metaphor for thinking about the self as a multiple and decentered system. Thirdly, working with children using new generations of simulation games, robots and virtual pets, and with children experimenting with online life on the Internet, Turkle argues that children see computational objects as psychological machines.

Birgit Richard and Jutta Zaremba ("Gaming with Grrls: Looking for Sheroes in Computer Games") trace the characteristics, contradictions, and potentials of the virtual heroines in computer games, such as Lara Croft (in *Tomb Raider*), Xena and Gabrielle (in *Xena*), Leeloo (in *The Fifth Element*), and a number of female characters in *The Nomad Soul*. The authors describe how their reception causes highly various reactions and classifications, especially among the female audience, ranging from "female enemy number one" to "postfeminist icon." This obvious discrepancy is, according to the authors, comparable to the paradigm shift that feminists see in fashion: it is no longer regarded as a manipulative instrument for the realization of male power fantasies, but can provide instruments for visual self-realization. The authors make a distinction between those virtual characters that are products created for commercial interests, and those that (also) have an autonomous potential that could be developed by the users.

Jo Bryce and Jason Rutter ("Gendered Gaming in Gendered Space") argue that analysis of the relationship between gender and computer gaming generally focuses on content analysis at the expense of broader understandings of gaming. The authors examine computer games through gendered game content, gaming spaces, and gaming activities, and they argue that despite the self-perpetuating myth of computer gaming as a male-only activity, there is increasing evidence of female gaming. This suggests the need to examine the relationship between gender and gaming in greater depth and within everyday contexts. The authors argue that gaming developments demonstrate that computer gaming is an increasingly social, public, and multigendered leisure activity.

Arguing that the video game industry privileges young and male gamers who are "universalized" under the sign of whiteness, historian of popular culture Anna Everett ("Serious Play: Playing with Race in Contemporary Gaming Culture") examines race matters in the short history of video games. At stake is the way in which video and computer games reinforce, reject, or alter iconographical representations, which we know from other media texts. Everett examines the ways games might be thought to replicate attitudes about racial difference or, on the other hand, subvert and refuse racist stereotypes in character designs.

Cursed as history is with a double identity—no imaginable set of "historical" representations can do justice to the fullness of "history" as past—William Uricchio ("Simulation, History, and Computer Games") examines the claims and implications of historical simulation games. Taking interactivity to be one of the distinguishing characteristics of computer games, the author argues that the interaction between a present-day player and the representation of a historically specific world seems to challenge any notion of a unique configuration of historical "fact" and "fixity." Exploring the relationship of computer games to the larger cultural processes of understanding the historical, Uricchio refers to the parallel development of post-structuralist historiography (challenging notions of factuality and the authority of the historian) and computer games (empowering the users, enabling them to organize their own texts). Together, these two practices coincided to give both theory and form to a new way of organizing historical experience and historical identity.

VI. Games as a Social Phenomenon

Jeffrey Goldstein reviews research on video games and aggression ("Violent Video Games"). He looks critically at definitions and methods used in empirical studies of violent video games. He devotes special attention to laboratory experiments that attempt to establish the causal effects of violent video games on aggressive behavior. He concludes that research participants are not *playing* in the laboratory and that the measures used to determine aggressive behavior are of questionable meaning or validity. Research fails to take into account the voluntary nature of play, the many attractions of violent entertainment, and the highly social nature of the computer game experience.

The question of video game addiction is addressed by Mark Griffiths and Mark N. O. Davies ("Does Video Game Addiction Exist?"). Can video games be addictive? Griffiths and Davies consider definitions of addiction and whether these can be applied fairly to playing video games. The *Diagnostic and Statistical Manual of Mental Disorders* of the American Psychiatric Association has been adapted for application to video game addiction. If games have the potential to become addictive, which individuals are most likely to be at risk for video game addiction? The authors review research on health issues related to video games. They conclude that evidence of serious adverse effects on health is rare. Nevertheless, some individuals may have a predisposition to addictive-like behaviors, and these youth should be monitored in such a way that early intervention can succeed.

Although participatory media culture isn't limited to the so-called new interactive media, Joost Raessens ("Computer Games as Participatory Media Culture") argues that computer games, as one of the most successful digital media systems, bring about an influential participatory turn in culture. The author examines three domains of participation in computer gaming: interpretation (the different reading strategies to interpret computer games), reconfiguration (the actualization of game elements that are engineered by the designer), and construction (the creative creation of new game elements). The author finishes his chapter with a discussion of participatory media culture from a political-ideological perspective.

Jan-Willem Huisman and Hanne Marckmann ("I Am What I Play: Participation and Reality as Content") argue that Dutch multimedia company IJsfontein proceeds from two important elements: participation and "reality as content." By participation, they mean offering users more than merely a preprogrammed choice by letting them participate in building the game themselves (as in *Typotoons*). Distancing themselves from the quest for realism in visual design, IJsfontein tries to design reality as content in a threefold way: by giving real elements a place in the content of the game (as in *Masters of the Elements*), by mingling the virtual and the real world (as in *Biotoons, Emergency Stop*), and by exploring the way games can be taken out of the virtual world to give them a place in our daily reality using location-based technology (as in *Road Quiz Show*).

Against the background of a history that highlights some key moments when the desire to play games

and hacking converged, Anne-Marie Schleiner ("Game Reconstruction Workshop: Demolishing and Evolving PC Games and Gamer Culture") explores the phenomenon of game modification, also referred to as "game patching." Her analytical lenses culled from her research into gamer culture, gender representation in computer games, game mods as a hacker art form, and her recent forays into the military-fetish boyland of the popular mod *Counter-Strike*. The author draws a general map of game engine structure, parts of which may be opened to players for modification, and locates the modifiable game within an ecosystem of modders, players, and network topologies.

Living in a world of stories and defining participation as their creation and dissemination, Douglas Rushkoff ("Renaissance Now! The Gamers' Perspective") thinks of the proliferation of interactive media as an opportunity for renaissance: the ability to rethink and redesign our world using entirely new rule sets. The author summarizes the way in which the power of one-way media such as television to program *us*, was broken respectively by the remote control, the video game joystick and the computer mouse, keyboard and modem. Venturing out onto the Internet in search of other fans and user groups to discuss and share secret codes and abilities, gamers might be today's most likely candidates to helm a do-it-yourself (DIY) renaissance in our relationship to stories as well as the reality they mean to describe and influence: both are open source, up for discussion, and ripe for reprogramming.

Notes

1. Because Internet addresses may change, readers can access outdated websites via www.archive.org.

Part I

Computer Games

SLOTS OF FUN, SLOTS OF TROUBLE: AN ARCHAEOLOGY OF ARCADE GAMING

Erkki Huhtamo

By gosh—it is a pinball machine!
—Steve "Slug" Russell, one of the creators of
Spacewar

In *The pilgrim in the microworld* (1983), an early, unjustly neglected analysis of electronic gaming,[1] the sociologist and musician David Sudnow compares his struggle to master *Breakout* with an Atari home video game console to his long-term efforts to learn to play the piano:[2]

Before, the piano was the quintessential human instrument. Of all things exterior to the body, in its every detail it most enables our digital capacities to sequence delicate actions. Pushing the hand to its anatomical limit, it forces the development of strength and independence of movement for fourth and fifth fingers, for no other tool or task so deeply needed. This piano invites hands to fully live up to the huge amount of brain matter with which they participate, more there for them than any other body part. At this genetically predestined instrument we thoroughly encircle ourselves within the finest capabilities of the organ. (Sudnow, 1983, p. 26)

Sudnow's encounter with video games, which soon developed into an addiction, gave an impetus to a book that is unique. It is still the most detailed description of the psychophysical bind created between the player and the game (and, by implication, the user and the computer). Hardcore gamers rarely feel the need to conceptualize their experiences. Sudnow, however, does exactly this, profiting from his double background as an academic researcher of social interactions and a jazz pianist.[3] His detailed account is a mixture between a diary of addiction and recovery, a phenomenological study, and a self-referential literary work, reminiscent—as Grahame Weinbren has suggested—of Samuel Beckett (Weinbren, 2002, p. 182).[4] Sudnow makes intriguing observations about the medium that

had come to preoccupy his mind and his fingers so unexpectedly:

Punctuate a moving picture? I'm no painter and don't dance in mirrors. But here I could watch a mysterious transformation of my movements taking place on the other side of the room, my own participation in the animated interface unfolding in an extraordinary spectacle of lights, colors, and sounds. Improvised painting, organized doodling, with somebody doodling against you to make sure you keep doing it. (Sudnow, 2001, p. 23)

Although primarily concerned with describing and analyzing the author's own relationship with *Breakout*, *The pilgrim in the microworld* also inspires the reader to think about the cultural background of electronic gaming. For if human history has been cultivated, as Sudnow suggests, "through speech and the motions of fingers ... the tiniest not biggest actions," video gaming may not be an unprecedented phenomenon. At the very least, it would be linked with the tradition of using keyboards, from playing the piano to tapping the keys of a "Hughes machine" (a telegraphic apparatus with piano-like keyboard) or the typewriter. However, Sudnow does not elaborate on the historical and cultural ramifications of his observation. In fact, the "keyboard tradition" can be considered part of a wider phenomenon, that of interfacing humans with artefacts of all kinds. Although the history of such interfacing goes back thousands of years, its significance began to grow enormously in the nineteenth century as a result of the industrial revolution and its social, economic, and cultural consequences. The introduction of large-scale machine production was accompanied by an avalanche of different devices that provided amusement, including gameplay. Although often mechanically simple (at least if judged against twenty-first-century standards), and limited in their interactive potential, such devices prepared the ground for future applications such as electronic arcade games. How, why, when, and where this happened is a challenge for scholars. What is needed is an "archaeology of gaming."

Looking Backward: Beyond Game History

This chapter is a contribution to the cultural and historical mapping of electronic gaming. Its basic premise is at least seemingly simple: electronic games did not appear out of nowhere; they have a cultural background that needs to be excavated. The existing literature on the history of video games has done little toward achieving this goal. In fact, the (hi)story is usually told in a remarkably uniform fashion, built around the same landmarks, breakthroughs, and founding fathers (not a word about mothers!). The history of coin-operated arcade video games is routinely said to begin with the appearance of Nolan Bushnell's *Computer Space* (1971) and *Pong* (1972), that of home games with the introduction of Magnavox Odyssey (1972), the first video game console for domestic use, conceived by Ralph Baer, with Bushnell another founding father.[5] The main predecessor to these landmarks has been identified in *Spacewar*, associated with the name of Steve "Slug" Russell, but actually created by a group of student-hackers at MIT in the early 1960s, and subsequently improved collectively by other students at the computer science departments of various American universities throughout the 1960s.[6] The main argument concerning the "prehistory" of electronic games has centered around the status of *Spacewar*—was it really the first video game? Although most seem to agree, there are those who claim that this honor really belongs to a simulation called *Tennis for Two*, created on an analog computer by the physicist William Higinbotham at the Brookhaven National Laboratory in 1958.[7] Most game historians also have something to say about the emergence of computing as a precondition for the video game phenomenon, yet few of them venture further than that. Stephen L. Kent includes a summary description of the history of mechanical arcade games in his massive volume *The ultimate history of videogames*, yet in most cases "prehistorical" information, if any, has been included "from duty," rather than from a critical urge to establish (and question) the links with the past.

The current state of writing on game history could be called its "chronicle era." Books such as Leonard Herman's *Phoenix: The fall and rise of videogames*, Van Burnham's *Supercade*, Steven L. Kent's *The ultimate history of videogames*, and Rusel DeMaria's and Johnny

I. Wilson's *High score!* are mainly concerned with amassing and organizing data.[8] Whereas Herman focuses on the development of game hardware, Van Burnham's overwhelmingly visual *Supercade* celebrates the games themselves, trying to delineate the elements of a "game aesthetics." DeMaria and Wilson have organized their volume around numerous "minihistories" of game companies. None of the histories published so far develops a critical and analytic attitude toward its subject. This can perhaps be explained by external factors. Game historians such as Steven L. Kent, Leonard Herman, and Van Burnham (introduced as a "video game junkie" in the sleeve) are all roughly the same age (in their early 30s), and became familiar with electronic games in their childhoods in the 1970s. The same goes for J. C. Herz, Alain and Frédéric Le Diberder, and Steven Poole, whose books deal with gaming history as well, although not as their main goal.[9] All these writers belong to the first generation that grew up with electronic games; for them gaming became a powerful formative experience. This is both their strength and their weakness. It is a strength, in that the writers are all gamers familiar with their field, and observing it with the eyes of a fan and an insider.[10] It is a weakness, in that they often lack critical distance to their topic and are unable to relate it to wider cultural framework(s), including contemporary media culture.

In this chapter, I excavate some cultural and historical issues relevant for a critical assessment of the emergence of games as an interactive medium. My main emphasis will be the background of electronic games as a manifestation of the human-machine relationship. Although I am fully aware of the complexity of electronic games as a cultural hybrid, I have chosen not to deal with certain of their historical "ingredients," such as motives from earlier forms of gaming and play and the oral and literary traditions of storytelling. As Gillian Skirrow pointed out in her pioneering study "Hellivision: An Analysis of Video Games" (1986), ancient myths and fables often manifest themselves in games, both in their subject matter and their narrative deep structures. This raises intricate questions about the migration of myths across time, space, and various "media." It also leads to questions about the roles and functions of myths embodied in games, literature, cinema, and other cultural forms. I leave these issues for cultural anthropologists and literary scholars to explore. Instead, I present the outline of an archaeology of gaming in public spaces, particularly in game arcades. Thus I leave issues such as domestic and nomadic (mobile, portable) gameplay to a future article. The interplay between public and domestic media consumption is an important issue that deserves a full treatment elsewhere. Although the same games are often adapted from one platform to another, the playing context makes a difference, influencing the nature of the experience, often in relation to other media forms.[11]

As an interactive medium, the roots of electronic gaming go back to the time of the industrial revolutions of the nineteenth and early twentieth century. Connecting humans and machines was a central cultural, economic, and social issue of the time. The introduction of machines as a new source of power and rationalized mass production led to an intense and long-lasting debate. An impressive overview of the dimensions of this debate is provided by Humphrey Jennings' *Pandemonium* (1987), an extraordinary collage of textual fragments. The book tells the story of the coming of the machine entirely by means of quotations from contemporaries, realizing one of Walter Benjamin's dreams. The use of machines for productive purposes in factories and offices provided a background for the appearance of other kinds of machines, meant for amusement and relaxation. To start with, I sketch the cultural background for the emergence of these "useless" machines. I then concentrate on the public amusement machines—often known as coin-ops or slot machines—dealing with their cultural roles and analyzing the modes of human-machine relations they introduced. There is a wealth of factual information available, thanks to collector-writers such as Nic Costa and Richard M. Bueschel, but far less cultural analysis.[12] Very few writers have elaborated on the relationship between early coin-operated machines and video arcade games.[13]

In the final section I reflect on the significance of these "media archaeological" findings for contemporary media culture and electronic gaming in particular, pointing out connecting links across the fabric of the twentieth-century culture. Although my emphasis is on the ways in which electronic gaming can be related to preceding cultural formations, I am not claiming that the "nature" of video games could be exhaustively explained by the phenomena covered in this essay. There are other influential developments that have been left out, including the impact of the technologies meant for domestic production and consumption. I am not trying to say that phenomena identified in contemporary media culture could be fully explained by looking toward the past. Electronic games and the roles they play in contemporary culture have much that is unique and unprecedented. Yet, to correctly assess their "uniqueness" media-archaeological excavations of the past may prove to be helpful. All cultural processes consist of interplay between continuity and rupture, similarity and difference, tradition and innovation; only their mutual proportions and emphases vary. Critical cultural analysis should take both dimensions into account.

"The Animal Machine ... Chained to the Iron Machine"

The notion of a close, near-symbiotic relationship between the human and the machine is often thought to be the product of contemporary culture, saturated by all kinds of devices, both stationary and mobile. As arguably the most widespread application of interactive media, electronic games may seem the ultimate fulfillment of this idea, both in good and in bad. Yet the discourse on linking humans with machines goes further back in time. When it emerged, it was often formulated in a negative sense, seen as a dark side effect of progress. The issue emerged in a world that was undergoing dramatic changes, related to industrialization and mechanization. Beginning in the late eighteenth century, the introduction of steam-powered and mechanical machines into workshops and factories changed the nature of work.[14] In the earlier system of mercantile production, much work had been distributed to skilled craftsmen, who could work from their homes. Not only did they retain their privacy, they could also more or less define their own working pace. With the new machinery, this relative independence disappeared. The workers were gathered at centralized factories where they had to submit themselves to the predefined rhythms and routines of the workplace. The value of skilled workforce began to diminish. Already in the early nineteenth century, the factory itself was felt to turn into one huge machine, with the workers becaming its parts. Around 1815, visiting the mechanized shoe manufactory of "that eminent, modest, and persevering mechanic, M. Brunel," Sir Richard Phillips saw such a human-mechanical machine-hybrid in function:

Every step in it is effected by the most elegant and precise machinery; while as each operation is performed by one hand, so each shoe passes through twenty-five hands, who complete from the hide, as supplied by the currier, a hundred pair of strong and well-finished shoes per day. All the details are performed by ingenious application of the mechanic powers, and all the parts are characterized by precision, uniformity, and accuracy. As each man performs but one step in the process, which implies no knowledge of what is done by those who go before or follow him, so the persons employed are not shoemakers, but wounded soldiers, who are able to learn their duties in a few hours. (Phillips, 1817, cit. Jennings, 1987, pp. 137–138)

Not only skilled, but even healthy workers were eliminated. Their role as "gears" in the factory-machine was given to crippled soldiers. In a way the machinery compensated for the deficiencies of their mutilated bodies, serving as a "prosthesis." Although employing former soldiers could be interpreted as a philanthropic gesture, it might also have been motivated by purely economic motives: the idea of using the cheapest and the most loyal (stable) workforce available. Already in the first half of the nineteenth century, social observers began to pay attention to the fact that workers were in the process of being turned into machines (or machine parts). James Phillips Kay wrote in 1832 about the working conditions in the cotton mills of Manchester: "Whilst the engine runs the people must work—men, women, and children are yoked together with iron and steam. The animal machine—breakable in the best case, subject to a thousand sources of suffering—is chained fast to the iron machine, which knows no suffering and no weariness." (Kay, 1832, cit. Jennings, 1987, p. 185).

"The animal machine ... chained fast to the iron machine" appeared in other sectors of society as well. From the second half of the nineteenth century, office workers were gradually subordinated to the principles of mechanization as well. They were forced to spend their time tied to new office machines—mechanical calculators, "electric pens" and typewriters, copying machines (or "mimeographs"), dictating machines, telephone switchboards. The workdays were divided into repetitive routines developed after the factory model. As Adrian Forty (1986) explains, the new rationalized ideology of office work was totalitarian in nature and found expression on all levels from the largest to the smallest elements, including specially designed office furniture and automated timecard devices. It is not surprising that the extensive linking of the human with the machine became the subject of fantasies and parodies. Devices such as mechanical "shaving mills," torturing machinelike photographers' chairs and feeding machines for workers (featured later in Chaplin's *Modern Times*, 1936) were imagined. Eccentric applications inspired by the factory assembly line were proposed,

often with a satirical touch. Although some of them displayed liberatory potential, releasing the worker from one's toiling, most implied a tightening bondage to the machine. One such idea was the automatic "spanking machine," able to administer a beating simultaneously to a whole row of culprits, tied to the steam-powered apparatus, side by side, their bottoms exposed![15] (figure 1.1).

As a controversial social issue, the bonding of the worker to the machine also received scientific attention, leading to theories such as the "Science of Work" and "Taylorism."[16] These theories tried to give the issues raised by the widespread use of machines in working life a scientific basis. They concentrated on the worker, whose body and its motions were submitted to an intensive analysis. A central aim was to define the optimal body language that would enable the worker to perform with maximum efficiency. Chronophotographic studies, such as those by Étienne-Jules Marey and Georges Demenÿ, served a similar function: by freezing the movements of the body, captured in a series of successive photographs, gestures and motions could be submitted to an "objective" scientific analysis.[17] There were deep contradictions underlying these theories. The supporters of the scientific approach claimed that educating the worker to use his or her body "scientifically" according to the defined principles, prevented it from becoming exhausted, making the worker's life easier. The critics of mechanization countered by claiming that the proposed methods merely dehumanized the worker, turning him or her into a machine (or a machine part). As Mark Seltzer has shown, the need to adapt to the monotonous rhythms of the machine often led to psychological disorders known as "pathological fatigue" or "the maladies of energy" (Seltzer, 1992, p. 13).

From Automata to Automatic Machines
In the second half of the nineteenth century, a line of different machines appeared. In many ways they were the antithesis of the production machines in the factories and offices. The new machines were used voluntarily, outside the working hours. They were placed in all imaginable public places: street corners, bars, newsstands, department stores, hotel lobbies, waiting rooms at railway stations, amusement parks, seaside resorts, and trade fairs. Eventually they found their way into penny arcades designed for the purpose. Particularly from the 1880s on, many different types of machines were developed: vending machines, "trade stimulators," gambling machines, strength testers, fortune-telling

| Figure 1.1 |

The automated spanking machine—humans chained to the machine for discipline. A nineteenth-century Victorian fantasy (source unknown), Erkki Huhtamo's archive.

machines, electric shock machines, games machines, automated miniature theatres (or "working models"), viewing and listening machines, automatic scales.[18] These devices have come to be known by the generic terms "slot machines," "coin machines" or "coin-operated machines" (coin-ops), referring to their basic principle of operation. Whatever the mode of interaction, the user begins the session by inserting a coin in a slot. The machine gives something in return: a postcard, candy or cigar, a "therapeutic" electric shock, a receipt with one's weight or fortune, a visual or musical performance, an amusing joke, a psychologically or socially encouraging experience, an opportunity to train one's skills, enjoy a sharp-shooting session or—last but not least—a possibility to turn one's initial investment into a shower of coins.

In spite of their variety, on the basis of their mode of feedback, the slot machines fall broadly into two categories that could be labelled "automatic" and "proto-interactive." These labels are necessarily anacronistic. In the late nineteenth and early twentieth centuries, the word "automatic" was often applied to any kind of coin-operated machine. The word obviously emphasized the fashionable novelty of these devices, associating them with technological progress and the march of the machines in society. Evoking the ancient tradition of automata (to be discussed later), it also referred to a situation where a human operator had been replaced by a mechanized system; whatever the mode, the com-

munication took place between a human user and a machine as the partner. An arcade advertising "Automatic Amusements" could contain an eclectic array of machines with many different user interfaces and modes of operation, all activated by the visitor him or herself (Pearson, 1992, p. 4). For an archaeology of gaming, however, the division "automatic"- "proto-interactive" makes sense. It helps us decipher the operational and cultural logic of these machines, and gives us clues about the cultural *modus operandi* of their electronic and digital successors.

According to our classification, in the case of an "automatic machine," the user's role is limited to a momentary, simple, noncontinuous action: inserting a coin, perhaps pushing a button or pulling a lever, and then maybe opening a box or lifting a cover. Examples of such machines are vending machines, mechanical miniature theatres, fortune-telling machines, music boxes, and "automated phonographs," the predecessors of jukeboxes. After initiating the action, the user picks up a product or merely experiences the machine in operation. The duration of the experience varies. Picking up a cigar or a chocolate egg from a "coin fed" vending machine only takes an instant, whereas viewing or listening machines provide the user a somewhat longer scopic or auditive experience. It is important to note that after the initial action, the latter part of the experience is passive. The person enjoying the spectacle does not affect its nature in any way. The presentation has a predefined course of action and duration. When it is over, the user can repeat it by inserting another coin, or just walk away.

The automated experiences provided by such devices were preceded by those offered by automata, human- or animal-like mechanical marvels that spoke, made music, or performed acrobatic stunts. Displayed by touring showmen and dime museums, such devices had astonished audiences for centuries. In addition to the technological simulation of life, their fascination must have been based on the distanced position assigned to the viewer. Direct interaction with the automaton was not allowed. The experience was mediated by a human, a showman who introduced, started, and interpreted the automaton's performance (and also collected the coins, sometimes aided by his monkey). In a way, the performing automaton created around itself a kind of "magic circle" the spectator was not allowed to enter. The classic automaton was also emphatically "useless." It was the opposite of a practical or productive machine, although its mechanism could be highly sophisticated (clockworks, etc.). An automaton performed its stunt to amaze, to raise money for its exhibitor, and perhaps advertise the skills of its maker (who often created "useful" things as well, such as clocks, and even mechanical looms). In their spectacular uselessness, the automata clearly differed from their successors, the prosaic, but highly performative industrial robots.

The way in which the emerging department stores appropriated the automata tradition in the late nineteenth century and metamorphosed it into their animated dioramas for the Christmastime window displays was a sign of the times. The animated diorama was now merely a teaser for the real consumeristic spectacle waiting behind it, inside the building. The window pane separated the spectators from the spectacle. The people standing on the sidewalk in front of the display had no direct control over it. They were supposed to be marvelling on the giant steps taken by commercial capitalism. The proliferation of automated slot machines in the cityscape took place simultaneously with this development. Here a user was given at least an illusion of agency, although within strictly predefined limits (which did not prevent people from treating the machines in subversive ways).[19] The user was at least seemingly allowed to enter the magic circle, negotiating the experience oneself by touching the machine physically, and, most importantly, by "penetrating" it by means of the coin. What was the psychological consequence of this action? Did it break the magic circle,

or actually enhance it by making the user a participant in its mysteries? It might be proposed that the introduction of coin-ops was merely an alternative strategy adopted by commercial capitalism. Instead of marvelling at an "untouchable" spectacle in the department store window, the proliferation of coin-operated automatons gave the hard-pressed consumers a temporary, and largely illusionary, feeling of being in command.[20]

Some automatic coin-op devices made efforts to re-create the magic circle of the display of automata by relocating it inside the device, often behind a display window. This is most evident in the case of the fortune-telling machines that contained life-sized animated figures enclosed in a glass case—these simulated fortune-tellers, "Princess Doraldinas" or "Zoltans," were essentially automata displayed in a new context.[21] Although coin-operated, their fascination was based on their "mysterious" agency and "independence." The case of the Automatic Phonograph is more complex. The phonograph, the first successful device for both recording and playing back speech and music, was invented by Thomas Edison in 1877, and put into the market in an improved version a decade later.[22] It became a great success as a stand-alone coin-operated version, often exhibited in public "Phonograph Parlors" (a predecessor of the game arcade). It was enclosed in a wooden cabinet with the phonograph mechanism—an attraction in its own right—visible behind a glass cover. The recording function was omitted. After inserting a coin, the listeners were connected with the device for a short time, wearing earphones and often leaning against the cabinet. Although this kind of contact may now seem insignificant, it anticipated later ways of spending time linked physically to a machine for the purpose of pleasure. With sounds from the earphones filling his/her head, the listener had entered a new virtual realm, another kind of magic circle. The experience could be lengthened by moving from machine to machine, with enough coins in one's pocket.

Proto-Interactive Machines

In the case of the proto-interactive machines, the human-machine relationship went further. Their operating principles were based on the user's repeated and continuous action to which the machine responded in various ways. The tactility of the relationship was essential: to activate the machine, one had to touch it by means of an interface. The gambling machines (later known as "one-armed bandits") were the simplest. Their operation was limited to inserting a coin and pulling a lever that made a set of reels (usually three) with graphic symbols spin inside the machine. The outcome of the game depended on the final combination of the symbols.[23] The operation was made very user-friendly to encourage repeated use. Gambling machines were meant to have a mesmerizing effect on the user, creating yet another kind of magic circle, an intensive feedback loop connecting the player and the device. Mechanical repetition was to induce psychological repetition, which at times manifested itself as compulsive behaviour. The goal was to make the user spend more and more coins at an increasing pace. The effectiveness of this formula is proven by the fact that it still is the basis of millions of slot machines in casinos around the world.

Gambling machines gave minimal opportunities for higher level interaction—the outcome of the game depended on chance, rather than on the quality of the player's actions. Using such machines was not far from the repetitive gestures the worker was forced to perform in a mechanized factory. One might question whether such machines deserve to be called proto-interactive at all; the user was, after all, merely the initiator of the process (and perhaps, in the end, the recipient of a reward). The interactive quality of stereoscopic viewing machines, such as the popular Whiting's Sculptoscope, did not get much further. After inserting a coin, the user peeked into an eyepiece and released a series of 3D cards one by one by pushing a button or pulling a lever. It was only possible to effect the duration of the viewing act, to choose for how long one wanted to stare at an individual card before introducing another. Another device, the Mutoscope, provided slightly more opportunities (figure 1.2). First introduced in 1897, it was a novelty peep show box for viewing "animated photographs."[24] Different from its motor-driven predecessor, Edison's Kinetoscope, the Mutoscope was hand-cranked.[25] The frames of the moving pictures had been copies on paper slips attached to a rotating cylinder. Viewers could freely adjust the cranking speed, and interrupt the session at any point to observe a particularly interesting frame (perhaps a half-naked lady). The only limitation was that the movement could not be reversed. Of course, this was an economic rather than a technical imperative. For just one coin, the user could not be allowed to spend too much time with the device; the profit had to be maximized.

An advertising booklet from 1897 clearly expressed the proto-interactive nature of the Mutoscope:

| Figure 1.2 |
Mutoscope, International Mutoscope Reel Co., 1920s. Erkki Huhtamo Collection, Society of Film History, Helsinki, Finland. Photo: Kai Vase/SEA

In the operation of the Mutoscope, the spectator has the performance entirely under his own control by the turning of the crank. He may make the operation as quick or as slow as fancy dictates ... and if he so elects, the entertainment can be stopped by him at any point in the series and each separate picture inspected at leisure; thus every step, motion, act or expression can be analyzed, presenting effects at once instructive, interesting, attractive, amusing and startling. (Nasaw, 1999, p. 133)

The expression "entirely under control" almost sounds like a flash-forward, an echo of the advertising slogans around interactive media. There was, however, an important difference: experiencing the voyeuristic offerings of the Mutoscope required no acquired mastery, a central quality of video games.[26] To view a Mutoscope reel one needed no more skill than for performing the simplified operations by the assembly line in a mechanized factory. Using a telephone switchboard or a typewriter was much more difficult. Strength testers and mechanical game machines took a step, although timid, toward incorporating mastery. Machines belonging to the first type only required physical strength to punch a boxing bag, to hold handles as an electric stream ran through your body, or to have an arm-wrestling match with Apollo or Uncle Sam. The anthropomorphic interfaces may in retrospect have been their most remarkable feature. Most of these machines involved the use of hands, thus antipating their growing importance on the field of interactive entertainments. The machine's interface often had painted or imprinted outlines of the hand(s), making the tactile connection visually explicit. Yet, anticipating the popular arcade game *Dance Dance Revolution* (Konami), there were also machines operated by one's feet. To excel in a more unexpected variant, the "Lion Head Lung Tester" (Mills, 1904), one needed to blow hard in a pneumatic tube to make a mechanical lion roar and flicker its eyes. Arcade video game makers have not explored this alternative, and probably never will.[27]

With mechanical sporting games, displays of skill began to replace the need for raw physical power. From the late nineteenth century on, many different types came to the market, pointing toward the immaterialization of the gaming experience. Among the most successful genres were the shooting games (hunting, target shooting). They were sometimes justified by patriotic slogans, such as Lord Salisbury's dictum "Every man should learn to shoot!" (Costa, 1988, p. 21). Coin-operated shooting games were an individualized and mechanized form of the shooting galleries, which were popular attractions at fairgrounds and fairs. For any moralist deploring the devastating effect of *Doom* or *Quake* on today's youth, this background should give something to think about. There were many machines that simulated sports, such as boxing, bowling, football, and horse racing. The player either participated in the sport simulation as him/herself or transferred his/her actions to miniature players (kind of proto-avatars) operating within the realm of the game. By being mutated to this new mechanical arena the actual sport genres were transformed. Many early games were for a single player, but multiplayer possibilities increased steadily. Although the interactive possibilities offered by these machines were limited, the ways they managed to create desire, pleasure, and involvement anticipated the intense user-relationships created by arcade video games. In this sense none was more successful than pinball, a mechanized version of the Victorian parlor game bagatelle.[28] Introduced in the 1930s, its golden age dawned after World War II,

helped both by new, more interactive features (the flippers) and the emergence of the postwar youth culture.

The Social Contexts of the "Counter-Machine"

David Nasaw has characterized the meaning of early slot machines by saying: "Here was the perfect diversion for city folk, a momentary break from routine that was so unobtrusive it could be seamlessly interwoven into the fabric of daily life" (Nasaw, 1999, p. 159). The same people who spent their days chained to the machines in factories and offices could gather around these different machines during their lunch breaks or in the evenings and during the weekends. They provided an escape that did not take the users too far from their duties in daily life. The experience provided by these machines was short, fleeting, ephemeral. Their colorful appearance, their fantastic forms, and the very fact that they were a new brand of the Machine, the guiding idea of the era, increased their appeal. The sociologist Yves Hersant has analyzed the nature of these new machines by contrasting them with the world of work:

They are all based on the negation of work, and it is particularly ironic that in its social context the slot-machine has reversed its capitalistic and industrial role, thereby consuming rather than producing wealth. It is clear that such a paradoxical instrument could be found only in a mechanically-orientated world, both as a by-product and a counter product of mechanics. (Hersant, 1988, p. 9)

Slot machines obviously fulfilled a therapeutic function by providing the user an opportunity to step outside the capitalistic idea of constant productivity and scientifically regulated work routines for a moment. The user could release one's tensions by beating a mechanical strongman in arm wrestling, shooting herds of mechanical animals, or merely immersing oneself into the erotic fantasies of the Mutoscope. He (and more rarely she) could look for social esteem denied in the rigid hierarchy of the workplace. For the growing crowd of office workers, machines such as strength testers could actually perform a paradoxical return to the world of physical toiling of which they had been increasingly alienated in the modern office. Yet in spite of their therapeutic value, it would be naive to assume that slot machines had been able to achieve a true liberation, even a momentary one. It is more likely that the "negation of work" that began when a user put his/her coin into one of these machines initiated a psychotechnical feedback loop that linked the working life and the spare time even more tightly together. The slot machines may have been "counter machines," but they were machines nevertheless, and functioned according to machine logic.

Analyzing discourses of bodies and machines in the late nineteenth and early twentieth century literature, Mark Seltzer has paid attention to a peculiar psychic disorder that manifested itself as machine induced neurastenia. As defined by Anson Rabinbach, neurastenia means "an ethic of resistance to work or activity in all its forms." (Rabinbach, 1992, p. 167). Much researched in the late nineteenth and twentieth century, it was identified as symptom of the fatigue caused by monotonous and repetitive work routines in mechanized factories. It would be tempting to associate the great success of proto-interactive coin operated machines with this same phenomenon. The overstimulated mind of a neurasthenic is unable to relax, except by being drawn to another kind of a machine. With machines and counter-machines filling one's life, there is no way to break out of the circle. Whether such a comparison makes sense or not, it is tempting to look for a modern example of a similar phenomenon from Japan, where millions of "salarymen" (white-collar workers) spend their evenings, and often even their lunch hours, in one the countless game centers, driving simulated cars or trains, or staring at the screen of a Pachinko machine, with its endlessly bouncing balls. In a collective society with strict work morale, interfacing with game machines has become simultaneously an obsession and an outlet.

Although they may not have been a remedy to the psycho-physiological problems caused by machine culture, the slot machines also had a social dimension. Just like the amusement parks that became popular in the late nineteenth century, slot machines provided opportunities for new forms of social interaction between the sexes. They were a common topic for discussion, and also an opportunity to make an impression on others, to try to improve one's self-esteem.[29] The social values activated by the slot machines were, in spite of the modernity of the phenomenon, mostly conservative. Devices such as gambling machines and strength testers did little to challenge the prevailing gender divisions. They belonged to the male territory. Gambling machines, located in bars, were rarely even seen by "decent" women. When it comes to the strength testers, women were usually assigned a passive role as observ-

ers, while the men punched the bag or swung the hammer. The Mutoscope was another device associated with the male user, mainly because of the erotic and voyeuristic content of many reels. Yet masculinity may also have been inscribed into the design of the machine. Linda Williams has noted the relationship between the physical turning of the crank of the Mutoscope (located on the frontside) and the action of male masturbation (Williams, 1995, p. 19). Partly because of its doubtful reputation, often commented on by satirical cartoonists, the Mutoscope has been left outside "serious" histories of the moving image, in spite of its phenomenal success and long-lasting cultural presence. If mentioned at all, it is presented as an early effort, a false path that was soon superceded by the mainstream of projected moving pictures. Until the end, Mutoscopes showed short clips, whereas the "real" film culture was associated with the feature film.

It could be claimed, however, that the world of slot machines may have been more heterogeneous than has been thought. Some studies about women's spare-time activities around the turn of the century imply that the situation was not necessarily so clear-cut. Feminist scholars such as Kathy Peiss and Lauren Rabinowitz have challenged earlier ideas about women's passive and distanced relationship to public amusements (Peiss, 1985; Rabinowitz, 1998). Particularly young working women (shop assistants, office ladies, factory workers) were looking for amusements from community halls, amusement parks, nickelodeons, or just city streets. They were searching for outlets from their somber living conditions and actively locating partners, thus subverting moral rules of the late Victorian era. The world of bars and saloons—the havens of gambling machines—were largely closed to women who were concerned about their reputation, but the sprawling urban environment must have offered women many opportunities to interact with coin-ops and other entertainment machines. One should not neglect the fact that women who had entered the working life as typists and telephone operators were often in more direct contact with the latest technology than males. Although, as Ellen Lupton has shown, they were relegated to the role of mediator and thus segregated from power and decision making, they would have been at ease with new machines, including coin-ops (Lupton, 1993).

Although there is at present little direct evidence about women's contact with slot machines, after reading Peiss's and Rabinowitz's studies it makes sense to assume that women used Mutoscopes and other coin-ops much more often than has been thought.[30] Some known photographs of women eagerly interacting with Mutoscopes point to this direction, although they fail to provide conclusive evidence.[31] The fascination exerted by slot machines could perhaps be compared to the pleasures provided by amusement park rides.[32] Yet the constitution of the subject position of these devices was quite different. Whereas slot machines required some form of conscious physical activity from the user, in the amusement park rides "[t]he person surrendered to the machine which, in turn, liberated the body in some fashion from its normal limitations of placement and movement in daily life" (Rabinowitz, 1998, p. 143). How did the forms of pleasure provided by these attractions differ from each other? Were the pleasures of proto-interactivity really very different from those provided by the "passive" sensations of the rollercoaster? These questions are important because they have been activated again in the context of interactive media, claimed to be categorically different from passive spectacles such as going to the movies or watching television.[33]

A group that was largely excluded from using early coin-ops, with perhaps the exception of simple vending machines on the streets, were children. This exclusion was inscribed into the user interfaces of many machines. Many strength testers required too much physical power for chidren to use them. Kineto-scopes, Mutoscopes, and other peepshow machines had their viewing hoods or control interfaces so high from the ground that a child would not have been able to reach them.[34] It is likely that many children became acquainted with these machines with the help of their parents, lifting them up to the viewing hoods and control devices. Because of the bad reputation of amusement arcades, this experience often took place in family-oriented amusement parks and fairgrounds, where proto-interactive devices where placed alongside other kinds of attractions, including merry-go-rounds, rollercoasters, ferris wheels, and traditional shooting and gaming galleries. The presence of these different types of attractions created an integrated experience, where submission and immersion took turns with active participation. During the twentieth century, the number of coin-operated devices that were either meant for children or could be operated by them because of their interface design steadily increased (figure 1.3). This seems to have reflected social changes, such as the loosening of the family control on children's pastime, the increasing amount of pocket money at their disposal,

| Figure 1.3 |
Children using a vending machine. Magic lantern slide, early twentieth century, Echer Slide Co., Dayton, Ohio. Erkki Huhtamo Collection, Los Angeles

and growing importance of human-machine interaction in daily life. More research on this topic is needed.

From the Penny Arcade to the Game Center

Early slot machines were placed in many kinds of public places, both indoors and outdoors. Like wall-mounted broadsides, billboards, and posters, they became one of the tokens of an urban landscape in transition. The novelty value of the coin-ops, which was reflected in many early cartoons poking fun at the devices as well as their users, gradually faded.[35] Although many machines were silently removed, others became a permanent feature of the modern city. They were so common and familiar that the city dwellers' relationships to them became "automated." To use one, one hardly needed to think about the entire operation. Although ever-present, the machines became invisible, like the ATMs today. This is probably also one reason for their nearly total absense from the cultural histories of the twentieth century.

Although the coin-ops were scattered in the city-scape, they were also concentrated in penny arcades. Beginning in the 1890s, such arcades were found in many cities, but also at amusement parks, midways (the entertainment areas of public expositions), and seaside resorts. Although some arcades were touring attractions, connected to a railway show or a touring circus, many of them were located in storefronts, converted to accomodate the new "automatic amusements." Many of these were modest, operating mainly during the winter season and housing the repertories of touring showmen.[36] Yet there were also arcades that were permanently installed. They presented themselves as a new kind of entertainment that tried to attract a general "respectable" audience. David Nasaw has listed the offerings of an exceptionally luxurious early arcade, the Automatic One Cent Vaudeville emporium in New York City.[37] Most early penny arcades would have contained similar items, although in smaller quantities and in less grandiose settings:

Inside, the long narrow arcade extended a block south to the 13th Street. It was lit with chandeliers and hundreds of large white-frosted bulbs; the floor jammed with the latest and most luxurious collection of automatic coin-in-the-slot machines available anywhere. For the sporting crowd, there were punching bags to compare your punch with Corbett's, Jeffries', Fitzsimmons', or Terry McGovern's; shooting-gallery rifles; weights to pull; hammers to pound; stationary bicycles and hobby-horses. There were also automatic amusement machines that dispensed cards with your fortune, your horoscope, or your future wife's picture; metal embossers that spit out "Your name in Aluminum"; "automatic" gum, candy, and peanut machines; coin-in-the-slot phonographs with the Floradora Sextet, Sousa's Band, and comic monologues; and more than 100 peep-show machines. (Nasaw, 1999, p. 157)

On offer here was a true multimedia, multi-interface and multisensory experience, made even more attractive by the fact that the presence of media technology in the home was still very limited. Such arcades were, however, not an absolute novelty. The concept penny arcade evokes the popular nineteenth-century shopping arcades (or "passages"), considered by Walter Benjamin as one of the earliest signs of urban modernism (Benjamin, 1983). From the first half of the nineteenth century, such arcades had contained, in addition to shops and boutiques, also novelty amusements, such as dioramas and cosmoramas. For shoppers, such attractions were just another kind of commodity, an experience to buy.[38] Some shows even adapted the idea of the arcade to their own purposes. Cosmoramas, for example, were peepshow "arcades," consisting of rows of magnifying lenses inserted into the walls. Viewers peeped at illuminated views, often with sensational subject matter, through the lenses. The popularity of cosmoramas—P.T. Barnum's mighty

American Museum had one—inspired all kinds of improved spectacles.[39] One of them was the Kaiser Panorama, a European-wide network of stereoscopic peepshow arcades that operated for several decades from the 1880s on.[40] Although the idea of gathering Edison's Automatic Phonographs and Kinetoscopes into public phonograph and kinetoscope parlors has often been treated as a cultural innovation, it was just an adaptation of an existing tradition.[41] The novelty was in turning this tradition "automatic," or, in other words, coin-operated. The cosmoramas and other early arcade amusements had usually been noninteractive. The images were for viewing only, and a fee paid at the entrance.

In spite of their huge and immediate popular appeal, penny arcades were often considered morally questionable, accused of being breeding-grounds for vice and even for infectious diseases. Penny arcades attracted a socially mixed crowd, including women. They were seen as dark and gloomy. The attitudes toward them had much in common with those associated with the earliest cinemas, known as "nickelodeons".[42] Like the penny arcades, many nickelodeons also operated in converted store fronts. Sometimes both were combined, with cinemas opened in the back rooms of the penny arcades (the association between pennies and nickels is not a coincidence). To enter the room, the spectators would have to walk through the penny arcade itself, filled with proto-interactive machines, above all Mutoscopes. The arcade would function as a waiting room (a kind pre-show) for the cinema experience, thus reenacting an already old tradition.[43] From a theoretical point of view, a tension was created between these two modes of consuming moving images—the hand-cranked peepshows and the screen projection. These two forms soon went to different directions, although some slot machines remained in the lobbies of cinema theatres. The co-existence of game centers and cinema multiplexes in shopping malls has brought them together again.

Although it is commonly agreed that both early penny arcades and nickelodeons attracted a mixed audience, its exact constitution is still open to debate. Particularly enthusiastic users for the penny arcades were certainly adolescent boys (when they managed to sneak in). Popular illustrations, including cartoons and postcards, often show delighted youngsters peering into the Mutoscope.[44] According to a contemporary observer, a sign displayed in Samuel Swartz's arcade in Chicago, "For Men Only," "attracts the small boy like a magnet" (Nasaw, 1999, p. 154). This was often considered a social problem, for which solutions were sought. Tinkering with wireless transmitters and radio sets was promoted as a good domestic hobby for boys at least partly to keep them away from the streets. For women, penny arcades were also consided unsuitable, although signs saying "For Women Only" were sometimes displayed next to some attractions (no doubt to stir the curiosity of men as well). As Kathy Peiss and Lauren Rabinowitz have demonstrated, young working women often disregarded reproaches and entered "forbidden" places. Considering penny arcades as a zone for men only seems a false generalization that fails to account for the variety of their audiences and attractions.

With the advent of the movie palace era in the 1910s, the cinemas managed to whitewash their public image. In spite of the fashionable "high class" penny arcades, their general reputation got even worse in the eyes of moral reformers and authorities. During the Great Depression of the 1930s, often considered the golden age of the penny arcade in the United States, these places provided unemployed men affordable opportunities to spend time. Interacting with an arcade game or trying one's luck with a gambling machine, often disguised as an "innocent" machine, such as a candy or cigarette dispenser, made one forget the harsh realities for a while. A common objection against slot machines was their association with gambling and organized crime. The authorities often adopted tough measures, forbidding slot machines and instituting laws against gambling. As Marshall Fey's history of the slot machine demonstrates, the trajectory of the fight against these machines is equally long as their history itself. Symbolic manifestations included the wrecking parties organized by the authorities as public stunts for the media.[45] Perhaps the most famous episode took place in 1934, when New York City's mayor Fiorello La Guardia himself posed for the press, holding a hammer with a large pile of wrecked machines.[46] Similar gestures had often been seen in propagandistic photographs from the Prohibition Era in the 1920s, only now slot machines had taken the place of the barrels and bottles of illegal alcohol. One might also recall the book burning rituals organized by the Nazis, another attempt to "purify" the society. When the Philippines' president Ferdinand Marcos forbid arcade video games in 1981 and publicly destroyed them with his hammer, he actually reenacted a well-established cultural model (Le Diberder & Le Diberder, 1998, p. 8).

The slot machine industry defended itself by changing its focus from games of chance to games of skill. Instead of money, the successful player would be rewarded by immaterial values such as additional games or high scores displayed in the arcades. Pinball played a crucial role in this transformation. Although it was based on the nineteenth-century bagatelle and existed already in the 1930s, its heyday began in the late 1940s. In 1947, an engineer named Harry Mabs, working for Gottlieb, invented "flipper bumpers," little paddles used to sling the ball back to the gamefield (Kurtz, 1991, p. 56). Flippers were first used in a pinball machine named Humpty Dumpty, which became a model for countless later models. In this improved form, pinball became one of the symbols of postwar youth culture. Pinball machines appeared in bars or revamped game arcades, the inheritors of penny arcades. The typical players were now younger than earlier, males in their teens and twenties (sometimes in the company of their girlfriends, who were occasionally allowed to play).

Arcades, with pinball as their centerpiece, became part of a lifestyle that encouraged bonding among youth and served as a safety zone against the repressive values of both the family and the workplace. Playing became a way of being in two places at the same time (bilocation): entering into an intense relationship with an enclosed microworld and remaining at the same time part of a group of peers in the surrounding physical space. Pinball provided an opportunity to show one's mastery for oneself and others and to attain fame and acceptance within the gaming subculture. This situation was symbolically embodied in Tommy, the protagonist of The Who's rock opera (1968), later a successful musical. Tommy is a new kind of (anti)-hero, a neglected, mistreated and autistic youth, a "deaf, dumb, and blind kid," whose creativity and communicativeness are expressed through a single channel: his phenomenal ability to play pinball. "Standing like a statue," he becomes "part of the machine," according to the lyrics of "Pinball Wizard."[47] Similar figures have since appeared in the discourses around arcade video games, including films such as Nick Castle's The Last Starfighter (1984), a story about a small-town boy, whose one special skill, his mastery in arcade games, leads him to become an intergalactic warrior. The emergence of such topoi seems to indicate that continuities between predigital and digital gaming cultures may be more important than discontinuities.

Video game arcades were direct descendants of the game parlors. The transition that took place during the 1970s was gradual. Mechanical and digital game machines often existed side by side, as photographs from the era demonstrate. There existed a continuity rather than a rupture between electromechanical slot machines and video game machines. Not only were the physical interfaces, such as joysticks, simulated guns, steering wheels, and so on, often used in earlier games; many game genres, such as driving simulators, shooting games, and sport and fighting games, already existed in predigital arcades. This connection has been symbolically expressed in a story about Steve "Slug" Russell, one of the creators of *Spacewar*. Russell is said to have exclaimed, many years after working on the game, as if struck by a sudden revelation: "*By gosh—it is a pinball machine!*"[48] As can be expected, video game arcades inherited their predecessors' bad reputation. Parents' groups and authorities concerned with the sanity and morality of the youth voiced loud criticism. The widely publicized prejudices against arcade video games and the arcades themselves were probably one of the reasons for the breakthrough of home gaming: parents bought video game consoles for their children to keep them away from those diabolic places. In the early 1980s, game centers launched campaigns to clean their image. Yet the efforts to turn the arcade experience into a form of family entertainment did not please the hardcore gamers who had grown up in the "seedy caves." According to J. C. Herz, after the "destruction" of video game arcades, their real continuity can be found from the realms of networked role-playing games on the Internet, at least when it comes to the sense of community and atmosphere (Herz, 1997, pp. 58–59).

Conclusion: Beyond Cryptohistory

Slot machines have been almost totally neglected by cultural historians and media scholars.[49] Even historians of popular culture usually mention them only in passing, without analyzing them, or placing them into their original cultural contexts. The existing literature has been written almost exclusively by collectors and coin-op enthusiasts. The current state of things does not do justice to the long-lasting popularity and wide cultural impact of these machines. One reason for the *damnatio memoriae* is no doubt their near-ubiquity. When a phenomenon becomes too familiar and commonplace, it in a way turns invisible; we no longer pay attention to it. As counter-machines opposed to work, productivity, and progress, slot machines have been considered trivial, an ephemeral form of spending (or wasting) one's time and money. The *damnatio* goes even further: not only have coin-ops been seen as trivial, they have been considered harmful as well, worth prosecution rather than praise. Of course, none of

this provides an excuse for neglecting them, for slot machines are, to borrow an expression from Siegfried Giedion, an essential part of the "anonymous history" of our time (Giedion, 1969). They have been a veritable laboratory for designing and testing forms of human-machine relationship. Perhaps it is only with the emergence of interactive media as a major cultural and economic force that their significance gradually becomes clear.

I have tried to show that excavating the past makes sense when trying to explain phenomena such as arcade video gaming with seemingly very short histories. Such an approach helps counter the claims frequently made by industry publicists and corporate "cryptohistorians," who like to represent electronic gaming as something unprecedented, a unique phenomenon heralding an imminent transition into a culture of interactivity.[50] Of course, such claims are not totally unfounded. There is much unique, and perhaps even revolutionary, in the games themselves and in their nearly worldwide appeal. It also has to be admitted that we are probably witnessing only the first stages in a development that will attain much more massive dimensions and proceed into directions we cannot at present conceive. Gaming in public spaces such as game centers will be only one aspect of the game culture, alongside the use of domestic devices, mobile personal gaming platforms, and networking. This chapter has been deliberately limited to an "archaeology of arcade gaming," trying to identify its outlines and the forms of human-machine relationships associated with slot machines. Without pretending that arcade video games and game arcades themselves could be entirely accounted for by reference to the past, it should be clear that many of their incredients are found, albeit in rudimentary form, already in nineteenth-century developments.

The missing thread that should be woven into this narrative is, of course, the archaeology of games played at home and in various intermediate spaces with personal games machines. Isn't *this* something unprecedented? Once again, there is a history of proto-interactive devices for domestic use, covering a great number of nineteenth-century "philosophical toys," such as the phenakistiscope and the zoetrope, early media machines, including the phonograph, and an even greater variety of miniature theatres and other role playing environments. Nor should one neglect wireless transmitters/receivers and radio kits that have been widely available since the early twentieth century. These devices were not used for gaming, but they provided boys with an opportunity for personal tinkering with technology (Douglas, 1992, pp. 44–59). Such activities anticipated coding and hacking—important aspects of the video and computer game culture from the outset. The history of commercial media also knows attempts to turn existing mass media channels into (pseudo)interactive experiences, including the 1950s children's television program *Winky Dink and You*. As these examples show, electronic gaming cannot be traced back to any single source. It emerges from a slowly evolving, complex web of manifold cultural threads and nodes. What is clear is that this web began to develop a long time before anything like "digital interactive media" existed.

Notes

1. I use the concepts "electronic games" and "electronic gaming" in this chapter as conceptual umbrellas, covering phenomena variously referred to as "arcade games," "video games," "console games," "TV games," and "computer games." There is much confusion in the use of terminology. By "arcade games," I understand stand-alone games (enclosed in dedicated cabinets) played in public arcades or locations. By "video games," I mean games played with a dedicated console connected with a CRT, most often a TV set. The concepts "console game" and "TV game" are more or less synonymous with a "video game." The concept "TV game" (*terebi geimu*) is frequently used in Japan. A "computer game" is a game played with the personal computer, either off-line or online. There is much overlapping among these categories; numerous games are available for arcades, consoles, and PCs. An alternative to "electronic games" could be "digital games," but the first mentioned seems culturally more established. The leading industry event in the field is known as Electronic Entertainment Expo (E3, Los Angeles), which is organized by the former Interactive Digital Software Association (IDSA), now known as the Entertainment Software Association (ESA). This seems to further emphasize the interchangeability of the words "electronic" and "digital" (although they by no means mean the same thing). The industry has more and more often shown signs of replacing the word "games" with "entertainment."

2. *Breakout* was first released as an arcade game by Atari in 1976, and later as a console version. According to a well-known story, it is said to have been designed in four days and nights by Steve Wozniak at the request of his friend, Steve Jobs. Jobs had been given the task of designing a new game in the tradition of *Pong* by Atari's founder Nolan Bushnell. The purpose of the game was to destroy a brick wall (on the top part of the screen) by slowly knocking out the bricks one by one by means of a paddle moving horizontally in the bottom of the screen. Jobs and Wozniak became founders of Apple Computer (see Van Burnham, 2001, p. 137). About the legends around the making of *Breakout*, see also Steven L. Kent, 2001, pp. 71–73.

3. Before *Pilgrim in the microworld*, Sudnow had already edited an academic anthology called *Studies in social interaction* (1972) and written the highly acclaimed *Ways of the hand: The organization of improvised conduct* (1978). In this book, anticipating *Pilgrim in the microworld*, Sudnow meticulously describes and conceptualises his process of learning to play the piano. In his motto, Sudnow quotes Martin Heidegger: "Every motion of the hand in every one of its works carries itself through the element of thinking, every bearing of the hand bears itself in that element." (p. ix). *Ways of the hand* has been recently republished in a revised form (2001)—*Pilgrim in the microworld* deserves to be reprinted as well.

4. I would like to thank Grahame Weinbren for focusing my attention on Sudnow's book.

5. As an exception to the rule, DeMaria and Wilson refer to a coin-operated version of *Spacewar* called *Galaxy War*, which appeared at Stanford University campus in the early 1970s. The authors think the game may have been available even before *Computer Space* and *Pong*, which would make it the first arcade video game. No conclusive evidence is given (DeMaria & Wilson, 2002, p. 13). Baer has recently written forewords to Van Burnham's *Supercade* (2001) and to Wolf, 2001, which further consolidates his mythologized status as a founding father.

6. Stewart Brand (1974) gives a valuable rare, early account about the culture around *Spacewar*.

7. Herman, 6–7; Burnham, 28; DeMaria & Wilson, pp. 10–11. The game was displayed on a tiny oscilloscope screen and ran on an analog computer. Two special control boxes, predecessors of the joystick, were created. Kent dismisses the status of Higinbotham's game because it

remained an isolated case and had no impact. It was not known by pioneers such as Steve Russell (*Spacewar*) or Ralph Baer (Magnavox Odyssey) (Kent, 2001, p. 18).

8. Kent's book is the most exhaustive chronicle to date, based on original interviews with over five hundred game designers, producers and executives. It is a massive and detailed, albeit somewhat naive "polylogue" that relies to a great extend on direct quotations. Another data collection, focusing on arcade machines and games, is Sellers, 2001. The "fan" in the title quite clearly also addresses the author, who begins his introduction: "I lost my video-game virginity at the age of six during an otherwise unmemorable afternoon at Cannonsburg Ski Area outside of Grand Rapids, Michigan. The game was *Breakout*, it was early 1977 and my mind was ready to explore the world beyond *Mister Mouth* and *Hungry Hungry Hippos*" (p. 10). The description has some affinities with discourses on religious conversion.

9. The European contributors (Le Diberder and Poole) are easily the culturally and theoretically most sophisticated ones. They also devote some space to the European game industry, which is almost totally missing from the American-Japanese perspective of the American writers.

10. As Mark J. P. Wolf has reminded, games are a difficult subject for study. Whereas it is easy to view a film or a television program, going through all the levels of a video game is a time consuming task, that requires practice and often special skills. See Wolf, 2001, p. 7. This may be one reason why so many early studies on electronic gaming kept a definitive distance to "hands-on" approaches, dealing with gaming as a general phenomenon; at most, the researchers had peeped at the games from behind the gamers' (often children's) shoulders.

11. Sudnow found this out when he realized that *Breakout*, the game he had been attempting to master (to play it through repeatedly, based on his acquired mastery) on a home console, was originally an arcade game. An important principle behind arcade games is their coin-op logic: while depending on the gamer's mastery, the game also has to contain some randomizing factors that will increase the likelihood that the gamer needs to insert a new coin from time to

time. In a sense, Sudnow's quest for an absolute mastery of *Breakout* was misguided from the beginning, influenced by his background as a pianist. With piano, one can really learn to master a certain piece and repeat the performance over and over again.

12. For basic data, see Costa, 1988 (well written, but unfortunately not annotated), Bueschel, 1998; Bueschel and Gronowski, 1993; Fey, 1997.

13. See, however, Slovin, 2001, p. 139. Compare, Kent, 2001, pp. 2–3.

14. A classic account of this process is Giedion, 1969.

15. Cartoonists also imagined mechanical "photographer's chairs," that resembled ghastly torturing instruments. The idea of tying the person to be photographed to a mechanical contrivance had a basis in reality. Photographers often used head and neck stands to help people remain motionless when the picture was taken. The idea of freezing the subject was taken much further in prison photography. Inmates understood that having a photograph taken would help in their identification and surveillance. They tried to move their heads so that the photographs would be blurred. Special chairs with straps were created to immobilize the prisoner. This naturally also brings to mind the electric chair, invented in the 1880s for permanent immobilization of the inmates who had been given a death sentence.

16. See Rabinbach, 1992. About psychotechnical research applied to female office workers in Germany, see also Gold and Koch, 1993.

17. Marey's and Demenÿ's work also aimed at creating the perfect soldier: an effective and tireless killing machine. They received ample financing from the French army, who felt the need to improve its performance after being defeated in the Franco-Prussian war of 1870–1871. About Marey's work, see Braun, 1992.

18. A good way to gain an idea of the great variety of these machines is to peruse Bueschel, 1998. The book contains plenty of basic information and hundreds of color photographs. According to Nic Costa, the number of patent applications for coin-operated devices grew from three in 1883 to 139 in 1887, etc. By the mid 1890s, more than a thousand patent applications for such devices had been received by the British Patent Office (Costa, 1988, 11).

19. The history of subversive treatment of coin-op machines is as long as that of the machines themselves. Using fake coins is the most well-known trick, but there were many others, all the way to the well-known tilting of the pinball cabinet for enhanced performance. See Costa, 1988, p. 19.

20. The word "automaton" was used about coin-op machines. In 1895, *De Natuur* wrote: "At the present time we are being inundated with automatons. If this continues, the time will come when all the arts and crafts will be performed by machines which, at the cost of a coin, be it large or small, will be at everybody's service." (quoted in Costa, 1988, p. 16). Because of widespread mistreatment, most automatic machines only dispensed cheap items or gave small rewards.

21. Another inheritor of the automata tradition, also placed behind a sheet of glass are the animated dioramas shown by many department stores in their show windows around Christmas.

22. For a general history, see Charbon, 1977. On the background of the phonograph, see Gitelman, 1999.

23. The ultimate source of information on gambling machines is Fey, 1997. The author's grandfather was the famous slot machine manufacturer and inventor Charles Fey, the creator of the original Liberty Bell (1899), the model for countless slot machines up to the present.

24. On the invention of the Mutoscope, see Hendricks, 1964. For its early history, see Bueschel & Gronowski, 1993, pp. 91–100.

25. This decision may be partly explained as an effort to avoid patent infringement. The Kinetoscope and the Mutoscope were largely the work of one man, William Kennedy Laurie Dickson, who left Edison's company after the development of the Kinetoscope. Edison tried to find new applications for his electric technology, which may explain why the Kinetoscope used an electric motor to run the film. Mutoscope relied on a different principle, that of the flip book, which had been known since the 1860s. But Mutoscope was also more reliable and could be shown in places where electricity was not available. Kinetoscope soon disappeared from the market, whereas the Mutoscope became a great success that lasted until 1950s, and even later.

26. About the notion of mastery in video games and interactive media, see Weinbren, 2002.

27. Bueschel, 1998, p. 119. With twenty-first-century hygienic standards the popularity of pneumatic blowing machines in the late nineteenth and early twentieth century seems almost surreal.

28. About the history of pinball, see Colmer, 1976.

29. This strangely resembles the peculiar gym culture in today's Southern California. Gym card holders certainly exercise with all kinds of machines, but this act serves all kinds of symbolic goals, some of them conscious, some not. Gyms are places to display one's body, to socialize, and to create business relationships.

30. At the Musée Mécanique in San Francisco's Cliff House there is a slot machine that must have appealed to working women. It is the automated typewriter that functions as a fortune-telling machine. It is easy to imagine an office lady, chained to her typewriter all day long, pushing her coin into the slot of this machine. She does not have to do anything else—the typewriter types automatically for her.

31. A great example, captioned "'Living Pictures' on the pier, 1912" shows a row of four Mutoscopes outside on the pier, with two women peering into the machines. There are no men in the picture. Coe and Gates, 1977, 90.

32. King Vidor's classic silent film *The Crowd* (1929) provides a vivid picture of the willingness of the working women to immerse themselves into the new mechanized amusements.

33. About theme park rides, see Huhtamo, 1995, pp. 159–186.

34. The International Mutoscope Reel Company began at some point, probably in the 1920s or later, to manufacture special "kiddie stands" that would enable a child to use the machine. Such stands were special accessories. Still, their existence shows that the company began to acknowledge the importance of children as potential users.

35. In cartoons, the coin-ops seemed capable of performing any imaginable tasks. Graphic artists and humorists imagined "automatic dentists," "automatic conscience clearers," "automatic arbitration," "automatic warm water washstands," etc. They also showed people trying these machines, and being ridiculed by the crowd

observing the operation. For examples, see Costa, 1988, pp. 14, 10.

36. Some penny arcades operated in the cities during the winter season, but were taken again on tour in the spring. They were hybrids of a stationary and nomadic attraction.

37. The "Automatic One Cent Vaudeville" was the enterprise of Adolph Zukor (later CEO of Paramount Pictures) and Morris Kohn. See Nasaw, 1999, p. 157.

38. The same arcades often contained showrooms for printers and toysellers, who specialized in optical toys, an important predecessor to moving images and also electronic games.

39. The first Cosmorama is said to have been opened by the abbot Cazzara in Paris in 1808. See Campagnoni, 1995, p. 87.

40. The Kaiser Panorama (later known also by other names) was the invention of the German August Fuhrmann (1844–1925). It was based on earlier stereoscopic viewing arcades. The prehistory of the gaming arcade is very rich and complex. It cannot be fully detailed here.

41. The first phonograph parlor was opened by The Ohio Phonograph Company in Cleveland on September 15, 1890. The listening machines were often lined along the walls of the premise, reenacting the arrangement of the Cosmorama (also known as "Cosmorama Rooms"). Peeping at images was replaced by listening to sounds. The intimacy of the peephole was replaced by the aural intimacy provided by the earphones. See Musser and Nelson, 1991, pp. 38–39.

42. For original documents related to this debate in the early twentieth century, see Harding and Popple, 1996, pp. 68–71. Several documents attack "mutoscopic" outrages, although defences are also included.

43. This arrangement can already be found from Etienne-Gaspard Robertson's Fantasmagorie show in Paris in the 1790s. Fantasmagorie, or Phantasmagoria, was a form of magic lantern show. Before entering the hall itself, the audience often spent time in an antechamber looking at mechanical and optical curiosities and perhaps observing a popular scientific demonstration. This tradition continues in the preshows of many theme park rides today. For Robertson, see Levie, 1990.

44. However, there is only one example of this in Bottomore, 1995, p. 171. There are several cartoons showing middle-aged men peering into the Mutoscope (see pages 40–43).

45. A case in point, in France all slot machines (appareil à sous) were forbidden in 1937. According to Jean-Claude Baudot, they were still forbidden in the 1980s, although in less extreme form. There were ways to by-pass the laws. See Baudot, 1988, p. 19.

46. See Fey, 1997, pp. 111, 137. Slot machines were forbidden in New York City from 1934 until May 1976. See Colmer, 1976, p. 37.

47. "He stands like a statue / Becomes part of the machine / Feeling all the bumpers / Always playing clean / He plays by intuition / The digit counters fall / That deaf, dumb and blind kid / Sure plays a mean pinball" (words and music by Pete Townshend).

48. Levy, 1984, p. 65. For Stewart Brand, Russell told that his main source of inspiration was the series of science fiction books called the Lensman by E. E. "Doc" Smith. See Brand, 1974, p. 55.

49. Unfortunately, much of the evidence about the slot machine users' attitudes has disappeared without a trace, not being considered worth recording. We know the machines and the companies quite well, but not what people thought about them.

50. About the notion of cryptohistory as applied to media production, see Schiffer, 1991, pp. 1–2.

References

Baudot, J. C. (1988). *Arcadia: Slot machines of Europe and America*. Tunbridge Wells, Kent: Costello.

Benjamin, W. (1983). *Charles Baudelaire: A lyric poet in the era of high capitalism*. Harry Zohn. transl. London: Verso.

Bottomore, S. (1995). *I want to see this Annie Mattygraph. A cartoon history of the movies*. Pordenone: Le giornate del cinema muto.

Brand, S. (1974). *II Cybernetic frontiers*. New York: Random House.

Braun, M. (1992). *Picturing time. The work of Etienne-Jules Marey (1830–1904)*. Chicago: University of Chicago Press.

Bueschel, R. M. (1998). *Collector's guide to vintage coin machines*, 2d ed., Atglen, PA: Schiffer Publishing.

Bueschel, R. M., & Gronowski, S. (1993). *Arcade 1. Illustrated historical guide to arcade machines*, vol. 1. Wheat Ridge, CO: Hoflin Publishing Ltd.

Burnham, V. (2001). *Supercade. A visual history of the videogame age, 1971–1984*. Cambridge, MA: MIT Press.

Campagnoni, D. P. (1995). *Verso il cinema. Macchine spettacoli e mirabili visioni*. Torino: UTET Librería.

Charbon, P. (1977). *Le phonographe à la Belle Epoque*. Brussels: S.P.R.L. Sodim.

Coe, B., & Gates, P. (1977). *The snapshot photograph: The rise of popular photography, 1888–1939*. London: Ash & Grant.

Colmer, M. (1976). *Pinball: An illustrated history*. London: Pierrot Publishing.

Costa, N. (1988). *Automatic pleasures: The history of the coin machine*. London: Kevin Francis Publishing Limited.

DeMaria, R., & Wilson, J. L. (2002). *High score! The illustrated history of electronic games*. Emeryville: McGraw-Hill Osborne Media.

Douglas, S. J. (1992). Audio outlaws: Radio and phonograph enthusiasts. In J. Wright (Ed.), *Possible dreams: Enthusism for technology in America*. Dearborn, MI: Henry Ford Museum & Greenfield Village.

Fey, M. (1997). *Slot machines: A pictorial history of the first 100 years*. Reno: Liberty Belle Books.

Forty, A. (1986). *Objects of desire: Design and society, 1750–1980*. London: Thames and Hudson.

Giedion, S. (1969). *Mechanization takes command. A contribution to anonymous history*. New York: W. W. Norton.

Gitelman, L. (1999). *Scripts, grooves, and writing machines: Representing technology in the Edison era*. Stanford: Stanford University Press.

Gold, H., & Koch, A. (Eds.). (1993). *Fräulein von Amt*. Munich: Prestel-Verlag.

Harding, C., & Popple, S. (1996). *In the kingdom of shadows: A companion to early cinema*. London: Cygnus Arts & Fairleigh Dickinson University Press.

Hendricks, G. (1964). *Beginnings of the Biograph*. New York: The Beginnings of the American Film.

Herman, L. (1998). *Phoenix: The fall and rise of videogames*. Sd: Rolenta Press, Union, N.J.

Hersant, Y. (1988). Introduction. In J.-C. Baudot, *Arcadia. Slot machines of Europe and America* 7–11. Tunbridge Wells, Kent: Costello.

Herz, J. C. (1997). *Joystick nation*. Boston: Little, Brown and Company.

Huhtamo, E. (1995). Encapsulated bodies in motion: Simulators and the quest for total immersion. In S. Penny (Ed.), *Critical issues in electronic media*. Albany: State University of New York Press.

Jennings, H. (Ed.). (1987). *Pandemonium: The coming of the machine as seen by contemporary observers 1660–1886*. London: Picador/Pan Books.

Kay, J. P. (1832). *The moral and physical conditions of the working classes employed in the cotton manufacture in Manchester*. In H. Jennings (Ed.), (1987), *Pandemonium: The coming of the machine as seen by contemporary observers 1660–1886*. London: Picador/Pan Books.

Kent, S. L. (2001). *The ultimate history of video games*. Roseville, CA: Prima Publishing.

Kurtz, B. (1991). *Slot machines and coin-op games*. London: The Apple Press.

Le Diberder, A., & Le Diberder, F. (1998). *L'univers des jeux vidéo*. Paris: La Découverte.

Levie, F. (1990). *Etienne-Gaspard Robertson. La vie d'un fantasmagore*. Bruxelles: Les Editions du Préambule et Sofidoc.

Levy, S. (1984). *Hackers: Heroes of the computer revolution*. New York: Dell Publishing.

Lupton, E. (1993). *Mechanical brides: Women and machines from home to office*. New York: Princeton Architectural Press.

Musser, C., & Nelson, C. (1991). *High-class moving pictures. Lyman H. Howe and the forgotten era of traveling exhibition, 1880–1920*. Princeton: Princeton University Press.

Nasaw, D. (1999). *Going out: The rise and fall of public amusements*. Cambridge, MA: Harvard University Press.

Pearson, L. F. (1992). *Amusement machines*. Princes Risborough, Buckinghamshire: Shire Publications.

Peiss, K. (1985). *Cheap amusements: Working women and leisure in turn-of-the century New York*. Philadelphia: Temple University Press.

Phillips, R. (1817). *A morning walk from London*. In H. Jennings (Ed.), (1987), *Pandemonium: The coming of the*

Erkki Huhtamo

machine as seen by contemporary observers, 1660–1886. London: Picador/Pan Books.

Rabinbach, A. (1992). *The human motor: Energy, fatigue, and the origins of modernity*. Berkeley: University of California Press.

Rabinowitz, L. (1998). *For the love of pleasure: Women, movies and culture in turn-of-the-century Chicago*. New Brunswick, NJ: Rutgers University Press.

Sellers, J. (2001). *Arcade fever: The fan's guide to the golden age of video games*. Philadelphia: Running Press.

Schiffer, M. B. (1991). *The portable radio in American life*. Tucson: University of Arizona Press.

Seltzer, M. (1992). *Bodies and machines*. New York: Routledge.

Skirrow, G. (1986). Hellivision: An analysis of video games. In C. McCabe (Ed.), *High theory/low culture*, pp. 115–142. Manchester: Manchester University Press.

Slovin, R. (2001). *Hot circuits*. In M. Wolf (Ed.), *The medium of the video game*, pp. 137–154. Austin: University of Texas Press.

Sudnow, D. (1972). *Studies in social interaction*. New York: The Free Press.

Sudnow, D. (1983). *Pilgrim in the microworld: Eye, mind, and the essence of video skill*. New York: Warner Books.

Sudnow, D. (2001). *Ways of the hand: The organization of improvised conduct*. Cambridge, MA: MIT Press.

Weinbren, G. (2002). Mastery (Sonic c'est moi). In M. Rieser & A. Zapp (Eds.), *New screen media: Cinema/art/ narrative*. London: BFI.

Williams, L. (1995). Corporealized observers: Visual pornographies and the "carnal density of vision." In P. Petro (Ed.), *Fugitive images: From photography to video*. Bloomington: Indiana University Press.

Wolf, M. J. P. (2001). *The medium of the video game*. Austin: University of Texas Press.

2

THE HISTORY OF THE VIDEO GAME

Steven Malliet and Gust de Meyer

To summarize the history of the video game in a single chapter is by no means a self-evident assignment. Although the games industry is much younger than the film, literature, or pop music industries, it nonetheless entered its fifth decade in 2003. A brief glance at the number of games produced between 1962 and today clearly indicates that it is impossible to discuss this topic with the help of a timeline of all games ever produced; there simply are too many. Therefore we have chosen to divide video game history into a number of separate periods, each with its own specific tendencies and characteristics. Our primary objective is to provide an improved insight into the video game phenomenon that we know today, the enumeration of independent historical events is of secondary importance.

Prehistory: 1958–1972

Even though 1962 is frequently cited as "the year when the first video game was produced," it is not true that before 1962 there was no such thing and afterwards suddenly there was. Like other media, such as film or recorded music, it is difficult to connect the emergence of the video game to one brilliant inventor who started from scratch and decided it was time to invent something new.

Instead we should consider the early period, which we like to refer to as "the prehistory of the computer game," a period of experimentation, a period in which a number of people from a variety of backgrounds, whether stimulated by one another or not, made their own contribution to what would eventually become a new form of popular culture. We must remember that a number of cultural and scientific traditions had already prepared the ground for the development of the video game. There was the amusement industry with pinball machines and board games on the one hand, and the rapid development of computer technology on the other. In this section we will first say a few words on the early forerunners and then take a closer look at the three "godfathers" of the computer game.

The Forerunners: Willy Higinbotham, Game Traditions, and Computer Technology
Computer and *game* first went hand in hand in 1958, at the Brookhaven National Laboratory, a research institute of the American government. For the open day of this company, one of the engineers, Willy Higinbotham, proposed to do away with the traditional statistics and corporate presentations used each year and come up with something more exciting to show the visitors (Hunter, 2000). He converted an oscilloscope (a machine that transforms vibrations into a wavelike motion on a screen) into a kind of pinball game. A speck of light moved across the screen and with the help of two boxes with push buttons one could control the curve it followed. He considered his creation an abstract simulation of the game of tennis, and aptly named it *Tennis for Two*. He had not foreseen game aspects such as "who scores the point?" or "what is the score?" Higinbotham was not interested in the possible applications of his invention. He saw it as an attractive way to demonstrate the operation of a piece of technology, no more, no less. Subsequently, he did not patent his invention.

One of the interesting aspects of Higinbotham's creation was the interaction between player(s) and machine. He managed to make a scientific instrument attractive for a nonscientific audience, simply by obscuring its complexity and making it easy to manipulate. The interactive possibilities that he foresaw were closely related to the mechanical amusement tradition that already existed in his country in the form of pinball and slot machines. The popularity of such machines depended on the same principle: players got a limited amount of control (by operating several buttons or pulling an automatic arm), but the game could still go an unlimited number of ways (Yesterdayland, 2000). Higinbotham did not explicitly incorporate the aspect of reward (a second important element of such games) into his machine; he left this to the imagination of the players.

Steven Malliet and Gust de Meyer

This brings us to the second set of forerunners of the video game: the tradition of board games and children's games such as hide and seek or cops and robbers, in which (part of) reality is represented in a simplified, iconic way, and players are expected to use their imagination to play their part in this world. Those who play *Monopoly* are supposed to dive into the world of capitalism, and those playing *Stratego* will consider themselves generals for the duration of the game. In the early seventies, with the advent of *Dungeons and Dragons* (1974, created by Gary Gygax and Dave Arneson), an extreme variant of such games emerged: the so-called "fantasy role playing game." In those games, the players enter a wholly imaginary environment and work out the storyline with the help of several standard plots. Although at the time, already some text-based adventure games existed (e.g., *Star Trek*, 1967; *Hunt the Wumpus*, 1971), fantasy role playing games have exercised a considerable influence on the structure of a variety of future computer games. Aspects such as a complex object system, or the creation of a fantasy world governed by its own social and economic rules, have now become a standard ingredient in many console and computer games, and can be directly traced back to the rules described in the manuals of *Dungeons and Dragons* and its followers.

In essence, a video game is nothing more or less than a special kind of computer program. This automatically brings us to a third forerunner: the development of computer technology, which accelerated enormously in the 1940s and 1950s (LaMorte & Lilly, 1999). A number of important inventions, such as transistor memory in the late 1940s and the first chips in the late 1950s, resulted, in the early 1960s, in the early forerunners of today's computers. These machines were still bulky and expensive. By today's norms they had very limited storage and processing capacities, and were predominantly found in universities. Since those days, the technical foundations for computers have improved rapidly and this evolution is still going strong. Over the past forty years, the continuous development of computer technology has served as the driving force behind the ever-increasing sophistication of video games. Little wonder, then, that this force will serve as a red thread throughout our argument.

The Inventors: Steve Russell, Ralph Baer, or Nolan Bushnell?

When investigating the question of who should be considered the true inventor of the video game, three names pop up repeatedly: Steve Russell, Ralph Baer,

and Nolan Bushnell (Hunter, 2000; GameSpy Staff, 2002). A heated discussion will usually follow concerning which of the three made the most essential contribution and can consequently be considered the founding father. We do not consider it our task to answer the question here. We limit ourselves to briefly considering each of the three men, leaving it up to the reader to pick his or her favorite.

Steve Russell, the first of the three, was a student at the renowned Massachusetts Institute of Technology (MIT) in January 1962, when he developed *Spacewar* for the PDP-1 mainframes that were available there.[1] In contrast with his predecessor Higinbotham, he explicitly intended to create an application for entertainment (Hunter, 2002). Soon, many varieties of the game's code spread amongst universities across America. Technically speaking, *Spacewar* came down to the constant appearance and disappearance of flashes of light on the screen, comparable to some of today's screensavers. Russell's greatest merit was to incorporate a game element into this light show by making two of those specks look like spaceships, which could be controlled by two different players. The other specks were stars that figured merely as decoration. In the middle of the screen was a cross representing a black hole. The task of a player was twofold: to prevent your spaceship from crashing into the black hole, and to fire torpedoes to destroy your opponent before he was able to destroy you. Technically speaking, *Spacewar* can be seen as the first *computer game*, simply because it was the first "game" that was programmed on a "computer." Moreover, because the game contained both a simulation and an action element, it laid the foundation for a number of different genres that would follow in the 1970s and 1980s.

The second man on the list, Ralph Baer, came from a completely different background. When he introduced his innovations in 1966, he was a well-respected, forty-four-year-old engineer at an electronics company, Saunders Associates (Hunter, 2002). Baer, an immigrant from Nazi Germany, was intrigued by the possibilities of the medium of television, which had already entered the living rooms of some 40 million families across the United States. He designed a device that could be connected to his TV, which would allow him to play a kind of ping pong game on the screen. The game itself strongly resembled Willy Higinbotham's creation of almost a decade before, but contained a number of game elements that were missing in *Tennis for Two*. Baer did not stop there, and in 1967, he developed a new television game, this time a hockey simulation. In 1968, he even thought up a system that could bring his games to living rooms by cable, just like television programs. Cable companies did not fancy the idea, and, even though Baer managed to obtain no fewer than seventy-five patents, his plans were shelved for a couple of years (Hunter, 2002). Baer's innovative contributions did not involve the nature of computer games—even in those days the controlled movement of a ball or puck across a screen was nothing new—but they involved the possible applications that he foresaw for his games. He can be considered the founder of the in-home video game: his idea that computer games could penetrate the privacy of the home was proof of great vision.

The most famous, but without doubt also the most controversial, name on the list of founding fathers is Nolan Bushnell. When he was young, Bushnell was a fervent chess player and a gamer avant-la-lettre. He enjoyed Japanese thinking games such as *Go*, and he worked in an amusement park. In university he encountered *Spacewar* and used it as the basis for *Computer Space* (figure 2.1), a game he developed in 1970 (Jacobi, 1996; Hunter, 2002). As a game, *Computer Space* was not too innovative, but nevertheless it constituted breakthroughs in a number of areas. First of all, it was not a computer game for the mainframes at university, or a video game to play at home on the television, but a machine in the pinball tradition. Bushnell took advantage of the dramatic reduction in price and size of computer chips in the late 1960s and used them to market the first arcade videogame. Second, *Computer Space* introduced a practical, profit-oriented way of thinking that was unprecedented in the video games sector until then. Bushnell fitted his game with an extensive visual layout to make it more attractive, and he made no secret of the fact that the main purpose of this game was simply making money.

| **Figure 2.1** |
Computer Space (Nutting Associates, 1971): The first arcade game

Bushnell's strategy was less successful than expected; the instructions were too complicated, and the public massively ignored *Computer Space*. The idea of attracting players by means of a colourful closet and a range of simple controlls, was there, however, and it was Nolan Bushnell himself who brought it to perfection two years later. His new arcade game, *Pong*, was the simplest possible game and the instructions could hardly be misunderstood: "Avoid missing ball for high score," or, in other words, "no prior knowledge needed to enjoy the game." *Pong* was not the only ping pong game around at the time, but it was the first serious games hit, and it gave the go-ahead for a booming industry.

This game also made Nolan Bushnell's contribution to the development of videogames rather controversial, to say the least, as Ralph Baer recognized his own ping-pong game in *Pong* and sued Nolan Bushnell for copyright violation (Hunter, 2002). However, from a historical point of view, this dispute is of no great significance. It suffices to say that Bushnell managed to break ground that none of his predecessors had broken before. He managed to take video games out of the sphere of scientific research and bring them to the general public. His role in the evolution of video games is therefore comparable to the role of the Lumière brothers in the evolution of motion pictures. Technically speaking, Bushnell can be considered the founding father of the arcade video game.

The Birth of an Industry: 1973–1977

The mid-seventies, more specifically the years 1976–1977, are known as the time when America first massively fell for video games. Both the console market, based on the ideas of Ralph Baer, and the arcade market, following Nolan Bushnell's footsteps, took off and quickly realized excellent sales figures. This same period witnessed some important innovations, both technically and contentwise, which contributed to setting the standards for future platforms and genres. In this section we will take a closer look at the technical and economic aspects of both markets, and mention a number of important games to illustrate some major content-related innovations.

The Industry Develops Through Different Channels: Arcades versus Consoles

Arcades: Atari Against the Rest After a dispute with Nutting Associates, the firm that took care of the production and distribution of his *Computer Space*, Nolan

Bushnell decided that he no longer wished to be dependent on a third party to publish a game. Together with his business partner Ted Dabney, he established Atari (X, 2001b). They delineated well-considered and efficient policies, and quickly became the largest arcade manufacturers. The success of *Pong*, their first game in 1972, inspired many other companies to give the video games market a try and launch their own versions of the game. Due to, among other things, aggressive licensing politics, which contractually prohibited all Atari distributors to distribute machines of other companies, Bushnell and company managed to establish a quasi-monopoly around 1974, at which time their main competitors were small companies operating on a local scale. In 1976, perhaps fifteen companies were active on the arcade market, but on a national level only one had sales figures approaching Atari's, namely Midway, owned by Bally, a pinball producer (Brown, 1998). With his company operating at an ever-growing scale, Bushnell found himself forced to sell Atari to Warner in that same year (Seitz, 2001). By the end of 1977, Atari controlled about 70 percent of the coin-operated market in the United States.

The industry's growth between 1972 and 1978 went hand in hand with the evolution of the hardware of the platforms on which these arcades ran. Although games such as *Pong* and *Computer Space* were operationally still far from actual computers, some important innovations helped to close the gap around 1976. The game *Tank*, which was launched in 1974 by Kee Games (a daughter company of Atari), constituted a major technical breakthrough (Yesterdayland, 2000). It was the first game to use ROM chips to store graphics, making them far more accurate. The use of separate ROM chips for graphics can be seen as an early precedent of the graphics cards known today. Another milestone is the game *Gun Fight*, which was marketed by Midway in 1975. In this game, microprocessors replaced the cumbersome and sluggish chips that had been prevalent up to then (Yesterdayland, 2000). This considerably accelerated the processing of instructions. The game also introduced a number of peripheral devices, such as an early joystick and a number a fake guns, two devices that would become common gadgets in the console and arcade markets.

Home Consoles: Atari Cashes in on the Work of Others
At the end of this period, Atari also dominated the home console market, which built on Ralph Bear's ideas. This, however, turned out to be more time-consuming and difficult than taking over the arcade

market. Both technically and economically speaking, the home console had to come a long way between 1972 and 1978.

In the early 1970s, Ralph Baer's ideas were finally appreciated at their true value. Electronics giant Magnavox recognized the enormous potential, and bought a license from Baer for manufacturing a home console (Hunter, 2002). The result is the Odyssey, which came out in 1972. It is a simple device, which, like the arcades of the time, was far removed from the game computers we know today. It was a fully analogue system, which meant that the possibilities for image formation and game variety were rather limited (Brown, 1998). In addition, the difference between "console" and "game" did not exist yet: all possible games (meaning some twelve variations on the same ball and paddle theme) were programmed in the hardware itself. It was impossible to buy a new game and connect it to the Odyssey. A final limitation of the Odyssey was that it used only a fraction of the possibilities that the TV set had to offer: there was no sound, and the games were black and white. This last problem was overcome by introducing colorful plastic covers that could be placed over the screen. By today's standards, the Odyssey can be considered a marginal console at best. It was nonetheless quite popular and it took some time before new and better consoles were marketed. For this reason the arcades were initially the Odyssey's largest competitor.

In 1974, Atari took the plunge onto the home console market when it launched Home Pong, a console that did not differ greatly from the Odyssey. Other companies followed, resulting in a whole series of ball and paddle games that each offered a slight variation on the original concept: some introduce a digital console, some allow four players to play at once, others add color or sound to the game (Brown, 1998). It was not until the end of 1976 that a true turnaround came about with the introduction of two highly innovative new consoles: the Studio II by RCA and the Channel F by Fairchild. Both were so-called programmable consoles: the code of a game was not built into the hardware, but the consoles were "real" computers that listened to a language of predetermined instructions (Brown, 1998; Hunter, 2002). Using this language, programmers could develop games for these consoles and store the code on external data carriers. The Studio II and the Channel F introduced the cartridge system: separate data carriers (the cartridges), sold separately, that contained the game's source code and could be connected to the appropriate consoles. They also started a trend that would run as a red thread through-

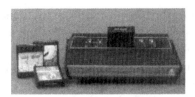

| Figure 2.2 |
The Atari VCS

out the history of home consoles: consoles are genuine computers, and each and every improvement in computer technology will almost directly influence the quality of the available games.

As we saw in the Ralph Baer–Nolan Bushnell conflict, and as we will see repeatedly throughout this chapter, it was not necessarily the technically most innovative console that would eventually have the largest impact. In 1977, when Atari launched its Atari 2600 (or Atari VCS; figure 2.2), which was quite similar to the Studio II and Channel F, the RCA and Fairchild machines, innovative as they were, were pushed to the background. Partly thanks to a range of ingenious games and partly thanks to strong management, the 2600 managed to leave its competitors far behind and enter the history books as the first modern home console (X, 2001a). All later consoles use a structure similar to the one used in 1977, but merely add refinements made possible by technological progress. Despite its name (VCS stands for Video Computer System), Atari's console was not an actual computer. There was no keyboard, and all peripheral devices were aimed at making games easier to play. The 2600, for example, was equipped with primitive joysticks and a number of turning buttons, specifically designed for ball and paddle games (X, 2001a; Brown, 1998).

The Contents: The Foundations for a Number of Genres
Largely due to limitations imposed by the hardware, most games in the 1970s were variations on the *Pong* concept, games in which players control a paddle and have to maneuver a ball as well as possible. As we will discuss later, this overproduction of ball and paddle games was largely responsible for the crisis that the industry faced in the late 1970s. The introduction of better chips opened the door for other, more innovative games. Some of the new games laid the foundation for genres that would become very big in the future. We will list the most important ones.

The 1974 game *Tank* constituted a major technical breakthrough. Contentwise too, this game introduced a number of innovations (Yesterdayland, 2000). Two players each control a tank in a maze littered with mines. The winner is the one who destroys the other or forces him to drive onto a mine. Both graphically and game playwise, *Tank* meant a large step forward: the tanks no longer looked like a collection of dots (as in *Computer Space* and its many relatives) or abstract geometrical figures (like the rectangles in *Pong*) but they were well-outlined, solid figures. Moreover, *Tank* introduced the "kill-or-be-killed" element that would return in a range of later games. Danger was lurking behind every corner and the players had to think fast and efficiently to finish the game successfully. *Tank* is the forefather of the many "shoot 'em ups" that were to be produced in the years to come.

As far as navigation and screen set-up is concerned *Tank* used a number of principles that Atari had been working on for *Got'cha*, a game that was produced a year earlier and proved highly innovative, despite its simplicity. *Got'cha* is classified as the first "maze game" and is considered the main predecessor of subsequent classics such as *Pac-Man* (Yesterdayland, 2000). It was a two-person game that was based on the "cat-and-mouse" principle: player number one, the "catcher," had to get a hold of the other, and player number two, the "runner," had to prevent this from happening. Both players were able to move horizontally and vertically through a maze on the screen. This possibility to move in two directions already existed in *Computer Space*, but was a large step forward from games such as *Pong*.

Also in the genre of sports simulations Atari came up with a number of innovative games: *World Cup Football* (1974) laid the foundation for a whole generation of soccer games, and *Grand Track 10* and *Grand Track 20* (both 1974) were milestones in the development of racing simulators. Other games worth mentioning are *Space Race* (1973, again by Atari), a forerunner of the subsequent platform and obstacle games, and *Death Race* (1976), by Midway. This last game was a racing simulator, with the added bonus that drivers could score additional points by running over live creatures (the "Gremlins") as they crossed the road. *Death Race* was the first game that startled parents, politicians, the media, and other authorities because of its explicitly violent character.

1978–1982: A First Crisis Awakens the Industry

The year 1978 was a turning point in the history of the computer game. For the first time, the young industry was not making any progress and many companies were suffering heavy losses. Rather than being the end, this crisis created space for a number of creative new-comers, predominantly from Japan, guiding the video games industry into its golden years.

Crisis

Christmas of 1977 meant the beginning of an unexpected end for many companies in the games industry. There was a spectacular drop in games sales, right when growth had been expected. The home console market was hit hardest, but the arcade market did not go unscathed. In 1978–1979 a number of important players were forced to seriously reduce, or even stop, the production of their consoles: the Channel F disappeared in 1978, the Studio II in 1979, and the Odyssey slowly passed into oblivion (De Meyer, Malliet & Verbruggen, 2001, p. 58). The only player that (more or less) managed to survive was Atari. Even though the 2600 shared in some of the blows (the number of consoles sold was still growing, but games sold rather poorly), Warner's daughter company managed to maintain itself thanks to her strong position in the arcade market (X, 2001a).

A second reason why Atari managed to survive the crisis while all its competitors got into rather serious trouble, was related to the nature of the crisis. The drop in sales figures was a result of the state the market was in: there was an oversupply of consoles (hardware), and a shortage of innovative games (software). During this period Atari was the company that introduced the most creative games. It was therefore less vulnerable to the public's decreasing interest. The crisis did, however, affect Atari's dominance in the market as space was created for new, more innovative companies. This helped to make the period of 1979–1982 one of unprecedented bloom and creativity.

The Japanese Invasion

Until 1978, the Americans dominated the world of video games. Then things changed. Many Japanese companies, which had long been active in different sectors in their own geographical area, started to focus on computer games. They soon managed to greatly influence the games scene in the United States and Europe by introducing a number of technical and content-related innovations that set new, lasting standards.

It is not a coincidence that this impulse for innovation came from Japan (Costello, 1991, pp. 114–117; Sheff, 1993, pp. 12–33). For one, Japan had a long tradition of game machines, and pachinko, the Japanese version of the pinball machine, was, to put it mildly, wildly popular. Furthermore, during the mid 1970s a

considerable market for video games had developed, initially by importing arcade machines from America, and later, when it became apparent that additional variations on the *Pong* concept did not really pose a threat to the pachinko machines, by coming up with new games. Around 1976, there were already many games companies, the most important ones being Taito and Namco. Both of these companies gained a firm foothold in the United States during the late 1970s, early 1980s, and were soon followed by fellow-Japanese companies such as Nintendo, Universal, Konami, Sega, and Tehkan.

Taito: Space Invaders On June 5, 1978, Taito, a Japanese company established by Belorussian immigrant Michael Kogan, released *Space Invaders*. The game caused a true mania and was the first computer game to become more popular than the local pachinkos (Poole, 2000, pp. 33–34). American company Midway noticed the enormous potential of the game and bought a license to manufacture the game and distribute it on the western market. Here too, *Space Invaders* was a great success. Already in 1981, the game had swallowed more than four billion coins, an average of one game per inhabitant of the earth.

The success of *Space Invaders* can, for a large part, be explained by the nature of the game itself. It contained a number of elements that were completely new, or that were a perfection of techniques that had been peripheral beforehand. First of all the game used a narrative structure, albeit a primitive one (Yesterdayland, 2000). Referring to the body of science fiction ideas that existed, a simple story was told of a swarm of aliens that came to conquer the earth and it was up to the player to stop them from getting a stronghold on this planet. The player was given a mission, which created the feeling of being the hero in a great adventure.

In addition, the aspect of reward took a large step forward. *Space Invaders* was a game without an end (Poole, 2000, p. 37). When the player had neutralized the first swarm of aliens, a second would come that moved slightly faster than the one before, and so on. The rhythm of the game would build to the point that it became impossible for the player to keep up and the game would stop. There was no upper limit to the number of points that a player could score, and as a result players could keep on playing indefinitely, always finding a new challenge in having to do better than the time before.

Third, *Space Invaders* used sound in a functional way: the rhythmical bass-based soundtrack, which sped up with the rhythm of the game, was an integral part of the game experience (Poole, 2000, p. 36). Before *Space Invaders*, sounds in video games had generally been used as padding or a subordinate bonus, but afterwards game developers could no longer afford to ignore this aspect.

The success of *Space Invaders* invited other companies to market their own copies of the game, which were, more often than not, cases of genuine piracy (Yesterdayland, 2000). Europe, for example, witnessed the introduction of such games as *UFO Invaders* or *Space Commanders*. The practice of copying or reproducing the source code of a game already existed in the early years of the videogame business (e.g., the different *Space War* or *Pong* clones in the 1960s and 1970s). It was, however, not until the 1980s that piracy assumed such dramatic proportions that enormous amounts of money would disappear into the illegal circuit (De Meyer, Malliet & Verbruggen, 2001, pp. 145–147).

Namco: Pac-Man and the Rise of the Maze Game
Space Invaders unleashed a true flood of space war games, which would only be counterweighed some two years later. Again the answer came from Japan; it was a game that depended more on friendliness and humor than on violence and threat and it was called *Pac-Man*. The game, which was developed in 1980 by a team of eight at Namco in Japan, was launched in 1981. In that year alone, more than a hundred thousand *Pac-Man* arcade machines were sold (De Meyer, Malliet & Verbruggen, 2001, p. 138). The success of *Pac-Man* can be explained both from a content perspective and from a social standpoint.

With respect to content, *Pac-Man* was the perfection of the maze game genre. By using bright colors, funny names for the opponents, happy background music, and animation breaks between the levels, the developers wanted to create a feel-good atmosphere (Jacobi, 1996). The game was relatively simple: a pizza-like figure, called Pac-Man, enters a maze in which he has to eat as many little balls as possible. He is being chased by a number of ghosts that do not try to kill him, but merely send him back to the starting point. Pac-Man could walk in four directions only, so controls were quite easy.

Pac-Man entered history books as the first game that managed to draw the female population into arcades (Herz, 1997, p. 132). Previously only teenage boys had populated the arcades, satisfying their macho impulses by playing the role of a trigger-happy space explorer. With its cartoonlike contents, *Pac-Man* took

a different route and opened doors that had previously remained closed for video games. The game was not only found in dark arcades, but soon also made its way into more neutral surroundings such as restaurants and bars. An entire media hype came into being surrounding Namco's ball-eating creature. Pac-Man appeared on t-shirts, in newspapers, and on television; he could be found on snack wrappers, lunch boxes, and plastic bags; he got little brothers and sisters, uncles and cousins; and he became the hero in innumerable follow-up games. Pac-Man became the first star of the video game era, giving the industry a new, less violent image (Poole, 2000, pp. 159–160).

Nintendo, Universal, and Sega: The Rise of the Climbing Games Space games here, maze games there: the early 1980s seemed to offer something for everyone. Two other Japanese firms, which refused to market clones and derivatives of games that already existed, disagreed. Sega and Nintendo have always been known to impulsively go their own way, and this was already obvious in the early 1980s, when they developed another new genre: the climbing or obstacle game.

Climbing games built on the theme of maze games, but focused on different aspects. First of all, players did not just wander around a maze, but had to go from start to finish in as little time as possible. Often they would start at the left bottom of the screen and end at the top right. Spatially there was a clear direction and line in these games. On their way from the bottom to the top, players would collect points, but these were secondary to the final goal of reaching the finish alive. This usually came down to trying to dodge all kinds of obstacles (ranging from ladders and barrels to speeding cars) encountered on the way up. The first climbing games were based on principles of reward similar to those in *Space Invaders*: upon reaching the end of one level, the game starts anew, but with a slightly increased level of difficulty.

Space Panic, the first climbing game to enter the market, was introduced by Universal (another Japanese arcade manufacturer) in 1981. The game introduced a screen composed of platforms, scaffoldings, and ladders, and combined these with the alien-theme of *Space Invaders* (Hunter, 2000). By far the most famous and influential climbing game, though, was Nintendo's *Donkey Kong*, which also came out in 1981. *Donkey Kong* set the norm that would be copied by numerous imitators: using a screen composition similar to *Space Panic*, the manufacturers proved to be clever in presenting a wide variety of obstacles that ranged anywhere from being "quite possible" to being "too hard" (Yesterdayland, 2000). The game also introduced two figures, one virtual and the other human, that would return to play an important role in the history of the computer game. The first, the virtual figure, was the main character of the game. Initially his name was just "Jumpman," but later on he would be called "Mario," and reappear in a large number of highly innovative games. The second, the human, was the developer of the game: Shigeru Miyamoto. Miyamoto, an industrial designer by training, had been working at the development department of Nintendo since 1977. He was put in charge of the development of a new game in 1981, and *Donkey Kong* was the result. The success of this game (which meant the breakthrough of Nintendo on the American arcade market) considerably strengthened Miyamoto's position within Nintendo and gave him a large degree of creative freedom (Sheff, 1993, pp. 52–53). The games he developed in the 1980s, as we will show later, became some of the most essential video-games ever.

A final important climbing game was *Frogger*, developed by Konami in 1981, and distributed in the United States by Sega. The game differed from the usual ladders-and-scaffoldings concept (as had been elaborated in games such as *Donkey Kong* and all its clones) in that it worked vertically rather than diagonally. A frog, positioned at the bottom of the screen, had to get to the top as quickly as possible, running into a variety of obstacles on the way, such as roads and rivers. Altogether *Frogger* had a more realistic touch than most other climbing games, due to the more "natural" environment it imitated (Yesterdayland, 2000).

During this period Sega introduced another important game: *Zaxxon* (1982). *Zaxxon*, a space war game, introduced a new way to construct the screen that would later become very popular in god games and adventure games: the use of the isometric perspective (Poole, 2000, p. 133; Yesterdayland, 2000). We will discuss the isometric perspective further.

America's Reaction

In the meantime, things had not come to a standstill in the United States. The most important games companies, with Atari in the lead, realized that producing good and innovative games had gradually become the norm and a must for companies that aspired to commercial success. We shall see that two strategies became popular: the Atari strategy, which implied coming up with better games yourself, and the Midway strategy, which consisted of importing and distributing the more successful games from Japan.

Atari: Asteroids, Adventure, and Battlezone Following the disappointing years of 1978 and 1979, Atari became very productive again in 1980. It managed to produce a number of influential games and, just as a number of the Japanese companies mentioned above, laid the foundations for some influential techniques and genres.

The first one was *Adventure*, a game developed in 1979 for the 2600. Though visually rather primitive (a king, for example, was depicted by a crown, just as in chess), it was the first adventure game that used graphics, instead of being text-only (Jacobi, 1996). With respect to the narrative, the games followed the traditional quest-structure: a player is placed in an imaginary world and has to complete a task. In this game the player's task is to find a golden goblet and return it to the castle of the king, without being killed by one of the three dragons. Both the search motive and the narrative structure became prototypical of the organization of any adventure game. It is therefore not surprising that the whole genre was named after the first game in its kind.

On the arcade market, Atari scored some successes with a number of games that were not really innovative (i.e., closely related to *Computer Space* and *Space Invaders*), but contained a number of interesting novelties. *Asteroids*, a *Computer Space* clone, was the first to provide the possibility of breaking through the flat enclosure of the screen: the spaceship could disappear on one side of the screen and reappear on the other and instead of being a rectangular plane the screen represented a cylinder-like space (Poole, 2000, p. 130). *Lunar Lander*, a game in which the player had to land a spaceship on the moon's surface as safely as possible, relied more on strategic thinking than on speed and firepower, thus becoming somewhat of an odd-one-out in the world of space games (Yesterdayland, 2000).

In 1981, Atari marketed one of the graphically most forward-looking games of all times, *Battlezone*. *Battlezone* introduced an image processing technique that would, in the 3D era, come to be a kind of Holy Grail. Because a discussion of the visual principles used in Battlezone is most appropriate when we discuss the games of the 1990s, we will postpone further analysis of this game until later.

Midway: Imports from Japan Whereas Atari mainly invested in producing new games to compete with the Japanese, Midway took another turn. Instead of com-

peting with the Japanese firms, it made licensing deals with them, becoming a manufacturer and distributor of Japanese products. In the 1970s, this method had already proven quite successful on a number of occasions (*Gun Fight*, licensed by Taito, being the most important example), but from *Space War* on it became clear that this way of working could be highly profitable. Midway's name is often associated with games such as *Galaxian* (1980) that had initially been developed by Japanese companies (Namco in this case).

Williams and Defender: Horizontal Scrolling In the early 1980s, a new manufacturer entered the American arcade market: the Chicago-based Williams company. Just like Bally, this company had been active (and highly innovative) in the pinball market for many years. Encouraged by the success of games such as *Pong*, Williams entered the arcade market in the 1970s. They remained a second rate player until early 1981, when they came to the foreground with a game called *Defender*, which was developed by their own staff (under the supervision of Eugene Jarvis).

Defender differed from the average space battle game. In contrast with *Space Invaders* and its many relatives, the action did not take place vertically, but horizontally (Poole, 2000, pp. 130–131). The player would fly his spaceship from left to right (or vice versa) above a moon landscape to shoot as many aliens as possible. An important novelty was that the enclosure of the screen was opened; the world of the game was no longer limited to the world that one could see on the screen. When the player reached the side of the screen, the landscape would move, allowing the spaceship to fly to places that were initially invisible. At the top of the screen was a map, keeping the player informed about the location of the spaceship in the entirety of this virtual world.

Where *Asteroids* already suggested that off-screen action was possible (by having the spaceship disappear and reappear on opposite ends of the screen), *Defender* was the first game to actually use it (Poole, 2000, p. 131). To use this navigation technique for this purpose was as innovative as the principle itself. *Defender* was the first game to use "scrolling": the landscape zoomed by the spaceship, making the movement of the spaceship more pronounced. Scrolling became the video game equivalent of panning movements in film, and proved to by highly suitable for games that required lots of speed and action on the screen.

Just like *Lunar Lander*, *Defender* is an example of how, at that point in time, games moved away from

the principle of "the faster you move and shoot, the more points you score." Strategic thinking became more and more important. The aliens in *Defender*, for example, were equipped with a limited form of AI (Artificial Intelligence) and there were a number of different tactics that players could use to eliminate certain enemies as efficiently as possible.

Cinematronics and Space War: The Level System In addition to Williams, another American firm came into being: Cinematronics, from El Cajon, California, near San Diego. In 1977, before *Space Invaders* had even been launched, Cinematronics had already scored a hit with a space war game, aptly named *Space Wars* (not to be confused with *Spacewar*, Steve Russell's first game). Cinematronics owed its success largely to the original make-up of the game's cabinet, and thus to the way the machine was presented visually in the arcade halls. But contentwise, too, *Space Wars* offered some novelties (Yesterdayland, 2000). The game was equipped with different degrees of difficulty: there were separate levels for beginners, experienced players, and experts, which helped to attract a wider range of players. Just like *Battlezone*, *Space Wars* used a vector beam screen instead of the regular pixel-based raster screen.[2] This technique allowed the lines to be drawn much more smoothly, but it limited the use of colors.

Content Innovations: The State of Affairs
The hectic description of innovative games presented in the previous paragraphs points to a number of general tendencies. We can say that the period discussed above is dominated by three different genres: maze games (after the model set by *Pac-Man*), climbing and obstacle games (á la *Donkey Kong*), and space wars (the *Space Invader* genre). Having noted this, it is remarkable that almost all genres known today already existed in a prototypical form in the early 1980s.

Grand Prix Monaco (Sega, 1979) and *Pole Position* (Namco, 1982) are examples of simulation games that managed to break through in the arcades. In the console market a number of soccer and basketball simulations did well. Simulation games became more and more realistic due to increased computing power and the use of ever-improving content-related techniques, such as the use of perspective to display depth on the screen (Herz, 1997, pp. 29–30). The genre of the graphical adventure game got off the ground, in the wake of games such as *Adventure* (Atari, 1978), that was a logical succession to traditional text-based, narrative computer games. A number of titles followed that, despite their limited graphics and narratives, managed to find an opening in the console and (especially) the game computer market. We should remember *Wizard of Wor* (Midway, 1981) and *Venture* (Exidy, 1981), which both incorporated the adventure theme into a maze game. This period also saw the rise of the role-playing game. A number of computer games were created, based on the rules of *Dungeons and Dragons*, with *Akalabeth* (California Pacific, 1979), and its successors, the first two games in the *Ultima* series (California Pacific, 1980, and Sierra, 1982) as key examples. Also worth mentioning are the games in the Epyx *Dunjonquest* series: *The Temple of Apshai* (1979), *Hellfire Warrior* (1980), or *The Curse of Ra* (1982). Finally we should make notice of a founding father in the genre of thinking games (*Qix*, by Taito in 1981) and a number of primitive "first-person shooters" (*Battlezone* and *Tempest*, both by Atari in 1981).

It is interesting to see how these different genres each found their way into different market segments. We already mentioned that adventure games scored well on the home markets. Arcades turned out to be suitable for action and simulation games, whereas maze and climbing games were predominantly found on handhelds.

Technical Innovations: The Evolution of the Home Console and the Rise of Handhelds

Home Consoles: Atari, Mattel, and Coleco In the period 1977–1982 a whole range of consoles saw daylight that were similar to the Atari VCS. With the exception of the Mattel Intellivision, they were eight-bit systems that used higher screen resolutions and faster internal connections to graphically outperform Atari's console.

The first system that truly attacked Atari's monopoly position was Mattel's Intellivision in 1979 (figure 2.3). Intellivision stood for intelligent televi-

sion, a name that the console, graphically speaking, absolutely lived up to. The console was built around a sixteen-bit processor and contained a much more complicated chip structure than any of the other game computers and consoles of the time (Brown, 1998).

The launch of the Intellivision was followed by a period of fierce competition between Mattel and Atari (Brown, 1998). This battle was fought both on the hardware and the software front. Both companies would regularly introduce new technical gadgets to give their respective machines the competitive edge, simultaneously trying to produce as many quality games as possible. Atari had an extensive arcade department at its disposal and managed to convert a large number of games for use on the 2600. Mattel followed a different route. It specialized in sports simulations, a genre in which its superior graphical capacities truly paid off, and made lots of deals with sports clubs and associations (such as the NBA) to use the names of the players and teams in their games.

In June 1982, a third competitor entered the battlefield: the Colecovision by Coleco (figure 2.3). The console, which was an eight-bit system, was presented as being less mainstream than its two competitors and managed to obtain a solid market share by converting a number of lesser-known, but nonetheless good arcade games (Brown, 1998). In 1983, Coleco even sold more consoles than the other two companies. In 1982, Atari introduced its new console: the Atari 5200. This system contained a number of improvements compared to the 2600, without truly causing a graphical revolution.

During the early 1980s Atari, Mattel, and Coleco dominated the console market and they did not tolerate much competition from others. The story of the Channel F 2 (the successor of the revolutionary 1976 system) was typical of the situation: again Fairchild's console did not manage to get a grip on the market, and it disappeared as suddenly as it had appeared.

| Figure 2.3 |
Atari's competitors: The Intellivision (left) and the Colecovision (right)

Handhelds The honor of having produced the first-ever handheld goes to toy manufacturer Milton Bradley (MB) for producing *Simon* in 1974. *Simon* was actually a cross between a true video game (controlled by a computer program) and a regular mechanical toy. The game consisted of a platform with four buttons, each button producing a specific sound. The player could (re)produce melodies by pressing a certain combination of buttons in a certain rhythm.

A few years later, Mattel marketed a number of handheld sports simulations. These miniature systems were graphically greatly inferior to the consoles of the time and the available batteries could only guarantee fifteen minutes of playing pleasure. Owing to these two factors, handhelds had a rather slow start in the late 1970s.

In 1980, Nintendo started its "Game & Watch" series, causing the great turnaround for handhelds. Inspired by the miniaturization of calculators, the Japanese company used LCD screens that allowed the device to be kept small. Although the first Game & Watch games used only one screen, there were two screens after 1982. Although Nintendo ran into similar problems as Mattel several years earlier (most importantly the still limited graphical capacity), it managed to create a market for its product for a number of reasons. The Game & Watch series did not, at first, aim to produce graphically challenging games such as sports simulations, but marketed adaptations of climbing and obstacle games. Nintendo marketed these games as the cheap and handy counterpart of the expensive consoles that were sometimes difficult to control. It was largely this positioning that gave the handhelds a big push in the right direction (Sheff, 1993, pp. 110–112). The biggest successes in the Game & Watch series were a number of conversions of *Donkey Kong* and cartoons such as *Mickey Mouse* and *Popeye*.

Game Computers: Apple, Commodore, and the Rest What the 1960s had been for computers in general, the 1970s were for the *personal* computer. As chips became ever smaller and cheaper, it became possible to market compact computers for a reasonable price (LaMorte & Lilly, 1999). Additionally, companies such as IBM finalized techniques such as the floppy disk system. In the 1970s, IBM as well as MITS[3] launched their first "personal computers" (the term PC was introduced in 1981, before which these machines had been referred to as *microcomputers*). For the evolution of video games, however, two other companies that brought out their own microcomputers were of great importance: Apple and Commodore.

Steve Jobs, a friend and former colleague of Nolan Bushnell, and Steve Wozniak established Apple in 1976 (Hunter, 2002). That same year saw the marketing of their first microcomputer, the Apple I. Between 1976 and 1983, as many as five different computers were launched, the Apple II becoming most popular (Patterson, 2000). Distinguishing themselves from other microcomputers thanks to their graphical capacities, Apple computers were highly suitable as a platform for video games. The most famous Apple games of the time were adventure games such as the *Zork* and *Ultima* series.

Commodore, a company that originally produced typewriters and calculators, produced a series of microcomputers during the late 1970s and early 1980s. Like Apple computers, they were user-friendly and relatively inexpensive. In scientific circles, Commodore computers were considered inferior machines, and, just like Apple, Commodore sold most computers to a gamer public. Commodore also produced a whole sequence of computers, most importantly the PET (1977), the VIC-20 (1981) and the Commodore 64 (1982) (X, 2002a). On the games market they scored with conversions of hits such as *Frogger*, *Pac-Man*, and *Battlezone*. Because Commodore managed to offer good visual quality for a relatively low price, it reached a large public and positioned itself as a counterpart to the expensive consoles, just like the handhelds.

At the time, microcomputers offered a number of advantages over consoles. Although all machines were 8-bit systems, the Apple and Commodore machines had somewhat more processing power than the consoles produced by Atari, Mattel, and Coleco. Additionally, they offered broader functionality. Many youngsters were introduced to the world of computers and programming languages by writing their first simple computer programs for the C-64 or the Apple II. Consequently, it is not a great surprise that certain console manufacturers tried to enter the home computer market. With the Odyssey II, Magnavox was the first to market a console with a keyboard, partly closing the gap between the two formats (Brown, 1998). It was, however, still a specialized gaming console, and it could not be considered a real computer. Atari, on the other hand, developed an entire series of machines with their own operating systems that would run applications in addition to games. Among them were the Atari 400 and the Atari 800 (both 1979) (Brown, 1998). In the early 1980s, a number of improved versions followed, namely the Atari 600 XL and the Atari 1200 XL. Although the Atari sequence and the Odyssey II were responsible for decent sales figures, they never posed a serious threat to the popular consoles and game computers of the time.

Innovations in the Industry: The Declaration of Independence of Developers

In the early period of video game history, companies such as Atari and Magnavox took care of all aspects of the development of a game, from conception to distribution. Throughout the 1970s and especially during the 1980s, this situation changed. We already indicated that many Japanese companies relied on American distributors to run their operations overseas. Companies such as Midway are examples of the gradual disconnection of production and distribution.

This period witnessed a remarkable increase in the number of independent developers who produced games for a specific format and marketed these games without any involvement of the hardware manufacturer. The most famous example is Activision, a company that was established by a number of programmers that left Atari with a thorough knowledge of the programming language for the Atari 2600. They developed games for the 2600 and marketed them without any Atari involvement (Hunter, 2000). Another example is Imagic, established by former Mattel employees that developed games for the VCS and the Intellivision.

Before long, distributors, console manufacturers, and developers started to collaborate. Each of the three parties benefited from a quick and efficient division of labor and exchange of information. Developers needed the technical specifications of the different consoles, distributors needed a license for using and distributing the source codes, and the console manufacturers saw the economic value of their console rise with the increased availability of good games. In the long run, this change in the market structure was to have a positive influence on the games industry as a whole.

1983–1989: A Second Crisis Guides the Industry into the Nintendo Era

Early in 1983, not even five years after the first crisis, the industry went into a second recession. This crisis was more radical than the previous one, as it was deeply rooted in the 1982 market situation. Its effects had far-reaching consequences for the structure of the different market segments. Despite the economic shift, technological progress continued, however, and genres that had taken shape in the years before were developed further.

1983–1985: Crisis

In the mid 1980s, the industry was faced with a large setback: sales figures went down from $3 billion in 1982 to $2 billion in 1983, and made a free fall in the years 1984 ($800 million) and 1985 ($100 million) (De Meyer, Malliet & Verbruggen, 2001, p. 58). In three years' time, turnover went down by 96 percent, to a level below that of 1979. The crisis was due to the overproduction of software, rather than to the overproduction of hardware (as in 1978). Too many games were available. The console market especially contributed greatly to this problem, as Atari, Mattel, and Coleco were trying to compete by spewing out as many games as possible. The market was flooded with too many average games and too many poor variations on the same concept, and the public massively lost interest in computer games. Certain companies responded to the crisis by dumping their games at extremely low prices, causing a domino effect that would not come to a standstill until 1986.

Again a large number of companies ran into serious problems. The games industry faced some hectic years characterized by takeovers, changes in corporate structure, disputes, and eventually the rise of a new superpower.

Mattel's games department was taken over by Odd-Lot Trading, a company specialized in second-hand trade, and was renamed Intellivision Inc. Toy manufacturers Milton Bradley (MB) and Hasbro, both active in the arcade market, fused, and swallowed Coleco in 1988. Warner sold 60 percent of Atari's arcade department to Namco, one of its competitors, and 75 percent of its console and computer department to Jack Traniel, the former CEO of Commodore. Corporate disputes were a frequent phenomenon: in 1982, Coleco sued Atari for monopoly formation. Some time later, Mattel did the same, also accusing Atari of stealing trade secrets from Mattel employees. In turn, Atari sued its former employee Nolan Bushnell, for breaking past agreements. And finally Coleco, Atari, and Nintendo started fighting over the rights to produce *Donkey Kong* for game computers (De Meyer, Malliet & Verbruggen, 2001, pp. 67–68).

The situation stabilized around 1986. Turnover gradually started to climb again and several market segments began to show a new structure. The big winner was Nintendo, the company that had already scored big with *Donkey Kong* in the early 1980s. In the second half of the 1980s, Nintendo would be the absolute leader in the console and handheld market (Selnow, 1987, pp. 23–24).

The Console Market: Nintendo Dominates, Sega and Atari Compete

Nintendo: The Famicom, the NES, and Shigeru Miyamoto Not paying any heed to the general malaise in the United States, Nintendo put a new console on the market in 1983: the Famicom. It was another eight-bit system, but thanks to its separate processor for graphics, it meant a large step forward with respect to image processing. In Japan, the console soon became a big hit. The success was largely due to a game called *Mario Bros.*, which (re)wrote some of the rules of how a good console game had to be put together (Sheff, 1993, pp. 36–54).

Shigeru Miyamoto, the man who had been responsible for *Donkey Kong*, also developed *Mario Bros.* The game had the same main character as *Donkey Kong*, a plumber called Mario, who was now forced to share the spotlight with his brother Luigi. Mario quickly became a true video game star, just like Pac-Man a few years earlier. He became the figurehead of Nintendo and everything the company stood for. In contrast with Pac-Man, Mario was not an abstract disc, but an actual person with a family and a job. His appearance was inspired by cartoons in the Japanese manga tradition, giving Mario a high cuteness factor that helped set Nintendo's reputation as the video game equivalent of Disney (Horwitz & Miller, 2001).

As a game, *Mario Bros.* leaned heavily on the existing climbing and obstacle games, such as *Donkey Kong* and *Joust* (1982, Williams). Similar to those games, the players would start at the bottom of the screen and would gradually climb to the highest of a number of platforms. The game could also be played in multiplayer mode: two players each controlled one of the two brothers and they had to cooperate to finish the game. Furthermore *Mario Bros.* used a new reward system: instead of playing the same game over and over again at ever-increasing speeds, the players would enter new levels. Upon reaching the end of a screen, they had to start again at the bottom, but in a slightly different setup: new opponents, new obstacles, sometimes even a new goal. The level system was still rather rudimentary, but in the years to come it would develop into a fixed ingredient in many games in the platform and obstacle genre.

This brings us to the next game in the Mario sequence, *Super Mario Bros.* (1985), also developed by Shigeru Miyamoto. The game made optimal use of the Famicom and was much more complex than the first Mario game. It became one of the most essential platform games ever. *Super Mario Bros.* combined techniques that up to that point had only been used separately in specific genres. The game also realized Shigeru Miyamoto's vision of the computer game as an interactive cartoon.

The level system was taken to new heights as *Super Mario Bros.* consisted of no fewer than eight worlds, spread out over thirty-two levels. The game's movements were both horizontal and vertical: Mario moved from left to right (using the scrolling technique used in the space war games), but at the same time he had to climb all kinds of platforms, pillars, hills, and the like. During his search for the princess he would run into a wide scope of opponents (each of a different species, name, and intelligence) and he could eat certain "power-ups" to increase in strength. The highly detailed background had, up to that point, occurred mainly in simulation games.

In 1986, *Super Mario Bros.* was the game that managed to revive the American games industry. This year saw the release of the Famicom in the United States under the name of Nintendo NES, and the accompanying large-scale advertisement campaign surrounding Mario caused the public to run back to the stores to buy video games in large numbers. The NES was a true hype, making Nintendo the biggest player on the video games market for the next five years (Sheff, 1993, pp. 139–150).

In Nintendo's Footsteps: Atari Licks Its Wounds, Sega Gets a Foot in the Door With *Super Mario Bros.*, Nintendo not only created a very influential game, but also laid the foundation for a completely new business model (Sheff, 1993, p. 67). Due to the growing demand for NES games, and the increased complexity of the games, it became impossible for Nintendo to be responsible for the development of all of its games. This resulted in greater cooperation between console owners and developers. Thanks to the immense popularity of the NES, Nintendo was in quite a favorable negotiating position, the result being that whoever wanted to develop a game for the NES was not allowed to do business with any other companies for the duration of their agreement. In addition, there was Nintendo's policy to give the highest priority to the quality of the games produced, rather than to the number of games produced. Nintendo's name had to be a guarantee for good games, and consequently this company did not walk into the same trap as its predecessors Atari, Mattel, and Coleco had done.

The "big three" of the beginning of the decade had a hard time recovering from the crisis and never managed to step out of the shadow of the NES. The successor of the Intellivision, the INTV III came onto the market, and although it accounted for considerable sales figures (in 1986, it registered more than $6 million worldwide), it wasn't able to step out of the shades of Nintendo (Brown, 1998). In 1984, Coleco stopped the production of the Colecovision and entered the game computer market, albeit with little success (Brown, 1998). Atari was the only one of the three that managed to keep up with the pace of its Japanese counterparts, even though it was only a shadow of the superpower it was in the 1970s. The Atari 7800 was a console that was technically comparable to the NES, but contentwise, Atari completely lost track. It kept on bombarding the market with old arcade conversions and did not manage to appeal to the new, young crowd that Nintendo had managed to reach (Brown, 1998).

Nintendo's biggest competitor turned out to be another upcoming company, called Sega. This Japanese arcade-king became involved in the American console market in 1986, when it launched the Sega Master System: another 8-bit system, which was technically slightly superior to the NES (X, 2002b). Sega had to content itself with a second place, though, as the best game developers already had exclusive agreements with Nintendo, forcing Sega to score with games from their own arcade department.

Handhelds: The GameBoy Revolution

On the handheld market, Nintendo's dominance was even more absolute. The company had already been the biggest player with the Game & Watch series, but caused a true revolution in 1989 when they launched the GameBoy. The GameBoy was for the handheld what the Channel F and the Intellivision had been for the console: it introduced the cartridge system and greatly increased the graphical possibilities of the format (X, 2002b). Technically, the GameBoy was the first true "handheld game computer" and it used the same chip structure that is still found in today's handhelds.

Paradoxically, it was a very simple game called *Tetris* (developed in 1985 by Russian mathematician Alexei Pajitnov) that brought about the breakthrough of the GameBoy. After a legal battle that dragged on for several months, Nintendo obtained the rights to develop this game for its handheld, and used *Tetris* as the top game for the GameBoy (Jacobi, 1996; Sheff, 1993,

pp. 174–192). Tetris went on to become one of the most popular video games of all time. This was a great surprise, because it deviated in all possible ways from what would be considered a "hip" game. To explain the success, a psychological theory was developed that claimed that the game satisfied the fundamental human need to create order in a world full of chaos. Furthermore, *Tetris* proved that a scoring system could greatly contribute to the attractiveness of a computer game, and that complexity and violence are not necessary ingredients of a good game. Whatever the case may be, *Tetris* meant the breakthrough of the puzzle game, a genre that had existed for years, but had never been considered a fully fledged complement of the climbing games or space wars.

Game Computers and Adventure Games

Initially, game computers had been considered an important cause for the crisis that occurred in the mid 1980s. Graphically they were more powerful, they had a broader functionality, and their price was comparable to that of the better consoles. The argument was that PCs were inherently better than consoles and therefore it was pointless to buy one. If we look at the second half of the 1980s, however, we see that game computers and consoles simply developed along different routes, rather than interfering with each other.

Especially after the arrival of the Amiga (Commodore, 1986), the Macintosh (Apple, 1984), and a whole sequence of IBM PCs (1981, 1983, 1985), personal computers were indeed ahead of the consoles of the time with respect to processing capacity (LaMorte & Lilly, 1999; Brown, 1998). The games that helped make these computers so popular, however, differed from the typical console games. During the 1980s, PCs turned out to be more suitable for games built up around a story requiring a lot of memory activity and controlled by keyboard or mouse.

"Keep Searching": Adventures, Quests, and Rambles

The honor of having thought up the first graphically controlled adventure game goes to a woman, Roberta Williams (X, 1994). In 1979, she and her husband Ken Williams started a small development company called Sierra-On-Line. In 1983, they created *King's Quest*, an adventure game with an unprecedented graphical capacity. The game used the sixteen-color image processing techniques of the time to display the game's world in great detail. The main character (a knight called Graham) was no longer an icon on an abstract screen, but a colorful silhouette in a colorful environment. He could be directed using the cursor key, and players could type commands to make him perform certain actions. This form of interaction often led to frustration (as it sometimes took hours to find the appropriate command for a certain action), but it was highly influential during the mid 1980s. Sierra-On-Line produced two sequels (*King's Quest II* and *III*), and a range of other games (*Space Quest I–III*, *Leisure Suit Larry I–III*, and *Police Quest I–III*) that all worked in a similar way.

Sierra-On-Line was the sole supplier of adventure games until Lucasfilm Games (later renamed Lucas-Arts) employee Ron Gilbert developed a new navigation technique in 1987 (GameSpy Staff, 2002; Roschin, 2002). This was the "point-and-click" technique, which allowed the player to communicate with the game using the mouse rather than the keyboard. The point-and-click technique signified a radical break with the conventional way of working. Instead of specifying left/right and up/down with the cursor keys, it sufficed to click somewhere on the screen and the computer would move the character to the designated location on the screen. This technique turned out to be very suitable for games in which the player had to do a lot of exploring, but was less appropriate for games that depended on quick action. It introduced a kind of intuitive storyline to the adventure genre and it did away with text commands once and for all.

Toward the end of the 1980s, LucasArts became known as an important developer of point-and-click adventure games, consecutively producing *Maniac Mansion* (1987), *Indiana Jones and the Last Crusade* (1989), and *The Secret of Monkey Island* (1990). All these games combined a quick rhythm with a good dose of comedy. Sierra-On-Line, too, successfully switched to the new formula and produced many (some would say, too many) follow-ups in the *Quest* and *Larry* series.

"Everybody's God to Me": Strategy Games

With the emphasis shifting to story telling and the introduction of the point-and-click technique, the 1980s provided a breeding ground for one of the most addictive genres ever: the strategy game. This genre is inextricably linked to a technique introduced by *Zaxxon* in 1982. *Zaxxon* used isometric perspective, a way to build up the screen that was greatly undervalued at the time and was only recognized for its full potential later. In games using the isometric perspective, the action does not take place parallel to the edges of the screen, but at an angle of about 30°, a technique creating the optical illusion that some of the objects could jump out of the plane (Yesterdayland, 2000). Literally speaking, the isometric perspective was not a perspective in the true sense of the word, because distant objects were just as large as those in the foreground and all lines on the screen were parallel.

The isometric perspective introduced a new way of looking at things, namely the third-person total overview. As opposed to regular (frontal) third-person points of view, the player would get the impression that the playing field was an endless plain. The player would be somewhere at the top right corner and could observe everything in its totality. Between 1989 and 1990, three groundbreaking games were developed that managed to incorporate this total overview as a functional game element: *Populous* (Peter Molyneux, 1989), *SimCity* (Will Wright, 1988), and *Civilization* (Sid Meier, 1990). The narrative of these three games was totally different from the quest structure that was most common at the time (GameSpy Staff, 2002). The player does not control an individual character, but an entire population. The aim of the game is to bring your people to the highest possible level of development by making strategic decisions. You were almost literally an almighty god in the game's world. By now it is commonly accepted that *Populous*, *SimCity* and *Civilization* laid the foundation for a totally new genre: the strategy game, or "god game" (as they were also known at the time).

The Legend of Zelda

Before we move on to the arcades, we would like to point out that in the 1980s, adventure and role playing games were not exclusively available for the PC. Adventure stories were also developed for consoles, and we can be especially grateful for *The Legend of Zelda*, yet another creation of Shigeru Miyamoto, which was brought out for the NES in 1986.

At first sight, *Zelda* looked like a crossover between a platform game, à la *Mario* (on which the controls were based), a searching game, à la *King's Quest* (on which the storyline was based), and a role playing game in the tradition of *Ultima* or *The Temple of Apshai* (on which the character structure was based). It was especially this last characteristic that made *Zelda* a somewhat exceptional game in the console market. The player had to solve all kinds of puzzles and earn power-ups, just as in many other games. In *Zelda*, however, the impression existed that these activities were not an end in themselves, but small steps toward a greater good, namely building up a strong character. Therefore, *The Legend of Zelda* meant a major breakthrough of the role playing game genre to a mass audience.

"Beat Me Out of It": Arcades, the Violence, and the Reputation

In the 1980s, arcades clearly fell behind PCs and consoles. Even though the Japanese Amusement Machine Manufacturer's Association (JAMMA)[4] standard for arcade architecture and the introduction of laser discs signified considerable steps forward, this format was unable to follow the pace of its two competitors. Arcades managed to survive mainly because their games attracted a rather specific, but dedicated target audience.

The 1980s formed the heyday of the traditional "beat 'em ups," a genre based on different martial arts movies. Players had to control a fighter as quickly and inventively as possible in order to beat as many opponents as possible. The one who could beat the most opponents or stay alive the longest scored the most points. Beat 'em ups, with *Street Fighter* (Capcom, 1987) and *Double Dragon* (Technos, 1987) as two prime examples, extensively used the scrolling technique and required large amounts of skill (Yesterdayland, 2000). They appealed to a specific audience and aroused a lot of worried reactions from parents, politicians, the media, and other authorities in the conservative 1980s (Le Diberder & Le Diberder, 1993, pp. 149–158). The criticism was mainly based on the "dark" milieu in which arcade games were generally played and the interactive way these games dealt with violence. Passively experiencing violence on television was already considered extremely harmful, and this obviously applied all the more to games that "taught" youngsters to violently knock down all opposition they encountered.

1990–1999: The War of the Bits

Technological innovation has always been the force pushing video games to new heights. The cartridge system in the 1970s and the PC and the increasing screen resolutions in the 1980s greatly influenced the entire video game industry. However, when comparing these developments to those that took place in the 1990s,

they were little more than careful steps in an evolution that would soon go out of control.

During the 1990s, the bit capacities of PCs as well as consoles grew exponentially. New methods of visual processing were developed allowing computer generated images to achieve an unprecedented level of precision. Existing genres mainly improved quantitatively; year after year games became more complex and average playing time increased. In addition, the money flow generated by computer games grew to such a level that at the beginning of the twenty-first century, the turnover of the games industry exceeded that of the film industry (*USA Today*, May 23, 2002).

A detailed description of everything that happened in this period could fill an entire chapter, or even a book of its own. This is why we have decided to limit ourselves to describing only the most fundamental changes with respect to the periods already been discussed. We will first describe how the industry entered this chaotic acceleration, both technically and economically; then we will take a closer look at some of the content-related changes.

"Stop This Crazy Machine": The Story of an Industry Unleashed

The 1989 Mega Drive, Sega's answer to Nintendo's Entertainment System, is generally seen as the instigator of the "war of the bits" (figure 2.4). The machine, named Genesis in the United States, was built around a 16-bit processor, and technically speaking it was superior to the NES (X, 2002b). Sega used these capacities to produce a number of fast, rhythmical games. We remember *Sonic the Hedgehog* (1991) and *Virtua Racing* (1992), but also lesser-known games such as *Toejam and Earl* (1993), games that were aimed at the teenager market. "More Rock and Roll, Less Disney" seemed to be Sega's motto. Sonic the Hedgehog (from the game of the same name) became the sparkling opponent of "good old" Mario, and gave Sega an image that turned out to be quite lucrative (Horwitz & Miller,

| Figure 2.4 |
The instigators of the "war of the bits": The Nintendo Super NES (left) and the Sega Mega Drive (right).

2001). In 1991, after five years of Nintendo dominance, Sega's Mega Drive finally overtook the NES as the best-selling console.

Nintendo's reaction came that same year. The NES was succeeded by the Super NES (figure 2.4), also a 16-bit system, which was equivalent to the Mega Drive with respect to processing power (X, 2002b). Games such as *Super Mario World* (1991), *Donkey Kong Country* (1994), and a number of RPGs in the *Dragon-Quest* and *Final Fantasy* series had highly detailed graphics and extensive virtual worlds. Whereas Sega focused on rhythm and game structure, Nintendo turned out to be an accomplished producer of technical tours-de-force with respect to landscapes, background images, and the like. Both competitors raced neck-and-neck, which had great consequences for the market structure (Games Investor Staff, 2004).

With Nintendo losing its comfortable monopoly position, it was unable to uphold its strict licensing politics. Game developers had more freedom, a fact that was further enhanced by a whole range of programs and devices that became available to simplify programming in the different programming languages. As the production and distribution processes became increasingly more complex, a third player entered the market, namely the game publisher (De Meyer, Malliet & Verbruggen, 2001, p. 154). Traditionally, publishing had been the task of a separate division of producers or developers, but now a number of companies stood up that specialized in publishing games for others.

Even though a number of other 16-bit systems were available at the time (i.e., the TurboGraphics by NEC, and the Neo*Geo by SNK from Japan—both impressive consoles with disappointing games), the big two did not run into serious competition until 1994, when Sony introduced the revolutionary PlayStation, a console that had everything necessary to sweep the market. Equipped with a 32-bit processor, the Play-Station technically took another large step forward (X, 2002b). Due, in part, to an intensive cooperation with developers such as Namco and Squaresoft, Sony's machine managed to live up to the expectations. In two years, Sony sold more than 30 million PlayStations and more than 200 million games around the world (De Meyer, Malliet & Verbruggen, 2001, p. 150).

One of the most important innovations introduced by the PlayStation was the fact that the console no longer used (specialized) cartridges, but read its games from the general CD-ROM format. This method, which Sega and others had previously tried, offered many advantages, but had one major disadvantage. On the one hand, the PlayStation was an "all-around" machine. It could be used as a CD-ROM player, providing an extra incentive for many people to buy one. Furthermore, the capacity of a CD-ROM is vastly larger than that of a cartridge. On the other hand, Sony spoon-fed the software piracy industry by using the CD-ROM format, and it became easier than ever to produce illegal copies of video games.

Initially PlayStation's fiercest competition came from two consoles that each meant the beginning of the (slow) end of two manufacturers: the Atari Jaguar (1993) and the Sega Saturn (1994). The first of the two can be considered Atari's final attempt to renew its grip on a market that had escaped its clutches several years earlier. With the Jaguar, the first 64-bit console ever, it had a superior console at its disposal, but the games Atari produced predominantly scored criticism (Jacobi, 1996; X, 2002b). Sega's Saturn, a 32-bit machine just like the PlayStation, was a different story, typical for Sega's future. It was an excellent console, nobody doubted that, and they came out with some beautiful games that, according to some, were better than those for the PlayStation, but it just never managed to come close to Sony's sales figures. Several erroneous marketing and management decisions were held responsible for this lack of success (Games Investor Staff, 2004).

Nintendo fared a little better with its introduction, in response to the PlayStation, of the Nintendo 64. This console pushed the capacities of game computers to an even higher level. Sales figures were not as expected however, mainly because Nintendo had decided to stick to the cartridge format instead of making the move toward the CD-Rom as a carrier of its games software. For reasons of efficiency and compatibility, many developers preferred the PlayStation and the Sega Saturn as their favorite platform. The Nintendo 64 was forced to thrive on conversions of older games, and suffered a shortage of new games (Horwitz & Miller, 2001). Another problem for the Nintendo 64 was caused by the PlayStation already being present in millions of living rooms and having already saturated a large part of the market.

A final console that was launched in the 1990s was Sega's Dreamcast, the successor of the Saturn. The story of this console is even more astonishing than that of its predecessor. The Dreamcast was not just a console with slightly enhanced capacities, it was technically vastly superior to any of its competitors, with a 128-bit processor, the capability to connect the console to the Internet, unprecedented storage capacity, and so on. Sega also published a number of excellent games to accompany the console. Still, sales did not live up to the expectations by a long shot, yet again thanks to a variety of economic reasons. In 2001, Sega decided to stop producing the Dreamcast and to leave the console market for good.

Different Formats: Different Forms Evolve at Different Rates

The console market was subject to a hectic succession of developments, and the question arises how the other market segments evolved. When trying to answer this question, it becomes apparent that each market segment developed at a different pace. Most techniques that the consoles rely on are based on PCs and computer technology; it is therefore no surprise that this sector evolved at least as rapidly. Handhelds and arcades, by contrast, fell behind during the 1990s, each for their own specific reasons.

Without going into too much detail, it is safe to say that the capacity and applicability of PCs developed at an astonishing rate. With the Pentium series (by Intel) and the PowerPC (by IBM, Apple, and Motorola) in the lead, a number of architectural standards were developed that served as the model for many powerful machines (Patterson, 2000). As in consoles, the PC's bit rates increased immensely, and the rate at which the processors could process instructions skyrocketed. From the second half of the 1990s on, the PC world was largely dominated by Microsoft, which managed to monopolize the commercial market with the Windows operating system. Due to the success of Windows and the increasing power of PCs in general, the position of Apple and Commodore machines on the game computer market gradually eroded. Ever-increasing processing capacity eliminated the difference between "serious PCs," predominantly aimed at data processing applications, and "recreational PCs," which specialized in graphical applications.

Another breakthrough in the field of home computing was the rapid rise of the Internet in the 1990s, which became an important element in the recreational applicability of computers.

The format of the handheld evolved at a more moderate pace. Although many competitors entered the market, some of them with relatively advanced machines, Nintendo managed to maintain a good grip on the market. The Atari Lynx (as early as 1987), the NEC TurboExpress (1990), and the Sega GameGear (1991) had a color screen, whereas the GameBoy was a black-and-white machine. Furthermore, the latter two were technically much stronger then Nintendo's hand-

held (X, 2000b). Both had been designed as a compact version of their bigger brothers (the TurboGraphics and the Master System, respectively). These handhelds were also regularly supplied with quality games, but still neither became a commercial success. Once again the reasons were bad timing and the wrong marketing strategy.

If we disregard the Virtual Boy (1995), an experiment with handheld virtual reality that was not quite compact enough to actually be considered handheld, Nintendo did not introduce the GameBoy's successor until 1998. This was the GameBoy Color, which was almost literally what its name suggested: a GameBoy with a color screen. Architecturally it was almost identical to its predecessor, except for a faster (32-bit) processor, and some additional memory capacity (X, 2000b).

Because the GameBoy mainly scored with platform-based action games (after the classics from the 1980s), there was no need for drastic innovations. Nintendo's comfortable position in the handheld market throughout the 1990s can be held responsible for the limited evolution of the handheld format during this period.

Throughout the 1990s, arcades continued to be pushed to the background. With their increased capacities, growing graphical quality and the possibility to be connected to a network, consoles and PCs took over the role of main supplier of action games (Jacobi, 1996). This development coincided with a reduction in the number of arcades due to the increasingly strict legislation concerning gambling and game machines that was adopted in many countries. The arcade as a format for video games is more and more becoming an icon of a time long gone, for which there is little place in the current landscape.

3D Takes Over

The previous two sections reveal the clear tendency that the success of a format or a company depended more on the content of the games that were produced, than on the rapid succession of technical innovations. It is therefore no surprise that the 1990s also witnessed a number of changes with respect to content.

"Blood on the Tracks": Violent Action in a 3D-World

In 1992, a developer called ID Software shocked the world by introducing *Castle Wolfenstein 3D*. The commotion that this PC game aroused not only stemmed from its highly violent content, but also from the fact that the action took place in a world that was totally three-dimensional (Poole, 2000, p. 136). In contrast with earlier games that already used perspective or an isometric standpoint, this did not just mean that there was depth in the images. 3D meant that the player could actually manipulate and explore the image. In *Wolfenstein 3D* each wall existed in three dimensions, and it was possible to walk around it. This possibility did not exist in any of the two-dimensional games produced before.

The technique that was used to program *Wolfenstein 3D* was the perfected and refined form of the technique that was used ten years earlier for *Battlezone*. Central to this technique is the use of "polygons." The objects on the screen are no longer prints of images that are displayed, but transformations of a mathematical model. Inside the computer, the objects on the screen are a collection of polygons (usually triangles or rectangles) in a three-dimensional coordinate system. The graphics of a primitive 3D game, such as *Battlezone*, give a good idea of what this is like. One can clearly see how the tanks and rocks are little more than a number of points connected by lines.

As can be seen by looking at the graphics of the two games, *Wolfenstein 3D* employed far more advanced techniques than *Battlezone*, but in the end it comes down to the exact same principle. In *Wolfenstein* the visible figures consisted of far more polygons and were therefore visualized far more accurately. They were also colored, and looked less naked and skeleton-like than the tanks in *Battlezone*. At the time of *Wolfenstein 3D*, PCs were also sufficiently powerful to produce more fluent visual transitions, to add shadow, and so on.

With successors such as *Doom I* (1993), *Doom II* (1994), *Quake I* (1996), *Quake II* (1997), and *Quake III* (1999), ID Software further perfected their 3D-exploration techniques, and built (on its own) the foundation for a new genre: the first-person shooter (FPS) (GameSpy Staff, 2002). In addition to their dimensionality, FPS games differed from the beat 'em ups from the 1980s in a number of ways. They were the first genre to use a first-person standpoint, which managed to directly involve the player in the game. They required the player to be quite skillful, and eventually reached a very high level of realism. The levels of violence put on screen surpassed those seen in most karate or boxing games, mainly because it was portrayed rather expressively; it is self-evident that first-person shooters were the subject of fierce criticism throughout the 1990s.

Another innovation introduced by ID was the possibility of online gaming. *Quake* was the first game that could be played over the Internet, giving players the opportunity to fight real opponents, instead of computer-driven characters (Morris, 1999). Games like *Doom* and its successors also allowed players to become co-authors of the in-game world. Programming languages like QuakeC were distributed and documented over the Internet, and whoever was able to master those languages had the possibility of writing new worlds for the game, or of making new skins[5] for his or her character. Some of these additions, not created by the original team of developers but by enthusiastic fans, have grown to lead a life of their own, available as add-ons or modulations (mods) to the original game (e.g., *Urban Terror*, which is an extension of *Quake III: Arena*).

3D in Other Genres: Sports Games and Action Adventures Among the major genres that had been established during the 1980s, there were two that gained considerably from the new image processing techniques: simulation and adventure genres.

In the 1990s, simulation games, and sports simulations in particular, became quite lucrative for many companies. With realism and "congruence with human intuition" being important criteria for such games, working with polygons was a perfect technique for developers. Especially toward the late 1990s, as bit rates increased, the popularity of sports simulations grew considerably. Electronic Arts, a game publisher that grew tremendously thanks to such series as *NBA Basketball*, *NHL Hockey* and *FIFA Soccer*, even established a daughter company that fully concentrated on sports simulations (De Meyer, Malliet & Verbruggen, 2001, p. 74). Another important game in this genre, receiving much praise for its astonishing levels of realism, was the *Gran Turismo* racing simulator (Polyphony Digital, 1998).

The adventure genre, too, embraced 3D technology. In many cases this resulted in sluggish games lacking the primitive charm of before. One game, however, forced a breakthrough, forming the beginning of a genre that combined adventure and action in a 3D environment. This game was *Tomb Raider*, developed by Core and published by Eidos in 1996. The success of *Tomb Raider* depended less on content-related innovations than on the game's heroine: the by-now legendary Lara Croft. In no time, Lara Croft became a role model, a sex symbol, for some even a symbol of feminism. She became the front-woman of the games industry, and, like Pac-Man fifteen years earlier, lent it a less violent character. In many circles she still elicited a lot of criticism, though, mainly for the size of her breasts. Although the succes of *Tomb Raider* was largely due to its heroine, the game nevertheless managed to pave the way for a range of 3D adventure games that gave the player a third-person point-of-view.

RPG's and Strategy Games: Two-Dimensionality Lives On Not all adventure games accepted the 3D action direction. Games such as the popular *Myst* series (Cyan, 1992, 1998) mainly continued working on the puzzle aspect; point-and-click technique, too, was also still common. Two other genres that did not switch to three-dimensionality were the RPGs and the strategy games. Mainly working on developing complex narrative structures, both underwent a number of necessary changes, but in contrast with the shooters and action games discussed above, they only used the new techniques at a later stage of development to include sophisticated graphics. For the designers of these games, developing an interesting storyline was the first priority.

Role playing games specialized in constructing a complex set of rules that would allow the player to build up his own character. These rules were, among others, based on handbooks from the fantasy role playing milieu (Costello, 1991, p. 214; Poole, 2000, p. 53). Graphically speaking they developed into two subgenres: the PC games, which used the point-and-click technique, and the console games, which stuck to using cursor keys or a joypad. In the PC game category we remember *Diablo* (Blizzard, 1996) and *Baldur's Gate* (Black Isle, 1998), the latter of which especially received extensive praise for approaching the *Dungeons and Dragons* experience so closely (De Meyer, Malliet, & Verbruggen, 2001). By far the most famous console RPGs were the *Phantasy Star* series for the Sega consoles and the *Final Fantasy* series, initially for the SNES and later for the PlayStation. Games in these series consistently grew in size and often used short films or "cut scenes" to support the storyline. This approach was regularly criticized for pushing the interactivity of a game to the background (De Meyer, Malliet & Verbruggen, 2001, p. 59).

Strategy games, too, did not immediately jump to 3D graphics, but paid a lot of attention to the storyline. Just as the RPGs, this genre split up in two groups: the god game, following in the footsteps of *Populous* and *Civilization*, and the real-time strategy game that incorporated elements of the RPGs. God games saw their storylines expand in so far that there were more and more ways for the player to steer the game in different directions. It is important to point at the violence that

sneaked into many of these games, often as a simple solution to complicated challenges. We think of games such as *Age of Empires* (Microsoft, 1997) and the successors in the *Civilization* series. A new genre that flourished during the 1990s was the real-time strategy game that can best be described as a crossover between a god game and an RPG. Real-time strategy games shared their controls with god games; as a player you controlled a large group of people and some supplies that you had to use as efficiently as possible. Often you would be the general of a large army. The storyline, however, resembled that of the RPGs. Frequently the aim of the game was to beat some evil (historical) superpower and to prevent the world from coming to an end. Real-time strategy games required the player to be able to take certain strategic decisions, thinking quickly and efficiently, because, no matter what decision the player made, the rest of the game would continue. Enemies had high levels of Artificial Intelligence, which would regularly make gameplay rather difficult. *Herzog Zwei* (Technosoft, 1989) and *Dune II* (Westwood, 1992) are the pioneers of this genre (Geryk, 1998). The true classics followed a little later with the *Warcraft* (Blizzard, 1994, 1995) and the *Command-and-Conquer* series (Westwood, 1995, 1996).

The Future: PlayStation2, X-Box, GameCube, and Beyond

To summarize everything that happened in the 1990s in a limited number of pages was anything but self-evident. And, considering the tendencies of the past years, it is even more difficult to predict what we can expect in the future. As a starting point we will use the three consoles that, for now, constitute the latest generation, and we will look at some of the promises they will have to realize in the years to come.

At the moment, the market is dominated by the PlayStation2, launched by Sony in 2000 and a big success from day one, just like its predecessor. In many countries the demand for the new console was so high that Sony had trouble producing enough new machines. It was not until 2001 that the situation stabilized, and by then more than 50 million families worldwide owned a PlayStation2. Technically speaking, the PlayStation2 is the first console that truly outperforms the PC format. The machine can process more than 60 million polygons per second[6] and offers spectacular possibilities for game programmers. In 2002, new releases such as *Gran Turismo 3* and *Fifa 2002* have shown the tip of the iceberg of what can be expected of game consoles in the future, and it is indeed impressive.

There are two competitors to the PlayStation: the X-Box, by Microsoft (a newcomer on the console market), and the GameCube, by old-timer Nintendo. Both competitors have managed to surpass the PlayStation2 graphically (Tyson, 2002), and bring us yet another step closer to realizing the game programmer's dream of processing 100 million polygons per second. Recent sales figures have shown, however, that these technical capacities are no guarantee for an immediate domination of the market. Although at the time of writing, the amount of games available for both consoles has already surpassed a hundred, it is still the PlayStation2 that accounts for the largest share of console sales (MCV Magazine, July 26, 2002; August 30, 2002). Since the launch of its competitors, the Sony console has managed to outsell the GameCube at a ratio of 1.5/1 (meaning that for every GameCube sold, on average, 1.5 PlayStation2s are sold), and to outsell the X-Box at a ratio of 2.6/1.

Although the X-Box and the GameCube have entered a market that is already largely saturated by the PlayStation2, the graphical capacities of both consoles have raised expectations concerning the contents of future games. High on the wish list of many developers, manufacturers, and publishers are working out a framework for online gaming, the breakthrough of virtual reality, and an increased integration of different forms of entertainment. Before we end our history, we would like to briefly discuss each of these three dreams.

With respect to online gaming, the industry can build on a formula that has already proved successful. From the mid 1990s on, many first-person shooters have expanded to include multiplayer modes, mainly aimed at network-based play. These games allow multiple (clans of) players to battle each other in a virtual 3D world. A very popular game in this respect is *Counter-Strike*, a multiplayer extension of *Half-Life*, which was published in 1999 by Valve. Role playing games, too, have been exploring the possibilities of online gaming for a couple of years. "Massive Multiplayer Online Role Playing Games," or MMORPGs, which have almost become a genre in their own right, are in fact no more than endlessly long RPGs, where, in addition to the computer-generated characters, players can also run into human players.

Both online shooters and online RPGs already have large followings, but there is still a lot of room for future development. Online players with a slow network connection will often be frustrated while playing online tournaments such as *Counter-Strike*, because their characters will not respond fast enough to their commands or controls. With the increased worldwide availability of broadband network connections, these technical issues are, however, more and more becoming of secondary importance, shown in the current succes of such MMORPGs as *Everquest* or *Ultima Online*. The three largest consoles of the moment seem to envisage the potential of the Internet, as the X-Box, the Game-Cube, and the PlayStation2 are all equipped with a network connection. They do not only see a future in multiplayer games, but also, for example, in creating worldwide databases for high scores in certain games (Antoja, 2001).

A second challenge for the future is virtual reality. Even though the theories and concepts behind VR were already been developed back in the 1980s, there has not yet been a practical application that has appealed to a wide audience. In certain ways, VR is the logical successor of the polygon model, as it takes the same idea a step further. The impression that, as a player, you are actually *inside* the game, which is created by the first-person standpoint, will only be amplified by the so-called "immersion" that goes along with VR. As a player you will no longer be confined to a screen, but you will be involved in the game with several senses at the same time.

Integration and synergy are coming. Different forms of entertainment will, as they say, grow toward one another, both with respect to content and hardware. When we look at the PlayStation2, we see that in addition to being a game console, it is also very popular as a DVD player, and soon probably also as a home computer. Many companies in the entertainment industry are playing with taking this concept a step further: they see computer, television, stereo system, and game console all together into one "all-around" multimedia machine (Antoja, 2001). Contentwise, they see a future in melding more and more media into one integrated style.

There is no doubt that technology will keep on moving. According to many gamers and executives, the industry should not focus on this evolution alone, however. When push comes to shove, the contents of the available games will always be the crucial determinant of success, and one should always keep economic market forces in mind. If there is one thing to learn from the foregoing history, it is the fact that the games industry only needs a few years to completely change its appearance. Therefore, we have to be very careful in drawing any premature conclusions and we cannot end

Steven Malliet and Gust de Meyer

this chapter with a big closing remark that says it all. We do hope, however, that we have offered an improved insight into the ups and downs of this new form of popular culture.

Notes

1. The PDP (Program, Data, Processor) was the first computer equipped with a monitor and a keyboard to be commercially exploited. It was introduced by Digital Equipment in 1960. By the standards of those days, it was a very compact and user-friendly machine, but compared with today's personal computers it looks very awkward. As a consequence of their size and their price, PDPs were only used at universities and research companies (Polsson, 2002).

2. In systems making use of a vector beam monitor, images are not stored in the memory as a collection of *pixels*, each with their specific color information, but as a collection of *lines*, determined by the coordinates of their beginning point and ending point. The laser beam that is built in a vector beam monitor does not continuously scan every pixel that constitutes the screen (this is what happens in a regular cathode ray tube), but draws straight lines between two given coordinates on the screen.

3. Micro Instrumentation Telemetry Systems, a company that was better known in those days than it is now, is credited for having made the first commercially succesful personal computer, the MITS Altair. More than two thousand of these machines were sold in 1975 (Patterson, 2000; LaMorte & Lilly, 1999).

4. Arcade machines that follow the JAMMA hardware guidelines are no longer bound to one single game: it becomes relatively easy to insert a new piece of hardware that contains another game, without having to change the entire cabinet. Because of this property, the JAMMA standard meant to the arcade market what the cartridge system had meant to the console market (IGN Entertainment Staff, 2002).

5. The "skin" of a player's character refers to how that character is actually visualised on the screen: the color of its hair, the clothes it is wearing, its size, etc. Traditionally players had to choose between a range of preprogrammed skins, with a male vs. a female appearance, a muscled vs. a wizardlike appearance, and so on as the major options.

6. The number of polygons a console can process per second is often used as a measure of its graphical capacity. It places a boundary on the level of detail of the 3D graphics within a game.

References

Antoja, E. (2001). *The internet impact on the coin-up industry.* Presentation at the Eurotechno conference, Brussels. Oct. 5, 2001.

Brown, D. (1998). *Classic home video games museum.* gamesmuseum.h-body.org.

Costello, M. J. (1991). *The greatest games of all time.* New York: John Wiley & Son.

De Meyer, G., Malliet, S., & Verbruggen, D. (2001). *Videogame lexicon.* Diegem, Belgium: Kluwer.

GameSpy Staff. (2002). *GameSpy's 30 most influential people in gaming.* archive.gamespy.com/articles/march02/top30/61/index.shtm.

Games Investor Staff. (2004). *The games industry: Past, Present and Future.* www.gamesinvestor.com/History/history.htm.

Geryk, B. (1998). *A history of real-time strategy games.* www.gamespot.com/gamespot/features/all/real_time.

Herz, J. C. (1997). *Joystick nation. How videogames ate our quarters, won our hearts, and rewired our minds.* Boston: Little, Brown, and Company.

Horowitz, J., & Miller, S. (2001). *The history of Nintendo.* www.videogames.com/features/universal/hist_nintendo.

Hunter, W. (2000). *The dot eaters—Classic videogame history.* www.emuunlim.com/doteaters.

Hunter, W. (2002). *The history of video games: From "Pong" to "Pac-Man."* www.designboom.com/eng/education/pong.html.

IGN Entertainment Staff. (2002). *IGN lexicon.* games.ign.com/lexicon.html.

Jacobi, S. (1996). *The history of videogames: An independent study.* home.nycap.rr.com/poetwarrior/game.htm.

LaMorte, C., & Lilly, J. (1999). *Computers: History and development.* www.digitalcentury.com/encyclo/update/comp_hd.html.

Le Diberder, A., & Le Diberder, F. (1993). *Qui a peur des jeux vidéo?* Paris: La Découverte.

Morris, S. (1999). *An examination of emerging forms of production and participation in multiplayer first-person-shooter gaming.* www.game-culture.com/articles/onlinegaming.html.

Patterson, J. (2000). *The history of computers during my lifetime.* www.pattosoft.com.au/jason/Articles/HistoryOfComputers.

Polsson, K. (2002). *Chronology of personal computers.* www.islandnet.com/~kpolsson/comphist.

Poole, S. (2000). *Trigger happy. The inner life of video-games.* London: Fourth Estate.

Roschin, O. (2002). *What's happening to adventure games?* ps2.mobygames.com/featured_article/feature,13/section,57.

Seitz, L. K. (2001). *Classic videogaming nexus.* home.hiwaay.net/~lkseitz/cvg/nexus/nexus.cgi?Topic=Features&Feature=1.

Selnow, G. W. (1987). The fall and rise of video games. *Journal of Popular Culture, 21,* 53–60.

Sheff, D. (1993). *Game over. Nintendo's battle to dominate videogames.* London: Hodder & Stoughton.

Tyson, J. (2002). *How videogame systems work.* www.howstuffworks.com/video-game.htm.

Yesterdayland. (2000). *Arcade games.* www.yesterdayland.com/popopedia/shows/categories/arcade/.

X. (1994). *History of King's Quest.* members.aol.com/KQswst104/history.html.

X. (2001a). *Atari planet.* www.holyoak.com/atari/.

X. (2001b). *Big history of the arcade.* dragonsden.emuunlim.com/ddhistory.htm.

X. (2002a). *Commodore history.* amiga.emugaming.com/commodore.html.

X. (2002b). *Games consoles.* www.gameconsoles.com/home_framed.htm.

3

FUTURE OF GAMES: MOBILE GAMING

Justin Hall

Whereas social play is a constant possibility, initiated by curious people through a chance smile or a shared bench, most electronic gaming is a dedicated pastime. People must take time to be deliberately engaged with their machines. The advent of mobile communications devices with the power to play could merge gaming and communication into a constant state of machine-mediated social exchange.

Every Environment

Before, electronic games had a context: played on a TV in the "family room" or a computer in a darkened bedroom corner. When mobile communications machines are harnessed for games, they present a new gaming environment, literally every environment. A game might likely follow you into the bathroom. It might interrupt a meeting. It could occupy you under the table during a family dinner, or in bed late at night while your partner is sleeping. There are portable game systems now that make this kind of pervasive electronic play possible, but they are single-function devices. Mobile communications devices follow us into circumstances where electronic games might not have been previously available or appropriate, making opportunities for electronic gaming essentially constant and ubiquitous.

Because they can share in our lives, available near constantly for interconnected play, these electronic game experiences are disposable, subject to the unpredictable demands of real life, so at once the games are always present and negligible. They are for passing moments, not the object of focused attention. These situations beg simple games that can be played and forgotten: play in the moment, play that might happen just before an arriving train, or secretly to pass time during an overlong mass.

The first generation of wireless games reflects this situation. In contrast to the involving worlds available for exploration inside the plastic boxes made for digital distraction, early mobile phone games have been ex-

ceedingly casual. The first widespread mobile phone game, *Snake* from Nokia, was a single-player puzzle game the likes of which had been seen as early as the 1981 Apple II and perhaps earlier. *Snake* ordered the collective human finger to chase food and sidestep growing obesity. It came included with Nokia's popular handsets, so it was a most accessible mobile entertainment experience: a way to challenge the thumbs.

Elementary distraction was about all you could hope for with early handsets. In the United States and Europe, mobile phone games involving story, evolved choice, or other people were hamstrung by tiny, pokey hardware and stuttering wireless data connections.

Sorcery

Matthew Bellows software tested the likes of *Cutthroats* and *Hitchhiker's Guide to the Galaxy* at grandfather text-only game-maker Infocom. Later working in business development at an e-commerce startup, he felt the lure of electronic entertainment as the later-day Internet calcified. In 2001, he co-founded a website about mobile gaming called Wireless Gaming Review: "The motto of the site was 'Two Worlds Colliding,' which was meant to evoke the potential and the inevitability of combining 700 million cellphones with \$20 billion per year in global video game expenditures." The web supported this niche approach to publishing; his site for curious mobile gamers supports reviews, chat, and a database of wireless games. Bellows hosted conversation about a game medium with a distributed experience and games often simple enough to keep from needing much support from other players, creating a gaming community that otherwise had little to draw it together.

In 2001, the users at Wireless Gaming Review voted *Sorcery* the best use of the wireless gaming medium. Published for the wireless web by Digital Bridges, *Sorcery* had originally been a gamebook: branching narrative detailed in page flipping, the end of each section provides a choice in page numbers. For the wireless version, the branching narrative was an enumerated series of choices following the text. This transition from book to electronic entertainment put a stop to metagaming, according to *Sorcery* book game designer and wireless game consultant Steve Jackson (this Steve Jackson works for Lionhead studios in England; he's occasionally confused with Steve Jackson of *G.U.R.P.S.*, *Illuminati*, *Car Wars*, and Secret Service raid fame, whose company is the Texas-based Steve Jackson Games). In a January 2002 email interview, Jackson says working with a processor "stops people cheating! In Sorcery gamebook you could always test out all the options using your fingers as bookmarks. In Sorcery WAP your decision is final." Here the constraints of the mobile phone platform serve immersion. The wireless form severs some gamer appendages, here literally the fingers, keeping them from poking into the game's structure.

When a similar sort of game is produced for a computer, save and load is expected without fail, because any game with consequences must invariably give the player a chance to experiment with permutations. With nearly all computer games, the player can save their game before a difficult or binding moment, play through, and then reload if they are unsatisfied with the outcome. Save/Load is a design affordance created to comply with player expectations of a seemingly controllable computer world. If there are plenty of virtual possibilities, I might feel my $50 in computer entertainment software has been wasted if I cannot iteratively recompile my experience throughout. And if the game proposes to go on for dozens of hours, then I may well end up saving and loading dozens of times.

Most games of the adventure ilk give players the chance to visit and revisit the many plot lines in the game by use of readily reloadable games; with *Sorcery*, the player's progress is only saved along the way to keep communications disconnections from interrupting play. Notably, the mobile platform has an award-winning role-playing game of some complexity that doesn't afford much permutation exploration. A computer or console adventure/role-playing game would be a major departure if it proposed that players should have to live with the consequences of their play. But somehow the expectation of metagame management has been adequately dispensed of as the scale of the game shrinks. In spite of these constraints, *Sorcery* was voted best around; to quote the *Sorcery* review from WGR: "Once you start moving around, you discover that the world of *Sorcery* is incredibly rich. I've played

the game through three times and I'm still finding new stuff to do. There are very few PC games that can hold my attention that well." One wonders if the suspension of the save/reload mechanic in *Sorcery* forced the author of the review to pay more attention to the game than he or she has given most PC games: immersion through restraint.

The idea that self-denial and constraint might lead to greater engagement for enthusiastic gamers runs entirely counter to the general spirit of ejaculation common in the gaming industry. The mobile entertainment platform otherwise seems to pour icy cold water on gaming's groin.

The Romero

John Romero has been widely hailed an exemplar and representative of the spirit that created modern teenage male stimulation. By turns proud and humbled, Romero was a game designer and programmer on the team that created *Castle Wolfenstein 3D*, *Doom*, and *Quake* at ID Software in Texas. ID Software was a fantasy itself, a small staff of wealthy long-haired geek proto-boys driving highly modified, brightly colored European power sports cars that were barely street legal. ID co-founder and programming wiz John Carmack recent funded his own amateur spaceflight development effort called Armadillo Aerospace. *Castle Wolfenstein 3D* was the first modern first-person shooter, the model for immersion: players stalk halls while being stalked, hunter and hunted; pixellated visions of pure evil charge in above the swinging gun dominating the lower half of the screen. This iteration of tag with guns became the first means by which masses of worldwide citizenry inhabited 3D virtual worlds. These 3D worlds invariably require the next generation of computer hardware, spawning a spiral in processing power and graphics hardware that has catered to an enthusiastic hardcore market of fevered young men who are now the face of this postmodern entertainment.

Romero's career followed first-person shooters up to a fantastic apex, the height of game making celebrity. A story "A game boy in the cross hairs" from the May 23, 1999 Sunday *New York Times Magazine* shows Romero with a wide black mane of hair, a cocky glower on his face. He was running late on his work on *Daikatana*, a first-person shooter that was to top the previous works by offering more depth of story, fantastical art, "kewler" weapons, more environments—the infinite expansion of the world inside the computer that this boy had imagined. Or, as it was put in a print advertisement for *Daikanata*, "Suck It Down."

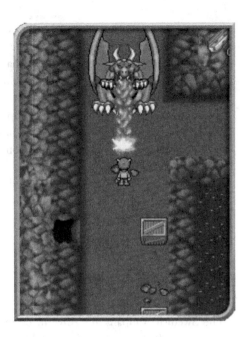

| Figure 3.1 |
Hyperspace Delivery Boy

Thrown Back

For Romero, *Hyperspace Delivery Boy* is a bit of a throwback. Similarly, other game companies have decided that nostalgia may be a convincing way to sell this new medium. These game experiences offer a bridge to players who look at the small screen in their pocket and still crave something more vivid, like what they see from their couch or in their computer.

Home video games were born in America and raised in Japan. Similarly, the mobile phone reached adolescence on this Asian island, where teenagers were carrying strobing pink flashing sticker adorned color screen camera-enabled *keitai* while their American brethren were still contemplating black and white brickphones available in either dark gray or dark green.

Many of the early mobile games in Japan took advantage of color, Java-enabled handsets to offer familiar arcade experiences. Users could visit Taito or Namco online to download java versions of *Pac-Man*, *Galaga*, and *Arkanoid*. These games are perfect miniature versions of what some may remember from now shuttered arcades, replete with sound effects. Astonishing upon first glance and inspiring for laggard American and European mobile phone users, they are in fact a retrograde action, whereby the future of mobile games is put on hold while nostalgia is sold.

And the project was sucked down, famously, in electronic gaming's most thoroughly observed fall from grace. Romero's cockiness was increasingly lambasted in the gaming press as delays mounted. When it emerged years later, three years after the ad proclaiming "Suck It Down," *Daikatana* was almost an afterthought to what had been a lively circus of celebrity developed through critique.

It was telling when Romero emerged from the *Daikatana* debacle, cut his hair, sold his canary yellow Ferrari, and turned instead to making simple games. His first release from 2001, *Hyperspace Delivery Boy* (figure 3.1) was built for PocketPC, a wallet-sized personal digital assistant and communications device platform. It was not exactly wireless, but built to be played in a liminal space outside of the heated confines of deep computer graphical worlds.

Hyperspace Delivery Boy has more in common with the roots of PC gaming, notably that Carmack and Romero both made games where tiny men run and jump through 2D space to avoid obstacles, shoot foes, and win prizes. A humbled Romero was eager for the design constraints presented by small screens, game products more manageable and much faster. Four years to design a box on the shelf, or a few months to design something for download. It may not necessarily be the entire future of games, but it was more immediately gratifying.

The millions of potential mobile phone game players made them attractive targets for game companies looking to revitalize themselves. One of the major PC and video game publishers in the West, THQ, announced their wireless division in 1998. THQ Wireless launched in part with two efforts: one, they would be producing games for the mobile phone based on the WWF, North America's World Wrestling Federation (starting with *WWF: Mobile Madness*) and second, they would be reproducing Intellivision titles for mobile gamers.

Born in 1980, the Intellivision was one of the first machines that brought pixellated playmates into family free time. *Utopia*, *Sea Battle*, and *Night Stalker* were some of their popular titles; most of their games you might have seen the likes of elsewhere; every early console had a maze-based dot-chewing game, a driving game, a game of shooting and dodging floating space rocks. There would appear to be very few ideas available in the game industry once you strip out variance in themes. But subtle differences in game architecture can earn fond memories. Intellivision titles on mobile phones are history recast and recompiled, nostalgia for those going slowly into wireless. These games were made small and compact by modern standards.

Still *Astrosmash!*, the first Intellivision/THQ release, required some fine tuning to make what had been built for an entire afternoon on a couch fit into ten minutes on a train platform. *Astrosmash!* for a mobile phone becomes more difficult more quickly than its cartridge-based progenitor.

Some companies bank that themes (such as nostalgia or wrestling) will help sell interactive mobile phone entertainment. Busy thirty-somethings might be happy to revisit *Q-Bert* in their pocket. If middle-aged men don't yet game with their thumbs, maybe they await the right golf sim. Working women? Marketing doesn't seem to know. Perhaps a proliferation of possible themes and identities will elevate the phone to a first class distraction, something all kinds of customers would turn to, to purchase entertainment. You can find pink plastic shells and strobing blue antennae to customize, so wouldn't some folks like to have their phone engage them through wrestling, shopping, or memories?

Perhaps, but these pocket friends and human interconnectors will not fulfill their potential to carry the merry bouncing spirit of the world unless they evolve not just their stories but also their form. As legions grab their phones in moments of desperate boredom, they might find themselves participating only in the first stage of mobile human entertainment evolution. These early offerings may beckon gaming strangers to play on these little machines, when other more sophisticated games might be lurking behind simple exteriors. Still, Romero doesn't see it that way entirely, writing in a January 2002 email, "The main thing that's going on right now is licensing of old Atari and Intellivision titles—you know, the 2600 stuff and other blocky-ass games like that. Those are perfect for the lame US hardware that we have right now and someday we'll get to use REAL cpus and hardware!" His PC muscle twitching, still he looks forward to more complexity afforded by processing power.

It's easy to look at a mobile phone today and lament all the ways that it isn't as fit for fun as a Game-Boy, let alone a video game console or a computer. Mobile phone buttons are tiny and poorly placed. The screens are pinched and small. Battery life is short. Too many mobile devices are still black and white, sadly enforcing a nostalgic quality on these modern multimedia terminals.

Greg Costikyan is an articulate New York–based game designer who has worked in nearly all modern gaming mediums, from wargames, board games, and role-playing games to video and computer games. He has tested many schemes for human entertainment, and still he can be effusive about the potential for mobile gaming. For Costikyan, the characteristics of wireless, handicapped but communicating, will force new forms of electronic game design. "Phones are inherently networked devices, so multiplayer is feasible, and maybe mandatory" (from an April 2001 interview "Unplugging Games" posted on the mobile analysis web site The Feature).

The preverbal game of tag or hide-and-go-seek may be about the oldest human multiplayer game. One game lauded in the early days of mobile entertainment was based directly on tag, offering the chance to reach out and touch someone with more loaded consequences.

Tag—You're Dead

The Swedish company It's Alive made its name on its first game *BotFighters*. *BotFighters* blew a few minds around the world as it was the first entertaining use of "location based" technology, using a phone's physical position on communications networks to allow players to track and kill each others' virtual personas. In this case, the virtual personas were robots, selected from a website prior to play and customized with "robucks" earned by dispatching opponents. Technology anthropologist Howard Rheingold spent an evening with some BotFighters in Stockholm in late 2001; he wrote about it in his 2002 book *SmartMobs*:

At a quarter to midnight on one of those late spring evenings when night falls around ten o'clock, I found myself cruising greater Stockholm with four devotees of a game that involves virtual persona, mocking text messages, location-sensing technology, junk food, and continuous banter. They call themselves "the Mob." By their own gleeful confessions, they spend too much of their time chasing game opponents around Stockholm. They first met when three of them ganged up to track down the fourth and destroy his "bot" [a software robot that represents the player]. After the virtual battle, the four exchanged good-natured insults via SMS, decided to meet face to face, and instantly became a self-styled gang.

Joel Abrahamsson picked me up in front of my hotel after finishing his day's work as a system administrator for a Swedish web-hosting firm. He looked up from his mobile phone long enough to greet me. "Oh hell!" was the next thing he said. "My bot got shot." The opponent, Abrahamsson informed me, was less than 400 meters away—perhaps one of the people we could see in the small park in front of my hotel. "Now he is demeaning me by SMS! He better hope he leaves the area before my gang gets here." A small Volvo stopped at the curb and I jammed in with four young men, all of whom cordially but fleetingly looked up from their phones to greet me. (Howard Rhinegold, *SmartMobs*, chapter 1: Shibuya Epiphany, p. 18)

Their cackling elation in the dark huddled around their mobile phones might have seemed to Rheingold like the first telling signs of some new social configurations evolving in conjunction with technology.

BotFighters seemed to signal the arrival of a *sui generis* form of mobile gaming. Journalists and researchers were happy to see some unusual human-computer mediated interaction within the environment. All of a sudden you might be playing a game with your mobile phone when you hadn't chosen to do so; the game might creep into your life. Still, virtual robot combat spawned by a flurry of twenty-cent SMS messages only appeals to a certain dedicated set of gamers. This first example of pervasive gaming is particularly paranoia inducing; *BotFighters* makes you a potential victim as readily as a potential hunter: any random passer-by might suddenly take a deadly interest in you. To quote promotional literature from It's Alive, "In the future, games will surround you and be a part of your everyday life. You're always connected to the game, and it's not always easy to tell reality from fiction. We call this *pervasive gaming*." And so Rheingold saw the victorious side of *Assassin* on mobile phones. Whereas real world face-to-face point-and-kill makes for an edgy mobile phone game, location-based technologies should invariably migrate to scavenger hunts and social permutation play. These less invasive location-based game forms could invite some nontraditional gaming folks to use their phones for social play in their immediate environment.

Those Swedes with fancy gear fused to their fingernails did not necessarily need another medium in which to slay, but it is provocative to see that you can inspire people to virtually hunt, using the urban landscape, if you give them access to each other. Players of *BotFighters* are consensually participating in a collective death-stacking rush, and it's endless, because the robots-representing-players are simply stripped of their battery power and forced to start the robot-rebuilding process again. So you have repetitive group activity toward tearing each other down.

This is not much different than the games that have ruled PC online multiplayer gaming, at least those games in the first-person shooter ilk. The goal of most introductory sessions of *Quake* and *Unreal* is to kill the other, more and faster. But even these most primitive fight-or-flight games have evolved. Prior to the North American mobilization against "terror," a user-created game "mod" (modification) of *Half-Life* (a popular first-person shooter) took over as the most popular online multiplayer game. *Counter-Strike* emphasizes team play with competing objectives (terrorism versus terrorist suppression), a fairly far cry from the indiscriminate killing favored by *Counter-Strike*'s predecessors. Perhaps the gamers who took up their mice and keyboards to stalk death in blood-splattered computer corridors have found they can manage tasks of increasing complexity.

Beast of Burden

Searching for increasing complexity in mobile games, it might be best to first seek out an appropriate mentor. Danielle (*nee* Daniel) Bunten Berry designed games for computers in the early 1980s. Although she created some compelling single-player adventures, her notable contributions to video gaming involved pre-Internet multiplayer, when multiple players explicitly meant multiple joysticks. In a 1998 eulogy posted on Happy Puppy, Greg Costikyan wrote about Berry's game design, "She saw that, however engaging play with a machine might be made, it was ultimately void, because it created no engagement with other people." Or, in Berry's own words from her personal website, "No one on their death bed ever said 'I wish I had spent more time alone with my computer!'" Her games today appear simple, with blocky characters walking around in solid-color two-dimensional top-down worlds. But this simplicity belies the thick multiplayer potential. Offer Bunten's 1983 *M.U.L.E.* on an emulator today and many gamers will be tapping away heatedly, two decades after she created *M.U.L.E.* for the Atari 800.

Players have landed on a planetary colony. By using the game's namesake "Multiple Use Labor Element" units to harvest a combination of food, energy, and mineral resources, the players contribute to the health of the colony. *M.U.L.E.*'s economy of resource consumption, harvesting, and supply managed by competative auction makes for ample entanglement between players. The genius of *M.U.L.E.* lies in the cooperative, playful economy where everyone contributes to the colony. There was a remake of *M.U.L.E.* in the works, in which Dani Berry was asked to add guns and bombs to the game. She refused. This game doesn't need the stakes of death and destruction to make for lively multiplayer.

To long for *M.U.L.E.* itself on a mobile phone is nothing more than another throwback. Still, the ideals within that simple space-trading game are legend precisely because they harness human entertainment time for lively cooperative competition. The game, relegated still to emulators, is largely the play material for literate game geeks who would know to seek it out and make it run. But games made in the spirit of *M.U.L.E.* are more likely to gain a sizeable and secular audience for multiplayer gaming on mobile phones. There's a lively sense of human-to-human play there that transcends metaphor and medium. Building may be more inviting to nontraditional gamers than death. Recent PC MMORPGs and Sega's *Phantasy Star Online* have proven that maintaining virtual life online appeals to a great many gamers.

Online All the Time

Everquest and the other multiplayer online role-playing games are the current societal exemplar for video game addiction. Professionals and married couples lose themselves in these fantasy kingdoms for hours a week. These are largely online communities. They are message boards and chat rooms with costumes and chat and some distraction. They are expansive 3D environments where people can build up persistent characters and enjoy some interaction. They add the hierarchy and interaction of other beings to the struggles to develop oneself in a finite virtual world.

Players and the curious commonly complain about the time required to maintain an active and evolving identity in a massively multiplayer online role-playing game. This is the function of any lively online community; frequent participation is required to keep up on community matters. But in most MMORPGs, the gameplay is dominated by time-on-task, where the players who can devote the most hours to the game develop strong characters. Folks with other engagements might find their avatars in the game world are weak compared with those avatars that belong to players with less balanced or busy lives. Some job-holding professionals have hired virtual babysitters for their online characters—high school kids paid to devote hours to developing online power and status for people that can only spare game time on the weekends.

All this is artificial and secondary to the enjoyment of the game experience. Clearly the chance to manage characters in a persistent fantasy world online appeals. Because the game world might be accessible anywhere anytime so it would seem that the immense time demands for modern multiplayer games make the mo-

bile phone a ready target—instead of spending four hours a night hunting basilisks on the desert plains, you could instead steal ten minutes here and twenty minutes there to dispatch any ready foes. This might give online multiplayers the chance to flexibly engage the game mechanic for character advancement. But the human interaction aspect of multiplayer online role-playing games could suffer. Players dropping in for ten minutes of gaming and then leaving could fracture the communal aspects of MMORPGs that are obviously so compelling. Perhaps a new form of conversation in MMORPGs would emerge from these mobile players. The first multiplayer role-playing game for mobile phones essentially ditched human communication by relegating it to a separate piece of software.

Samurai Romanesque

Samurai Romanesque is an online multiplayer role-playing game available to mobile phone subscribers of NTT DoCoMo's popular i-mode service in Japan. The game was developed by Dwango, the Japanese subsidiary of a Houston company established in the early 1990s to coordinate modem-based multiplayer for ID Software's popular first-person shooters, before the Internet made multiplayer a relatively trivial matter. The North American parent company went out of business before it could make the transition to Internet multiplayer game brokering, and so the Japanese subsidiary was left to make its way developing multiplayer technology and mobile phone games. In *Samurai Romanesque*, short samurai characters with large heads wander in a small screen vision of feudal Japan (figure 3.2). Compared with prior MMORPGs it is quite rudimentary, largely a string of mini-arcade games with social networking deliberately hobbled to comply with rules from Japanese phone provider NTT DoCoMo.

The game consists of three types of Java applications ("appli") downloaded into the mobile phone handset. The training applications are a squat samurai

| Figure 3.2 |
Samurai Romanesque

veneer applied to vintage arcade games, relying primarily on hand-eye coordination, through which you can boost particular character statistics and resources for later use in the regular game (another appli). For example, one training exercise called "the Landing game" would be familiar to anyone who has played with the black and white forerunners of mobile electronic entertainment, the Nintendo Game & Watch: Little men drop bales of hay and bombs from atop a wall; you run underneath with a basket on your head. Can you catch all the bales but not the bombs?

All this training is manifested in the main appli, where the proper electronic role playing takes place. In graphics reminiscent of 8-bit Nintendo or GameBoy titles, your shrunken samurai wanders through villages in feudal Japan. There are over a thousand villages in the game, and in each of them there might be some local event, a festival or some special food you can taste. It's sight-seeing in a small window—the events are rendered with some small picture and text in Japanese. According to Sachiko Kurokawa at Dwango, it should take six real-world months of gameplay to see all the sights in *Samurai Romanesque*.

In each village, you might find a shop, a teacher, a drunken belligerent looking for a fight, and maybe a wife. The lifespan of your character in the game is around forty days of game play. After that time, your character passes away. But you can perpetuate your legacy in the game world through procreation with one of the female characters you might meet in your travels.

In addition to the computer-coordinated nonplayer characters, you'll see many other small figures wandering the landscape alongside you. But you can't communicate with them in the main game. There are public bulletin boards in the game world where you can post messages composed of preselected words and phrases provided by the game. Occasionally as you wander between villages you'll have random battles. If it's not against a red or blue computer soldier, you're battling another thumbing *Samurai Romanesque* gamer. But they'll remain anonymous, in accordance with NTT DoCoMo's policies forbidding introductions between strangers visiting official content sites on their mobile phone networks. There is a third application provided for chat and conversation. Here you can talk strategy, tell stories, or do battle as your character. However, you can't arrange to meet, chat, or duel with a specific friend or foe in the chat appli, only with other random *Samurai Romanesque* gamers.

One of the first visions of the interconnected whole of mobile gaming is this, a feudal world full of voiceless *Pokemon*-scale characters. The pocket monsters in this case are gamers mingling with archetypes from Japanese tradition, the drunken buffoons, wise old men, pretty young maidens, and brave but lonely samurai who typify some modern images of old Japan. And each player is expected to play that, a samurai wandering in an online world, where he—always he—is passed constantly by other diminutive characters. These are the other players—just out of reach but still visible as a part of the same ether play space, connected in pockets and traincars throughout this island nation.

That the characters are slight and cuteified might only be uniquely Japanese but it is important to note here that anything must be shrunk to fit on these sorts of screens. It is the shorthand of expression evolved into a pervasive media mode in Japan: the tiny body and larger head. The gestures of the face must be written larger than the flailing of the limbs. Heads teetering on top of squat or skinny frames serve expression, emotion that can be read from a distance, or within a few pixels.

Although pixel granularity is another technological benchmark at the mercy of feverish technicians all over the world, the need to fashion avatars that can fit in our pockets and represent us in the immediate wireless future continues apace in other applications. Online avatars that we can train to travel in virtual worlds and even seek out their own relationships still require dedicated attention, perhaps nagging at our consciousness overmuch because they are ever-ready, never sleeping, seldom self-directed.

Two lives, or more—with the phone, one's own personal communications could be enough of a full-time pursuit. Already, these communications form the most popular form of mobile entertainment. It's not terrifically interactive, but in these early days of mobile technology, the most popular software is "personalization" software. Machines inherently lack a sense of play; we bring of ourselves and our culture to the machines to "personalize" them.

Personalization—Communications Score Keeping

What will come of communications technology if we continue to mingle machine and flesh? The dumb terminal phone in a pants pocket or purse will draw juice from an animated animal-human companion. We'll lift our faces from the info troughs to discover we're armored in green plastic caked with hair, old blood, and metal bits, a cyborganic mess shrink-wrapped in shiny pink or blue. Already Britney Spears and other pop fabrications can be commandeered to serve as your voice mail greeting. The J-Phone T06 from Toshiba sold in Japan in late 2001 came with Ulala standard. This purple-haired orange-skirted lady broadcasts intergalactic news in *Space Channel 5*, a popular console dancing game from Sega.

Here on this phone Ulala was not meant for play as a protagonist *per se* but as a phone intermediary and companion. As people call and email you, she keeps track. If enough friends engage your device, you "unlock" her greater powers; she will do special dances during which you can arrange her on your screen so you can watch her short skirt swoosh up over her orange pixel panties. The phone comes to tease you about the minutes you've already spent online, or plays into your perception of your popularity.

It's not a game in the sense of discreet events designed to test skill. But it is a game in the same sense as the game commentary software *Progress Quest*. In *Progress Quest*, players are asked to pick a few attributes about themselves, arbitrary fantasy-game designations. After you create your Trans-Kobold Inner Mason or a Double Hobbit Ur-Paladin, the game proceeds through simple text quests, combat, and item acquisition without any control or input from you—role-playing autopilot. This is a simplified play mechanic lifted from the likes of *Diablo*, the popular online treasure-hunting and monster slaying game that requires an endless flurry of clicking to drive relatively decisionless play. Likewise, our phone, our personal communications are a game we would play anyhow, even if nobody was keeping score.

Why keep score? It feeds a feeling of achievement and turns this constantly accompanying technology reflective. If I'm attentive to grooming my phone, my phone will increasingly come to resemble me. It's a merging of *The Sims* and technology, where we raise our devices as our digital children, our spawn reflecting us. This is the game, to create characters in our phones. And there are many minds planning to bring some sort of breeding game to the mobile phone; something along the lines of *Pokemon*, where characters are fed by your attention to technology and are then shared with or measured against other proximate personalized technology fans.

Better this sort of game than a story game for role playing. A role-playing game appeals to a small market of dedicated narrative trackers, people who can follow and pay attention to these fantastical threads. But as a Japanese friend reported, she loses track of story games when she returns to the rest of her life. She was happier

with simple pattern recognition through her phone. So there's always *Tetris* on the small screen, the deceptively simple game that made the GameBoy a bestselling piece of video game hardware. But between *Tetris* and *Everquest* is a middle path game that might make players of all of us. One vision involves value added to personal communications: All wireless exchanges could be a massively multiplayer online role-playing game.

My mascot contacts your mascot, and because neither one of us is present, our mascots mediate for us, exchanging information for each other that we can then absorb when we return to machine attention. We compose our mascots in our image, or as our ideal, an integrated sense of online self-awareness. And so do we adventure through information space, calling and emailing our friends to add to their score maintained by their phone, as we expect them to do the same for us.

Calling this the commoditization of human relationships is futile. Better to think of all as data. All of the human exchanges made media between small machines might be intermediated. By adding elementary machine accounting we create a data space where gameplay could occur.

Still, a literal recasting of your life in the virtual world would not be a game. There must be some break between real and virtual, some liminal space where play and manipulation can occur. The degree of this break and the interface between your mobile-mediated human communications is the play balancing task of the next generation of mobile game developers.

Simply connecting people and machines, keeping track of their communications, is paranoia-inducing perhaps. But leaving the dataforms open, however, could be a revolutionary act. If anyone was permitted to make metaphors for our personal communications, how many people might come up with some sort of viral fun that could infect our time and the space between us to make something insightful or whimsical? The possibilities are nearly visible in the air, as all interceding space is literally data-capable. One has only to look at the myriad uses of the Internet to see a human playspace made of what was first a United States Department of Defense failsafe. In this case, it has already been proven in Japan and Northern Europe that if you give people a wireless playspace, they will make someone else some money as they spend increasing portions of their social lives there.

By far the most popular application of mobile phones at the turn of the millennium is short messaging. Where are you? What are you doing? Are you available? I'm bored. These messages form the vast bulk of the information exchanged in wireless dataspace. Adding some game mechanism to this rapid fire short personal personnel tracking could turn communications into play, perhaps similar to Blizard's *Diablo*: rapid and indiscriminate accumulation and manipulation of intangible resources. The game merely marks time, channels rote activity into digital reinforcement. Life: thank you for playing. It's the feeling that all of life's activities, the banal ones, the insignificant ones, are now part of a system of accumulating value, adding a layer of meticulous data tracking—if not challenging, at least geekable.

That a game would have access to this information and could parse it in a timely fashion might be asking a lot from devices that still cannot maintain the average mobile phone call during a drive across town. It is the domain of the gamer and the theoretician to dream out this far into the field of mobile entertainment. And "mobile" is increasingly a blurred distinction, with laptops, personal digital assistants, connected watches, and Internet kiosks seemingly reproducing themselves and joining the information cacophony. In the future, the data exchange chatter among machines will outpace the few words exchanged by sentient flesh.

There will always be entertainment products for people who can disengage from socializing. What do we stand to gain from turning mobile devices into oddsmakers and scorekeepers for personal growth and development? To imagine a literal digitally driven collective play is perhaps over-whimsical. But already all of life and interaction is an exchange, a game of sorts. James P. Carse argues in his book *Finite and infinite games* a sort of gnomic approach to life—gnomic, in that we are consistently playing with the rules and structure of the games in our society and some success comes both from playing within and with those rules. Those who succeed, a Carse reader is encouraged to believe, are those who are aware of the metagame and are not too invested in the outcome.

We could see a mobile technology-connected society where the metagame is a mobile application or series of protocols specified by the mobile operators and their anointed software smiths. There is only one large game, and the victory conditions and players and moments of entertainment happen in temporary arrangements within the confines of that over-game. The channels between all of minds, the playspaces where we iterate our social relations and develop ourselves during "downtime" work within strictures specified by technology and technologists. Looser rules

manipulatable by broader creative minds should make for a more play-full society. Encouraging human play should relieve the stress probable when our lives are always-on online. What more does game-tracking add to the interconnected digital? Perhaps the very enshrinement of nonefficient human values, amid the commoditization of human communication: ameliorating the increasing technological mediation of our relationships.

Part II

Design

4

GAME DESIGN AND MEANINGFUL PLAY

Katie Salen and Eric Zimmerman

We have only to watch young dogs to see that all the essentials of human play are present in their merry gambols. They invite one another to play by a certain ceremoniousness of attitude and gesture. They keep to the rule that you shall not bite, or not bite hard, your brother's ear. They pretend to get terribly angry. And—what is most important—in all these doings they plainly experience tremendous fun and enjoyment. Such rompings of young dogs are only one of the simpler forms of animal play. There are other, much more highly developed forms, including regular contests and beautiful performances before an admiring public.

...

Even it its simplest forms on the animal level, play is more than a mere physiological phenomenon or a psychological reflex. It goes beyond the confines of purely physical or purely biological activity. It is a significant function—that is to say, there is some sense to it. In play there is something "at play" which transcends the immediate needs of life and imparts meaning to the action. All play means something. (Huizinga, 1955, p. 446, emphasis added)

Johan Huizinga is one of the greatest scholars of play in the twentieth century. His groundbreaking book, *Homo Ludens*, is a unique investigation of the role of play in human civilization. The title is a play on *Homo sapiens*, translated as *Man the Player*. According to Huizinga, play and games, which have been maligned in recent history as trivial and frivolous, are in fact at the very center of what makes us human. "Play is older than culture," as Huizinga puts it, and *Homo Ludens* is a celebration of play that links the visceral, combative nature of contest directly to war, poetry, art, religion, and other essential elements of culture. *Homo Ludens* is, in many ways, an attempt to redefine and elevate the significance of play.

Huizinga's vision of play offers a perfect point of departure for our development of the concept of meaningful play. Let us begin with a close reading of one section of the opening passage from *Homo Ludens*:

"It [play] is a significant function—that is to say, there is some sense to it. In play there is something "at play" which transcends the immediate needs of life and imparts meaning to the action. All play means something."

Huizinga emphasizes the fact that all play *means* something, that there is "sense" to play, that it transcends. The idea that "all play means something" is a wonderfully complex statement we can interpret in a variety of ways. In fact, all of the following are possible readings of the text:

• Huizinga says that play is a *significant function*. Does this mean that play is an important (and possibly unrecognized) force in culture—that it is significant in the way that art and literature are? Or does he mean that play *signifies*—that it is a symbolic act of communication?

• He mentions that there is *some sense* to play. Does he mean that play isn't solely chaotic, but is instead an event that can be understood and analyzed if one looks closely enough? Or is he implying that sense itself (the opposite of nonsense) is something intrinsically related to play?

• There's the complex statement: *In play there is something "at play."* Does Huizinga mean that there is always something deeper "at play," which constitutes any instance of play we observe in the real world? Or that in play something is always in motion, never fixed, and in a constant state of transformation?

• This "at play" quality of play *transcends the immediate needs of life*. Does the word "transcend" imply something spiritual? Or does Huizinga simply mean that play creates an artificial space beyond that of ordinary life?

• The same "at play" characteristic of play *imparts meaning to the action*. Does the fact that play is always "at play" relate to the meaning of the action? Or does it imply that play must be understood as one element of a more general system out of which meaning grows?

• The passage concludes with the sentence, *All play means something.* But what does play mean? To who or what is it meaningful? What is the process by which meaning emerges from play?

These are complex and multilayered questions, lacking definitive answers. In some sense, each of the interpretations posed are implied in Huizinga's statement, and all of them point to key aspects of play and play's participation in the creation of meaning. These important questions, and their possible answers, contain all of the main themes of this essay. We will, in the pages that follow, investigate the intricate relationships among game design, play, and meaning.

Meaning and Play

Learning to create great game experiences for players—experiences that have meaning and are meaningful—is one of the goals of successful game design, perhaps the most important one. We call this goal the design of *meaningful play*, the core concept of our approach. This concept is so critical to the rest of this chapter that we are going to repeat ourselves: *the goal of successful game design is the creation of meaningful play.* Meaningful play is that concept which can address all of the "unanswerable" questions raised by Huizinga. It is also a concept that raises questions of its own, challenging assumptions we might have about the role of design in shaping play.

One of the difficulties in identifying meaningful play in games is the near-infinite variety of forms that play can take. Here are some examples:

• the intellectual dueling of two players in a well-met game of Chess
• the improvisational, team-based balletics of Basketball
• the dynamic shifting of individual and communal identities in the online role-playing game *Everquest*
• the lifestyle-invading game Assassin, played on a college campus

What do all of these examples have in common? Each situates play within the context of a game. Play doesn't just come from the game itself, but from the way that players interact with the game in order to play it. In other words, the board, the pieces, and even the rules of Chess can't alone constitute meaningful play. Meaningful play emerges from the interaction between players and the system of the game, as well as from the context in which the game is played. Understanding this interaction helps us to see just what is going on when a game is played.

One way of framing what players do when they play a game is to say that they are making choices. They are deciding how to move their pieces, how to move their bodies, what cards to play, what options to select, what strategies to take, how to interact with other players. They even have to make the choice whether or not to play!

When a player makes a choice within a game, the action that results from the choice has an outcome. In Chess, if a player moves a piece on the board, this action affects the relationships of all of the other pieces: one piece might be captured, or a king might suddenly find itself in check. In Assassin, if a player stealthily stalks her target and manages to shoot him with a dart gun, the overall game changes as a result of this action: a hit is scored, the victim is out for the rest of the game, and he must give *his* target name to the player that just shot him. In *EverQuest*, if you engage with and kill a monster, the stats and equipment of your character can change; and the larger game-world is affected as well, even if it simply means that for the moment there is one less monster.

Playing a game means making choices and taking actions. All of this activity occurs within a game system designed to support meaningful kinds of choice making. Every action taken results in a change affecting the overall system of the game. Another way of stating this point is that an action a player takes in a game results in the creation of new meanings within the system. For example, after you move a piece in chess, the newly established relationships between chess pieces gives rise to a new set of meanings—meanings created by the player's action.

Two Kinds of Meaningful Play

We define meaningful play in two separate but related ways. The first sense of meaningful play refers to the way game actions result in game outcomes to create meaning. Framing the concept in this way, we offer the following definition:

Meaningful play *in a game emerges from the relationship between player action and system outcome; it is the process by which a player takes action within the designed system of a game and the system responds to the action. The* meaning *of an action in a game resides in the relationship between action and outcome.*

Think about an informal game of "Gross-Out" played during an elementary school recess. One by one, players tell a gross-out story, each tale more disgusting than the last. When a story is finished the group spontaneously and collectively responds, confirming or denying the player's position as master of the playground, until such time that an even grosser story is told.

If we look at Gross-Out from the perspective of meaningful play, we see that a player takes an action by telling a story. The *meaning* of the action, as a move in a game, is more than the narrative content of the story. It is also more than the theatrics used to tell the story. The outcome of the storytelling action depends on the other players and their own voting actions. Meaningful play emerges from the collective action of players telling and rating stories. The *meaning* of the story, in the sense of meaningful play, is not just that Hampton told a whopper about his little brother eating a live beetle—it is that Hampton's story has beaten the others and he is now the undisputed Gross-Out king.

This way of understanding meaningful play refers to the way *all* games generate meaning through play. Every game lets players take actions, and assigns outcomes to those actions. We therefore call this definition of meaningful play *descriptive*, because it describes what happens in every game. This is our first understanding of meaningful play.

At the same time, some games create more meaningful play than other games: the design of some games generates truly meaningful experiences for players, whereas other, less successful game designs result in experiences that somehow fall short. Even if meaningful play is a goal that we strive to achieve in our games, sometimes we don't quite get it right. So, in addition to our descriptive understanding of meaningful play, which describes what happens in all games, we need something that will help us be more selective in determining when meaningful play occurs.

This is the second sense of meaningful play. Instead of being a description of the way games operate, it refers to the goal of successful game design. This sense of meaningful play is *evaluative*: it helps us critically evaluate the relationships between actions and outcomes, and decide whether they are meaningful enough within the designed system of the game:

Meaningful play occurs when the relationships between actions and outcomes in a game are both discernable and integrated into the larger context of the game. Creating meaningful play is the goal of successful game design.

The word "meaningful" in this sense is less about the semiotic construction of meaning (how meaning is made) and more about the emotional and psychological experience of inhabiting a well-designed system of play. In order to understand why some play in games is more meaningful than others, we need to understand the key terms in the definition: *discernable* and *integrated*.

Discernable

Discernable means that the result of the game action is communicated to the player in a perceivable way. In the following excerpt from *Game Design: Theory and Practice*, Richard Rouse III points out the importance of displaying discernable information to the player within the context of the game-world. His example looks explicitly at computer games where there is an obvious need to condense massive amounts of data into a representative form that can be clearly communicated to the player. The idea of discernable outcomes applies to all games, digital or otherwise. Rouse writes,

Consider a strategy game in which the player has a number of units scattered all over a large map. The map is so large that only a small portion of it can fit on the screen at once. If a group of the player's units happen to be off-screen and are attacked but the player is not made aware of it by the game, the player will become irritated. Consider an RPG where each member of the player's party needs to be fed regularly, but the game does not provide any clear way of communicating how hungry his characters are. Then, if one of the party members suddenly keels over from starvation, the player will become frustrated, and rightly so. Why should the player have to guess at such game-critical information? (Rouse, 2001, p. 141)

If you shoot an asteroid while playing a computer game and the asteroid does not change in any way, you are not going to know if you actually hit it or not. If you do not receive feedback that indicates you are on the right track, the action you took will have very little meaning. On the other hand, if you shoot an asteroid and you hear the sound of impact, or the asteroid shudders violently, or it explodes (or all three!) then the game has effectively communicated the outcome of your action. Similarly, if you move a board game piece on the board but you have absolutely no idea whether your move was good or bad or if it brought you closer to or farther away from winning—in short, if you don't know the meaning of your action—then the result of your action was not discernable. Each of these examples makes clear that when the relationship between an action and the result of that action is not discernable, meaningful play is difficult or impossible to achieve.

Discernability in a game lets the players know *what* happened when they took an action. Without discernability, the player might as well be randomly pressing buttons or throwing down cards. *With* discernability, a game possesses the building blocks of meaningful play.

Integrated

Another component of meaningful play requires that the relationship between action and outcome is *integrated* into the larger context of the game. This means that an action a player takes not only has immediate significance in the game, but also affects the play experience at a later point in the game. Chess is a deep and meaningful game because the delicate opening moves directly result in the complex trajectories of the middle game—and the middle game grows into the spare and powerful encounters of the end game. Any action taken at one moment will affect possible actions at a later moment.

Imagine a multi-event athletic game, such as the Decathlon. At the start of the game, the players run a footrace. What if the rules of the game dictated that winning the footrace had nothing to do with the larger game? Imagine what would happen: the players would walk the race as slowly as possible, trying to conserve energy for the other, more meaningful events. Why should they do anything else? Although one of them will win the footrace, it will have no bearing on the larger game. On the other hand, if the players receive points depending on how well they rank and these points become part of a cumulative score, then the actions and the outcomes of the footrace are well integrated into the game as a whole.

Whereas discernability of game events tells players *what* happened (*I hit the monster*), integration lets players know *how* it will affect the rest of the game (*If I keep on hitting the monster I will kill it. If I kill enough monsters, I'll gain a level.*) Every action a player takes is woven into the larger fabric of the overall game experience: This is how the play of a game becomes truly meaningful.

Meaningful play can be realized in a number of ways, depending on the design of a particular game.

There is no single formula that works in every case. In the example of the asteroid shooting game, immediate and visceral feedback was needed to make the action discernable. But it might also be the case that in a story-based game, the results of an action taken near the beginning of the game are only understood fully at the very end, when the implications play out in a very unexpected and dramatic way. Both instances require different approaches to designing meaningful play.

Meaningful play engages several aspects of a game simultaneously, giving rise to layers of meaning that accumulate and shape player experience. Meaningful play can occur on the formal, mathematically strategic level of a single move in Chess. It can occur on a social level, as two players use the game as a forum for meaningful communication. And it can occur on larger stages of culture as well, where championship Chess matches can be used as occasions for Cold War political propaganda, or in contemporary philosophical debates about the relative powers of the human mind and artificial intelligence.

The rest of this chapter elaborates on the many ways that game designers construct spaces of meaningful play for players. Among the many topics we might select, we cover three core concepts that form several of the fundamental building blocks of game design: *design*, *systems*, and *interactivity*.

Design

What is the "design" in *game design* and how is it connected to the concept of "meaningful play"? In answer to this question, we offer the following general definition of design: *Design is the process by which a designer creates a* context *to be encountered by a* participant, *from which* meaning *emerges.*

Let us look at each part of this definition in relation to game design:

• The *designer* is the individual game designer or the team of people that create the game. Sometimes, games emerge from folk culture or fan culture, so there may not be an individual designer or design team. In this case, the designer of the game can be considered culture at large.
• The *context* of a game takes the form of spaces, objects, narratives, and behaviors.
• The *participants* of a game are the players. They inhabit, explore, and manipulate these contexts through their play.
• *Meaning* is a concept that we've already begun to explore. In the case of games, meaningful play

is the result of players taking actions in the course of play.

This connection between design and meaning returns us to the earlier discussion of meaningful play. Consider a game of Tag. *Without* design we would have a field of players scampering about, randomly touching each other, screaming, and then running in the other direction. *With* design, we have a carefully crafted experience guided by rules, which make certain forms of interaction explicitly meaningful. *With* design a touch becomes meaningful as a "tag" and whoever is "It" becomes master of the domain. The same is true of computer games as well. As game designer Doug Church puts it, "The design is the game; without it you would have a cd full of data, but no experience" (Church, 1999).

Design and Meaning

When we ask what something "means," particularly in the context of design, we are trying to locate the value or significance of that instance of design in a way that helps us to make sense of it. Questions such as, "What does the use of a particular color mean on a particular product?" or "What does that image represent?" or "What happens when I click on the magic star?" are all questions of *meaning*. Designers are interested in the concept of meaning for a variety of reasons, not least of which is the fact that meaning is one of the basic principles of human interaction. Our passage through life from one moment to the next requires that we make sense of our surroundings—that we engage with, interpret, and construct meaning. This movement toward meaning forms the core of interaction between people, objects, and contexts.

Consider the act of greeting a friend on the street. A wave, a nod, a kiss on the cheek, a pat on the back, a warm hug, a firm handshake, and a gentle punch in the arm are all forms of interaction meaning, "Hello, my friend." As a participant in this scenario, we must make sense of the gesture and respond appropriately. If we fail to make sense of the situation, we have failed to understand the meaning of the interaction. Game designers, in particular, are interested in the concept of meaning because they are involved in the creation of systems of interaction. These systems then give rise to a range of meaning-making activities, from moving a game piece on a board, to waging a bet, to communicating "Hello, my friend" with other online characters in a virtual game world. This question of how users make sense of objects has led some designers, in recent years, to borrow insights and expertise from other fields. In particular, the field of semiotics has been instructive. Semiotics is the study of meaning and the process by which meaning is made. In the next few pages, we will take a slight detour into semiotics, in order to more carefully build our concept of meaningful play.

Four Semiotic Concepts

The American philosopher and semotician Charles S. Peirce defines a sign as "something that stands for something, to somebody, in some respect or capacity" (Pierce, 1958). This broad definition recognizes four key ideas that constitute the concept of a sign.

1. A sign represents something other than itself.
2. Signs are interpreted.
3. Meaning results when a sign is interpreted.
4. Context shapes interpretation.

A Sign Represents Something Other Than Itself A sign represents something other than itself; it "stands for something." The mark of a circle (O) in the game of tic-tac-toe, for instance, represents not only an action by player "O" (as opposed to player "X") but also the capture of a certain square within the game's nine-square grid. Or consider the interaction between two players in a game of *Assassin*. A tap on the arm might represent "death" or "capture," depending on the rules of the game. In either case, the tap is meaningful to players as something other than a tap.

This concept of a sign representing something other than itself is critical to an understanding of games for several reasons. On one hand, games use signs to denote action and outcome, two components of meaningful play. The marks of an "X" or "O" in tic-tac-toe or the taps on the arms of players in a game of Assassin are actions paired with particular outcomes; these actions gain meaning as part of larger sequences of interaction. These sequences are sometimes referred to as "chains of signifiers," a concept that calls attention to the importance of relations between signs within any sign system.

On the other hand, games use signs to denote the elements of the game world. The universe of Mario, for example, is constructed of a system of signs representing magic coins, stars, pipes, enemies, hidden platforms, and other elements of the game landscape. The signs that make up the game world collectively represent the world to the player—as sounds, interactions, images, and text. Although the signs certainly make reference to objects that exist in the real world, they gain their symbolic value or meaning from the relationship between signs within the game. We can illustrate the idea of signs deriving meaning from *within* the context of a game with an example drawn from the history of *Scrabble*.

In late 1993, a campaign was initiated against Hasbro, the company that owns and distributes Scrabble, requesting that the company remove racial or ethnic slurs from *The Official Scrabble Players Dictionary* (OSPD). This rulebook of playable or "good" words contained, at that time, words such as "JEW," "KIKE," "DAGO," and "SPIC." As a result of pressure from The Anti Defamation League and the National Council of Jewish Women, Hasbro announced that fifty to one hundred "offensive" words would be removed from the OSPD. As Stefan Fatsis writes in *Word Freak: Heartbreak, Triumph, Genius, and Obsession in the World of Competitive Scrabble Players.*

The Scrabble community went ballistic. A handful of players, notably some devout Christians, backed the decision. But a huge majority led by a number of Jewish players, accused Hasbro of censorship. Words are words, and banning them from a dictionary would not make them go away, they argued. Plus, the players tried to explain, the words as played on a board during a game of Scrabble are without meaning. In the limited context of scoring points, the meaning of HONKIE, deemed offensive in the OSPD, is no more relevant than the meaning of any obscure but commonly played word. (Fatsis, 2001, p. 149)

Within the context of a game of Scrabble, words are reduced to sequences of letters—they literally do not have meaning as *words*. Rather, the letters are signs that have value as puzzle pieces that must be carefully arranged according to the rules of spelling. Thus, although the sequence of letters H-O-N-K-I-E has meaning as a racial slur *outside* of the context of a game of Scrabble, *within* it the sequence has meaning as a six-letter play worth a number of points on the board. Within Scrabble the chain of signifiers represent words stripped of everything except their syntactical relationships. Outside of Scrabble, however, the words represent racial animosity.

Looking at chains of signifiers within a game means dissecting a game in order to view the system at a micro-level to see how the internal machinery operates. But entire games themselves can also be identified as signs. Viewing them from a macro—rather than micro—perspective allows us to look at games from the outside, seeing them as signs within larger sign systems. The game of Tic-Tac-Toe, for instance, could be seen as a sign representing childhood play, while the game of Assassin might stand for college mischief in the 1980s or the film *The 10th Victim*, which inspired the game.

Signs Are Interpreted Peirce's definition suggests that *signs are interpreted*; they stand for something *to somebody*. It was one of Saussure's fundamental insights that the meanings of signs are arrived at arbitrarily via cultural convention. The idea that the meaning of signs rests not in the signs themselves but in the surrounding system is critical to our study of games. It is people (or players), after all, who bring meaning to signs. As semiotician David Chandler notes,

There is no necessary reason why a pig should be called a pig. It doesn't look sound or smell any more like the sequence of sounds "p-i-g" than a banana looks, smells, tastes or feels like the sequence of sounds "banana." It is only because we in our language group agree that it is called a "pig" that that sequence of sounds refers to the animal in the real world. You and your circle of friends could agree always to refer to pigs as "squerdlishes" if you wanted. As long as there is general agreement, that's no problem—until you start talking about squerdlishes to people who don't share the same convention. (Chandler)

Chandler's point has resonance when we consider players as active interpreters of a game's sign system. Children playing tag during recess may change the sign for "home base" from game to game, or even in the middle of a game, if circumstances allow. A tree in the corner of the playground might be used one day, or a pile of rocks another. Although a home base does have to possess certain functional qualities, such as being a touchable object or place, there is nothing special about the tree or rocks that make them "home base" other than their designation as such by the players of the game. Thus signs are essentially arbitrary, and gain value through a set of agreed upon conventions. Because "there is no simple sign = thing equation between sign systems and reality, it is we who are the active makers of meanings" (Underwood).

Meaning Results When a Sign Is Interpreted Peirce's definition suggests that meaning results when a sign is interpreted; a sign stands for something, to somebody, *in some respect or capacity*. Although this may seem like an obvious point, it is important to note, for it calls attention to the outcome of the process by which signs gain value within a system.

If player A in a game of Rock-Paper-Scissors holds up three fingers in the shape of a "W" instead of two in the shape of a "V," she has failed to create a sign that has value, or meaning, within the rock, paper, scissors sign structure of the game. Player B might say, "What is that supposed to be?" in an attempt to infuse the sign with value within the system of the game. If player A responds, "Scissors," then player B has two choices. She can either accept the new sign as representative of "scissors" or she can reject the interpretation. If she accepts the new representation, the players have, in effect, added a new sign to the system; a sign that now means "scissors."

Context Shapes Interpretation   Context is a key component to our general definition of design. It also is a key component in the creation of meaning. Design is "the process by which a *designer* creates a *context* to be encountered by a *participant*, from which *meaning* emerges." This definition makes an explicit connection between context and meaning. When we speak of context in language we are referring to the parts of something written or spoken that immediately precede or follow a word or passage that serve to clarify its meaning. The phrase "I am lost," for example, can mean many different things depending on the context in which it is used. If a player of the text adventure game *Zork* says, "I am trying to install the game and I am lost," we understand that she is having a difficult time making sense of the game's installation instructions. If that same player were to say, "I am in the second chamber and I am lost," we can ascertain that she is actually playing the game, has lost her way, and needs help navigating the fictional game space. In each instance the phrase "I am lost" is given context by the words that follow.

We can also understand context in relation to the idea of *structure*, which in semiotics refers to a set of regulations or guidelines that prescribe how signs, or elements of a system, can be combined. In language, for example, we refer to structure as *grammar*. The grammatical rules of a sentence create a structure that describes how words can and cannot be sequenced. We might refer to these rules as *invisible structure*, as we are not always aware that they are there. In games, this concept of grammar takes the form of game rules, which create a structure for the game, describing how all of the elements of the game interact with one another. Structure (in language or games) operates much like context, and participates in the meaning-making process. By ordering the elements of a system in very particular ways, structure works to create meaning. The communication theorist David Berlo uses the following example to explain how structure supports interpretation:

Structure:

Most smoogles have comcom

We don't know what smoogles and comcom are, but we still know something about them: we know that a smoogle is something countable and can be referred to in the plural, unlike, say, water or milk. We know that smoogles is a noun and not a verb. We know that more than one smoogle is referred to in this sentence. We know that comcom is a noun and that it is a quality or thing which most smoogles are claimed to have. We still don't know what is referred to, but the formal properties of English grammar have already provided us with a lot of information. (Berlo)

Although the structure of any system does provide information that supports interpretation, context ultimately shapes meaning. In the following example, Berlo shows how structure and context work together to aid interpretation:

Context:

My gyxpyx is broken

From the structure of the language you know that gyxpyx is a noun. You know that it's something that it makes sense to refer to as broken.

One of its keys is stuck

Now we're getting a bit closer—a gyxpyx is maybe a typewriter, calculator, or musical instrument; at any rate it's something that has keys.

and I think it could do with a new ribbon, as well

Well, that pretty well clinches it. We're still left with the question of just what the difference is between a typewriter and a gyxpyx or why this person has the odd habit of referring to typewriters as gyxpyxes, but we can be reasonably sure already that a gyxpyx is something typewriter-like. (Berlo)

Berlo goes on to note that the meaning we have for gyxpyx comes partly from the structure. We know it is a noun and we know it can be broken, that it has keys and a ribbon. But structure can only take us so far in our search for meaning; context must often be called upon to complete the quest. Consider the experience of playing a game of Pictionary with friends. Much of the guessing that occurs early in a turn relies on structure to provide clues. A player attempting to draw "Frankenstein" may begin by drawing a head and eyes, as a means of establishing the structure of the human form. This structure helps players to make guesses like "eyes," "face," or "head," but it soon becomes clear that more information is needed. In response, the player at the drawing board may begin to create a context for the head by drawing a large body with outstretched "zombie" arms, stitch marks denoting surgical scars, and a Tesla coil crackling in the background. Although players might not initially understand what these marks represent (the stitches might just look like squiggly lines), the context created by the other elements of the drawing supply the marks with the meaning they would otherwise lack. Once the players recognize the context "zombie" or "monster," the stitch marks become "scars" and Frankenstein is brought to life.

This relationship between structure, context, and meaning tells us that the act of interpretation relies, in part, on the movement between known and unknown information. Players of Pictionary, for example, will often come across a sign for which they don't have a meaning (stitch marks) within the context of signs for which they do (zombie or monster). The meanings that are known and familiar generate other meanings due to the formal relations between the known and the unknown signs. Keep in mind that the actual elements that constitute structure and context are fluid. The drawing of a head might operate as structure early in the guessing period (if it is the first thing drawn), but when it serves to help identify the squiggles, it becomes part of context. It is critical that designers not only recognize but also facilitate the relationship between structure and context in the design of their games.

Sign Systems
Games can be characterized as a system of signs. The meaning of any sign (object, action, or condition) in a game arises from the context of the game itself—from a system of relations between signs. This is what we mean when we say that the design of a game is the design of a space of possibility—a space in which rules and play create carefully orchestrated instances of designed interaction.

In *Swords and circuitry: A designer's guide to computer role playing games*, Neal and Jana Hallford (2001) look closely at the way players learn what something "means" through interaction. They describe a player exploring a world in an adventure game. The player

comes across a button set into an otherwise featureless wall. The curious player pushes the button to see what happens, and a secret door opens. Pushing the button gives the player access to a new part of the game world. Hallford and Hallford note that by providing the player with this scenario—push button, open door—the game designer has given the player a "rule" about how the game world works. The action *push button* results in the outcome *open secret door*. Armed with this rule, the player should be able to use this knowledge throughout the game to make informed decisions about how and when to push buttons. The meaning of the button press seems to be both integrated and discernable, two qualities of meaningful play. The interaction is *discernable*, because we clearly see the secret door open as a result of the action of pressing a button. The interaction also appears to be *integrated*, as we feel like we have discovered a rule about how buttons operate in the game.

Hallford and Hallford then ask us to imagine the player in another location somewhere later in the game. The player spies yet another button along the edge of a wall. If the action > outcome meaning of the button were integrated, the player should expect that pushing the button will open a secret door. But when the player pushes the button a fireball of doom comes out instead.

What just happened? Why did the button unleash a lethal fireball, rather than open a secret door? Here is where Hallford's analysis ties directly to the concept of play and representation. They write,

If the designer hasn't provided some kind of clue about what sets this button apart from the door-opening variety, they've just violated a rule that's already been established by the game. The value of choice has been taken away from the player because they have no way of knowing whether pushing the button opens a door or whether it will do some catastrophic amount of damage. While this would certainly add a heightened degree of tension to the pushing of any buttons in the game, it really is nothing more than a way of arbitrarily punishing the player for being curious. Even worse, the value of the things that the player has learned are now worthless, making the winning of the game more a matter of chance than of acquired skill. (Hallford & Hallford, 2001, pp. 152–154)

When the meaning of an action is unclear or ambiguous, meaningful play in a game breaks down. How might meaningful play in this situation be reestablished? Hallford and Hallford suggest one way to remedy the situation is by adding a small visual detail that gives the player some idea of the consequences for pushing a particular type of button. Blue buttons consistently open secret doors. Red buttons unleash fireballs of doom.

This example shows how game meanings can be engineered to create meaningful play. Color-coding buttons to denote consequence establishes a system of meaning. Players are, over time, able to determine which buttons are "good" and "bad," and can make informed choices about their actions in the world. This system implicates the player directly, for the *meaning* of a button is only ever established through player interaction. As Hallford and Hallford (2001) note, this design strategy will also have the added bonus that players will pay a little closer attention to their environment to see if there is anything new found there that may lead to new kinds of experiences. They do so by creating a very specific set of conditions, or context, within which a particular object or action becomes meaningful in the course of play.

Making sense of signs relies, in part, on the movement between known and unknown information. Players in Hallford and Hallfords hypothetical adventure game, for example, might come across a sign for which they don't have meaning (red button) within the context of signs for which they do (blue button). Familiar meanings generate other meanings due to the formal relations between known and unknown signs. Players of a game gain information about the game world by *interacting* with it, by *playing* with signs to see what they might do or what they might mean. This element of play as a mechanism for sense-making is a critical concept for game designers.

Systems

The system is partly a memory of its past, just as in origami, the essence of a bird or a horse is both in the nature and order of the folds made. The question that must be answered when faced with a problem of planning or design of a system, is what exactly is the system? It is therefore necessary to know the nature of the inner structure before plans can be made.—Wolfgang Jonas

Games are intrinsically systemic: all games can be understood as systems. A system is "a group of interacting, interrelated, or interdependent elements forming a complex whole."[1] In a game of soccer, the players, the ball, the goal nets, the playing field, are all individual elements. When a game of soccer begins, these elements gain specific relationships to each other within the larger system of the game. Each player, for example, plays in a certain position on one of two teams. Different player positions have roles that interrelate, both within the system that constitutes a single team (goalie vs. forward vs. halfback), and within the system that constitutes the relationship between teams (the goalie guarding the goal while an opposing forward attempts to score). The complex whole formed by all of these relationships within a system comprises the game of soccer.

As systems, games provide contexts for interaction, which can be spaces, objects, and behaviors that players explore, manipulate, and inhabit. Systems come to us in many forms, from mechanical and mathematical systems to conceptual and cultural ones. One of the challenges of our current discussion is to recognize the many ways a game can be framed as a system. Chess, for example, could be thought of as a strategic mathematical system. It could also be thought of as a system of social interaction between two players, or a system that abstractly simulates war.

The Elements of a System

A *system* is a set of things that affect one another within an environment to form a larger pattern that is different from any of the parts. In his textbook *Theories of human communication*, Stephen W. Littlejohn identifies four elements that constitute a system (1989, p. 41):

- *The first is* objects—*the parts, elements, or variables within the system. These may be physical or abstract or both, depending on the nature of the system.*
- *Second, a system consists of* attributes—*the qualities or properties of the system and its objects.*
- *Third, a system has* internal relationships *among its objects. This characteristic is a crucial aspect (of systems).*
- *Fourth, systems also possess an* environment. *They do not exist in a vacuum but are affected by their surroundings.*

Let us take a detailed look at a particular game, Chess. We will first think about chess as a strictly strategic and mathematical system. This means considering Chess as a purely formal system of rules. Framed in this way, the four elements of the system of Chess are as follows:

- *Objects*: The objects in Chess are the pieces on the board and the board itself.

- *Attributes*: These are the characteristics the rules give these objects, such as the starting positions of each piece and the specific ways each piece can move and capture.
- *Internal Relationships*: Although the attributes determine the possible movements of the pieces, the internal relationships are the actual positions of the pieces on the board. These spatial relationships on the grid determine strategic relationships: one piece might be threatening another one, or protecting an empty square. Some of the pieces might not even be on the board.
- *Environment*: If we are looking just at the formal system of Chess, then the environment for the interaction of the objects is the play of the game itself. Play provides the context for the formal elements of a game.

But framing the game as a formal system is only one way to think about the system of Chess. We can extend our focus and think of Chess as a system with experiential dimensions as well. This means thinking of chess not just as a mathematical and logical system, but also as a system of interaction between the players and the game. Changing the way that we frame the game affects how we would define the four components of a system. Framed as an experiential system, the elements of the system of Chess are as follows:

- *Objects*: Because we are looking at Chess as the interaction between players, the objects of the system are actually the two players themselves.
- *Attributes*: The attributes of each player are the pieces he or she controls, as well as the current state of the game.
- *Internal Relationships*: Because the players are the objects, their interaction constitutes the internal relationships of the system. These relationships would include not just their strategic interaction, but their social, psychological, and emotional communication as well.
- *Environment*: Considering chess as an experiential system, the total environment would have to include not just the board and pieces of the game, but the immediate environment that contained the two players as well. We might term this the *context of play*. Any part of the environment that facilitated play would be included in this context. For example, if it were a play-by-email game of Chess, the context of play would have to include the software environment in which the players send and receive moves. Any context of play would also include players' preconceptions of Chess, such as

the fact that they think it is cool or nerdy to play. This web of physical, psychological, and cultural associations delineate—not the experience of the game—but rather the context that surrounds the game, the environment in which the experience of play takes place.

Lastly, we can extend our focus and think about Chess as a cultural system. Here the concern is with how the game fits in to culture at large. There are many ways to conceive of games as culture. For example, say that we wanted to look at the game of Chess as a representation of ideological values associated with a particular time and place. We would want to make connections between the design of the game and larger structures of culture. We would be looking, for example, to identify cultural references made in the design of the game pieces (What is the gendered power relationship between King and Queen implied in their visual design?); references made in the structure and rituals of game play (Was playing chess polite and gentlemanly or vulgar and cutthroat?); and references made to the people who play (Who are they—intellectuals, military types, or nerds?).

Note that there are innumerable ways of framing Chess as a cultural system. We could examine the complex historical evolution of the game. Or we could investigate the amateur and professional subcultures (books, websites, competitions, etc.) that surround the game. We could study the culture of Chess variants, in which Chess is redesigned by player-fans, or how Chess is referenced within popular culture, such as the Chess-like game Spock played on the television show *Star Trek*. The list goes on.

Framing Systems

Even though we were talking about the same game each time, as we proceeded from a formal to an experiential to a cultural analysis, our sense of what we considered as part of the system grew. In fact, each analysis integrated the previous system into itself. This integration is made possible by the hierarchical nature of complex systems.

Because of the hierarchical nature of the critical or complex system, with interactions over all scales, we can arbitrarily define what we mean by a unit: In a biological system, one can choose either a single cell, a single individual, such as an ant, the ant's nest, or the ant as a species, as the adaptive unit. In a human social system, one might choose an individual, a family, a company, or a country as the unit. No unit at any level has the right to claim priority status. (Bek, p. 492)

In a game system, as in a human social system or biological system, hierarchies and interactions are scalable and embedded as complexity theorist Per Bek points out in the quote above. Although no single framing has an inherent priority, there are specific relationships among the kinds of framings given here. The formal system constituting the rules of a game are embedded in its system of play. Likewise, the system of play is embedded in the cultural framing of the game. For example, understanding the cultural connotations of the visual design of a game piece still should take into account the game's rules and play: the relative importance of the pieces and how they are actually used in a game. For example, answering a cultural question, regarding the politics of racial representation would have to include an understanding of the formal way the core rules of the game reference color. What does it mean that white always moves first?

Similarly, when you are designing a game you are not designing just a set of rules, but a set of rules that will always be experienced as play within a cultural context. As a result, you never have the luxury of completely forgetting about context when you are focusing on experience, or on experience and culture when you're focusing on the game's formal structure. It can be useful at times to limit the number of ways you are framing the game, but it is important to remember that a game's formal, experiential, and cultural qualities always exist as integrated phenomena.

Open and Closed Systems

There are two types of systems, *open* and *closed*. In fact, the concept of open and closed systems forms the basis of much of our discussion concerning the formal properties of games and their social and cultural dimensions. This concept speaks not only to games themselves, but also to the relationships games have to players and their contexts. What distinguishes the two types of systems? Littlejohn writes, "One of the most common distinctions [in systems theory] is between closed and open systems. A *closed system* has no interchange with its environment. An *open system* receives matter and energy from its environment and passes matter and energy to its environment" (Littlejohn, 1989, p. 41).

What makes a system open or closed is the relationship between the system and the context, or environment that surrounds it. The "matter and energy" that passes between a system and its environment can take a number of forms, from pure data (a thermometer measuring temperature and passing the information to the system of a computer program that tries to predict the weather), to human interaction (a person operating and interacting with the system of a car in order to drive down a highway). In both examples the system is open because there is some kind of transfer between the system and its environment. The software system passes temperature information from the outside climate. The car system exchanges input and output with the driver in a variety of ways (speedometer, gas pedal, steering wheel, etc).

When we frame a game as a system it is useful to recognize whether it is being treated as an open or closed system. If we look at our three framings of Chess, which framings were open and which were closed?

- *Formal system:* As a formal system of rules, Chess is a closed, self-contained system.
- *Cultural system:* As a cultural system, Chess is clearly an open system, as we are essentially considering the way that the game intersects with other contexts such as society, language, history, etc.
- *Experiential system:* As an experiential system of play, things get tricky. Framing Chess as an experiential system could lead to an understanding of the game as either open or closed. If we only consider the players and their strategic game actions, we could say that once the game starts, the only relevant events are internal to the game. In this sense, the game is a closed system. On the other hand, we could emphasize the emotional and social baggage that players bring into the game, the distractions of the environment, the reputations that are gained or lost after the game is over. In this sense, the play of Chess would be framed as an open system. So framed as play, games can be either open or closed.

In defining and understanding key concepts like design and systems, our aim is to better understand the particular challenges of game design and meaningful play. Game designers do practice design, and they do so by creating *systems*. But other designers create systems as well—so what is so special about games? The systems that game designers create have many peculiar qualities, but one of the most prominent is that they are interactive, that they require direct participation in the form of play. The next section builds directly on our understanding of systems and design to tackle this confounding but crucial concept: the enigmatic *interactivity*.

Interactivity

The word "interactivity" isn't just about giving players choices; it pretty much completely defines the game medium.—Warren Spector [2]

Play implies interactivity: to play with a game, a toy, a person, an idea, is to interact with it. More specifically, playing a game means making choices within a game system designed to support actions and outcomes in meaningful ways. Every action that is taken results in a change affecting the overall system. This process of action and outcome comes about because players interact with the designed system of the game. Interaction takes place across all levels, from the formal interaction of the game's objects and pieces, to the social interaction of players, to the cultural interaction of the game with contexts beyond its space of play.

In games, it is the explicit interaction of the player that allows the game to advance. From the interactivity of choosing a path to selecting a target for destruction to collecting magic stars, the player has agency to initiate and perform a whole range of explicit actions. In some sense, it is these moments of explicit action that define the tone and texture of a specific game experience. To understand this particular quality of games—the element of interaction—we must more completely grasp the slippery terms "interactive," "interaction," and "interactivity."

The following model presents four modes of interactivity, or four different levels of engagement, that a person might have with an interactive system. Most "interactive" activities incorporate some or all of them simultaneously.

Mode 1. *Cognitive interactivity; or interpretive participation:* This is the psychological, emotional, and intellectual participation between a person and a system. Example: the imaginative interaction between a single player and a graphic adventure game.

Mode 2. *Functional interactivity; or utilitarian participation:* Included here: functional, structural interactions with the material components of the system (whether real or virtual). For example, that graphic adventure you played: how was the interface? How "sticky" were the buttons? What was the response time? How legible was the text on your high-resolution monitor? All of these characteristics are part of the total experience of interaction.

Mode 3. *Explicit interactivity; or participation with designed choices and procedures:* This is "interaction" in the obvious sense of the word: overt participation like clicking the non-linear links of a hypertext novel, following the rules of a board game, rearranging the clothing on a set of paper dolls, using the joystick to maneuver Ms. Pac-Man. Included here: choices, random events, dynamic simulations, and other procedures programmed into the interactive experience.

Mode 4. *Beyond the object-interactivity; or cultural participation:* This is interaction outside the experience of a single designed system. The clearest examples come from fan culture, in which participants co-construct communal realities, using designed systems as the raw material. Will Superman come back to life? Does Kirk love Spock?

But Is It "Designed" Interaction?

Interaction comes in many forms. But for the purposes of designing interactivity, it is important to be able to recognize what forms of interactivity designers create. As an example, compare the following two actions: someone dropping an apple on the ground and someone rolling dice on a craps table. Although both are examples of interaction proper, only the second act, rolling the dice, is a form of designed interaction.

What about this action has been designed? First, the dice, unlike the apple, are part of a system (a game) in which the interaction between the player and the dice is made meaningful by a set of rules describing their relationship. This relationship, as defined by the rules of craps, describes the connection between action and outcome—for example, "When the dice are rolled, a player counts the number of dots appearing on the face-up sides of the dice." Even this extremely simple rule demonstrates how the act of rolling has meaning within the designed interactive system of the game. Secondly, the interaction is situated within a specific context: a game. Remember that meaningful play is tied not only to the concept of player action and system outcome, but also to a particular context in which the action occurs.

The description of "someone dropping an apple on the ground," on the other hand, does not contain a designed structure or context. What conditions would have to be present to evolve this simple interaction into a designed interaction? The dropping of the apple does meet baseline criteria for interaction: there is a reciprocal relationship between the elements of this system (such as the person's hand, the apples, and the ground). But is it a designed interaction? Is the interactivity situated within a specific context? Do we have any ideas about what dropping the apple might "mean" as a form of interaction between a person and an apple? Do we have a sense of the connection between action and outcome?

No. All we know is that an apple has been dropped. What is missing from this description is an explicitly stated context within which the dropping of the apple occurs. If we were to change the scenario a little by adding a second player and asking the two participants to toss the apple back and forth, we move toward a situation of designed interaction. If we were to ask the two apple-tossers to count the number of times in a row they caught the apple before dropping it, we add an even fuller context for the interaction. The simple addition of a rule designating that the players quantify their interaction locates the single act of toss-catch within an overall system. Each element in the system is assigned a meaning: the toss, the catch, and the dropped toss. Even in the simplest of contexts, design creates meaning.

Interaction and Choice
The careful crafting of player experience via a system of interaction is critical to the design of meaningful play. Yet, just what makes an interactive experience "meaningful?" We have argued that in order to create instances of meaningful play, experience has to incorporate not just explicit interactivity, but meaningful *choice*. When a player makes a choice in a game, the system responds in some way. The relationship between the player's choice and the system's response is one way to characterize the depth and quality of interaction. Such a perspective on interactivity supports the descriptive definition of meaningful play presented earlier.

In considering the way that choices are embedded in game activity, we look at the design of choice on two levels: micro and macro. The *micro* level represents the small, moment-to-moment choices a player is confronted with during a game. The *macro* level of choice represents the way in which these micro-choices join together like a chain to form a larger trajectory of experience. For example, this distinction marks the difference between tactics and strategy in a game such as Go. The *tactics* of Go concern the tooth-and-nail battles for individual sectors of the board, as individual pieces and small groups expand across territory, bumping up against each other in conflict and capture. The *strategy* of the game is the larger picture, the overall shape of the board that will ultimately determine the winner. The elegance of the design of Go lies in its ability to effortlessly link the micro and the macro, so

that every move a player makes works simultaneously on both levels. Micro-interaction and macro-interaction are usually intertwined and there are, of course, numerous shades of gray in between.

Keep in mind that "choice" does not necessarily imply *obvious* or *rational* choice, as in the selection of an action from a menu. Choice can take many forms, from an intuitive physical action (such as "twitch" firing of a *Time Crisis* pistol) to the random throw of a die. Below are a few more examples of designed choices in games.

• *The choice of whether or not to take a hit in Blackjack.* A Blackjack player always has a clear set of choices: the micro-choice of taking or not taking a hit will have the eventual outcome of a win or a loss against the house. On the macro-level, each round affects the total amount of money the player gains or loses over the course of the game. Playing each hand separately, according to its probability of beating the house, is like tactics in Go. Counting cards, which links all of a players hands between rounds, is a more long-term, strategic kind of choice-making.

• *The choice of what to type into the flashing cursor of a text adventure.* This is a more open-ended choice context than the simple hit or pass of Blackjack. The micro-choice of typing in a command gives the player feedback about how the player moves through or changes the world. The choice to type the words "Move North" takes the player to another location in the game where different actions are possible—perhaps actions that will eventually solve the multipart puzzles which exist on the macro-level of game play. Even when a player tries to take an action that the program cannot parse (such as typing "grab rock" instead of "get rock"), it is meaningful: the outcome of bumping up against the limits of the program's parsing ability serves to further delineate the boundaries of play.

• *The choice of what play to call in a Football game.* This moment of game-choice is often produced collaboratively among a coaching staff, a quarterback, and the rest of the offensive players. There are a large number of possible plays to call, each with variations, and the choice is always made against the backdrop of the larger game: the score, the clock, the field position, the down, the strengths and weaknesses of both teams. The most macro-level of choices address the long-term movement of the ball across the field and the two teams' overall scores. The most micro-level of choices occur once the play is called and the ball is hiked: every offensive player has the moment-to-moment challenge of executing the play as the defensive team does its best to put a stop to it.

. As these examples demonstrate, choice making is a complex, multilayered process. There is a smooth transition between the micro- and macro-levels of choice making, which play out in an integrated way for the player. When the outcome of every action is discernable and integrated, choice making leads to meaningful play. Game designer Doug Church, in his influential essay "Formal Abstract Design Tools," outlines the way that these levels of choice transition into a complete game experience.

In a fighting game, every controller action is completely consistent and visually represented by the character on-screen. In Tekken, *when Eddy Gordo does a cartwheel kick, you know what you're going to get. As the player learns moves, this consistency allows planning—intention—and the reliability of the world's reactions makes for perceived consequence. If I watch someone play, I can see how and why he or she's better than I am, but all players begin the game on equal footing* (Church, 1999).

As Church points out, the macro-levels of choice making include not only what to do over the course of a game, but also whether or not you want to play a game, and against whom. If you are beaten in a fighting game that doesn't contain clear and meaningful play, you will never know why you lost and you will most likely not play again. On the other hand, if you know why your opponent is better than you are, your loss is meaningful, as it helps you assess your own abilities, gives you ideas for improvement, and spurs on your overall interaction with the game.

Choice Molecules

[The designers of Spacewar!, *a 2D graphical shooter dating back to 1962] identified action as the key ingredient and conceived* Spacewar! *as a game that could provide a good balance between thinking and doing for its players. They regarded the computer as a machine naturally suited for representing things that you could see, control, and play with. Its interesting potential lay not in its ability to perform calculations but in its capacity to represent action in which humans could participate.*—Brenda Laurel

The capacity for games to "represent action in which players participate" forms the basis of our concept of "choice." If we consider that every choice has an out-

come, then it follows that this action > outcome unit is the vehicle through which meaning in a game emerges. Although games can generate meaning in many ways (such as through image, text, sound, etc.), to understand the interactive nature of meaningful play, we focus on the kinds of meaning that grow from player interaction. At the heart of interactive meaning is the action > outcome unit, the molecule out of which larger interactive structures are built.

In order to examine this concept more closely we will look at the classic arcade game Asteroids, a direct discontent of Spacewar!. In Asteroids, a player uses buttons to maneuver a tiny spaceship on the screen, avoiding moving asteroids and UFOs and destroying them by shooting projectiles. The action > outcome interactive units of Asteroids are manipulated through a series of five player commands, each one of them a button on the arcade game's control panel: rotate left, rotate right, thrust, fire, and hyperspace. Within the scope of an individual game, possible player actions map to the five buttons:

1. *Press rotate right button:* spaceship rotates right
2. *Press rotate left button:* spaceship rotates left
3. *Press thrust button:* spaceship accelerates in the direction it is facing
4. *Press fire button:* spaceship fires projectile (up to four on the screen at a time)
5. *Press hyperspace button:* spaceship disappears and reappears in a different location (and occasionally perishes as a result)

Action on the screen is affected through the subtle (and not so subtle!) orchestration of these five controls. As the game progresses, each new moment of choice is a response to the situation onscreen, which is the result of a previous string of action > outcome units. The seamless flow that emerges is one of the reasons why Asteroids is so much fun to play. Rarely are players aware of the hundreds of choices they make each minute as they dodge space rocks and do battle with enemy ships—they perceive only their excitement and participation inside the game.

Anatomy of a Choice

Although the concept of choice may appear basic upon first glance, the way that a choice is actually constructed is surprisingly complex. To dissect our action > outcome molecule, we need to ask the following five questions. Together, they outline the *anatomy of a choice.*

1. *What happened before the player was given the choice?* What is the current state of the pieces on a gameboard, for example, or the level of a player's health? What set of moves were just finished playing out? What is the game status of other players? This question relates to both the micro and macro events of a game, and addresses the context in which a choice is made.

2. *How is the possibility of choice conveyed to the player?* On a game board, the presence of empty squares or a "draw pile" might indicate the possibility of choice, whereas choices in a digital game are often conveyed through the game's controls. In Asteroids, for example, the five buttons on the control panel communicate the opportunity for choice-making to the player.

3. *How did the player make the choice?* Did the player make a choice by playing a card, pressing a button, moving a mouse, running in the opposite direction, or passing on a turn? The mechanisms a player uses to make a choice vary greatly, but all are forms through which players are given the opportunity to take action.

4. *What is the result of the choice? How will it affect future choices?* A player taking action within a system will affect the relationships present in that system. This element of the anatomy of a choice speaks to the outcome of a player action, identifying how a single choice impacts larger events within the game world. The outcome of taking a "hit" in Blackjack impacts whether or not the player wants to take another hit, as well as the outcome of the game.

5. *How is the result of the choice conveyed to the player?* The means by which the results of a choice are represented to a player can assume many guises, and forms of representation are often related to the materiality of the game itself. In a game of Twister, for example, the physical positioning of bodies in space, conveys the results of choices; in Missile Command, the result of the choice to "fire" is conveyed by a slowly moving line of pixels, ending in an explosion; in Mousetrap, the mechanical workings (or non-workings) of the mousetrap convey the results of moving a mouse into the trap space. Note that step 5 leads seamlessly back to step 1, because the result of the choice provides the context for the next choice.

These are the five stages of a choice, the five events that transpire every time an action and outcome occur in a game. Each stage is an event that occurs internal or external to the game. *Internal events* are related to the systemic processing of the choice; *external* events are related to the representation of the choice to the

player. These two categories make a distinction between the moment of action as handled by the internal game state and the manifestation of that action to the player.

The idea that a game can have an internal event represented externally implies that games are systems that store information. Jesper Juul, in a lecture titled "Play Time, Event Time, Themability" (2001), describes this idea by thinking of a game as a state machine:

A game is actually what computer science describes as a state machine. It is a system that can be in different states. It contains input and output functions, as well as definitions of what state and what input will lead to what following state. When you play a game, you are interacting with the state machine that is the game. In a board game, this state is stored in the position of the pieces on the board, in computer games the state is stored as variables, and then represented on the screen.[3]

In Juul's example of a board game, the "internal" state of the game is immediately evident to the players in the way that the pieces are arranged on the board. In the case of a computer game, as Juul points out, the internal variables have to be translated into a representation for the player. The distinction between internal and external events helps us to identify and distinguish the components of a choice. Within the action > outcome molecule stages 1, 3, and 4 are internal events, and stages 2 and 5 are external events. These two layers of events form the framework within which the anatomy of a choice must be considered. To see how this all fits together, let us take an even closer look, in table 4.1, at the way choice is constructed in two of our example games, Asteroids and Chess.

Although all five stages of the action > outcome choice event occurred in both games, there are some significant differences. In Asteroids, the available choices and the taking of an action both involve static physical controls. In Chess, the pieces on the board serve this function, even as they convey the current state of the game. The internal and external states of Chess are identical, but in Asteroids, what appears on the screen is only an outward extension of the internal state of the software. Although the "anatomy of a choice" structure occurs in every game, each game will manifest choice in its own way.

This way of understanding choice in a game can be extremely useful in diagnosing game design problems. If your game is failing to deliver meaningful play, it is

Table 4.1
Asteroids and chess

	Asteroids	Chess
1. What happened before the player was given the choice? (internal event)	Represented by the current positions and trajectories of the game elements.	Represented by the current state of the pieces on the board.
2. How is the possibility of choice conveyed to the player? (external event)	The possible actions are conveyed through the persistent button controls as well as the state of the screen, as it displays the relationships of the game elements.	The possible actions are conveyed through the arrangement of pieces on the board, including the empty squares where they can move.
3. How did the player make the choice? (internal event)	The player makes a choice by pressing one of the five buttons.	The players makes a choice by moving a piece.
4. What is the result of the choice? How will it affect future choices? (internal event)	Each button press affects the system in a different way, such as the position or orientation of the player's ship.	Each move affects the overall system, such as capturing a piece or shifting the strategic possibilities of the game.
5. How is the result of the choice conveyed to the player? (external event)	The result of the choice is then represented to player via screen graphics and audio.	The result of the choice is then represented to player via the new arrangement of pieces on the board.

probably because is a break down somewhere in the action > outcome chain. Here is a sample list of common "failure states" and the way that they relate to the stages of a choice.

• *Feeling like decisions are arbitrary.* If you need to play a card from your hand and it always feels like it doesn't matter which card you select, the game probably suffers in stage 4, the affect of the player's choice on the system of the game. The solution is to make sure that player actions have meaningful outcomes in the internal system of the game.

• *Not knowing what to do next.* This can be a common problem in large digital adventure games, where it is not clear how a player can take action to advance the game. The problem is in stage 2, representing choices to the player. These kinds of problems are often solved with additional information display, such as highlights on a map, or an arrow that helps direct the player.

• *Losing a game without knowing why.* You think that you're about to reach the top of the mountain, when your character dies unexpectedly from overexposure. This frustrating experience can come about because a player has not sufficiently been informed about the current state of the game. The problem might be in stage 5, where the new state of the game resulting from a choice is not represented clearly enough to the player.

• *Not knowing if an action even had an outcome.* Although this sounds like something that would never happen, there are many examples of experimental inter-activity (such as a gallery-based game with motion sensor inputs) in which the player never receives clear feedback on whether or not an action was taken. In this case, there is a breakdown at stages 3 and 4, when a player is taking an action and receiving feedback on the results.

These examples represent only a small sampling of the kinds of problems a game's design can have. The anatomy of a choice is not a universal tool for fixing problems, but it can be especially useful in cases where the game is breaking down because of a glitch in the player's choice-making process.

Space of Possibility
Creating a game means designing a structure that will play out in complex and unpredictable ways, a space of possible action that players explore as they take part in your game. What possible actions might players take in the course of a game of Musical Chairs? They might push, shove, tickle, poke, or fight for their seat once the music stops and the mad scramble for chairs begins. The game designer must carefully craft a system of play in which these actions have meaning in support of the play of the game, and do not distract or interrupt its play.

But game designers do not directly design play. They only design the structures and contexts in which play takes place, indirectly shaping the actions of the players. We call the space of future action implied by a game design the *space of possibility*. It is the space of all possible actions that might take place in a game, the space of all possible meanings which can emerge from a game design. The concept of the space of possibility not only bridges the distance between the designed structure and the player experience, but it also combines the key concepts we have presented so far. The space of possibility is *designed* (it is a constructed space, a context), it generates *meaning* (it is the space of all possible meanings), it is a *system* (it is a space implied by the way elements of the system can relate to each other), and it is *interactive* (it is through the interactive functioning of the system that the space is navigated and explored).

The Magic Circle

This is the problem of the way we get into and out of the play or game ... what are the codes which govern these entries and exits?—Brian Sutton-Smith

What does it mean to enter the system of a game? How is it that play begins and ends? What makes up the boundary of a game? At stake is an understanding of the artificiality of games, the way that they create their own time and space separate from ordinary life.

Steve Sniderman, in his excellent essay "The Life of Games" notes that the codes governing entry into a game lack explicit representation. "Players and fans and officials of any game or sport develop an acute awareness of the game's 'frame' or context, but we would be hard pressed to explain in writing, even after careful thought, exactly what the signs are. After all, even an umpire's yelling of 'Play Ball' is not the exact moment the game starts." (Sniderman). He goes on to explain that players (and fans) must rely on intuition and their experience with a particular culture to recognize when a game has begun. During a game, he writes, "a human being is constantly noticing if the conditions for playing the game are still being met, continuously monitoring the 'frame,' the circumstances surrounding play, to determine that the game is still in progress, always aware (if only unconsciously) that the other participants are acting as if the game is 'on'" (Sniderman).

The frame of a game is what communicates that those contained within it are "playing" and that the space of play is separate in some way from that of the real world. Psychologist Michael Apter echoes this idea when he writes,

In the play-state you experience a protective frame which stands between you and the 'real' world and its problems, creating an enchanted zone in which, in the end, you are confident that no harm can come. Although this frame is psychological, interestingly it often has a perceptible physical representation: the proscenium arch of the theater, the railings around the park, the boundary line on the cricket pitch, and so on. But such a frame may also be abstract, such as the rules governing the game being played. (Apter, 1990, p. 15)

In other words, the frame is a concept connected to the question of the "reality" of a game, of the relationship between the artificial world of the game and the "real life" contexts that it intersects. The frame of a game is responsible not only for the unusual relationship between a game and the outside world, but also for many of the internal mechanisms and experiences of a game in play. We call this frame the *magic circle*, a concept inspired by Johan Huizinga's work on play.

Boundaries

What does it mean to say that games take place within set boundaries established by the act of play? Is this really true? Compare, for example, the informal play of a toy with the more formal play of a game. A child approaching a doll, for example, can slowly and gradually enter into a play relationship with the doll. The child might look at the doll from across the room and shoot it a playful glance. Later, the child might pick it up and hold it, then put it down and leave it for a time. The child might carelessly drag the doll around the room, sometimes talking to it and acknowledging it, at other times forgetting it is there.

The boundary between the act of playing with the doll and not playing with the doll is fuzzy and permeable. Within this scenario we can identify concrete play behaviors, such as making the doll move like a puppet. But there are just as many ambiguous behaviors, which might or might not be play, such as idly kneading its head while watching TV. There may be a frame between playing and not playing, but its boundaries are indistinct.

Now compare that kind of informal play with the play of a game—two children playing Tic-Tac-Toe. In order to play, the children must gather the proper materials, draw the four lines that make up the grid of the board, and follow the proper rules each turn as they progress through the game. With a toy, it may be difficult to say exactly when the play begins and ends. But with a game, the activity is richly formalized. The game has a beginning, a middle, and a quantifiable outcome at the end. The game takes place in a precisely defined physical and temporal space of play. Either the children are playing Tic-Tac-Toe or they are not.

There is no ambiguity concerning their action: they are clearly playing a game.

The same analysis can occur within the context of digital media. Compare, for example, a user's casual interaction with a toylike screensaver program to their interaction with a computer game such as Tetris. The screensaver allows the user to wiggle the mouse and make patterns on the screen, an activity that we can casually enter into and then discontinue. The entry and exit of the user is informal and unbound by rules that define a beginning, middle, and end. A game of Tetris, on the other hand, provides a formalized boundary regarding play: the game is either in play or it is not. Players of Tetris do not "casually interact" with it; rather, they are playing a game. It is true that a Tetris player could pause a game in progress and resume it later—just as two tennis players might pause for a drink of water. But in both cases the players are stepping out of the game space, formally suspending the game before stepping back in to resume play.

As a player steps in and out of a game, he or she is crossing that boundary—or frame—that defines the game in time and space. As noted above, we call the boundary of a game the *magic circle*, a term borrowed this from the following passage in Huizinga's book *Homo Ludens*:

All play moves and has its being within a play-ground marked off beforehand either materially or ideally, deliberately or as a matter of course.... The arena, the card-table, the magic circle, the temple, the stage, the screen, the tennis court, the court of justice, etc., are all in form and function play-grounds, i.e., forbidden spots, isolated, hedged round, hallowed, within which special rules obtain. All are temporary worlds within the ordinary world, dedicated to the performance of an act apart. (Huizinga, 1955, p. 10)

Although the magic circle is merely one of the examples in Huizinga's list of "play-grounds," the term is used here as shorthand for the idea of a special place in time and space created by a game. The fact that the magic circle is just that—a circle—is an important feature of the concept. As a closed circle, the space it circumscribes is enclosed and separate from the real world. As a marker of time, the magic circle is like a clock: it simultaneously represents a path with a beginning and end, but one without beginning and end. The magic circle inscribes a space that is repeatable, a space both limited and limitless. In short, a finite space with infinite possibility.

Enter In
Boundaries help separate the game from life. They have a critical function in maintaining the fiction of the game so that the aspects of reality with which we do not choose to play can be left safely outside.—Bernie De Koven

In a very basic sense, the magic circle of a game is where a game takes place. To play a game means entering into a magic circle, or perhaps creating one as a game begins. The magic circle of a game might have a physical component, like the board of a board game or the playing field of an athletic contest. But many games have no physical boundaries—arm wrestling, for example, doesn't require much in the way of special spaces or material. The game simply begins when players decide to play.

The term magic circle is appropriate because there is in fact something genuinely magical that happens when a game begins. A fancy Backgammon set sitting all alone might be a pretty decoration on the coffee table. If this is the function that the game is serving—decoration—it doesn't really matter how the game pieces are arranged, or if some of them are out of place, or even missing. However, once you sit down with a friend to play a game of Backgammon, the arrangement of the pieces suddenly becomes extremely important. The Backgammon board becomes a special space that facilitates the play of the game. The players' attention is intensely focused on the game, which mediates their interaction through play. While the game is in progress, the players do not casually arrange and rearrange the pieces, but move them according to very particular rules.

The Lusory Attitude
So far in the discussion of the magic circle we have outlined the ways that the interior space of a game relates to the real world spaces outside it, how the magic circle frames a distinct space of meaning that is separate from, but still references, the real world. What we have not yet considered is what the magic circle represents from the player's point of view. Because a game demands formalized interaction, it is often a real commitment to decide to play a game. If a player chooses to sit down and play Monopoly, for example, he cannot simply quit playing in the middle without disrupting the game and upsetting the other players. On the other hand, if he ignores this impulse and remains in the game to the bitter end, he might end up a sore loser. Yet, these kinds of obstacles obviously don't keep most people from

playing games. What does it mean to decide to play a game? If the magic circle creates an alternate reality, what psychological attitude is required of a player entering into the play of a game?

Games are curiously inefficient and challenging activities. To play a game is to take on a task that is not easy to accomplish. In his book *Grasshopper: Games, Life, and Utopia*, Bernard Suits uses the example of a boxer to explain this concept. If the goal of a boxing match is to make the other fighter stay down for a count of 10, the easiest way to accomplish this goal would be to take a gun and shoot the other boxer in the head. This, of course, is not the way that the game of Boxing is played. Instead, as Suits points out, boxers put on padded gloves and only strike their opponents in very limited and stylized ways. Similarly, Suits discusses the game of Golf:

Suppose I make it my purpose to get a small round object into a hole in the ground as efficiently as possible. Placing it in the hole with my hand would be a natural means to adopt. But surely I would not take a stick with a piece of metal on one end of it, walk three or four hundred yards away from the hole, and then attempt to propel the ball into the hole with the stick. That would not be technically intelligent. But such an undertaking is an extremely popular game, and the foregoing way of describing it evidently shows how games differ from technical activities. (Suits, 1990, p. 40)

What the boxer and the golfer have in common, according to Suits, is a shared attitude toward the act of game-playing, an openness to the possibility of taking such indirect means to accomplish a goal. "In anything but a game the gratuitous introduction of unnecessary obstacles to the achievement of an end is regarded as a decidedly irrational thing to do, whereas in games it appears to be an absolutely essential thing to do" (Suits, 1990, pp. 38–39). Suits calls this state of mind the *lusory attitude*. The lusory attitude allows players to "adopt rules which require one to employ worse rather than better means for reaching an end" (Suits, 1990, pp. 38–39). Trying to propel a miniature ball with a metal stick into a tiny hole across great distances certainly requires something by way of attitude!

The word "ludo" means *play* in Latin, and the root of "lusory" is the same root as "ludens" in "Homo Ludens." The lusory attitude is an extremely useful concept, as it describes the attitude that is required of game players for them to enter into a game. To play a game is in many ways an act of "faith" that invests the game with its special meaning—without willing players, the game is a formal system waiting to be inhabited, like a piece of sheet music waiting to be played. This notion can be extended to say that a game is a kind of social contract. To decide to play a game is to create—out of thin air—an arbitrary authority that serves to guide and direct the play of the game. The moment of that decision can be quite magical. Picture a cluster of boys meeting on the street to show each other their marble collections. There is joking, eye-rolling, and then a challenge rings out. One of them chalks a circle on the sidewalk and each one of them puts a marble inside. They are suddenly playing a game, a game that guides and directs their actions, that serves as the arbiter of what they can and cannot do. The boys take the game very seriously, as they are playing for keeps.

Their goal is to win the game and take marbles from their opponents. If that is all they wanted to do, they could just grab each other's marble collections and run. Instead, they play a game. Through a long and dramatic process, they end up either losing their marbles or winning some from others. If all that the boys wanted to do was increase the number of marbles in their collection, the game might seem absurd. But the lusory attitude implies more than a mere acceptance of the limitations prescribed by the rules of the game—it also means accepting the rules because the play of the game is an end in itself. In effect, the lusory attitude ensures that the player accepts the game rules "just so that the activity made possible by such an acceptance can occur" (Suits, 1990, p. 40).

There is a pleasure in this inefficiency. When you fire a missile in *Missile Command*, it doesn't simply zap to the spot underneath the crosshairs. Instead, it slowly climbs up from the bottom of the screen. To knock down a set of bowling pins, you don't carry the bowling ball down the lane; instead you stand a good distance away and let it roll. From somewhere in the gap between action and outcome, in the friction between frustrated desire and the seductive goal of a game, bubbles up the unique enjoyment of game play. Players take on the lusory attitude for the pleasure of play itself.

The magic circle can define a powerful space, investing its authority in the actions of players and creating new and complex meanings that are only possible in the space of play. But it is also remarkably fragile as well, requiring constant maintenance to keep it intact. The lusory attitude goes hand in hand with the magic circle: without the proper state of mind, the magic circle could not exist—and without the magic circle, the actions of the players would be meaningless. As a game is played, these powerful mechanisms feed each other, permitting meaning to emerge in a game.

We began this essay by discussing that wonderfully rich passage by Johan Huizinga in *Homo Ludens*. "All play means something," he writes, "in play there is always something 'at play' which transcends the immediate needs of life and imparts meaning to the action." Huizinga's words provoke deep questions. We have not, in the course of this brief space, had a chance to explore all of them fully. But we have outlined some of the concepts which have an impact on the design of meaningful play.

Afterword: Game Design in Context

The essay in this volume is based on selections from *Rules of play: Game design fundamentals*. In this afterword, we would like to put the essay in its proper context by outlining some of our larger concerns.

Our project is to understand games. That means all kinds of games: paper-based strategy games and first-person shooters, classical board games and glitzy gambling games; math puzzles and professional sports; austere text adventures and giggly teenage party games. Our goal is to link these diverse play activities within a common framework—a framework based in *game design*.

In *The study of games*, Brian Sutton-Smith writes, "Each person defines games in his own way—the anthropologists and folklorists in terms of historical origins; the military men, businessmen, and educators in terms of usages; the social scientists in terms of psychological and social functions. There is overwhelming evidence in all this that the meaning of games is, in part, a function of the ideas of those who think about them" (Sutton-Smith, 1971b, p. 438).

What meaning, then, does a *game designer* bring to the study of games? What does it mean to look at games from a game design perspective? First and foremost, it means looking at games in and of themselves. Rather than placing games in the service of another discipline such as sociology, literary criticism, or computer science, we study games within their own disciplinary space. Because game design is an emerging area, we often borrow from other areas of knowledge—from mathematics and cognitive science; from semiotics and cultural studies. We may not borrow in the most orthodox manner, but we do so in the service of helping to establish a field of game design proper.

We bridge theoretical and practical concerns by looking closely at games themselves, discovering patterns within their complexity that bring the challenges of game design into full view. But our work is not just

for game designers: our ideas have direct application in fields outside game design. Our concepts, models, and examples can be used by interactive designers, architects, product designers, and other creators of interactive systems. Similarly, our focus on understanding games in and of themselves can benefit the emerging academic study of games in fields as diverse as sociology, media studies, and cultural policy. Engagement with ideas, like engagement with a game, is all about the play the ideas make possible. Feel free to have fun. Even if you are not a game designer, we hope you have found something here that lets you play with your own line of work in a new way.

Notes

1. *The American Heritage® Dictionary of the English Language*, fourth edition. Boston: Houghton Mifflin Company, 2000.
2. Re:Play: Game Design + Game Culture. Online conference. 2000. www.eyebeam.org/replay.
3. Jesper Juul. Computer Games and Digital Textuality, conference at IT University of Copenhagen, March 1–2, 2001.

References

Apter, M. J. (1990). A Structural phenomenology of play: A reversal theory approach. In M. J. Apter & J. H. Kerr (Eds.), *Adult play*. Amsterdam: Swets & Beitlinger.

Avedon, E. (1971). *The study of games*. Canada: John Wiley & Sons.

Bek, P. Self-organized criticality: A holistic view of nature. In G. A. Cowan, D. Pine, & D. Meltzer (Eds.), *Complexity: metaphors, models and reality*. Cambridge: Perseus Books.

Berlo, D. Communication studies, cultural studies, media studies. http://www.cultsock.ndirect.co.uk/MUHome/cshtml/semiomean/semio1.html.

Chandler, D. Semiotics for beginners. www.aber.ac.uk/~dgc/semiotic.html.

Church, D. (1999). Formal abstract design tools. www.gamasutra.com.

De Koven, B. (1978). *The well-played game*. New York: Doubleday.

Fatsis, S. (2001). *Word freak: Heartbreak, triumph, genius, and obsession in the world of competitive Scrabble players*. Boston: Houghton Mifflin.

Hallford, N. & Hallford, J. (2001). *Swords and circuitry: A designer's guide to computer role playing games*. Premier Press.

Huizinga, J. (1955). *Homo ludens: A study of the play element in culture*. Boston: Boston Beacon Press.

Jonas, W. (1999). On the Foundations of a Science of the Artificial, Hochschule fur Kunst und Design Halle. http://home.snafu.de/jonasw/JONAS4-49.html.

Littlejohn, S. W. (1989). *Theories of human communication*, 3d ed. CA: Wadsworth Publishing Company.

Pierce, C. S. (1958). *Selected writings*. In P. O. Wiener (Ed.), New York: Dover.

Rouse, R. III (2001). *Game design: Theory and practice*. Word ware Publishing.

Sniderman, S. The life of games. http://www.gamepuzzles.com/tlog/tlog2.htm.

Suits, B. (1990). *Grasshopper: Games, life, and utopia*. Boston: David R. Godine.

Sutton-Smith, B. (1971a). Boundaries. In R. E. Herron & B. Sutton-Smith (Eds.) *"Child's play."* New York: John Wiley and Sons, Inc.

Sutton-Smith, B. (1971b). *The study of games*. Canada: John Wiley & Sons.

Underwood, M. Communication studies, cultural studies, media studies. http://www.cultsock.ndirect.co.uk/MUHome/cshtml/semiomean/semio1.html.

5

CLICK READING: SCREENWRITING AND SCREEN-READING PRACTICES IN FILM AND MULTIMEDIA FICTIONS

Isabelle Raynauld

The terms "multi" and "media" joined together have brought fresh air to many university departments and have encouraged governments to inject funds in a cultural phenomenon that might rime with profit. It has given artists new tools of expression, and information junkies a world to consume in a new and often bulimic way. Obviously this new medium, with its potential proficiency to integrate and maybe even digest its predecessors, is in high demand. However, one question haunts me: why do we seem to need—and not just want—this "new medium" so much? Why are so many scholars, artists, and writers so enthusiastic upon hearing such words as digital, cybernautes, arborescence, database, interactive fictions, multimedia, mediation (re-; trans-; inter-;)? And why are companies, industry money makers, and do-it-all people so seduced by the apparent powers of nonlinearity, navigation systems, and by the reader-spectator-user-writer's capacity to be drawn into an "immersive" participation? Are these reactions a sign that multimedia owns unifying commercial and artistic properties, or is the attraction due to the media's intrinsic quality to exude power?

Studying multimedia today feels as if we were all expecting this new medium to be able to take us to Pluto and back, inventing amazing and endlessly pleasurable stories and adventures along the way. Multimedia is essentially the promise of a differently mediated story. If no one disputes the fact that terms such as interactivity, virtual worlds, and agency are here to stay, their importance and their impact on the practice of screenwriting do not reach such wide-ranging unanimity. Many interested by the field of multimedia believe that merely questioning the nature and the impact of this new technology amounts to a contemptible refusal to embrace progress; they want to believe the new medium itself has opened the door to a revolution in storytelling practices.

However optimistic, technologically aware, and sincere this standpoint may be, film history can teach us a lot about apparent revolutions in narratives. In fact, cinema as a medium has gone through a number of radical transformations, brought on by technological and scientific innovations. At each step, many a skeptic did not hesitate to toot the horn of "real" cinema's demise. Indeed, classical cinema's future appeared to be quite dim as each innovation clustered itself to the medium, whether it is the emergence and development of montage, extended footage, the increased mobility of the camera, the introduction of sound and dialogue, the introduction of color, wide-screen formats, and 3D. Each change found someone, somewhere, declaring that the art of film was nearing its end; this was especially true during the transition from silent to talkies, a time full of apocalyptic prognostics and dire warnings. But as Marshall McLuhan insightfully summed up, every medium "reconfigures" the previous one.[1]

Generally speaking, reactions to the introduction of new technologies and scientific innovations are twofold. Experienced as radical transformations and as progress, a triumph of the new over the old, every technical improvement or innovation may seem to empower the artist. At the opposite end of the spectrum, they instill fear in others, who view them as threatening and dangerous, perils to be avoided at all costs. If cinema itself has often been portrayed as being in a state of crisis, we must not forget that its invention and development during the early days of the twentieth century also worried and troubled the proponents of another art form—theater—whose artists felt their mode of representation was being threatened.

These radically negative responses and sometimes violent reactions show that at each new step, creators, industrialists, critics, and intellectuals have had to come to terms with the mutations "their" medium was undergoing and, most importantly, have had to redefine the specificity of their practice and of their art. It is fascinating to discover how similar the reactions to games and to multimedia interactive fictions are to those voiced concerning photoplay screenwriting during cinema's early days. Most commentators rushed to criticize the awkwardness of early cinematic storytelling, as opposed to the sophistication of the literary novel and the classical theater.[2] In spite of these comments—which were sometimes at least partly justified but often utterly ungracious—screenwriting continued to evolve.

"Time Is Visible in All Places"[3]

If many technological novelties can be thought to be capable of bringing about a revolution in storytelling practices, in fact, only a few actually do. From a historical and theoretical perspective in film and in screenwriting practices, this chapter will address questions such as: What is the spectator's relationship to the storytelling process when it is multimediated in CD-ROM form? In what ways does a multimedia environment challenge our reading and writing habits and competencies? What happens to spectator identification in an interactive fiction or game? What impact has the invention of new technologies and scientific innovations had on screenwriting rules since the beginnings of cinema?

The Novelty Factor: Are We Taking Part in a Revolution?

Even though experiences of the past few years have revealed in no uncertain terms how disappointing, often frustrating, and deceiving the interactive fictions can be, the "fascination with technological interactivity"[4] is far from waning. The intense desire many share to witness and participate in the advent of a "mature electronic narrative art" is keeping academic research and creative projects going strong.

What does a medium and/or an art in gestation teach us about ourselves? What should we look at to learn new things from this moment in history? When early cinema studies became popular in the mid-eighties, the historians who saw newly (re)discovered early films were faced with a double challenge: they had to revisit—simultaneously—the notions of primitiveness *and* of novelty of the cinematograph; but most importantly they had to question their own modes of perception and ways of seeing. Multimedia fictions challenge us in a similar way, specifically because they have not yet produced what Janet Murray calls their works of maturity. In this chapter we will argue that it is our *relationship* to this emerging medium that is essential to analyze and confront. Multimedia fictions and electronic narratives are fascinating to study

right now in the way they point to the hopes, dreams, and expectations we—reader/users—project on them through the *apparently novel character of these technologies*.

How do we approach the multimediated story? With what knowledge and from what point of view do we apprehend this newcomer? Most importantly, how do we handle our own (in)competence and willingness to be and/or become a multimedia reader-spectator-user? By comparing historically film screenwriting principles to those used in multimedia, we will question how electronic narrative art plans (or not) its new reader's involvement in the fiction.

Let us clarify one last point before we begin the analysis per se: multimedia fictions should not be reduced to being looked at solely as interactive narrative; because if the medium's interactivity is interesting, the fact that "it has become a medium in its own right"[5] is where most fundamental issues take root.

What I wish to argue here is that, now, the medium is a promise—a promise to become more, a promise to change.

Who hasn't wished to see this new medium already offer more complex stories, more disorienting and dramatic situations (Laurel, 1993)? It's as if we were all waiting and hoping for "it" to always and already be something else.

The Spectator's Competence as a "New" User

In the early 1900s, what most intrigued and attracted the emerging film spectator was the fact that the black and white images were *moving*. Not that one could recognize a street corner or a familiar narrative, but that this new technology could indeed show *moving pictures*. A similar situation is happening with electronic art: the rules of reading and interpreting a multimedia fiction are as novel and enticing as is the promise of a "different" story. With every new CD we want to know quickly what we have to do and what kind of role we will get to play. Depending on our media literacy, just installing a game can be a challenge.[6] Personally, I find that what we discover and learn about the medium itself while we are clicking, dragging, and waiting, and the various types of interfaces one finds in the multimedia fiction CDs are what titillate the curiosity and desire to click on, first and foremost. Rarely has the content really stopped me in my path of discovering the interface. Just as in film, how a fiction is presented and told is two-thirds of the story.

In 1999, I was invited by the Film and Television Department of Utrecht University to give a seminar on interactive narratives.[7] During this course, I asked each student to discover and play with as many games and CDs they could get their hands on and to analyze them. What quickly became clear in this experiment is that the students were, 95 percent of the time, disappointed by their electronic narrative and/or fictional encounters with a game's or an interactive CD's invented world. This led me to think that recognizing (as many other users have done), most often with disappointment, that a story or a game wasn't yet offering a fulfilling experience in this new medium or feeling the content was somewhat "primitive," as early cinema spectators did about short silent black and white films, are important aspects to underline but they seem, a few years later, less essential to discuss.

Instead, I wish to question our capacity and/or resistance to discover and open ourselves to the way this new medium works: that is, if it *makes sense* or not, is empowered to make *meaning* and simultaneously empowers us to *perceive, understand,* and thus *experience it*, as a story, as an unraveled territory, fictional universe and/or as a game.

Similar to what happened with early cinema spectators whose viewing competencies developed with each new editing trick, our proficiency as multimedia spectators grows with each new object of experience. At every encounter with a new fictional CD-ROM, one is faced with a double reading/acknowledging task: to discover the interface's patterns and uniqueness and to want, or not, to enter the fictional world. The various interfaces are of immense interest in themselves because they refer to their own materiality, limitations, and often quickly fading novelty. Although having to "click read" a fiction is a fairly new practice, we are already hoping to be asked to do more. Early cinema spectators also acquired viewing skills at a quick pace. As early as 1903, spectators were already begging for more complex stories to be created for the cinematograph (Raynauld, 1990).

Looking at this new medium in a diachronic way, the question of the competency of the spectator faced with a new technology is crucial. More often than not, it is our own (in)competence that a new medium reveals. By demanding multimedia objects to mediate our stories in such a "new way," we are possibly trying to shadow our own (in)capacity to relate in an open minded fashion to this medium's capabilities, a medium that is still in its early stages of development. As the French semio-pragmatist Roger Odin has defined it, the notion of competence should be understood in a dynamic, synchronic, and diachronic way, meaning

that signification is possible only through the spectator's "competence" to create it (Odin, 1980). Early cinema evolved into feature-length sound colored stories because of public demand. Today, it is our way of looking, of reading, and of clicking that will enable the medium to go beyond "primitiveness." But before the art reaches maturity, and for it to actually grow, its own participants (creators, spectators, and analysts) also have to mature in the way they relate to, engage, and discover ways of understanding and of capturing "it."

Early cinema stories came from popular culture (vaudeville, comic strips, biblical sources), as well as from a known literary and theatrical repertoire. This familiarity with the content permitted the neophyte spectators to concentrate their energies on what this then new medium was bringing to a familiar narrative. It allowed them time to become *competent* film spectators. I still remember how impressed I was when I first did a 360° scroll in one of Zoe Beloff's interactive installations in her CD-ROM *Beyond* (1996)! The films shot at the end of the nineteenth century and during the first years of the twentieth century were considered "attractions,"[8] and the task of the filmmakers was to impress and dazzle the spectator with moving pictures. The novelty of film itself, as a new medium, was at the heart of their preoccupations. One hundred years later, we are at the same stage of development in multimedia narrative: discovering its materiality and potentialities, writers trying to anticipate the user's competencies with this different medium in order to offer engaging stories and universes to discover. Let us not forget that to this day, multimedia fictions are still sold with instruction manuals!

The Practice of Screenwriting

Scriptwriting is a manipulative art, whether in "old" or "new" media. Since 1897, every invention in film, every new technology both helped and slowed down the screenwriting strategies. In the early twenties, while some scripts pointed explicitly to the lack of the technology of sound, others fiercely resisted its advent. The same happened with developments in editing, coloring, and computerized special effects. When a writer creates a story in screenplay form, he or she spends as much time planning and imagining the future spectator's reactions, capacity to anticipate, and possible engagement in the story as imagining and creating a fictitious, hopefully compelling and convincing universe. Moreover, the screenplay writer has to know everything about the available technologies; if he doesn't, he might as well write a novel. Unfortunately, in the film business, if many writers have great ideas, few can actually imagine and use enough of the medium's unique capabilities and original modes of representation and of storytelling.

Screenwriting has always been about using other media and technologies of reproduction to communicate, in writing, a potential future story. Just as a screenwriter in 1906 needed to understand basic editing principles, the so-called interactive screenwriter has to be familiar with computer programming basics as well as have the desire to plan the future showing and telling of the story. If a multimedia writer needs to collaborate with a programmer, if not be a programmer, the screenwriting's core characteristic—that of being a written mapping and imagining of story(ies) and/or of paths made of fictional material—is the same. Just as the 1910 screenwriter had to think about what the spectator would perceive, understand, and experience, the interactive screenwriter has to be able to visualize where, how, when, and why the user will want or not to experience the story through this or that character or path. As much as we would like to think that our principles of storytelling and story writing have changed with the advent of this medium, I believe multimedia is still, even with all its attractiveness and its limits, only the latest new technology yet. The difference is it's *ours*. It's from *our* time. And our time is *now*.

How to click, wait, and scroll are all new (and already aging) ways of writing and reading that emulate new competencies from the writer as well as from the reader-user-navigator. The scriptwriter has the responsibility not only to know the medium's technical possibilities and limitations, but to script out the navigator's reading-playing journey and script out the character's strengths and the story's pitfalls. And how new a scriptwriter's job is that? Since Georges Méliès wrote the *Trip to the Moon* screenplay (1902), writers have been trained to imagine and anticipate what a spectator might want to see and know, to regulate the flow of information. Scripting a multimedia fiction is still about how the spectator will or will not accept to immerse him or herself in a story.

Screenwriting Principles

What did early screenwriting principles look like at the turn of the century? As early as 1910, the principles underlying budding screenwriting techniques resemble incredibly those recommended in current interactive multimedia writing practices. To illustrate this point, let's compare some of these precepts, written, respectively, in 1913 and in 1996.

Photoplay, in a word, is not an adaptation of another branch of literary work, but is possessed of a technique all its own. There are, of course, the broad basic rules of literary construction and dramatic development, applicable to all forms of literature, whether written or verbally expressed, but in the past few years the art of the photoplays has been possessed of a technique that is applicable only to writing of picture plays and to no other form. (Sargent, 1913, p. 41)

Every art form strives for a sense of unity. A script works as a whole.... It means constructing your story in a way that will give it form, focus, momentum, clarity. It means finding ways to help your audience "get with" your story, and involving your audience *all along the way. It means crafting your story into dramatic form. Since this action is dramatic and visual (not expressed through dialogue), it pushes the story forward.* (Sargent, 1913, p. 88)

Multimedia refers to an environment. The distinctive characteristic of multimedia is interactivity. It is the mechanism that allows you to move between the various media. The fact of the media itself is not interesting (Blow away what preceded you.) The point is, if you're going to be scripting multimedia experiences, be mindful of the intense personal level on which your audience will be participating. The first lesson of this book is to never forget your audience. (Varchol, 1996, p. 43)

These quotes are only but a few of the numerous examples of contiguity between the rules "then" and the rules "now." In fact, the similarities are still so numerous it's disconcerting.

However "interactive" writers are asked to be, they are still, as were earlier screenwriters, constantly concerned with the spectator's emotional involvement: "The key is to involve the audience (user) emotionally. How do we do that in an interactive world?" (anonymous writer quoted in Varchol, 1996, p. 86). To this question Michael Utvitch, an interactive writer responded: "Involve them emotionally, involve them actually. Make them do things, solve problems, puzzles, respond to situations using their own judgment."[9] Notice the similitude in discourse between the two eras? Unquestionably, when scriptwriting a multimedia fiction one uses different technical steps than when writing a feature film screenplay;[10] however, both practices in both media share the same mandate: to involve the spectator emotionally in a fictional world: "The key to Myst is to lose yourself in this fantastic virtual exploration and act and react as if you were really there" (*Myst* user's manual, 1993). As we will see, how this *involvement* is achieved—whether you call it identification or agency—is by using fundamental storytelling principles.

In light of what precedes, which changes have really been profound and irreversible in terms of narrative structuring? It is not my intention here to label changes happening in an era or another as "progress" and/or "lack of progress" from what preceded; however, I do believe that drawing parallels between both turn of the centuries is not only essential to do but, from a theoretical point of view, extremely humbling. It permits us to eliminate superfluous adjectives while concentrating on factual differences.

What Multimedia Promises and Plays With

As stated earlier, multimedia is, for now, a promise. Thus, the next section of this chapter analyzes multimedia fictions edited on CD-ROMs as a set of promises the fictions implicitly make. One can use most of the principles identified and described hereafter to discuss and question how other interactive practices function, make sense. This section should be used as a tool to question multimedia projects and products and not as a closed system of interpretation and of understanding. Moreover, when certain principles fail to shed new light on the way a specific game or web practice functions, I offer counterexamples to think about.[11] Also, for obvious reasons of space, I chose only a few but hopefully representative examples of fictional CD-ROMs, which I then classified in two main genres: first, those that explicitly promise a story (as a game and/or as an exploration) and second those that offer a fictional universe or environment (not to be confused with a virtual one that is implicit in all electronic documents). The opening sequence of a CD should minimally (when it works well!) contain at least: (1) an explicit invitation to enter the fiction—such as the prologue in *Myst* where a narrator introduces you to the fictional world;[12] (2) an implicit reading-navigating contract (how and where to click, drag, and find), and (3) the implicit design of the user's potential role in this story and or universe: adventurer, detective, warrior, discoverer, victim, and so on.

We will refer to the user's manual presentation texts often because they give us an unequivocal window to look through for the discussion of generic classifications of these "new" fictions.

Promise of Being Part of the Story

Interactive games promise an immersive experience, but first and foremost they promise a story. "Computer games, for instance, are experienced by their players as narratives."[13]

Let's start with the best known and apparently still most popular electronic game in the world: The *Myst* trilogy (*Myst I*; *Riven*; *Myst III*). The emphasis is mine.

You are about to be drawn *into an amazing alternative reality. The entire game was designed from the ground up to draw you in with little or no extraneous distractions on the screen to interfere with the feeling of* being there. *Myst is not linear, it's not flat, and it's not shallow. This is the most depth, detail and reality you've ever experienced in a game. Myst is real. And like real life, you don't die every five minutes.... The key to Myst is to lose yourself in this fantastic virtual exploration and act and react as if you were really there.* (*Myst* user's manual, 1993)

Each version contains eloquent and laudatory introduction texts about the magnificent and mysterious powers of immersion. *Myst* advertises itself as being a game of choices in which the user can become the author: "Myst: The surrealistic adventure that will become your world." The user's manual stresses the user's freedom to explore the world: "Moving around in Myst is incredibly intuitive," and the Official Strategy Guide focuses on the promise of nonlinearity: "Of course the structure of Myst isn't linear: you can visit the four Ages in any order."[14] Again in the user's manual: "Myst is not linear, it's not flat, it's not shallow." However, it also warns that "some locations are not accessible. Clicking in those locations will have no effect, and indicate that the location is not important."! (p. 3) In fact, moving around in *Myst* is often a punitive experience. It definitely tests your endurance to accept rebuttals. You're there all right, and you're trapped!

On a different level, the opening sequence of *Myst I* strikes us as being a linking metaphor and homage to previous media: the book and the film:

I realized the moment I fell into the future that the book would not be destroyed as soon as I had planned. It continued falling into the starry expanse of which I had glimpsed an

Isabelle Raynauld

eclipse. I tried to speculate where it might have landed. I must admit however that such conjecture is futile. Still questions about whose hands might one day hold my Myst *book are unsettling to me. I know my apprehensions might never be allayed. And so I close realizing that perhaps the ending has not yet been written.*[15]

Not only does the prologue borrow completely from film codes of representation (blackness, authoritative male voice-over, background music, dramatic overture with a book falling in deep space), it is structured as a film introduction: as you hear a voice-over address you implicitly, the all empowered omniscient narrator invites you to enter the fiction by explaining that a long lost book has just been found again:

You have just stumbled upon a most intriguing book, a book titled Myst. *You have no idea where it came from, who wrote it, or how old it is. Reading through its pages provides you with only a superbly crafted description of an island world. But it's just a book, isn't it? As you reach the end of the book, you lay your hand on a page. Suddenly your own world dissolves into blackness, replaced with the island world the pages described. Now you're here, wherever here is, with no option but to explore....*[16]

The narrator invites you to gain access to the story by writing it yourself—"the ending is not yet written." Some users have since done this: see the *Myst Journal* by Christopher Josephes on the web site (www.visi. com/~cpj1/myst). You may enter under certain conditions: you have to learn the rules of the game but most importantly, you have to play by the rules. "Don't trash!" Any subversive behavior will just keep you trapped in a repetitive world. If you play by the rules, the story becomes in fact your own journey—your click reading—through forty hours of promised entertainment: clicking, dragging, waiting, puzzle solving:

If you hit a wall: Don't trash! If you're not sure what to do next, clicking everywhere won't help. Think about what you know already, and ask yourself what you need to know, collect your thoughts and piece them together. Think of related items or places you've seen, think of information you've been given, pay close attention to everything you see, don't forget anything. But most importantly—think of what you would do if you were really there. Remember, there is always the sealed envelope if you need it, but ...[17]

Needless to say, one must let go of old fashion needs of abandonment to a storyteller until the story reaches its dramatic climax. Here, the ending—if and when you ever reach it—is definitely not the payoff. This didn't stop the creators from designing a sequel to *Myst* in *Riven*. If *Myst* promised fictional access to the "adventurous" user, *Riven* ironically—unconsciously?—puts the user in the prisoners' role. As you start the game you are singled out in a prison-like set and your first clickings quickly take you inside a prison cell: suddenly the bars close on you and you see the action from the prisoner's point of view! The interfaces metaphor went from the film and the written world to those of a carceral environment. No wonder the user's manual promises an "immersive experience." In the message from the creators, you are urged to "shut the door, turn down the lights, turn up the sound, sit in a comfortable chair, and let yourself be drawn into the world of Riven. And, for goodness sake, use a pair of headphones or a good pair of speakers!" On the following page is the proverb that should inspire our experience: "Lose your questions and you will find your answers" (p. 10), the notions of control given to the user and the promise of moving freely through a story are here superbly acted out by the designers. *Riven* traps you in its folds. "The life of a screenwriter of an interactive film is much better than the life of a Hollywood writer because by making an interactive script, you build a better mousetrap, you become indispensable. Because you know how it all fits together long before the rest of them do" (Michael Kaplan, quoted in Varchol, 1996, p. 3).

How revealing is such a statement? Doesn't a "Hollywood writer" also know "how it all fits together" before the spectators do? What, exactly, is interactive fiction? Upon closer review, the interactivity enthusiast just might find cause for concern.

Promise of Choice

Interactivity is the parent of all choices. But let's be immediately clear and synthetic about the notion of interactivity: (1) interactivity is neither a new nor contemporary process, it has always existed; (2) interactivity is an act of communication that affects the other's response, such as in a dialogue between two consenting individuals; (3) interactivity did not "invent" nonlinearity. In fact, nonlinear narratives have always existed, regardless of the medium of representation used to communicate them (whether it is literature, film, or photos). On the contrary, linearity is at the heart of the very nature of some of today's multimedia interactive documents (on CD-ROMs); (4) interactive stories are still pseudo-interactive: offering multiple programmed choices is very different from offering a space of exchange, possibility of transformation for both the sender and the receiver.

In fact, CD-ROM based fictions are much more "hyper selective"[18] than they are interactive. Interactivity is the implementation of a series of choices that have been tried, tested, and planned beforehand. Interactive fiction is created and designed to implicate the spectator and make him believe that the story being told is custom-made for him or her—and most importantly *by* him or her to become, through an avatar, the main character of the story.

In the realm of interactive fictions, although a variety of choices are offered to the participant-reader, access to the final *outcome* is strictly forbidden. In fact, for example, the French CD-ROM called *Les croisades* (1997) (The Crusades) severely punishes curiosity. Fundamental information—the very heart of the narrative—may only be accessed if one follows a specific course of action. If one tries to venture off the beaten path, so to speak, through what may be perceived by the player as clever assumptions designed to outplay others in the resolution of problems posed by the application, one is invariably returned to square one.

If this frustrating situation is often at play with fictional interactive CD-ROMs, the game industry quickly found ways to make money by offering gamers publications describing short cuts, solutions, and tips to gain immortality or skip sections. Gamers also advise each other, for better or for worse! However, the point I wish to make now is that in terms of the promise of choice, the narrative structures, whether they are arborescent, pearllike, or clustered based are still, in fact, of a profoundly linear nature—even when multiple endings are offered. Despite its outward appearance and encouragements to get lost or to err in the various areas of the fiction,[19] the plot—when plot there is—fulfills all the requirements of classical narrative of exposition, development, and resolution. The "choices," are more often than not delaying strategies that, hopefully, one will find entertaining or truly puzzling (no pun intended here!).

One of the main differences between interactive fictions and a classical narrative film structure does lie in the fact the user must make a series of choices within a funnellike, "degressive" structure (where his options tend to be narrowed down as the story progresses). A number of digressions (time and space allotted to action sequences, subplots, misleading clues, and red herrings) are destined less to propel the action, but mainly to slow down, distract, and most importantly keep the reader occupied during forty or so hours.

Although the film spectator does not have to physically take action, he or she does, however, have to formulate a set of hypothesis and make inferences based on the information provided by the narrative. Although the narrator may mislead the film spectator and withhold information, as is often the case in suspense movies, he ultimately is the one who decides when and how to satisfy the spectator's curiosity. Tensions are then released and the experience of catharsis ensues. In CD-ROM based interactive fictions, the spectator-player-reader can be led to believe he or she is the master of the character's fate. The interactive story will exhort you to find this or that or else something terrible will happen to the hero. Also, many games allow you to be the character, to endorse the role of the adventurer, the discoverer, the problem-solver, the visitor, the warrior. This type of involvement, when it happens, functions on the same principles of identification and of suspension of disbelief. This promise of control of the hero's whereabouts is, of course, an illusion, a programmed deception. In those interactive fictions on CD-ROMs, the user is never as free as the advertising would like him to believe, as his choices are most often quite limited.[20]

In this regard, Luc Courchesne's CD-ROM *Portrait One* CD[21] illustrates pseudo-interactivity wonderfully. It mimics a conversation between the user and a character, Marie, who is looking straight at you, her face in full frame. When you click under her face, lines of basic human dialogue appear. She will ask you your name, what you want to know about her. She offers lines in French, English, or German. She will "say" things such as: "Excuse me?" "Why are you staring at me?" "Do we know each other?" Each interaction offers you two or three choices to move on in the conversation with Marie. Of course, eventually, you won't have anything new to say to each other and the CD's exploration is completed. If this "conversation" possesses the appearances that an actual interactive dialogue is happening, *Portrait One* gives us an artistic representation of interactivity as a prescribed, preplanned encounter, multiple choice or not. Just as we feel that we are meeting Marie, the exchange is and feels artificial. Interactivity is represented and staged (mise-en-scène) as a deception condemned to a Sisyphean faith of having to be replayed in a forever repetitive loop. *Portrait One* simultaneously offers the ironically tautologic chance to *interactively dialogue* with

Isabelle Raynauld |

Marie while demonstrating the forever inscripted and prescripted impossibility to achieve a fully interactive exchange. If *Portrait One* were to be really interactive, it would have to offer a "real" dialogue between Marie and the user, such as people experience while chatting. A chat is interactive, but interactive narratives on CD-ROM aren't, strictly speaking, inter-active.[22] I have to admit I wish they would truly be, although technically it still seems to be impossible. What the CD-ROM *Portrait One* offers is a scripted dialogue of multiple choices that portrays a fictional encounter between a young woman named Marie and an unknown user: the stranger in front of her she refers to being the player.

From a theoretical perspective, real or at least functional interactivity is based on the presence of reciprocal actions; although it is first and foremost an activity that influences and changes the development of the narrative, it does not fundamentally modify its ending. In CD-ROM based narratives such as *Myst*, the interactive story is already mapped out. The driving force behind its structure is the process of causality: if A, then B. Such logical reasoning is in itself of a linear kind, element B being contingent to the fulfillment of element A. If the expectations of the "ideal" reader-participant (Eco, 1985) as imagined by the writer correspond to a specific set of dramatic rules, they also correspond to the rules of classical logic that stipulate that if A is equal to B and B is equal to C, then A is also equal to C. Hence, the weblike structure does not engulf the story but the participant, by giving the impression, through dead end leads and erroneous assumptions that he or she may get lost.

I distinguish between "interactive narrativity" and "interactive zones." To explain this I will describe the *Liquidation* CD-ROM (figure 5.1). To achieve (pseudo-)interactive narrativity, the profound structure has to be linear and degressive. Events, characters, and situations are scripted with a hierarchical value attached to them. This process ensures that the user will ultimately discover a story with a beginning, middle, and end. It also permits one to distinguish the essential, nonnegotiable clicks from the secondary, superfluous ones, and from the main narrative versus the interactive zones that are in fact digressions from the main plot. Interactive writing foresees the links between sequences and maps out the arborescent structure that will permit the "interactive navigation." How, when, and where the reader will explore and discover the documented story is what interactive scriptwriting is all about.

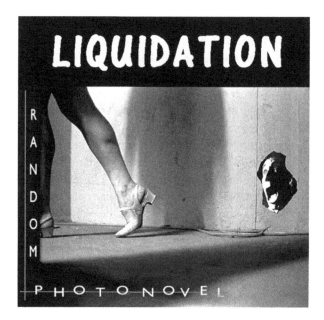

| Figure 5.1 |
Liquidation cover

Whereas classical narrative cinema prides itself on an editing structure based on transparency and the illusion or impression that the narratives it produces seem to "tell themselves," promoters of interactive fictions sell the illusion that the reader is the writer, that it is he or she who in the end, tells the tale. The CD's descriptive leaflets promise that with interactivity, the user will in fact be in charge of the story. The CD-ROM *Liquidation*, by Michel Lefebvre (writer), Eva Qunitas (photographer), and Alain Bergeron (software designer), is worthy of notice in this regard. Presented as a "random photonovel," the CD-ROM *Liquidation*[23] is advertised as a plurimedia work made of eighteen hundred photographs, four hours of soundtrack, and dialogues with twenty-five interpreters:

A scientific formula, which was to liquidate world debt, has been stolen from Ricard Enterprises! Thus begins the story of Liquidation, *a plurimedia work. The title is also the theme of this photo romance that casts both a critical and playful eye on our lives and cities, where endless accumulation leads to endless liquidation. After having completed a printed version in 1995 and a web-radio version of this work in 1998 the authors now present a CD-ROM version of this random fiction.* Proman, *custom software designed by Alain Bergeron, uses combinatorial functions to randomly choose photos, display effects, text and sound according to the viewing duration chosen by the user (15 to 120 minutes). Although the interface allows for a sequential viewing, the CD-ROM version of*

Liquidation *can best be likened to a film that changes every time it is seen.*[24]

Liquidation stands out from other CDs because of its capacity to offer two types of stories and thus two types of navigation: one is totally random and you click, scroll, and discover chaotically elements of the fiction. This way of discovering the story is what the authors describe as seeing a different film every time. However, you also have the possibility to choose a predetermined time of screening (20, 25, or 120 minutes) during which you cannot interact and you are "told" a story with a beginning, middle, and end. Whether it is the short or the long version of the story it supposedly offers a coherent story structure. However, because *Liquidation* is designed with software that works on the random combination of words, texts, images, and sounds, the story is at the image of its written text originator: completely poetic, it is for the most part narratively incoherent. If some events are definitely more important than others and seem to belong to the principal story line, each transformation—whether it is major or secondary—brings a new quality to what preceded. If we all agree that causality is inseparable from narrativity, *Liquidation*'s story structure definitely challenges the generic definition of what causality is and can mean. Here, if a main event eventually leads to another important event, the outcome is often more poetic than dramatic and only remotely narrative. I would describe *Liquidation* as a *computer generated automatist story.* Moreover, what gives *Liquidation* its extra charm is that the dialogues are made of a very large number of words and sentences that combine randomly to make up dialogue lines that are as strange and evocative as the surrealist's automatic poetry of the twenties. The software used here can randomly combine nouns, verbs, and adjectives while respecting basic grammatical rules. Thus the sentences, in a way, make sense. It gives the verbal exchanges between the characters a very unique tone and style.

Far less deceiving in its promises than other multimedia fictions, *Liquidation* not only openly embraces previous media, but is like an homage to what preceded it. The sequential scenes have a film noir esthetic to them while being made of still photographs, just as in a photo novel; meanwhile the dialogue lines appear in text and remind us of comic strip iconography. Acted out theatrically, the lines are totally poetic and often absurd. The auto-ironic drama of *Liquidation* is due to the combinatory design that gives this CD-ROM a remarkable uniqueness and style. The writer Michel Lefebvre showed me his 250-page screenplay: it looks like a genealogical tree from hundreds of generations! The story structure was conceived following a hierarchical principle; built as a tree with a trunk and branches, the author had to attribute a value (on a scale of 1 to 5) to each character, every element of the story, and to parts of dialogue lines. This hierarchy is what permits the story to navigate between main and secondary events. The still photos that make up the photo novel are led by the combinatory software and can only pair up with dialogue lines and sounds *in a random order,* thus creating a new viewing experience every time. In the sequential mode where the navigator can actually interact, the software recombines written words, spoken lines, and images in a different, unpredictable way each time. The experience is absolutely surprising but not at all engaging emotionally. The spectator witnesses this random ballet and appreciates the overall poetry or not.

Promise of Contact

Then how does the reading experience—that is, interactive navigation—distinguish itself from the experience of film viewing? Because most electronic narratives still rely heavily on cinematographic modes of representation to create and mediate their fictional worlds to us, comparing film vs. multimedia is not aimed at creating a hierarchy of media; it is a valid comparison because each acts as a *revelator* of the other's specificities. One medium can exist insofar as he (she) is not the other. If the two viewing-reading experiences offer a certain number of similarities, they are also in certain aspects undoubtedly very different. One of those differences is the type of contact one may have with an electronic story. Let us look at how *Ceremony of Innocence,* based on the *Griffin and Sabine Trilogy* by Nick Bantock. Notice how many tactile expressions are used to invite the user into *Ceremony of Innocence.* Interactive stories are trying to appeal to all the senses. When you choose a CD, it's as if it lights up and cries out "See me! Feel me! Touch me! Hear me!". Moreover, they single out an individual instead of a crowd, promising that your unique touch can make a difference. Let's look at the cover presentation of the CD-ROM *Ceremony of Innocence.* It is necessary to quote the long introduction as a whole, as its phrasing and packaging of the product is implicitly a definition of an "interactive fiction." Also notice how it exemplifies the "promise" rhetoric:

The mysterious correspondence of Griffin and Sabine. Featuring Paul Mc Gann, Isabella Rossellini and Ben Kingsley. 1997. Progressing through Ceremony of Innocence: Movement through the story of Griffin and Sabine is a fluid experience—you can propel yourself along through the narrative, or linger and go back to places that move you or stimulate you. There are many things to discover; don't expect to find everything on an initial viewing. You may want to revisit cards and letters you have seen, to understand the layers of the story more fully and to enjoy the interaction again. Finding things and progressing through the cards and letters in Ceremony of Innocence is accomplished through a variety of mouse movements and interaction—this is a part of the discovery. Your cursor will behave in a number of different ways; sometimes it will disappear and remain invisible. You may find yourself in control of an object or character. Pointing and clicking will sometimes, but not always produce the desired result. Try clicking and dragging objects, and slowly rolling over objects to reveal their content and character. Progress at your own pace. There will be certain times between cards and letters when you will see and hear very little—relax—the mail will arrive. [Instructions leaflet] ... Revisiting and continuing play: You will then be shown a menu screen displaying all of the cards and letters you have viewed. These are divided into three sections, which correspond to the three acts in Ceremony of Innocence.[25]

The advertised promise that your touch will move the story along, that your witty sense of puzzle solving will guide you into an unknown realm of wonderful narrative pleasures never experienced before are persuasive arguments that entice us to open the box and try the CD. Unlike a film or a book, multimedia fictions invite the user to *experience* them more than to *follow* them. Why do we crave multimedia fictions? Why do we even accept the advertisement, believe the hype, and venture into the narratives they propose?

Promise of Discovery

All fiction makes the implicit promise that its navigator will discover a new, untraveled world. Zoe Beloff's *Beyond* is very interesting in this regard. Although it is an indefinable CD-ROM in many regards, her invitation to the user isn't unlike *Myst*'s: they both play with the "mysterious world" hook to reel their spectator in.

In a playful spirit of philosophical inquiry, *Beyond* (1997) explores the paradoxes of technology, desire, and the paranormal posed since the birth of mechanical reproduction: the phonograph severing the voice from the body, photography capturing the soul, and cinema resurrecting the dead.[26]

Far from being a construction of deceiving clues and destinations that only aim at slowing down the user's journey in the CD to keep him "entertained" longer, *Beyond* truly asks you to surrender to it. Navigation here is similar to entering a private house by yourself and having license to search rooms, open drawers, read the occupant's personal notes and diaries, and even hear her commenting on herself in a ghostlike, often screeching voice, that's hard to understand. The author shared with me that she did this on purpose to force the user to get close to the machine. *Beyond* gives you the uneasy feeling of being lost in someone else's interior world; you are also faced with your own resistances or impulses to voyeurism.[27]

Promise of Exploration of Time and Space in a Universe

Daniel Canty's CD-ROM adaptation of Alan Lightman's novel *Einstein's dreams* is a beautiful and convincing approach to so-called interactivity.[28] While exploring each dream dated between April and June 1905, you will encounter many moments of grace when it truly feels like the cursor is giving life to the text-sound-image representations. In the June 28 dream, "Time is a flock of nightingales," and you can suddenly start drawing flocks of white birds that appear, erase each other, leave, and reenter the screen. This visualization illustrates Einstein's notion that "the past shifts." Conceived as individual interfaces, similar to *Ceremony of Innocence*, *Einstein's Dreams* offers different types of interactions with each dream. Although *Einstein's dreams* (the novel) was written by Lightman as a daydreaming journey on the definition of time according to Einstein, what struck me is how many of the reflections about time can actually be applied directly to what multimedia is offering right now. Here are but a few quotes: "Time passes but little happens" (May 4, 1905); "With no memory each touch is the first touch." "The passage of time brings increasing order." The June 20 dream is one of the most enlightening ones to read while thinking about what kind of experience a multimedia interactive fiction actually offers: "In this world, there can be no right or wrong. Right and wrong demand freedom of choice, but if each action is already chosen, there can be no freedom of choice. In this world, no person is responsible. Each person is free in a world without freedom." *Einstein's Dreams* June 5 is also significant: "Who can say if an event happened fast or slow, causally or without cause, in the past or in the future? Who can say events happen at all?"[29]

This stillness and unrealness of sets and events in interactive games and fictions is part of an important discomfort the user feels after a while. In the French CD *Les Croisades: Conspiration au Moyen-Orient* (1997, script by Al Harawi), a computerized man is cutting trees in a computerized forest. If you don't click out of there fast enough, you see that the sequence is a loop: trees regrow, the man cuts them again, in the exact same way and with the exact same artificialness. Time is imprisoned in this redundant sequence and your own sense of time spent in the game becomes distorted, moving in stillness.

Who can believe in this enough to abandon himself as if he/she were "really there?" That's one claim *Einstein's Dreams* doesn't make. You are not invited in a supposedly real world; you are invited into a creation that explores notions of time, space, and man's place in the universe. The only other CD that has those intellectual and stylistic qualities is Chris Marker's *Immemory* (1997), which invites you to explore numerous planes of memory: being an self-portrait of Marker by Marker, *Immemory* refers simultaneously to five types of memories: personal, the filmmaker's memory of his own work, the filmmaker's memory of social and political events, the actual historical events, and the user's own memory of his/her journey in Marker's CD.

Another subtle quality of *Einstein's Dreams* is that although mostly avoiding redundancy, the structure nonetheless lets you keep track of your journey, each visited dream making a connective line with other explored stars in the galaxy.

It created linear time in a nonlinear environment. It is the only CD-ROM I know I have ever completed. This feeling of closure is essential to the feeling of satisfaction (which we will develop on in the next section). Most users need closure because it's rewarding. However, most CDs are experienced for a while (night after night, a whole summer, a week, a few hours) but are rarely explored exhaustively.[30] Some are abandoned because of the numerous inherent difficulties designed and put in the user's way to slow down the journey; others are never traveled far because the proposed universe itself is devoid of interest. If the interface happens to also be dull and too simplistic, frustration kicks in quickly. As the multimedia artist Henry Kuo summed it up in no uncertain terms:

A lot of people have complained about the controls being too hard in Wipeout, *and PSYGNOSIS is supposedly fixing them in the sequel,* Wipeout LX. *Well, I say, anyone who couldn't handle the original game should just stick to* Pole Position, *and stop convincing these game companies to make these games so fucking easy that any fucking moron could play it. If you want to be good at a game, you must understand the laws of nature based inside that video game, and allow your mind to enter into it and become whatever it is you are controlling, and only then will you gain the basis for a true understanding of what a video game is.*[31]

Promise of Involvement: Promise of Being (Given a Role)

In light of this, we can ask ourselves the following three questions: (1) How is spectator identification achieved in a multimedia document? (2) Is this medium offering a new type of writing practice, or a new kind of reading experience? (3) In what ways has spectator participation and involvement in the fiction changed with regards to his or her expectations about each "new technology?" Relying on the works of Umberto Eco, Roland Barthes, Christian Metz, Hans Robert Jauss, Gérard Genette, and Roger Odin, we will explore the concept of spectator identification in a screenplay and comment on his or her expectations about the story. Literary theory and semiology, transposed and adapted to the study of the screenplay (whether it be cinematic or interactive), afford very useful and powerful tools that enable us to understand how spectator identification is constructed.

A screenwriter has to be able to create a strong enough world that it will permit the suspension of disbelief to happen. Without that infamous storytelling mechanism, the process of identification cannot kick in and thus the experience of the viewer can never really attain high levels of narrative contentment. Without our full abandonment in a story and our trusting engagement in a situation, a climax is hard to reach.

With this in mind, what novelty these projects do offer is the concept of the reader-participant, which entails another type of satisfaction. Whereas the film script has to be written to satisfy the needs of both the film director and the future spectator, the interactive script is structured to encourage the active intervention of the reader-participant, with regards to the itinerary he or she will have to follow—whether he or she likes it or not—to get to the end of the story. In *Einstein's Dreams*, one quickly ends up identifying with the cursor. The clicking process is in itself a representation of your reading abilities and patterns and how the dreams unfold for you are totally dependent on your cursor's sense of discovery and touch. In the May 5 dream titled "Cause and effect are erratic:" "Each touch has no past or future, each kiss is a kiss of immediacy."

Promise of Making the Reader a Potential Writer-Participant of the Story

The fundamental difference between screenwriting for the cinema and scripting an interactive document resides less in the writing process than in the (programmed) reading experience ("reading" in the Barthesian sense). As we have seen, the basic principles of writing have not changed as much as some have stated or implied. The same rings true as far as the rules of drama are concerned: the transformations multimedia has brought about are still a far cry from being revolutionary. However, what has changed from film to CD-ROM based fiction is the reading experience itself and the way in which a reader approaches the text at hand. The shift can be summed up as a progression from simply watching to actually doing, or as Greimas would put it, from watching to "make something happen" (a literal translation from the French: "*faire faire*"). Whereas a film script anticipates the reactions and the expectations of the "ideal" spectator, the multimedia script prompts the reader-spectator to live out the narrative by making a series of choices.

If a film encourages spectator participation by making him or her make inferences about what will happen next, the multimedia document brings the spectator's participation to a different level, as he or she must act out these inferences. *Myst*'s user manual constantly reminds that the user, when lost should:

Think of related items or places you've seen, think of information you've been given, pay close attention to everything you see, don't forget anything. But most importantly— think of what you would do if you were really there. Remember, there is always the sealed envelope if you need it, but . . .[32]

Thus, the reader-participant must literally navigate through the story in order for it to be "told" to him. The tale, far from narrating itself, must be *found out* by the reader-participant through a series of deductions and inductions that are to be lived out through a very real manipulation of the actual machine. The manipulation grants him or her access to the medium, and to the actual storytelling procedures.

The age-old question of the film spectator's alleged passivity is creeping back into the spotlight. Other than exploring, discovering, and accumulating information, what must the reader-participant of a CD-ROM based fiction do in order to get to the heart of the narrative?

He or she must learn the rules of the game, so to speak, and get accustomed to the internal functions of the proposed "environment" (Cotton and Oliver, 1993). It is *only* by learning these rules that the reader-participant will be able to move forward in the narrative, and at a faster pace. In order to gain access to the narrative it seems the reader must (re)learn to read every time he or she tackles a new CD-ROM based story. The narrative structure integrates these rules and uses them as the driving force behind the story.

I would argue further: the interface *is* the story. In many interactive fictions the interface itself is more interesting to explore and discover than the content and the story it actually wants to mediate and take us into. Our own way of discovering this interface becomes our reading, our story, and, most importantly here, our *experience*.

What happens to the process of identification when one can never really feel a story is being told but that instead one has to search and look for it? As we have said earlier, as a reader or spectator (of a film, a novel, a play) makes inferences, establishes links between sequences in order to understand the plot, and is generally curious about the outcome of the story, so does the interactive reader.

The main difference between the two viewing experiences is in the physical manipulation of the material: the clicking. Making choices while interpreting a text isn't new; breaking away from a prefixed temporal ordering of sequences is. But let's not get overly enthusiastic yet! The multimedia fiction introduces a structure where the reader-participant is afforded the possibility of ordering the sequences as he or she sees fit—however, to a limited degree, as choices are also limited by the length/space available on the CD.

Furthermore, however active this mode of reading may seem at first, it actually short circuits a crucial element of storytelling: causality. Causality is completely dependent on montage (editing of apparently heterogeneous story fragments). The most important consequence of this aborted causality resides in the experience of catharsis. More than a few reader-participants have experienced at least a slight degree of frustration and disappointment upon completing interactive narratives. It seems the time and effort required to see them through are a rather steep price to pay. Contrary to what satisfaction he or she may feel at the end of a well-written novel or well-crafted film— expectations being somewhat different—the reader-participant may feel let down, discovering the story was not written in a truly interactive fashion, as promised at the beginning of the game; as we have previously seen, there is no real interactivity. In addition, the reader-participant may be disappointed because he or she did not lose himself in the story as he or she might have, had the story told itself. Because the reader-participant has had to actively play—and work—to resolve the problems proposed by the narrative, to order the sequences and ultimately to understand the plot, the spectator is constantly reminded of his or her own status: that of a spectator who is prompted to act, following a specific set of guidelines.

I wish to argue that the "click reading process" creates a constant effect of distancing. Constantly reminded of our own reading trajectory, with its errors and misleading clues (which translate into impatience), it's as if the story was taken over by its enablers (the clickable links)—just as in a brechtian *mise en scène* the actor supplants the character, thus rendering him, dramatically speaking, an impotent protagonist. After a few minutes or hours of narrative perdition within a web of frustrating and punitive digressions, one is tempted to click = to quit reading = playing. Perpetually disengaged from the narrative by the interface, instead of feeling you're part of the story, you feel out of place, not unlike the experience of watching *Lady in the Lake* (Robert Montgomery, 1947), a feature-length film shot entirely from the subjective point of view of the main character. The effect, although somewhat novel (in 1947) and interesting at first glance, quickly becomes tedious. What that film has taught us is that if you don't see the character's entire body and face at least once in the film, you'll notice the camera moves but will be unable to feel for him and, needless to say, to identify with him. Going back to my own experience of the Montgomery film, the awfully awkward and distorted kiss to the camera lens is one memorable anticathartic viewing experience I am not about to forget! Just as it failed to operate in the *Lady in the Lake*, suspension of disbelief, the mechanism that enables the spectator or reader to truly appreciate the tension created by the narrative and its ultimate cathartic outcome, is still for now absent from all the interactive fictions we have had access to.

All narrative fiction is *designed* with a specific set of rules and guidelines. These rules may be slightly modified from time to time because of technological changes and innovations. Indeed, theater, the printing press, photography, cinema, then sound cinema have all had an impact on the way stories were and are told. Truth be said, we must admit that the most solid and fundamental principles of storytelling date back to Aristotle. Whether one speaks now of a revolution or not, that fact cannot be disputed. Consequently, we consider that if there are distinctions to learn from comparing the practice of screenwriting for the cinema and for interactive media, the real change resides in what the screenwriter will allow the spectator to know, see, and understand, in the manner the reader-participant-spectator will *enter* the narrative and deem it *believable* or not, and, last but not least, if it is worthy of being experienced or not. Now the time has come to click and quit.

Notes

1. Marshall McLuhan (1995).
2. Isabelle Raynauld (1990).
3. Alan Lightman (1993). *Einstein's dreams*. Warner Books, p. 33.
4. Henry Jenkins and Janet Murray, 1999, pp. 35–57.
5. Ibid.
6. I wish to thank a Ph.D. student who followed my seminar on technologies and screenwriting at the University of Montreal, Éric Alloi, for the many insightful comments he offered after reading this chapter.
7. Many thanks to William Uricchio, Joost Raessens, and Frank Kessler for this invitation.
8. See Tom Guning (1989).
9. M. Utvitch, as quoted by Varchol 1996, p. 90.
10. For a visual understanding, just have a look at one of the 250 *Liquidation* script pages.
11. I wish to thank Daniel Canty (multimedia writer-director), Michel Lefebvre, and Eva Quintas (Agence Topo), Alain Mongeau director of multimedia research at Ex-centris in Montreal, Michel Laforest, and Daniel Cholette for sharing their thoughts, collections of CDs and for the ensuing discussions around them. Special thanks go to screenwriter Simon St-Onge for his careful and insightful reading of an earlier version.
12. Prologue in the game *Myst*, 1993.
13. Manovich, 2001, p. 221.
14. *Myst: The official strategy guide*. Prima Communications, Inc., 1993.
15. Prologue in *Myst*.
16. Ibid.
17. M. Henderson. (1993). *Myst Journal*, p. 6.

Isabelle Raynauld

18. Expression coined by P. C. Bélanger in *Le système vidéoway: Modalités d'adoption d'un système interactif de télévision*, (M.A.). Montréal, Université de Montréal, 1991.

19. As Éric Alloi argued about *EverQuest* and *Afternoon*.

20. This comment does not apply or include role playing games because they function on a completely different level with a different set of rules that deserve to be analyzed on their own. For a variety of multimedia CD-ROMs, go to: www.agencetopo.qc.ca/vitrine.

21. Luc Courchesne: *Portrait One*, Karlsruhe, ZKM Zentrum fur Kunst und Medientechnologie, 1995.

22. I want to remind the readers that this chapter focuses on interactive CD-ROMs: the degree of interactivity of MUDs or that of other fictional experiences on the web or between users on the net deserve a separate analysis and are not included here.

23. Presentation document of the CD-ROM *Liquidation*. Productions Sous le Manteau, Canada, 2001. Before becoming a CD-ROM, *Liquidation* started as a web-audio fiction (1998); it then became a multimedia projected installation and was later designed as a random photonovel. For the genesis of this project go to: www.agencetopo.qc.ca/liquidation. From 1994 to 2000, the writer Michel Lefebvre worked on the photo novel *Liquidation*, and has accompanied its metamorphosis from one medium to the other: book, radio, website, and CD-ROM. He is now working on a multiuser project.

24. The software is called La calembredaine; conceived and produced by Alain Bergeron and Myriam Cliche in the early 1980s by the Société de Conservation du Présent in Montreal to create random poetry. Contact: loplop@loplop.com.

25. *Ceremony of innocence*, 2001.

26. Cover presentation of the CD-ROM *Beyond*, by Zoe Bellof.

27. Other CDs deserve further analysis such as: Julia Hayward, *Miracles* in *Reverse* (an interactive work in progress); and Chris Marker's *Immemory*. I have commented on Marker's in two papers given respectively at the Universities of Utrecht in the Netherlands and Paris III in 1998–1999.

28. June 20 dream, written text in *Einstein's Dreams*, CD-ROM by Daniel Canty, 1999.

29. Idem.

30. Since I started teaching this topic in university, I must have had 150 students given assignments to analyze fictional CD-ROMs. Only one student ever finished *Myst!* All the others complained of the lengthy experience, of getting bored, frustrated, and discouraged.

31. Henry Kuo in *Red Landscapes*, CD-ROM, 1999.

32. *Myst*'s user manual, p. 6.

References

Aristotle. (1858). *Poétique*. Éd.Librairie Philosophique de Ladrange, Paris.

Barthes, R. (1973). *Plaisir du texte*. Paris: Seuil.

Bélanger, P. C. (1991). *Le système vidéoway: Modalités d'adoption d'un système interactif de télévision* (MA). Montréal, Université de Montréal.

Cotton, B., & Oliver, R. (1993). *Understanding hypermedia: From multimedia to virtual reality*. London: Phaidon Press.

Eco, U. (1985). *Lector in fabula*. Grasset: Paris.

Gunning, T. (1989). The cinema of attractions: Early film, its spectator and the avant-garde. In T. Elsaesser & A. Barker (editors), *Early Film*. London: BFI.

Jauss, H. R. (1978). *Pour une esthétique de la réception*. Paris: Gallimard.

Jenkins, H., & Murray, J. H. (1999). Before the holodeck: Tracing Star Trek through digital media. In G. Smith (Ed.), *On a silver platter: CD-ROMS and the promises of a new technology*. pp. 35–57 New York: New York University Press.

Laurel, B. (1993). *Computers as theater*. Reading, MA: Addison-Wesley.

McLuhan, M. (1995). *Essential McLuhan*. Concord, Ontario: Anansi Press.

Manovich, L. (2001). *The language of new media*. Cambridge, MA: MIT Press.

Murray, J. (1997). *Hamlet on the holodeck? The future of narrative in Cyberspace*. New York: Free Press.

Odin, R. (1980). L'entrée du spectateur dans la fiction. In J. Aumont & J. L. Leutrat (eds.), *La théorie du film*. Paris: Albatros.

Odin, R. (1988). Du spectateur fictionnalisant au nouveau spectateur approche sémiopragmatique. *Iris*, 8, cinéma et narration 2. Paris: Méridien-Klincksieck.

Odin, R. (1990). *Cinéma et production de sens.* Paris: A. Colin.

Raynauld, I. (1990). *Le scenario de film comme texte: histoire, théorie et lecture(s) du scenario de Méliès à Duras et Godard*; Ph.D. dissertation, Université de Paris VII, 1990.

Raynauld, I. (1997). Written stories of early cinema: Screenwriting practices in the first twenty years in france. In *Film history, an international journal.* New York: American Museum of the Moving Image.

Raynauld, I. (1999). Du scénario de film aux scénarios multimédia dits interactifs: étude des pratiques d'écriture scénaristique. *Cinémas*, Le scénario. Montréal.

Raynauld, I. (1991). Le scénario a toujours été en crise, *CinémAction*, 61.

Raynauld, I. (1999). The arborescent structure in multimedia screenwriting. Université d'Amsterdam, Conférence, 1995.

Sargent, E. (1913). *The technique of the photoplay.* New York: The Moving Picture World.

Varchol, D. J. (1996). *The multimedia scriptwriting workshop.* San Francisco: Sybex.

6

COMPUTER GAMES AND LEARNING: DIGITAL GAME-BASED LEARNING

Marc Prensky

Although computer and video games are most often thought of as pure entertainment, it is important to understand that they are enormously powerful learning tools as well. Realizing this will not only help us to design better games, but will allow us—using computer games as a medium that can express many different messages—to create effective new learning opportunities and tools for those raised on a heavy computer and video game diet from an early age.

In this chapter I shall explore the *learning dimensions* of computer games. In doing so I shall refer to the phenomenon I am talking about here—putting games and learning together—as *digital game-based learning*.[1]

My aims here are to help clarify the rich and complex relationship between computer games and learning, and to highlight computer and video games' enormous potential for helping people to learn more effectively in the future. In so doing, I will address the following:

1. Why might we *want* or *need* to consciously design and use games as vehicles for learning "serious" (i.e., nongame) content and subject matter?
2. What learning *already happens* when a person plays a computer or video game designed purely for entertainment—whether consciously or partially or totally unbeknownst to the player?
3. *How* do we design learning games that create rigorous learning of given academic or training material and, at the same time, appeal to players?
4. *Where are we* today in the process of creating digital game-based learning? What has been done so far and how successful has it been? How can we do better? What will the future hold?

Why Use Games for Learning?

Play is our brain's favorite way of learning things.
—Diane Ackerman

Anyone who makes a distinction between education and entertainment doesn't know the first thing about either one.
—Attributed to Marshall McLuhan

Why might we want or need to consciously design and use computer and video games for learning "real-world" (i.e., nongame) content and subject matter? There are two key reasons:

- Our learners have changed radically.
- These learners need to be motivated in new ways.

All digital game-based learning is based on these two key premises. Let us examine them in more detail.

The first premise that today's *learners have changed in some fundamentally important ways*. Growing up with digital technology, of which computer and video games are a major part, has dramatically—and, importantly, *discontinuously*—changed the way people raised in this time think and process information. These changes have been so enormous that today's younger people have, in their intellectual style and preferences, *very different minds* from their parents and, in fact, *all* preceding generations.

The second premise is that *computer games can provide a new way to motivate today's students to learn*. One of the growing problems facing *all* formal learning, whether classroom, online, distance, or "e-," is *keeping students motivated*—motivated enough to stick with the learning process to the end of a class, lesson, session, course, semester, or degree. Motivation is important because learning requires putting out effort. However, the things that were effective in motivating learners in past do not motivate the learners of today. We need something new.

Fortunately, we now have a generation that when growing up deeply experienced, for the first time in history, a radically new form of play—computer and video games. As this new form of entertainment has radically shaped their preferences and abilities, it has absorbed their time and effort to an extent never before seen. The typical student has now played thousands of hours of video games before graduating from college. The engagement power of electronic games for this generation (and those to come) may be, if used correctly, the biggest learning motivator we have ever seen.

How Learners Have Changed

It is interesting to me that so few have observed that *our students are no longer the people our educational system was designed to teach*. Today's students have not just changed incrementally from those of the past, nor simply changed their slang, clothes, body adornments, or styles, as has happened between generations previously. A really big discontinuity has taken place. One might even call it a "singularity"—an event that changes things so fundamentally that there is absolutely no going back. This so-called "singularity" is the arrival and rapid dissemination of digital technology in the last decades of the twentieth century.

Today's students—kindergarten through college —represent the first generation to grow up with this new technology. They have spent their entire lives surrounded by and using computers, video games, digital music players, video cams, cell phones, and all the other toys and tools of the digital age. Today's average college grads have spent fewer than five thousand hours of their lives reading, but more than ten thousand hours playing video games and another ten on their cell phones (not to mention twenty thousand hours watching TV).[2] Computer games, email, the Internet, cell phones, and instant messaging are integral parts of their lives.

It is now clear that as a result of this ubiquitous digital environment and the sheer volume of their interaction with it, today's students think and process information fundamentally differently from their predecessors. These differences go far further and deeper than most educators suspect or realize. "Different kinds of experiences lead to different brain structures," says Dr. Bruce D. Berry of Baylor College of Medicine.[3] It is very likely that our students' brains have physically changed—and are different from those of their parents—as a result of how they grew up. But whether or not this is *literally* true, we can say with certainty that their *thinking patterns* have changed. I will get to *how* they have changed shortly.

What should we call these "new" students of today? Some refer to them as the N-(for Net)-gen or D-(for digital)-gen. But the most useful designation I have found for them is *Digital Natives*. Our students today are all "native speakers" of the digital language of computers, video games, and the Internet.

So what does that make the rest of us? Those of us who were not born into the digital world but have, at some later point in our lives, become fascinated by and adopted many or most aspects of the new technology are, and always will be compared to them, *Digital Immigrants*.

The importance of the distinction is this: As Digital Immigrants learn—like all immigrants, some better than others—to adapt to their environment, they always retain, to some degree, their "accent," that is, their foot in the past. The "Digital Immigrant accent" can be seen in such things as turning to the Internet for information second rather than first, or in reading the manual for a program rather than assuming that the program itself will teach us to use it. Today's older folk were socialized differently from their kids, and are now in the process of learning a new language. And a language learned later in life, scientists tell us, goes into a different part of the brain.

There are hundreds of examples of the Digital Immigrant accent. They include printing out your email (or having your secretary print it out for you—an even "thicker" accent); needing to print out a document written on the computer in order to edit it (rather than just editing on the screen); and bringing people physically into your office to see an interesting website (rather than just sending them the URL). I'm sure you can think of one or two examples of your own without much effort. My own favorite example is the "Did you get my email?" phone call. Those of us who are Digital Immigrants can, and should, laugh at ourselves and our accent.

But this is not a joke. It's deadly serious, because the single biggest problem facing education today is that our Digital Immigrant instructors, who speak an outdated language (that of the predigital age), are struggling to teach a population that speaks an entirely new language.

This is obvious to the Digital Natives. School often feels pretty much as if we've brought in a population of heavily accented, unintelligible foreigners to lecture them. Ever since *Pong* arrived in 1974, our kids have been adjusting or programming their brains to the speed, interactivity, and other factors in computer and video games, much as their parents the boomers reprogrammed their brains to accommodate TV. But when they get to school they have to "power down."

The "mind alterations" or "cognitive changes" caused by the new digital technologies and media have led to a variety of new needs and preferences on the part of the younger generation, particularly—although by no means exclusively—in the area of learning. In fact, says one observer, "Linear thought processes that dominate educational systems now can actually retard learning for brains developed through game and Web-surfing processes on the computer." (Moore, 1997)

Ten Ways Digital Natives Are Different

Exactly *how* are the Digital Native learners different as a result of the technology and games they grew up with? Here are ten examples.

Twitch Speed versus Conventional Speed

"Twitch speed" is the rate that a game player's thumbs move up and down on the controller. Because of games and other experiences (such as MTV), the Digital Natives have had far more experience at processing information quickly than their predecessors, and are therefore better at it. Of course, humans have *always* been capable of operating at faster than "normal" speeds—think of airplane pilots, race-car drivers, and speed-reading guru Evelyn Wood—but this ability has now moved into a generation at large, and at an early age. A big problem Digital Natives face is that, after MTV and video games, they essentially hit a brick wall—short of piloting a jet, little in real life moves that fast. Traditional school feels to them like a depressant. We see the Digital Natives' need for speed manifesting itself in a number of ways, including a demand for a faster pace of development, less "time-in-grade," and shorter lead times to success. We need to create learning experiences that maintain the pace and exploit the Digital Natives' facility with twitch speed while adding content that is important and useful. Digital game-based learning is one of the ways we can do this.

Parallel Processing versus Linear Processing

Digital Natives grew up doing their homework while watching TV and doing almost everything while wearing a Walkman. Most of these people feel much more comfortable than their predecessors doing more than one thing at a time. At least some of this comes from games—Patricia Greenfield of UCLA (1984) cites parallel processing as a "cognitive requirement of skillful video game playing." It turns out our attention does not necessarily have to be limited to only one thing at a time, because the mind can actually process many tracks at once (or in very quick succession) and often has quite a bit of "idle time" from its primary task that can be used to handle other things. "There is no question that people can learn to do quite a bit of parallel

processing in certain job situations, such as a lot of military jobs," says Susan Chipman.[4] Today it is common to see young computer artists creating complex graphics while listening to music and chatting with co-workers, young business people having multiple conversations on the phone while reading their computer screens and email, and securities traders managing multiple screens of information simultaneously. On today's cable TV news, the anchor person takes up only a small corner of the screen, the remainder being filled with sports statistics, weather information, stock quotes, and headlines, all presented simultaneously.

We need to be thinking of additional ways to enhance parallel processing for the Digital Natives to take advantage of this now more highly enhanced human capability. We can feed Digital Natives much more information at once than has been done in the past. As in their games, having all the information at their fingertips—numbers, video, links, simultaneous conversations, with the ability to move seamlessly between them—is the Digital Native's nirvana.

Random Access versus Linear Thinking

Digital Natives were the first to experience hypertext and "clicking around" in their games and on the web. As a result, "they develop hypertext minds," says William Winn.[5] "They leap around. It's as though their cognitive structures were parallel, not sequential." Another reports that the Digital Native takes in and outputs information differently—typically from multiple sources and occurring in a less sequential manner. This new random access information structure has increased the Digital Natives' awareness of and ability to make connections, has freed them from the constraint of a single path of thought. Although some fear that unbridled hyperlinking may make it more difficult for these people to follow a linear argument and to do some types of deep or logical thinking, what has been lost in linearity may have been made up for by a greater ability to perceive, and think in, structure and patterns. "Our electronically configured world," wrote Marshall McLuhan "has led us to move from the habit of data classification to the mode of pattern recognition. We can no longer build serially, block-by-block, step-by-step, because instant communication insures that all factors of the environment and of experience coexist in a state of active interplay" (1967, p. 9).

Graphics First versus Text First

In previous generations, graphics were generally illustrations, accompanying the text and providing some kind of elucidation. For today's Digital Natives, the relationship is almost completely reversed: the role of text is to elucidate something that was first experienced as an image. Since childhood, these people have been continuously exposed to television, and computer and video games that put high-quality, highly expressive graphics in front of them with little or no accompanying text. The result has been to acutely sharpen their visual sensitivity. They find it much more natural than their predecessors to begin with visuals, and to mix text and graphics in a richly meaningful way.

Video games figure importantly in Greenfield's explanation of a worldwide rise of what she terms "visual intelligence" (1984). It is linked to the other changes as well, because, in her words, "pictorial images, in general, tend to elicit parallel processing."

This shift toward graphic primacy in the younger generation raises some thorny issues with regard to textual literacy and depth of information. Our challenge is to design ways to use this shift to enhance comprehension, while still maintaining the same or even greater richness of information in the new visual context.

Connected versus Stand-Alone

The Digital Natives have been raised with, and become accustomed to, the worldwide connectedness of email, broadcast messages, bulletin boards, usegroups, chat, multiplayer games, and instant messaging. The games generations' connectedness is both synchronous and asynchronous—any time, anywhere, at almost no cost. For Digital Natives, there are people who can be contacted, spoken to and played with—somewhere in the world—24/7/365.

The connectedness of the Digital Natives has made them much less constrained by their physical location and more willing to work in the so-called "virtual teams" that are becoming more useful in a variety of education settings and businesses. Some claim that this leads to depersonalization, as people meet, chat, play, and even work on the web without ever seeing each other or knowing the other person's name or gender. But people who do this often find it enormously liberating and fun to be freed of all the effects of "lookism" and other prejudices. Moreover, as a result of their connected experience, Digital Natives tend to think differently about how to get information and solve problems. When a Digital Native wants to know something, he or she typically searches the web and possibly posts his question to a bulletin board, contacting thousands of people, rather than relying on only one or two "authorities."

Active versus Passive

A striking cross-generational difference can be observed when people are given new software to learn. Older folks almost invariably want to read the manual first, afraid they won't understand how the software works or that they'll break something. Digital Natives rarely even think of reading a manual. They just play with the software, hitting every key if necessary, until they figure it out. If they can't, they assume the problem is with the software, not with them—software is *supposed* to teach you how to use it. This attitude is almost certainly a direct result of growing up with electronic games where each level and monster had to be figured out by trial and error, and each trial click could lead to a hidden surprise. The games were designed to teach you as you go, as Greenfield was one of the first to point out. We now see much less tolerance among the Digital Natives for passive situations such as lectures, classrooms, and meetings. Nike's slogan "Just do it" (which began in 1988!) hits this generational change squarely on the head (Greenfield, 1984).

Payoff versus Patience

One of the biggest lessons the games generation learned from playing all those hours of video games is that if you put in the hours and master the game, you will be rewarded—with the next level, with a win, with a place on the high scorers' list. What you do determines what you get, and what you get is worth the effort you put in. Computers excel at giving feedback, and the payoff for any action is typically extremely clear. A key outcome of this is a huge intolerance on the part of Digital Natives for things that don't pay off at the level expected. Digital Natives make payoff versus patience decisions every minute. "Why should I bother?" they constantly ask. The challenge is to understand just how important these payoff versus patience trade offs are, and to find ways to offer Digital Natives meaningful rewards now, rather than advice about how things "will pay off in the long run."

Fantasy versus Reality

Another striking aspect of the games generation is the degree to which fantasy elements, both from the past (medieval, *Dungeons & Dragons* imagery), and the future (*Star Wars*, *Star Trek*, and other science fiction imagery) pervade their lives. This phenomenon has certainly been encouraged by games and technology. Although young people have always indulged in fantasy play, the computer has by its nature made this easier and more realistic, in many ways bringing it to life. Network

technology allows people not only to create their new fantasy identities, but also to express them to others and join in fantasy communities and games such as *EverQuest*. Rather than admonish Digital Natives to "grow up and get real" and abandon their rich fantasy worlds, we need to search for new ways to combine fantasy and reality to everyone's benefit.

Play versus Work

Although often derided in the press as intellectual slackers, in reality the Digital Natives are very much an intellectual problem-solving-oriented generation. Many types of complex logic, challenging puzzles, spatial relationships, and other demanding "thinking" tasks are built into the computer and video games they so enjoy. They spend more on such electronic games than on going to the movies; and unlike for many Digital Immigrants, getting a complex PC to run can be a fun way to spend their time. Some have argued that play and games are good preparation for work. For today's Digital Natives play *is* work to a large extent, and work is increasingly seen in terms of games and game play. The fact that the "real life" games are very serious does not make the player's approach any different than the way he or she approaches game software. Achievement, winning, and beating competitors are all very much part of the ethic and process.

Technology as Friend versus Technology as Foe

Finally, growing up with computers has engendered an overall attitude toward technology in the minds of the Digital Natives that is very different from that of their elders (Tapscott, 1998). To much of the older generation, technology is something to be feared, tolerated, or at best harnessed to one's purposes. To the Digital Native, the computer is a friend. It's where he or she has always turned for play, relaxation, and fun. It's something they *know*—the huge generational reversal in technical skill, where parents must turn to their children for help in using their expensive equipment, is now legendary. To Digital Natives, owning or having access to a networked, game-enabled computer feels almost like a birthright—and certainly a necessity.

Attitude

In addition to all of the above, a defining characteristic of the Digital Native is "attitude"—an irreverent, often sarcastic, tell-it-like-it-is, don't-try-to pull-the-wool-over-my-eyes way of looking at things. This attitude is captured in many of their games and especially in Jellyvision's game series *You Don't Know Jack*. ("What were

you *thinking?*") Attitude may have originated as a reaction to all the commercials and other television that Digital Natives grew up with. But however it started, it is certainly now part of their language ("Duh!") and almost a *sine qua non* for communicating with them effectively. In fact, *not* having attitude—or, worse, doing it wrong—is definitely part of the "Digital Immigrant accent" and is sure to be mocked.

In all these ways—and there are many others—the Digital Natives are *cognitively different* from their predecessors. There is strong scientific evidence from neuroscientists and social psychologists on brain plasticity and malleability to back this up.[6]

Digital Natives accustomed to the twitch speed, multitasking, random-access, graphics first, active, connected, fun, fantasy, and quick payoff world of their video games, MTV, and Internet feel *bored* by most of today's approaches to learning, well-meaning as they may be. Worse, the many skills that new technologies *have* actually enhanced, such as parallel processing, graphics awareness, random access, and so on—that have profound implications for their learning—are almost totally ignored by educators.

All these cognitive differences, resulting from years of "new media socialization" and profoundly affecting and changing the generations' learning styles and abilities, cry out for new approaches to learning with a better "fit" for the Digital Natives. Although certainly not the only way, computer and video games provide one of the few structures we currently have that is capable of meeting many of the Digital Natives' changing learning needs and requirements. This is the key reason why digital game-based learning is beginning to emerge and thrive.

Why It Works

In today's education, the process of learning is rarely the motivating or engaging factor. Although there are clearly some situations in which Digital Natives find learning interesting and are eager to remain engaged in the learning process (say a course in computers, or how to get a higher income), there are many more situations in which they do and are not. Their motivation to exert the effort needed to learn typically comes externally, from punishment and rewards.

Game playing, of course, is just the opposite. The main reason people play games is because the process of game playing *is* engaging. So engaging, in fact, that I would argue that computer and video games are possibly the most engaging pastime in the history of mankind. These games bring together combination of motivating elements not found together in any other medium:

- They are a form of fun. That gives us *enjoyment and pleasure*.
- They are form of play. That gives us *intense and passionate involvement*.
- They have rules. That gives us *structure*.
- They have goals. That gives us *motivation*.
- They are interactive. That gives us *doing*.
- They are adaptive. That gives us *flow*.
- They have outcomes and feedback. That gives us *learning*.
- They have win states. That gives us *ego gratification*.
- They have conflict/competition/challenge/opposition. That gives us *adrenaline*.
- They have problem solving. That sparks our *creativity*.
- They have interaction. That gives us *social groups*.
- They have characters and story. That gives us *emotion*.

Because of all these factors, combining games and learning can potentially add enormously to the motivation of students to learn what they may not be otherwise motivated to learn, and increase their engagement in the learning process. How? For a start, fun in the learning process creates relaxation. It enables them to put forth effort without resentment. Play has a deep biological, evolutionarily important function, which has to do specifically with learning—it is nature's way of making it engaging for both humans and animal children learn (Hillis, 2000). "Children are expected to play because we recognize (perhaps unconsciously) the fundamental utility of games as an educational tool," says Chris Crawford, noted game designer (Crawford, 1980).

Games provide the formal, structured way we harness and unleash all the power of fun and play in the learning process. Games engage and motivate us through their goals and our struggle to achieve them, through the decisions we make and the feedback we get from them, through the opponents and challenges we have to overcome, and through the emotions and connections with others we feel when playing. It is this powerful stuff that keeps kids glued to their computers and consoles for those countless hours.

Consciously combining all this engaging power of computer games with a set of interactive learning processes (that can take several different forms depending on the learning goals) is what creates digital game-based learning. The key of course, is to manage how the two are put together into a whole package. Another big part of the picture is *how that package is used* as part of a learning process. In most cases, digital game-based learning isn't designed do an entire training or teaching job alone, and is often part of larger educational initiatives and approaches, often including teachers and other types of learning. But increasingly, the game portion is taking up a more up-front, more primary, larger role in the process.

A final requirement—and this is no different than any learning—is that the content and the learner be well matched. If they are not, little or no learning will happen with any method.

Should Learning Be *Fun*?

I have spoken a lot about "fun" in the learning process. Should learning be fun? Not everyone thinks so. A. P. Herbert has said, "People must not do things for fun. We are not here for fun. There is no reference to fun in any act of Parliament." (2001). Clifford Stoll, in his book *High Tech Heretic* (1999) says, "I may be old fashioned, but learning is hard work." Yale Professor David Gelertner calls education "the hardest work most of us will ever do."[7]

Digital game-based learning doesn't dispute this. What it takes issue with in "hard work" is not the "hard" part—no one seriously disputes that effort and energy is involved in learning. And *all* of the best games are hard to master. The change, rather, is in the word "work." Learning, as great teachers have known throughout the ages, does not feel like work when you're having fun. The MIT Media Lab's term for this is "hard fun" (taken from the comment of a third-grader) (Negroponte, 1996, p. 196). Digital game-based learning can certainly be hard fun. But at its very best, even the hard part goes away, and it becomes *all* fun, a really good time from which, at the end, you have gotten better at something, through a process that Doug Crockford of LucasArts has referred to as "stealth learning."[8] As the keen motivator of people Dale Carnegie observed, "People rarely succeed unless they have fun in what they are doing" (1964).

Not Everyone "Gets It"

Yet although digital game-based learning has been slowly making its way into education and training for over twenty years—for kids as "edutainment" and for adults as simulation and military games—many managers and leaders in the education world still do not fully accept its premises and utility. Many of these people are strong believers in "traditional" learning—the essentially nineteenth-century methods of rote learning, telling, and testing, and so on. One of the most frustrating things for digital game-based learning advocates is to bump heads with such people, many of whom are the potential purchasers of these products, who just "don't get it."

It is important that we help those raised on traditional educational and training theory understand that because digital technology *is* such a discontinuity, much, if not most of the data collected and the theories formulated in the past about how people think and learn no longer apply. This is one reason why our entire learning system, which worked well for hundreds of years, is breaking down. The "stuff" to be learned can no longer be just "told" to today's learners. It must be learned *by* them, through questions, discovery, construction, interaction, and, above all, fun. Digital game-based learning is a great way for these leaders to begin to create this. Although certainly not the only way, it represents one of the first effective and doable means to alter the learning process in a way that appeals to, and excites, Digital Natives.

Effectiveness

But how effective is it? Many criticize today's learning games, and there is much to criticize. But if some of these games don't produce learning it is not because they are games, or because the concept of game-based learning is faulty. It's because *those particular games are badly designed*.

As anyone who has ever looked at the problem of measuring "true learning" knows, it is no easy task. The real measure of learning is behavior change—would this individual, when faced with an identical or similar problem in the future, do something different (mentally or physically) from before? Because we can never know this until it happens, the proxy that we typically use to measure learning is the test: a series of questions, problems, and hypotheticals that let the learner demonstrate, although in a somewhat artificial context, the new behaviors and approaches they have learned. (When observing and measuring behaviors is possible, this is a better way to determine effectiveness.)

So what people really want to know is: are the test scores the same as with the other methods of learning? Although there have only been a few head-to-head comparisons between digital game-based learning and alternatives conducted in this way, the studies that have been done show that learning games that are well designed do produce learning, and lots of it, by and while engaging players.

The Lightspan Partnership, now part of Plato Learning, which created PlayStation games for curricular reinforcement in elementary school, measured that when one strips out the recesses and the lunch and the in-between times, a typical 9–3 school day actually consists of about three hours of instruction time.[9] So if they could get kids to play their games for six hours over a weekend, and the games were only 50 percent educational, they'd effectively add a day a week to their schooling. This would, they hoped, be reflected in higher test scores. Lightspan conducted studies in over four hundred individual school districts and performed a meta-analysis of all of them. They found increases in vocabulary and language arts of 24 and 25 percent respectively over the control groups, whereas math problem solving and math procedures and algorithms scores were 51 and 30 percent higher.[10]

Click Health, which made games to help kids self-manage their health issues, did clinical trials funded by the National Institutes of Health. They found, in the case of diabetes, that kids playing their games (as compared to a control group playing a pinball game) showed measurable gains in self-efficacy, communication with parents, and diabetes self-care. And more important, urgent doctor visits for diabetes-related problems declined 77 percent in the treatment group (Lieberman, 1998).

Scientific Learning's *Fast ForWard* game-based program for retraining kids with reading problems conducted National Field Trials using sixty independent professionals at thirty-five sites across the United States and Canada. Using standardized tests, each of the thirty-five sites reported conclusive validation of the program's effectiveness, with 90 percent of the children achieving significant gains in one or more tested areas.[11]

Over and over it's the same simple story. Practice—time spent on learning—works. People don't like to practice. Games capture their attention and make it happen. And of course they must be practicing the right things, so design is important.

The U.S. military, which has a quarter of a million eighteen-year-olds to educate every year, is a big believer in learning games as a way to reach their Digital Natives. They know their volunteers expect this: "If we don't do things that way, they're not going to want to be in our environment."[12] What's more, they've observed it working operationally in the field. "We've seen it time and time again in flying airplanes, in our mission simulators," practical-minded Department of Defense trainers say. They are, in fact, perplexed by educators who say "We don't know that educational technology works—we need to do some more studies." "We know the technology works," they retort. "We just want to get on with using it."[13]

Today's educators with the most crucial learning missions—teaching the handicapped and the military—are already using custom designed computer and video games as an effective way of reaching Digital Natives. In the end, much of the reason comes down to one simple thing: *time spent on the task*. Computer and video and games are incredibly powerful and effective learning tools, mainly because of the thousands of hours kids spend playing them.

But perhaps the most important reason why we can say for sure that digital game-based learning works as a learning tool is that *all games already cause players to learn*. Let's look now at *what* the players of computer and video games are already learning.

What Players Learn from Playing Computer and Video Games

Some observers express the opinion that computer and video games are "mindless," that kids don't learn anything beyond hand-eye coordination from the thousands of hours they spend playing video games. Others assert that although players may learn about the game (e.g., how to use a Pokeball on a Squirtle), they learn nothing about real life from these games. Still others express the opinion that violent video games "teach our kids to kill."

All of these positions are, I think, wrong. For *whenever* one plays a game—video, computer or otherwise—and *whatever* game one plays, learning happens constantly, whether the players want it to, and are aware of it, or not. And it is not just about the game that players are learning, but "about life." Learning about life is one of the great positive consequences of all game playing. Learning takes place every time one plays, in every game, continuously and simultaneously, on several levels. One need not even be paying much conscious attention. But we do have to pay some attention in order to analyze how and what players learn.

Five Levels of Learning in Games

I will focus here on five levels in which learning happens in video and computer games. My goal is not to be exhaustive, and it's quite clear that these levels intertwine.

I'll call these five levels the "How," "What," "Why," "Where," and "When" levels of game learning. There are no doubt more sophisticated names for them, but I'd prefer to avoid jargon as much as possible. Because I think these five levels apply, to a greater or lesser extent, to all game players, at any age, I will generally not distinguish here between older kids and younger kids, except in one or two specific instances. However, I think this distinction is sometimes useful, and can be broken down even further.

Let us examine what kids actually learn about real life from the video and computer games with which they spend so much of their time.

Learning Level 1: **Learning How** The most explicit level of learning that takes place as one plays a video or computer game is that one is learning *how* to do something. As one plays, one learns, gradually or quickly, the moves of the game. One learns how the various characters, pieces, or anything else, can move, and what you can make them do. One learns how to drag tiles to build up a virtual city or theme park. One learns how to protect oneself in a fighting game and what weapons to use to defeat your enemies. One learns how to train a creature and make it evolve and fight. One learns how to use weapons. And of course one learns the physical manipulations of the controllers involved in doing all this.

An additional, nonconscious message that one learns playing a game, of course, is that in video and computer games *one has control* of what goes on on the screen, unlike when watching movies or TV. Even infants learn this and are fascinated by this ability to control the screen. Many of us have watched infants and toddlers sit moving the mouse and watching the screen with glee for long periods. This is, it seems to me, real world learning.

What else do players learn about the real world at the *How* level? If the games are pure fantasy, then the explicit "how to do it" moves may be pretty useless in the schoolyard or workplace. But learning how to flip *Tetris* pieces may enhance their mental spatial processing abilities, which could help them on a real world nonverbal test.

The more a game simulates anything in the real world, the more one learns about how to do things in that world. One early computer game, *Life and Death* was about doing an appendectomy—in great detail, from diagnosis to surgery. The game was designed by a surgeon, and had a skillful player been called upon to do an emergency operation, I bet that he or she would have acquitted his or herself reasonably well.

Designers of simulation games pride themselves on the games' becoming ever more realistic and "lifelike." One may not be able to learn to do everything—there are kinesthetic cues, for example that you need to learn in a real airplane simulator or on a real horse—but what you *can* learn how to do is huge, and still vastly under-explored. Can you learn to monitor and use the controls and gauges of a real life airplane or train? Can you learn your way around a real-life oil platform? Can you learn via a game to trade financial instruments? To manage a theme park? To aim a gun and be stealthy? You bet you can. And gamers often choose their games because they are interested in learning these things.

Typically in games, players not only learn how to do these things in terms of knowing the procedures, but they also practice them over and over, until the learning is internalized and becomes second nature. Game critic Dave Grossman (1999) highlights the aiming accuracy of a young mass killer, which he attributes to such practice, which may, in fact be the case. But just because one learns *how* to do something, it doesn't mean one has learned *when or whether one should* do it. I will get to this later.

The *How* level also extends deeper, to more transferable learning, by enhancing *non-game-specific skills*. Heavy video and computer game players learn how to parallel process and multitask because they have to in order to succeed at the game. They learn how to take in many sources of information at once, such as the zoomed view, the overall view, the rear view mirror in a driving or flying game. Through practice in games they get better at integrating these perspectives simultaneously into a single world view. They learn how to incorporate peripheral information, a skill that has been shown to be enhanced by computer game-playing as well.

So, for example, we can ask "What, at the *How* level, does a kid learn about real life from playing *Poké-mon*?" Principally, I think, he or she learns how to use and manage a large database of information. (He or she learns this, of course, nonconsciously, and without thinking of it at all in those terms.) This is a quite socially useful type of learning that we could easily apply to other large bodies of information such as to real plants and animals, or geographic data, if the context were as compelling!

Before we leave this first level, we should ask: "How do we know the learning at the *How* level actually takes place?" This is easy: we can observe it. People who practice something over and over learn it and get better. This is common knowledge.

So at just the *How* level, the video or computer game player learns quite a bit. But we have barely even scratched the surface of the learning that goes on in video and computer games.

Learning Level 2: **Learning What** At the next level of learning in video and computer games, players learn about *what* to do in any particular game (and, equally important, what *not* to do). In other words they learn the rules. The rules of any game teach you what is possible and/or doable in the game environment, and video and computer games are no exception. The very process of game-playing can be viewed as learning to understand the "rules code," according to Sherry Turkle of MIT (1995).

Prior to the advent of computer and video games, players typically learned the rules of a game before they started playing it. However this is typically not true in electronic games—in these games the rules are built in to the programming, and you learn them as you play. Players typically learn the rules by trial and error, by playing and finding out what they can and can't do, rather than by reading the list ahead of time. One finds out by playing, for example whether a shooting game allows you to attack someone on your own team, or whether a simulation game allows you to do destructive (or self-destructive) acts.

Some critics have found video and computer rules to be "restrictive," and therefore limiting of learning. But an interesting feature of many video and computer games is that you can frequently *change* the built-in rules, by using the easily findable codes—known, to the dismay and misunderstanding of adults, as "cheat codes"—which are part of most games and passed around from player to player via the web, magazines, and word of mouth. These codes give you extra weapons, lives, power, and so on that let you essentially alter the rules.

So game players learn rules aren't necessarily fixed, but can be changed, and that games provide different challenges with different resources at your command.

What do a video game's rules teach kids about real life? Plenty! Above all, I think, they make a player, no matter what his or her age, reflect—at least subconsciously—and compare the game to what they already know about life. Players are constantly comparing the rules of whatever game they are playing to what they have learned elsewhere about life. When there is a conflict, players ask themselves "Is this a dumb rule," or

"Is it a rule that is good for the game even though it is dumb one in life?" Game players constantly ask themselves, "Are the rules of this game fair, accurate, etc., in terms of what I know?" And the more the rules do reflect the real world kids know, the more they believe the games reflect reality, and vice versa.

How do we know this comparison happens? Because games with wildly unfair or inaccurate rules get quickly identified by players as "bogus" and don't get played very much. If the rules were that small, under-equipped forces could defeat superior forces (except by stealth, guerilla, or other special tactics) no one would accept them. If *Sim City* allowed you to build a modern city without electricity, no one would care. Game designers spend a lot of time tweaking the rules of games to make them seem reasonable—this is known as "balancing" a game.

Gamers of all ages often argue heatedly whether game rules reflect the real world. This happens in terms of physics (e.g., "What is the true trajectory of a missile in space?"); it happens in terms of the reality the game is modeling ("Could a person really sustain that hit and live?"); and it happens in terms of human behavior ("Would an opponent actually do or say that?") among other things. And the rules of games certainly get applied to real life. That's why the Duke Of Wellington could say that "The battle of Waterloo was won on the playing fields of Eton."

Direct examination of game rules is a component of "metagaming," or "thinking outside the game." Part of metagaming is about asking "What rule changes would make the game better?" and then implementing those changes. In video and computer games designers and players are constantly trying to tweak the rules to improve the game.

And before we leave the *What* level, there is also some learning that goes on in video and computer games about rules in general, such as "What if we break them?" Kids learn to shout "That's not fair!" or "You can't do that" at a very early game-playing age, and this is precisely what they are learning about.

So, we've already seen a great deal of learning in video and computer games, much of which applies readily to the real world. But still, we are not even *close* to all the learning that goes on in these activities.

Learning Level 3: **Learning Why** A third level of learning in video and computer games is learning *why* you do something. Players learn the strategy of a game as they play it (which, of course, depends on, and flows from, the rules).

Successful players learn that in some games and situations to succeed you need to attack openly, and in others stealthily. They learn in some games you need to horde and be selfish, in others you need to cooperate, and that in some there are multiple winning strategies. They learn that small pieces have more power when used as a group. They learn that "combination moves" are more effective than single moves. They learn that buying everything in sight or building as fast as you can either works or doesn't. They learn that reserving some of your resources for defense can be important. They learn that some bosses need to be attacked in groups. They learn that hitting the head or the torso with a weapon is a more effective way to hurt someone than hitting an arm or leg. They learn that eyes and underbellies are vulnerable. They learn to keep their guard up, be prepared, and not attack until they have amassed the force required.

These, it seems to me, are all real-life lessons. Game strategy (and tactics) are full of such learning about real life, like the rules, the strategy in games needs to be lifelike for the games to make sense, even if the characters, such as Pokémons, are purely imaginary. Again, players are always making their unconscious comparisons. They know from life, for example, that a hierarchy of strength among species typically depends on size. If a smaller character can defeat a bigger one, they know he has to have something—strength, endurance, weapons, spells—that makes him more powerful.

Militaries have been aware for millennia that strategy can be learned by playing games, and recently they have adapted and adopted video and computer games to their own learning needs far ahead of the curve. To help their people learn better and faster, they use a combination of existing off-the-shelf games, specially modified games, and games specifically commissioned from game-makers. All branches of the U.S. military use video and computer games for learning at all levels from recruit to commander. Military video and computer games are used to learn squad-based teamwork, flying, safety, shooting, submarining, commanding multibranch forces, and countless other things. The Air Force now just takes it for granted that its pilot candidates have used every military flight simulator game there is. They expect these people to have learned not so much "how" to fly a plane, but why—what are the *strategies* for fighting in one. That sports and business strategy and tactics can be learned by playing video and computer games hopefully needs little or no explanation. It is now commonplace.

Just as in the other levels, there are also deeper *Why* lessons that are learned from video and computer games as well. Among these important and valuable real-life lessons are:

- Cause and effect.
- Long term winning versus short term gains.
- Order from seeming chaos.
- Second-order consequences.
- Complex system behaviors.
- Counterintuitive results.
- The value of persistence.

All this, and still two more learning levels to come!

Learning Level 4: **Learning Where**   The "Where" level is the "context" level, as in learning about where you are. This level encompasses the huge amount of *cultural* learning that goes on in video and computer games. Psychologists tell us that games are one means through which kids learn to understand their world. At the *Where* level, the player learns about the world of the game and the values it represents. He or she acquires cultural metaphors and images to use in describing the real world. It is on this level that kids learn, both consciously and nonconsciously as they play, their games' *ideas.*

Video and computer games certainly reflect the big ideas—or *myths*—of our culture: right versus wrong. Good versus evil. Victory versus defeat. Skill versus luck. Our desire to help. Our striving to rise. "[A player learns] to handle myth, lore … danger, betrayal, the fact that there's always someone bigger and more powerful than you are, and the existential inevitability that—even if you kill the bad guys and save the girl—eventually you will die," wrote one observer (Katz, 1999). Players learn through their games to handle cultural relativity, and deal with different peoples and roles. They learn that on one planet, in one society, in one world you can't do X, even though it may be perfectly normal in their own world. They learn their culture's ideas about achievement and leadership. It's at this level that game playing kids can learn that enemies are hard to defeat, but that if you persevere and learn enough, you *can* defeat all the enemies and beat the game.

Many thinkers, from Plato to McLuhan, have described our games as a reflection of our society. Those who deplore violent games, for example, might take a look at the statistics that show that American society—despite what some might like to think—is still a reasonably violent and not especially law abiding one, with a higher percentage of its population incarcerated than anywhere on earth. As with other forms of expression, video and computer games reflect and interpret the culture(s) and subculture(s) in which they are created. They reflect the ideas and fantasies of their makers—their heroes, their villains. Game players learn this. They learn to identify with the game characters, and with the cultures they inhabit.

Do kids playing video games really *learn* these things? I have watched young kids signing in to a game that requires a name, fight over who gets to be Link, the hero of the *Zelda* games. Link is their hero, the person they want to be. The qualities he possesses—courage, the desire to search, explore, overcome all enemies, and get to the end to save the princess—are the ones they want to possess. Game learning goes right into kids' language and concepts; one writer reports a six-year-old Nintendo player referring to his teacher as "the boss" (Provenzo, 1991).

For better or for worse, kids use video and computer games as a filter through which to understand their lives. This is not so different from the past, where their hero and filter for interpreting life might have come from a story (e.g., "I want to be Lancelot"). But one big difference between games and stories is that kids learn they have *control* over this life.

One of the most effective game techniques for transmitting the *Where*—that is, the contextual information—is *immersion*. It seems that the more one feels one is actually "in" a culture, the more one learns from it—especially nonconsciously. With recent improvements in graphics, sound, smells, and "force feedback" controllers, video and computer games have become incredibly immersive. (Soon there'll be appropriate food or gum to chew, I predict.) Language teachers are especially aware of how much learning goes on in immersive situations. So it is not surprising that the many immersive games are causing kids to learn a lot.

Because no simulation is ever perfect, and designers must make choices, the learning in these immersive worlds is *extremely controllable by the designers*, via what the designers choose to amplify, and what they decide to reduce. For example, if the designers amplify the difficulty of defeating enemies in order to increase the challenge or prolong the game, the message the player will get is that "enemies are hard to defeat." Kids will learn whatever messages are in the game.

And this is the importance of the fifth, and most important, learning level of all.

Learning Level 5: **Learning When and Whether**

We have now arrived at the ultimate level, the *When* and *Whether* level of learning. The learning at this level is the deepest, most interesting learning that goes on in video and computer games. For it involves the *nonconscious emotional* messages—the "subtext," as actors say. It is the level where game players learn to make *value-based* and *moral decisions*—decisions about whether doing something is right or wrong. It is therefore the most problematic of the learning levels, and the one that causes the most controversy.

The mechanisms for creating the learning at the *When / Whether* level range from the extremely simple and obvious to the most complex and subtle. At the simplest level, learning comes through the game's amplification of certain factors (through repetition and other means) and reduction of others, as we have already seen. At more complex levels it comes through the use of allegory and symbols, and through the manipulation of images, situations, sounds, music, and other emotion-producing effects and combinations of effects, just like a novel or movie.

It is hard to argue, I think, that the combination of "amplification" and "emotional" cues in certain games doesn't lead players to learn that the answer to "Is it OK to kill this character?" *in the game context* is "Yes." But to me the more important question is "Are kids also learning this about real life?" Do they generalize these messages to the actual world they live in?

I would argue that they don't, at least not in our society. Just as with the rules, game players are constantly cross-checking, automatically and nonconsciously (and occasionally consciously as well) with whatever else they know or have heard for consistency. Messages that are consistent get accepted, messages that are in conflict get further examination.

So in a warped culture where killing was encouraged, the messages in a killing game could indeed, I think, encourage a young player to kill in real life. But in a culture such as ours, where the message "do not kill" is profoundly a part of our cultural context, people—even kids—think more than twice about whether to do it in real life, unless they are already severely disturbed (although here we many have to distinguish the very youngest children). My friend the game designer is right when he says, "We have to be careful about buying into the rhetoric of people who blame *Doom* for Columbine and ignore the fact that those guys were building pipe bombs in their garage and their parents never noticed." We will always have kids on the edges, who do not get society's message from their parents or elsewhere. But they are the exception.

An excellent illustration of this consistency checking comes via a player who told me that one lesson he had learned from games is that "in a video game, it's usually more fun to be the outlaw or bad guy." This would, of course, also be true in life, were there no restrictions. But he, like most players, gets the message that the penalties society imposes make it a lot less fun later on, and so he is not an outlaw in real life.

This comparison of the *When / Whether* learning in the game with the *When / Whether* learning in the rest of life is the reason why shooting games can help kids learn how to aim, without their learning to kill. To really learn the latter, a player would have to to overcome an awful lot of disconnects with the messages he or she hears in the rest of life—at least in civilized countries. I think it is certainly in the public interest to keep these counter-messages as frequent and strong as possible, because as reality and simulation blur (and games are not the only place where this is happening), we get help keeping them straight. This has important implications for policy makers.

Positive or Negative?

So I hope that it is clear that players learn a lot from the computer and video games they play. By now the idea that people who play these games, especially people who play them a great deal as so many kids do, learn from them will not cause very much disagreement. But it is worth taking a minute to discuss an area where there is a great deal of fundamental disagreement. That is whether the learning in computer and video games is positive or negative for games players—especially those who are kids—and for the society they live in. The major concerns of those who think the learning in video and computer games is negative are, I think, as follows:

- At the *How* level, people are concerned that kids are learning how to do "inappropriate" things (such as aim guns accurately).
- At the *What* level, people are concerned that the rules of the video games are too restrictive, that games don't give kids enough room for their imaginations.
- At the *Why* level, people are concerned that the strategies for winning many of the games contain too much violence, too many "cheats," and many other undesirable elements.
- At the *Where* level, people are concerned that kids are being socialized to be loners, misogynists, and social deviants.

- At the *Whether* level, people are concerned that kids are learning to be "amoral killers."

Although all these concerns should be listened to, I do not think they are as valid as the critics claim. There are many appropriate things to do in video games. And even for those things the critics dislike, the games are, in the opinion of many, a useful defuser. Every day games are becoming *less* restrictive and more open to players' imaginations and personalities, with many more open-ended toylike elements that kids can use to exercise their own imaginations and tell their own stories. Newer games have multiple winning strategies. So-called "cheats" are, in reality, only alternative games. As network technology proliferates, video and computer games are quickly going back to the social orientation that games have always had. Video games are becoming more open to girls, and girls are becoming more open to video games. And tons of other messages exist, and more can be created, to counter the "killing is the answer" message that some games may impart to a small number of players.

The problem for me with all the nay-sayers' arguments is that they generally ignore all the positive learning that goes on, and, more importantly, *could go on*, in video and computer games. In my view, this far overwhelms any negatives.

Designing Games as Learning Tools

One wonders whether there's any limit to what can be done in merging the addictive elements of computer games with effective instruction.
—Bob Filipczak

Is it possible to take all the engagement of computer and video games and all the kinds of learning that go on when one plays them, and design computer games that produce reliable learning of given academic or training material? This has been the Holy Grail of many educators almost ever since there were computer games. However, many of the initial attempts produced—to be charitable—mixed results. Designers and players of entertainment-oriented computer and video games—and therefore the computer and video games companies—typically turn up their noses at anything that even smacks of education or learning—and with some justification. Most of the educational and learning "games" marketed under the heading of "edutainment," are hardly real games from the perspective of consumer game designers.

With only a few notable exceptions (see the end of this chapter), what are sold as "learning games" are not real games at all in the commercial sense, but rather short multimedia pieces containing problems to be found and solved, with varying amounts of graphics and animated rewards for getting problems right. These edutainment games have little in common with the exciting and challenging thirty to one hundred-hour experiences of *Quake, Unreal, Roller Coaster Tycoon, The Sims, Command and Conquer, Black and White*, and the gamut of sports games.

Why is this the case? In the opinion of one game designer, the "instructional designers" brought into the creation of a learning game because they supposedly know how to get people to learn, typically "suck the fun out" of any game they get their hands on. Although learning games can fail as real games in many ways, the failure happens mostly commonly in their lack of gameplay—the fun things that the player gets to decide, control, and do. Although this is not as much true for the preschool set, who, in my experience, enjoy many of the edutainment offerings available, it becomes increasingly true once kids get their hand on real entertainment games in consoles, arcades, movie theaters, and so on.

Why It's Hard

Although it is definitely possible to combine the fun of a real game with educational content, it is certainly not easy. The reason it's not easy is this: When a designer sits down to create an entertainment game (a new one, as opposed to a sequel), he or she starts, ideally with a blank slate and a single goal. The designer's "prime directive" is to make something that will engage players for as much time as possible, usually thirty, sixty, even a hundred or more hours. The designer invents all the content of the game—worlds, characters, puzzles—to help reach that goal. In the process of designing the game any element or idea can be accepted into the game if it furthers the goal of engagement, rejected if it doesn't. At the end of the process one can—and publishers often do—write a book about the game's content, often to help players understand the world in the game and succeed in it.

In educational games, on the other hand, the book of content is sitting on the desk before the designer even starts, and the game has to somehow be about that book. So the designer has at least two prime directives to follow simultaneously, to be engaging and to follow the book (i.e., be accurate). He (or she) can't just go about jiggling a concept here, changing a fact there, because it will enhance the game. And to make matters even harder, in addition to the two masters of engagement and accuracy, there is a third master, effectiveness. Does the game cause people to learn?

How do we deal with this three-headed problem? The answer, I suggest, is with *gameplay*. Of the major elements that make a computer or video game—the graphics the player sees (known as the "eye candy") and the actions the player takes (known as the gameplay)—it is the gameplay that really makes the difference between bad games, good games, and great games. Game players do expect great graphics, but the world is littered with failed, pretty games. Yet many games with little or no eye-candy but great gameplay, such as *Pong*, *Asteroids*, and its early arcade cousins, and of course *Tetris*, live on as classics. Over 200 million eye candy–poor GameBoys have been sold in the world. Any game designer will tell you gameplay is *much* more important than eye candy, and many of them wait eagerly for the day when graphics are so good that designers can forget about improving them in every game and go back to concentrating on creating exciting gameplay.

How does this help us in designing "Educational Games that Don't Suck" (the title of a well-attended session I held at a Game Developers Conference)? It challenges us as digital game-based learning designers to take whatever material is our starting point and design a series of great gameplay experiences to get it across. Although our games will certainly involve graphics and even characters, it is what the gameplay has those characters do and, more important, has *you, the player, do* that really counts. One great advantage of this approach is that it can potentially bring our costs way down, because state-of-the-art graphics take up by far the greatest part of any game's budget.

How Do We Combine Gameplay and Learning?

How can two so seemingly disparate phenomena as good gameplay and effective, rigorous learning (because that's what we want, of course) be combined? The answer, happily, is, in a great variety of ways.

It is useful to think of digital game-based learning along the two dimensions that need to be combined to make it work: Gameplay / engagement and Learning, as figure 6.1 shows.

If an electronic learning product delivers both low gameplay and low learning, it is probably "traditional" computer-based training (CBT) or "e-Learning"

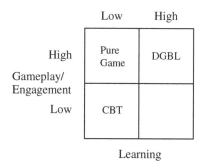

| Figure 6.1 |
Digital game-based learning–quadrant

(lower left quadrant). "Pure" (i.e., consumer) games typically deliver high gameplay but no learning of "traditional" educational content (upper left quadrant). Digital game-based learning occupies the high gameplay and high learning upper right quadrant. And I have yet to see something, online or elsewhere, that is really high learning with low engagement. I think it is a "null" category that just doesn't exist.

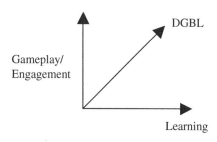

| Figure 6.2 |
Digital game-based learning–two-dimensional process

But even within the digital game-based learning quadrant, there can be a lot of variation. Each dimension is a continuum, and each project has a different amount of both learning and engagement. Ideally, you want to move out continuously on a 45° line balancing the two. Although there might be reasons in a given case to lean more towards one or the other, I'm not sure this is a good idea, although I have always thought it would be nice to have a slider as part of the interface, so the user could choose his or her own mix between learning and engagement based on their mood at the time (figure 6.2).

As we design learning games, we have to continually consider both the gameplay and learning dimensions. Not enough emphasis on learning and we risk sliding into being just a game; not enough emphasis on gameplay and we risk falling into CBT. It is much better to think about keeping both dimensions high than to think about trading them off, as some suggest we need to do.

So our *process* in creating digital game-based learning is the following: (1) Find or create a game with great gameplay that will engage our audience. (2) Find the learning activities and techniques that will teach what is required (doing each with the other in mind), and then (3) successfully blend the two. (We also need to take into account the political context, the technology, and the resources available, but that is outside the scope of this chapter.)

Understanding Your Players

Let us begin, as any game designer would, with our audience. Most learners will be excited when they hear you are designing a game for them, but they will also be skeptical. So much learning is boring and done *to* learners, that people need to be clear that the game is being made to engage them and that ideally they have a real say in its design. In the end, the audience will quickly determine whether the game is engaging, and if it isn't, they will basically ignore it or throw it away, wasting a lot of your effort, time, and money. So we begin by considering our particular type of audience, from whom we will select a representative group to work with.

In some fortunate situations we may have an audience that is reasonably homogeneous. *The Monkey Wrench Conspiracy*, for example, was designed for a relatively homogeneous audience of mechanical engineers, over 95 percent of whom are young (twenty to thirty years old) male and experienced gamers. The military's *Joint Force Deployment* was designed for a relatively homogenous group (at least in their training) of mid-level military unit commanders. Other games have been designed specifically for people with MBAs and/or strategy backgrounds. Still others have been aimed at highly competitive professionals, or at a particular type of student. But some audiences are not as easy. We often need to face the reality of fairly diverse audiences for any given type of learning. When this is true, among the most important variables that make a difference to choosing a type of digital game-based learning are:

- age
- gender
- competitiveness
- previous experience with games.

If the audience is diverse along one or more of these dimensions, there are alternative strategies for dealing with creating games for such groups:

1. Seek a "lowest common denominator" game style, a game format that appeals to both men and women, or to both competitive and noncompetitive employees. Among game formats that may serve this purpose are detective games, adventure and puzzle games, and strategy games.

2. Create more than one game, for example, one more competitive and one more cooperative. The commercial *Virtual World* game centers in America began by offering two games—a highly aggressive shooting game and a much less aggressive racing game. Games 2train has created a template in which the user can choose from among eight different games to learn the same content.

3. Provide a nongame alternative for those in the audience who are not engaged by the game you choose. This is valuable in every case.

Of course, the danger with the first strategy is that it may involve too much compromise, resulting in a game that pleases no one. The second may be too expensive. In such cases the third alternative, building the best game you can for the most people, but allowing those who don't like the game to learn another way, may be the best solution.

One of the most important things one can do in designing digital game-based learning is to get representatives of the audience involved very early on in the process. This can be done through focus groups, informal interviews, and/or by including audience members on the design team. More than anything else, player input and preferences will determine the game's ultimate acceptance and success.

Selecting a Game Style

The types of games we have to choose from to engage our audience include all the standard categories of computer games: action, adventure, fighting, puzzle, role-playing, simulation, sports, and strategy. Selecting a game style from these categories can be done in a number of ways. There may be a commercial game you are aware of (for children or adults) that immediately makes sense in terms of the content. However, it is best not to stop with the games you know, but to look at a wide variety of options, to speak with a lot of gamers, and especially to play as many games as possible. The variety of gaming experiences between, say, *The Sims*, *Alpha Centauri*, *Baldur's Gate*, and *Roller Coaster Tycoon*, for example, is very wide. The reason these and other "hit" games are good models, is that their gameplay is proven. However, it is also possible, if you have a good idea, to create an entirely new game from scratch combining gameplay elements from many, but you must be very careful to make the gameplay great. In the words of Ashley Lipson (creator of the legal game *Objection!*), "To be an entertaining and educational game, it must first be a game, and only then, a teacher" (Lipson, no date).

Game Elements?

A number of people studying games have come up with lists of game "elements" to put into a learning game to make it successful. In 1981, in a paper entitled "What Makes Computer Games Fun?" Tom Malone provided a checklist of elements for designing enjoyable educational experiences whose overall categories are *challenge, fantasy,* and *curiosity.*

Robert Ahlers and Rosemary Garris, of the U.S. Navy's Submarine School, have come up with a longer list of "critical characteristics for fun learning and game play," including imaginary situation, rule-governed, goals specified, competitive/cooperative, progressive difficulty, sound effects, dynamic graphics, user control, outcome uncertainty, simulated danger, performance feedback, high response rates, and informational complexity.

This is helpful information. But the trouble with an elements approach is that although these elements are indeed found in good games, just having a list of elements does not guarantee you a good game—that's one reason why there are so many boring and ineffective "learning games" that thought they were "doing it right." A better approach is to look at the games that work and try to capture these games' style of putting the elements together successfully. (Of course if you *can* design a completely original game that has all the elements and great gameplay, more power to you!)

Do not take this phase of the process lightly—consider many options. The type of game you finally choose, and your skill in integrating it with the learning, will determine the level of engagement. Find the potential game styles that will engage, consult, and reconsult your audience.

Offering a Choice

We don't all like the same game, so offering the player options is often a good idea. One option is to give users a choice of more than one game, and/or a nongame alternative or path through the material to the endpoint as well. I have found this latter strategy, giving users a choice of not playing, to be very important, particularly

if they have the option of opting in and out whenever they choose. This probably relates not only to the fact that some people may prefer not to play games or may not like the game you have, but also to the fact that one of the defining characteristics of play is that it is free— you don't *have* to do it, you can opt out.

The option of having more than one game may sound difficult, but in some instances it is not. It is not that hard to create parallel interfaces that allow you to create content once and have it flow into a number of game formats, offering the player a choice of style.

Understanding Your Content

Second in the process, not because it is less important, but because game-based learning in the audience comes first, you need to consider the kind of learning you are trying to make happen, and select your interactive processes for doing so (the steps can also be done in parallel). "Learning doesn't happen incidentally," says one psychologist. "You have to set out to teach those specific skills."[14] There are many different kinds of content to learn and the types of content and learning require different methodologies. The types of content will also have an effect on your choice of game.

Whatever your subject, you should begin by looking generically at the different kinds of learning content you want to teach to see what kinds of learning are really going on, such as learning knowledge (facts), skills, judgments, behaviors, theories, reasoning, process, procedures, creativity, language, systems, observation, or communication. For any subject there will no doubt be more than one, and probably many. We can then take the different kinds of games, and line them up against these requirements. Then we can decide if our game (and its subgames) can support these types learning, and iterate as required.

Table 6.1 shows types of things to learn, and some of the options for learning them through gameplay.

Choosing Your Learning Activities and Techniques

For the "learning" part of digital game-based learning, one can employ many interactive activities techniques that have been shown to work both in nongame forms of interactive learning such as CBT and in digital games (in many cases, that's where the CBT designers got them!). Additionally, we can and should invent new interactive learning techniques as they are needed. Continuous addition of new interactive activities and learning techniques to our repertoire will make digital game-based learning increasingly effective as time goes on.

Table 6.1
Types of learning and potential games styles

"Content"	Examples	Learning activities	Possible Game Styles
Facts	Laws, policies, product specifications	questions memorization association drill	game show competitions flashcard type games mnemonics action, sports games
Skills	Interviewing, teaching, selling, running a machine, project management	Imitation Feedback coaching continuous practice increasing challenge	Persistent state games Role-play games Adventure games Detective games
Judgement	Management decisions, timing, ethics, hiring	Reviewing cases asking questions making choices (practice) feedback coaching	Role play games Detective games Multiplayer interaction Adventure games Strategy games
Behaviors	Supervision, self-control, setting examples	Imitation Feedback coaching practice	Role playing games
Theories	Marketing rationales, how people learn	Logic Experimentation questioning	Open ended simulation games Building games Constructing games Reality testing games
Reasoning	Strategic and tactical thinking, quality analysis	problems examples	Puzzles
Process	Auditing, strategy creation	System analysis and deconstruction Practice	Strategy games Adventure games
Procedures	Assembly, bank teller, legal	imitation practice	Timed games Reflex games
Creativity	Invention, Product design	play	Puzzles Invention games
Language	Acronyms, foreign languages, business or professional jargon	Imitation Continuous practice immersion	Role playing games Reflex games Flashcard games
Systems	Health care, markets, refineries	Understanding principles Graduated tasks Playing in microworlds	Simulation games
Observation	Moods, morale, inefficiencies, problems	Observing Feedback	Concentration games Adventure games
Communication	Appropriate language, timing, involvement	Imitation Practice	Role playing games Reflex games

From *Digital Game-Based Learning* (McGraw-Hill, 2001).

Among the activities and learning techniques used in digital game-based learning (and games) are:

• *Practice and feedback.* Computers are very good at presenting a series of problems and keeping track, statistically, of how people answer them. Used poorly, this is often labeled "drill and kill." Yet practice and feedback has its place in digital game-based learning because it can be, in the right contexts, an excellent way of learning things that require lots of repetitive practice. (Anyone who denies there are such things should go out and learn to play a musical instrument.) Examples can include facts (e.g., anatomy), physical skills (e.g., typing), and reflex skills (including many aspects of language). Practice and feedback has become a lot more acceptable with the advent of adaptive programming techniques, which shift the difficulty level of the tasks or problems on the fly depending on how the user is doing.

• *Learning by doing.* Most who reject "telling" as a methodology want to replace it with "learning by doing." This works well for digital game-based learning, because "doing" is one of the things both the computer and games are especially good at—we inter*act* with them. (When was the last time you played a game that spent a lot of the time "telling" you anything.) Of course, there is doing, and there is doing. The "drill and kill" is, of course, one form of "doing." Exploring, discovery, and problem solving are others. The common element is *active participation and decision making* by the learner.

• *Learning from mistakes.* In this interactive learning technique, a user moves toward his or her goal until he or she comes to a "failure point" and then gets some kind of feedback. Of course, this is *precisely* what happens in many games. Anyone who has ever tried and failed over and over again to solve a puzzle in an adventure game or to beat a boss in an action game or get somewhere in a flying simulation knows that doing and failing—trial and error—is often a successful way to learn. It is something games are full of because it gives players the motivation to keep trying. One difference between games and learning applications is the way the feedback comes. In most learning apps, it is through some form of telling, be it video-based war stories, coaching, or written feedback. In most games feedback comes via action: something happens. You die. You lose. Your company fails. You go back to the beginning. You are mocked. Designing feedback to be less learninglike and more gamelike is often a big paradigm shift and challenge for digital game-based learning designers. Game designers almost always make the failure consequences interesting, and often fun.

• *Goal-oriented learning.* Some interactive learning designers distinguish learning that is fact oriented (learning *about* something) from leaning that is goal oriented (learning to *do* something). Those who use the term "goal-oriented" or "goal-based" learning have adopted a concept that has been in games since the beginning. A goal is a key element of a game; it's what makes free play *into* a game. The goals in a game, which players usually consider worth reaching, are what give players the incentive to push on through repeated failure.

• *Discovery learning and guided discovery.* Discovery learning is based on the idea is that you learn something better if you find it out for yourself, rather than having it told to you. In learning applications, discovery learning usually implies some sort of problem to solve, which is usually accomplished by searching through data or structures for pieces or clues. This is yet another kind of learning that has a long history in games—discovery learning is what many games, and

certainly all adventure games, are all about. Discovery learning can be frustrating to some people, particularly those who are very linear in their approach and thinking, so some learning designers *structure* the discovery, retaining the need for the player to discover the *solutions* for themselves, but giving the players a very clear idea at any time of the *problem* they need to solve, rather than letting them work even that out for themselves, as in many games. Structured or not, discovery learning is better for some things than others.

• *Task-based learning.* Traditional learning of systems and procedures (i.e., "how to do something") typically starts with conceptual explanations and demonstrations and only then moves on to problems or tasks one actually does. Task-based learning is a different approach, a variation of learning by doing. Here the approach is to skip (or greatly truncate) the generalized explanations and go straight to a series of tasks or problems that build on each other and gradually increase in difficulty. By doing the tasks, with strong specific guidance and modeling, the user gradually learns the skills. A potential downside of this methodology is that users may learn less of the theory behind the skills, although this can be made available as well in a number of ways.

• *Question-led learning.* Although questions are most often used in interactive learning applications as some form of test (pre, post, mastery, etc.) they can also be a form of learning. Attempting to respond as best you can to a question whose answer you don't know forces you to think about the information and reason among the answers, rather than just being told the response. Question-based learning is traditionally associated with one particular type of game, the quiz or trivia game. The fact that these types of games are so popular in the world, and so easily grab people's time and attention, makes them obvious vehicles for digital game-based learning.

• *Situated learning.* Situated learning sets the learning in an environment that is similar to where the learning material will be applied in the future. According to this approach, when students learn in such an environment they benefit not only from the learning material that is taught but also from the culture that is in that environment, the vocabulary used, and behavior associated to that environment. This obviously marries well with immersive style games.

• *Role playing.* Role playing is often used as a strategy in interactive training, particularly for skills such as interviewing, communication coaching, sales, and the like. Role playing, of course, is so much a part of games that it has its own genre, role-playing games, or RPGs.

One of the differences between role playing in training and role playing in games is that training role plays tend to be much shorter and more structured than those in games, which are often multihour, multiday, or even openended.

- *Constructivist learning.* Building on the work of Jean Piaget, the MIT Media Lab has long championed a kind of learning they call "constructivist." What they mean by this is first, that we learn best when we actively construct ideas and relationships in our own minds based on experiments we do, rather than being told; and second, that we learn with particular effectiveness when we are engaged in constructing personally meaningful physical artifacts. Games in which players construct worlds use this approach, which takes discovery learning even farther.

- *Multisensory learning.* The original ideas of including multiple senses in the learning process began in language learning. This type of learning is also related to theories of "multiple intelligences." The introduction of new technologies such as locatable sound and force feedback have greatly increased the game and learning options in this area.

- *Learning objects.* The idea of learning objects grows out of object-oriented programming, where pieces of a program are built as stand-alone units with input and output "hooks" to link them together in whatever order is needed for the particular larger task at hand. The concept is to design pieces of content and, hopefully, certain interactions that are independent, and then to hook them up in whatever sequence needed. Learning objects fit nicely with games, which are becoming much more object-oriented themselves.

- *Coaching.* Coaching is a growing part of interactive learning applications. Although this was formerly a role left almost entirety to the instructor, designers are now finding ways to build useful coaches into learning programs. Coaching has also existed in games for a long time. It often comes from various characters in the game that you happen across as you are madly searching around, or that you encounter when you have hit a failure point.

- *Intelligent tutors.* An "intelligent tutor" is able to look at a learner's responses, decide why he or she made the error, and give specific feedback, usually based on an inference engine with a cognitive model from expert problem solvers. Essentially, the tutor compares a user's behavior to that of an expert. The tutor understands most common misconceptions and tries to correct them early on, as well as giving problems and hints to mediate the misconceptions. Second

generation intelligent tutors add the ability not only to go out and find the information the user needs, but to filter it and present it in the ways that are most helpful.

You should be consider and use all of the above techniques as necessary as you design your learning.

In the end, the learning and the gameplay must be merged. There are a number of structures to consider when doing this. I present them here as a series of choices, but in reality none are purely binary "either-or" choices; one must find an appropriate place on each continuum.

Learning Game Structures: Different Means for Different Ends

Intrinsic versus Extrinsic Games

In 1981, Tom Malone published a second landmark paper based on his doctoral research. It was entitled "Towards a Theory of Intrinsic Motivation" (Malone, 1981b). In it, Malone made the argument that there are two main categories of learning games: intrinsic and extrinsic. In an intrinsic game, Malone argued, the content is an integral part of the game structure. His example is a math game, where things go up as you get to higher quantities and down as they are lower. A more contemporary example is a flight simulation game, where the game itself is about flying a plane, or *Sim City*, where you learn the rules of urban development by trying and succeeding or failing. Most simulation-type games fall into this category.

Extrinsic games, on the other hand, are games where the content and the game structure are less tightly linked, or not linked at all. The paradigm here is the question or trivia game, where the questions can be about any subject, but the game remains essentially the same. Bingo, *Jeopardy!* and other often-used training games fit into the extrinsic model.

Which model, intrinsic or extrinsic, is better? Proponents of each will give you reasons why theirs is superior, and this is a highly controversial topic among digital game-based learning designers. "Intrinsic games," says one designer, "may provide the most powerful learning experiences technology can support. These are perhaps the most noble and worthwhile applications of technology in the learning field."[15] Another argues that "the real power is when you capture the rules at an algorithm level and have people understand them through constant exposure to different circumstances and then they really know the rules."[16] By contrast, anyone who's ever used a typing game to relieve boredom knows it can be fun *and* help you learn.

I believe that both intrinsic and extrinsic games have their value in different situations. The trade-off is that although intrinsic games enhance certain kinds of learning and add to the engagement, they are typically created on a custom basis and are therefore more costly and often difficult to change or update. Extrinsic games, although lacking the learning power that may come from tightly linking the content into the game, lend themselves well to templatization and rapid content changes, often at lower cost. Remember that intrinsic/extrinsic is not an either/or proposition, but rather a continuum. There are a number of states between the two, one of which I refer to as loosely linked.

Tightly Linked Games versus Loosely Linked Games

This view of learning games is somewhat similar to the intrinsic/extrinsic classification, but is actually a different perspective. A tightly linked game is one constructed specifically around a fixed set of content. The content is built in to the game, and knowing the content is vital to succeeding in and winning the game. A tightly linked game can still be extrinsic, and the entire game might be able, with a fair amount of effort, to be repurposed for other content. A detective game where the clues are pieces of information about the product might be an example.

A loosely linked game, on the other hand is one where the content is essentially separate from the game, but there are hooks in the game that bring the two together, and send the player from the game to the content and back again. In repurposing the game to new content, only the hooks must be changed, not the whole game. An example of a loosely linked game is the *Monkey Wrench Conspiracy*, a task-based learning game where the tasks, which are done outside the game in the software to be learned, are initiated by encountering flashing objects, which although part of the story line, can easily be changed to add, eliminate, or change a task.

Like extrinsic games, loosely linked games often allow content to be changed much more easily than tightly linked games. That means you would use them in situations where, say, the content was still in development, or changing rapidly. A tightly linked game is better for incorporating unchanging content.

Hard-Wired Games versus "Engines," "Templates," or "Shells"

The ultimate tightly linked game is the so-called hard-wired game. Here the designers and programmers sit down with the goal of building only this particular game. Reusability is not a consideration. Everything in the game is designed and optimized around the game, the content, and the player experience. In many ways, if done well, this will produce the best game of all, just as a custom tailored suit is likely to look and fit better. But it is a very expensive way to do things.

The opposite of the hard-wired game is the template, or shell. In this approach the content, be it text, graphics, video clips, or whatever, sits somewhere external to the game and is "read-in" or "called" by the program at the appropriate time and displayed on screen. This allows the construction of "content editor" software, where a trainer or teacher can just type in various pieces of the content, which are automatically displayed in the correct place in the game.

An approach between hard-wiring and pure templates is to use what programmers refer to as an "engine." An engine can be, for example, the software that lets you run around a three-dimensional world realistically, not walking through walls and encountering objects and things that move and have various properties. Such an engine can underlie or drive equally well either a shoot em up such as *Doom*, *Quake*, or *Unreal*, or a nonviolent, more politically correct game such as *Straight Shooter!* from Games2train. A number of game engines are available commercially—game companies often amortize the large expense of developing them by licensing them to other companies for other games. The latest *Doom*, *Quake*, and *Unreal* engines are all on the market (typically at high prices for commercial use), as are many individually developed versions.

Some vendors often take the trouble to turn what were originally custom-developed, hard-wired games *into* engines, so they can resell them in a number of different contexts (this is also referred to as "templatizing" a game.) In this case, the *interactions* in the game make up the engine, and all the graphics and words change according to the new context.

The least happy result of all comes when a game is hard-wired not because it makes sense to do things in a unique way from a design or programming perspective, but because the designers or programmers are inexperienced with games and just plunge ahead building it as they go without considering reusability. This can happen either because they don't think they have to make things reusable, or because they don't know how to, or both. For maximum flexibility and reusability, hard-wiring should be avoided as much as possible in a final product. Prototypes, however, are often built hard-wired because doing so is faster and cheaper in this very limited case.

Reflective Games versus Action Games

There are a number of genres of games, ranging from action to role playing to strategy. One of the differentiating characteristics among these types of games that has an important bearing on digital game-based learning design is the *degree of reflection* they allow, because reflection is an important part of the learning process (for certain things) that is often under-included. Non-stop action games (aka "twitch" games), offer the least opportunity for reflection in themselves, whereas role playing, adventure, simulation, strategy, and puzzle games often proceed at a slower pace and offer more built-in reflective "space." (There are, nevertheless twitch puzzles, such as *Tetris* and *Devil Dice*, as well as less reflective real time strategy games.)

In role playing games, one typically gets to make choices in various types of dialogues, which provide reflection points. Adventure games, where one goes around finding objects that allow you to solve puzzles, also give time for reflection around "how do I solve this—what do I need?" Simulation games, such as "running a company" sims, often allow one to make decisions at your leisure, although some do provide "real time" time constraints, and strategy, and god games often give one all the time in the world to make up and change one's mind.

Does this mean we can or should never use a twitch game as part of digital game-based learning? Not necessarily. The important thing is that the gameplay be suited to the content, and there be the right balance of action and reflection in the final product. Too much action, and there's no time to reflect. Too much reflection, and it can get boring. We need to find the flow path between the two. This is part of *pacing*, which is so important to novels, movies, games, and all devices meant to hold our attention.

Synchronous (Real-Time) Games versus Asynchronous (Turn-Based) Games

The distinction between real-time and turn-based (aka synchronous and asynchronous) games is important to digital game-based learning in at least two ways. In a single player mode, a player must pause a real-time game, or put it into a pause state to interrupt it, either for reflection or to do something else. This usually involves saving the game-state (everything that is happening) at that point. Some games—for example with virtual pets—do not allow this, and the game continues whether or not one is playing. Stop playing long enough and one loses. In a turn-based game, on the other hand—Chess for example, but also many strategy games—the machine will wait forever for a player to figure out his or her next move, unless one is playing by the clock.

The distinction between synchronous and asynchronous becomes even more important in multiplayer games. A game where everyone is playing with or against each other at the same time—say a real-time battle or a competitive business simulation—can be very interesting, but for learning it can usually only happen when learners are in the same situation at the same time, such as in a class, orientation, offsite, and so on. When this is not the case, turn-based games, which allow each player to play whenever he or she has the time, may be a better solution. A turn-based game, though, may lack some of the immediate excitement of a real-time game, so the engagement has to be produced in other ways, such as a real interest in the outcome and other types of gameplay such as highly meaningful decisions.

Single Player Games versus Multiplayer versus Massively Multiplayer

Games today can be either single player, multiplayer on the same computer (such as some *You Don't Know Jack* games), two or multiplayer over a network or the Internet, or massively multiplayer with hundreds, thousands, or potentially even millions playing either at once, or on an in-and-out basis.

Most digital game-based learning to date has been single player, except in the military, where the goal has always been to link people. One issue for multiplayer games is getting the people together in real time. In consumer games this is often done via a virtual "lobby" where you first go when you want to play. When enough people are there for a game it starts, and in some games people can join while the game is ongoing. Another option for large multiplayer games is the "persistent state" game.

Session-Based Games versus Persistent-State Games

Session-based games exist only as long as the initial players are playing. Although the game may be able to be paused and resumed, it pauses for all players at the same time. When somebody wins, the game is over, and must be played again. In persistent-state games, on the other hand, the world of the game never goes away. Each player moves in and out of it as they wish, but like the real world, it continues. In persistent-state games such as *Ultima Online* or *EverQuest* (they tend to be role playing games) you can build up skill and experience over time, which has obvious implications for learning. Because the world is always continuing, and opportunities may come and go, there can also be penalties for *not* playing, but this too, has clear connections to real life.

Video-Based Games versus Animation-Based Games

Another interesting choice that designers of learning games must make is whether whatever representations of characters and places they include will be video or animation based. These are two very different styles, often reflecting whether or not the designers have a video background. The advantage of using video is absolute realism. Its disadvantages include size of the "assets," which are large and limit what can be put on a CD or sent over the Internet, and limits on interactivity, because the scenes needed to be prerecorded and play out when they are chosen by the player's choices. Both of these limitations have been overcome to some degree by proponents; the first by better compression and streaming methods, and the second by techniques for cutting videos into pieces as short as one or two seconds, and assembling video sequences on the fly. An additional issue to consider with video is that if any changes need to be made, the video may need to be re-shot, necessitating reassembling the same cast, sets, lighting conditions, and more. If much time has elapsed, the actors may have aged considerably!

Animated characters and graphics, on the other hand, allow designers a great deal of freedom. They can be made to look and sound any way you want. They never become "unavailable," like live actors. Their behaviors and actions can be programmed. "If I want a character to storm out," says a developer "I can just hit the 'storm out' key."[17] Animated characters and graphics are less expensive and, of course are totally lacking in ego (although that's not necessarily true of their creators).

Which to use in a digital game-based learning project? Of course it depends, but here are a couple of factors to consider. First, animated characters are fast approaching real ones in the details of what they can do (their voices, which are recorded actors, have always been real; computer generated voices are at present only good for robots.) If you look at football or soccer games on today's advanced consoles, you will see almost TV-like characters. However, in their total nuances, it is important to remember that these characters will never (at least not in our lifetimes) be perfectly like real people. Yet there is an interesting trade-off between specificity and universality that is explained well by Scott McCloud (1993) in his book *Understand-*

ing Comics. As McCloud explains, the more abstract a character is (the most abstract face being a circle), the easier it is for us to identify ourselves with it. As we get more and more photorealistic, characters take on identities that are more and more specific and become more difficult for us to project ourselves onto. So in some cases video, which is totally photorealistic (i.e., it's a photo) may, actually *hinders* player identification with a character. This may or may not be important in a specific instance. If the perspective of the game is first-person (through your eyes) and you never see yourself, it may not matter. If it is "over the shoulder," where you do see yourself continually as you play, it may.

Some find that using animation improves gameplay. You can fit so many more possibilities on the same CD. Says one developer, "My product is animation based, my competitor's product is video-based. My game has thousands of potential paths, theirs has one."[18] But others feel the technique of chopping the video into very small chunks and assembling them on the fly as needed produces similar results that are more lifelike.[19]

Narrative-Based Games versus Reflex-Based Games

Another interesting question is how much story to include in the game. Should it be like a movie, with an "inciting incident" at the start that makes you want to see the conclusion, and complex character development along the way? Or should it be a series of unconnected scenarios, puzzles, or interactions in a game-like context. The answer here depends on what you are trying to accomplish. The more you want to create something that is long-term and builds, the more story is a useful motivator. The alternative, of course, is to have lots of ever-increasing levels of puzzle difficulty, as in *Tetris*.

Although narrative and characters add emotional impact to a game, it is worth noting that there are many categories of content where reflex action, that is, the ability to react very quickly to a stimulus, is what is important. Language learning is one example (How are you? Fine.) Legal objection is another. Acronyms are a third. For such content, reflex-based games, where the computer rapidly presents stimuli (with or without a story-based context) and judges and times responses, can often provide a good, fun, solution.

Evaluating Your Work in Progress: Digital Game-Based Learning Principles

As you create your digital game-based learning, how do you go about evaluating what you are doing, so that you can make in-course corrections and iterations? Is there a set of digital game-based learning principles, things that any effective digital game-based learning would have to include?

Below is a short list of such principles. Following these concepts will enable you to take any subject matter and design a successful game-based learning experience on the computer. Although I could have phrased them as prescriptions ("Users should ..."), I think they work better as questions for you to keep asking yourself throughout the entire creation process. I suggest you put them on your wall and reflect on them as you are considering, designing, building, testing, and rolling out digital game-based learning.

1. Is this game fun enough that someone who is *not* in its target audience would want to play it (and would learn from it)?

2. Do people using it think of themselves as "players" rather than "students" or "trainees"?

3. Is the experience addictive? Does it produce great "word of mouth" among users? Do users rush out after they try it and tell their colleagues or classmates, "You've got to try this—it's way cool." Do users want to play again and again until they win, and possibly after?

4. Are the players' skills in the subject matter and learning content of the game—be it knowledge, process, procedure, ability, etc.—significantly improving at a rapid rate, and getting better the longer he or she plays? Does the game encourage reflection about what has been learned?

Notice the *order* of the above. Fun (i.e., gameplay) first, learning second. Others have "fun" on their lists, but generally much further down. The result is that many programs that purport to be game-based learning really aren't—they are just someone's theories of learning or some dry simulation dressed up with game-like graphics. Believe me, users know the difference.

Where Are We and Where Do We Go From Here?

The process of creating digital game-based learning is certainly well on its way. There are scores, and sometime hundreds of examples—of varying quality, to be sure—already built for K–12 education, postsecondary education, business and the military (see www.socialimpactgames.com for a list). Digital game-based learning is marching into the consumer gaming world as well. No longer confined to pure fantasies,

commercial computer and video games are beginning to contain content that students or other learners might need to know. A growing number of commercial games, such as *Start Up*, *Aviation Tycoon*, *Pizza Tycoon*, *Wall Street Trader*, and even *Sim City* are filled with content that can be very useful for certain types of education and business training. Games such as *Age of Empires* have much historically correct content that can potentially be used in schools. The military expects budding pilots to be proficient at consumer military flight simulator games.

Still, the fact is that most commercial games would require major revision to make them fully useful as either education or training that could replace other types of learning. But the process has begun, *because it works*. Although as yet far from mainstream, digital game-based learning is becoming an alternative, with amazing and increasing success, in a large number of areas. Almost all genres and styles of games have been used for learning. A new learning paradigm—learning via play—is gradually emerging:

- Preschoolers learn the alphabet and reading through computer games.[20]
- Elementary students learn the K–6 curriculum on Playstations.[21]
- Computer chess becomes a big part of K–12 curriculums.[22]
- Typing ("keyboarding") games are high-selling software products.[23]
- High-schools students play a multiplayer online game to learn electoral politics.[24]
- Financial traders use computer games to hone their skills.[25]
- Policymakers play a *Sim City*–style game to understand the health care system.[26]
- Business executives play at running simulated humor resources departments and oil refineries.[27]
- Engineers use a consumer-style videogame to learn new CAD technology.[28]
- Military trainees fight realistic battles in video game-like simulators.[29]

True digital game-based learning—learning that feels exactly like a "real game"—is finally beginning to emerge. Some examples include:

The Typing of the Dead: An action-packed game for the Sega Dreamcast in which mummies attack you and you must type phrases more and more quickly and accurately in order to stay alive.

The Monkey Wrench Conspiracy: A first-person shooter game for learning to use CAD software.

Joint Force Employment: A real-time strategy game put out by the Office of the Joint Chiefs to teach local commanders in chief and their staffs to combine land, air, sea, and space forces effectively in combat.

Objection!: A twitch game for lawyers in which you have only seconds to decide whether each sentence a witness says is "proper" or should be objected to, and if the latter, for which of a dozen reasons.

Qin: An adventure-style game for learning about ancient China.

There is no doubt that even as I write many more of these "true" learning games are already in development.

The Future of Digital Game-Based Learning

With demographics clearly on its side, the future of digital game-based learning is likely to be a bright one. By 2025, there will be almost no one left in the educational system—student, teacher, or administrator—who has not played computer games pretty much all his or her life.

I expect that by then the learning world will resemble the games world in many ways, with a wide variety of choices and styles of effective learning games for every subject, and users getting to decide (in conjunction with teachers) which approach, style, and learning game they want to play to learn the material.

For me, this is the promise of digital game-based learning:

• That motivation will finally be found for learning the subjects and content that are the most difficult to teach or train—either because they are extremely dull and dry or extremely complicated, or both—and to get people to train themselves.

• That small groups of trainers, teachers, content experts, and game designers working together will create experiences that will radically improve the learning, and ultimately the competence and behavior of thousands, and potentially millions of learners—not only entire companies, but entire industries, grade levels, even countries and populations, and that this will ultimately affect the market value of companies, and perhaps even nations.

• That the free market will create, through a user-evaluated process of marrying the engagement-driven, experience-centered, "fun" approach of the interactive entertainment and games world with effective techniques for teaching the material that students and workers are required to learn, a phenomenon of highly effective learning "hits," that move through target populations at the epidemic speeds of best-selling novels, movies, or games, leaving a lasting educational impact.

• That eventually any individual trainer, teacher, or educator will have at his or her disposal the tools and colleagues to work with to create such phenomena, and that "talent will out," with successful, effective instruction no longer being confined to those a single fantastic teacher or trainer can reach in person, but to all the learners in his or her entire potential target market, worldwide. Such target markets could be all sales people, all managers, all third graders, all elementary school students, all math students, all college-level chemistry students, etc.

• That, consequently, there will be training and learning brands based not just on publishers, but also on authors and designers, subjects and styles, as there are in books, movies, and games.

• That this user-driven learning phenomenon will not only move from company to company and school to school nationally, but will be worldwide, like movies and videogames.

• That the Internet, the wireless networks, and their successors will not just be the conduit for boring courses that people are forced to take or force themselves to suffer through. Rather they will be a competitive forum, much like the games and movie businesses, where talent, creativity, and the ability to hold the audience and deliver a compelling experience is what wins, where the best combination of game play, learning methodology and eye candy is what people seek.

• That we will have a learning world tomorrow, like the games and movies worlds of today, where there are both classic learning hits and exciting newcomers; where a plethora of magazines and reviewers cover what's in development and help learners choose the very best; where makers create their experiences with the goal of holding their audience and being successful in learning, and thereby making money and attracting capital; and where learners look forward to the next release as eagerly as they wait for an upcoming game, console, or movie.

All this is not only possible, but it is definitely coming. Some of it is already here.

We are fortunate, I think, to find ourselves at the beginning of something very new and powerful. Digital game-based learning is like the auto industry in 1890, airplanes in 1910, and computers in 1950. Visionaries then would have been able to paint a picture of phenomena just getting started, with a lot of promise. They could have cited only a relatively few pioneering instances, several of which had failed. Yet in each case, within less than a single lifetime, huge numbers of ordinary people around the world were doing previously unimaginable things: controlling vehicles moving at over sixty miles per hour a few feet apart over vast interconnected highway systems; flying to anywhere in the world in only hours often on a minute's notice; accessing—in seconds, at little cost—the entire network of human information and knowledge from little boxes in their laps.

I believe it will be the same with digital game-based learning. Long before the readers of this book grow old, digital game-based learning—or, more precisely, its infinitely more sophisticated successors—will be totally taken for granted as the way people learn.

Why? Because to be effective with tomorrow's learners, the "fun" component of all learning will have to go through the roof. Because digital game-based learning is enormously versatile, it is adaptable to almost any subject, information, or skill to be learned, and, when used correctly, it is extremely effective.

There is also a strong economic argument. A large and potentially hugely profitable opportunity exists to combine the multitrillion-dollar worldwide entertainment business with the multitrillion-dollar worldwide learning business. Although this may currently seem anathema to educators who see learning as a serious activity, and a strange business proposition to entertainment executives focused single mindedly on the commercial mass market, it makes perfect sense to today's learners. The key premise of digital game-based learning is that by marrying the engagement of games and entertainment with the content of learning we can fundamentally improve the nature of education and training for the world. *This is something people want, and, I think, will pay for.*

So congratulations! In finishing this chapter you have made it to the high scorers' list of those who now understand more about games and learning.

Notes

1. For more, see Prensky 2001.
2. These numbers are intended purely as "order of magnitude" approximations; they obviously vary widely for individuals. They were arrived at in the following ways:

   a. *Video games:* Average play time: 1.5 hours/day (Source: "Interactive Videogames, *Mediascope*, June 1996) It is likely to be higher five years later, so 1.8×365 days $\times 15$ years $= 9,855$.

   b. *TV:* "Television in the Home," 1998: Third Annual Survey of Parent and Children, Annenburg Policy Center, June 22, 1998, gives the number of TV hours watched per day as 2.55. M. Chen, in the *Smart Parents Guide to Kid's TV* (1994), gives the number as 4 hours/day. Taking the average, 3.3 hours/day $\times 365$ days $\times 18$ years $= 21,681$.

   c. *Reading:* Eric Leuliette, a voracious (and meticulous) reader who has listed online every book he has ever read (www.csr.utexas.edu/personal/leuliette/fwtablehome.html), read about 1,300 books through college. If we take 1,300 books $\times 200$ pages/book $\times 400$ words per page, we get 10,400,000,000 words. Read at 400 words/that gives 260,000 minutes, or 4,333 hours. This represents a little over 3 hours/book. Although others may read slowly, most have read far fewer books than Leuliette.

3. Dr. Bruce D. Berry, Baylor College of Medicine.
4. Dr. Susan Chipman, Researcher, Office of Naval Research.
5. William D. Winn, director of the Learning Centre at the University of Washington's Human Interface Technology Laboratory.
6. For a summary of this information, see www.twitchspeed.com/site/Prensky%20%20Digital%20Natives,%20Digital%20Immigrants%20-%20Part2.htm.
7. David Gelertner, in *Online Learning Magazine*.
8. Reported by Noah Falstein.
9. From John Kernan, CEO, The Lightspan Partnership.
10. "Evaluation of Lightspan. Research Results from 403 schools and over 14,580 students," February 2000, CD ROM.
11. Scientific Learning Corporation, National Field Trial Results (pamphlet). See also Merzenich et al., 1996 and Tallal et al., 1996.
12. Office of Readiness and Training, Department of Defence, The Pentagon, Private Briefing.
13. Ibid.
14. Dr. Ray Perez, cognitive psychologist, Department of Defense.
15. Michael Allen, President, Allen Communications.

16. Clark Aldrich, SimuLearn. Analyst emeritus, The Gartner Group.
17. Richard Barkey, CEO, Imparta, Ltd.
18. Ashley. S. Lipson, Esq. CEO, TransMedia, Inc.
19. Ed Heinbockel, CEO, Visual Purple, Inc.
20. Through programs such as *Sesame Street Letters*, *Jumpstart Learning Games ABC's*, and *Jumpstart Phonics, Toddlers*, and *Preschool*.
21. The Lightspan Partnership.
22. Art Fakazis, "A Look at Chess in the Public Schools," online at www.zome.com/kasparov/chessinschool.asp.
23. *New York Times*, December 31, 1998.
24. AOL's *Election 96* and *Reinventing America*, created by Crossover Technologies and funded by the Markle Foundation.
25. *Straight Shooter!* by Games2trai for Bankers Trust Company.
26. *Sim Health*, by Thinking Tools. Funded by the Markle Foundation.
27. Training simulation from Andersen Consulting, *Sim Refinery* for Chevron from Thinking Tools.
28. *The Monkey Wrench Conspiracy*, by Games2train for think3 software.
29. For example, SIMNET tank simulators.

References

Carnegie, D. (1964). *How to win friends and influence people*. New York: Simon & Schuster.

Crawford, C. (1980). The art of computer game design. http://www.vancouver.wsu.edu/fac/peabody/game-book/Coverpage.html.

Goode, E. (2000). How culture molds habits of thought. *New York Times*, August 8.

Greenfield, P. M. (1984). *Mind and media: The effects of television, video games and computers*. Cambridge, MA: Harvard University Press.

Grossman, D., & Di Gaetano, G. (1999). *Stop teaching our kids to kill*. New York: Crown.

Herbert, A. P. (2001). Misleading cases: Rez v.Haddock [Is it a free country?] http://www.kmoser.com/herbert/herb05.htm. In *Uncommon law: Being 66 misleading cases*. International Polygonics, Ltd.

Hillis, D. (2000). Address to the Game Developers Conference, March.

Katz, J. (1999). *Peter Applebome:* Two words behind the massacre, *New York Times*, May 2.

Lee Hotz, R. (1998). How culture molds habits of thought. *Los Angeles Times*, October 18.

Lieberman, D. A. (1998). Health education video games for children and adolescents: Theory, design and research findings. Paper presented in Jerusalem, International Communications Associations.

Lipson, A. S. The inner game of educational computer games. Self-published paper, no date.

Malone, T. W. (1981a). What makes computer games fun? *Byte*, December.

Malone, T. W. (1981b). Towards a theory of intrinsic motivation. *Cognitive Science, 4*, 333–369.

McCloud, S. (1993). Understanding comics, the invisible art. Amherst, MA: Kitchen Sink Press.

McLuhan, M., & Fiore, Q. (1967). *The medium is the message: An inventory of effects*. New York: Bantam Books.

Merzenich, M. M., Jenkins, W. M., Johnston, P., Schreiner, C., Miller, S., & Tallal, P. (1996). Temporal processing deficits of language-learning impaired children ameliorated by training. *Science, 271*, 27–28.

Moore, P. (1997). Inferential Focus Briefing, September 30.

Negroponte, N. (1996). *Being digital*. New York: Vintage Books.

Prensky, M. (2001). *Digital game-based learning*. New York: McGraw-Hill.

Provenzo, E. F. Jr. (1991). *Video kids*. Cambridge: Harvard University Press.

Stoll, C. (1999). *High tech heretic*. New York: Macmillan.

Tallalm Miller, Bedi, Byma, Wang, Hagarajan, Schreiner, Jenkins, & Mezenich (1996). Language comprehension in language learning impaired children improved with acoustically modified speech. *Science, 271*, 77–84.

Tapscott, D. (1998). *Growing up digital: The rise of the net generation*. McGraw-Hill.

Turkle, S. (1995). *Life on the screen*. New York: Simon & Schuster.

Part III

Reception

7

COGNITIVE EFFECTS OF VIDEO GAMES

Sandra L. Calvert

My eleven-year-old nephew Sean and I are playing a race-car video game. He races around the board, passing cars and moving his hands at lightening speed. I struggle along at the end of the pack. Sean, who is able to watch me play as he is winning the game against the computer (who is providing more competition than I am), begins to give me some verbal guidance about how to use my joystick. At one point, he even says, "Turn around, Aunt Sandy—you're going the wrong way!"

Sean is able to multitask and win a complex game, requiring skills of attention, memory, concentration, and planning while coaching and teaching me to play at the same time. How does he do it?

American children spend approximately six hours each day with media (Roberts et al., 1999). Although most of this time is currently spent viewing television, an increasing amount of time is invested in interactive technologies, including video games (Rideout et al., 1999). Video games are often children's first experiences with computer information technologies (Calvert, 1999). The popularity of gaming at home, often with other peers, now extends to online interactions with known and unknown competitors. Although the specific amount of time that children in other cultures spend with electronic games may be less than their American counterparts, the ways that children learn from media should be consistent across cultures.

Using an information-processing model that is sensitive to developmental differences in learning, I address the following questions: Who plays video games? How do children interact with, and think about, video games? What kinds of skills are needed to extract information from these games, and what kinds of skills does game playing cultivate? Why do boys gravitate to these games more than girls, and what is the potential impact of differential interest for children's development?

Who Plays Video Games?

For video games to impact children's development and cognitive skills, children must first play them. The kinds of video games available for children to play are as follows: (1) general entertainment, a story or game with no fighting or destruction; (2) educational, in which children learn about new ways to use information; (3) fantasy violence, in which the theme is to fight and avoid being killed; (4) human violence, in which the goal is to fight and avoid being killed as a human character; (5) nonviolent sports, sports games without fighting; and (6) violent sports, sports game with fighting (Funk & Buchman, 1995). Game play has now moved from consoles to online interactions with characters moving fluidly between offline and online spaces. In addition, virtual reality games provide three-dimensional versions of games for children to immerse themselves in (Calvert & Tan, 1994). These innovations, particularly the virtual reality game, may make gaming an increasingly realistic experience for children.

Boys are the overwhelming players of video games, typically spending twice as much time gaming as girls (Buchman & Funk, 1996). Gaming is a core part of boys' friendships and socialization experiences (Wartella, O'Keefe, & Scantlin, 2000). Boys primarily play fast-action games that include a considerable amount of violent content as well as sports games (Funk, Germann, & Buchman, 1997; Gailey, 1996; Wright et al., 2001). Girls, by contrast, prefer spatial games such as *Tetris*, fantasy genres, educational games, and games with traditional feminine themes such as *Barbie Fashion Designer* (Funk et al., 1997; Gailey, 1996; Subramanyam et al., 2001; Wright et al., 2001). Gaming is a much less important facet of girls' friendships and socialization than that of boys.

Video game play increases from ages two to seven (Huston et al., 1999), but then decreases as children grow older (Buchman & Funk, 1996). For instance, fourth-grade girls spent approximately five and a half hours per week of gaming compared to only about three hours per week for eighth-grade girls. Although the overall levels of game play was higher than that of girls, boys showed similar declines in play as age increased. Specifically, fourth-grade boys spent approximately nine and a half hours per week playing games, compared to only five hours per week by the eighth grade (Buchman & Funk, 1996).

Sean, my nephew, is at peak performance as a gamer. He has played games for several years by age eleven, and he knows the games well. He prefers action games, selecting a nonviolent sports game for us to play.

Does playing video games facilitate the development of children's cognitive skills, particularly visual and spatial skills? Or does playing video games impede the development of children's cognitive skills, particularly verbal linguistic skills?

Development and Information Processing Theory

Two major developmental theories are useful in understanding how and what children learn from playing video games. The first is information processing theory. The second is developmental theory grounded in the work of Piaget (1962) and Bruner, Olver, and Greenfield (1968). Both theoretical perspectives view children as active processors of information.

Information processing theory, which grew out of the developmental theories of Piaget and Bruner, is actually a group of theories that are based on how information flows through a "human" computer. These information-processing activities include perception, attention, representation and memory, and output. This chapter will integrate both theories into one framework, with the developmentalists primarily contributing to the section on representation and memory.

Perception

Perception involves the initial intake of information. In media research, one useful approach to the study of information intake is Berlyne's (1960) theory of perceptual salience. In Berlyne's approach, certain qualities of the environment are likely to trigger attention and interest because they have survival value for the organism. These perceptually salient qualities include movement, contrast, change, incongruity, complexity, and surprise.

In the predominantly visual medium of television, Huston and Wright (1983) examined perceptually salient qualities in relation to production techniques.

These production techniques include *action*, how much movement there is in the production; *pacing*, how quickly scenes and characters change; *visual and auditory special effects*, the violation of real-life events through surprising and incongruous visual events and sounds; *foreground music*, loud music that appears in the absence of dialogue; and *character vocalizations*, nonhuman incongruous sounds made by characters. Nonsalient production features involve *dialogue*, in which characters talk to one another meaningfully, but often without features that easily attract attention.

These same perceptually salient features are also the hallmark of video game presentations. That is, perceptually salient features such as rapid action, loud music, rapid pacing, and visual and audio effects characterize video games with nonsalient features such as dialogue being used sparingly.

Using principles embodied in video games, Malone (1981) theorized that challenge, fantasy, and curiosity were key elements for a theory of intrinsically motivating instruction. Variable levels of challenge included goals that were personally meaningful as well as uncertain outcomes, the latter embodying the salient quality of surprise. Fantasy included those that were created by the player as well as by the game maker. Curiosity included sensory curiosity such as audio and visual effects, a direct link to both Berlyne's theory of perceptual salience and the production features that embody those qualities. Malone (1981) found that boys preferred action, whereas girls preferred musical rewards.

Visual Attention

Video games use perceptually salient features to move children to the next phase of information processing: visual attention. Perceptually salient forms are important, in part, because they attract attention to certain content (Calvert, 1999). Initially, this attraction can be involuntary, based in large measure on the survival value that attention to certain features brings to the developing child. This is called the *salience function* of features. Over time, however, children learn that certain features signal and mark important content for further processing. This is called the *marker function* of features (Calvert et al., 1982).

In video game play, sound effects often signal and mark the presence of important content. For instance, a sound informs knowledgeable players that they are about to enter a new level of the game or that a certain event is about to happen. It is through prior experience in playing the game that players gleam nuances of meaning from such experiences. Through temporal contiguity with these sound effects, children are primed for the next sequence of game play.

Video games also require sustained attention to the task in order to succeed, as well as the ability to look at the proper areas of the screen. Few empirical studies have examined the role of visual attention in video games, apparently presuming that the player will automatically attend in order to win. One exception is in a body of work by Patricia Greenfield.

Allocation of attention to the correct areas of a task may be affected by video game play. Greenfield, deWinstanley, Kilpatrick, and Kaye (1994) examined divided attention, as indexed by response time, for college students who had to locate a target on a computer screen. Experienced video game players were similar to novices when the target appeared in a high probability location on the computer screen; however, the experienced players responded faster than the novices when the target was in a low probability location on the screen. In a second experiment, the authors demonstrated that five hours of practice with a video game called *Robotron* improved response time for the low probability location. These findings suggest that attention is actually guided by memories, that is, schemas, developed by previous game play.

As attention becomes more automatic at a task, scarce attentional resources are freed up that allow the player to perform multiple tasks at the same time, or multitasking. So one reason that my nephew Sean is able to play video games well and coach me simultaneously is because he knows what to do at the game; his attention is automatically directed to parts of the game needed to win.

Representation and Memory
McLuhan (1965) argued that television was unique in its form, not its content. That is, the same information could be presented in a book, on the radio, or on television, but how it was presented, and potentially represented, varied with the medium.

Video games are also presented in the unique audiovisual forms that first appeared with film and television. However, there are new ways of getting the content in video games that were not part of early media experiences. More specifically, children must now interact with content, not just observe it. This shift to interactive experiences provides very direct ways for children to control and to receive responsive feedback from media.

Through experience, children construct schemas, learned expectations that guide perceptions, memories, and inferences about content. These schemas can vary in the form in which they represent content and their repeated use over time can cultivate the development of visual and spatial skills. As they grow older, children develop metamemory skills that enable them to know about their knowing. At this abstract level, children become quite skilled at creating and articulating strategies, such as how to win video games.

Developmental theorists have been instrumental in putting forth a framework for understanding how children think differently at different points in development (Bruner, Olver, & Greenfield, 1968; Piaget, 1962). In Bruner et al.'s (1968) system, which was based in Piaget's earlier work, children represent information in: (1) enactive (with the body), (2) iconic (visual), and (3) symbolic (verbal) modes of thought. These levels of representation progress from enactive to iconic to symbolic, moving from very concrete to increasingly abstract ways of thinking about information.

Enactive representation, the first level of retaining information, involves representing information with the body. Young children, for instance, initially turn their head from side to side to avoid eating undesirable foods. That back and forth motion becomes an enactive representation for the concept "no." Enactive representations remain a part of thought, particularly in representing what it feels like to hit a baseball or throw a Frisbee. The body knows how to do these activities through the muscles.

In video game play, I've observed a child who physically jumped when he wanted his *Mario Brother*'s character to jump over an obstacle. His body knew what he wanted his character to do (Calvert, 1999). Similarly, in playing a virtual reality game such as *Dactyl Nightmare*, adolescents may have developed enactive representations of events, such as pulling the trigger of a gun. That is, they knew how it felt to pull the trigger of a gun and that feeling was retained and represented in their body (Calvert & Tan, 1994). Similarly, Sean's muscles knew what it felt like to operate his joystick when he played video games with me.

Iconic representation, the second level of representation, involves the use of concrete symbols such as visual pictures, to remember events. It is in this tier of representation that video game research has focused.

Video game play frequently activates cognitive skills by calling upon the player to construct mental representations of space in order to win the game. Repeatedly playing video games may cultivate visual spatial skills.

Studies of children and adults who are expert video game players demonstrate that they mentally construct maps as they interact with the game, even if they have never viewed a map of the game drawn for them (Greenfield, 1994). In pilot studies, Greenfield found that boys and college students could either draw or reported the use of mental maps of a video game called *Castle Wolfenstein.*

These mental maps are constructed through the activities of game players. More specifically, computer games frequently require the user to move from one screen to another through branching techniques. As the player practices and becomes proficient at the task, he or she is developing an iconic, schematic mental construction of the space. For instance, in *Castle Wolfenstein,* the player moves through several rooms and has to exit through particular doors from each room to reach the ultimate destination: freedom! Although it is clear that expert players of such games are more proficient at these visual-spatial skills, it is unclear if they were initially more proficient at creating mental maps or if they developed the skill through playing the game.

Playing computer games can cultivate (i.e., develop) visual-spatial skills. Greenfield, Brannon, and Lohr (1994) first performed a naturalistic study in which they went to a video parlor and waited for college students to complete *The Empire Strikes Back,* a game requiring the player to navigate through three-dimensional space from a two-dimensional representation. The experimenters then asked the players to perform a mental paper-folding task, a test of visual-spatial skills. Those students who were extremely proficient on the computer game were more proficient on the mental paper-folding task than were less successful computer game players. The results suggest that visual-spatial skills are associated with expertise in the spatial skills area.

In an experimental follow-up of this naturalistic study, Greenfield, Brannon, and Lohr (1994) exposed college students to the video game *The Empire Strikes Back* for an hour or two. Although short-term exposure did not improve students' performance on the paper-folding task, long-term exposure did predict performance. That is, the more frequently students had participated in computer games, the better they performed at the paper-folding task. This study suggests that long-term exposure to computer games is central to understanding their impact on the development of children's visual-spatial skills.

In another study of spatial performance (Okagaki & Frensch, 1994), older adolescents played the game *Tetris* for six hours. *Tetris* calls upon and cultivates rapid rotation of objects and placement of blocks. Compared to a control group, video game players were faster at mental rotation and spatial visualization. Men performed more quickly than women did on complex mental rotation tasks, but not on simple visual rotation tasks.

Boys such as Sean, who spend many hours each week playing video games, construct visually based schemas that allow them to anticipate the game layout and moves that they must make. His game playing has become so automatic that he can simultaneously instruct me as he carries out complex mental and motor activities involved in successful game performance.

Symbolic modes of thought, the most abstract way of representing information, involves using words or other abstract symbols that are arbitrary and do not have a direct link to the information that is being represented. There are numerous complaints that visual media, including video game play, are replacing verbal ways of thinking about information, leading to an illiterate society. To date, there is no firm evidence that an erosion of verbal skills has taken place due to experiences with visual media. Instead, it appears that video game play cultivates the development of visual spatial skills, an underutilized skill in American culture.

Sean has abstract metamemory skills that allow him to think about strategy, to plan his game so that he will be successful. He has developed the abstract as well as the concrete skills that are needed for successful gaming.

Output

The evidence suggests that the way that information comes into the information processing system is often similar to how it is encoded and represented. Therefore, how that information is remembered may also be modality specific. Visually presented information may be remembered in a visual form and verbally presented information may be remembered best in a verbal form (Calvert, 1999).

Preliminary evidence suggests that playing video games may cultivate iconic modes of information processing and subsequent output. In a cross-cultural study by Greenfield and colleagues (1994), college students from the United States and Italy interacted with one of six video games. Prior qualities, such as being a male, being an experienced video game player, and being American, positively affected pretest scores on scientific-technical discovery skills. After short-term exposure to video games for two and a half hours, all participants playing discovery games improved their decoding of graphs depicting scientific-technical information more than the control groups.

Participants also used iconic diagrams rather than written words to represent their memories during retrieval tasks. These visual diagrams paralleled the presentation of the task they had experienced, suggesting that information is best remembered in the form in which it was initially experienced. The findings suggest that computers can cultivate the use of iconic modes of expression.

Sean's output is smooth, fluid video game play as he maneuvers every turn and overcomes every obstacle. Through practice, he has become an expert at a visually based activity.

The Cultivation of Visual and Spatial Skills

Although visual skill development typically generalizes best to similar rather than more distant cognitive skills, there is some evidence that visual processing skills have improved during the twentieth century (Subramanyam et al., 2001). Consider the case of IQ scores.

IQ tests comprise school-like items because they were originally designed to predict success and failure in the French school system. During the twentieth century, children's performance on the visual subcomponents of IQ tests increased, a finding known as the Flynn effect (1994). Greenfield (1998) argued that these improvements in visual scores parallel and are probably caused, in part, by children's use of visual media, including video game play, because computer games develop many of the same nonverbal skills that are tested on the Stanford Binet and Weschler IQ tests (Greenfield, 1998). For example, the spatial visualization skill developed by playing *Tetris* is similar to the Object Assembly subtest of the Weschler IQ Test (Subramanyam et al., 2001). Because of these informal learning experiences, visual IQ performance may have actually increased over time. The implication is that visual interactive games are becoming informal learning tools that cultivate iconic ways of thinking about information. These visual skills, in turn, may be useful in occupations such as computer programming that require visual spatial thinking and visual forms of representation for successful performance.

Will Sean's IQ scores show increases in visual-spatial subscores because of his video game play? Will other children who play video games show increases in these subcomponents of IQ tests?

Gender Differences in Cognitive Skills

If, as the literature suggests, certain kinds of video game play increase visual and spatial skills, then getting girls to play games that cultivate this kind of skill may be important in their cognitive development. If researchers can get girls to play video games, do their spatial skills improve?

Subrahmanyam and Greenfield (1994) attempted to reduce gender differences in visual-spatial skills by exposing ten- and eleven-year-old children to a maze-based video game called *Marble Madness* for two and one-fourth hours. Children were initially pretested on spatial skills. A control group played a word game on the computer, while the experimental group played *Marble Madness*. Finally, children were posttested on two of the three original pretests. Boys were initially better on the visual-spatial tasks. After exposure to the computer games, however, girls who had received treatment in visual-spatial tasks had caught up to the boys in visual-spatial skills. Although girls performed as well as boys in the more general spatial task after video game exposure, boys continued to outperform girls at the video game. So even if I practice and improve my visual-spatial skills, Sean will probably continue to outperform me at video game play.

Kafai (1995) took a different tack in addressing the gender differences in video game play. Instead of having children play another person's game, she had children create their own games. Boys created games that were very much like the action and violent games that they played every day. Themes of good triumphs over evil were prevalent in their games, where players often fought off evil bad guys to achieve their goals. By contrast, girls' games had more variability in themes and in outcomes and rarely had evil characters. For instance, girls tried to avoid a spider or ski down a slope without taking a spill. Many of these "girl" games were nonviolent in focus and had treasures as a reward. All children constructed physical spaces as a setting for their game. Girls' games typically took place in real-life settings such as ski slopes and airports, whereas boys' games took place in imaginary places such as haunted houses, space stations, and "Funland." The characters of boys' games tended to be boys, whereas girls left the gender of the character flexible. Finally, the feedback of boys' games was violent; players were often killed and lost the game when they made mistakes. In contrast, the feedback of girls' games was rarely violent; players could continue the game if they made mistakes. So maybe there is hope for my video game play—I just need to create my own video game and I will have the advantage!

Conclusion

Computer games are often children's first entry into the world of interactive media. Boys like Sean are most interested in playing video games, and they reap the cognitive benefits of video game play, particularly the cultivation of visual-iconic and spatial representation skills. Such playful experiences can cultivate the skills that are necessary for successful navigation along the information highway as well as prepare children for later occupational skills in areas such as engineering and computer programming. Where our school system ends, our informal gaming environments begin, providing lessons in the visual skills needed to excel in many technical careers.

References

Berlyne, D. (1960). *Conflict, curiosity, and arousal.* New York: McGraw Hill.

Bruner, J., Olver, R., & Greenfield, P. M. (1968). *Studies in cognitive growth.* New York: Wiley.

Buchman, D., & Funk, J. (1996). Video and computer games in the '90s: Children's time commitment and game preference. *Children Today, 24,* 12–15.

Calvert, S. L. (1999). *Children's journeys through the information age.* Boston: McGraw Hill.

Calvert, S. L., Huston, A. C., Watkins, B. A., & Wright, J. C. (1982). The relation between selective attention to television forms and children's comprehension of content. *Child Development, 53,* 601–610.

Calvert, S. L., & Tan, S. (1994). Impact of virtual reality on young adults' physiological arousal and aggressive thoughts: Interaction versus observation. *Journal of Applied Developmental Psychology, 15,* 125–139.

Flynn, J. R. (1994). IQ gains over time. In R. Steinberg (Ed.), *Encyclopedia of human intelligence.* New York: Macmillan.

Funk, J., & Buchman, D. (1995). Video game controversies. *Pediatric Annals, 24,* 91–94.

Funk, J., Germann, J., & Buchmann, D. (1997). Rating electronic games in the United States. *Trends in Communication, 2,* 111–126.

Gailey, C. (1996). Mediated messages: Gender, class, and cosmos in home video games. In I. Sigel, P. Greenfield, & R. Cocking (Eds.), *Interacting with video: Vol. 11. Advances in applied developmental psychology.* Norwood, NJ: Ablex.

Greenfield, P. M. (1994). Representational competence in shared symbol systems: Electronic media from radio to video games. In R. R. Cocking & K. A. Renninger (Eds.), *The development and meaning of psychological distance.* Hillsdale, NJ: Erlbaum.

Greenfield, P. M. (1994). Video games as cultural artifacts. *Journal of Applied Developmental Psychology, 15,* 3–12.

Greenfield, P. M. (1998). The cultural evolution of IQ. In U. Neisser (Ed.), *The rising curve: The long-term gains of IQ and related measures.* Washington, DC: The American Psychological Association.

Greenfield, P. M., Brannon, C., & Lohr, D. (1994). Two-dimensional representational movement through three-dimensional space: The role of video game expertise. *Journal of Applied Developmental Psychology, 15,* 87–104.

Greenfield, P. M., deWinstanley, P., Kilpatrick, H., & Kaye, D. (1994). Action video games and informal education: Effects on strategies for dividing visual attention. *Journal of Applied Developmental Psychology, 15,* 105–124.

Greenfield, P. M., Camaioni, L., Ercolani, P., Weiss, L., Lauber, B. A., & Perucchini, P. (1994). Cognitive socialization by computer games in two cultures: Inductive discovery versus mastery of an iconic code? *Journal of Applied Developmental Psychology, 15,* 59–86.

Huston, A. C., & Wright, J. C. (1983). Children's processing of television: The informative functions of formal features. In J. Bryant & D. R. Anderson (Eds.), *Children's understanding of television: Research on attention and comprehension.* New York: Academic Press.

Huston, A. C., Wright, J. C., Marquis, J., & Green, S. (1999). How young children spend their time: Television and other activities. *Developmental Psychology, 35,* 912–925.

Kafai, Y. (1995). *Minds in play.* Hillsdale, NJ: Erlbaum.

Malone, T. (1981). Toward a theory of instrinsically motivating instruction. *Cognitive Science, 4,* 333–369.

McLuhan, M. (1965). *Understanding media: The extensions of man.* New York: McGraw Hill.

Okagaki, L., & Frensch, P. A. (1994). Effects of video game playing on measures of spatial performance: Gender effects in late adolescence. *Journal of Applied Developmental Psychology, 15,* 33–58.

Piaget, J. (1962). *Play, dreams, and imitation in childhood.* London: Routledge & Kegan Paul.

Rideout, V., Foehr, U., Roberts, D., & Brodie, M. (1999). *Kids and the media @ the new millennium. Executive summary.* Menlo Park, CA: Kaiser Family Foundation. http://www.kff.org.

Roberts, D. F., Foehr, U. G., Rideout, V. J., & Brodie, M. (1999). *Kids and media @ the new millennium.* Menlo Park, CA: Kaiser Family Foundation.

Subrahmanyam, K., & Greenfield, P. M. (1994). Effect of video game practice on spatial skills in boys and girls. *Journal of Applied Developmental Psychology, 15,* 13–32.

Subramanyam, K., Greenfield, P. M., Kraut, R., & Gross, E. (2001). The impact of computer use on children's and adolescents' development. *Journal of Applied Developmental Psychology, 22,* 7–30.

Wartella, E., O'Keefe, B., & Scantlin, R. (2000). *Children and interactive media: A compendium of current research and directions for future research.* A report to the Markle Foundation.

Wright, J. C., Huston, A. C., Vandewater, E. A., Bickman, D., Scantlin, R., Kotler, J., Caplovitz, A., Lee, J., Hofferth, S., & Finkelstein, J. (2001). American children's use of electronic media in 1997: A national survey. *Journal of Applied Developmental Psychology, 22,* 31–47.

8

CHILDREN'S SOCIAL BEHAVIOR DURING VIDEO GAME PLAY

Robyn M. Holmes and Anthony D. Pellegrini

One factor that has clearly influenced children's life experiences, including their play and play preferences, is technology (Calvert, 1999). That children are comfortable interacting with electronic media and the appeal of video games is undeniable (Kafai, 1996). Advances in technology and an expanding and prosperous global economy have made computers and video games accessible to children around the world. Electronic games became a part of American culture in the 1970s and now enjoy a global distribution (Funk, Germann, & Buchman, 1997).

In the United States, the video game industry was revitalized in the mid 1980s by the introduction of the Nintendo game system. Sales increased from $100 million to several billion dollars within a few years. Other cultures, particularly those in South East Asia, are experiencing similar trends (Hyun & Lee, 1994; Takeuchi, 1994). The demand for the newest game system, Sony's PlayStation2, created a buying frenzy on several continents. This system was so desirable, hopeful buyers joined waiting lists months in advance and stood in line for hours, trying to obtain a system for a holiday present. Demands for the product were extraordinary and supplies were scarce. In some instances, product shortages in retail stores caused public disturbances.

There is a genuine necessity to investigate the effects of video game playing on children given its emergence as a favorite leisure activity in the United States and other cultures (Funk, Germann, & Buchman, 1997; Takeuchi, 1994). There have been several recent works on this topic. For example, Calvert (1999) explored children's interactions with electronic media; Cassell and Jenkins (1998) investigated the impact of gender on video game playing; and Greenfield and Cocking's (1996) edited volume contains empirical and theoretical chapters on children's interactions with video media. However, research has yet to explore the immediate and long-term effects of playing these games on children's behavior (Dietz, 1998; Dill & Dill,

1998; Funk, Germann, & Buchman, 1997; Griffiths, 2000).

Parents, teachers, researchers, and policymakers have expressed concern about the omnipresent nature of these games. In 1984, Dominick reported that approximately nine out of ten children in the United States had some playing experience with these games. Some children may even spend countless hours at home and in friends' homes engaged in this type of play (Funk, Germann, & Buchman, 1997), and the new transportable game devices have made it possible for children to play video games anywhere and any time. Children's social behavior, particularly social interaction and aggression (Gailey, 1996; Kafai, 1996) is a major concern about children's video game playing.

Adult perceptions of children's social behavior include concerns about social isolation and children's social interactions. Some parents see video games as a solitary form of play that inhibits social interaction (Goldstein, 1994). However research by Bonnafont (1992) with French school children suggests that video game playing actually increases social contact and interactions among children. He noted that sharing knowledge about a game and game equipment facilitates social interaction and contact between children who play these types of games. Kubey and Larson's (1990) study with American school age children yields supportive evidence that video games are often played with companions. The first author's observations of watching children play these games and experiences as a player support these findings. Children often form social groups while watching the players. This facilitates social contact and verbal interaction among the children as they share information about "cheats" and learn strategies to win the game.

The issue of the relationship between aggression and video game playing, particularly video game play with aggressive themes, has been at the forefront of video play research (Griffiths, 1999, 2000). The majority of these studies have been concerned with whether or not play exposure is harmful. In particular, these studies have examined whether playing video games with aggressive/war themes is related to aggressive behavior in children. The notion that playing these types of games is correlated with aggressive behavior stems from the application of social learning theory to this play medium.

Social learning theory (e.g., Bandura, 1977, 1986) has heavily influenced both the course and the interpretation of findings from research on video game play. The preponderance of studies that employ a social learning position have examined the relationship between playing violent or aggressive video games and children's subsequent aggression (e.g., Anderson & Dill, 2000; Anderson & Morrow, 1995; Graybill, et al., 1987; Klemm, 1995; Schutte, et al., 1988; Scott, 1995; Wiegman & van Schie, 1998).

In this tradition, several researchers have postulated a relationship between viewing media violence and an increase in children's aggressive inclinations. This is extended to video game playing. Thus similar to television viewing, viewing these games should relate to aggression (Boyatzis, Matillo, & Nesbitt, 1995; Eron, 1982; Paik & Comstock, 1994; van Evra, 1990). Irwin and Gross (1995) suggest that aggressive themes and actions are prevalent in many video games (see also Provenzo, 1991), and that these are similar to those that occur in televised programming.

As Goldstein (1995) noted, comparisons between television viewing and video game play may be unacceptable and misleading for several reasons. First, in television viewing the viewer can be inactive, detached, and engaged in another task. In contrast, video game playing requires active involvement (see also Scott, 1995; Griffiths, 1991, 1999; Calvert, 1999; Kinder, 1996; see Sutton-Smith, 1997 for an alternative perspective).

Finally, video games allow for social interactions via simultaneous or alternate playing formats to occur between players. In effect, playing video games is a social activity that often involves cooperation between and among players (Goldstein, 1994). In contrast, television viewing is often a solitary activity even when others are physically present. One can view television with several people present without ever engaging in interactions.

Although much of the research links experiences with violent video games and subsequent aggression, virtually no research has described the extent to which children are aggressive or cooperative while they play

these games. This level of description is necessary to establish a proximal relation between games and aggression before we make distal statements about the effects of video games and aggression.

Descriptions of children's behavior while playing video games can broaden our understanding of the impact of playing these games on children's behaviors and social interactions. Following social learning theory, if these games are expected to increase children's aggressive behavior, then presumably children should exhibit this behavior while participating and playing these kinds of games.

In the first study presented in this chapter, we examined the impact of playing video games on children's behavior while they were playing and how these interactions vary by age and sex (Holmes & Pellegrini, 1997). In the second study, we again explored the effect of aggressive and nonaggressive video games on children's aggression while playing the games and how aggression would vary by sex (Pellegrini & Holmes, 1999). Also in the second study, we examined the relation between playing video games with aggressive themes and subsequent aggressive behavior. It was expected that playing video games with aggressive themes would elicit negative responses in the children, whereas playing video games with nonaggressive themes would elicit either positive or neutral responses (see, e.g., Cooper & Mackie, 1986; Funk, 1992; Irwin & Gross, 1995).

For the substance of our descriptions of children's social interactions while playing video games, we chose to analyze specific nonverbal and verbal behaviors. Previous studies that have explored the link between playing violent video games and aggression have employed standardized surveys to measure aggressive thoughts (Calvert & Tan, 1996), recorded children's physical and verbal aggressive behavior toward objects and people after exposure to these games (Silvern & Williamson, 1987), and proposed hypothetical situations in which children could punish or reward for positive and negative behavior (Cooper & Mackie, 1986).

In our studies we chose to focus upon previously unexplored nonverbal and verbal behaviors. We included facial expressions because they are indicative of emotional responses (Izard, 1971, 1977), social distance because it reflects comfortableness (Hall, 1959), and verbal behaviors that were reflective of the quality, direction, and content of the children's speech. These observational categories will give breadth to the descriptions we compile on the impact of playing video games on children's social interactions and behaviors.

Children's Behavior during Play

Based upon existing research that suggests a relation between playing video games with aggressive themes and subsequent aggressive behavior, it was expected that playing video games with aggressive themes would elicit negative responses in the children. In contrast, playing video games with nonaggressive themes would elicit either positive or neutral responses (see, e.g., Cooper & Mackie, 1986; Irwin & Gross, 1995). Such game conditions were expected to vary by age and sex.

For example, the majority of video game studies were conducted with older children and young adults (e.g., Anderson & Dill, 2000; Buchman & Funk, 1996; Funk, 1993; Scott, 1995) who presumably have had more exposure to video game playing than younger children and should demonstrate less aggression as a consequence of increasing cognitive maturity. Based upon their cognitive and social skills, it was expected that younger children would elicit more negative responses than older children in both aggressive and nonaggressive video games. This was partially attributable to: (1) their inexperience as players, (2) an inability to resolve any frustration that arose during play, and (3) difficulty in cooperating and sharing while playing.

With respect to sex, it was expected that boys would demonstrate more negative behaviors than girls in playing video games with aggressive themes. This was thought to be partially due to American socialization experiences in so far as boys are socialized to be more competitive, aggressive, and adventurous than girls (see Maccoby, 1980; Williams & Best, 1990). In comparison, it was anticipated that the nature and content of nonaggressive video games would promote more positive and neutral responses in both boys and girls.

Sixty-six children in a New Jersey day care program participated in this study. Twenty-nine of the children were between five and seven years of age, and thirty-seven were between eight and ten years of age. These age ranges were selected on the basis of Piaget's (1955) ages for preoperational and concrete operational cognitive development.

Materials A SuperNintendo (NES) video game system was connected to a 13-inch Samsung color television. The video game system was equipped with two control pads that afforded simultaneous play for two players. Ten Nintendo video game cartridges were used. Five had aggressive themes, and five had nonaggressive themes. The games with aggressive themes were *SuperMario, Super Mario Brothers 3, Power Rangers, MegaMan X3,* and *MegaMan X7.* Commonalities in these games included fantasy violence, the player assumes a character role, and the player competes against and combats opponents or evil characters. The player has the ability to hit, punch, kick, jump, or use weapons with the intention of destroying the opponent. We used Nintendo company ratings and Funk's (1993) work on categorizing video games as guidelines for classification in each video game case.

The games with nonaggressive themes were *Kirby's Avalanche; We're Back, Mickey Mania, Scooby Doo,* and *Mario Kart.* A commonality with these games was that the player was involved in a competition that does not involve physical contact with an opponent. Rather, themes involve competition in a variety of scenarios such as problem, solving, treasure hunts, and car races. All play was video recorded.

The children were escorted individually to the area (classroom or gymnasium spaces) where the game machines and video cameras were located. During play, the two children were seated side by side, approximately 30 cm apart and 1.2 meters in front of the game system. Children were asked prior to play if they had ever played the game before. All had had prior experience. In addition, parental consent forms contained a list of the video game selections. All were found to be acceptable and most parents noted whether their child(ren) had previously played these games. Therefore in this study, there were no practice sessions for play.

Children were selected randomly from each class to participate. Within each class, children were randomly paired in their playing dyads. There were thirty-three playing dyads. One child was the target child and played in all conditions. The other dyad partner was randomly assigned and pair composition changed by sex and playing condition. Dyad age ranges never exceeded six months. When there was no mate in a particular class grade, children were paired chronologically with same-age children. This occurred in six of the dyads. Every attempt was made to avoid the pairing of friends. Some pairings inevitably contained children who were familiar to each other since they were classmates.

Children were videotaped in four timed intervals, each six minutes in duration. Six minutes was selected as the playing interval based upon pilot tests and the range of playing intervals utilized by previous researchers (e.g., Garvey, 1990; Graybill, Kirsch, & Esselman, 1985; and Graybill et al., 1987). In these cases playing times ranged from six to eight minutes. Each interval contained one playing condition. There were:

Robyn M. Holmes and Anthony D. Pellegrini |

(1) same sex partner nonaggressive theme; (2) opposite sex partner, nonaggressive theme; (3) same sex partner, aggressive theme, and (4) opposite sex partner, aggressive theme. At the end of each timed interval, the researchers changed the video cartridges. Order of theme and partner were counterbalanced to account for any order effects. Cameras remained in full view of the children at all times during video recording.

Analyzing the Videos

Video recordings were coded in thirty-second intervals every minute for each six-minute interval. The observational categories were: (1) facial (measured as facial expression), (2) touch (measured as direction of movement between players), (3) verbal content (what was said during play), and (4) verbal interaction (the direction of a child's speech). All categories contained four levels of responses: positive, neutral, negative, and mixed. For the facial category, smiling was coded as positive, no expression was coded as neutral, and frowning was coded as negative. For touch, moving toward a player was coded as positive, no movement was coded as neutral, and moving away from a player was coded as negative. For verbal content, helpful comments and pleasant remarks were coded as positive, no comments of any kind were coded as neutral, and cynical or critical remarks were coded as negative.

For verbal interaction, talking to another player was coded as positive, talking to the monitor was coded as neutral, and talking to one's self was coded as negative. Although this is a common occurrence in children's play interactions (see e.g., Vygotsky, 1978) notions of private speech, talking to the self was coded as negative because it lacked social interaction between the players.

Each child of the pair (target and other) was coded independently by two coders, the first author and a research assistant, in the following manner. First, coding categories were mutually exclusive. Second, frequencies were obtained by coding every relevant behavior that occurred in a specific category during a given interval. Each category was coded separately. Inter-rater reliability was assessed by randomly selecting six coding sheets from each child for comparison. All reliability scores are based upon comparisons of exact behaviors. Ten one-minute intervals were selected from each child for comparison for each game condition and behavioral category. Reliability was statistically measured using the Pearson r correlation coefficient. Reliability for all measures was $\geq .90$. See Holmes and Pellegrini 1997 for details.

Table 8.1

Means for observational categories and levels of response

Categories	Positive	Neutral	Negative	Mixed
Facial Expression	4.09	6.05	1.59	.79
Touch	2.07	8.07	.56	.58
Verbal Content	7.16	2.87	.55	1.40
Verbal Interaction	5.55	2.88	1.33	2.40

Results are presented for the effects of age, sex, and condition on each of the four levels of responses (1 = positive, 2 = neutral, 3 = negative, and 4 = mixed) for each of our observational categories (facial, touch, verbal content, and verbal interaction). Table 8.1 summarizes these.

There were significant effects for facial expression, touch, verbal content, and verbal interaction.

Neutral was the facial expression observed significantly more than any other. Positive facial expressions were more frequent than either negative or mixed facial expressions. For touch, the results were the same as for facial expression: neutral was the greatest, and positive was greater than both negative and mixed.

For verbal content, positive was the greatest and neutral was greater than negative and mixed. For verbal interaction, positive was again the greatest category, but neutral, negative, and mixed were not significantly different from each other.

In only one case was there a statistical interaction. This occurred for verbal content: sex × level of response where boys were significantly more positive than girls.

The results of this study suggest that children's interactions around video games, despite the content of those games was positive or neutral. The positive facial expression indicates clearly that children are having fun. The neutral facial expressions probably reflect children's intense engagement with the game. Neutral expressions are indicative of concentration, although they could alternatively indicate boredom.

That the touch categories were predominantly neutral supports the notion that children are not aggressing towards each other. Of course the artificiality of the situation would have inhibited aggression, but the high incidence of positive touches suggest a more positive scenario. Boys are more likely to offer more positive comments when playing than girls are. This may be a consequence of play competency. Boys tend to play video games more than girls (e.g., Buchman & Funk, 1996; Cassell & Jenkins, 1998) and thus are more likely to be more competent players than most girls. Perhaps boys offer more positive comments in an attempt to help the other player become more skilled.

In comparison to boys, the interaction of sex × condition × level of response for verbal content for girls suggests that girls are more positive in their interactions when playing with a same-sex partner in an aggressive game than when playing either with a same-sex partner in a nonaggressive game or an opposite sex partner in a violent game. This may be partially attributable to the notion that girls play video games less often than boys and prefer those with nonviolent themes (Buchman & Funk, 1996; Cassell & Jenkins, 1998; Dietz, 1998). Thus they may be more likely to help in this condition and more likely to compete in nonaggressive games with a same-sex partner. The findings of the present study suggest that children's interactions during video game play are decidedly positive despite the content of those games.

Aggression While Playing Video Games

Pellegrini and Holmes (1999) explored social interaction using facial expressions, social distance and body contact, and various kinds of verbal behaviors. With respect to social interactions, it was expected that aggressive video games would elicit more negative behaviors in each of these categories and nonaggressive games would elicit more positive (prosocial or cooperative) or neutral behaviors.

With respect to sex, it was expected that boys would demonstrate more negative behaviors than girls while playing video games with aggressive themes. This was thought to be partially due to socialization experiences in so far as boys are socialized to be more competitive, aggressive, and adventurous than girls (e.g., Williams & Best, 1990). In addition, research has documented the fact that boys are more physically aggressive than girls are, and this appears to hold true cross-culturally (Maccoby, 1980). However, it is also acknowledged that aggression is a stable characteristic in children (Huesmann, Lagerspetz, & Eron, 1984), and intra- and inter-individual differences exist along this behavioral dimension.

These sex differences in aggression are reflected in children's video game preferences. Boys find games with violent and male dominated themes more appealing than girls do (Dietz, 1998; Goldstein, 1998). Additionally, girls were not attracted to the "kill" actions in these games (Cassell & Jenkins, 1999; Kafai, 1996). Thus it was anticipated that the nature and content of nonaggressive video games would promote more positive and neutral responses in both boys and girls.

| Figure 8.1 |
Golden Eye/007

Seventy children from grades two through five participated in this study. The children ranged in age from six to eleven years.

In the non-video condition, children played the board game *Operation*. In this game, players take on the role of doctor and engage in simulated surgery. They are required to remove pieces from a cartoonlike human body in simulated surgery using a tweezers. The captions alongside the body parts are humorous. Water on the knee is depicted as a bucket that the players must remove from the knee area. Players draw from a deck of cards. Each card yields information about the specific surgery that they are required to perform, and the fee that they will receive if the piece is removed successfully. A buzzer sounds (red light on the patient's nose lights simultaneously) if the player hits the rim of the body cavity and does not remove the piece successfully. The game was used an alternative to video game play and is suited for two players.

For the video conditions, we employed a Nintendo 64 video game system. The video game system had two control pads that afforded independent and simultaneous play in the two-player format.

Two Nintendo 64 game cartridges were used. The first was the aggressive game *Golden Eye/007* (figure 8.1). The ESRB rating is listed as "T," suitable for teens and adults. The game involves stalking and destroying an opponent. Griffiths (1999) categorized this kind of game as a shoot 'em up because it involved killing via shootings (p. 210). Although figures are animated, they are lifelike. Violence is realistic and once killed, the opponent's screen is covered in red symbolic of bloodshed.

| Figure 8.2 |
Waverace

The second game was *Waverace* (figure 8.2). The ESRB rating of this game is "KA," suitable for all ages from kids to adults. In this game, the player was involved in a competition that did not require physical contact with the opponent. Rather, the games involved competition and nonphysical problem solving in a variety of scenarios that required the player to maneuver a jet ski through an obstacle course. Griffiths (1999) classified this type of game as a "racer" because it involved sports simulations.

In addition to ESRB ratings, Funk's (1993) work on video game categorization was used as guidelines for the video game ratings for aggressive and nonaggressive thematic content. Games in all conditions contained an element of surprise and outcomes were determined by skill.

Children were selected randomly from each class to participate. Within each class, children were randomly paired in same-sex, same-age dyads. There were twenty-two male and thirteen female dyads. Dyad partners were randomly assigned and pairs remained in tact over the course of the study through all game conditions. Dyad age ranges never exceeded five months.

The children were escorted individually to the area (classroom or gymnasium spaces) where the game systems and video cameras were located. During play, the two children were seated side by side approximately 30 cm apart and 1.2 meters in front of the monitor. The children held the control pad in their hands or rested them on their lap or the table (figure 8.3).

| Figure 8.3 |
Children playing

Prior to play, children were asked if they had previous experience with playing video games and the particular selected games. Children's experiences with this medium were supported by parental report for game familiarity, ratings, and ownership. The parental consent form contained a list of possible video game selections for parental approval. Most parents noted whether their child(ren) had previously played with these games. Children unfamiliar with the games were allowed to practice with each game for five minutes.

Three timed intervals, fifteen minutes in duration, were videotaped. The fifteen-minute playing interval was selected based upon past behavioral and video play research with similar age children (e.g., Cooper & Mackie, 1986; Garvey, 1990; Graybill, Kirsch, & Esselman, 1985; Graybill et al., 1987). Playing time in previous studies has ranged from four to twenty minutes.

Each interval contained one playing condition. They were (1) same-sex partner, nonaggressive video game; (2) same-sex partner, aggressive video game, and

(3) same-sex partner, nonvideo condition. Children were exposed to each condition at one-week intervals to control for carry over effects. Order of presentation was varied to account for order effects.

Analyzing the Videos

Video recordings were coded in one-minute intervals every minute for each fifteen-minute interval. The observational categories were (1) facial expression, selected because they are indicative of emotional responses (e.g., Izard, 1971, 1977) and are a highly salient observable behavior. (2) Touch, operationally defined as the social distance and contact that occurred between players. According to Hall (1959), smaller distances are indicative of intimate contact, whereas greater distances are indicative of less intimate contact. (3) Verbal content, operationally defined as the quality of what was said during play. These contained examples of negative criticisms, verbal praise, helping, positive comments, and speech with no affective content. The verbal content category can be described as prosocial and negative speech. (4) Verbal material, including speech containing general comments, and remarks about the game and the players. The facial expression code was the measure of affect. (5) Verbal interaction, operationally defined as the direction in which the child speaks, for example toward or away from the other player or to the self. For the facial expression category, smiles were coded as positive, frowns as negative, and no facial expression as neutral. Descriptions of facial expressions were taken from Izard (1971, 1977) and ethological studies (McGrew, 1972). For example, a smile had to contain turned up mouth corners. Facial expressions could be directed at the monitor or other child. Facial expressions as an indicator of affect were also simultaneously coded with the touch and verbal content, interaction and material categories.

For touch, movement toward and away from another child was coded simultaneously with negative, positive, and neutral affect (facial expression). Distinguishing between aggressive and cooperative behaviors was essential to the study's goals, and making the distinction between touch toward another person that was aggressive and touch that was cooperative was difficult to do simply on the basis of body movement. This additional information was obtained by employing affect. Thus facial expression (affect) was coded simultaneously along with touch to help clarify the meaning of the players' contact. For example, a behavior was coded as negative touch if a player moved away from another player while displaying an angry face.

Coding for verbal content was adapted from linguistic coding procedures utilized by Garvey (1990) in children's play. Thus helpful comments and pleasant remarks were coded as positive; no comments of any kind were coded as neutral, and cynical or critical remarks were coded as negative. Verbal content focused upon the quality of the communication. Verbal material referred to specific speech interactions that centered on general comments about the game and remarks about the player and/or game. Because it was important to the study's goals to distinguish between aggressive and cooperative behaviors, verbal material was also coded for positive, neutral, and negative affect using facial expressions. Verbal interaction focused upon the direction of the speech and included talking to another player, the monitor, and the self. These were also coded simultaneously for negative, positive, and neutral affect in order to distinguish clearly between aggressive and cooperative behaviors. Reliability for all measures exceeded $r = .90$.

The Effects of Aggressive and Nonaggressive Games on Children's Aggression while Playing

It was hypothesized that video games with aggressive themes would produce more negative behaviors than either those with nonaggressive themes or the nonvideo condition during actual game playing. To initially examine this hypothesis, positive, negative, and neutral behaviors for all three game conditions were collapsed across all dependent variables to yield an overall mean for each behavioral response category (positive, negative, neutral) across the three game conditions. This was viewed as a conservative approach to look for an overall effect before subsequent, individual analyses were conducted. Overall means appear in table 8.2.

Surprisingly, the overall means for neutral and positive responses are greater than those for negative responses across all game conditions with neutral behaviors greater than positive behaviors in all game conditions.

The Effect of Aggressive and Nonaggressive Games on the Children's Social Interactions

The question of whether game condition would affect the children's social interactions during play was explored and paired t-tests revealed the following: for positive behavioral responses, the nonvideo produced the most responses. For negative behavioral responses, the nonaggressive video game produced the most responses, but the other two conditions did not differ. Finally, for neutral behavioral responses, each game

Table 8.2
Overall means for neutral, positive, and negative behaviors across game condition

Behavioral Response	G1 Aggressive	G2 Nonagg	G3 Nonvideo	Game Condition Overall
Neutral	169.81[a]	230.51[b]	252.29[c]	217.54
	(50.92)	(57.01)	(45.34)	(51.09)
Positive	118.64[a]	113.83[a]	160.17[b]	130.88
	(56.69)	(48.89)	(53.95)	(53.17)
Negative	40.20[ab]	47.59[b]	38.12[a]	41.97
	(28.81)	(40.97)	(25.14)	(31.64)

[a] G1 is aggressive video play; G2 is nonaggressive video play; and G3 is nonvideo play.
[b] Means with different alphabet superscripts are significantly different at $p < .05$.

condition was different from the other. Aggressive video play (G1) produced the least amount of neutral responses followed by nonaggressive video play. The nonvideo condition produced the most neutral responses.

Sex Differences by Game Condition
For sex, it was hypothesized that boys would demonstrate more negative behaviors in playing aggressive games than girls would and that both boys and girls would demonstrate more positive and neutral behaviors in the other conditions. Contrary to expectations, girls produced more overall negative behaviors than the boys did. Also, girls produced more positive and neutral behaviors than boys did, although these did not reach statistical significance.

Further analyses revealed the following. For the nonaggressive video game, girls produced more positive responses than boys did. Interestingly, G1, the aggressive video game produced an almost equivalent positive response for boys and girls. In short, girls seemed to enjoy the aggressive video game as much as the boys did. No other differences were found.

Contrary to expectations, aggressive video play did not produce the most negative types of behaviors. In fact, girls produced significantly more negative behaviors than boys did in all conditions. For example, in the nonaggressive video condition (G2), girls produced almost four times as many negative responses as boys did. In the aggressive condition (G1), girls produced almost twice as many negative responses as boys did.

Finally, the nonaggressive video game produced the most neutral responses for girls. Boys produced the least amount of neutral behaviors in the aggressive video condition. Both boys and girls produced

the most neutral responses for the nonvideo game condition.

Interestingly, the boys do not appear to drive any of our findings. Contrary to expectations, the girls are primarily responsible for the observed effects. For example, it was anticipated that boys would demonstrate more negative behaviors than girls did in the aggressive video game condition. In addition, it was expected that the nonaggressive and nonvideo conditions would produce more positive behaviors for the dependent variables.

However, the following findings emerged. For example, girls demonstrated more negative facial expressions in the nonaggressive video condition than boys did, and more neutral expressions, than the boys did in this condition. Also, girls produced more neutral conversation in the aggressive and nonaggressive video condition than the boys did. In addition, girls were more likely to produce conversation with negative material more so than the boys were in the nonaggressive video game condition. Finally, boys conversed positively about the game in the nonvideo condition, more than the girls did, yet this condition also produced more negative speech to the self for boys.

The findings from this sample of children suggest that children's dyadic interactions during video game play, despite the content of those games was positive. However, these findings contrast with the reported findings of studies that have examined the effect of playing video games with violent themes on children's subsequent aggressive behavior. For example, Irwin and Gross (1995) concluded that children's aggression recorded during free play increased after exposure to video games with violent content. In a related study, Silvern and Williamson's (1987) reported an increase in aggression for boys after exposure to their conditions, whereas girls demonstrated more social behaviors than boys did.

The difference in findings may be partly explainable by the time the observations were conducted. For example, the previous studies all examined children's behavior after exposure to video game playing. In contrast, the current study examined children's social behavior while they were playing video games and support findings from our earlier study (Holmes & Pellegrini, 1997).

Another factor that may partially explain the findings of the current study is the dependent variable. Selection of the observational categories was based upon an ethological tradition. For example, facial expressions were used as an indication of emotion, and social distance was used to indicate body contact. Another viable explanation may be linked to the children's perceptions of a video game's content. For example, research suggests that children are able to distinguish "real war" from "war play" or playing with war toys (see e.g., Goldstein, 1995; Wegener-Spohring, 1988). Rather it is adults who impose meaning upon the children's play. Perhaps in video game play, the children, as players recognize that this is just "play" and not real violence.

With respect to emotion, the positive facial expression indicates clearly that children are having fun in all game conditions. The high frequencies for the non-video condition may be partially explained by the choice of game. Children often smiled when surprised by the game's buzzer, and the game lends itself to taboo humor about the human anatomy. The high frequencies of neutral facial expressions probably reflect children's intent engagement with the game. Neutral expressions are indicative of concentration, although an alternative explanation could be linked to boredom.

The fact that children do not engage in a great deal of coded conversation while playing probably reflects their level of concentration. However, when speech is analyzed for content, children conversed positively about the game they were playing in all conditions. This suggests that these types of games may actually foster positive or prosocial kinds of interactive behavior in the children who play them (e.g., Gailey, 1996; Goldstein, 1994). Interestingly, the video game playing conditions promoted more self-directed speech with positive affect than the nonvideo condition did.

With respect to sex differences, girls exhibited more negative behaviors in the nonaggressive video condition. It is possible that this is due in part to the features of the game. Several possible explanations exist. For example, this game required good eye-hand coordination and the literature suggests that boys are better at these types of games than girls are (Keller, 1992). It is also possible that this game may not have been appealing to the girls (Goldstein, 1998; Subrahmanyam & Greenfield, 1998).

Boys exhibited more positive facial expressions during aggressive play than girls did. Thus the expected negative behaviors associated with aggressive play did not emerge. This may be a consequence of play competency. Playing video games is a domain dominated primarily by boys who often have more experience with and are more competent players with this medium than girls are (e.g., Funk & Buchman, 1996; Cooper & Mackie, 1986). In addition, boys may have been having more fun, as research suggests they find games with ag-

gressive themes more appealing than girls do (Dietz, 1998; Goldstein, 1998).

Finally, girls exhibited more speech with negative content and more self-directed negative speech than boys did. Because the latter occurred primarily in the nonaggressive video condition, it might be that this game (which requires good hand-eye coordination) may have been difficult and thus frustrating for the girls (see Griffiths, 2000). Thus this finding may be a result of play competency, because research has documented that girls tend to play video games much less than boys do (Funk & Buchman, 1996).

Given the small and socioeconomically and ethnically homogeneous sample, the present findings cannot be extended to a broader population of children. In addition, other social factors such as child popularity, status, and familiarity with classmates and how these may have impacted upon behavior were not systematically assessed. Finally, idiosyncratic and cultural or ethnic differences are acknowledged though not considered to be influential due to ethnic homogeneity of the sample and the ethic groups are all subgroups of American culture.

However, the present findings do suggest that children's interactions during video game play are decidedly positive despite the content of those games. Contrary to previous studies, game content does not appear to foster aggressive behavior in children while they are playing. These findings contrast sharply with the reported negative, short-term effects of playing aggressive video games on children's aggressive behavior. In addition, it appears as though player competency and the features of the game may be partly responsible for how children behave while they are playing video games.

This study contributes to current research by exploring the impact of game content on children's behavior while they are playing. These findings address the immediate impact of video game playing on children' aggression and social interactions. Because most existing studies have address the short-term effects of playing video games on children's behavior, those that address immediate and long-term effects are sorely needed (e.g., Griffiths, 1999).

One might also expect that these findings could have practical implications. For example, video game play could perhaps be utilized to promote cooperation, participation, and positive interactions between the sexes. As Thorne (1993) noted, children of both sexes segregate and come together under various situational contexts. Video game play may provide a context for

Robyn M. Holmes and Anthony D. Pellegrini |

positive interactions between the sexes that could help teach children problem solving and spatial skills.

Conclusion

As Griffiths (1999, 2000) noted, the majority of studies on the relationship between video game play and aggressive behavior have produced ambiguous findings and failed to establish a relationship between these two variables. The one consistent finding seems to suggest that exposure to video games with aggressive content/ themes does seem to produce short-term effects for aggression in young children. However, alternative explanations for this finding have not been pursued. Our studies have explored children's social interactions *while* they are playing and seem to suggest that children's behavior is positive or neutral across a variety of games. We suggest that the content of these games may be related to the behaviors children socially construct while playing them. Our preliminary findings suggest that aggressive video game play does not necessarily lead children to behave in negative ways. Future studies may wish to explore different observational categories, such as diversity and socioeconomic status, as possible variables. More research in this area is sorely needed as researchers seek to understand the relationship between playing video games and the immediate, short-term, and long-term effects of this play medium on children's behaviors and social interactions.

Acknowledgment

This work was supported in part by a Grant-in-Aid-for-Creativity award from Monmouth University to R. M. H.

References

Anderson, C., & Dill, K. (2000). Video games and aggressive thoughts, feelings, and behavior in the laboratory and life. *Journal of Personality & Social Psychology, 78*, 772–790.

Anderson, C., & Morrow, M. (1995). Competitive aggression without interaction: Effects of competitive versus cooperative instructions on aggressive behavior in video games. *Personality & Social Psychology Bulletin, 21*, 1020.

Bandura, A. (1986). *Social foundations of thought and action: A social cognitive theory*. Englewood Cliffs, NJ: Prentice Hall.

Bandura, A. (1977). *Social learning theory*. Englewood Cliffs, NJ: Erlbaum.

Bonnafont, E. (1992). *Video games and the child*. Paper presented at a seminar on Myths and Realities of Play. London, England.

Boyatzis, C., Matillo, G., & Nesbitt, K. (1995). Effects of "The Mighty Morphin Power Rangers" on children's aggression with peers. *Child Study Journal, 25*, 45–55.

Buchman, D., & Funk, J. (1996). Video and computer games in the '90s: Children's time commitment & game preference. *Children Today, 24*, 12.

Calvert, S. (1999). *Children's journeys through the information age*. New York: McGraw-Hill.

Calvert, S., & Tan, S. (1996). Impact of virtual reality on young adults' physiological arousal and aggressive thoughts: Interaction versus observation. In P. Greenfield & R. Cocking (Eds.), *Interacting with video* (pp. 67–82). Norwood, NJ: Ablex.

Cassell, J., & Jenkins, H. (1998). *From Barbie to Mortal Kombat: Gender and Computer Games*. Cambridge, MA: MIT Press.

Cooper, J., & Mackie, D. (1986). Video games and aggression in children. *Journal of Applied Social Psychology, 16*, 726–744.

Dietz, T. (1998). An examination of violence and gender role socialization in video games: Implications for gender socialization and aggressive behavior. *Sex Roles, 38*, 425–442.

Dill, K., & Dill, J. (1998). Video game violence: A review of the empirical literature. *Aggression & Violent Behavior, 3*, 407–428.

Dominick, J. (1984). Videogames, television violence, and aggression in teenagers. *Journal of Communication, 34*, 136–147.

Eron, L. (1982). Parent-child interaction, television violence, and aggression in children. *American Psychologist, 37*, 197–211.

Funk, J. (1993). Reevaluating the impact of video games. *Clinical Pediatrics, 32*, 86–90.

Funk, J. (1992). Video games: Benign or malignant? *Journal of Developmental and Behavioral Pediatrics, 13*, 53–54.

Funk, J., & Buchman, D. (1996). Children's perceptions of gender differences in social approval for playing electronic games. *Sex Roles, 35*, 219–231.

Funk, J., Germann, J., & Buchman, D. (1997). Children and electronic games in the United States. *Trends in Communication*, 111–127.

Gailey, C. (1996). Mediated messages: Gender, class, and cosmos in home video games. In P. Greenfield & R. Cocking (Eds.), *Interacting with video* (pp. 8–23). Norwood, NJ: Ablex.

Garvey, C. (1990). *Play: The developing child*. Cambridge: Harvard University Press.

Goldstein, J. (1998). Immortal kombat: War toys and violent video games. In J. Goldstein (Ed.), *Why we watch: The attractions of violent entertainment* (pp. 53–68). New York: Oxford University Press.

Goldstein, J. (1995). Aggressive toy play. In A. Pellegrini (Ed.), *The future of play theory* (pp. 127–147). Albany, NY: SUNY Press.

Goldstein, J. (1994). Sex differences in toy play and use of video games. In J. Goldstein (Ed.), *Toys, play, and child development* (pp. 110–129). New York: Cambridge University Press.

Graybill, D., Kirsch, J., & Esselman, E. (1985). Effects of playing violent versus nonviolent video games on the aggressive ideation of aggressive and non-aggressive children. *Child Study Journal*, *15*, 199–205.

Graybill, D., Strawniak, M., Hunter, T., & O'Leary, M. (1987). Effects of playing versus observing violent versus nonviolent video games on children's aggression. *Psychology—A Quarterly Journal of Human Behavior*, *24*, 1–8.

Greenfield, P., & Cocking, R. (Eds.) (1996). *Interacting with video*. Norwood, NJ: Ablex.

Griffiths, M. (2000). Video game violence and aggression: Comments on "Video game playing and its relations with aggressive and prosocial behavior" by O. Wiegman and E. van Schie. *British Journal of Social Psychology*, *39*, 147–149.

Griffiths, M. (1999). Violent video games and aggression: A review of the literature. *Aggression & Violent Behavior*, *4*, 203–212.

Griffiths, M. (1991). Amusement machine playing in childhood and adolescence: A comparative analysis of video games and fruit machines. *Journal of Adolescence*, *14*, 53–73.

Hall, E. (1959). *The silent language*. Garden City, NY: Doubleday.

Holmes, R. M., & Pellegrini, A. (1997). *Children's social behavior during video game play with aggressive and non-aggressive themes*. Paper presented at the International Toy Research Conference, Angouleme, France.

Huesmann, L., Lagerspetz, K., & Eron, L. (1984). Intervening variables in the TV-violence-aggression relation: Evidence from two countries. *Developmental Psychology*, *20*, 746–775.

Hyun, O., & Lee, H. (1994). A survey analysis of elementary school children's use of home video games. *Korean Journal of Child Studies*, *15*, 55–68.

Irwin, A., & Gross, A. (1995). Cognitive tempo, violent video games, and aggressive behavior in young boys. *Journal of Family Violence*, *10*, 337–350.

Izard, C. (1977). *Human emotions*. New York: Plenum.

Izard, C. (1971). *The face of emotions*. New York: Appleton-Century Crofts.

Kafai, Y. (1996). Gender differences in children's constructions of video games. In P. Greenfield & R. Cocking (Eds.), *Interacting with video* (pp. 39–66). Norwood, NJ: Ablex.

Keller, S. (1992). *Children and Nintendo*. Eric Reproduction Document No. ED 405069.

Kinder, M. (1996). Contextualizing video game violence: From Teenage Mutant Ninja Turtles 1 to Mortal Kombat 2. In P. Greenfield & R. Cocking (Eds.), *Interacting with video* (pp. 25–37). Norwood, NJ: Ablex.

Klemm, B. (1995). Various viewpoints on violence. *Young Children*, *50*, 53–63.

Kubey, R., & Larson, R. (1990). The use and experience of the new video media among children and young adolescents. *Communication Research*, *17*, 107–130.

Maccoby, E. (1980). *Social development*. New York: Harcourt, Brace & Jovanovich.

McGrew, W. (1972). *An ethological study of children's behavior*. New York: Academic Press.

Paik, H., & Comstock, G. (1994). The effects of television violence on antisocial behavior: A meta-analysis. *Communication Research*, *21*, 416–459.

Pellegrini, A., & Holmes, R. (1999). *Video games and social interaction in young children*. Paper presented at the 2[d] International Toy Research Conference, Halmstad, Sweden.

Piaget, J. (1955). *The language and thought of the child.* New York: World.

Provenzo, E. (1991). *Video kids: Making sense of Nintendo.* Cambridge, MA: Harvard University Press.

Schutte, N., Malouff, J., Post-Gorden, J., & Rodasta, A. (1988). Effects of playing video games on children's aggressive and other behaviors. *Journal of Applied Social Psychology, 18,* 454–460.

Scott, D. (1995). The effect of video games on feelings of aggression. *The Journal of Psychology, 129,* 121.

Silvern, S., & Williamson, P. (1987). The effects of video game play on young children's aggression, fantasy, and prosocial behavior. *Journal of Applied Developmental Psychology, 8,* 453–462.

Subrahmanyam, K., & Greenfield, P. (1998). Computer games for girls: What makes them play? In J. Cassell & H. Jenkins (Eds.), *From Barbie to Mortal Kombat: Gender and computer games* (pp. 46–71). Los Angeles: California State University Press.

Sutton-Smith, B. (1997). *The ambiguity of play.* Cambridge, MA: Harvard University Press.

Takeuchi, M. (1994). Children's play in Japan. In J. Roopnarine, J. Johnson, & F. Hooper (Eds.), *Children's play in diverse cultures* (pp. 51–72). Albany, NY: SUNY Press.

Thorne, B. (1993). *Gender play: Boys and girls at school.* New Brunswick, NJ: Rutgers University Press.

Van Evra, J. (1990). *Television and child development.* Hillsdale, NJ: Lawrence Erlbaum.

Vygotsky, L. (1978). *Mind in society.* Cambridge, MA: Harvard University Press.

Wegener-Spohring, G. (1988). War toys and childhood aggression. *Play & Culture, 1,* 35–47.

Wiegman, O., & van Schie, E. (1998). Video game playing and its relations with aggressive and prosocial behaviour. *British Journal of Social Psychology, 37,* 367–378.

Williams, J., & Best, D. (1990). *Sex and psyche: Gender and self viewed cross-culturally.* Cross-Cultural Research and Methodology Series, Vol. 13. Newbury Park, CA: Sage.

9

PSYCHOLOGICAL EFFECTS OF VIDEO GAMES

Barrie Gunter

The history of media developments is littered with examples of new forms of entertainment being introduced, attaining widespread popularity, and also attracting public concern because of their strong appeal to so many. Computer games proved to be no exception to this rule. As their popularity grew, so too did the level of anxiety about the possibly deleterious psychological effects of playing these games. A number of critics claimed that computer games had a corrupting influence on young people. These games were accused of glorifying violence and encouraging antisocial behavior. Twenty years ago, the U.S. Surgeon General, C. Everett Koop, was quoted as saying that there was "nothing constructive in the games.... Everything is eliminate, kill, destroy!" (Mayfield, 1982).

In addition to potentially harmful psychological effects, stories emerged of computers games' addictive qualities (Anderson & Ford, 1986). Thus, regularly playing computer games could cultivate a compulsion to continue playing and to display, in consequence, a diminished interest in other activities. To cease playing might result in withdrawal symptoms (Soper & Miller, 1983). Some identified physical consequences of regular computer game playing, such as tendonitis, and skin and muscle problems (Loftus & Loftus, 1983).

Not all the news about computer games was bad. Some showed positive psychological benefits accruing from involvement with these games, not least that they may contribute toward young people's computer literacy or at least a greater ease with computer technology. Computer games could also be devised with educational benefits such as vehicles for the learning of factual knowledge and experiences through which a variety of cognitive skills could be acquired (Greenfield & Lave, 1982; Rogoff & Lave, 1984; Scribner, 1986).

This chapter will examine evidence relating to all these different kinds of alleged psychological effects of computer games. Over the last quarter of the twentieth century, while most attention focused on the potential harms that these games might cause among young players, there was also a more limited, but nonetheless important, recognition of positive benefits. Although excessive playing with these games should be discouraged in the same way as excessive behavior in other contexts, much naturally occurring computer game playing takes place in healthy social contexts and can produce positive cognitive benefits.

Despite these optimistic sentiments, it is equally true that research into computer game playing is still at a fairly early stage of development. The research to date has not always yielded consistent findings and its contribution to our understanding of the impact of these games remains limited because of methodological issues that have still not been fully resolved (Sherry, 2001).

Computer Games, Occupation of Time, and Addiction

Computer and video games involve a time commitment that one can regard as a type of "effect." Playing with these electronic games has become a widespread and popular pastime among millions of children and teenagers. Much game playing initially took place in public spaces such as arcades, but today players can enjoy most electronic game playing almost anywhere, through various hardware systems such as hand-held games, personal computers, and home video consoles. The devotion of time to playing these games can vary with age and with the nature of the individual. Carried to an extreme, it may signify that a player has become dependent or even addicted to electronic game playing. Furthermore, although some cite computer games as contributing toward social isolation for some individuals, they can also provide opportunities for those who are already shy and isolated to enter new (electronic) social networks.

The notion that using computers can become either a compelling habit or even an addictive behavior that takes over a person's life and is difficult to kick has been the focus of interest since computers and computer programming began to achieve prominence in various walks of life in the 1970s. One view was that computer programming could generate endless fascination for some people and cast an almost narcotic spell over them (Martin & Norman, 1970). Furthermore, computer users attracted a rather disparaging image of dishevelled individuals with obsessive personalities and lacking in social skills (Weizenbaum, 1976).

This computer dependency was regarded as compulsive behavior driven by the programmer's power to control the computer. The same pattern was later observed among arcade game players. Compulsively playing early electronic games was regarded as potentially problematic where those games had violent themes (Weizenbaum, 1976). Further, computer game dependency was seen as particularly harmful where it occurred among children. Some writers argued that children learned nothing useful from playing computer games and that their constant use engendered greater introversion and social withdrawal (Levy, 1984; Waddilove, 1984).

Another side effect of severe computer game dependency was that young players could be driven to take more and more extreme measures to feed their habit. Loftus and Loftus (1983) reported one case involving a thirteen-year-old boy in Des Moines, Iowa, who became a serial burglar in order to support his *Pac-Man* habit. Other observers commented on cases of youngsters stealing money to play arcade games or to buy new games cartridges for home video games (Klein, 1984; Keepers, 1990; Griffiths & Hunt, 1993). Others went without food, by forfeiting their lunch money to pay for video games (McClure & Mears, 1984) or played truant from school to spend time playing computer games (Keepers, 1990; Griffiths & Hunt, 1993). Researchers have also found signs of withdrawal symptoms such as increased irritability when some are unable to play (Griffiths & Hunt, 1993; Rutkowska & Carlton, 1994).

There has been research with adults and children to find out whether computer addiction or dependency really occurs and what form it takes. Evidence for addiction or dependency stems from an indication that playing computer or video games eats into time spent with other activities to an extreme degree. Thus, any findings that indicate that computer or video game playing does not submerge all other pursuits tend to weaken the argument for the games having addictive qualities.

There have been conflicting opinions offered as to why computer or video games may generate dependency. One factor may be found in the inherent nature of the games themselves (Loftus & Loftus, 1983), which are interactive and therefore very involving. They offer challenges and varying levels of difficulty that encourage players to engage repeatedly to display increased competence and control.

In-depth research has indicated, however, that although a small proportion of people may shows signs of computer game dependency, it is a fairly harmless reaction (Shotton, 1989). Subsequent to this research, though, electronic games were constructed with increasingly sophisticated formats and realistic graphics. The skills required for competent play also developed further, opening up the possibility that such games could prove to be more involving than earlier versions giving them the power to generate a more powerful psychological dependence among players (Gunter, 1998).

Computer Games and Cognitive Effects

Computer games have been linked to a number of cognitive effects, both positive and negative. Researchers have found negative associations between academic achievement and playing electronic games. However, computer games also impart certain cognitive skills of a generic kind (e.g., spatial skills) and of a more specific nature (e.g., computer literacy). Electronic game formats have also been applied successfully in occupational training contexts.

Initial observations about computer games and cognitive performance centered on the negative rather than positive benefits electronic game playing could have. Some suggested that computer game playing took children and teenagers away from participating in more educational or sporting pursuits (Egli & Meyers, 1984; Professional Association of Teachers, 1994). Contrary indications emerged elsewhere, however, with evidence that computer game players may in fact be encouraged to read a great deal by the very large numbers of magazines targeted at players (Griffiths, 1996) and by findings that computer game players may be more likely than nonplayers to engage in sports (Phillips et al., 1995).

Empirical evidence has emerged that computer games can yield direct and positive effects for players both in terms of knowledge acquisition and cognitive skills development. Early research produced equivocal findings on links between reported computer game playing and school performance. In one case, access to a computer outside schools was found to have no link with academic performance (Dominick, 1984); in another instance, evidence emerged of a negative link (Braun et al., 1986), and then again of a positive link (Lockheed, Nielson, & Stone, 1983).

The growing use of computing in schools initially came under fire for displaying a lack of purposiveness and academic justification, poor quality software, and for showing a gender bias toward boys (Nairman, 1982; Sanders, 1984; Seidel, Anderson, & Hunter, 1982). Notwithstanding these criticisms, the use of computers was defended elsewhere for having many positive benefits (Gibb et al., 1983). Microcomputers and their accompanying software were reported to engage and cultivate particular kinds of complex spatial cognitive learning (Ball, 1978; Jones, 1981; Kennedy, Bittner, & Jones, 1981; Lowery & Knirk, 1983).

Quite apart from the intentional use of computers as learning instruments in computer-assisted instruction contexts, an educational potential was observed even for mainstream recreational electronic game playing. Computer and video games were able to invoke cognitive skills that were not only necessary to play these games successfully, but could also prove to be transferable to other learning situations and information processing contexts (White, 1992; Greenfield, 1994).

Computer game scenarios can provide contexts that can enhance memory for certain types of content. Young children, aged four to seven years, show better memory for pictures displayed during a computer game than when presented in a lesson format (Oyen & Bebko, 1996). The effectiveness of computer games in enhancing learning and memory for subject matter depends critically on the degree to which the to-be-learned material is integrated with the fantasy component of the game (Lepper, 1982). In examining this phenomenon further, Oyen and Bebko (1996) distinguished between "exogenous" games, in which the learning content was only arbitrarily linked with the fantasy component of the game, and "endogenous" games in which the to-be-learned content is intrinsically interrelated with the game itself. In their study, an endogenous game produced better subsequent picture content recall than did an exogenous game. One reason for this effect is that computer games can make learning more interesting (Corno & Mandinach, 1983).

Computer games can pose challenges to children that require them to utilize specific cognitive skills, but in a context that makes learning fun. Such games work best if they present a clearly defined goal or objective for the child to achieve, and offer enough uncertainty regarding outcomes at different points in play to provide a real challenge. Computer games can teach physical coordination skills, decision making, following directions, and numerical and word recognition skills (Ball, 1978). They can also cultivate an ability to divide visual attention between different tasks or aspects of a task (Greenfield et al., 1994).

Cross-national research with American and Italian undergraduates compared the cognitive skills acquisition of experienced and novice players with a computer game called *Evolution* (Greenfield et al., 1994a). This relatively nonviolent game comprised six different levels of play, with each one introducing a new set of rules and patterns of play. Male and female players were given an opportunity to practice playing the game on their own, to do so following some initial instruction and advice on how to play, or while answering questions about their experience with the game at regular intervals during play itself. The transfer of learned skills was tested via an educational computer game designed to teach the logic of computer circuitry. In this the students received a number of video demonstrations, on each of which they subsequently answered questions.

Students who were already experts at playing computer games performed well on the test of cognitive skill, especially if they had had some opportunity to play the *Evolution* game first. Even novice players, however, benefited from playing the computer game and appeared quickly to acquire essential skills that assisted them in playing with the later educational computer game. Knowledge of the computer game was acquired through practice and trial and error rather than by being told how to play it. The conditions under which the students received prior advice did not assist them in mastering the game. There were differences, however, between experts and novices in how effectively they responded to advice about game play strategies. Experts benefited from pre-playing advice about rules and strategies of the game, whereas novices did not. It seems likely that experts already had well-developed schemas relevant to game playing, which enabled them to relate to and adapt the advice given to this new computer game. In contrast, periodic questioning about the computer game task during breaks in the initial learning procedure did help novices to acquire relevant skills and to transfer them to a subsequent task. This procedure helped in the mastery of visual aspects of the game in particular, and this seemed to be the key to effective game play.

Skill in spatial representation is one example of everyday cognitive skills utilized and developed by computer games and other computer applications (Greenfield, 1983). Such skills allow individuals to deal with complex visual problems by being able to imagine objects in three dimensions in the mind through a kind of mental rotation of the entities observed, to imagine the relative movements of objects, to interpret and predict the unfolding of patterns, and to encode more rapidly information about visual forms (Lohman, 1979; Linn & Peterson, 1985). These skills are built up over time, and computer representations of visual fields have been found to serve as effective training tools in this context (Lowery & Knirk, 1983; Small & Small, 1982).

Playing computer games such as *Targ* and *Battlezone* was found to erode initial gender-related differences in spatial orientation, spatial visualization, and eye-hand coordination skills. Although men initially scored higher on these skills than women, after several hours of playing these games, these gender differences disappeared (Gagnon, 1985).

In another set of practice studies, Pepin and Dorval (1986) and Dorval and Pepin (1986) provided eight sessions of training on the computer game *Zaxxon* (each session included five games) to seventy undergraduate students. They also provided training to 101 twelve-year-olds, although the children received fewer practice sessions because of time constraints. A control was given the pretest and posttest with no computer game training. Among the adults, both men and women gained significantly in visual spatial skills following training on *Zaxxon*. Among the children, they observed no such changes. In the latter case, the youngsters had greater computer game playing experience than the adults, leaving less room for significant improvement after such a limited number of further playing sessions.

Other research has found strong support for the view that computer game playing can improve spatial skills performance (Forsyth & Lancy, 1987; McClurg & Chaille, 1987; Subrahmanyam & Greenfield, 1994). Children and teenagers aged ten to sixteen years, in particular, showed spatial skills benefits from playing computer games (McClurg & Chaille, 1987; Miller & Kapel, 1985).

Cognitive skills improvements occur not just with educationally oriented programs designed to pose mental challenges, but also in response to playing more action-oriented games that tend to prove more popular especially with young games players (Forsyth & Lancy, 1987; Greenfield et al., 1994b; Hayes, Lancy, & Evans, 1985; Lancy & Hayes, 1988).

Greenfield, Brannon, and Lohr (1994) tested whether computer games could contribute to developing spatial representational skills required for humans to "interface" effectively with computer technology. American undergraduate students took part in a study that examined the relationship between skills levels in playing a three-dimensional action arcade video game, *The Empire Strikes Back*, and the skills needed to complete a mental paper-folding task.

In *The Empire Strikes Back*, the game gives the player the perspective of a starship pilot flying through space. The player's task is to shoot enemy ships while avoiding asteroids and enemy fire so as to accumulate points and advance in difficulty level. The game requires players to navigate through three-dimensional space, represented on a two-dimensional screen. The test of visual-spatial skills, mental paper folding, was also one that demanded visualizing three-dimensional movement from a two-dimensional display. The key difference between the video game and paper folding was that the former was dynamic, involving a lot of movement, whereas the latter was static.

Performance in playing the video game was correlated with ability to complete the mental paper folding task in one study. In a second study, there was no short-term effect of playing the video game on mental paper folding ability, but some evidence did emerge that in the long-term, video game expertise could be beneficial to this kind of task. Practice was needed over an extended period of time to cultivate these skills.

As the way in which these games are played has been examined more closely, it has become apparent that they involve a range of cognitive skills that can become very acutely developed in individuals who are well-practiced in computer game play. Computer games are not simply an appealing pastime for young people, they may serve as an introduction to the world of computers. Furthermore, they have been found to cultivate certain categories of cognitive skills that are important in the context of other types of computer use. Indeed, some of the mental and information processing skills acquired through playing computer games may be transferable to other domains of experience. Far from impeding the intellectual growth of young people, computer games may be able to stimulate it. Although excessive computer game play, to the neglect of other pursuits—mental or physical—is not a habit that should be condoned, there do, nevertheless, seem to be some positive and beneficial side effects to young people's involvement with these games.

Computer Games and Social Behavior Effects

Playing computer games has been linked to positive and negative social effects. Negative effects research represents an extension of the media violence literature, with video game playing allegedly giving rise to arousal that might instigate aggression, imitative aggressive behavior, or simply the reduction of prosocial behavioral tendencies (Friedrich-Cofer & Huston, 1986; Gauntlett, 1995). Personality has also been invoked as a mediator of these effects. On a more positive note, constructive social skills effects can be achieved via computer games that are designed to produce these effects.

Many video games have violent themes and therefore often require aggressive performance by participants (Dominick, 1984; Loftus & Loftus, 1983). In many video games, players must shoot or harm their symbolic opponents in order to win. Violence is, in fact, a theme that pervades many of the most popular games, with games such as *Streetfighter*, *Mortal Kombat*, and *Tomb Raider* being among the best and most widely played examples. Some researchers have concluded that playing violent computer games can invoke increased aggression among players (Anderson & Ford, 1986; Ballard & Wiest, 1995; Irwin & Gross, 1995; Schutte et al., 1988; Silvern & Williamson, 1987). Other researchers have failed to find evidence for such a link (Cooper & Mackie, 1986; Graybill, Kirsch, & Esselmen, 1985; Graybill et al., 1987; Scott, 1995; Winkel, Novak, & Hopson, 1987). One literature review concluded that there is clear evidence of a causal relationship between playing computer games and aggression (Dill & Dill, 1998). Another reviewer argued that the research to date has been fraught with methodological problems and that no clear conclusion can be drawn (Griffiths, 1999).

Concern about the possible effects of computer games with violent themes stems from two main developments. First, they represent one of the most popular forms of entertainment among children and adolescents. Significant majorities of boys (88 percent) and girls (64 percent) in the United States in middle-class homes report playing computer games regularly (Funk, 1993), and many of these players express clear preferences for games with themes of human or fantasy violence (Sherry, 2001). Second, fighting games (e.g., *Mortal Kombat*, *Streetfighter*, *Tekken*) and first-person shooters (e.g., *Quake*, *Doom*, *Marathon*) have increased the level of violence over earlier games with faster and more graphic depictions of human violence.

A number of theories have been offered to explain the effects of violent computer games. These theories mostly derive from research on television violence and include social learning, neo-associative networks, arousal, and catharsis. Although games share some characteristics with television, the medium is different in important ways (Dominick, 1984). Television viewing is a passive experience, whereas playing with computer games is highly active, requiring intense concentration and physical activity. Television viewers can break concentration and still follow the story. Computer game players cannot break concentration, except during programmed rest periods. Computer game violence tends to be highly abstract, as opposed to the realistic violence on television. Studies of television and film violence have shown that greater post-viewing aggression may result from viewing more realistic or realistically perceived violence on screen (Atkin, 1983; Berkowtiz & Alioto, 1973).

The most frequently cited mechanism by which computer games may result in aggressive behavior is social learning theory (Alman, 1992; Brusa, 1988; Chambers & Ascione, 1987; Graybill et al., 1985; Hoffman, 1995). Social learning theory posits that behavior is learned through imitation of attractive rewarded models (Bandura, 1994). Proponents of this theory for computer games argue that electronic games should have particularly powerful effects due to the high attention levels of players and the active identification of players with characters on the screen. It has been further argued that game players are rewarded directly for enacting symbolic violence and therefore may transfer the learned aggression to the outside world (Winkel, Novak, & Hopson, 1987).

According to the general arousal model, exciting media experiences can give rise to a heightened, nonspecific drive state (Tannenbaum & Zillmann, 1975). This arousal will enhance any preferred behavioral response. Because computer games with violent themes can generate such arousal, aggressive behavior could be enhanced if prompted subsequent to playing (Ballard & West, 1995; Brusa, 1988; Calvert & Tan, 1994; Winkel, Novak, & Hopson, 1987).

The neo-associative networks model calls upon Berkowitz's notion of priming effects whereby cues in media violence may lead to subsequent aggression due to the priming of semantically related informational nodes in memory (Berkowitz, 1984; Berkowitz & Rogers, 1986). In the case of computer games, priming effects theory would suggest that exposure to violent games will prime a series of nodes associated with violence and aggression. In other words, playing with violent material generates hostile thoughts (Jo & Berkowitz, 1994) that might in turn promote aggressive responding under the right circumstances (Anderson & Ford, 1986; Anderson & Morrow, 1995; Hoffman, 1995).

A more positive effects notion derives from the catharsis hypothesis, which posits that violent media content can be used as a safe outlet for aggressive thoughts and feelings. Thus, an angry person may become less so as a consequence of playing a violent computer game (Calvert & Tan, 1994; Graybill, Kirsch, & Esselman, 1985; Graybill et al., 1987; Kestenbaum & Weinstein, 1985; Silvern & Williamson, 1987).

Some have raised methodological questions about research on computer games and aggression. One problem is whether the studies to date have external validity with findings that can be generalized to the outside world. Studies have varied in the treatment strength of violent computer game stimuli presented to experimental participants. The types of violent game stimuli have varied between simulated boxing (Graybill, Kirsch, & Esselman, 1985; Graybill et al., 1987), symbolic representations of bombs and missiles (Cooper & Mackie, 1986), and players shooting directly at robots and other objects on screen (Graybill et al., 1987). Later studies featured games with graphically more realistic, human-like characters (Ballard & Wiest, 1995; Irwin & Gross, 1995).

Studies have varied also in the length of treatment effect. In some cases, post-viewing measures of aggression have been taken after as little as five minutes of play, whereas in other cases, participants might be allowed to play for well over an hour. It is important to consider whether short duration of play might give rise to frustration in players who wish to play for longer or boredom for players required to play for longer durations and whether such feelings might become confounded with the experimental treatment (Sherry, 2001).

There have also been a variety of different measures of post-playing aggression used. These measures have varied from actual behavior (aggression observed during free play, or in terms of willingness to help or hurt others) to paper-and-pencil measures of aggressive feelings. This can make it difficult to ascertain whether the observed findings support the popular claim that computer games with violent themes represent a danger to society. Do computer games cause people to *act*

aggressively or to *feel* aggressive, or both? Choice of outcome measures has both theoretical and social consequences. Paper-and-pencil measures of hostility may reflect priming of associated nodes, but priming may not result in actual aggressive behavior. Behavioral measures such as aggression during play and willingness to help or hurt others may be more socially significant.

A recent meta-analysis of the research evidence on this subject has begun to shed further light on what might be key trigger factors. Sherry (2001) re-analyzed and compared the results from twenty studies of computer games and post-playing aggression. Three factors emerged as important indicators in this research: graphic realism of violence, length of treatment, and nature of outcome measure. Games with human or fantasy violence gave rise to stronger post-playing aggression effects than did games that were sports related. Assuming no difference in arousal levels between these types of games (though this is not proven), this could indicate evidence in support of the notion of priming of associative networks and the generation of aggressive thoughts by the violent cues in computer games with violent themes. The size of post-playing aggressive effects was negatively related to playing time, when controlling for age of players. Some studies may therefore have measured an initial arousal effect that falls off dramatically after extended play. Longer play periods may give rise to boredom. The social implication of this finding is that children and adolescents who play electronic games in long stretches may transfer less aggression from the game playing situation to the external world than those playing for relatively brief durations.

Finally, average aggression effect size for paper-and-pencil measures was somewhat larger than that for behavioral measures. This finding indicated that playing computer games with violent themes may give rise to enhanced aggressive thoughts or feelings, but these are not necessarily acted upon (Sherry, 2001).

Computer Games and Health

Finally, playing computer games has been related to health risk and benefits. Health risks include physical conditions that follow from excessive playing and also psychological effects upon those at risk of epilepsy and players with already disturbed personalities. Social health risks have also been considered in the form of social dependence on computer games and withdrawal from real social networks. More positively, computer games have been used in therapeutic contexts and as health education vehicles.

Physical and Psychophysiological Health Issues

The medical profession has voiced a number of concerns about computer game playing. According to Loftus and Loftus (1983), players reported new kinds of aches and pains. Rheumatologists have described cases of "Nintendinitis" and "Space Invaders' Wrist," in which players have suffered skin, joint, and muscle problems from repeated button hitting and joystick pushing on game machines. In a survey by Loftus and Loftus, 65 percent of (arcade) video game players examined complained of blisters, calluses, sore tendons, and numbness of fingers, hands, and elbows directly as a result of their playing.

There have also been a number of case studies that have reported some of the adverse effects of playing (nonarcade) computer and video games. These have inclded wrist pain (McCowan, 1981), neck pain (Miller, 1991), elbow pain (Bright & Bringhurst, 1992), tensynvitis (also called "Ninteninitis") (Reinstein, 1983; Brassington, 1990; Casanova & Casanvoa, 1991; Siegal, 1991), peripheral neuropathy (Friedland & St. John, 1984), enuresis (Schink, 1991), encoprisis (Corkery, 1990), epileptic seizures (Rushton, 1981; Dalquist, Mellinger, & Klass, 1983; Hart, 1990), and even hallucinations (Spence, 1993).

Some of these adverse effects were quite rare and "treatment" simply involved cessation of playing of the games in question. In the cases involving enuresis and encoprisis, the children were so engaged in the games that they simply did not want to go to the toilet. In these particular cases, they were taught how to use the game's "pause" button.

Several cases have been reported of epileptic seizures among children and teenagers following computer game play. These cases, though rare, resemble others in which seizures have been brought on by the fluttering of faulty television screens (e.g., Gastaut, Regis, & Bostem, 1962; Stefansson et al., 1977). One early observation of this phenomenon with computer games occurred with a seventeen-year-old boy playing a game called *Astro Fighter*, which was judged to have the right size, brightness, and frequently changing images, to cause seizures in susceptible individuals. In this case, the subject suffered epileptic attacks on two separate occasions after playing this particular game for twenty to thirty minutes (Rushton, 1981).

Dahlquist and his colleagues (1983) reported a case of a fifteen-year-old boy with no previous history of seizures. He played computer games regularly for one year before seizures began. On one occasion, the boy appeared to be in a daze with his hand twitching while playing a game called *Combat*. A month or so later, the boy had a further seizure while playing a *Pac-Man* computer game. Subsequently he developed a sensitivity to bright sunlight flickering through trees while being driven along a tree-lined road (Dahlquist, Mellinger, & Klass, 1983).

A further published case of computer game-induced seizure involved a thirteen-year-old girl who had been playing a Nintendo game for three hours with only a short break. At a particularly rapid phase in the game, she reported feeling strange, and then had a two- to three-minute seizure (Hart, 1990). It appears that certain shifting patterns of images and light in computer games can trigger seizures in photosensitive individuals. These cases, fortunately, are rare, but medical professionals have nevertheless given out warnings that computer games may be capable of causing these reactions among children and teenagers who have a low tolerance for flashing lights and rapidly moving and changing images.

Social Health Issues

Other speculative negative aspects of video game playing that have been reported include the belief that computer game play is socially isolating and prevents children from developing social skills (e.g., Zimbardo, 1982). One researcher has reported that computer game players use the machines as "electronic friends" (Selnow, 1984). However, this does not necessarily mean that players play these games instead of forming human friendships and interacting with their peer groups. Indeed, some of the young people surveyed by Selnow indicated that going to video game arcades represented an important aspect of their social life. These arcades were meeting places and places to go to observe other people and to learn how people behave when with others.

This impression that video game arcades represent an important social environment was reinforced elsewhere. Colwell, Grady, and Rhaiti (1995) reported that heavy video game players tended to see their friends more often outside school than did nonplayers, and had a need to see their friends on a regular basis. In fact, no difference has been found between high and low frequency video game players in terms of their inherent sociability (Rutkowska & Carlton, 1994). Frequent players tend to enjoy just as many friendships and contacts with friends as do less frequent players (Phillips et al., 1995).

The social aspect of computer and video games can be experienced at home just as much as in arcades where online games are played. Multi-user domains (MUDs) represent a broad class of online adventure games in which two or more participants can interact in fantasy virtual worlds that they can even help to create. By the mid 1990s, one estimate calculated that there were three hundred such games worldwide (Pavlik, 1996), with scenarios ranging from medieval villages to science fiction settings. Some observers and participants recognize MUDs as a major attraction among computer games players (Quittner, 1994). Their allure has much to do with the psychological and social experience afforded by playing with MUDs. Regular users can establish relationships with other players, and through their involvement in MUDs can become members of virtual communities (Rheingold, 1993).

The MUD program represents a set of tools with which users can create a social and cultural environment in which to enjoy a rich and varied range of communications with other people. The anonymity that players enjoy, unless they choose voluntarily to give this up, leads to less inhibited communications than found in the real world. Players feel freer to speak their minds and vent their feelings without holding back as they probably would in face-to-face interactions with others (Kiesler & Sproull, 1986; Kiesler, Siegel, & McGuire, 1984). Such disinhibition can be manifest in terms of greater aggressiveness and hostility or as greater friendliness and intimacy (Reid, 1995). In such a computer-mediated environment, participants lack the nonverbal cues they would normally experience in real world environments when communicating with others, which often function to temper verbal and physical behaviors (Rice & Love, 1987). This observation is challenged, however, by the fact that MUD users have developed nonverbal cues and signals even with text-based communications, and a lexicon of symbols that carry emotional connotations has been created for use alongside verbal language.

Social and Therapeutic Value of Computer Games
The rapid evolution of new technologies on the home entertainment front has brought a proliferation of new computer-based games that some therapists have adopted as tools in the therapeutic process. Such games can be especially effective with young and adult patients, serving as an excellent way to establish a rapport with the therapist and to control and shape behavior (Spence, 1988; Gardner, 1991).

Computer games can be used as training aids for certain cognitive and perceptual-motor disorders (Lynch, 1981). These disorders can appear in patients who have been in accidents, have had strokes, or who have simply been born with such problems. Loftus and Loftus (1983) reported the case of a teenage girl who suffered brain damage after being involved in a car accident. This damage manifests itself in terms of a sudden inability to spell (spelling dyspraxia). Computer game therapy was used on a twice-weekly basis to treat the disorder. This mostly involved playing a game called *Hangman*, in which two people guess letters in a word. If they guess a correct letter, there is no penalty. If an incorrect letter appears, another portion of the "hangman" is added on. After two months of this treatment, the dyspraxia problem was significantly reduced.

According to Gardner (1991), using computer games in his psychotherapy sessions provided common ground between himself and his client and provided excellent behavioral observation opportunities.

During the mid 1980s, researchers found that computer games could facilitate cooperative behavior among children and be used to reinforce desirable conduct within educational settings (Stein & Kochman, 1984; Salend & Santora, 1985). There have been a number of innovative uses of computer games in therapeutic contexts. "Video game therapy" was used by Lynch (1981, 1983) for various types of mental disorder (e.g., stroke patients). Not only can computer game performance be compared between patients and "normals," but video game playing can be used as a training aid to some cognitive and perceptual-motor disorders. Further to this, Szer (1983) reported the case of using video game playing as physiotherapy for someone with an arm injury, and Phillips (1991) reported the case of using a hand-held video game (Nintendo *GameBoy*) to stop an eight-year-old boy picking at his face. In this latter case, the child had enurodermatitis and scarring due to continual picking at his upper lip. Previous treatment had included a brief behavior modification program with food rewards for periods free of picking, and the application of a bitter tasting product to the child's fingers. These failed to work, so Phillips recommended the use of a hand-held computer game that was a psychologically rewarding experience and kept the boy's hands occupied. After two weeks the affected area had healed, and at a two-month follow-up, Phillips reported no problems related to the child's continued use of the game.

Computer games have been applied to the treatment of young people with a variety of handicaps.

Horn, Jones, and Hamlett (1991) examined the effectiveness of a video game format in training three children, aged between five and eight years, with multiple handicaps (e.g., severely limited vocal speech acquisition) to make scanning and selection responses similar to those needed to operate communication aids manufactured to assist them with their speech difficulties. The video scanning and selection game systematically shaped their behavior that involved selecting from among a number of boxes containing words. Playing this game produced improvements in the ability of the children to perform this task, which was subsequently found to transfer well to the application of a similar skill needed to operate a communication device.

Computer games may provide a distraction or an escape from worry and painful situations or feelings, having both physical and psychological benefits for young people. There are also many reports (e.g., Kolko & Rickard-Figueroa, 1985; Redd et al., 1987; Vasterling et al., 1993) that computer games have been used as a diversion from the side effects of cancer chemotherapy during childhood and that such distraction tasks can reduce the amount of pain killers children need.

Evidence has also emerged that computer games can alleviate feelings of anxiety. In one study, physiological and psychological measures of anxiety were taken of female college students, around half of whom were preclassified as having highly anxious personalities, and half as being relatively calm. Although the high-anxiety women were more likely to report being anxious throughout the experiment, physiological measures of skin conductance revealed that their arousal level actually decreased while they were playing a video game. For nonanxious women, no such effect was observed (Naveteur & Ray, 1990). Spence (1988) is another advocate of the therapeutic value of video games, incorporating them into his repertoire of behavior management techniques.

Other reports of the application of commercially available computer software to the therapeutic context indicate positive results. Some recommend computer games for their capabilities to provide distinctive help in overcoming certain therapeutic problems in a form of treatment to which adolescents will readily respond. Such computer-based games have recently been found to offer satisfactory treatment solutions for even quite complex therapeutic problems among adolescent patients. One such illustration was the development of an adventure-based computer game for the treatment of adolescents with difficulty controlling sudden impulses to behave in unusual or antisocial ways (Clarke & Schoech, 1994).

Video adventure games and games involving fantasy role playing can be effectively used to train adolescents to deal with real-life situations, by creating scenarios that may not exist in the adolescent's own experience. Mystery computer games can be used with good results when working with groups of adolescents suffering psychiatric problems. The group can learn by observing and modeling the behavior of group leaders as well as by participating in the development of successful problem-solving strategies (Favelle, 1994).

Even with young children, successful therapeutic applications have been reported. In one study, an ordinary office personal computer loaded with a role playing game, an electronic play program, a program that combined a simple word processor with a collection of pictures to produce cartoon-type stories, and a game of explanation suitable for pre-schoolers was used to conduct play therapy with children (Kokush, 1994). Throughout, the software applied was low cost and commercially available. Case examples illustrated the use of such PC-based programs in a small, private practice. The therapeutic progression of the young clients and their relationship with the therapist were described. Successful treatments were reported, but not without problems along the way. On balance, however, computer-based games were found to be a useful addition to the therapeutic tool-kit of the child therapist.

Other Psychological Applications

Computer games and simulations have been developed to assist promotional and educational campaigns aimed to put across social and health-related messages to children and adolescents. Bosworth (1994) reported the use of these technologies in a comprehensive health promotion campaign aimed at adolescents. They were used to attract the attention to young people to BARN (Body Awareness Resource Network) as well as to hold their interest across the duration of the campaign. This program comprised six topic areas: AIDS, alcohol, other drugs, body management, human sexuality, smoking, and stress management. Quiz games challenged players to test their knowledge on a topic. Simulations challenged users to apply health information in nonjudgemental, hypothetical situations. The games played an important part in turning young people's attention on to this health campaign and worked equally well among frequent and infrequent computer game players.

Cahill (1994) reported on research with *Health Works*, a prototype AIDS education program developed by the new York State Department of Health for schoolchildren aged between eleven and fourteen years. Health Works featured state-of-the-art interactive computer video programs and animated graphics on five stand-alone computer stations, housed in a customized mobile unit. Between January 1989 and June 1992, *Health Works* was visited by more than 17,000 students at 172 schools in New York State, including New York City. Cahill analyzed results concerning its impact for over thirty-eight hundred New York City students.

The findings revealed that computer games can take students beyond straightforward factual learning to a deeper involvement with the subject matter, having a much more powerful impact on strength of learning and likelihood of adoption of recommended health-related behaviors. The *Health Works* visits to schools served as booster sessions for classroom AIDS education.

Another computer-based program was developed around the same time to campaign against drug use. Oakley (1994) described the development and utilization of *Smack*, a computer-driven game for teenagers, which addressed drug abuse. The game was developed to illustrate to teenagers the negative consequences associated with drug use. The game was comprised of simulations requiring teenagers to make decisions regarding drug use and to respond to the consequences of such decisions. It was found that the program reinforced the anti-drug attitude of teens who were not inclined toward drug use.

Other games have been developed to assist with the moral development of young people and the rehabilitation of those who have already become offenders. Sherer (1994) described the development and application of a computerized therapeutic simulation game for raising the moral level of adolescents or to re-socialize those who had already got into trouble. The effects of the game on moral development were determined by a moral development measure. The level of moral development of thirteen teenagers who participated in this exercise and fourteen others who served as a comparison group, all aged fifteen years, was measured before and after exposure to the therapeutic game. Participants met for sixteen weekly, two-hour sessions in which the first hour was spent playing with the computer game followed by a further hour of discussion. Two out of five indices of moral development were found to show improvements as a result of playing with the computer game. Counsellors reported that the teenagers had been stimulated by the computer game experience, and the teens themselves enjoyed the games and thought they were relevant to the issues being addressed.

A computer simulation game called *Busted* was designed as part of a program to reduce antisocial behavior in young offenders. The aim of this game was to raise delinquents' awareness of their own conduct and the consequences of antisocial behavior for victims, and to work on these youngsters' interpersonal skills when dealing with other people. The rehabilitation program using this game ran for three to four weeks, during which it was played once or twice a week for around one and a half hours a time by three to six players. The game set up scenarios in which players had to take decisions, make choices, and receive the consequences of those choices. Firm conclusions about the effectiveness of *Busted* have not yet been reached and its evaluation is still continuing. A preliminary evaluation conducted in two high school classrooms yielded positive results, with both boys and girls showing a degree of enthusiasm for the game and claiming to have learned something from it. Teachers also reportedly found the program useful. Whether it can produce longer term attitudinal and behavioral changes remains to be seen. Nevertheless, this project represents one more illustration of the way computer games are being applied to problems relating to children's and adolescents' social and moral development (Sherer, 1994).

Computer games can have both positive and negative health implications. Clinical observations have revealed that certain types of computer games, coupled with intensive playing of them, can give rise to adverse physiological reactions, causing epileptic seizures among individuals with such a predisposition as well as producing physical strains, aches, and pains deriving from bad posture or repetitive movements during play. Counterbalancing these problems, however, is evidence that playing video games can have positive benefits for youngsters in the sense of boosting feelings of self worth and in the context of treating behavioral disorders. As with many other forms of home entertainment, computer games need to be used sensibly in a carefully managed fashion. Where they represent part of a social scene for young people, their use seems to be generally controlled and related to positive feelings about self. Where they are used as a social distraction and a form of escape or withdrawal from social contact, they represent part of an undesirable behavioral syndrome that needs to be discouraged.

References

Alman, R. E. (1992). *Video games: Interaction vs. observation as sources of social learning.* Unpublished master's thesis, Michigan State University, East Lansing.

Anderson, C. A., & Dill, K. E. (2000). Video games and aggressive thoughts, feelings, and behavior in the laboratory and in life. *Journal of Personality and Social Psychology, 78,* 772–790.

Anderson, C. A., & Ford, C. M. (1986). Affect of the game player: Short-term effects of highly and mildly aggressive video games. *Personality and Social Psychology Bulletin, 12,* 390–402.

Anderson, C. A., & Morrow, M. (1995). Competitive aggression without interaction: Effects of competitive versus cooperative instructions on aggressive behavior in video games. *Personality and Social Psychology Bulletin, 21,* 1020–1030.

Atkin, C. (1983). Effects of realistic TV violence vs. fictional violence on aggression. *Journalism Quarterly, 60,* 615–621.

Ball, H. G. (1978). Telegrams teach more than you think. *Audiovisual Instruction,* May, 24–26.

Ballard, M. E., & Wiest, J. R. (1995). *Mortal Kombat: The effects of violent video technology on males' hostility and cardiovascular responding.* Paper presented at the biennial meeting of the Society for Research in Child Development, Indianpolis, Indiana.

Bandura, A. (1994). The social cognitive theory of mass communication. In J. Bryant & D. Zillmann (Eds.), *Media effects: Advances in theory and research* (pp. 61–90). Hillsdale, NJ: Lawrence Erlbaum Associates.

Berkowitz, L. (1984). Some effects of thoughts on anti-and prosocial influences of media events: A cognitive-neoassociation analysis. *Psychological Bulletin, 95,* 410–427.

Berkowitz, L., & Alioto, J. (1973). The meaning of an observed event as a determinant of its aggressive consequences. *Journal of Personality and Social Psychology, 28,* 206–217.

Berkowitz, L., & Rogers, K. H. (1986). A priming effect analysis of media influences. In J. Bryant & D. Zillmann (Eds.), *Perspectives on media effects* (pp. 57–81). Hillsdale, NJ: Lawrence Erlbaum Associates.

Bosworth, K. (1994). Computer games and simulations as tools to reach and engage adolescents in health promotion activities. *Computers in Human Services, 11*(1–2), 109–119.

Brassington, R. (1990). Nintendinitis. *New England Journal of Medicine, 322,* 1473–1474.

Braun, C. M., Goupil, J., Giroux, J., & Chagnon, Y. (1986). Adolescents and microcomputers: Sex differences, proxemics, task and stimulus variables. *Journal of Psychology, 120,* 529–542.

Bright, D. A., & Bringhurst, D. C. (1992). Nintendo elbow. *Western Journal of Medicine, 156,* 667–668.

Brusa, J. A. (1988). Effects of video game playing on children's social behavior (aggression, cooperation). *Dissertation Abstracts International-B, 48*(10), 3127.

Cahill, J. M. (1994). Health works: Interactive AIDS education video games. *Computers in Human Services, 11*(1–2), 159–176.

Calvert, S., & Tan, S. L. (1994). Impact of virtual reality on young adult's physiological arousal and aggressive thoughts: Interaction versus observation. *Journal of Applied Developmental Psychology, 15,* 125–139.

Casanova, J., & Casanova, J. (1991). Nintendinitis. *Journal of Hand Surgery, 16,* 181.

Chambers, J. H., & Ascione, F. R. (1987). The effects of prosocial and aggressive video games on children's donating and helping. *Journal of Genetic Psychology, 148,* 499–505.

Clarke, D., & Shoech, D. (1994). A computer-assisted therapeutic game for adolescents: Initial development and comments. *Computers in Human Services, 11*(1–2), 121–140.

Colwell, J., Grady, C., & Rhaiti, S. (1995). Computer games, self-esteem, and gratification of needs in adolescents. *Journal of Community and Applied Social Psychology, 5,* 195–206.

Cooper, J., & Mackie, D. (1986). Video games and aggression in children. *Journal of Applied Social Psychology, 16,* 726–744.

Corkery, J. C. (1990). Nintendo power. *American Journal of Diseases in Children, 144,* 959.

Corno, L., & Mandinach, E. B. (1983). The role of cognitive engagement in classroom learning and motivation. *Educational Psychologist, 18,* 88–108.

Dahlquist, N. R., Mellinger, J. F., & Klass, D. W. (1983). Hazards of video games in patients with light-sensitive epilepsy. *Journal of the American Medical Association, 249,* 776–777.

Dill, K. E. (1997). Violent video game and trait aggression effects on aggressive behavior, thoughts, and feelings, delinquency, and world view. *Dissertation Abstracts International-B, 59*(07).

Dill, K. E., & Dill, J. C. (1998). Video game violence: A review of the empirical literature. *Aggression & Violent Behavior, 3,* 407–428.

Dominick, J. R. (1984). Videogames, television violence, and aggression in teenagers. *Journal of Communication, 34,* 136–147.

Dorval, M., & Pepin, M. (1986). Effect of playing a video game on measure of spatial visualisation. *Perceptual and Motor Skills, 62,* 159–162.

Egli, E. A., & Meyers, L. S. (1984). The role of video game playing in adolescent life: Is there a reason to be concerned? *Bulletin of the Psychonomic Society, 22,* 309–312.

Favelle, G. K. (1994). Therapeutic applications of commercially available computer software. *Computers in Human Services, 11*(1–2), 151–158.

Fling, S., Smith, L., Rodriguez, T., Thornton, D., Atkins, E., & Nixon, K. (1992). Video games, aggression, and self-esteem: A survey. *Social Behavior and Personality, 20*(1), 39–45.

Forsyth, A. S., & Lancy, D. F. (1987). Simulated travel and place location learning in a computer adventure game. *Journal of Educational Computing Research, 3,* 377–394.

Friedland, R. P., & St. John, J. N. (1984). Video-game palsy: Distal ulnar neuropathy in a video-game enthusiast. *New England Journal of Medicine, 311,* 58–59.

Friedrich-Cofer, L., & Huston, A. H. (1986). Television violence and aggression: The debate continues. *Psychological Bulletin, 100,* 364–371.

Funk, J. (1993). Reevaluating the impact of video games. *Clinical Pediatrics, 32,* 86–90.

Gagnon, D. (1985). Video games and spatial skills: An exploratory study. *Educational Communication and Technology Journal, 33,* 263–275.

Gardner, J. E. (1991). Can the Mario Bros. help? Nintendo games as an adjunct in psychotherapy with children. *Psychotherapy, 28,* 667–670.

Gastaut, H., Regis, H., & Bostem, F. (1962). Attacks provoked by television and their mechanism. *Epilepsia, 3,* 438–445.

Gauntlett, D. (1995). *Moving experiences: Understanding television's influences and effects.* London: John Libbey.

Gibb, G. D., Baily, J. R., Lambirth, T. T., & Wilson, W. P. (1983). Personality differences between high and low electronic games users. *Journal of Psychology, 114,* 159–165.

Graybill, D., Kirsch, J. R., & Esselman, E. D. (1985). Effects of playing violent versus non-violent video games on the aggressive ideation of children. *Child Study Journal, 15,* 199–205.

Graybill, D., Strawniak, M., Hunter, T., & O'Leary, M. (1987). Effects of playing versus observing violent versus non-violent video games on children's aggression. *Psychology: Quarterly Journal of Human Behavior, 24,* 1–7.

Greenfield, P. (1983). Video games and cognitive skills. In S. S. Baughman and P. D. Claggett (Eds.), *Video games and human development: A research agenda for the 80's.* Cambridge, MA: Harvard Graduate School of Education.

Greenfield, P. M. (1994). Video games as cultural artifacts. *Journal of Applied Developmental Psychology, 15*(1), 3–12.

Greenfield, P. M., Brannon, G., & Lohr, D. (1994). Two-dimensional representation of movement through three-dimensional space: The role of video game expertise. *Journal of Applied Developmental Psychology, 15*(1), 87–103.

Greenfield, P. M., Camaioni, L., Ercolani, P., Weiss, L., et al. (1994a). Cognitive socialization by computer games in two cultures: Inductive discovery or mastery of an iconic code. *Journal of Applied Developmental Psychology, 15*(1), 59–85.

Greenfield, P. M., & Lave, J. (1982). Cognitive aspects of informal education. In D. Wagner & H. Stevenson (Eds.), *Cultural perspectives on child development* (pp. 181–207). San Francisco, CA: Freeman.

Greenfield, P. M., de Winstanley, P., Kilpatrick, H., & Kaye, D. (1994b). Action video games and informal education: Effects on strategies for dividing visual attention. *Journal of Applied Developmental Psychology, 15*(1), 105–123.

Griffiths, M. (1999). Violent video games and aggression: A review of the literature. *Aggression & Violent Behavior, 4*, 203–212.

Griffiths, M. D., & Hunt, N. (1993). *The acquisition, development and maintenance of computer game playing in adolescence*. Paper presented at the British Psychological Society, London Conference, City University, December.

Gunter, B. (1998). *The effects of video games on children: The myth unmasked*. Sheffield, UK: Sheffield Academic Press.

Hart, E. J. (1990). Nintendo epilepsy. *New England Journal of Medicine, 322*, 1473.

Hayes, B., Lancy, D. F., & Evans, B. (1985). Computer adventure games and the development of information-processing skills. In G. H. McNick (Ed.), *Comprehension, computers, and communication* (pp. 60–66). Athens, GA: University of Georgia Press.

Hoffman, K. (1995). Effects of playing versus witnessing video game violence on attitudes toward aggression and acceptance of violence as a means of conflict resolution. *Dissertation Abstracts International, 56*(3), 747.

Horn, E., Jones, H. A., & Hamlett, C. (1991). An investigation of the feasibility of a video game system for developing scanning and selection skills. *Journal of the Association for Persons with Severe Handicaps, 16*(2), 108–115.

Irwin, A. R., & Gross, A. M. (1995). Cognitive tempo, violent video games, and aggressive behavior in young boys. *Journal of Family Violence, 10*, 337–350.

Jo, E., & Berkowitz, L. (1994). A priming effect analysis of media influences: An update. In J. Bryant & D. Zillmann (Eds.), *Media effects: Advances in theory and research* (pp. 43–60). Hillsdale, NJ: Lawrence Erlbaum Associates.

Jones, M. B. (1981). Videogame for performance testing. *American Journal of Psychology, 94*, 143–152.

Keepers, G. A. (1990). Pathological preoccupation with video games. *Journal of the American Academy of Child and Adolescent Psychiatry, 29*, 49–50.

Kennedy, R. S., Bittner, A. C. Jr., & Jones, M. B. (1981). Video-game and conventional tracking. *Perceptual and Motor Skills, 53*, 310.

Kestenbaum, G. I., & Weinstein, L. (1985). Personality, psychopathology and developmental issues in male adolescent video game use. *Journal of the American Academy of Child Psychiatry, 24*, 329–337.

Kiesler, S., Seigel, J., & McGuire, T. W. (1984). Social psychological aspects of computer-mediated communications. *American Psychologist, 39*, 1123–1134.

Kiesler, S., & Sproull, L. (1986). Reducing social context cues: Electronic mail in organizational communication. *Management Science, 32*(11), 1492–1512.

Kirsh, S. J. (1998). Seeing the world through *Mortal Kombat*-colored glasses: Violent video games and the development of a short-term hostile attribution bias. *Childhood, 5*, 177–184.

Klein, M. H. (1984). The bite of Pac-Man. *Journal of Psychohistory, 11*, 395–401.

Kokush, R. (1994). Experiences using a PC in play therapy with children. *Computers in Human Services, 11*(1–2), 141–150.

Kolko, D. J., & Rickard-Figueroa, J. L. (1985). Effects of video games on the adverse corollaries of chemotherapy in paediatric oncology patients. *Journal of Consulting and Clinical Psychology, 53*, 223–228.

Lancy, D. F., Cohen, H., Evans, B., Levine, N., & Nevin, M. L. (1985). Using the joystick as a tool to promote intellectual growth and social interaction. *Laboratory for the Comparative Study of Human Cognition Newsletter, 7*, 119–125.

Lancy, D. F., & Hayes, B. L. (1988). Interactive fiction and the reluctant reader. *The English Journal, 77*, 42–46.

Lepper, M. R. (1982). *Microcomputers in education: Motivational and social issues*. Paper presented at the American Psychological Association, Washington, DC, August.

Levy, S. (1984). *Hackers: Heroes of the computer revolution*. New York: Anchor Press/Doubleday.

Lin, S., & Lepper, M. R. (1987). Correlates of children's usage of videogames and computers. *Journal of Applied Social Psychology, 17*(1), 72–93.

Linn, M. C., & Peterson, A. C. (1985). Emergence and characterization of sex differences in spatial ability: A meta-analysis. *Child Development, 56*, 1479–1498.

Lockheed, M. E., Nielson, A., & Stone, M. K. (1983). *Some determinants of microcomputer literacy in high school students*. Paper presented at American Educational Research Association, Montreal, April.

Barrie Gunter

Loftus, G. A., & Loftus, E. F. (1983). *Mind at play: The psychology of video games*. New York: Basic Books.

Lohman, D. F. (1979). Spatial ability: A review and reanalysis of the correlational literature. Tech. Rep. No. 8, Palo Alto, CA: Stanford University Aptitude Research Project.

Lowery, B. R., & Knirk, F. G. (1983). Micro-computer video games and spatial visualization acquisition. *Journal of Educational Technology Systems*, *11*, 155–166.

Lynch, W. J. (1981). *TV games as therapeutic interventions*. Paper presented at the American Psychological Association, Los Angeles, August.

Lynch, W. J. (1983). *Cognitive retraining using microcomputer games and commercially available software*. Paper presented at the Meeting of the International Neuropsychological Society, Mexico City, February.

Martin, J., & Norman, A. R. D. (1970). *The computerized society*. London: Penguin.

Mayfield, M. (1982). Video games only fit for old. *USA Today*, November 10, p. 1.

McClurg, P. A., & Chaille, C. (1987). Computer games: Environments for developing spatial cognition? *Journal of Educational Computing Research*, *3*, 95–111.

McClure, R. F., & Mears, F. G. (1984). Video game players: Personality characteristics and demographic variables. *Psychological Reports*, *55*, 271–276.

McCowan, T. C. (1981). Space Invaders wrist. *New England Journal of Medicine*, *304*, 1368.

Miller, D. L. G. (1991). Nintendo neck. *Canadian Medical Association Journal*, *145*, 1202.

Miller, G. G., & Kapel, D. E. (1985). Can non-verbal puzzle-type microcomputer software affect spatial discrimination and sequential thinking skills of 7th and 8th graders? *Education*, *106*, 160–167.

Nairman, A. (1982). Women, technophobia and computers. *Classroom Computer News*, *2*(3), 23–24.

Naveteur, J., & Ray, J.-C. (1990). Electrodermal activity of low and high trait anxiety subjects during a frustration video game. *Journal of Psychophysiology*, *4*(3), 221–227.

Oakley, C. (1994). Smack: A computer driven game for at-risk teens. *Computers in Human Services*, *11*(1–2), 97–99.

Oyen, A. S., & Bebko, J. M. (1996). The effects of computer games and lesson contexts on children's mnemonic strategies. *Journal of Experimental Child Psychology*, *62*(2), 173–189.

Pavlik, J. (1996). *New media and the information superhighway*. Boston, MA: Allyn and Bacon.

Pepin, M., & Dorval, M. (1986). *Effect of playing a video game on adults' and adolescents' spatial visualization*. Paper presented at the annual meeting of the American Educational Research Association, San Francisco, CA., April.

Phillips, C. A., Rolls, S., Rouse, A., & Griffiths, M. (1995). Home video game playing in schoolchildren: A study of incidence and patterns of play. *Journal of Adolescence*, *18*, 687–691.

Phillips, W. R. (1991). Video game therapy. *New England Journal of Medicine*, *325*(17), 1256–1257.

Professional Association of Teachers. (1994). *The street of the Pied Piper: A survey of teachers' perceptions of the effects on children of the new entertainment technology*. Derby, UK: Author.

Quittner, J. (1994). Johnny Manhattan meets the Furrymuckers. *Wired*, March, 92.

Redd, W. H., Jacobsen, P. B., DieTrill, M., Dermatis, H., McEvoy, M., & Holland, J. C. (1987). Cognitive-attentional distraction in the control of conditioned nausea in paediatric cancer patients receiving chemotherapy. *Journal of Consulting and Clinical Psychology*, *55*, 391–395.

Reid, E. (1995). Virtual worlds: Culture and imagination. In S. G. Jones (Ed.), *Cybersociety: Computer-mediated communication and community* (pp. 164–183). Thousand Oaks, CA: Sage.

Reinstein, L. (1983). De Quervain's stenosing tenosynovitis in a video games player. *Archives of Physical and Medical Rehabilitation*, *64*, 434–435.

Rheingold, H. (1993). *The virtual community: Homesteading on the electronic frontier*. New York: Simon and Schuster.

Rice, R. E., & Love, G. (1987). Electronic emotion: Socio-emotional content in a computer-mediated communication network. *Communication Research*, *1491*, 85–108.

Rogoff, B., & Lave, J. (Eds.). (1984). *Everyday cognition: Its development in social context*. Cambridge, MA: Harvard University Press.

Rushton, B. (1981). Space Invader epilepsy. *The Lancet, 1*, 501.

Rutkowska, J. C., & Carlton, T. (1994). *Computer games in 12–13 year olds' activities and social networks.* Paper presented at the British Psychological Society Annual Conference, April.

Salend, S., & Santora, D. (1985). Employing access to the computer as a reinforcer for secondary students. *Behavioral Disorders*, November.

Sanders, J. S. (1984). The computer: Male, female or androgynous? *The Computing Teacher*, April, 31–34.

Schink, J. C. (1991). Nintendo enuresis. *American Journal of Diseases in Children, 145*, 1094.

Schutte, N., Malouff, J., Post-Gordon, J., & Rodasta, A. (1988). Effects of palying video games on children's aggressive and other behaviors. *Journal of Applied Social Psychology, 18*, 451–456.

Scott, D. (1995). The effect of video games on feelings of aggression. *Journal of Psychology, 129*, 121–132.

Scribner, S. (1986). Thinking in action: Some characteristics of practical thought. In R. J. Sternberg & R. K. Wagner (Eds.), *Practical intelligence: Nature and origin of competence in the everyday world* (pp. 13–30). Cambridge, UK: Cambridge University Press.

Seidel, R. J., Anderson, A. E., & Hunter, B. (Eds.). (1982). *Computer literacy.* New York: Academic Press.

Selnow, G. W. (1984). Playing video games: The electronic friend. *Journal of Communication, 34*, 148–156.

Sherer, M. (1994). The effect of computerized simulation games on the moral development of youth in distress. *Computers in Human Services, 11*(1–2), 81–95.

Sherry, J. L. (2001). The effects of violent video games on aggression: A meta-analysis. *Human Communication Research, 27*(3), 409–431.

Shotton, M. (1989). *Computer addiction?: A study of computer dependency.* London: Taylor and Francis.

Siegal, I. M. (1991). Nintendonitis. *Orthopaedics, 14*, 745.

Sigel, I. E., & Cocking, R. R. (1977). Cognition and communication: A dialectic paradigm for development. In M. Lewis & L. A. Rosenblum (Eds.), *Interaction, conversation, and the development of language: The origins of behavior* (vol. 5, pp. 207–226). New York: Academic Press.

Silvern, S. B. (1986). Classroom use of video games. *Education Research Quarterly, 10*, 10–16.

Silvern, S. B., Lang, M. K., & Williamson, P. A. (1987). Social impact of video game play. *Meaningful play, playful meaning: Proceedings of the 11th annual meeting of the Association for the Anthropological Study of Play.* Champaign, IL: Human Kinetics.

Silvern, S., & Williamson, P. (1987). The effects of video game play on young children's aggression, fantasy and prosocial behavior. *Journal of Developmental Psychology, 8*, 449–458.

Small, D., & Small, S. (1982). The experts' guide to beating *Asteroids, Battlezone, Galazian Ripoff,* and *Space Invaders. Creative Computing, 18*(1), 18–33.

Soper, W. B., & Miller, M. J. (1983). Junk time junkies: An emerging addiction among students. *School Counsellor, 31*, 40–43.

Spence, J. (1988). The use of computer arcade games in behavior management. *Maladjustment and Therapeutic Education, 6*, 64–68.

Spence, S. A. (1993). Nintendo hallucinations: A new phenomenological entity. *Irish Journal of Psychological Medicine, 10*, 98–99.

Stefansson, B., Darby, C. E., Wilkins, A. J., et al. (1972). Television epilepsy and pattern sensitivity. *British Medical Journal, 2*, 88–90.

Stein, W., & Kochman, W. (1984). Effects of computer games on children's cooperative behavior. *Journal of Research and Development in Education, 18*, 1.

Subrahmanyan, K., & Greenfield, P. M. (1994). Effect of video game practice on spatial skills in girls and boys. *Journal of Applied Developmental Psychology, 15*(1), 13–32.

Szer, J. (1983). Video games as physiotherapy. *Medical Journal of Australia, 1*, 401–402.

Tannenbaum, P. H., & Zillmann, D. (1975). Emotional arousal in the facilitation of aggression through communication. In L. Berkowitz (Ed.), *Advances in experimental social psychology, vol. 8* (pp. 149–192). New York: Academic Press.

Vasterling, J., Jenkins, R. A., Tope, D. M., & Burish, T. G. (1993). Cognitive distraction and relaxation training for the control of side effects due to cancer chemotherapy. *Journal of Behavioral Medicine, 16*, 65–80.

Waddilove, K. (1984). The case for cost effective chalk. *The Guardian*, March 20, p. 11.

Weizenbaum, J. (1976). *Computer power and human reason*. San Francisco: W.H. Freeman and Company.

White, W. B. Jr. (1992). What value are video games? *USA Today Magazine*, March, p. 74.

Winkel, M., Novak, D., & Hopson, H. (1987). Personality factors, subject gender and the effects of aggressive video games on aggression in adolescents. *Journal of Research in Personality, 21*, 211–223.

Zimbardo, P. (1982). Understanding psychological man: A state of the science report. *Psychology Today, 16*, 15.

10

THE THERAPEUTIC VALUE OF VIDEO GAMES

Mark Griffiths

Until recently, most reported effects of video games centered on the alleged negative consequences. These included video game addiction (e.g., Griffiths & Hunt, 1995, 1998), increased aggressiveness (e.g., Griffiths, 1998), and the various medical and psychosocial effects (Griffiths, 1996). However, there are abundant references to the positive benefits of video games in the literature, including brief overviews (e.g., Lawrence, 1986; Griffiths, 1997). Despite research into the more negative effects, for over twenty years, researchers have been using video games as a means of researching individuals. Many of these reasons also provide an insight as to why games may be useful therapeutically. For instance:

· Games are a natural part of human behavior. Using video games as a measurement tool, the researcher achieves the relaxation and ease that can be essential to successful experimentation.

· Video games can assist children in setting goals, ensuring goal rehearsal, providing feedback, reinforcement, and maintaining records of behavioral change.

· Researchers can use video games when examining individual characteristics such as self-esteem, self-concept, goal-setting, and individual differences.

· Video games are fun and stimulating for participants. Consequently, it is easier to achieve and maintain a person's undivided attention for long periods of time (Donchin, 1995).

· As research tools, video games are very diverse and attract participation by individuals across many demographic boundaries (e.g., age, gender, ethnicity, educational status; Washburn & Gulledge, 1995).

· Video games also allow participants to experience novelty and challenge.

· Video games also allow participants to engage in extraordinary activities and to destroy or even die without real consequences (Washburn & Gulledge, 1995).

· Video games can be useful because they allow the researcher to measure performance on a very wide variety of tasks, and can be easily changed, standardized, and understood.

· Video games may help adolescents regress to childhood play (because of the ability to suspend reality in videogame playing)

Research dating back to the early 1980s has consistently shown that playing computer games (irrespective of genre) produces increases in reaction times, improved hand-eye coordination, and raises players' self-esteem. What's more, curiosity, fun, and the nature of the challenge also appear to add to a game's therapeutic potential. This chapter will concentrate on the reported therapeutic benefits of video game playing. Some evidence suggests that important skills may be built or reinforced by video games. For example, video game playing can improve spatial visualization ability (i.e., mentally rotating and manipulating two- and three-dimensional objects) (Subrahmanyam & Greenfield, 1994). However, video games were more effective for children who started out with relatively poor skills. It was therefore suggested that video games may be useful in equalizing individual differences in spatial skill performance.

Many people seem surprised that video games have been used innovatively in a wide variety of therapeutic and medical contexts. As we shall see during the course of this chapter, "video game therapy" has been used successfully in rehabilitation for stroke patients, people with traumatic brain injuries, burns victims, wheelchair users, Erb's palsy sufferers, children undergoing chemotherapy, children with muscular dystrophy, and autistic children.

Video Games as Physiotherapy and Occupational Therapy

Video games have been used as a form of physiotherapy and/or occupational therapy with many different groups of people (e.g., those who are physically handicapped, learning disabled, emotionally disturbed, etc.).

Much has been written about how boring and repetitive exercises are if someone is attempting to recover from or cope with a physical ailment. Introducing video games into this context can be of huge therapeutic benefit. As we shall see, the same appears to be true for more complex psychological abnormalities.

Video games have been used innovatively as a form of physiotherapy for arm injuries (Szer, 1983), in training the movements of a thirteen-year-old child with Erb's palsy (Krichevets et al., 1994), and as a form of occupational therapy to increase hand strength (King, 1993). For instance, King (1993) showed that video games could be used in an occupational therapy setting to increase hand strength among patients with just three-minute "exercise" periods on computer games. Video games have also been used as therapeutic interventions to promote and increase arm reach in persons with traumatic brain injury (Sietsema et al., 1993). This paper reported the use of a computer game (described as an occupationally embedded intervention) to promote and increase arm reach in people with traumatic brain injury. The study showed that the game produced significantly more range of motion in all of their twenty participants.

Therapeutic benefits have also been reported for wheelchair users, burn victims, and muscular dystrophy sufferers. More specifically, some wheelchair users find regular exercise programs too difficult physically or psychologically, and many find that using standard arm crank or roller systems monotonous. O'Connor and colleagues (2000) looked for ways that individuals with spinal cord injuries would be motivated to exercise on a regular basis. As a consequence, they developed an interactive video game system (*Gamewheels*) that provided an interface between a portable roller system and a computer. This system enabled wheelchair users to play commercially available video games, and their results demonstrated improved physical fitness in a sample of people with spinal cord injuries, spinal cord diseases, amputations, nerve diseases, and multiple sclerosis. Most of their participants (86 percent) reported that they would like a *Gamewheels* system for their home.

Adriaenssens and colleagues (1988) reported the use of video game playing as an exercise program to facilitate the rehabilitation of upper-limb burn victims (using a variety of large to smaller joysticks). This technique not only helped overcome initial therapy resistance but also encouraged and shaped movement of the hand, wrist, and elbow by providing feedback for the desired performance while also offering a distrac-

tion from pain. Finally, video games were also used as a respiratory muscle training aid for young patients with Duchenne Muscular Dystrophy (Vilozni et al., 1994).

Using video games in almost all these differing contexts capitalizes on a number of interrelated factors. One of the most important is the person's motivation to succeed. Furthermore, video games have advantages over traditional therapeutic methods that rely on passive, repetitive movements and painful limb manipulation (i.e., they focus attention away from potential discomfort).

Video Games as Distractors in the Role of Pain Management

Studies have shown that cognitive/attentional distraction may block the perception of pain. The reasoning is that distractor tasks consume some degree of the attentional capacity that would otherwise be devoted to pain perception. Video game playing offers an ideal way to analyze the role of distraction in symptom control in pediatric patients. Redd at al. (1987) argue that the main reasons for this are:

1. Video games are likely to engage much of a person's individual active attention because of the cognitive and motor activity required.
2. Video games allow the possibility to achieve sustained achievement because of the level of difficulty (i.e., challenge) of most games during extended play.
3. Video games appear to appeal most to adolescents.

Video games have also been used in a number of studies as "distractor tasks." For instance, one study (Phillips, 1991) reported the case of using a handheld video game (*Nintendo GameBoy*) to stop an eight-year old boy picking at his face. The child had neurodermatitis and scarring due to continual picking at his upper lip. Previous treatments (e.g., behavior modification program with food rewards for periods free of picking and the application of a bitter tasting product to the child's fingers) had failed, so therapists used a handheld videogame to keep the boy's hands occupied. After two weeks, the affected area had healed. Another creative use of video games has been to help increase sitting tolerance for people with lower back pain (Butler, 1985).

There are also a number of studies (e.g., Kolko & Rickard-Figueroa, 1985; Redd et al., 1987; Vasterling et al., 1993) that have demonstrated that video games can provide cognitive distraction during cancer chemotherapy in children. All these studies have reported that distracted patients report less nausea prior to chemotherapy and lower systolic pressure after treatment (when compared with controls). Such distraction tasks also reduce the amount of painkillers needed. There are many practical advantages for using video game therapy for pediatric patients during chemotherapy treatment. Redd et al. (1987) argue that:

1. Video game playing can be easily integrated with most chemotherapy administration procedures.
2. Video games represent a more cost-effective intervention than many traditional behavioral procedures such as hypnosis and relaxation.
3. Video games can be played without medical supervision.

To date there has been no long-term follow-up to such interventions and it is unclear whether patients eventually tire of such games. Therefore, researchers need to explore factors such as novelty, game preference, and relative level of challenge. This pain management technique utilizing video games has also been applied successfully to children undergoing treatment for sickle cell disease (Pegelow, 1992). As mentioned in the previous section, the studies by Adriaenssens et al. (1988) and O'Connor et al. (2000) on burns victims and wheelchair users claimed that success was in part due to the distraction from pain.

Finally in this section it is worth noting that one report alerted doctors that children may mistake patient-controlled analgesia (PCA) devices for video game consoles. Blunt, Hastie, and Stephens (1998) reported the case of a seven-year-old boy with Ollier's disease undergoing an operation whose pain was managed via a PCA pump. On the third day following his operation, the boy's PCA usage escalated from zero to a total of seventy-four demands during a four-hour period. Upon questioning it became clear that the boy had been playing a video game and he had mistakenly been pressing his PCA pump as if it had been a video game!

Video Games and Cognitive Rehabilitation

Video games have been used as a rehabilitation aid among various groups of people. Fisher (1986) argued that computers (including video games) have the potential to aid cognitive remediation. Areas that can be helped include perceptual disorders, conceptual thinking, attention, concentration, memory, and difficulties with language. A number of researchers have studied these ideas empirically. For instance, Larose and colleagues (1989) carried out a study to test the hypothesis that computer games may be an efficient therapeutic tool in a cognitive rehabilitation program. Sixty participants who showed attention difficulties with or without cerebral dysfunctions participated in a twelve-hour training program based on intensive use of a video game. Analyses showed improvement for the experimental group on scanning and tracking variables, notwithstanding the nature of their particular dysfunctions. Other studies have successfully used video games in rehabilitation programs to improve sustained attention in patients with craniocerebral trauma (Lawrence, 1986; Funk, Germann, & Buchman, 1997), and as a training and rehabilitation aid to cognitive and perceptual-motor disorders in stroke patients (Lynch, 1983).

Other authors have advocated the use of video games as a cognitive rehabilitation aid (attention, perceptual spatial abilities, reasoning, memory) to assist patients who have had brain damage to regain lost function (Lawrence, 1986; Skilbeck, 1991). Video games have also been used to increase spatial visualization (Dorval & Pepin, 1986). However, more recent research by Subrahmanyam and Greenfield (1994) has suggested that spatial skills are only improved in those whose skills were very weak to begin with but unlikely to improve skills for those with average or above-average spatial abilities.

Video Games and the Development of Social and Communication Skills among the Learning Disabled

Video games have also been used in comprehensive programs to help develop social skills in children and adolescents who are severely retarded or who have severe developmental problems such as autism (e.g., Gaylord-Ross et al., 1984; Sedlak, Doyle, & Schloss, 1982). Case studies such as those by Demarest (2000) are persuasive. Demarest's account of her own autistic seven-year old son reported that although he had serious deficiencies in language and understanding, and social and emotional difficulties, video game playing was one activity at which he was able to excel. This was ego-boosting for him and also had a self-calming effect. Video games provided the visual patterns, speed, and storyline that help children's basic skills development. Some of the therapeutic benefits Demarest (2000) outlined were language skills, mathematics and reading skills, and social skills.

Horn, Jones, and Hamlett (1991) used video games to train three children with multiple handicaps (e.g., severely limited vocal speech acquisition) to make scan and selection responses. These skills were later transferred to a communication device. Other researchers have used video games to help learning disabled children in their development of spatial abilities (Masendorf, 1993), problem-solving exercises (Hollingsworth & Woodward, 1993), and mathematical ability (Okolo, 1992a). Other researchers have offered critiques on how best to use computer technology for improved achievement and enhanced motivation among the learning disabled (e.g., Blechman, Rabin, & McEnroe, 1986; Okolo, 1992b).

Video Games and Impulsivity/Attention Deficit Disorders

There are now a few studies that have examined whether video games might be able to help in the treatment of children with impulsive and attentional difficulties. Kappes and Thompson (1985) tried to reduce impulsivity in incarcerated juveniles (ages fifteen to eighteen years) by providing either biofeedback or experience with a video game. Impulsivity scores improved for both conditions. Improvement was also noted in negative self-attributions and in internal locus of control. The authors concluded that the most likely explanation for the improvement in both experimental conditions was the immediate feedback. Clarke and Schoech (1994) also used video games to help adolescents learn impulse control. They used a video game for four weeks with four subjects (eleven to seventeen years) diagnosed with impulse control problems. After the experimental trial, the participants became more enthusiastic and cooperative about treatment.

New research (Pope, 2001; Wright, 2001) suggests video games linked to brainwave biofeedback may help children with attention deficit disorders. Biofeedback teaches patients to control normally involuntary body functions such as heart rate by providing real-time monitors of those responses. With the aid of a computer display, attention-deficit patients can learn to modulate brain waves associated with focusing. With enough training, changes become automatic and lead to improvements in grades, sociability, and organizational skills. Following on from research involving pilot attentiveness during long flights, a similar principle has been developed to help attention-deficit children stay focused by rewarding an attentive state of mind. This has been done by linking biofeedback to commercial videogames. In their trial, Pope and Palsson (2001; cited in Wright, 2001) selected half a dozen *Sony PlayStation* games and tested twenty-two girls and boys

between the ages of nine and thirteen who had attention deficit disorder. Half the group got traditional biofeedback training, the other half played the modified video games. After forty one-hour sessions, both groups showed substantial improvements in everyday brainwave patterns as well as in tests of attention span, impulsiveness, and hyperactivity. Parents in both groups also reported that their children were doing better in school. The difference between the two groups was motivation. The video game group showed fewer no-shows and no dropouts. The researchers do warn that the "wrong kinds of video game" may be detrimental to children with attention disorders. For instance, "shoot 'em up" games may have a negative effect on children who already have a tendency toward short attention and impulsivity. They also state that the technique is an adjunct to drug therapy and not replacement for it.

Video Games and the Elderly: Therapeutic Benefits

One could perhaps argue that video game manufacturers have done very little to target older people as prospective video game users. This might be different if they were aware that there is a growing body of evidence that video games may have beneficial therapeutic effects for the elderly. Given that video game playing involves concentration, attention, hand-eye coordination, memory, decision-making, and speed reactions, the activity may be of great benefit to this particular cohort. Researchers working in this area have postulated that the intellectual declines that are part of the natural aging process may be slowed (and perhaps counteracted) by getting the elderly involved as active users of technology (Farris et al., 1994). For instance, a game as simple as *Tetris* can engage the mind in an enjoyable problem-solving exercise. The same enjoyable pleasures that occur when any of us master a new computer skill may have therapeutic value to both young and old. Learning something new on the computer results in a sense of accomplishment and satisfaction that invariably creates a feeling of well-being. Technology with the aged can therefore foster greater independence and can be put to therapeutic use. Dustman, Emmerson, Laurel, and Shearer (1992) showed that video games could increase reaction times among the elderly after an eleven-week period of video game playing.

McGuire (1984, 1986) examined the effectiveness of video games in improving self-esteem among elderly long-term care residents. In one wing of the institution, researchers made video games available for an eight-week period. Residents of a second wing did not have the opportunity to play them and were used as a control group. Results showed that the video game group exhibited significant improvement in self-esteem. Other researchers have found similar results. For instance, Goldstein and colleagues (1997) reported that (noninstitutionalized) elderly people improved reaction times, self-esteem, and positive sense of well-being, as a result of playing video games for five hours a week for five weeks. However, there was little improvement in cognitive performance compared with controls. Riddick, Spector, and Drogin (1986) examined the impact of video game play on the emotional states and affiliative behavior of elderly nursing home residents. The experimental group had an opportunity to play video games three times per week for up to three hours per session, over a six-week period. In comparison to the control group, the experimental group underwent significant changes in their arousal state and affiliative behavior.

Weisman (1983) suggested that video games may have a role to play in meeting clients' needs for fun and mental stimulation and in enhancing self-esteem. He reported that moderate mental and physical impairments did not prevent fifty nursing home residents from participating in four video games that were especially adapted for this population. Further research by Weisman (1994) on the institutionalized elderly found that computer and video game use was found to be a valuable learning and diagnostic tool. The author urged practitioners to investigate the possibilities of using video games in their work with the elderly.

Farris et al. (1994) suggested that older adults can benefit significantly from ongoing education, and that computers can be valuable tools in this process. They advocate the use of computers for long- and short-term memory functioning. They reported a study using the video game *Memory of Goblins*. This game was developed primarily for use in the assessment of working memory but can also train working memory. Conclusions were difficult to draw from this particular study, but there is evidence to suggest that the impact of computer use among the elderly population can be profound. Ryan (1994) also used the *Memory for Goblins* video game to assess memory skills among various groups. Preliminary results with older users suggested they find it novel and interesting although there appeared to be little effect on improvement of working memory.

Hollander and Plummer (1986) reported the use of a hands-on microcomputer experience in forty-one senior adults. Over a three-week period, video games

served as a therapeutic and rehabilitative tool, as well as a form of social and educational enrichment. Results indicated that thought-provoking games (*Trivia* and *Hangman*) held the participant's highest level of attention, and were perceived as exciting and stimulating. Schueren (1986) also analyzed the value of video games as an activity program for geriatric populations in skilled nursing home facilities. It was concluded that video game playing may be a successful small group recreational activity for those residents with adequate eye-hand coordination, vision and mental functioning. Researchers proposed suggestions for equipment adaptations to correct problems of poor visual clarity and awkward manipulation of controls.

Given this small but growing body of evidence, there is clearly a need for more research on video game use among this particular group of people. There are many areas that researchers need to explore in more detail including elderly use of technology in general, the use of computers and video games to develop and strengthen memory skills, intergenerational computing projects (teaming seniors with school aged students), and the use of computers and video games to assess cognitive functions. Many older adults may be receptive to using technology if introduced to it in a comfortable environment. If introduced in the right way, technology (including video games) may become a major hobby and interest in the lives of the elderly, and may also be of therapeutic value.

Video Games in Psychotherapeutic Settings

Therapists working with children have long used games in therapy and games as therapy in sessions with their young patients (Gardner, 1991). Play has been a feature in therapy since the work of Anna Freud (1928) and Melanie Klein (1932), and has been used to promote fantasy expression and the ventilation of feeling. The recent technological explosion has brought a proliferation of new games that some therapists claim to be an excellent ice-breaker and rapport builder with children in therapy and behavior management (e.g. Spence, 1988; Gardner, 1991). Research in the mid 1980s had already suggested that video games may actually facilitate cooperative behavior and reinforcement in more educational settings (e.g., Strein & Kochman, 1984; Salend & Santora, 1985).

Lawrence (1986) advocates using video games in the treatment of psychological problems during therapy. In an overview, he reported that there had been approximately two dozen efforts in the published literature to deliver counselling or other psychological intervention services by computer. Although not concentrating on video games specifically, he did refer to games, computer-aided instruction, biofeedback, and behavior therapy. He concluded that computers (including games) could make meaningful contributions to the treatment of psychological problems.

Gardner (1991) claimed that the use of video games in his psychotherapy sessions provided common ground between himself and his child clients, and provided excellent behavioral observation opportunities. According to Gardner, such observations allowed him to observe:

1. The child's repertoire of problem-solving strategies
2. The child's ability to perceive and recall subtle cues as well as foresee consequences of behavior and act on past consequences
3. Eye-hand coordination
4. The release of aggression and control
5. The ability to deal with appropriate methods of dealing with the joys of victory and frustrations of defeat in a more sports oriented arena
6. The satisfaction of cognitive activity in the involvement of the recall of bits of basic information
7. The enjoyment of mutually coordinating one's activities with another in the spirit of cooperation

Gardner went on to describe four particular case studies that used video games to support psychotherapy. Although other techniques were used as an adjunct in therapy (e.g., storytelling, drawing, other games), Gardner claimed it was the video games that were the most useful factors in the improvement during therapy. Gardner's contention is that clinical techniques tend to change as a function of the trends of the times, though the goals remain the same. Slower paced and more traditional activities such as those outlined above may lengthen the time it takes to form a therapeutic relationship as the child may perceive the therapist not to be "cool" or "with it."

Spence (1988) is another advocate of the therapeutic value of video games and has incorporated them into his repertoire of behavior management techniques. Spence believes that video games can bring about changes in a number of areas and provided case study examples:

1. *Development of relationships:* Used video games to provide the basis to develop a therapeutic relationship. The video games gave an acceptable "middle ground"

for both parties to "meet," which provided an enjoyable experience that could be shared. Relationships become close and trusting.

2. *Motivation:* Used video games as "bargaining counters" to motivate children to do things. This simply involved negotiating with an individual for a set period of work time or tasks in return for a set period of time playing video games.

3. *Cooperative behavior:* Used video games to develop social skills and cooperation in individuals by making them share a computer with peers. Through the medium of video games, individuals developed friendships that fostered cooperation.

4. *Aggressive behavior:* Used video games to "take the heat out of situations," i.e., individuals played video games when they were angry so that they inflicted "damage" on the video games' characters rather than human beings.

5. *Self-esteem:* Used video games as a measure of achievement to raise self-esteem. Because video games are skill based and provide scores, they can be compared and provide a basis for future goals. Beating personal high scores raised self-esteem in the individual.

As Spence's brief summaries show, the benefits are similar to those Gardner (1991) outlined. Similar techniques have also been advocated for behavioral management of exceptional children (Buckalew & Buckalew, 1983).

Olsen-Rando (1994) reported on the development and initial assessment of a video game version of the *Talking, Feeling, and Doing Game.* The game was developed by Richard Gardner, M.D., in order to facilitate the therapeutic process for those children who are inhibited, constrained, or resistive, or as an alternative therapeutic tool for children who are not characterized as resistive and thus freely reveal information. The game provides children an opportunity to talk about themselves in a way that is less anxiety provoking than traditional methods of eliciting information about their underlying psychodynamics. Unfortunately, this was a descriptive account only and contained no evaluation. Similarly, Kokish (1994) described the use of a personal computer loaded with various video games to aid play therapy with children, outlining case studies and making reference to the fact that learning to use the computer as a play therapy tool was more difficult and slower than expected.

Favelle (1994) also described some therapeutic applications of computer software and video games in work with both individuals and groups. The applications described were used with adolescents at a psychiatric treatment center and involved using commercially available software and video games. An adventure-fantasy game and a role playing game were described as helpful in work with individuals. This is because the importance and utilization of fantasy in play was expressed. A mystery computer game was presented as useful when working with groups. The author concluded that video games have useful therapeutic value if applied by skilled professionals, and suggested that further research would result in improvements to computer-assisted therapy.

Sherer (1994) described the development and application of a computerized therapeutic simulation game for the purpose of raising the moral level of youth in distress. The effects of the video game on moral development were determined by a moral development measure. The level of moral development of a research group (n = 13) and a control group (n = 14) were measured before and after exposure to the therapeutic video game, using total of five indices of moral development. Two of these, Moral Stage and Punishment, revealed a positive effect on the participants.

There is some research suggesting that video games can be useful when evaluating schizophrenics in their attitudes and responses (Samoilovich et al., 1992). To do this, Samoilovich et al. (1992) investigated the initial attitude of ten chronic, defected schizophrenic patients to a computer video game session. Six of them enjoyed the experience and wanted to repeat it. Cooperation and performance were compared by means of video games and a standard psychometric test (WAIS). Video game performance correlated with the execution test IQ more than with the verbal test IQ. The authors also claimed that video games can be used for psychological testing, motivation, and reward, and to evaluate psychomotor activity.

It has also been suggested that some psychiatric patients who are socially undisciplined may be reachable with computers and video games (Matthews et al., 1987). Studies were reported that explored the usefulness of computers with chronic psychiatric patients. In one study, video games were made available to patients, and one-half showed an active interest. The second study showed a neutral relationship between patients' social communication skills and their involvement with video games. Thus, some patients who were socially intractable may be reachable with computers. The researchers argued that the computer can effectively automate many tasks normally undertaken by clinicians and that the computer may have special advantages over the clinician for some purposes.

Video Games and Health Care

In randomized clinical trials, it has been reported that children and adolescents improved their self-care and significantly reduced their use of emergency clinical services after playing health education and disease management video games (Brown et al., 1997; Lieberman, 2001). Three games were investigated: *Bronkie the Bronchiasaurus* for asthma self-management; *Packy & Marlon* for diabetes self-management; and *Rex Ronan* for smoking prevention. In these interactive video games, children and adolescents assume the role of a main character who also has their chronic condition or is battling the effects of smoking and nicotine addiction. Children who used them for one week (smoking prevention) to six months (diabetes self-care) increased their resolve not to smoke, markedly improved their ability to manage their asthma or diabetes, and reduced by as much as 77 percent, on average, their urgent or emergency care visits related to their illness.

Electronic games have also been used to enhance adolescents' perceived self-efficacy in HIV/AIDS prevention programs (Cahill, 1994; Thomas, Cahill, & Santilli, 1997). Using a time travel adventure video game format, researchers provided information and opportunities for practice discussing prevention practices to high-risk adolescents. Video game playing resulted in significant gains in factual information about safe sex practices, and in the participants' perceptions of their ability to successfully negotiate and implement such practices with a potential partner.

Video games and simulations have been used extensively in a comprehensive health promotion for adolescents. For instance, Bosworth (1994) used these strategies to attract adolescents to BARN (Body Awareness Resource Network), as well as helping to hold interest. In each of the six topic areas (AIDS, Alcohol and Other Drugs, Body Management, Human Sexuality, Smoking, and Stress Management), video game quizzes challenged users to test their knowledge on a topic. Simulations challenged users to apply health information in hypothetical situations. Video games were a more important factor in the selection of BARN for younger users than for older users. BARN game users were not more likely than nongame users to be users of other computer or video games, nor did game users engage in more risk taking behaviors (e.g., alcohol and other drugs) than nongame users. Similar types of health promotion video games have been used successfully for drug use (Oakley, 1994), alcohol (Resnick, 1994a), marijuana (Henningson, Gold, & Duncan, 1986), sexual behavior (Starn & Paperny, 1990), life choices (Thomas, 1994), and antisocial behavior (Resnick, 1994b). One of the major problems with this area is that reported positive effects from video games in a health promotion context is that almost all of the video games evaluated were specially designed rather than those that were already commercially available. This does raise questions about the utility of generally commercial games in helping health promotion activities.

Conclusion

It is clear from the preceding overview that in the right context, video games can have a positive therapeutic benefit to a large range of different subgroups. Videogames have been shown to help children undergoing chemotherapy, children undergoing psychotherapy, children with particular emotional and behavioral problems (ADD, impulsivity, autism), individuals with medical and health problems (Erb's palsy, muscular dystrophy, burns, strokes, movement impaired), and the elderly. In terms of video games being distractor tasks, it seems likely that the effects can be attributed to most commercially available video games. However, as with the literature on video games aiding health promotion, one of the major problems is that reported positive effects in other instances were from specially designed video games rather than those that were already commercially available. It is therefore hard to evaluate the therapeutic value of video games as a whole. As with research into the more negative effects, it may well be the case that some video games are particularly beneficial, whereas others have little or no therapeutic benefit whatsoever. What is clear from the empirical literature is that the negative consequences of video game playing almost always involve people who are excessive users. It is probably fair to say that therapeutic benefits (including such things as self-esteem) can be gained from moderate video game playing.

Clearly there are many areas for future research and development in this area as most of the field is disparate in terms of positive therapeutic consequences. There is also a need to examine closely the factors that facilitate therapeutic benefits in the first place. This is because benefits (such as educational learning) depend on other factors than the nature of the video game itself. For instance, psychologists have shown that working cooperatively can speed up the time taken to do problem-solving tasks but are slowed down when they are done competitively. Also, psychologists have found that girls who do problem-solving tasks together with other girls tend to cooperate, whereas boys compete against each other. For those video games reliant on strategy and problem solving, such findings may have implications for therapeutic potential.

One unexplored area in video game research is people's attitudes toward playing. How a person thinks about a particular game—or video game playing in general—may actually affect the therapeutic value. For instance, one could speculate that when it comes to video games, there are three different types of people. The first type is the *technophobe* who thinks that video games are (literally) a complete waste of time and want nothing to do with them whatsoever. Technophobes would probably take every opportunity to be critical of them on a matter of principle and therefore gain little therapeutically. The second group of people are the *technosceptics* who use and enjoy the technology but are not convinced that it is a vital therapeutic tool, although there may be some therapeutic uses in some circumstances. The final group are the *technoromantics* who raise people's expectations about the capabilities and potential of computer games and who sing their praises at every available opportunity. It is these individuals who may benefit most therapeutically from video games.

Video games do seem to have great positive therapeutic potential in addition to their entertainment value. Many positive applications in education and health care have been developed. There has been considerable success when games are specifically designed to address a specific problem or to teach a certain skill. However, generalizability outside the game-playing situation remains an important research question.

References

Adriaenssens, E. E., Eggermont, E., Pyck, K., Boeckx, W., & Gilles, B. (1988). The video invasion of rehabilitation. *Burns, 14,* 417–419.

Benedict, J. O. (1990). A course in the psychology of video and educational games. *Teaching of Psychology, 17,* 206–208.

Blechman, E. A., Rabin, C., & McEnroe, M. J. (1986). Family communication and problem solving with boardgames and computer games. In C. E. Schaefer & S. E. Reid (Eds.), *Game play: Therapeutic use of childhood games* (pp. 129–145). New York: John Wiley & Sons.

Blunt, D., Hastie, C., & Stephens, P. (1998). More than he Nintended? *Anaesthesia and Intensive Care, 26*, 330–331.

Bosworth, K. (1994). Computer games and simulations as tools to reach and engage adolescents in health promotion activities. *Computers in Human Services, 11*, 109–119.

Brown, S. J., Lieberman, D. A., Germeny, B. A., Fan, Y. C., Wilson, D. M., & Pasta, D. J. (1997). Educational video game for juvenile diabetes: Results of a controlled trial. *Medical Informatics, 22*, 77–89.

Buckalew, L. W., & Buckalew, P. B. (1983). Behavioral management of exceptional children using video games as reward. *Perceptual and Motor Skills, 56*, 580.

Butler, C. (1985). Utilizing video games to increase sitting tolerance. *Archives of Physical Medicine and Rehabilitation, 66*(8), 527–527.

Cahill, J. M. (1994). Health works: Interactive AIDS education videogames. *Computers in Human Services, 11*(1–2), 159–176.

Clarke, B., & Schoech, D. (1994). A computer-assisted game for adolescents: Initial development and comments. *Computers in Human Services, 11*(1–2), 121–140.

Demarest, K. (2000). Video games—What are they good for? http://www.lessontutor.com/kd3.html.

Donchin, E. (1995). Video games as research tools: The Space Fortress game. *Behavior Research Methods, Instruments, & Computers, 27*(2), 217–223.

Dorval, M., & Pepin, M. (1986). Effect of playing a video game on a measure of spatial visualization. *Perceptual and Motor Skills, 62*, 159–162.

Dustman, R. E., Emmerson, R. Y., Laurel, A., Shearer, D., & Dustman, T. J. (1992). The effects of videogame playing on neuropsychological performance of elderly individuals. *Journal of Gerontology, 47*, 168–171.

Farris, M., Bates, R., Resnick, H., & Stabler, N. (1994). Evaluation of computer games' impact upon cognitively impaired frail elderly. *Computers in Human Services, 11*(1–2), 219–228.

Favelle, G. K. (1994). Therapeutic applications of commercially available computer software. *Computers in Human Services, 11*(1–2), 151–158.

Fisher, S. (1986). Use of computers following brain injury. *Activities, Adaptation & Aging, 8*(1), 81–93.

Freud, A. (1928). *Introduction to the technique of child analysis* (L. P. Clark, trans.). New York: Nervous and Mental Disease Publishing.

Funk, J. B., Germann, J. N., & Buchman, D. D. (1997). Children and electronic games in the United States. *Trends in Communication, 2*, 111–126.

Gardner, J. E. (1991). Can the Mario Bros. help? Nintendo games as an adjunct in psychotherapy with children. *Psychotherapy, 28*, 667–670.

Gaylord-Ross, R. J., Haring, T. G., Breen, C., & Pitts-Conway, V. (1984). The training and generalization of social interaction skills with autistic youth. *Journal of Applied Behavior Analysis, 17*, 229.

Goldstein, J., Cajko, L., Oosterbroek, M., Michielsen, M., van Houten, O., & Salverda, F. (1997). Video games and the elderly. *Social Behavior and Personality, 25*, 345–352.

Griffiths, M. D. (1996). Computer game playing in children and adolescents: A review of the literature. In T. Gill (Ed.), *Electronic children: How children are responding to the information revolution* (pp. 41–58). London: National Children's Bureau.

Griffiths, M. D. (1997). Video games and clinical practice: Issues, uses and treatments. *British Journal of Clinical Psychology, 36*, 639–641.

Griffiths, M. D. (1998). Video games and aggression: A review of the literature. *Aggression and Violent Behavior, 4*, 203–212.

Griffiths, M. D., & Hunt, N. (1995). Computer game playing in adolescence: Prevalence and demographic indicators. *Journal of Community and Applied Social Psychology, 5*, 189–194.

Griffiths, M. D., & Hunt, N. (1998). Dependence on computer game playing by adolescents. *Psychological Reports, 82*, 475–480.

Henningson, K. A., Gold, R. S., & Duncan, D. F. (1986). A computerised marijuana decision maze: Expert opinion regarding its use in health education. *Journal of Drug Education, 16*(3), 243–261.

Hollander, E. K., & Plummer, H. R. (1986). An innovative therapy and enrichment program for senior adults utilizing the personal computer. *Activities, Adaptation & Aging, 8*(1), 59–68.

Hollingsworth, M., & Woodward, J. (1993). Integrated learning: Explicit strategies and their role in problem solving instruction for students with learning disabilities. *Exceptional Children, 59*, 444–445.

Horn, E., Jones, H. A., & Hamlett, C. (1991). An investigation of the feasibility of a video game system for developing scanning and selection skills. *Journal for the Association for People With Severe Handicaps, 16*, 108–115.

Kappes, B. M., & Thompson, D. L. (1985). Biofeedback vs. video games: Effects on impulsivity, locus of control and self-concept with incarcerated individuals. *Journal of Clinical Psychology, 41*, 698–706.

King, T. I. (1993). Hand strengthening with a computer for purposeful activity. *American Journal of Occupational Therapy, 47*, 635–637.

Klein, M. (1932). *The psychoanalysis of children*. London: Hogarth.

Kokish, R. (1994). Experiences using a PC in play therapy with children. *Computers in Human Services, 11*(1–2), 141–150.

Kolko, D. J., & Rickard-Figueroa (1985). Effects of video games on the adverse corollaries of chemotherapy in pediatric oncology patients. *Journal of Consulting and Clinical Psychology, 53*, 223–228.

Krichevets, A. N., Sirotkina, E. B., Yevsevicheva, I. V., & Zeldin, L. M. (1994). Computer games as a means of movement rehabilitation. *Disability and Rehabilitation: An International Multidisciplinary Journal, 17*, 100–105.

Larose, S., Gagnon, S., Ferland, C., & Pepin, M. (1989). Psychology of computers: XIV. Cognitive rehabilitation through computer games. *Perceptual and Motor Skills, 69*, 851–858.

Lawrence, G. H. (1986). Using computers for the treatment of psychological problems. *Computers in Human Behavior, 2*, 43–62.

Lieberman, D. A. (2001). Management of chronic pediatric diseases with interactive health games: Theory and research findings, *Journal of Ambulatory Care Management, 24*, 26–38.

Lynch, W. J. (1983). Cognitive retraining using microcomputer games and commercially available software. Paper presented at the Meeting of the International Neuropsychological Society, Mexico City.

Masendorf, F. (1993). Training of learning disabled children's spatial abilities by computer games. *Zeitschrift für Pädagogische Psychologie, 7*, 209–213.

Matthews, T. J., De Santi, S. M., Callahan, D., Koblenz-Sulcov, C. J., & Werden, J. I. (1987). The microcomputer as an agent of intervention with psychiatric patients: Preliminary studies. *Computers in Human Behavior, 3*(1), 37–47.

McGuire, F. A. (1984). Improving the quality of life for residents of long term care facilities through video games. *Activities, Adaptation & Aging, 6*(1), 1–7.

McGuire, F. A. (1986). *Computer technology and the aged: Implications and applications for activity programs*. New York: The Haworth Press.

Oakley, C. (1994). *Smack*: A computer driven game for at-risk teens. *Computers in Human Services, 11*(1–2), 97–99.

O'Connor, T. J., Cooper, R. A., Fitzgerald, S. G., Dvorznak, M. J., Boninger, M. L., VanSickle, D. P., & Glass, L. (2000). Evaluation of a manual wheelchair interface to computer games. *Neurorehabilitation and Neural Repair, 14*(1), 21–31.

Okolo, C. (1992a). The effect of computer-assisted instruction format and initial attitude on the arithmetic facts proficiency and continuing motivation of students with learning disabilities. *Exceptionality, 3*, 195–211.

Okolo, C. (1992b). Reflections on "The effect of computer-assisted instruction format and initial attitude on the arithmetic facts proficiency and continuing motivation of students with learning disabilities." *Exceptionality, 3*, 255–258.

Olsen-Rando, R. A. (1994). Proposal for development of a computerized version of talking, feeling and doing game. *Computers in Human Services, 11*(1–2), 69–80.

Pegelow, C. H. (1992). Survey of pain management therapy provided for children with sickle cell disease. *Clinical Pediatrics, 31*, 211–214.

Phillips, W. R. (1991). Video game therapy. *New England Journal of Medicine, 325*, 1056–1057.

Porter, D. B. (1995). Computer games: Paradigms of opportunity. *Behavior Research Methods, Instruments, & Computers, 27*(2), 229–234.

Redd, W. H., Jacobsen, P. B., DieTrill, M, Dermatis, H., McEvoy, M., & Holland, J. C. (1987). Cognitive-attentional distraction in the control of conditioned nausea in pediatric cancer patients receiving chemotherapy. *Journal of Consulting and Clinical Psychology, 55*, 391–395.

Resnick, H. (1994a). Ben's Grille. *Computers in Human Services*, *11*(1/2), 203–211.

Resnick, H. (1994b). Electronic technology and rehabilitation: A computerised simulation game for youthful offenders. *Computers in Human Services*, *11*(1/2), 61–67.

Riddick, C. C., Spector, S. G., & Drogin, E. B. (1986). The effects of videogame play on the emotional states and affiliative behavior of nursing home residents. *Activities, Adaptation & Aging*, *8*(1), 95–107.

Ryan, E. B. (1994). Memory for goblins: A computer game for assessing and training working memory skill. *Computers in Human Services*, *11*(1–2), 213–217.

Salend, S., & Santora, D. (1985). Employing access to the computer as a reinforcer for secondary students. *Behavioral Disorders*, November 1985.

Samoilovich, S., Riccitelli, C., Scheil, A., & Siedi, A. (1992). Attitude of schizophrenics to computer videogames. *Psychopathology*, *25*, 117–119.

Schueren, B. (1986). Video games: An exploration of their potential as recreational activity programs in nursing homes. *Activities, Adaptation & Aging*, *8*(1), 49–58.

Sedlak, R. A., Doyle, M., & Schloss, P. (1982). Video games—a training and generalization demonstration with severely retarded adolescents. *Education and Training in Mental Retardation and Developmental Disabilities*, *17*(4), 332–336.

Sherer, M. (1994). The effect of computerized simulation games on the moral development of youth in distress. *Computers in Human Services*, *11*(1–2), 81–95.

Sietsema, J. M., Nelson, D. L., Mulder, R. M., Mervau-Scheidel, D., & White, B. E. (1993). The use of a game to promote arm reach in persons with traumatic brain industry. *American Journal of Occupational Therapy*, *47*, 19–24.

Skilbeck, C. (1991). Microcomputer-based cognitive rehabilitation. In A. Ager (Ed.), *Microcomputers and clinical psychology: Issues, applications and future developments* (pp. 95–118). Chichester: Wiley.

Spence, J. (1988). The use of computer arcade games in behavior management. *Maladjustment and Therapeutic Education*, *6*, 64–68.

Starn, J., & Paperny, D. M. (1990). Computer games to enhance adolescent sex education. *Journal of Maternal Child Nursing*, *15*(4), 250–253.

Strein, W., & Kochman, W. (1984). Effects of computer games on children's co-operative behavior. *Journal of Research and Development in Education*, *18*, 1.

Subrahmanyam, K., & Greenfield, P. (1994). Effect of video game practice on spatial skills in boys and girls. *Journal of Applied Developmental Psychology*, *15*, 13–32.

Szer, J. (1983). Video games as physiotherapy. *Medical Journal of Australia*, *1*, 401–402.

Thomas, D. L. (1994). Life choices: The program and its users. *Computers in Human Services*, *11*(1–2), 189–202.

Thomas, R., Cahill, J., & Santilli, L. (1997). Using an interactive computer game to increase skill and self-efficacy regarding safer sex negotiation: Field test results. *Health Education and Behavior*, *24*, 71–86.

Vasterling, J., Jenkins, R. A., Tope, D. M., & Burish, T. G. (1993). Cognitive distraction and relaxation training for the control of side effects due to cancer chemotherapy. *Journal of Behavioral Medicine*, *16*, 65–80.

Vilozni, D., Bar-Yishay, E., Shapira, Y., Meyer, S., & Godfrey, S. (1994). Computerized respiratory muscle training in children with Duchenne Muscular Dystrophy. *Neuromuscular Disorders*, *4*, 249–255.

Washburn, D. A., & Gulledge, J. P. (1995). Game-like tasks for comparative research: Leveling the playing field. *Behavior Research Methods, Instruments, & Computers*, *27*, 235–238.

Weisman, S. (1983). Computer games for the frail elderly. *The Gerontologist*, *23*(4), 361–363.

Weisman, S. (1994). Computer games for the frail elderly. *Computers in Human Services*, *11*(1/2), 229–234.

Wright, K. (2001). Winning brain waves: Can custom-made video games help kids with attention deficit disorder? *Discover*, *22*. http://www.discover.com/mar_01/featworks.html.

Part IV

Games as an Aesthetic Phenomenon

11

GAMES, THE NEW LIVELY ART

Henry Jenkins

Another important element is a belief that creators are artists. At the same time, however, it's necessary for us creators to be engineers, because of the skill required for the creations.
—Shigeru Miyamoto

Why can't these game wizards be satisfied with their ingenuity, their $7 billion (and rising) in sales, their capture of a huge chunk of youth around the world? Why must they claim that what they are doing is "art"?... Games can be fun and rewarding in many ways, but they can't transmit the emotional complexity that is the root of art.
—Jack Kroll

Let's imagine games as an art form. I know, I know—for many of us in contact with the so-called real arts, the notion sounds pretentious. It also makes developers who are former computer science majors edgy, because it challenges assumptions that games are founded upon technology. Still, it's a useful concept. It's especially useful when we start to think about the mediocre state of our profession, and about ways to elevate our aims, aspirations, and attitudes.
—Hal Barwood

Over the past three decades, computer and video games have progressed from the primitive two-paddles-and-a-ball *Pong* to the sophistication of *Final Fantasy*, a participatory story with cinema-quality graphics that unfolds over nearly a hundred hours of game play, or *Black and White*, an ambitious moral tale where the player's god-like choices between good and evil leave tangible marks on the landscape.[1] The computer game has been a killer app for the home PC, increasing consumer demand for vivid graphics, rapid processing, greater memory, and better sound. One could make the case that games have been to the PC what NASA was to the mainframe—the thing that pushes forward innovation and experimentation. The release of the Sony Playstation2, the Microsoft X-Box, and the Nintendo Game Cube signaled a dramatic increase in the resources available to game designers.

In anticipation of these new technological breakthroughs, people within and beyond the game industry began to focus attention on the creative potentials of this emerging medium. Mapping the aesthetics of game design, they argued, would not only enable them to consolidate decades of experimentation and innovation but would also push them forward toward greater artistic accomplishment. Game designers were being urged to think of themselves not simply as technicians producing corporate commodities but rather as artists mapping the dimensions and potentials of an emerging medium; this reorientation, it was hoped, would force them to ask harder questions in their design meetings and to aspire toward more depth and substance in the product they shipped. At the same time, the games industry confronted increased public and government scrutiny. If you parsed the rhetoric of the moral reformers, it was clear that their analogies to pollution or carcinogens revealed their base-level assumption that games were utterly without redeeming value, lacking any claim to meaningful content or artistic form. Seeing games as art, however, shifted the terms of the debate. Most of these discussions started from the premise that games were an emerging art form, one that had not yet realized its full potentials. Game designer Warren Specter, for example, told a *Joystick 101* interviewer, "We're just emerging from infancy. We're still making (and remaking!) *The Great Train Robbery* or *Birth of a Nation* or, to be really generous, maybe we're at the beginning of what might be called our talkies period. But as Al Jolson said in *The Jazz Singer*, "You ain't heard nothing yet!" (Squire). In this context, critical discussions sought to promote experimentation and diversification of game form, content, and audience, not to develop prescriptive norms.

These debates were staged at trade shows and academic conferences, in the pages of national magazines (such as *Newsweek* and *Technology Review*) and newspapers (such as *The New York Times*), and in online zones aimed at the gaming community (such as *Joystick101* and *Gamasutra*). Game designers, policy makers, art critics, fans, and academics all took a position on the question of whether computer games could be considered an art form and what kinds of aesthetic categories made sense for discussing them.

Games increasingly influence contemporary cinema, helping to define the frantic pace and model the multidirectional plotting of *Run Lola Run*, providing the role-playing metaphor for *Being John Malkovich*, encouraging a fascination with the slippery line between reality and digital illusions in *The Matrix*, inspiring the fascination with decipherment and puzzle solving at the heart of *Memento*, and even providing a new way of thinking about Shakespearean tragedy in *Titus*. Game interfaces and genres have increasingly surfaced as metaphors or design elements in avant garde installations. Matthew Barney, currently the darling of the New York art museum world, transformed the Guggenheim into a giant video game for one of his *Cremaster* films, having his protagonist battle their way up the ramps, boss by boss.[2] If critics, like Kroll, were reluctant to ascribe artistic merit to games, artists in other media seemed ready to absorb aspects of game aesthetics into their work. At high schools and colleges across the country, students discuss games with the same passions with which earlier generations debated the merits of the New American Cinema or the French New Wave. Media studies programs report that a growing number of their students want to be game designers rather than filmmakers.

At the same time, academics were finally embracing games as a topic worthy of serious examination—not simply as a social problem, a technological challenge, a cultural phenomenon, or an economic force within the entertainment industry, but also as an art form that demanded serious aesthetic evaluation.[3] Conferences on the art and culture of games were hosted at MIT, the University of Southern California, the University of Chicago, and the University of West England. As academics have confronted games, they have often found it easier to discuss them in social, economic, and cultural terms than through aesthetic categories. The thrust of media studies writing in recent years has been focused around the category of popular culture and been framed through ideological categories, rather than in terms of popular art, a concept that car-

ried far greater resonance in the first half of the twentieth century.

My goal here is not to argue against the values of applying concepts and categories from cultural studies to the analysis of games, but rather to make the case that something was lost when we abandoned a focus on popular aesthetics. The category of aesthetics has considerable power in our culture, helping to define not only cultural hierarchies but also social, economic, and political ones as well. The ability to dismiss certain forms of art as inherently without value paves the way for regulatory policies; the ability to characterize certain media forms as "cultural pollution" also impacts how the general public perceives those people who consume such material; and the ability to foreclose certain works from artistic consideration narrows the ambitions and devalues the accomplishments of people who work in those media. I will admit that discussing the art of video games conjures up comic images: tuxedo-clad and jewel-bedecked patrons admiring the latest *Streetfighter*, middle-aged academics pontificating on the impact of Cubism on *Tetris*, bleeps and zaps disrupting our silent contemplation at the Guggenheim. Such images tell us more about our contemporary notion of art—as arid and stuffy, as the property of an educated and economic elite, as cut off from everyday experience—than they tell us about games.

The Lively Criticism of Gilbert Seldes

What I want to do in the following pages is revisit one important effort to spark a debate about the aesthetic merits of popular culture—Gilbert Seldes' *Seven Lively Arts* (originally, published in 1924)—and suggest how reclaiming Seldes might contribute to our current debates about the artistic status of computer and video games. Adopting what was then a controversial position, Seldes argued that America's primary contributions to artistic expression had come through emerging forms of popular culture such as jazz, the Broadway musical, vaudeville, Hollywood cinema, the comic strip, and the vernacular humor column.[4] Although some of these arts have gained cultural respectability over the past seventy-five years (and others have died out entirely), each was disreputable when Seldes staked out his position. Seldes wanted his book to serve two purposes: first, he wanted to give readers fresh ways of thinking about and engaging with the contents of popular art; second, he wanted to use the vitality and innovation of these emerging forms to challenge the "monotonous stupidity," "the ridiculous postures," and "stained glass attitudes" of what we might now call middlebrow culture (Seldes, 1957, p. 193).

Readers then were skeptical of Seldes's claims about cinema for many of the same reasons that contemporary critics dismiss games—they were suspicious of cinema's commercial motivations and technological origins, concerned about Hollywood's appeals to violence and eroticism, and insistent that cinema had not yet produced works of lasting value. Seldes, on the other hand, argued that cinema's popularity demanded that we reassess its aesthetic qualities. Cinema and other popular arts were to be celebrated, Seldes insisted, because they were so deeply imbedded in everyday life, because they were democratic arts embraced by average citizens. Through streamlined styling and syncopated rhythms, they captured the vitality of contemporary urban experience. They took the very machinery of the industrial age, which many felt dehumanizing, and found within it the resources for expressing individual visions, for reasserting basic human needs, desires, and fantasies. And these new forms were still open to experimentation and discovery. They were, in Seldes's words, "lively arts."

My thinking about Seldes's value for reflecting on game aesthetics first took shape when I was sitting in the audience at the USC Interactive Frictions conference and heard two panels back to back, one composed of digital artists, the other of game designers. The first discussion was sluggish and pretentious; the artists were trying—without much success—to describe what the computer brought to their art, but they kept falling back on high modernist and early postmodernist categories. I knew exactly what they were going to say before they opened their mouths. On the other hand, the game designers were struggling to find words and concepts to express fresh discoveries about their media; they were working on the very edge of the technology, stretching it to its limits, and having to produce work that would fascinate an increasingly jaded marketplace. They were keeping on the top of their toes trying to learn not only from their own production practices but from each other. I scribbled on my notepad, "If art enlivens and commerce deadens, then how do we explain the immediacy of this panel and the dullness of the previous one?" I suddenly flashed on Seldes's characterization of the attitude that dominated the art institutions and criticism of the early twentieth century: "What is worthwhile must be dull. We suffer fools gladly if we can pretend they are mystics" (Seldes, 1957, p. 264).

Games represent a new lively art, one as appropriate for the digital age as those earlier media were for the machine age. They open up new aesthetic experiences and transform the computer screen into a realm of experimentation and innovation that is broadly accessible. And a public that has otherwise been unimpressed by much of what passes for digital art has embraced games. Much as the salon arts of the 1920s seemed sterile alongside the vitality and inventiveness of popular culture, contemporary efforts to create interactive narrative through modernist hypertext or avant garde installation art seem lifeless and pretentious alongside the creativity and exploration, the sense of fun and wonder, that game designers bring to their craft. As Hal Barwood explained to readers of *Game Developer* magazine in February 2002, "Art is what people accomplish when they don't quite know what to do, when the lines on the road map are faint, when the formula is vague, when the product of their labors is new and unique" (Barwood, 2002). Art exists, in other words, on the cutting edge, and that was where games had remained for most of their history. The game designers were creating works that sparked the imagination and made our hearts race, and they were doing so without the safety net that inherited modernist rhetoric provides for installation and hypertext artists. They can offer no simple, straightforward justification for what they are doing or why they doing it except by way of talking about "the fun factor," that is, the quality of the emotional experience they offer players.

Although his writing was impressionistic and evocative, rather than developing a systematic argument or framework, one can read *The Seven Lively Arts* as mapping an aesthetic of popular culture, one that is broadly enough defined to be useful for discussing a wide range of specific media and cultural practices, including many that did not exist at the time he wrote the book. Seldes drew a distinction between the "great arts," which seek to express universal and timeless values, and the "lively arts," which seek to give shape and form to immediate experiences and impressions. "Great" and "lively" arts differed "not in the degree of their intensity but in the degree of their intellect" (Seldes, 1957, p. 272). Seldes, in fact, often showed signs of admiring the broad strokes of the popular arts—where the needs for clarity and immediate recognition from a broadly defined audience allowed "no fuzzy edges, no blurred contours"—over the nuance and complexity of great art (p. 228). Seldes consistently values affect over intellect, immediate impact over long term consequences, the spontaneous impulse over the calculated effect. Seldes defined art through its affective force, its ability to provoke strong and immediate reactions. As popular artists master the basic building block of their media, they developed techniques enabling them to shape and intensify affective experience. Creativity, Seldes argued, was all bound up with our sense of play and with our demands to refresh our sensual apparatus and add new energy to our mental life, which was apt to become dulled through the routine cognition and perception of everyday life. He wrote, "We require, for nourishment, something fresh and transient."[5]

From the start, games were able to create strong emotional impressions—this accounts for the enormous staying power with consumers. An early game of *Pac-Man* or *Asteroids* could provoke strong feelings of tension or paranoia. The works of Shigeru Miyagawa represented imaginative landscapes, as idiosyncratic and witty in their way as the *Krazy Kat* comic strips or Mack Sennett comedies Seldes admired. Seldes wrote at a moment when cinema was starting to consolidate what it had learned over its first three decades of experimentation and produce works that mixed and matched affective elements to create new kinds of experiences. One could argue that recent games, such as *Deus X*, *Grand Theft Auto 3*, or *Shenmue*, represent a similar consolidation of earlier game genres, whereas games such as *The Sims*, *Majestic*, *Rez*, or *Black & White* are expanding the repertoire of game mechanics and by doing so, expanding the medium's potential audience.

The great arts and the lively arts shared a common enemy, the "bogus arts," the middlebrow arts, which sought to substitute "refinement of taste" for "refinement of technique," and in the process, cut themselves off from the culture around them (Seldes, 1957, p. 223). The popular arts, he warned, often promised more than they could deliver; their commercial imperative required that they leave us somewhat unsatisfied and thus eager to consume more, but in their straightforward appeal to emotion, they do not "corrupt." Middlebrow culture, however, often seduces us with fantasies of social and cultural betterment at the expense of novelty and innovation. Seldes wanted to deploy the shock value of contemporary popular culture to shake up the settled thinking of the art world, to force it to reconsider the relationship between art and everyday life.

At a time when the United States was emerging as a world leader, Seldes wanted to identify what he felt was a distinctively American voice. He protested, "Our life is energetic, varied, constantly changing; our art is imitative, anemic" (Seldes, 1957, p. 300). Contempo-

rary intellectuals, he felt, had accepted too narrow a conception of what counted as art, seeing America as a new country that had not yet won the approval of its old world counterparts. Their search for refinement constituted a "genteel corruption," a "thinning out of the blood," which cut them off from what was vital in the surrounding culture. European artists, he suggested, had often revitalized their work by returning to folk art traditions, but operating in a new country with few folk roots, American artists would need to find their vitality through a constant engagement with what was fresh and novel in popular culture. As Seldes explained, "For America, the classic and the folk arts are both imported goods.... But the circumstance that our popular arts are home-grown, without the prestige of Europe and of the past, had thrown upon them a shadow of vulgarity, as if they were the products of ignorance and intellectual bad manners" (p. 299).

Seldes wrote at a time when American dominance over popular culture and European dominance over high culture were taken for granted. The aesthetics of contemporary game design, however, operates in a global context. One would have to concede, for example, that our current game genres took shape as a conversation between Japanese and American industries (with plenty of input from consumers and creators elsewhere). Increasingly, American popular culture is responding to Asian influences with the rise in violence in mass market entertainment a property of heightened competition among Japan, India, Hong Kong, and Hollywood for access to international markets. Action elements surface not only in games, but also in film, television, and comics, because such elements are more readily translated across linguistic and national boundaries.

The need to appeal to a mass consumer, Seldes insisted, meant that popular artists could not give themselves over to morbid self-absorption. Creating works in media that were still taking shape, popular artists were not burdened with a heritage but had to constantly explore new directions and form new relationships with their publics. The lively arts look toward the future rather than the past. Similarly, game designers work in a commercially competitive environment and within an emerging medium. Thus, they must continually push and stretch formal boundaries in order to create novelty, while they also have to insure that their experimentation remains widely accessible to their desired audience. The context is dramatically different when one turns their attention to middlebrow art, which often wants to build on well-established traditions rather than rely on formal experimentation, or high art, which can engage in avant-garde experimentation accessible only to an educated elite.

Seldes wrote during an era of media in transition. The cinema was maturing as an expressive medium—making a move from mere spectacle toward character and consequence, from a "cinema of attractions" to a classical storytelling system.[6] A decade earlier, many intellectuals might have freely dismissed cinema as a parlor entertainment, whose primary content consisted of little more than chase scenes and pratfalls. A decade later, few would have doubted that cinema had earned its status as one of the most important contemporary arts. Seldes's respect for cinema's popular roots set him at odds with many contemporary critics who saw the refinement of narrative techniques as essential for the maturation of the medium. Cinema, Seldes argued, "was a toy and should have remained a toy—something for our delight" (Seldes, 1957, p. 288). For Seldes, cinema was not an art despite slapstick; it was an art because slapstick had helped us to realize that the fullest potentials of motion pictures lay in their ability to capture motion and express emotion. "Everything in slapstick was cinematographic," Seldes proclaimed, remaining deeply suspicious of filmmakers such as Thomas Ince or D. W. Griffith, who he feared had sought to impose literary and theatrical standards alien to cinema's core aesthetic impulses (p. 16). He explained, "The rightness of the spectacle film is implicit in its name: the screen is a place on which things can be seen and so long as a film depends on the eye it is right for the screen" (p. 18).

The maturing of the cinematic medium may well have been what enabled Seldes to recognize its artistic accomplishments. However, in aspiring toward cultural respectability, cinema ran a high risk of losing touch with its own primitive roots. Seldes sounded a warning that would seem familiar to many contemporary observers of video and computer games, suggesting that the cinema was confusing technological enhancement with aesthetic advancement, confusing the desire to reproduce reality for the desire to create an emotionally engaging experience. What had given filmgoers the "highest degree of pleasure," he argued, was "escaping actuality and entering into a created world, built on its own inherent logic, keeping time to its own rhythm—where we feel ourselves at once strangers and at home" (Seldes, 1957, p. 288).

Newsweek's Jack Kroll sparked heated debates in the gamer community when he argued that audiences will probably never be able to care as deeply about pixels on the computer screen as they care about characters in films: "Moviemakers don't have to simulate human beings; they are right there, to be recorded and orchestrated.... The top-heavy titillation of *Tomb Raider*'s Lara Croft falls flat next to the face of Sharon Stone.... Any player who's moved to tumescence by digibimbo Lara is in big trouble" (Kroll, 2000). Yet countless viewers cry when Bambi's mother dies, and World War II veterans can tell you they felt real lust for *Esquire*'s Vargas girls. We have learned to care as much about creatures of pigment as we care about images of real people. Why should pixels be different? If we haven't yet cared this deeply about game characters (a debatable proposition as the response to Kroll's article indicated), it is because the game design community has not yet found the right techniques for evoking such emotions, and not because there is an intrinsic problem in achieving emotional complexity in the medium itself. Kroll, like the respectable critics of early cinema whom Seldes battled, assumes that realism is necessary in order to achieve a high degree of emotional engagement. The art of games may not come from reproducing the world of the senses. As Steve Poole has written,

Whereas film—at least naturalistic, "live-action" film— is tied down to real spaces, the special virtue of video games is precisely their limitless plasticity. And only when that virtue is exploited more fully will video games become a truly unprecedented art—when their level of world-building competence is matched with a comparable level of pure invention. We want to be shocked by novelty. We want to lose ourselves in a space that is utterly different. We want environments that have never been seen, never been imagined before. (Poole, 2000)

As I visit game companies, I see some of the industry's best minds struggling with this challenge. As they search for answers, they will need to avoid the temptation to import solutions over wholesale from cinema and other more established arts. Independent game designers, such as Eric Zimmerman, have argued that games need to return to a garage aesthetic, stripping aside fancy graphics and elaborate cinematics, to reclaim the core elements that make games distinctive from other expressive media. Protesting that games are more than simply "mutant cinema," Zimmerman warns that "mistaken attempts to apply the skills and methods of Hollywood to the world of electronic gaming resulted in CD-ROMs bloated with full-motion video sequences and lacking meaningful gameplay."[7] Similarly, Seldes warned that long intertitles substituted literary for cinematic values, seeking to "explain everything except the lack of action," and resulting in scenes devoid of visual interest (Seldes, 1957, p. 286). The result was movies that no longer moved. Zimmerman and others warn that extended cinematics, often the favored means of adding narrative and character to games, cuts the player off from the action and thus sacrifices those elements of interactivity that make games games. One could argue that a similar tension is at the heart of the ongoing debates among game scholars between the so-called narratologists and the ludologists. The ludologists fear that the narratologist want to impose an alien aesthetic sensibility onto games and thus cut the medium off from its basic building blocks in game play. Games should not achieve aesthetic recognition by giving themselves over to "cinema envy," they warn, but should remain true to their roots. Seldes's concept of the lively arts may, in fact, offer us a way out of this binary, because he focuses primarily on the kinetic aspects of popular culture, aspects that can operate inside or outside a narrative frame. Poole arrives at a similar conclusion:

A beautifully designed video game invokes wonder as the fine arts do, only in a uniquely kinetic way. Because the video game must move, it cannot offer the lapidary balance of composition that we value in painting; on the other hand, because it can move, it is a way to experience architecture, and more than that to create it, in a way which photographs or drawings can never compete. If architecture is frozen music, then a video game is liquid architecture. (Poole, 2000, p. 226)

Memorable Moments

What Seldes offers us might be described as a theory of "memorable moments," a concept that surfaces often in discussions with game designers but only rarely in academic writing about the emerging medium. Writing about the German Expressionist film, *The Cabinet of Dr. Caligari*, Seldes praises not its plot but its lingering aftertaste: "I cannot think of half a dozen movies which have left so many clear images in my mind" (Seldes, 1957, p. 19). Or later in the book, he writes about the pleasures of finding peak experiences within otherwise banal works: "A moment comes when everything is exactly right, and you have an occurrence—it may be something exquisite or something unnameably gross; there is in it an ecstasy which sets it apart from everything else" (p. 186). Such peak experiences seem fully

within reach of contemporary game designers in a way that the development of complex causally integrated yet open-ended narratives or psychological rounded yet fully interactive characters are not. If games are going to become an art, right now, rather than in some distant future, when all of our technical challenges have been resolved, it may come from game designers who are struggling with the mechanics of motion and emotion, rather than those of story and character.

As game designers evaluate games on the basis of their emotional appeal, their criteria often emphasize moments of emotional intensity or visual spectacle—the big skies that can suddenly open before you when you ride your snow board in *SSX*, the huge shots in a hockey game when the puck goes much further than it could possibly do in real life, the pleasure of sending your car soaring off a cliff or smashing through pedestrians in *Grand Theft Auto 3*. Increasingly, games enable us to grab snapshots of such moments, to replay them and watch them unfold from multiple angles, and to share them with our friends, pushing them to see if they can match our exploits and duplicate accomplishments. Game companies encourage their staffs to think of their designs in terms of the images on boxes or in previews, the way that the demo is going to look on the trade show floor. Yet this may be to reduce the concept of memorable moments down to eye candy or spectacle, something that can be readily extracted from the play experience, something that can be communicated effectively in a still image. Other game designers would contest this understanding of the concept, arguing that memorable moments emerge when all of the elements of the medium come together to create a distinctive and compelling experience.

Often, in games, those memorable moments don't simply depend on spectacle. After all, spectacle refers to something that stops you dead in your tracks, forces you to stand and look. Game play becomes memorable when it creates the opposite effect—when it makes you want to move, when it convinces you that you really are in charge of what's happening in the game, when the computer seems to be totally responsive. Frequently, the memorable moment comes when the computer does something that follows logically from your actions, yet doesn't feel like it was prescribed and preprogrammed. As *Deus X* designer Warren Spector explains, "Great gameplay comes, I think, from our ability to drop players into compelling situations, provide clear goals for them, give them a variety of tools with which they can impact their environment and then get out of their way. . . . That has to be so much more compelling for players—thrilling even—than simply guessing the canned solution to a puzzle or pressing a mouse button faster than a computer opponent can react" (Squire, 2001).

Seldes was one of a number of early twentieth-century writers who sought to better understand the "mechanics of emotion" that shaped popular entertainment. The Italian futurist Flippo Marinetti saw within the variety theater "the crucible in which the elements of an emergent new sensibility are seething," describing it as an art that had "only one reason for existing and triumphing: incessantly to invent new elements of astonishment" (Marintetti, 1971). The Soviet film theorist Sergei Eisenstein developed a theory of "attractions," a term he saw as broad enough to encompass any device—whether formal, narrative, or thematic—that could solicit powerful emotions from a spectator, arguing that film and theater should seek their inspiration from the circus and the music hall (Eisenstein, 1974). Inspired in part by Pavlovian refloxology, they tried to document and master basic "surefire" stimuli that could provoke a predictable emotional response from the spectator and then to streamline their works, cutting out anything that would obscure or retard that affective impact. Eddie Cantor warned, "A comedian in vaudeville ... is like a salesman who has only fifteen minutes in which to make a sale. You go on stage knowing every moment counts. You've got to get your audience the instant you appear."[8] Theater critic Vadim Uraneff explained in 1923, "the [vaudeville] actor works with the idea of an immediate response from the audience: and with regard to its demands. By cutting out everything—every line, gesture, movement—to which the audience does not react and by improvising new things, he establishes unusual unity between the audience and himself" (Uraneff, 1923).

Game designers engage in a similar process as they seek to identify "what's not in the game," that is, to determine what elements would get in the way of the game mechanic or confuse the player. Game designers speak of "hooks" that will grab the consumers' attention and keep them playing, a concept that would have been familiar to vaudeville showman and circus barkers. Longtime game designers refer back to the challenges of developing games that played well in the arcades, which offered a compelling experience that could be staged in less than two minutes, and ramped up to an emotional high that would leave the player reaching for another quarter. Early console games also demanded economy, given the limited memory capacity of the early systems.[9] However, as consoles have developed greater capacity and thus enabled lengthier and more complex game experiences, some fear that game designers are adding too many features that get in the way of the core mechanics. The lengthy cut scenes of narrative exposition and character back-story, which academics praise for their aesthetic advancements, are often received with hostility by serious gamers because they slow down the play and result in a relatively passive experience. A great deal of effort goes into the first few minutes of game play, in particular, to insure that they offer a solid emotional payoff for the player rather than ending in frustration: an early moment of mastery or movement is to spark their appetite for bigger and better things to come.[10]

Play as Performance

Seldes and other early twentieth-century critics saw the emotional intensity of popular culture as emerging from the central performer, who "commanded" the spectator's attention through mastery of his or her craft. Seldes writes about the "daemonic" authority of Al Jolson: "He never saves up—for the next scene, or the next week, or the next show.... He flings into a comic song or three-minute impersonation so much energy, violence, so much of the totality of one human being, that you feel it would suffice for a hundred others" (Seldes, 1957, p. 175). His contemporary, Robert Lytell, described the characteristics of the best revue performers:

Human horsepower, size, electricity, energy, zingo.... These people have a fire in their belly which makes you sit up and listen whether you want to or not, which silences criticism until their act is over, and you can start thinking again.... They seize you and do pretty nearly anything they want with you and while it is going on, you sit with your mouth open and laugh and laugh again. (Lytell, 1925, p. 156)

Such comments reflected the performer-centered aesthetic of vaudeville and the Broadway revue. One might well understand the pleasures of gameplay according to performance criteria but as we do so, we need to understand it as a pas de deux between the designer and the player. As game designer David Perry explains, "A good game designer always knows what the players are thinking and is looking over their shoulders every step of the way" (Perry, 2000). The game designer's craft makes it possible for the players to feel as if they are in control of the situation at all times, even though their game play and emotional experience is significantly sculpted by the designer. It is a tricky balancing act, making the player aware of the challenges they confront, and at the same time, insuring they have the resources necessary to overcome those challenges. If the gameplay becomes transparently easy or impossibly hard, the players lose interest. The players need to feel they can run faster, shoot more accurately, jump further, and think smarter than in their everyday life and it is this expansion of the player's capacity that accounts for the emotional intensity of most games. I still recall the first time I grabbed the controls of *Sonic the Hedgehog*, got a good burst of speed, and started running as fast I could around the loop-the-loops, collecting gold coins, and sending all obstacles scattering. I am not an especially good game player, yet I felt at that moment totally invincible, and everything in the game's design—the layout of the space, the properties of the character, the selection of the soundtrack—contributed to giving me that sense of effortless control, that release from normal constraints.

As many observers have noted, we don't speak of controlling a cursor on the screen when we describe the experience of playing a game; we act as if we had unmediated access to the fictional space. We refer to our game characters in the first person and act as if their experiences were our own. James Newman has argued that we might understand the immediacy of game play not in terms of how convincing the representation of the character and the fictional world is but rather in terms of the character's "capacity" to respond to our impulses and desires. A relatively iconic, simplified character may produce an immediate emotional response; a relatively stylized world can nevertheless be immersive. Once we engage with the game, the character may become simply a vehicle we use to navigate the game world. As Newman explains:

Lara Croft is defined less by appearance than by the fact that "she" allows the player to jump distance x, while the ravine in front of us is larger than that, so we better start thinking of a new way round.... Characters are defined around game play-affecting characteristics. It doesn't matter that it's a burly guy—or even a guy— or perhaps even a human. That the hang glider can turn faster is a big deal; this affects the way the game plays. This affects my chances of getting a good score. (Newman, 2001)

A number of game designers have reminded me that Shigeru Miyamoto, whom many regard as the

medium's first real master, designs his games around verbs, that is, around the actions that the game enables players to perform. He wants each game to introduce a new kind of mission, making it possible for the consumer to do something that no other game has allowed before. A close examination of Miyamoto's games suggests, at the same time, that he designs a playing space that at once facilitates and thwarts our ability to carry out that action and thus creates a dramatic context in which these actions take aesthetic shape and narrative significance.

Many contemporary games seek to expand that sense of player mastery beyond the game space, encouraging players to dance to the rhythm, to shake maracas, twist turntables, beat drums, as the domestic space or the arcade space become performance spaces. The spectacular and performative dimensions of these games are summarized by this player's account of his experience of being a *Dance Dance Revolution* devotee:

The first song starts and finishes, and I did well. I hear a man ask me "How in the hell do you do that?" I just laugh and pick the next song, a harder one. I can hear people milling around behind me and I can see their reflection on screen. I hear whispers of "wow," and "damn!" The song ends. I hear a woman shout "Wooooo!" I turn and smile. Her and her friend blush and turn away.... Of course, Friday and Saturday nights are the big days to show off. Big crowds, loud crowds, and occasionally rowdy, mean crowds. These are the days for the big dogs, and competition is tough. Very hard songs are done, and feet fly like hummingbird wings.... But you take the good with the bad, and it's still fun when you get a good, loud reaction, and there's more than "boots" to it. There's that feeling when you finally beat that tough song, or when you help a buddy learn to play. It still boils down to just having fun, whether the crowd cheers or not. (Dikarika, 2002)

Here, the player gets to enjoy the same kind of experience that fueled Jolson or Cantor's performances— the pleasure of intense and immediate feedback from an engaged audience. At the same time, the game instructs the performance, giving the kinds of structured feedback that enables players to quickly master the necessary skills to impress friends and strangers alike.

The designers of *Frequency* and *Rez*, two recent music-making games, have sought to expand the sensory experience available to players. Both games start with the sensation of traveling at high speeds down winding tunnels of light and color. As we move through these stylized but representational spaces, our interactions help to shape the sound and rhythm of their techno-based soundtracks. As we get into the spirit of the game, we stop thinking simply in terms of our physical movements and become more in tune with the pulse of the music. Such games start to blur the line between play and performance, creating a context where even novice musicians can start to jam and advanced players can create complex and original musical compositions. *Frequency* designer Alex Rigopulos describes the trajectory of a player through his game:

When a gamer starts to play Frequency, he plays it using the gaming skills he already has: the ability to react to symbolic visual information with a precisely timed manual response.... What we noticed again and again in play testing was that there is a certain point at which novice players stop playing entirely with their eyes and start playing with their ears (or, rather, their "internal ears"): they start to feel the musical beat; then, as a stream of gems approaches, they look at the oncoming stream, "imagine" in their ears what that phrase will feel like or sound like rhythmically, and begin to "play the notes" (rather than "shoot the gems"). As soon as players cross this threshold, they begin excelling much more rapidly in the game.[11]

Rez's designers have suggested that they based their designs on the theories of abstract artist Wassily Kandinsky: "*Rez* is an experience, a fusion of light, vibration and sound completely immersed in synaesthesia" (BBC News, 2002). Here, the game controller vibrates and even develops the rhythm of a heart beat in response to the player's actions, creating yet another dimension to what is a complex multimedia experience.

These games build on the excess kinetic energy that has always surrounded gameplay. Watch children play games and they sway with the movement of the figures on the screen, bouncing with the action, totally engaged with the moment. One could argue that such responses reflect the degree of control they feel over what happens on the screen. We speak not just of controlling the characters but of "owning" the space of the game. It is even more interesting to observe the responses of people watching them play, because they also mimic the actions occurring on the screen, even though their actions have no consequences on the gameplay. Cinema has never achieved this same visceral impact, unless we are talking about the kind of fairground attractions that are designed to give us the sen-

sation of driving down a racetrack or riding a rollercoaster. People do sometimes feel like they are about to fall out of their seats when watching an IMAX image, for example. Games routinely create the same degree of immersion without having to totally surround us. Sometimes they achieve it by the use of first person perspective, but one can have the same sensation watching an early *Mario Brothers* game that relies totally on third-person point of view and a relatively iconographic landscape. One could argue that it is our knowledge of the interactive potential of games that produces these kinetic effects, yet I have observed similar kinds of behavior from people watching pre-recorded clips from games, suggesting that the response has as much to do with the visual presentation of the action as any real-time engagement with the controller.

Expressive Amplification

David Bordwell makes a similar argument about the Hong Kong action film:

We need no special training to grasp vigorous, well-structured movement. More exactly, it's not so much that we grasp it as that it grabs us; we respond kinesthetically, as when we tap our toes to music, or hammer the air at a basketball game. These films literally grip us; we can watch ourselves tense and relax, twitch or flinch. By arousing us through highly legible motion and staccato rhythms, and by intensifying their arousal through composition and editing and sound, the films seem to ask our bodies to recall elemental and universal events like striking, swinging, twisting, leaping, rolling. (Bordwell, 2000, p. 244)

By now, the aesthetics of the action movie and the video game are hopelessly intertwined: game aesthetics have clearly and directly shaped the emergence of the genres Bordwell discusses, and at the same time, game designers have consciously internalized lessons from filmmakers such as Akira Kurosowa, James Cameron, and John Woo. As game criticism emerges as a field, it will need to address not only the stories that games tell, or the kinds of play that they facilitate, but also the formal principles that shape our emotional responses to them. Bordwell's account of the Hong Kong martial arts movie, here, suggests two intertwined factors: first, the ways that commonly staged actions appeal to bodily memories, and second, the ways that various aesthetic devices can intensify and exaggerate the impact of the actions, making them both more legible and more intense than their real world counterpoints.

Bordwell describes this second process as "expressive amplification" (Bordwell, 2000, p. 232). Action film directors combine circus acrobatics and special effects with rapid-fire editing and stylized sound effects to amp up the intensity of a fight sequence. Similarly, game designers use movement, camera angle, sound effects, and other devices to exaggerate the impact of punches or to expand the flight of a skateboarder. The protagonists in *Jet Grind Radio* run riot through the streets of a futuristic Tokyo, sliding up and down ramps or along rails at high speeds, their in-line skates sending out a shower of sparks, the sounds of the cops' boots pounding right on their heels and the crackle of the police radio breathing down their necks. Here, we see "expressive amplification" at work. We take pleasure not simply in the outcome of the player's actions but the style with which they/we execute them.

Games and Silent Cinema

This brings us back to what Seldes had to say about the cinema. The police in *Jet Grind Radio* display the exaggerated dignity and one-track thinking we associate with the Keystone Cops, as they hurl themselves onto the protagonist and end up in a heap, face down on the asphalt. Silent cinema, Seldes argued, was an art of expressive movement. He valued the speed and dynamism of Griffith's last minute races to the rescue, the physical grace of Chaplin's pratfalls, and the ingenuity of Buster Keaton's engineering feats. He argued that each silent performer developed their own characteristic way of moving, their own posture, and their own rhythm, which defined them for the spectator the moment they appeared on the screen. Chaplin "created his own trajectory across the screen which was absolutely his own line of movement" (Seldes, 1957, p. 37). This distinctive way of moving occurred through stylization, reducing screen action to simple units of action, which could recur across a broad range of narrative situations. Moviegoers came to love the slight bounce in Chaplin's walk, the daintiness of his hands, his slightly bow-legged stance. James Agee would make a similar claim in his essay, "Comedy's Greatest Era," describing the unique personalities on screen as emerging from a rhetoric of comic clichés:

The man who could handle them properly combined several of the more difficult accomplishments of the acrobat, the dancer, the clown, and the mime. Some very gifted comedians, unforgettably Ben Turpin, had an immense vocabulary of these clichés and were in part so lovable because they were deeply conservative classicists

and never tried to break away from them. The still more gifted men, of course, simplified and invented, finding out new and much deeper uses for the idiom. They learned to show emotion through it, and comic psychology, more eloquently than most language has ever managed to, and they discovered beauties of comic motion which are hopelessly beyond the reach of words.[12] (Age, 1974, p. 439)

Games also depend upon an art of expressive movement, with characters defined through their distinctive ways of propelling themselves through space. Game designers have had to reduce character down to a limited range of preprogrammed expressions, movements, and gestures, but as they have done so, they have produced characters, such Mario and Luigi or Sonic, who are enormously evocative, who provoke strong emotional reactions.

The art of silent cinema was also an art of atmospheric design. To watch a silent masterpiece such as Fritz Lang's *Metropolis* is to be drawn into a world where meaning is carried by the placement of shadows, the movement of machinery, and the organization of space. If anything, game designers have pushed beyond cinema in terms of developing expressive and fantastic environments that convey a powerful sense of mood, provoke our curiosity and amusement, and motivate us to explore. The German expressionists had to construct the world's largest sound stage so that they could insure that every element in their shot was fully under their control. Game designers start with a blank screen: every element is there because they choose to put it there and so there is no excuse for elements that do not capture the imagination, shape our emotions, or convey meanings. Game designers are seeking inspiration from stage design, amusement park "imagineering," and postmodern architecture as they develop a better understanding of spatial design. Across a range of essays, I have made the case that games might best be discussed through a spatial aesthetic, one that sees the art of game design as a kind of narrative and affective architecture, as linked in important ways to the art of designing amusement park attractions (Jenkins, 2002). I have argued that games compensate their players for their loss of mobility across real world spaces, at a time when children enjoy diminished access to real world play spaces (Jenkins, 1998). With Kurt Squire, I have expanded that analysis to look more closely at the ways that a range of games create spaces that encourage our exploration and that are well-designed as staging grounds for conflicts (Squire & Jenkins, 2002).

Many of the most memorable moments in the silent films Seldes discussed centered on the struggles of characters against spatial features. Consider, for example, the extended sequence in *Safety Last*, where Harold Lloyd must climb the side of a building, floor by floor, confronting a series of obstacles, and ends up hanging from the hands of a clock face. To be sure, some of the sequence's fascination has to do with the photographic basis of cinema—the fact that Lloyd is actually hanging several stories off the ground (a stunt rendered all the more remarkable by the fact that Lloyd is missing a few fingers from one of his hands). Yet the scene also depends on a challenge-mastery-complication structure remarkably similar to that found in contemporary games: the higher Lloyd climbs the more intense the risk and the more likely he is to fall. Will future generations look back on *Tomb Raider's* Lara Croft doing battle with a pack of snarling wolves as the twenty-first-century equivalent of Lillian Gish making her way across the ice floes in *Way Down East*?

In making these analogies, I am not necessarily advocating that games should become more cinematic, any more than Seldes felt cinema should become more theatrical or literary. Game designers should study a wide range of different arts, searching not only for what they have done best but also for what they have failed to achieve, for those "roads not taken" that might be more fully realized within a game aesthetic. Game designers will need to experiment with the broadest possible range of approaches and styles, breaking with the still somewhat limited conventions of the existing game genres in some cases and deepening our appreciation of their potentials in others. In the end, games may not take the same path as cinema. Game designers will almost certainly develop their own aesthetic principles as they confront the challenge of balancing our competing desires for storytelling and interactivity. As Spector explains: "The art in gaming lies in the tension between the elements we put in our game worlds and what players choose to do with those elements. The developers who get that—the ones who aren't just making expensive, sophisticated pick-a-path books or movies where you get to determine what the next shot is—are the ones who will expand the boundaries of this new art form" (Squire & Jenkins, 2002).

It remains to be seen whether games can provide players the freedom they want and still provide an emotionally satisfying and thematically meaningful shape to the experience. Some of the best games—*Snood* and *Tetris* come to mind—have nothing to do with storytelling. For all we know, the future art of games may look more like architecture or dance than cinema.

Mode of Production

If we are to see games accepted as a contemporary art form, game designers are going to have to stop using "market pressures" as an excuse for their lack of experimentation. True, game designers need to ship product, and that can place serious limitations on how much innovation can occur within a single game. Yet it is worth remembering that all art occurs within an economic context. The Hollywood filmmakers of the 1920s and 1930s often produced five to seven feature films per year, but somewhere in that rush to the marketplace, they nevertheless came more fully to realize the potentials of their medium and developed what has withstood the test of time. Seldes describes popular art in terms of a careful balance between convention and invention: convention insures accessibility, invention novelty. What keeps the lively arts lively is that they are the site of consistent experimentation and innovation. No sooner are genre conventions mapped than popular artists start to twist and turn them to yield new effects. The constant push for emotional immediacy demands a constant refinement of the art itself, keeping creators on their toes and forcing them to acknowledge audience response into their creative decision making.

Seldes worried whether the conditions that had led to an enormous flowering of popular arts in the early twentieth century could be sustained in the face of increasingly industrialized modes of production. He blamed the studio system for much of what was wrong with contemporary cinema, yet he ended the book with a prediction that the costs of film production are likely to decrease steadily as the core technology of film production becomes standardized, thus returning filmmaking to its artisan roots. He predicts, "The first cheap film will startle you; but the film will grow less and less expensive. Presently it will be within the reach of artists.... The artists will give back to the screen the thing you have debauched—imagination" (Seldes, 1957, p. 289). Several decades later, in his book, *The Great Public*, Seldes would be even more emphatic that the rise of corporate media had strangled the aesthetic experimentation and personal expression that had enabled these lively arts to exist in the first place (Seldes, 1950). With the coming of sound, the costs of film production had increased rather than decreased, further consolidating the major studios' control over the filmmaking process, and thus delaying by several decades the rise of independent cinema he had predicted.

What does this suggest about the future of innovation in game design? For starters, the basic apparatus of the camera and the projector were standardized by the turn of the century, enabling early filmmakers to focus on the expressive potential of the medium rather than continuing to have to relearn the basic technology. Game designers, on the other hand, have confronted dramatic shifts in their basic tools and resources on average every eighteen months since the emergence of their medium. This constant need to respond to a shifting technological infrastructure has shifted attention onto mastering tools that could otherwise have been devoted to exploring the properties and potentials of the medium. Second, despite a pretty rigorous patents war, the early history of filmmaking was marked by relatively low barriers of entry into the marketplace. Although many film histories still focus on a small number of key innovators, we now know that the basic language of cinema emerged through widespread experimentation among filmmakers scattered across the country and around the world. The early history of computer games, by contrast, was dominated by a relatively small number of game platforms, with all games having to pass through this corporate oversight before they could reach the market. The proliferation of authoring tools and open-source game engines have helped to lower barriers of entry into the game marketplace, paving the way for more independent and smaller game companies. In such a context, those emerging companies have often been forced to innovate in order to differentiate their product from what was already on the market. The rise of the girls' game movement, for example, can be explained in terms of female-run start-ups seeking to expand the game market in order to create a niche for their product in the face of competition with larger corporations.

At the same time as these new delivery technologies have loosened the hold of the platform manufacturers over game content, the cost of game development for those platforms has dramatically increased. We have seen rising technical standards that make it difficult for garage game designers to compete. Some have worried that the result will be an increased focus on blockbuster games with surefire market potential and the constant upgrading of popular franchises. What would contemporary cinema look like if it supported a succession of summer popcorn movies but could not support lower budget and independent films? The situation is not totally hopeless. The sheer size of some of the major game publishers has encouraged them to diversify game design and content. A company such as Electronic Arts, for example, draws on profits from its cash cow sports games to sustain a variety of smaller boutique companies, such as Maxis or Bullfrog, which are producing some of the most original and genre-breaking content.

The Value of Criticism

How can we insure the continued creative evolution of games? What will games look like as a mature art form, given the extraordinary shifts it has undergone over the past few decades? What modes of production or forms of authorship will insure the diversification necessary to expand the core gaming market to reach a broader public? Seldes was quite clear that sustained and rigorous criticism of the lively arts was the key to their long-term development. Such criticism must start from a sympathetic position, one that takes the popular arts on their own terms, one that respects the defining properties of specific media and genres. This criticism offers a measure of success quite independent from, but every bit as important as, the results of the box office. As he explains, "The box office is gross; it detects no errors, nor does it sufficiently encourage improvement" (Seldes, 1957, p. 303). Criticism encourages experimentation and innovation; commercial pressures insure accessibility. The lively arts grow through a careful balancing between the two.

The nature and value of these aesthetic experiments warrant close and passionate engagement not only within the games industry or academia, but also by the press and around the dinner table. Even Kroll's grumpy dismissal of games has sparked heated discussion and forced designers to refine their own grasp of the medium's distinctive features. Imagine what a more robust form of criticism could contribute. We need critics who know and care about games the way Pauline Kael knew movies. We need critics who write about them with that same degree of wit, wisdom, and passion. Early film critics played vital functions in documenting innovations and speculating about their potential. As a new medium, computer games demand this same kind of close critical engagement. We have not had time to codify what experienced game designers know, and we have certainly not yet established a canon of great works that might serve as exemplars. There have been real creative accomplishments across the first three decades of game design, but we haven't really sorted out what they are and why they matter.

The problem with many contemporary games isn't that they are violent but that so many of them are banal, formulaic, and predictable. Thoughtful criticism can marshal support for innovation and experimentation in the industry, much as good film criticism helps focus attention on neglected independent films. At the present time, game critics represent a conservative force on aesthetic innovation, with most reviews organized around pre-existing genre preferences. They are also mostly organized around technical elements as opposed to the game's emotional impact or its aesthetic statement. It is hard, in many cases, for truly innovative games to get the attention of consumers, though the success of products such as *The Sims* suggest it is certainly not impossible.

Thoughtful criticism could even contribute to our debates about violence. Rather than bemoaning "meaningless violence," we should explore ways that games could not simply stage or simulate violence but offer us new ways to understand the place of violence within our culture. Moreover, game criticism may provide a means of holding the game industry more accountable for its choices. In the wake of the Columbine shootings, game designers are struggling with their ethical responsibilities as never before, searching for ways of appealing to empowerment fantasies that don't require exploding heads and gushing organs. A serious public discussion of this medium might constructively influence these debates, helping identify and evaluate alternatives as they emerge.

As Seldes grew older, his initial enthusiasm for the "daemonic" force of popular art gave rise to growing concerns that it could be used negatively to shape public opinion and he became a key supporter of Frederic Wertham's campaign to regulate comic books (Seldes, 1950). Seldes's career trajectory—from defender of *Krazy Kat* to persecutor of E.C. horror comics—suggests the ambivalence at the heart of his celebration of the lively arts. We should recognize that ambivalence within our own response to games as an emerging medium and use our criticism to debate the merits of different approaches to representing violence in games (Cain & Jenkins, 2002). The goal should be the creation of a context that supports more thoughtful game content rather than the promotion of censorship.

As the art of games matures, progress will be driven by the most creative and forward thinking minds in the industry, those who know that games can be more than they have been, those who recognize the potential of reaching a broader public, of having a greater cultural impact, of generating more diverse and ethically responsible content, and of creating richer and more emotionally engaging content. But without the support of an informed public and the perspective of thoughtful critics, game developers may never realize that potential.

Notes

1. The core argument in this chapter initially took shape as remarks presented at the Video and Computer Games Come of Age conference, jointly sponsored by the MIT Comparative Media Studies Program and the Interactive Digital Software Association. It was presented as a talk at various venues, including the Game Developers Conference, The Electronic Entertainment Exposition, Queensland Institute of Technology, and the University of Western England-Bristol. It was expanded and published as "Art form for the Digital Age," in *Technology Review*, September-October 2000, and subsequently reprinted in an abbreviated form in the *New York Times* Arts and Entertainment Section. I am grateful for the feedback it has received in these various venues. I am especially thankful to advice on this current revision from Kurt Squire, Alex Chisholm, Philip Tan Boon, Eric Zimmerman, and Kevin Johnson, as well as the insights of the larger Games to Teach team and the great variety of people in the games industry who have volunteered their time to help us with our efforts.

2. For more on Matthew Barney and his relationship to the aesthetics of popular culture, see Henry Jenkins, "*Monstrous Beauty and the mutant aesthetic: Rethinking Matthew Barney's Relationship to the Horror Genre,*" http://web.mit.edu/21fms/www/faculty/henry3/horror.html.

3. For example, see Wardrip-Fruin & Harrigan (in press), King & Bain (2002), and *Game Studies*.

4. For a useful overview of Seldes's contributions to American arts and letters, see Kammen 1996. Note that although he borrowed the concept of the Seven Arts from the classical tradition, the book remains ambiguous about how to break down the topics he discusses into seven distinct traditions. What one takes from Seldes is less a taxonomy of popular arts than a way of understanding the relationship of popular, middlebrow, and high art.

5. Seldes's arguments about sensory restoration need to be understood in the context of larger discourses about sensation and expression at the turn of the century. For an overview of those discussions, see Singer 2001 and Jenkins 1992.

6. These shifts have attracted considerable scholarly attention within film studies circles. For a useful overview of these historical traditions, see Elsaesser & Barker 1990.

7. See Lantz & Zimmerman 1999. Also, see Zimmerman 2002: "Games suffer from cinema envy. What passes for 'realism' in games is an awkward and unimaginative use of 3D computer graphics. It's time for game developers to stop trying to replicate the pleasures of film. Games need to find their own forms of expression, capitalizing on their unique properties as dynamic, participatory systems."

8. See Eddie Cantor in Mullet, 1924.

9. For a useful discussion of the aesthetics of early video games, see Burnham & Baer 2001.

10. I am indebted to the participants of the Comparative Media Studies–Electronic Arts Creative Leaders workshop series for these insights into the game design process.

11. Alex Rigopulos, email correspondence with the author, March 1, 2002.

12. See more on Agee's theory of comic performance in Jenkins & Brunovska Karnick 1995.

References

Agee, J. (1974). Comedy's greatest era. In G. Mast & M. Cohen (Eds.), *Film theory and criticism*. New York: Oxford University Press.

Barwood, H. (2002). The envelope please. Game Developer, February.

BBC News. (2002). Gamers set for sensory overload. http://news.bbc.co.uk/hi/english/sci/tech/newsid _1846000/1846561.stm.

Bordwell, D. (2000). *Planet Hong Kong: Popular cinema and the art of entertainment*. Cambridge, MA: Harvard University Press.

Burnham, V., & Baer, R. H. (2001). *Supercade*. Cambridge, MA: MIT Press.

Cain, J., & Jenkins, H. (2002). I'm gonna git medieval on your ass: A conversation about violence and culture. In H. Postner (Ed.), *Culture of violence*. Amherst: University of Massachusetts Press.

Dikarika. Tales from a DDR addict. Joystick 101. http://www.joystick101.org/?op=displaystory&sid= 2002/1/12/133339/317.

Eisenstein, S. (1974). Montage of attraction. *Drama Review*, March.

Elsaesser, T., & Barker, A. (1990). *Early cinema: Space-frame-narrative*. London: BFI.

Game Studies. http://www.gamestudies.org/.

Jenkins, H. (1992). *What made pistachio nuts?: Early sound comedy and the vaudeville aesthetic*. New York: Columbia University Press.

Jenkins, H. (2002). Game design as narrative architecture. In N. Wardrip-Fruin & P. Harrigan (Eds.), *First person*. Cambridge, MA: MIT Press.

Jenkins, H. (1998). Complete freedom of movement: Video games as gendered play spaces. In J. Cassell & H. Jenkins (Eds.), *From Barbie to Mortal Kombat: Gender and computer games*. Cambridge, MA: MIT Press.

Jenkins, H., & Brunovska Karnick, K. (1995). Acting funny. In H. Jenkins & K. Brunovska Karnick (Eds.), *Classical hollywood comedy*. New York: Routledge/AFI.

Kammen, M. G. (1996). *The lively arts: Gilbert Seldes and the transformation of cultural criticism in the United States*. Oxford: Oxford University Press.

King, L., & Bain, C. (2002). *Game on*. London: Barbican.

Kroll, J. (2000). Emotional engines? I don't think so. *Newsweek*, February 27.

Lantz, F., & Zimmerman, E. (1999). Checkmate: Rules, play and culture. Merge. http://www .ericzimmerman.com/acastuff/checkmate.html.

Lytell, R. (1925). Vaudeville old and young. New Republic, July 1, p. 156.

Marintetti, F. T. (1971). The variety theatre. In M. Kirby (Ed.), *Futuristic performance*. New York: Dutton. (pp. 179–186).

Miyamoto, S. (2000). In M. Saltzman (Ed.), *Game design secrets of the sages* (2nd Ed.). Indianapolis: Macmillan.

Mullet, M. B. (1924). We all like the medicine "Doctor" Eddie Cantor gives. American Magazine, July, pp. 34ff.

Newman, J. (2001). On being a tetraminoe: Mapping the contours of the videogame character. Delivered at the International Game Cultures Conference. Bristol, England.

Perry, D. (2000). In M. Saltzman (Ed.), *Game design secrets of the sages* (2nd Ed.). Indianapolis: Macmillan.

Poole, S. (2000). *Trigger happy: Videogames and the entertainment revolution*. New York: Arcade Publishing.

Saltzman, M. (2000). *Game design secrets of the sages* (2^d Ed.). Indianapolis: Macmillan.

Seldes, G. (1950). *The great audience*. New York: Viking.

Seldes, G. (1957). *The seven lively arts*. New York: Sagmore Press.

Singer, B. (2001). *Melodrama and modernity: Early sensational cinema and its contexts*. New York: Columbia University Press.

Squire, K. Educating game designers: An interview with Warren Spector. http://www.joystick101.org/?op=displaystory&sid=2001/5/23/155255/302.

Squire, K., & Jenkins, H. (2002). The art of contested spaces. In L. King & C. Bain (Eds.), *Game on*, London: Barbican.

Uraneff, V. (1923). Commedia dell' arte and American vaudeville. *Theatre Arts*, October, p. 326.

Wardrip-Fruin, N., & Harrigan, P. (2004). *First person*. Cambridge, MA: MIT Press.

Zimmerman, E. (2002). Do independent games exist? In L. King & C. Bain (Eds.), *Game on*. London: Barbican.

Genres

12

GENRE AND THE VIDEO GAME

Mark J. P. Wolf

The idea of categorization by genre, and the notion that there are certain conventions present in each genre, has been used in the studies of literature and film and has proven to be a useful way of looking at both. The idea of genre has not been without difficulties, such as defining what exactly constitutes a genre (or a subgenre), overlaps between genres and hybrids of them, works occurring in multiple genres simultaneously (and thus what the criteria are for genre membership), the role of the audience's experience in determining genre, and the fact that the boundaries of genres and even genres themselves are always in flux as long as new works are being produced.[1]

And genre study differs from one medium to the next. Thomas Schatz, in his book *Hollywood genres*, outlines some distinctions between literary and film genre studies. He also notes that genre study in the past often focused on subject matter and neglected the role of the audience. He writes,

Genre study may be more "productive" if we complement the narrow critical focus of traditional genre analysis with a broader sociocultural perspective. Thus, we may consider a genre film not only as some filmmaker's artistic expression, but further as the cooperation between artists and audience in celebrating their collective values and ideals. In fact, many qualities traditionally viewed as artistic shortcomings—the psychologically static hero, for instance, or the predictability of the plot—assume a significantly different value when examined as components of a genre's ritualistic narrative system. (Schatz, 1981, p. 15)

One could easily substitute "video game" for "film" in the above quote; video games' heroes are certainly more static than film ones, and plots are often even more predictable. And most of all, the interactive experience of playing a video game is even more of a "cooperation between artists and audiences," who go

beyond "celebrating collective values" by applying those values to the activity found in game play itself.

Video game genre study differs markedly from literary or film genre study due to the direct and active (in a physical as well as mental sense) participation of the audience, through the surrogate player-character who acts within the game's diegetic world (insofar as it has one), taking part in the central conflict of the game's narrative. In regard to narrative, Schatz describes the general plot structure of the genre film as:

establishment *(via various narrative and iconographic cues) of the generic community with its inherent dramatic conflicts;*
animation *of those conflicts through the actions and attitudes of the genre's constellation of characters;*
intensification *of the conflict by means of conventional situations and dramatic confrontations until the conflict reaches crisis proportions;*
resolution *of the crisis in a fashion which eliminates the physical and/or ideological threat and thereby celebrates the (temporarily) well-ordered community.* (p. 30)

Apart from the fact the video games often do not have happy endings (games usually end with a player-character's death), Schatz's four terms describe the action of most video games. If a film genre represents a "range of experience" for the audience as Schatz argues, video games fit the description even more closely. In some ways, player participation is arguably the central determinant in describing and classifying video games, moreso even than iconography. From the earliest times when video games were classified into genres, first by the companies that made and marketed them and game reviewers, and later in works such as Chris Crawford's 1982 *The art of computer game design*, the player's experience and the activities required for gameplay (commonly referred to as "interactivity") have largely provided the basis for video game genre delineation.

Iconography versus Interactivity

In his essay "The idea of genre in the American cinema," Ed Buscombe lists three areas in which genre elements may appear in film: iconography, structure and theme (1970, pp. 33–45). Although iconography and theme may be applicable to narrative-based video games, other games such as *Tetris* and *Ataxx* are abstract to the point where little or no narrative exists, and some games, such as *Video Pinball* and *Scrabble* are patterned after relatively nonnarrative activities, and do not contain much in the way of diegetic worlds populated by characters. Although the ideas of iconography and theme may be appropriate tools for analyzing Hollywood films as well as many video games, another area, interactivity, is an essential part of every game's structure and a more appropriate way of examining and defining video game genres.

Just as different forms of dance (foxtrot, waltz, ballet, jazz) are defined by how the dancers move rather than how they look, an examination of the variety and range of video games reveals the inadequacy of classification by iconography of even narrative-based games. Although some video games can be classified in a manner similar to that of films (we might say that *Outlaw* is a western, *Space Invaders* science fiction, and *Combat* a war game), classification by iconography ignores the fundamental differences and similarities that are to be found in the player's experience of the game. *Outlaw* and *Combat*, both early games for the Atari 2600, are very similar in that both simply feature player-characters maneuvering and shooting at each other in a field of obstacles on a single, bounded screen of graphics, with cowboys in one game and tanks in the other. In a similar vein, Activision's *Chopper Command* for the Atari 2600 is essentially a version of *Defender* with helicopters replacing the spaceships. Conversely, an iconographic analysis of *Space Invaders*, *Spaceward Ho!*, *Defender*, and *Star Wars*, as well as many other games, would consider them all "science fiction," even though they vary widely in player experience. As narrative games grow more complex and cinematic, we will be able to apply iconographic and thematic generic classifications from film more usefully, but interactivity will always be an important factor in the way we experience the games.

Genres based on interactivity also avoid some of the problems found in literary and film genres. In "Genre and critical methodology," Andrew Tudor points out that in relying on theme for the determination of genre, one is confronted with the difficulties in isolating a film's (or rather, film author's) intentions (Tudor, 1976). In a video game, there is almost always a definite objective that the player strives to complete (or find and complete, as in the case of *Myst*), and in doing so very specific interactions are used. Thus the intention, of the player-character, at least, is often clear and can be analyzed as a part of the game. The game's objective is a motivational force for the player, and this, combined with the various forms of interactivity present in the game, are useful places to start in building a set of video game genres. The object of the game can be multiple or divided into steps, placing the game in more than one genre, just as a film's theme and iconography can place a film in multiple genres (the film *Blade Runner*, for example, fits both science fiction and hard-boiled detective genres). The main objective in *Pac-Man* by which a player gains points and advances levels, for example, is the eating of the yellow dots. In order to do so successfully, the player-character must avoid the pursuing ghosts, and also navigate a maze. Thus although *Pac-Man* may be primarily classified (according to the terms below) as a "Collecting" game, we may also classify it as an "Escape" or "Maze" game, albeit secondarily. By beginning with the interaction required by the game's primary objective, we can start to divide the wide variety of video games into a series of interactive genres.

Interactive Genres for Classifying Video Games

The following list of genres based on interactivity can be used in conjunction with the existing taxonomy of iconographically or thematically based genres (like those of film) when attempting to categorize video games. The genres below take into consideration the dominant characteristics of the interactive experience and the games' goals and objectives, and the nature of the game's player-character and player controls. Also, certain genres listed here (Diagnostic, Demo, Educational, Puzzle, Simulation, and Utility) contain programs that are arguably not "games," but because they appear as cartridges or discs in a form similar to game cartridges and discs (and are treated as such by many game collectors), and because they sometimes contain game-like elements (such as *Mario Teaches Typing*), I have included them here for the sake of completeness. As genres grow and expand, they inevitably begin to break up into a series of subgenres (for example, the Shooting genre could include subgenres such as the first-person shooter, side-scrolling shooter, vertical shooter, and so on). A list of all the subgenres contained in each genre, however, is beyond the scope of this chapter, and would more than double its length.

In the culture surrounding the video game, certain generic terms are already established and in use among players, and the proposed list of terms below reflects these terms and distinctions. Some of these genres overlap commonly used genres of moving imagery (such as Adaptation, Adventure, Chase), whereas others, such as Escape, Maze, or Shooting, are specific to video games and reflect the interactive nature of the medium. These genre terms regard the nature of interactivity in the game itself rather than ask whether the game is single-player, multiple-player, or designed to be playable over a network. Due to the different types of action and objectives that can occur in a single game, games can often be cross-listed in two or more genres. Also, some games, such as *M*A*S*H* or *Rebel Assault*, feature different sequences or scenarios each of which can be categorized into different genres. Video games used as examples here include arcade video games, home video games, home computer games, and in a few cases, networked games. The format of this list is patterned after the Library of Congress Moving Imagery Genre-Form Guide compiled by Brian Taves (chair), Judi Hoffman, and Karen Lund, whose work was the inspiration and model for this list. I decided to use their list as a model not only because it was rigorous enough to be accepted and used at the Library of Congress, but also due to the way it attempts to articulate the genres it describes by examining the differences that demarcate individual genres relative to one another, seeking to divide the field of moving imagery forms in such a way so as to be as inclusive and exhaustive as possible, rather than setting up finite and absolute criteria for genre membership. Thus the following genres below tend toward inclusion, with some genres (i.e., Demo, Diagnostic, Utility) that are arguably not "games," as noted above.

Genres covered in this list are: Abstract, Adaptation, Adventure, Artificial Life, Board Games, Capturing, Card Games, Catching, Chase, Collecting, Combat, Demo, Diagnostic, Dodging, Driving, Educational, Escape, Fighting, Flying, Gambling, Interactive Movie, Management Simulation, Maze, Obstacle Course, Pencil-and-Paper Games, Pinball, Platform, Programming Games, Puzzle, Quiz, Racing, Rhythm and Dance, Role-Playing, Shooting, Simulation, Sports, Strategy, Table-Top Games, Target, Text Adventure, Training Simulation, and Utility.

Abstract

Abstract games have nonrepresentational graphics and often involve an objective that is not oriented or organized as a narrative. Often the objective involves construction or visiting or filling every part of the screen (as in *Tetris*, *Qix*, *Pipe Dream*, or *Q*bert*), or destruction or emptying of the screen (as in *Breakout* or *Pac-Man*). Characters appearing in abstract games may be anthropomorphic in design (such as Q*bert), but usually do not attempt to represent real world animals or people or their behaviors. Abstraction is, of course, a matter of degree, though it is usually possible to discern whether or not the game was intended to be deliberately representational. For example, despite their simple, blocky graphics, early Atari 2600 games such as *Basketball* or *Street Racer* attempt to represent people and race cars, which is reflected not only in their design but in their interaction within the game. Nor should the term be used for games that are adaptations of games existing in different media, such as *Checkers* or *Othello*, which are adaptations and thus representations of games from other media.

Examples include *Arkanoid*; *Amidar* (with Collecting); *Ataxx*; *Block Out* (with Puzzle); *Breakout*; *Marble Madness*; *Pac-Man* (with Collecting, Escape, and Maze); *Pipe Dream*; *Q*bert*; *Qix* (with Collecting); *Super Breakout*; *Tempest* (with Shooting); *Tetris* (with Puzzle).

Adaptation

These games are based on activities adapted from another medium or gaming activity, such as sports, table-top games, board games, card games, or games whose action closely follows a narrative from a work existing in another medium, such as a book, short story, comic book, graphic novel, or play. This involves such questions as how the original work is changed to allow for interactivity and the completion of an objective, or in the case of adapted games, how the original activity changes as a result of being adapted. This term should not be used for games that use the same characters as existing works in another medium but make no attempt to follow (even loosely) plots or imitate activities found in those works. Home video games and computer games may also be adaptations of arcade video games, in which case they are usually reduced in graphic detail, complexity, or speed when compared with the original. In a few cases, arcade games, such as *Computer Space* (1971), are adaptations of mainframe computer games. This term should only be applied to Simulation games when they are adapted from games or gaming activities in other media.

See also Sports, Table-Top Games, Board Games, Card Games, Pencil-and-Paper Games, and Simulation.

Examples include, adapted from card games: *Casino, Eric's Ultimate Solitaire, Ken Uston Blackjack/Poker*. Adapted from cartoons: *Spy vs. Spy, The Simpsons*. Adapted from comic books: *Spiderman, X-Men, Teenage Mutant Ninja Turtles*. Adapted from film: *Tron, Star Wars, Krull, Muppet Treasure Island*. Adapted from pencil-and-paper games: *Hangman, Tic-Tac-Toe*. Adapted from sports: *American Football, Atari Baseball, Hot Shots Tennis*. Adapted from table-top games: *Pong, Sure Shot Pool, Virtual Pool*. Adapted from television game shows: *Family Feud, Jeopardy, Joker's Wild, Password, The Price is Right, Tic-Tac-Dough, $25,000 Pyramid, Wheel of Fortune*.

Adventure

Adventure games are set in a "world" usually made up of multiple, connected rooms or screens, involving an objective that is more complex than simply catching, shooting, capturing, or escaping, although completion of the objective may involve several or all of these. Objectives usually must be completed in several steps, for example, finding keys and unlocking doors to other areas to retrieve objects needed elsewhere in the game. Characters are usually able to carry objects, such as weapons, keys, tools, and so on. Settings often evoke a particular historical time period and place, such as the middle ages or Arthurian England, or are thematically related to content-based genres such as Science Fiction, Fantasy, or Espionage. This term should not be used for games in which screens are only encountered in one-way linear fashion, such as the "levels" in *Donkey Kong*, or for games such as *Pitfall!* that are essentially limited to running, jumping, and avoiding dangers (see Obstacle Course). Nor should the term be used to refer to games such as *Dragon's Lair, Gadget*, or *Star Trek: Borg*, which do not allow a player to wander and explore its world freely, but strictly limit outcomes and possible narrative paths to a series of video sequences and linear progression through a predetermined narrative (see Interactive Movies).

For adventure games that are primarily text-based, see Text Adventure. For related games similar in theme to adventure games, see also Obstacle Course and Interactive Movies.

Examples include *Adventure* (for the Atari 2600); *E.T. The Extraterrestrial* (with Adaptation); *Haunted House, Krull* (with Adaptation); *Myst* (with Puzzle); *Raiders of the Lost Ark* (with Adaptation); *Spy vs. Spy* (with Adaptation); *Superman* (with Adaptation); games in the *Tomb Raider* series; *Venture*; games from the *Daggerfall* series; games from the *Ultima* series.

Artificial Life

These games involve the growth and/or maintenance of digital creatures of some sort, which can "die" without the proper care by the player. Often growth and the "happiness" or "contentedness" of the characters are the goals of the game. (Whether or not all such programs constitute "games" in debatable.) The term should not be used for games that deal with the allocation of resources or games that are primarily concerned with management (see Management Simulation).

Examples include *AquaZone, Babyz, Catz, Creatures, Dogz, The Little Computer People, The Sims* (with Management Simulation).

Board Games

This category includes games that are an adaptation of existing board games (see Adaptation) or games that are similar to board games in their design and play even if they did not previously exist as board games. Games of this genre include either classic board games such as chess, checkers, or backgammon, or trademarked ones such as *Scrabble* or *Monopoly*. This term should not be used for games adapted from games such as pool or table tennis, in which physical skills are involved (see Table-Top Games), nor for games adapted from games that require only paper and a pencil to play, such as *Hangman* or *Tic-Tac-Toe* (see Pencil-and-Paper Games), nor for games adapted from games that are primarily card-based and do not use a board (see Card Games). Three games made by Philips/Magnavox, *Conquest of the World, Quest for the Rings*, and *The Great Wall Street Fortune Hunt*, required a board game to be used along with the video game itself.

It is not necessary to cross-list with Adaptation, as this is implied in Board Games. Most Board Games can also be cross-listed with *Strategy*.

Examples include *Backgammon, Battleship, Clue, Conquest of the World, The Great Wall Street Fortune Hunt, Monopoly, Othello, Quest for the Rings, Scrabble, Stratego, Video Checkers, Video Chess*.

Capturing

In Capturing games, the primary objective involves the capturing of objects or characters that move away from and try to evade the player-character. This may involve stopping the object or character (as in *Gopher* or *Keystone Kapers*), or closing off their access to an escape route (as in *Surround* or in the light cycle section of the arcade game *Tron*). This term should not be used for games in which objects or characters do not move (see Collecting) or do not actively try to avoid the player-character (see Catching), nor should it be used for Strategy games (such as Chess and Checkers) involving the capturing of pieces that are controlled by the player, but which are not player-characters directly representing the player in the game.

It is not necessary to cross-list with Chase, as this is implied in Capturing. Many games with more than one player can be cross-listed with Escape, as game play often involves player-characters alternately trying to capture one another and escape from one another. Capturing objectives also occur briefly in some games; for example, in *Pac-Man* after eating a power pill when the ghosts can be chased and eaten, or the capturing of criminals in *Superman*.

Examples include *Gopher*, *Hole Hunter*, *Keystone Kapers*, *Surround* (with Escape); *Take the Money and Run*, *Texas Chainsaw Massacre*, the light cycle game in *Tron*.

Card Games

These games are adaptations of existing card games, or games that are essentially like card games in that they are primarily card-based (such as various solitaire computer games). Although most Card Games use the standard four-suit deck, some games use specialized cards (such as *1000 Miles*, a shareware game that is an adaptation of Parker Brothers' *Milles Bornes* racing card game). This term should not be used for Trivia Games, which are primarily question-and-answer games.

It is not necessary to cross-list with Adaptation, as that is implied in Card Games. Many card games which involve betting can also be cross-listed with Gambling.

Examples include *1000 Miles* (with Racing); *Blackjack* (with Gambling); *Casino* (with Gambling); *Eric's Ultimate Solitaire*; *Ken Uston Blackjack/Poker* (with Gambling); *Montana*; *Video Poker* (with Gambling).

Catching

In Catching games, the primary objective involves catching objects or characters that do not actively try to evade the player-character. If the objects or characters are in motion, it is usually along a predetermined path and independent of the movements of the player-character. In some cases the player-character can affect the motion of the objects or characters (such as in *Stampede*, where the player-character can nudge the cattle forward), but at no time do the objects or characters try to actively avoid the player-character. This term should not be used for games in which objects or characters do not move (see Collecting) or games in which they actively try to avoid the player-character (see Capturing). Nor should the term be used for games that require timing in order to use moving objects, such as the moving logs in *Frogger*, or the swinging vines in *Pitfall!*, nor for Sports games with balls which are thrown, bounced, or caught, as these objects are used and reused but not "caught" and removed from the game.

Examples include *Alpha Beam with Ernie* (with Educational), *Big Bird's Egg Catch*, *Circus Atari*, *Fishing Derby*, *Lost Luggage*, *Stampede*, *Quantum*, and games 21 through 27 in *Street Racer*.

Chase

See Catching, Capturing, Driving, Escape, Flying, and Racing.

Collecting

The primary objective in Collecting games involves collecting objects that do not move (such as *Pac-Man* or *Mousetrap*), or the surrounding of areas (such as *Qix* or *Amidar*). Often scoring in these games is determined by the number of objects collected or areas bounded. "Collecting" here can mean simply running over or hitting objects, which then disappear (as the dots in *Pac-Man*, or the balloons in *Prop Cycle*). This term should not be used for games in which objects or characters sought by the player-character are in motion (see Catching) or games in which they actively try to avoid the player-character (see Capturing). Nor should the term be used for games that require the use of objects (such as keys, currency, or weaponry) that are only indirectly used in the attainment of the game's objective. Some games involve collecting pieces of an object that can be assembled once all the pieces are found, such as the bridge in *Superman* or the urn in *Haunted House*, although these games often have objectives that involve more than simply collecting, and so should not be considered as belonging to this genre.

Examples include *Amidar* (with Abstract); *Mousetrap* (with Maze and Escape); *Pac-Man* (with Maze and Escape); *Spy vs. Spy* (with Combat and Maze); *Prop Cycle* (with Flying); *Qix* (with Abstract).

Combat

Combat games are games which involve two or more players, or one player and a computer-controlled player, shooting some form of projectiles at each other, and in which all players are provided with similar means for a fairly balanced fight. These games usually emphasize maneuverability and sometimes the outwitting of the opponent. This term should not be used for Shooting games in which the two sides are clearly unequal or not evenly balanced, nor for Fighting games that do not involve shooting. Although these games may range in the appearance of their content, for example, cowboys in *Outlaw*, tanks or planes in *Combat*, or paddles in *Warlords*, the basic play of the game, shoot the opponent while avoiding getting shot, remains essentially the same.

For related games, see Fighting and Shooting.

Examples include *Battletech*; *Battlezone*; *Combat*; *Dactyl Nightmare*; *Outlaw*; *Spy vs. Spy* (with Collecting and Maze); *Warlords*.

Demo

Demos include cartridges, discs, or downloads designed to demonstrate games or a game system. Such cartridges were primarily used in store displays to demonstrate games. Although they may not contain complete games themselves, these cartridges have the same appearance as game cartridges and are sometimes collected and traded as game cartridges, and they are often included in listings of cartridges. As discs or downloads, Demos allow a player to try out a game for free without buying the full-sized game.

It is not necessary to cross-list these with Utility, as that is implied in Demo.

Examples include *ADAM Demo Cartridge*, *Dealer Demo* (Bally Astrocade), *Demonstration Cartridge* (RCA Studio II), *Music Box Demo* (Coleco ADAM).

Diagnostic

Diagnostic cartridges are designed to test the functioning of a system. Although they are not games themselves, these cartridges have the same appearance as game cartridges and are sometimes collected and traded as game cartridges, and they are often included in listings of cartridges.

It is not necessary to cross-list these with Utility, as that is implied in Diagnostic.

Examples include *Diagnostic Cartridge* (Identification number FDS100144) for the Atari 5200 system, *Diagnostic Cartridge* (Identification number CB101196) for the Atari 7800 system, *Final Test Cartridge* (Coleco ADAM), *Super Controller Test Cartridge* (Coleco ADAM).

Dodging

In dodging games, the primary objective is to avoid projectiles or other moving objects. Scoring is often determined by the number of objects successfully dodged, or by the crossing of a field of moving objects that must be dodged (as in *Freeway* or *Frogger*). This term should not be used for games in which players avoid getting shot at and are able to shoot (see Combat and Shooting). In many games such as *Asteroids* or *Space Invaders*, avoidance of objects or projectiles is important for the player to remain in the game, but points are not awarded for merely avoiding them, and players usually have the option of shooting at obstacles, which is not the case in Dodging games.

Examples include *Dodge 'Em* (with Driving), *Freeway* (with Obstacle Course); *Frogger* (with Obstacle Course); *Journey Escape*; and some games in *Street Racer* (with Driving and Racing).

Driving

Driving games are based primarily on driving skills, such as steering, maneuverability, speed control, and fuel conservation. This term should not be used for games in which racing or winning a race is the main objective (see Racing), nor for games that are essentially obstacle courses in which a player's main objective is to hit or avoid touching a series of objects or characters (see Obstacle Course), unless driving skills are essential to play and to the winning of the game. In most cases, Driving games involve vehicles, whereas Obstacle Course games generally do not. Scoring in Driving games is often based on how fast a player completes a particular course, rather than whether or not an opponent is beat in a race, and these games are often single-player games.

Examples include *Dodge 'Em* (with Dodging); *Indy 500* (with Racing); *Night Driver*; *Pole Position* (with Racing); *Red Planet* (with Racing); *Street Racer* (with Dodging and Racing).

Educational

Educational games are designed to teach, with the main objective involving learning a lesson. Rather than being structured as a straightforward set of lessons or exercises, these programs are structured like games, with such elements as scoring, timed performances, or incentives given for correct answers. The degree to which these programs can be considered games varies greatly.

It is not necessary to cross-list these with Utility, as this is implied in Educational.

Examples include *Alpha Beam with Ernie* (with Catching), *Basic Math, Mario's Early Years: Fun With Numbers, Mario Teaches Typing, Math Blaster: Episode 1, Math Grand Prix, Morse, Number Games, Playschool Math, Spelling Games, Word Games.*

Escape

In escape games, the main objective involves escaping pursuers or getting out of some form of enclosure. Games can be open-ended, with the game ending when a player escapes from an enclosure or enters a place safe from the pursuers, or closed, in which a player escapes pursuers for as long as possible but always succumbs in the end (as in *Pac-Man*). This term should not be used for games in which the player-character battles the opponent instead of fleeing (see Combat and Shooting), nor for games such as *Adventure* or *Haunted House* in which the player-character is only occasionally pursued by characters.

Examples include *Pac-Man* (with Collecting and Maze); *Maze Craze* (with Maze); *Mousetrap* (with Collecting and Maze); *Ms. Pac-Man* (with Collecting and Maze); *Surround* (with Capturing).

Fighting

Fighting games involve characters who fight usually hand-to-hand, in one-to-one combat situations without the use of firearms or projectiles. In most of these games, the fighters are represented as humans or anthropomorphic characters. This term should not be used for games that involve shooting or vehicles (see Combat and Shooting), or for games that include fighting, such as *Ice Hockey*, but that have other objectives (see Sports).

Many Fighting games can also be cross-listed with Sports. For related games, see also Combat.

Examples include *Avengers, Body Slam, Boxing* (with Sports); games in the *Mortal Kombat* series, *Soul Edge,* games in the *Tekken* series, *Wrestle War.*

Flying

These games involve flying skills, such as steering, altitude control, takeoff and landing, maneuverability, speed control, and fuel conservation. This term should not be used for games in which shooting an opponent is the main objective (see Combat and Shooting), unless flying skills are essential to game play and to the winning of the game. Flying games can involve airplanes, birds, or spaceships, and movement can take place in the sky (as in *A-10 Attack* and *Prop Cycle*), through

caverns (as in *Descent*), or in outer space (as in *Starmaster* and *Star Ship*).

See also Combat, Shooting, Sports, and Training Simulation.

Examples include *A-10 Attack* (with Training Simulation); *Descent* (with Maze and Shooting); *F/A-18 Hornet 3.0* (with Training Simulation); *Flight Unlimited* (with Training Simulation); *Prop Cycle* (with Collecting); *Solaris; Starmaster* (with Shooting).

Gambling

Gambling games involve betting a stake, which increases or decreases the player's total assets in the following round. These games usually involve multiple rounds of betting, allowing a player's stakes or money to grow or diminish over time. This term should not be used for games in which betting does not occur, or for games in which wins and losses do not carry over into the following round.

See also Card Games and Table-Top Games.

Examples include *Blackjack* (with Card Games); *Casino* (with Card Games); *Slot Machine; Video Poker* (with Card Games); *You Don't Know Jack* (with Quiz).

Interactive Movie

These games are made up of branching video clips or other moving images, the branching of which is decided by a player's actions. Players are often called to make decisions at points in the game where the action stalls or loops, or during action sequences that allow player input that can stop or change the course of action while the video clip is running. Although the player may be given limited freedom of movement or action, revelation of the story is still largely linear in structure, with little or no variation possible in its overall sequence of events. This term should not be used for games that place a controllable player-character over video clip backgrounds, such as *Rebel Assault*, nor should the term be used to refer to games such as *Myst*, which allow a player to wander and explore its world freely, but still limit outcomes and possible narrative paths to a series of video sequences and linear progression through a relatively predetermined narrative.

Examples include *Dragon's Lair, Space Ace, Gadget, Johnny Mnemonic, Star Trek Borg.*

Management Simulation

In Management Simulation games, players must balance the use of limited resources to build or expand some kind of community, institution, or empire, while dealing with internal forces (such as the crime and pollution in *SimCity*), or external forces, such as those of nature or chance (such as natural disasters and monsters in *SimCity*, or planets that require various amounts of terraforming as in *Spaceward Ho!*), and often competition from other players as well. Single-player games are often open-ended, where the community or institution grows and develops over time and continues changing, whereas multiple-player games usually have the objective of dominating all of the other players, at which point the game ends. In some cases, these games can take on an educational function as well, for example, games found in museum displays that simulate supply and demand or other economic principles.

See also Educational and Utility games.

Examples include *Aerobiz*, *Caesar II*, Sid Meier's *Civilization*, *M.U.L.E.*, *Monopoly*, *Railroad Tycoon*, *SimAnt*, *SimCity*, *SimFarm*, *SimTower*, *Spaceward Ho!*

Maze

The objective of these games requires the successful navigation of a maze. What can be called a maze is, of course, a matter of degree, though it is usually possible to discern whether a configuration of rooms or hallways was intended to deliberately cause difficulties in navigation (consider, for example, the difference in complexity between the mazes found in *Berzerk*, *Pac-Man*, and *Doom*). Mazes may appear in an overhead view (as in *Pac-Man*), a side view (as in *Lode Runner*), or first-person perspective (as in *Doom*), or hidden from view (as in certain games in *Maze Craze*). In some cases, the player-character can alter the maze, such as opening or closing passageways (as in *Mousetrap*), or even digging holes or passageways (as in *Lode Runner* or *Dig Dug*). Some mazes, such as those found in *Lode Runner*, focus less on navigation and more on how to gain access to certain portions of the screen in order to achieve certain results or obtain objects. Often the player-character must navigate the maze under the pressure of pursuers, although this is not always the case. Mazes are also often imbedded within other games, such as the Blue Labyrinth in *Adventure*, or the underground maze of the Selenitic Age in *Myst*.

Examples include *Descent* (with Flying and Shooting); *Dig Dug*; *Doom* (with Shooting); *K. C. Munchkin* (with Collecting and Escape); *Lode Runner* (with Platform); *Maze Craze*; *Mousetrap* (with Collecting and Escape); *Pac-Man* (with Collecting and Escape); *Tunnel Runner*; *Tunnels of Doom* (with Adventure); *Ms. Pac-Man* (with Collecting and Escape); *Spy vs. Spy* (with Collecting and Combat); *Take the Money and Run*.

Obstacle Course

In Obstacle Course games, the main objective involves traversing a difficult path or one beset with obstacles, through which movement is essentially linear, often involving running, jumping, and avoiding dangers. This term should not be used for games that do not require more than simply steering down a clear path (see Driving) or avoiding objects or characters without a linear progression of movement (see Dodging), nor should it be used for games that involve chasing or being chased (see Chase), or shooting at opponents or getting shot at (see Combat and Shooting), nor for games with complex objectives (see Adventure), nor for games involving more than traversing a path of obstacles (see Platform).

Although Obstacle Courses are generally linear in design as far as the player-character's advancement through them is concerned, this degree of linearity can vary somewhat; for example, in games allowing a character to backtrack, or choose an alternate route.

Examples include *Boot Camp*, *Clown Downtown*, *Freeway* (with Dodging); *Frogger* (with Dodging); *Pitfall!*, *Jungle Hunt*.

Pencil-and-Paper Games

These are games that are adaptations of games usually played with pencil and paper (see Adaptation). This term should not be used for drawing or doodling programs (see Utility), or for games like those in the *Dungeons & Dragons* series, whose adaptations are very different from the version of the game played with pencil and paper.

It is not necessary to use this with Adaptation, as this is implied in Pencil-and-Paper Games.

Examples include *3-D Tic-Tac-Toe*, *Effacer: Hangman from the 25th Century*, *Noughts and Crosses*, *Tic-Tac-Toe*, and *Hangman*, which appears as a cartridge in several game systems.

Pinball

These games simulate a pinball game. Although these games could be considered Table-Top Games, there is a tradition of video pinball games and a wide enough variety of them to warrant categorizing them in a genre of their own.

It is not necessary to cross-list with Table-Top Games as that is implied in Pinball.

Examples include *Arcade Pinball*, *Astrocade Pinball*, *Electronic Pinball*, *Extreme Pinball*, *Flipper Game*, *Galactic Pinball*, *Kirby's Pinball Land*, *Midnight Magic*, *Pachinko!*, *Pinball*, *Pinball Challenge*, *Pinball Dreams*, *Pinball Fanta-*

sies, *Pinball Jam, Pinball Quest, Pinball Wizard, Power Rangers Pinball, Pro Pinball, Real Pinball, Sonic Spinball, Spinball, Super Pinball: Behind the Mask, Super Sushi Pinball, Thunderball!, True Pinball, Video Pinball.*

Platform

In Platform games, the primary objective requires movement through a series of levels, by way of running, climbing, jumping, and other means of locomotion. Characters and settings are seen in side view as opposed to top view, thus creating a graphical sense of "up" and "down" as is implied in "Platform." These games often also involve avoiding dropped falling objects, conflict with (or navigation around) computer-controlled characters, and often some character, object, or reward at the top of the climb that provides narrative motivation. This term should not be used for games that do not involve ascending heights or advancement through a series of levels (see Adventure), nor for games that involve little more than traversing a path of obstacles (see Obstacle Course).

For related games, see also Adventure and Obstacle Course.

Examples include *Crazy Climber, Donkey Kong, Donkey Kong Jr., Lode Runner* (with Maze), *Spiderman* (Atari 2600); *Super Mario Bros.* (with Collecting); *Warioland, Yoshi's Island.*

Programming Games

In Programming games, the player writes short programs that control agents within a game. These agents then compete and react to situations based on the player's programming. This term should not be used for games in which a player must learn to operate a machine, such as *Riven* (see Puzzle), nor for games in which the player controls the player-characters directly. Depending on what the programmed agents do, games may be able to be cross-listed with other genres.

Examples include *AI Fleet Commander; AI Wars, CoreWar; CRobots; Omega; RARS* (Robot Auto Racing Simulator); *Robot Battle.*

Puzzle

Puzzle games are games in which the primary conflict is not so much between the player-character and other characters, but rather in figuring out a solution, which often involves solving enigmas, navigation, learning how to use different tools, and manipulating or reconfiguring objects. Most often there is a visual or sonic element to the puzzles as well, or at least some verbal description of them. This term should not be used for

games that only involve the answering of questions (see Quiz). Many Text Adventures also contain Puzzles, and use text to describe their sights and sounds.

Examples include *The 7th Guest, Atari Video Cube, Block Out* (with Abstract), *Dice Puzzle, Hitchhiker's Guide to the Galaxy* (with Text Adventure), *Jigsaw, Myst* (with Adventure), *Rubik's Cube* (with Adaptation), *Sokoban, Suspended Animation* (with Text Adventure), *Tetris* (with Abstract).

Quiz

In Quiz games, the main objective is the successful answering of questions. Scoring is usually based on either how many questions are answered correctly, or on the amount of money players have after betting on their answers. Some of these games are adaptations of board games or quiz shows from television.

Games in which the player can place a bet on their answers should be cross-listed with Gambling.

Examples include *$25,000 Pyramid* (with Adaptation); *Fax; Jeopardy* (with Adaptation); *NFL Football Trivia Challenge '94/'95; Name That Tune* (with Adaptation); *You Don't Know Jack* (with Gambling); *Sex Trivia; Trivial Pursuit* (with Adaptation); *Trivia Whiz; TrivQuiz; Video Trivia; Wizz Quiz.*

Racing

In Racing games, the objective involves winning a race, or covering more ground than an opponent (as in *Slot Racers*). Often these games involve driving skills and can also be cross-listed with Driving. One-player games can be considered Racing if there are other computer-controlled cars or vehicles competing on the race track; however, if they are not competitive and act only as obstacles, use Driving.

It is not necessary to cross-list with Sports as this is implied in Racing. Although most of these games involve driving skills and can be cross-listed with Driving, some of them, such as *1000 Miles*, do not.

Examples include *1000 Miles* (with Card Games); *Daytona U.S.A.* (with Driving); *High Velocity* (with Driving); *Indy 500* (with Driving); *Mario Kart 64* (with Driving); *Math Grand Prix* (with Educational); *Pole Position* (with Driving); *Red Planet* (with Driving); *Slot Racers* (with Dodging); *Street Racer* (with Dodging and Driving); *Super GT* (with Driving).

Rhythm and Dance

In Rhythm and Dance games, gameplay requires players to keep time with a musical rhythm. These games may employ a variety of controllers beyond the usual video game hardware, including controllers simulating drums (as in *DrumMania*), turntables (as in *Beatmania*), guitars (as in *Guitar Freaks*), or even maracas (as in *Samba de Amigo*).

Examples include *Beatmania, Bust-a-Groove, Dance Dance Revolution, Guitar Freaks, PaRappa the Rapper, Pop 'n' Music, Samba de Amigo, Space Channel 5, Um Jammer Lammy, Vib-Ribbon* (with Obstacle Course).

Role Playing

In Role-Playing games, players create or take on a character with a developed persona, that often has a description often including specifics as species, race, gender, and occupation, and may also include various abilities, such as strength and dexterity, to limited degrees usually represented numerically. The games can be single-player, such as *Ultima III: Exodus* (1983), or multiple-player games such as those which are networked. This term should not be used for games such as *Adventure* or *Raiders of the Lost Ark*, in which identity is not emphasized or important.

Many networked games, including MUDs (multi-user dimensions), MOOs (MUD, object-oriented), and MUSHs (multi-user shared hallucination), fall into this category, although the degree to which they can be considered games may vary depending on the players and system operators, and whether or not objectives are set for the players and competition occurs.

Examples include *Anvil of Dawn, Diablo, Dragon Lore 2, Fallout, Mageslayer, Phantasy Star, Sacred Pools*, games from the *Ultima* series or *Dungeons & Dragons* series. Networked games include: *Interstate '76, Ivory Tower, JediMUD, Northern Lights, OutlawMOO, PernMUSH, RiftMUSH, Rivers of MUD, Sunflower, Unsafe Haven, VikingMUD, Zodiac*.

Shooting

Also known colloquially as shoot 'em up or shooters, Shooting games involve shooting at, and often destroying, a series of opponents or objects. As opposed to Combat games, which feature one-on-one battles with opponents of roughly equal attributes and means, Shooting games usually feature multiple opponents (the "'em" is short for "them") attacking at once (as in *Space Invaders* or *Galaga*) or multiple objects that can be destroyed (as in *Centipede*), which are often potentially harmful to the player-character (as in *Asteroids*). In many cases, the player-character and opponents of the player-character have unequal attributes and means, and do not even resemble one another (as in *Yar's Revenge*), and the games usually require quick reflexes.

Do not use this term for games such as *Stellar Track*, in which the player-character and opponents fire at each other, but in such a way that quick reflexes are not necessary (see Strategy). There are three common types of Shooting games: in one, the player-character moves horizontally back and forth at the bottom of the screen shooting upward while opponents moving around above shoot downward (as in *Space Invaders*); in the second, the character moves freely about the screen, encountering opponents from all sides (as in *Berserk* or *Robotron: 2084*); and the third features a first-person perspective (as in *Doom*). This term should not be used for fighting games that do not involve shooting (see Fighting), nor for games in which opponents are fairly evenly matched (see Combat), nor for games in which none of the objects the player-character fires upon can harm the player-character (see Target). In a few cases, the player-character is primarily defending rather than attacking, as in *Atlantis, Commando Raid, Missile Command*, and *Missile Defense 3-D*.

Examples include *Asteroids, Berserk, Centipede, Doom, Duckshot, Galaga, Millipede, Missile Command, Robotron: 2084, Space Invaders, Yar's Revenge, Zaxxon*.

Simulation

See Management Simulation and Training Simulation.

Sports

Sports games are adaptations of existing sports or variations of them.

There is no need to cross-list with Adaptation as this is implied in Sports. See also Driving, Fighting, Obstacle Course, Racing, and Table-Top Games.

Examples include *American Football, Atari Baseball, Bowling, Boxing* (with Fighting); *Fishing Derby* (with Catching); *Hot Shots Tennis, Golf, Human Cannonball* (with Target); *Ice Hockey, Madden Football 97, Miniature Golf, NHL Hockey 97, Pong* (with Table-Top Games); *Skeet Shoot* (with Target); *Track & Field, Summer Games, Video Olympics, RealSports Soccer, RealSports Tennis, RealSports Volleyball, SimGolf, Sky Diver, Tsuppori Sumo Wrestling, World Series Baseball '98*.

Strategy

Strategy games emphasize the use of strategy as opposed to fast action or the use of quick reflexes, which are usually not necessary for success in these games.

See also management simulation games such as *M.U.L.E.* and *Spaceward Ho!*, as well as many Board Games, Card Games, and Combat games.

Examples include *Ataxx* (with Abstract); *Checkers* (with Board Games), *Chess* (with Board Games); *Monopoly* (with Board Games); *M.U.L.E.* (with Management Simulation); *Othello* (with Board Games); *Spaceward Ho!* (with Management Simulation); *Stellar Track*.

Table-Top Games

Table-Top games involve adaptations of existing table-top games requiring physical skill or action (such as pool). This term should not be used for games involving little or no physical skill or action (see Board Games and Card Games), nor should it be used for games that cannot be played on a table-top of some sort (see Sports). For games that resemble pinball games, see Pinball.

It is not necessary to cross-list with Adaptation, as this is implied in Table-Top Games.

Examples include *Battle Ping Pong, Electronic Table Soccer!, Parlour Games, Pocket Billiards!, Pong* (with Sports), *Sure Shot Pool, Trick Shot, Virtual Pool*.

Target

In Target games, the primary objective involves aiming and shooting at targets that are not moving or in motion. Occasionally the targets may be harming the player-character's property (as in *Wabbit*). This term should not be used for games in which the player-character can be fired upon by opponents (see Combat, and Shooting), or games that do not involve shooting (see Catching and Collecting), nor for games in which the objects or characters actively elude the player-character (see Capturing).

Examples include *Air-Sea Battle, Carnival, Human Cannonball, Marksman/Trapshooting, Shooting Gallery, Skeet Shoot* (with Sports), *Wabbit*.

Text Adventure

Text Adventure games rely primarily on text for the player interface, and often for the description of the game's world and the action that takes place there as well. Some games may use images, but these are usually noninteractive illustrations that are not central to the play of the game. Games range from allowing free movement throughout the game's "world" (usually by commands such as "north," "south," "east," "west," "up," and "down") with a variety of options for interaction, to more linear, branching narratives. Players often are able to carry objects that are kept track of by an inventory function, and are able to converse with computer-controlled player-characters through a very limited vocabulary. Although some games may incorporate text-based informational screens (as in *Stellar Track*), rely on text for description (such as the books in the library in *Myst*), or even use text as a graphic element (such as *Rogue*), this term should only be used for games in which the players experience the world of the game primarily through text that describes the world of the game and the events occurring in it.

It is not necessary to cross-list these with Adventure because that is implied in Text Adventure. Multiple-player Text Adventures that are networked are considered to be Role-Playing games (see Role Playing). Almost all Text Adventures can also be cross-listed with Puzzle.

Examples include *The Hitchhiker's Guide to the Galaxy, Planetfall, Leather Goddesses of Phobos, Suspended Animation, Zork*.

Training Simulation

These are games or programs that attempt to simulate a realistic situation, for the purpose of training, and usually the development of some physical skill such as steering (as in driving and flight simulators). This term should not be used for simulations that focus on management (see Management Simulation) or the employment of strategy (see Strategy). These games can range from realistic simulations used by institutions, such as those used to train astronauts, tank drivers, or airline pilots, to simplified game-like approximations of them used mainly for entertainment, such as *Police Trainer* or *A-10 Attack*.

It is not necessary to cross-list with Utility or Simulation, as that is implied in Training Simulation.

Examples include *A-10 Attack*; *Comanche 3* (with Flying); *F/A-18 Hornet 3.0* (with Flying); *Flight Unlimited* (with Flying); *Police Trainer*; military and airline flight simulators; and driving simulations used in driver education.

Utility

Utility cartridges or programs have a purpose or function beyond that of entertainment, although they may be structured in a manner similar to games (such as *Mario Teaches Typing*) or contain elements of entertainment. Although they are often not games themselves, some of these programs have the same appearance as game cartridges and are sometimes collected and traded as game cartridges, and they are usually included in listings of cartridges.

See also Demo, Diagnostic, Educational, and Simulation.

Examples include *Basic Programming*, *Beginning Algebra*, *Beginning Math*, *Computer Programmer*, *Diagnostic Cartridge* (Identification number FDS100144) for the Atari 5200 system (with Diagnostic), *Home Finance*, *Infogenius French Language Translator*, *Mario Teaches Typing*, *Music Box Demo* (with Demo), *Number Games*, *Speed Reading*, *Spelling Games*, *Touch Typing*, *Word Games*.

Note

1. For anthologies devoted to the discussion of genre as it relates to film, see Grant, 1995 and Browne, 1998.

References

Browne, N. (Ed.). (1998). *Reconfiguring film genres: History and theory*. Berkeley: University of California Press.

Buscombe, E. (1970). The idea of genre in the American cinema. *Screen*, *11* (1970), 2, 33–45.

Grant, B. K. (Ed.). (1995). *Film genre reader II*. Austin, Texas: University of Texas Press.

Schatz, T. (1981). *Hollywood genres*. New York: McGraw-Hill, Inc.

Tudor, A. (1976). Genre and critical methodology. In B. Nichols (Ed.), *Movies and methods, volume I*. Berkeley: University of California Press, pp. 118–126.

13

THE ROLE OF ARTIFICIAL INTELLIGENCE IN COMPUTER GAME GENRES

John E. Laird and Michael van Lent

Although games have existed for thousands of years, the computer has greatly expanded the types of games we can play. The computer allows us to create and interact with completely new virtual worlds that previously existed only in our imagination. The computer is unique in its ability to create an almost infinite variety of challenges at many different time scales, from epic quests that take weeks to achieve, to moment to moment action where we know that if we play just a few more minutes, we will achieve new powers or unlock hidden secrets. The challenges usually arise directly from our *interaction* with the virtual environment, varying from the dramatic, such as struggling to leap over a bottomless chasm, to the mundane, such as attempting to create an unbroken line of bricks out of an unending supply of descending blocks. However, it is not just the challenge of a human vs. the world that enthralls us; it is also the challenge of competing and cooperating with another intellect. From the very first computer game, *Space War!*, where the player controlled a space ship and attempted to destroy another player's ship, the challenge has often been human versus human. What is unique to computer games is that we now have the technology to create games where the challenge of playing against another intellect is not restricted to playing another human. Computers can not only create challenging environments; they can also create challenging artificially intelligent (AI) characters (Woodcock, 2000). AI characters allow us to create games where the challenges stem not just from competition, but also from the social interactions with characters in populated virtual worlds. Despite the obvious connection between AI and computer games, the AI research community has only occasionally explored games as an application area (Agre & Chapman, 1987; McCarthy, 1998).

In this chapter, we explore the impact of AI on computer games. We start with an examination of the different game genres: action, role playing, adventure, strategy, simulation, sports, and racing. There are no hard and fast lines that delineate these genres, and many games straddle multiple genres. For example, there are strategy games (*Dungeon Keeper*) that allow the human to "jump into the body" of one of their units and play as if it is an action game. Also, there are action games where you must manage resources and multiple units (such as *Battlezone*). However, the genres provide a useful organization and different genres present the player with different environments, different challenges, and different roles for AI to enhance the game experience. Although each genre has its distinctive characteristics, there are some commonalities to the roles that AI plays in these genres. Figure 13.1 shows the connection between the genres and roles.

The second half of this chapter examines each of the AI roles in more detail, providing historical background on the AI techniques used for each role. For each role, we also examine the tension that exists between overall game play and the competence of the AI. In many cases, multiple levels of AI are needed to challenge the range of human players who vary from novice to expert. In order to provide a challenging opponent for human experts, the AI may finesse some of the rules that the human must play by. For each role, we also attempt to predict how AI in games will evolve in the future as both the power of the underlying hardware increases and we improve our understanding of artificial intelligence.

Game Genres

Action Games

Shortly after landing on an alien surface you learn that hundreds of your men have been reduced to just a few. Now you must fight your way through heavily fortified military installations, lower the city's defenses and shut down the enemy's war machine.—Quake II

Action games are one of the most popular game genres, and involve the human player controlling a character in

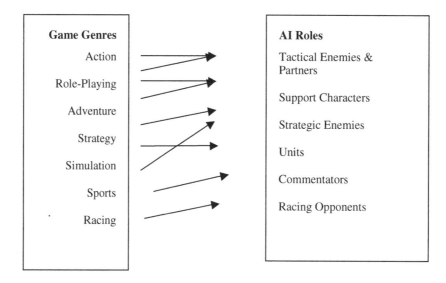

| Figure 13.1 |
Game genres and associated AI roles

a virtual environment, usually running around frantically using deadly force to save the world from the forces of evil. These games vary in the perspective that the human has of their character, be it first-person, where the human sees what the character would see, or third-person, where the player looks over the shoulder of the character. Popular examples include *Doom*, *Quake* (Keighley, 1999), *Descent*, *Half-Life* (Birdwell, 1999), *Tomb Raider*, *Unreal Tournament*, and *Halo*. In pure action games, AI controls the enemies, which are invariably alien monsters or mythical creatures. Realism in graphics has been the point of competition for these games; however, the graphics race seems to have run its course, with better AI becoming the point of comparison. Recent games have extended the genre so that the human player may be part of a team, including either human or AI partners. In all cases, it is the moment-to-moment reaction of the AI to the human that is most important, so the AI must be tactically savvy with little emphasis on strategy.

Role-Playing Games

Immerse yourself in a ... world where nations hang in the balance of your actions, dark prophecies test your resolve, and heroic dreams can be fulfilled at last.—Baldur's Gate

In role-playing games, a human can play different types of characters, such as a warrior, a magician, or a thief. The player pursues quests, collects and sells items, fights monsters, and enhances the capabilities of their character (such as strength, magic, quickness, etc.), all in an extended virtual world. Example games include *Baldur's Gate*, *Diablo*, and the *Ultima* series. Recently, massively multiplayer role-playing games have been introduced where thousands of people play and interact in the same game world: *Ultima Online*, *Everquest*, and *Asheron's Call*. In all types of role-playing games, some of AI characters play the same role of enemy as in action games; however, role-playing games include additional characters, such as traveling companions, shopkeepers, and villagers who increase the social aspects of the game. These additional, supporting characters expand the requirements of AI beyond just tactical enemies. Because of their open-ended nature, massively multiplayer games provide an additional opportunity to use AI as a generator of quests for human players to pursue.

Adventure Games

Aye, 'tis a rollicking piratey adventure that's sure to challenge the mind and shiver a few timbers!—The Curse of Monkey Island

Adventure games, and the related genre of interactive fiction, move even further away from action games, as they de-emphasize armed combat and emphasize story, plot, and puzzle solving. In these games, players must solve puzzles and interact with other characters as they progress through an unfolding adventure that is determined in part by their actions. Early adventure games, such as *Adventure* and *Zork* were totally text based, but more recent games sport 3D graphics (sometimes using the graphics engines developed for action games). Example games include the Infocom series, *King's Quest*, and many games from Lucas Arts, such as *Full Throttle*, *Monkey Island*, and *Grim Fandango*. AI can be used to create realistic goal-driven supporting characters that the player must interact with to further their progress in the game. One of the holy grails of interactive fiction is to have a computer director who can dynamically adjust the story and plot based on the actions of the human. The majority of these games have fixed scripts and use many tricks to force the human player through essentially linear stories. However, a few games, such as *Blade Runner*, have incorporated some autonomy and dynamic scripting into their characters and story line (Castle, 1998).

Strategy Games

Players must successfully construct and rule their medieval empire while engaging in real-time tactical warfare over land, sea, and air. —Warcraft

In strategy games, the human controls many units (usually military units, such as tanks, or the ever present alien war machines) to do battle from a god's eye view against one or more opponents. Strategy games include reenactments of different types of battles: historical (*Close Combat*, *Age of Empires*), alternative realities (*Command and Conquer*), fictional future (*Starcraft*), and mythical (*Warcraft*, *Myth*). The human is faced with problems of resource allocation, scheduling production, and organizing defenses and attacks. These games use AI in two roles: to control the detailed behavior of individual units, and as a strategic opponent that plays against the human. The AI requirements of the individual units differs from the enemies of action and role playing games. Units must often navigate through complex outdoor environments on their own as well as follow orders generated by the human or strategy level AI.

Simulation Games

You're in charge of creating an entire city from the ground up—and the sky's the limit. —SimCity 3000

Simulation games give the player godlike control over a simulated world. The human can modify the environment and, to some extent, its inhabitants. The entertainment comes from observing the effects of his or her actions on individuals, society, and the world. *Sim City* is the classic example of a simulation, or god game, where the human acts as mayor and the AI controls individual units or citizens of the simulated city. *The Sims* and the game *Black and White* are probably the most intriguing examples. In these games, the player creates individual characters (units) that have significant autonomy, with their own drives, goals, and strategies for satisfying those goals, but where god (the human player) can come in and stir things up both by managing the individual characters and their environment.

Sports Games

Welcome to Madden NFL 97, the game that captures the excitement of a 30 yard touchdown pass, the strategy of a well executed scoring drive, and the atmosphere of a crisp autumn afternoon in the stadium. —Madden NFL 97

Sports games cover almost every sport imaginable, from traditional team sports such as football or baseball, to individual sports, such as Olympic events. Many of the individual sports fall under racing games, such as car racing, boat racing, or snowboarding, which are covered in a separate genre below. Team sports games have the human play a combination of coach and player in popular sports, such as U.S. Football (Whatley, 1999), Basketball, Soccer, Baseball, and Hockey. Sports games use AI in two roles that are similar to the roles in strategy games. The first role is unit level control of the individual players where the human controls one key player, such as the quarterback, and the computer controls all the other members of the team. A second role is as the strategic opponent, in this case the opposing coach. One unique aspect of team sport games is that they also have a role for a commentator, who gives the play by play and color commentary of the game (Frank, 1999).

Racing Games

Gran Turismo 3 delivers the most realistic racing experience. Customizable vehicles handle different due to differences in horsepower, ride height, tire type or vehicle mass, just to name a few variables. —Gran Turismo 3

There are computer racing games for almost any vehicle or platform that a human can climb on: cars, trucks, motorcycles, boats, planes, skates, skateboards, and snowboards. Some of the first computer games involved racing cars, avoiding obstacles, and trying to beat a computer or human opponent. In racing games, the computer provides a simulation of a sport from a first- or third-person perspective. The human player controls a participant in the game who competes against other human or computer players. The AIs for a racing game are in a class by themselves because the goal in a racing game is so simple—stay on course and be the fastest to the finish line.

AI Roles

These genres use AI in a variety of ways. One might be tempted to think that an AI should always be constructed to model a human player as accurately as possible. Sometimes that is appropriate, but as we review each of the roles an AI character can play, we will see that often human-like behavior must be sacrificed because human-like behavior is still beyond the state of the art or because the game is more fun without it. In computer games, the real goal of the AI character is to enhance gameplay, and most of the time that entails being an opponent that fights up until then end and then loses.

Tactical Enemies and Partners

In action games, the main thrill is destroying the bad guys and, except for multiplayer games, the computer controls bad guys. In early action games, the computer-controlled enemies did little more than shoot wildly and run directly at the player. The enemies were challenging, not because of the complex tactics they used, but because of their superior numbers. Initially, some tactical enemies overcome their limited intelligence by "cheating," such as having the ability to see through walls or out of the back of their heads.

Navigation was not an issue in early games because the enemies were placed in locations that the human player had to traverse and the AIs could just run at the human. When navigation is required, it is done via nodes that are placed in the world that the AIs can see, but are invisible to the human player. The AI moves from node to node, whose placement guarantees that the AI will not have to avoid obstacles dynamically. Usually a level designer places the nodes by hand, although recently some games have software that automatically generates nodes. Nodes are used for more than pure navigation, with some nodes being marked as places for sniping or ambushing. In addition to following nodes, the AIs also are also able to interact with the items in their world, such as picking up weapons,

ammo, or health power-ups. In some games, the AI will have complex responses to player actions, such as picking up a grenade that has been thrown their way and throwing it back at the human player (*Return to Castle Wolfenstein*). Some tactical enemies will use cover during reloading to avoid being easy targets.

There is a continual tension between making the enemies more realistic and maintaining the game play experience. For most of these games, the human player fights against tens or hundreds of opponents, and if the AI opponent had anything close to the human's capabilities, the game would be impossible. The AI must be challenging and then, because of some failure or mistake, die gracefully before the onslaught of the human player. For example, in the game *Deus Ex*, the enemy AI characters have realistic models of a human's limited field of view, and must detect the player by "hearing" the sound of footsteps, door openings, and so on. Thus, these characters react to their environment much the way a human would. But if the AI characters use this information to the fullest to hunt down the human, the player would be "toast." To keep the realism high but still allow the player to win, the AI characters always give their position away by talking or making noise when they hear or see a glimpse of the player, saying such witty comments as "What was that?" or "Who goes there?" This alerts the player to the presence of the enemies, giving the player a chance to get that all-important first shot in. Moreover, the enemy characters *always* miss on the first couple shots, which further helps the human player beat the AI enemy.

In most action games, there is a multiplayer mode where it is every player—human or computer— fighting for itself. In these cases, the computer enemies should be as challenging as a human without obvious faults or disadvantages. It is easy to make the computer enemies challenging by giving them superhuman reaction times and aiming skills. Playing against these types of enemies forces the human player to adopt tactics that don't necessarily transfer to playing against other humans. Our own research (Laird & van Lent, 1999; Laird, 2000b) has concentrated on building enemies for *Quake II* that have the same strengths and weaknesses as human players. To beat them, you have to out-think them as much as you have to out-shoot them. Our *Soar Quakebot* is essentially a real-time expert system that has multiple goals and extensive tactics and knowledge of the game. It is built within the Soar architecture and has more than eight hundred rules. While exploring a level, it creates an internal model of its world and it uses that model in its tactics, to collect nearby weapons, ammo, and health, to track down an enemy, and to set ambushes. It also tries to anticipate the actions of human players by putting itself in their shoes (creating an internal model of their situation garnered from its perception of the player) and projecting what it would do if it were the human player. This changes the game from one of always trying just to get off the first shot, to a more strategic game of predicting the opponent's behavior, and at the same time, avoiding being too predictable yourself.

Building human-level enemies for these games requires solving many general AI problems and integrating the solutions into coherent systems. The enemies must be autonomous. They must interact with a complex dynamic environment, which requires reactive behavior, integrated planning, and common sense reasoning. As they advance, they will also need models of high-level vision that have the same strengths and weaknesses as humans. For example, if the human were in a dark room, the AI would be cheating if it could easily sense, identify, and locate the human. However, if the human is backlit by a bright hall, the AI enemy should easily sense and locate the human, but possibly not identify him. This is important for game play so that the same tactics and behaviors that work well with humans work well with AI enemies.

There are many other aspects of AI that are important to building intelligent enemies. Because of the extended geography of the environment, they must navigate, use path planning, spatial reasoning, and temporal reasoning. As the games become more complex, the AI will need to plan, counter-plan, and adapt to the strategies and tactics of its enemies, using plan recognition, opponent modeling techniques, and learning. Their responses need to be within the range of humans in terms of reaction times and realistic movement. One can even imagine adding basic models of emotions, where the enemies get "mad" or "frustrated" and change their behavior as a result.

Although the emphasis in many games is fighting *against* the computer, some games provide the player with teammates that help them fight against the overwhelming odds. Creating AI controlled partners involves many of the same research issues as tactical enemies. However, whereas enemy AIs emphasize autonomy, AI partners emphasize effortless cooperation and coordination between the human player and the AI partner. Current games restrict the human to using specific commands to interact with partners, such as defend, attack, and follow me—commands much more limited than used in human-to-human interactions. In

the extreme, this brings speech recognition, natural language processing, and even gesture recognition into the mix of future research issues that will need to be incorporated into computer games. The partner AI must coordinate its behavior, understand teamwork, model the goals of the human, and adapt to his or her style. Creating such partners can build on previous research in these areas, but must embed it within the context of all of the other cognitive activities involved in playing the game.

Support Characters

In adventure and role-playing games, support characters fill out the game world with interesting people for the player to interact with. Support characters are the merchants you buy equipment from, the tavern drunks you learn key clues from, the guard you must convince to unlock the gate, and the damsel in distress. Although they are some of the least sophisticated AI characters in today's computer games, they have the most promise to improve games and are the most interesting in terms of developing human-level AI. Today's support characters are very limited in their interactions with the player and very scripted in their behavior. Conversations with the player take the form of canned speeches by the support characters, usually text with corresponding voice-overs, interspersed with decision points at which the player can affect the direction of the conversation. Decision points present the player with a short list of phrases from which to choose their next utterance. The behavior of support characters is generally limited to a looping animation with a few scripted action sequences that are triggered by the player's actions. So the support characters stand in one place, continually chopping wood or drinking from their mug of ale, until the player initiates an interaction. During the scripted interaction, the support character may gesture to emphasize a point or even walk a short distance to hand the player an object. Once the interaction is over, the character returns to his or her looping behavior.

In a few games, such as in *Blade Runner* (Castle, 1998), the support characters have some limited autonomy and some simple goals, but they are extremely narrow goals supported by limited sets of behaviors. Unfortunately, most game developers aren't as interested in improving support characters as they are in improving AI for the other roles. The popularity of adventure games seems to be temporarily ebbing and, with the advent of massively multiplayer role playing games, human players are filling the role of support characters in role playing games. However, recent advances in research on human-computer interaction, social intelligence, and natural language interfaces may provide interesting new approaches to the AI for support characters. This is a promising area for AI research because, if done well, they will allow the characters in the game to interact socially with the player. One reason today's games are so violent is the lack of sophisticated support characters. Shooting at the player requires less complex AI than talking to the player. Socially intelligent support characters will help populate the games with interesting opportunities for interaction that guide the player along various plot lines. Each character will have a set of goals and beliefs about the world that the player must discover and utilize to obtain the assistance of that character. Perhaps after a long and harrowing quest the player will discover that the princess doesn't want to be rescued and the final challenge is resolving her conflicts with her father, the king.

Because these characters will exist in a virtual world and play the role of humans in that world, they provide a useful first step in research toward human-level AI (Brooks et al., 1999; Laird & van Lent, 2001). Support characters must interact with and adapt to the environment, to human players, and to other support characters. They must provide human-like responses, including realistic movement (Hayes-Roth & Doyle, 1998), personality, emotions, natural language understanding, and natural language generation. In order to do all this, and because these support characters most directly play the role of embodied virtual humans, they require a wide range of integrated AI capabilities.

Strategic Opponents

The tasks a strategic opponent performs can be divided into two categories: allocating resources and issuing unit control commands. In the popular real-time strategy game *Age of Kings*, for example, resources include food, gold, wood, and stone, which players gather from specific points on the map. Once gathered, players use these resources to build a wide variety of units, such as militia, archers, knights, and workers, as well as ships, and buildings—for example barracks, farms, walls, monasteries, and universities. Tailoring the allocation of resources simultaneously to support cultural development, defense and offense is half of the strategic opponent's job. The other half of the job is to develop offensive and defensive strategies and command the units that have been produced to implement those strategies. Units can be ordered to move in a variety of formations, attack enemy units and buildings, defend

friendly units or buildings, and perform a number of special actions. For example, monks can convert enemy forces so they change sides. Strategy games almost always include nonmilitary units that are used to gather resources, build new buildings, and repair damaged buildings. The resource allocation and unit control tasks cannot be controlled independently. The type of resources gathered and how they're spent must be guided by the needs of the strategic opponent's unit control strategy. Similarly, the unit control strategy must take into account the available resources to avoid selecting a strategy that requires unavailable resources.

Team sports games also use strategic opponents. Acting as the coach of the opposing team, the strategic opponents is again faced with the tasks of allocating resources and issuing unit control commands. In a U.S. football game, for example, resources take the form of players on the bench who must be allocated according to their strengths and weaknesses to support the coach's strategy. This strategy is implemented by the commands the coach issues to the players (units), generally in the form of selecting among a variety of passing and running plays. Strategic opponents for team sports games face an additional difficulty in that their style of play must match a real world team about which the human players are likely to be very knowledgeable.

In the past, most game developers resorted to static, predefined strategies and "cheating" to minimize the demands on the strategic opponent. The artificial intelligence for the strategic opponents generally took the form of a single hard-coded strategy created by the game designer. For real-time strategy games this would be a single attack plan, usually a mass frontal assault, executed periodically (for example, every ten minutes) with no regard for the human player's behavior. As with tactical opponents, these strategic opponents were designed to allow the human to win after a close and entertaining battle. Often this design goal was explicitly programmed into the strategic opponent's behavior. If the periodic attacks threatened to wipe out the human player, the strategic opponent would reduce the attacking force accordingly. Based on the belief that human players would lose interest after forty minutes of game play, at least one game company programmed the strategic opponent to destroy most of its own forces after thirty-five minutes of play. These behaviors gave the human players the perception that they had barely survived the strategic opponent's desperate, last-ditch attack, and as a result conquered the undefended base.

In sports games, the strategic opponent often utilized a fixed sequence of plays or would randomly select plays from the play library. Because most strategic opponents relied on a fixed strategy, they were predictable and easily beaten once their weaknesses were found.

To implement these predefined strategies the strategic opponents usually cheated in a number of ways. One form of cheating allowed the creation of extra units or resources from nothing to support the periodic attacks. Another form of cheating gave the strategic opponent complete knowledge of the map and the locations of the player's forces. This freed the strategic opponent from exploring the map and scouting the enemy to obtain this information. In most cases, players eventually detected that the strategic opponents were cheating, which destroyed the illusion that they were matching wits with a military genius or famous coach.

More recent strategic opponents have become more sophisticated. In many cases, cheating has been reduced or eliminated. As the players demand more varied opponents, game developers have given strategic opponents a library of strategic plans from which to choose. In strategy games, this library may consist of a small number of hard-coded attack strategies. By selecting a strategy that corresponds to the human player's plan, the strategic opponent can use its resources more effectively and require fewer cheat-provided resources. In addition, better path planning algorithms have made it much easier to include exploring and scouting as part of the strategic opponent's behavior. Recent sports games are going a step further by detecting patterns in the human player's behavior and giving the strategic opponent the ability to take advantage of these regularities. An AI who reacts to the player's behavior results in a more challenging and entertaining strategic opponent. In addition, it reduces the chance that the player will find and exploit weaknesses in the strategic opponent.

In the future, strategic opponents may be able to create new strategies specific to the opponent and situation. This will involve integrated planning, common sense reasoning, spatial reasoning, plan recognition, and counter-planning. One of the most important aspects of strategy creation is the coordination of multiple types of units into a cohesive strategy. Once a plan is created, the strategic opponent must determine how best to use limited resources to compose offensive and defensive forces appropriate to implementing the plan. This resource allocation can involve scheduling, constraint satisfaction, and temporal reasoning.

Units

In both strategy games and team sports games, the strategic opponent implements a strategy by issuing commands to a large number of units that make up their force. For example, in strategy games, the strategic opponent issues orders to worker units and military units. Commands to worker units specify what type of building to build or what type of resources to gather and from which site. Military units might be commanded to attack an enemy unit, defend against attack, or patrol along a specified path. In both cases, some intelligence is required on the part of the unit to carry out the strategic opponent's orders. The units must be able to plan a path, follow it to a selected location, and react to changes in their local environment such as the appearance of enemy units or depletion of resources.

In a team sports game, the strategic opponent might select a play or strategy for the entire team. That strategy defines a role and/or approximate path for each player involved in the play. As with strategy games, the individual units (players) must plan and follow paths and react to the opposing units. Because there is more variation between players than between military units (at least in a strategy game context), team sports games tend to place more of the decision-making responsibility on the units. Returning to the Football game example, the coach specifies a general play that may have a number of options when executed. The unit players, especially the quarterback, must decide which of these options to select, which receiver to throw to or which running lane to take, on the fly as the play unfolds. As with strategic opponents, units in sports games must conform to the user's knowledge of the style of the player that that unit represents.

Initially the primary focus of artificial intelligence development for units was path planning. Tens or hundreds of units are often active at the same time, and calculating a path for each unit to its goal around environmental obstacles is a computationally expensive procedure. Borrowing from the AI research community, game programmers discovered that the A* search algorithm is a powerful and efficient way to calculate these paths. To this day variations on the A* algorithm are still the primary path planning technology used in the game industry. A* is effective in avoiding static obstacles, but dynamic obstacles, such as other moving units, still present a problem. Recalculating each unit's path at every step to avoid all the other units is simply too expensive. As a result, early strategy games had frequent traffic jams at bottlenecks when groups of units moved together. This was often overcome by allowing units to pass through each other, avoiding unit collision and moving obstacles altogether. In these early strategy games, units typically ignore enemy units they discover unless explicitly ordered to attack them. These two problems could cause armies to get strung out due to a bottleneck and then parade past a single enemy unit, allowing it to destroy the whole army.

In more recent strategy games, units can be given commands defining how to react to enemy units. A unit set to attack may attack and follow any enemy it comes across until it kills or is killed. When set to defend, however, the unit might attack the enemy unit but would not follow it. These different behavior strategies are supported by a finite state machine that controls how the unit selects actions to execute a command. The different settings (attack, defend, etc.) simply modify the transitions within that unit's finite state machine. Another recent advance allows groups of units to move in formation. The player selects a group of units and specifies a formation. The units will then automatically organize themselves into that formation, with different types of units in appropriate places. For example, a group of swordsmen and archers will organize themselves in a box formation such that the archers are on the inside, protected by the swordsmen around the perimeter. Once in formation, the units will move as a group and try to avoid breaking formation. Formation organization and moving in formation requires some advanced path planning, teamwork, and careful scripting on the game developer's part.

As strategy games and team sports games continue to advance, the units in these games will continue to become more autonomous. The level of unit autonomy must be carefully balanced to allow users to maintain strategic and tactical control over their units while eliminating the tedious micromanagement of each unit. The move toward grouping units into formations and issuing group commands is a first step in this direction. Future areas of research for unit-level AI include case-based reasoning, teamwork, distributed planning and execution, and, as always, path planning. Because there can be hundreds of units active in a game at one time, the issues of computational and memory overhead are particularly important for unit AI (Atkin, Westbrook, & Cohen, 1999).

Racing Opponents

Opponents for racing games are some of the most pure applications of artificial intelligence in games. The AI must travel over a course, controlling a vehicle (which could be a car, a boat, a plane, or even a snowboard). The most primitive and earliest opponents for racing games followed a predefined circuit around the course at a set speed—they were essentially the rabbit that the greyhounds/players chase around the course. They were oblivious to the physics of the world, so they could move in ways and at speeds that were impossible for the human player to match. A simple extension to make them appear more realistic was to vary their speeds at predefined places around the course, such as slowing down in curves or over rough terrain and then speeding up in straightaways.

The next step was to have the AI-controlled vehicles obey the same physics as the players' vehicles, so they would spin out or crash if they took a corner too fast, and more generally have to race following the same rules as a human player. Controlling a vehicle can be quite complex, requiring the integration of domain-dependent planning to determine where the vehicle should attempt to be a few seconds from now using the appropriate tactics, real-time execution to attempt to get to that position, and real-time reaction to respond to the movements of other vehicles. To avoid these complexities, the AI for racing opponents almost invariably follows a recorded trace of the behavior of a human player. It is as if there is a line on the course that tells the AI where to go, what speed to use, and possibly any special maneuvers that should be performed.

Using a trace of human behavior solves some of the problems. However, racing games inevitably involve reacting to changes in the environment: another vehicle may be in the way and must be avoided, a power-up (an object that gives the racer special powers, such as enhanced speed or repairs to injuries) may appear, or the vehicle may be pushed off onto an alternative part of the course and need to switch to a new path. Thus, one of the complexities in using human traces is knowing how to balance blind trace following with pursuing dynamic goals that arise during the race. Usually there will be a set of prespecified cues that establish the behaviors that respond to the dynamic events and then once those behaviors are complete, the AI returns to following the trace.

Creating opponents whose behavior is based on human traces also makes it easy to create a variety of opponents at different skill levels with different styles—just record different humans with these different characteristics (or if you are on a restricted budget, a single human pretending to have different styles). In the limit, the behavior of world-famous expert racers can be recorded—similar to using motion capture for signature moves in sports games.

The different skill levels are an important part of making a racing game fun to play. If a human player must start out against an expert, he or she will be soundly beaten. Conversely, if there are only easy opponents to race against, the human player will quickly become bored as he or she gains experience. Although AI opponents with multiple skill levels is a successful and probably the dominant approach, it does require that the human continually choose the right level of competition—there will inevitably be races in which the human finds himself either far behind or far ahead of the AI competition. An alternative is to try to make every race a nail biter, where the human always has a chance to come back and win, no matter what mistakes they made early on. Moreover, if they have a great race, they are challenged up until the end. To provide this, many racing games have "rubber banding," where the AI systems slows down if it gets too far ahead and speeds up if it gets too far behind. Thus, the player is always in the heat of a race, and if the player has a strong finish, he or she will win.

What can we expect in the future for racing AIs? Racing AIs already provide excellent competition (some even include taunts during the race), but we can speculate that many future racing games will require AIs that can race over novel or dynamic terrain, where it is infeasible to create human traces for all of the possible paths. These AIs will probably incorporate limited planning where they analyze the course in front of them and pick a path and speed based on knowledge of the terrain they must traverse, performance characteristics of their vehicle, and its predicted interaction with the race course. Such reasoning is inherently more computationally intensive than current approaches, but as both consoles and PCs continue to marshal more and more processing power, the AI will get enough computational resources to use more complex approaches.

Commentators

One of the more unusual roles for AI in computer games is to simulate the play-by-play reporting during a sports game by having one or more computerized commentators. The role of the commentator is to observe the actions of the AI and the human and generate natural language comments suitable to describe the action (Frank, 1999). Although not necessary for the competitive aspects of the game, game players seem to enjoy having the background patter that highlights their successes and failures. Many sports games take their commentators very seriously, using established commentators, such as John Madden, not only to provide the play-by-play, but also to market the games. Hours of commentary is recorded and then played at the appropriate times during the game. Good commentary is extremely difficult because not only does it report on the specific action in the game, but it relates that action to current state of the game (where the ball is on the field, who is ahead, by how much, how much time is left in the game ...) and the teams' goals, often with a comment on the wisdom of the play selection. Thus, the exact same play can be a good call at one point in the game, but be a huge mistake in another. For example, in U.S. Football, if time is running out in the game and a team is behind by four points with the ball on the opponent's twenty-yard line, with fourth down and eight yards to go, the player might call a pass play in an attempt to win the game, and the commentators should acknowledge that he is forced to do this. If the player attempts to kick a field goal, that won't help win the game and the player should be chastised. However, if time is running out in the first half (but not the game), and a team is up by seven points, with the ball still on the opponent's twenty-yard line with fourth down and eight yards to go, the commentators should comment that the player is taking a huge risk by calling a pass play, but laud the human player if he attempts a field goal. The difficulties in creating good commentary are further complicated by the need to avoid repetition, which is difficult because to obtain high quality in the speech production, all of the phrases are prerecorded. There is nothing like hearing the same exact phrase more than once in a game to destroy the suspension of disbelief.

Conclusion

The focus of this chapter is the different roles AI plays in today's game genres. However, game developers are constantly searching for the next innovation that will revolutionize the industry. An example of this is the recent appearance of massively multiplayer online games, now the fastest growing game genre. New genres and new roles in existing genres will provide new opportunities for AI. AI story directors might construct stories on the fly, giving the player unlimited freedom in the game world. AI opponents might use fast planning algorithms to detect weaknesses in the player's defenses and create novel strategies and/or tactics specifically designed to exploit those weaknesses. Developers may teach, rather than program, AI opponents that learn to play the game and learn to adapt to the strengths and weaknesses of different players. Conversely, new advances in AI can open a door to new game genres and even new game paradigms (Stern, 1999). For example, speech recognition, natural language understanding, and speech generation could lead to a new class of games played via cellphone.

The existing roles for artificial intelligence, as well as future roles, share a common goal of providing the human player with an entertaining experience. Success and profitability requires careful balancing of a number of factors. The AI opponents must challenge the player while still allowing the player to taste victory. The AI characters must be believable with personality and a rich range of behaviors while still fitting into a game developer's budget and schedule. The AI enemies must be cunning and crafty in their tactics while still reacting in factions of a second.

Fortunately for gamers, game developers only need concern themselves with the results, or external appearance of believability, of the AI. Shortcuts, cheats, and other smoke and mirror techniques abound in commercial game development. In some cases, such as strategic opponents, the players discover the cheats. However, in most cases the players only see the resulting behavior that makes games so entertaining. With the goal of discovering the foundations and inner workings of intelligent behavior, AI research pays as much attention to the realism of the process as the realism of the result. With a few exceptions, game developers have generally found the techniques used by the research community to be too costly in terms of processor and memory demands. However, with the power of computers increasing almost daily and AI's new prominence as a point of competition for games, we believe AI research will soon play a role in commercial computer games (Laird, 2000a; Takahashi, 2000).

Acknowledgments

The authors are indebted to the many students and staff who have worked on the Soar/Games project, most notably Steve Houchard, Karen Coulter, Mazin Assanie, Josh Buchman, Joe Hartford, Ben Houchard, Damion Neff, Kurt Steinkraus, Russ Tedrake, and Amy Unger. Thanks to Doug Church and Lars Liden for educating us on AI and commercial computer games.

References

Agre, P. E., & Chapman, D. (1987). Pengi: An implementation of a theory of activity. *Proceedings of AAAI-87*, 268–272.

Atkin, M. S., Westbrook, D. L., & Cohen, P. R. (1999). Capture the flag: Military simulation meets computer games. *Papers from the AAAI 1999 Spring Symposium on Artificial Intelligence and Computer Games*, Technical Report SS-99-02, AAAI Press, 1–5.

Birdwell, K. (1999). The Cabal: Valve's design processing for creating Half-Life. *Game Developer*, 6(12), 40–50.

Brooks, R. A., Breazeal, C., Marjanovic, M., Scassellati, B., & Williamson, M. (1999). *The cog project: Building a humanoid robot*. New York: Springer-Verlag.

Castle, L. (1998). The making of Blade Runner, soup to nuts! In *Proceedings of the Computer Game Developers' Conference*, Long Beach, CA, 87–97.

Frank, I. (1999). Explanations count. *Papers from the AAAI 1999 Spring Symposium on Artificial Intelligence and Computer Games*, Technical Report SS-99-02, 77–80. AAAI Press.

Hayes-Roth, B., & Doyle, P. (1998). Animate characters. *Autonomous Agents and Multi-Agent Systems*, 1(1), 195–230.

Keighley, G. (1999). The final hours of Quake III Arena: Behind closed doors at id software. GameSpot, http://www.gamespot.com/features/btg-q3/index.html.

Laird, J. E. (2000a). Bridging the gap between developers and researchers. *Game Developer*, 7(8), 34.

Laird, J. E. (2000b). It knows what you're going to do: Adding anticipation to a Quakebot. *Papers from the AAAI 2000 Spring Symposium on Artificial Intelligence and Interactive Entertainment*, Technical Report SS-00-02, 41–50. AAAI Press.

Laird, J. E., & van Lent, M. (1999). Developing an artificial intelligence engine. *Proceedings of the Game Developers Conference*, San Jose, CA, 577–588.

Laird, J. E., & van Lent, M. (2001). Interactive computer games: Human-level AI's killer application. *AI Magazine*, 22(2), 15–25.

McCarthy, J. (1998). Partial formalizations and the lemmings game. http://www-formal.stanford.edu/jmc/lemmings.html.

Stern, A. (1999). AI beyond computer games. *Papers from the AAAI 1999 Spring Symposium on Artificial Intelligence and Computer Games*, Technical Report SS-99-02, 77–80. AAAI Press.

Takahashi, D. (2000). Artificial intelligence gurus win tech-game jobs. *The Wall Street Journal*, March 30, B14.

Whatley, D. (1999). Designing around pitfalls of game AI. *Proceedings of the Game Developers Conference*, San Jose, CA, 991–999.

Woodcook, S. (2000). Game AI: The state of the industry. *Game Developer*, 7(8), 24–32.

Storytelling

14

GAMES TELLING STORIES?

Jesper Juul

As questions go, this is not a bad one: Do games tell stories? Answering this should tell us both *how* to study games and *who* should study them. The affirmative answer suggests that games are easily studied from within existing paradigms. The negative implies that we must start afresh.

But the answer depends, of course, on how you define any of the words involved. In this chapter, I will examine different ways to discuss this. Lest this turns into a battle of words (i.e., who has the right to define "narrative"), my agenda is not to save or protect any specific term, but rather to say that we should allow ourselves to make distinctions.

The operation of framing something as something else works by taking selected notions of the source domain (narratives) and applying them to the target domain (games). This is not neutral; it emphasizes some traits and suppresses others. Unlike this, the act of *comparing* furthers the understanding of differences and similarities, and may reveal hidden assumptions.

The chapter begins by examining some standard arguments *for* games being narrative. There are at least three common arguments: (1) We use narratives for everything. (2) Most games feature narrative introductions and backstories. (3) Games share some traits with narratives.

The article then explores three important reasons for describing games as being nonnarrative: (1) Games are not part of the narrative media ecology formed by movies, novels, and theater. (2) Time in games works differently than in narratives. (3) The relation between the reader/viewer and the story world is different than the relation between the player and the game world.

The chapter works with fairly traditional definitions of stories and narratives, so as a final point I will consider whether various experimental narratives of the twentieth century can in some way reconcile games and narratives.

Telling Stories

Everything Is Narrative/Everything Can Be Presented as Narratives

The first argument is a compelling one, as it promises a kind of holistic view of the world: Because we use narratives to make sense of our lives, to process information, and because we can tell stories about a game we have played, no genre or form can be *outside* the narrative.

The problem is that this really is an a priori argument. Narratives may be fundamental to human thought, but this does not mean that everything *should* be described in narrative terms. And that something can be presented in narrative form does not mean that it *is* narrative.

Ideal Stories/Backstories

A more interesting argument centers on the fact that most games have a story written on the package, in the manual, or in intro sequences, placing the game in the context of a larger story (backstory), and/or creating an ideal story that the player has to realize.

If we play *Space Invaders* (Taito, 1977; figure 14.1), we are presented with an ideal story that we have to realize using skill. *Invaders* suggests a prehistory: an invasion presupposes a situation before the invasion. It is clear from the science fiction we know that these aliens are evil and should be chased away. So the title suggests a simple structure with a positive state broken by an external evil force. It is the role of the player to recreate the original positive state. This is, of course, a sequence often found in folk tales: an initial state, an overturning of this state, and a restoration of the state.

But it works in a different way. If we *play Space Invaders*, we find that we cannot actually restore the initial state; we cannot win, because every wave of aliens is followed by another. As players we are fighting to *realize* an ideal sequence of events, but the actual playing is not this sequence.

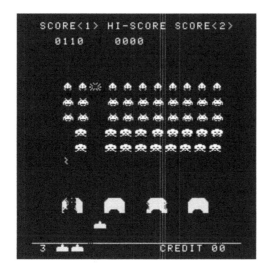

| Figure 14.1 |
Space Invaders (Taito, 1977)

Most modern, single player non-arcade games such as *Half-Life* (Valve Software, 1998) actually let you complete the game: through countless saves and reloads, it is possible to realize the ideal sequence that *Half-Life* defines. Obviously, only a microscopic fraction of the play sessions actually follow the ideal path, but *Half-Life* does succeed in presenting a fixed sequence of events that the player can then afterwards retell.[1] This means that some games *use* narratives for some purposes.

Similarities

The above *Space Invaders* example also means that games share some traits with narratives. Many games feature reversals such as movements from a lack to the lack being restored. Jens F. Jensen has used this trait of *Space Invaders* to argue that computer games, although being deviant, are narratives (1988).

Additionally, many games have quest structures, and most computer games have protagonists (though this is less common in nonelectronic games). As Janet Murray suggests in *Hamlet on the holodeck* (1997), such similarities would indicate that there is a promising future for digital storytelling and interactive narratives, that games and narratives are not very far apart.

It is also an oft-repeated but problematic point that players experience game sessions linearly, just like narratives (see also Aarseth, 1997, p. 2). I will return to this, but briefly note that this idea ignores the player's experience of being an active participant—this experience is so strong that most people will involuntarily change bodily position when encountering interactivity, from the lean backward position of narratives to the lean for-

ward position of games. And playing a game includes the awareness that the game session is just one out of many possible to be had from *this game*.

Is This It?

It is thus possible, in different ways, to view games as being in some way connected to narratives, but does this really answer the opening question? The preceding points would indicate that games and narratives do not live in different worlds, but can in some ways work together. A narrative may be used for telling the player what to do or as rewards for playing. Games may spawn narratives that a player can use to tell others of what went on in a game session. Games and narratives can on some points be said to have similar traits. This does mean that the strong position of claiming games and narratives to be *completely* unrelated (my own text, Juul, 1999 is a good example) is untenable.

But we also have to look at differences.

The Problem of Translation

I will now use narrative theory in an operation for which it was not intended. The basic problem of *the narrative* is the fact that a narrative can never be viewed independently, in itself. We can never see the story itself; we can only see it through another medium such as oral storytelling, novels, and movies. The classical argument for the existence of narratives is the fact that a story can be translated from one medium to another: "This transposability of the story is the strongest reason for arguing that narratives are indeed structures independent of any medium" (Chatman, 1978, p. 20).

Correspondingly, Peter Brooks says: "Narrative may be a special ability or competence that ... when mastered, allows us to summarise and retransmit narratives in other words and other languages, to transfer them into other media, while remaining recognisably faithful to the original narrative structure and message" (Brooks, 1992, p. 3–4).

This may seem somewhat unproblematic; we can never get everything between media, but at least something seems to get transported from medium to medium. A recounting of *Pride and Prejudice* the movie will be recognizable to somebody who has read the book.

Translating What?

This brings us to the problem of what we actually mean by saying that something can be translated from one medium to another. In a slightly limited view of narratives, narratives can be split into a level of discourse (the

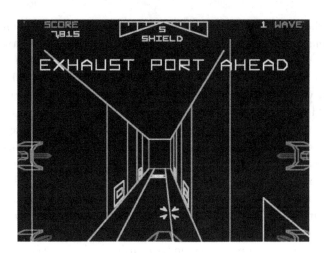

| Figure 14.2 |
Star Wars (Atari, 1983)

telling of the story) and the story (the story told). The story can then be split into two parts, *existents* (actors and settings) and *events* (actions and happenings) (Chatman, 1978, p. 19). A story can then be recognized by having the same existents (with the same names) and the same events; this is what we usually mean by talking of "the same story."

This can be used the other way, as a test of whether the computer game is a narrative medium. If the computer game is a narrative medium, stories from other media must be retellable in computer games, and computer games must be retellable in other media. On a superficial level, this seems straightforward because many commercial movies are repackaged as games—*Star Wars* is an obvious example. The other way around, games transferred into movies are less common, but examples include *Super Mario Brothers* (Jankel, 1993), *Mortal Kombat* (Anderson, 1995), and *Tomb Raider* (West, 2001). Upon further examination, we will find the situation to be much more complex.

From Movie to Game: Star Wars

The arcade game *Star Wars* (Atari, 1983; figure 14.2) is based on the George Lucas movie of the same name (1977). In the movie *Star Wars*, an army of rebels fights a heroic battle against the evil galactic empire. The dramatic peak of the movie is when the rebel army and the protagonist Luke Skywalker must attack the evil empire's new weapon, the Death Star. The *Star Wars* game consists of three phases, in all of which the player controls a spaceship from the inside, presumably as Luke Skywalker. The first phase takes place in space, where we fight hostile spacecraft. The second phase is on the Death Star, fighting different objects on the

Death Star surface. In the third phase, we fly through a tunnel in the Death Star to attack an exhaust port. This makes the Death Star explode. The first phase corresponds to an in-movie battle before Luke flies to the Death Star—except that the rebel fleet is absent. The second phase has no clear correlate in the movie. The third phase corresponds to a scene in the movie—again with the rebel fleet being absent. If you complete the mission, the Death Star explodes, so the game copies a small part of the movie.

The primary thing that encourages the player to connect game and movie is the title "Star Wars" on the machine and on the screen. If we imagine the title removed from the game, the connection would not be at all obvious. It would be a game where one should hit an "exhaust port" (or simply a square), and the player could note a similarity with a scene in *Star Wars*, but you would not be able to reconstruct the events in the movie from the game. The prehistory is missing, the rest of the movie, all personal relations. Possibly we are even missing the understanding that we are fighting a Death Star (whatever that is). Finally the most obvious: If you do not complete the mission, this is unlike the movie; if you complete the mission, another Death Star appears—which is also unlike the movie.

Thus, *Star Wars* the game cannot be said to contain a narrative recognizable from *Star Wars* the movie. Most characters from the movie are missing, and the few events that are included in the game have become simulations where the player can either win or fail. The same thing goes for the second batch of *Star Wars* games. *Star Wars: Racer* (Lucasarts, 1999) features the race sequence of *Star Wars: Episode I* (Lucas, 1999), but only that.[2]

From Game to Story

I will only briefly cover game-story translations, because they are fairly uncommon. If we look at the game *Mortal Kombat* (Midway Games, 1993), it is a fighting game (beat 'em up) where different opponents (humans or computer players) battle in an arena. It is thus a dynamic system that allows many different people to interact with many different outcomes. The *Mortal Kombat* movie is not a dynamic system, but a story with a specific set of characters entering a *Mortal Kombat* game and playing through with specific outcomes. The fairly nondescript game characters and open player positions become more detailed movie characters; the open simulation is converted into fixed events.

Correspondingly, if we recount a game of chess, our playing of the entire *Half-Life* game or a multiplayer game of *Starcraft*, the existents and events will be transferred, but not the dynamic systems.[3] Our retelling will not be a game, and in fact much of the vast journey that it takes to complete *Half-Life* would be excruciatingly dull if retold in any detail.

The concept of existents is best suited for physical games, where the number of manipulable elements is, at least in principle, finite. The problem is that programs are basically existent-creating machines. Computer games allow for the easy production of infinite numbers of existents; many action games in fact come with an infinite number of existents in the form of opponents. The other problem with the concept of existents is that in itself it does not specify what attributes of the existent are important, whereas game rules feature a strict hierarchy of important and unimportant features—Erving Goffman calls this the "rules of irrelevance" (Goffman, 1972, p. 19).

We should also note that most modern games feature cut-scenes, passages where the player cannot do anything but most simply watch events unfolding. Cut-scenes typically come in the form of introductions and scenes when the player has completed part of the game.

It is then possible to describe in a more general way how games get translated into narratives, and how narratives get translated into games, as table 14.1 shows.

Table 14.1
A table of narrative—game translations

Movies/Novels etc.	Game
Existent	Existent
	or
	Continuous production of existents (i.e. hordes of opponents)
Event	Event (cut-scene)
	or
	Simulation with multiple outcomes
Sequence of events	Selected events as events or simulations
	or
	Ideal sequence of events that the player has to actualize by mastering the simulations*
Character	Character (cut-scene)
	or
	Player position (game)

*The ideal sequence is much harder to actualize than the numerous non-ideal sequences—this is what makes it a game.

Note that both directions of the translation leave plenty of room for improvisation and carry many optional operations. In short, games based on movies tend to pick a few select action sequences, which are then simulated in game sequences—as we saw with *Star Wars*. Character description and development is either ignored or done in cut scenes (because this is too hard to implement in game form). Working from game to movie, the game is no longer a game, but is rather presented as specific game sessions, played by specific characters, with specific outcomes. The characters also tend to become more developed: *Tomb Raider*'s (Core Design, 1996) heroine Lara Croft acquires much more of a past and personality in the *Tomb Raider* movie.

Time, Game, and Narrative

Narrative is a ... double temporal sequence.... There is the time of the thing told and the time of the narrative (the time of the signified and the time of the signifier). This duality not only renders possible all the temporal distortions that are commonplace in narratives (three years of the hero's life summed up in two sentences of a novel or in a few shots of a "frequentative" montage in film, etc.). More basically, it invites us to consider that one of the functions of narrative is to invent one time scheme in terms of another time scheme.—Christian Metz (quoted from Genette, 1980, p. 33)

In the classical narratological framework, a narrative has two distinct kinds of time, the *story time*, denoting the time of the events told, in their chronological order, and the *discourse time*, denoting the time of the telling of events (in the order in which they are told). To read a novel or watch a movie is to a large extent about reconstructing a story on the basis of the discourse presented.

In a verbal narrative, the grammatical tense will neccesarily present a temporal relation between the time of the narration (narrative time) and the events told (story time). Additionally, it is possible to talk of a third time, the reading or viewing time (Genette, 1980, p. 34). Although movies and theatre do not have a grammatical tense to indicate the temporal relations, they still carry a basic sense that even though the viewer is watching a movie, now, or even though the players are on stage performing, the events told are *not* happening *now*. Bordwell writes, "there is the sense that the text before us, the play or the film, is the performance of a 'prior' story" (Bordwell, 1985, p. 15).

We cannot necessarily describe this as a specific temporal relation (hence "prior") but there is a funda-

| Figure 14.3 |
Doom II, level 2

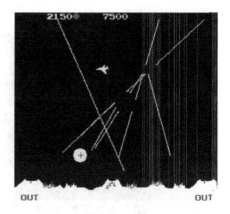

| Figure 14.4 |
Missile Command (Atari, 1980)

mental distance between the story time and discourse time. As Christian Metz notes in the above quote, narratives rely heavily on this distance or nonidentity between the events and the presentation of these events.

Time in the Computer Game

If we then play an action-based computer game such as *Doom II* (ID Software, 1994; figure 14.3), it is hard to find a distance between story time, narrative time, and reading/viewing time. We may find a representation, and as a player you try to reconstruct some events from this representation. The blocky graphics can be interpreted so far as the player controls a character, whose facial expression is represented in the bottom center. On the illustration this person has been cornered by a large pink monster, whose hostile intents are clear. Players are attacked by monsters; puzzles must be solved to get to the next level.

It is clear that the events represented cannot be *past* or *prior*, because we as players can influence them. By pressing the CTRL key, we fire the current weapon, which influences the game world. In this way, the game constructs the story time as *synchronous* with narrative time and reading/viewing time: the story time is *now*. Now, not just in the sense that the viewer witnesses events now, but in the sense that the events are *happening* now, and that what comes next is not yet determined.

In an "interactive story" game where the user watches video clips and occasionally makes choices, story time, narrative time, and reading/viewing time will move apart, but when the user can act, they must necessarily implode: it is impossible to influence something that has already happened. This means that *you cannot have interactivity and narration at the same time*. And this means in practice that games almost never perform basic narrative operations such as flashback and flash forward.[4] Games are almost always chronological.

This chapter is not about the intricacies of time in games (see Juul, 2004). Let us simply note that games may also have a speed that is not equal to the playing time—a day and night in the online multiplayer game *EverQuest* (Verant Interactive, 1999) takes seventy-two actual minutes to complete, and a game played in 2001 may be labelled as taking place in 1941. But playing a game requires at least points or periods of temporal convergence where the time of the game world and the time of the playing merge—and the player can actually *do* something.

The Player and the Game

The next question is less structural and more oriented toward the reader: How do the player and the game interact?

Movies and other stories are largely about humans (or anthropomorphic things) that the viewer/reader identifies with cognitively. It is basically boring to view/read fictions without anthropomorphic actors. This is not true for games. Games with no actors represented on screen have appeared throughout the history of the computer game.[5] Many of these have been extremely popular. An early example is *Missile Command* (Atari, 1980; figure 14.4), where a number of cities are attacked by missiles that you then have to destroy using rockets from three missile batteries. The player is not represented on screen as an entity or actor, but only sees the results of his or her actions. It would be possible to create a "job description" for the player—a soldier controlling missiles, a typical hero. It is harder to understand *Tetris* (Pazhitnov, 1985; figure 14.5), where you must combine a series of falling bricks.

Tetris does not have a visible actor either, and it does not seem possible to construct any actor

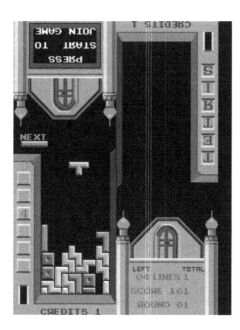

| Figure 14.5 |
Tetris (Atari's 1986 version)

controlling the falling bricks. "*Tetris—The Movie*" does not seem like a viable concept. But *Tetris* is incredibly popular, and nobody is disputing its status as a computer game.

But how can computer games be abstract and without points of identification, and yet be interesting? No matter how variable or even absent the protagonist in computer games, the player is always constant. The reader/viewer needs an emotional motivation for investing energy in the movie or book; we need a human actor to identify with. This is probably also true for the computer game, only this actor is always present—it is the player. The player is motivated to invest energy in the game because the game evaluates the player's performance. And this is why a game can be more abstract than a movie or a novel, because games involve the player in a direct way.

This discrepancy raises many issues. In a game, the player works to reach a goal. This goal has to mimic the player's situation. It seems, for example, that a game cannot have the goal that the player should work hard to throw the protagonist under a train.[6] As a player, the goal has to be one that you would conceivably want to work for.[7]

A Final Argument: The Avant Garde Fallacy

There is a final counter-argument to the points set forth here: The problem with my description of story

as having existents and events, my description of time, my description of the player/game relation as unique could be this: That I am ignoring the experimental narratives of the twentieth century, works that do not simply subscribe to the story/discourse duality, activate the reader much more, and do not have a sense of being past or prior. We can explore this with a few select examples.

Jean-Luc Godard's *Pierrot le fou* (1965) would serve as an example of a movie where it is hard to construct a coherent story due to numerous temporal skips and distancings, such as the actors addressing the camera. This foregrounding of the discourse has a sense of immediacy that would make it ripe for a game adaptation—if only we could figure what the game should be about.

During the creation of *Naked Lunch*, William Burroughs wrote the follow explanation to Allen Ginsberg: "The usual novel *has happened*. This novel *is happening*" (Burroughs, 1993, p. 375).

It may be obvious that the more open a narrative is to interpretation, the more emphasis will be on the reader/viewer's efforts *now*. The difference between the now in narratives and the now in games is that the first now concerns the situation where the reader's effort in interpreting obscures the story—the text becomes *all* discourse, and consequently the temporal tensions ease. The now of the game means that story time converge with playing time, *without the story/game world disappearing*.

Games rely on having goals that can be deciphered by the player and something obstructing the player's possibility of reaching the goals. Narratives are basically interpretative, whereas games are formal. Or, in cybertextual terms, stories have an interpretative dominant, whereas games have a configurative dominant (Eskelinen, 2001). Although readers and viewers are clearly more active than some theories have previously assumed, they are active in a different way.

The idea of using experimental narratives to answer the opening question suffers from the problem that the very emphasis on interpretation and ontological unstability that would make the narrative more immediate and thus closer to the game, in itself would make a game unplayable.[8]

Conclusion

I believe that: (1) The player can tell stories of a game session. (2) Many computer games contain narrative elements, and in many cases the player may play to see a cut-scene or realize a narrative sequence. (3) Games and narratives share some structural traits. Nevertheless, my point is that: (1) Games and stories actually do not translate to each other in the way that novels and movies do. (2) There is an inherent conflict between the *now* of the interaction and the *past* or *"prior"* of the narrative. You can't have narration and interactivity at the same time; there is no such thing as a continuously interactive story. (3) The relations between reader/story and player/game are completely different—the player inhabits a twilight zone where he or she is both an empirical subject outside the game *and* undertakes a role inside the game.

Even if this chapter has been somewhat structural in its orientation, I would like to state that I think we need to consider games as fairly formal structures that in complex ways spawn and feed player experiences. This means that we cannot afford to ignore the effect of interactivity. The nondetermined state of the story/game world and the active state of the player when playing a game has huge implications for how we perceive games. Even if we were to *play* only a single game session of a hypothetical game and end up performing exactly the same sequence of events that constitute *Hamlet*,[9] we would not have had the same experience as had we *watched Hamlet* performed. We would also not consider the game to be the same object as the play because we would think of the game as an explorable dynamic system that allowed for a multitude of sequences.

The narrative turn of the last twenty years has seen the concept of narrative emerge as a privileged master concept in the description of all aspects of human society and sign-production. Expanding a concept can in many cases be useful, but the expansion process is also one that blurs boundaries and muddles concepts, whether this is desirable or not. With any sufficiently broad definition of *x*, everything will be *x*. This rapidly expands the possible uses of a theory but also brings the danger of exhaustion, the kind of exhaustion that eventually closes departments and feeds indifference. Having established that everything is *x*, there is nothing to do except to repeat this point.

Using other media as starting points, we may learn many things about the construction of fictive worlds, characters ... but relying too heavily on existing theories will make us forget what makes games games, such as rules, goals, player activity, the projection of the player's actions into the game world, the way the game defines the possible actions of the player. It is the unique parts that we need to study now.

These are both descriptive and normative issues. It does not make much sense to describe *everything* in the same terms. It also is quite limiting to suppose that all cultural forms *should* work in the same way. The discussion of games and narratives is a relevant one and I can not hope to close it here. This chapter has argued for telling the difference.[10]

Notes

1. Note that multiplayer games rarely contain ideal sequences but rather allow the players to replay the same setting with new results—think of Chess or *Starcraft* (Blizzard Entertainment, 1998). As such they are very far from narratives. On the other hand, the retelling of a game session in a single player game (*"and then I ... and then I ... and then I ..."*) is less interesting than the retelling of a multiplayer game because the latter can include intrigues, lies, and deceit between people (*"We had agreed to combine forces on the eastern front, but only in the end did I realize that she was actually conspiring with Joe"*).

2. This also relates to the maturation of the game industry: The first *Star Wars* movie resulted in one computer game; the latest movie has spawned somewhere around ten different games on different platforms featuring different pieces of the movie or of the *Star Wars* universe.

3. The other major problem is that games are formalized and rule-bound; and as such much more fit for physics and firearms than existential problems, because the latter are not easily formalized (see Juul, 2000). This means that some events are very hard to create as dynamic systems.

4. Flash forward is more of a problem than flashback, because describing events in the future means that the player cannot do anything.

5. Traditional board and card games tend to be much more abstract than computer games.

6. The *Anna Karenina* example was presented by Marie-Laure Ryan (2001).

7. This does not rule out ironies, but all examples I know of work by putting the player in an *active* position doing things normally considered negative: Destroying houses and killing people in *Rampage* (Bally Midway, 1986), killing pedestrians in *Death Race* (Exidy, 1976) and *Carmageddon* (Sales Curve Interactive, 1997). I know

of no games where the goal of the player is to die or be destroyed.

8. This still leaves open numerous unexplored possibilities such as multiple contradictory goals, games of *Tetris* that cause the destruction of famous artworks in another window on the screen, etc. The point is that we should not expect (or demand) that game experiments mimic narrative experiments.

9. *Hamlet* is actually a poor choice for game adaptation because it (like many narratives) has several scenes where the protagonist is absent, and thus gives the audience more information than is available to the characters. Such common devices of knowledge and suspense are not in any obvious way implementable in a game format where audience and protagonist are the same person.

10. This chapter is based on a paper in *Game Studies*, 2001, *1* (1).

References

Aarseth, E. J. (1997). *Cybertext: Perspectives on ergodic literature*. Baltimore: Johns Hopkins University Press.

Bordwell, D. (1985). *Narration in the fiction film*. Madison: The University of Wisconsin Press.

Brooks, P. (1992). *Reading for the plot*. Cambridge, MA: Harvard University Press.

Burroughs, W. S. (1993). *The letters of William Burroughs 1945–1959*. Ed. by O. Harris. London: Penguin Books.

Chatman, S. (1978). *Story and discourse: Narrative structure in fiction and film*. Ithaca: Cornell University Press.

Eskelinen, M. (2001). *The gaming situation*. Paper presented at the Digital Arts and Culture conference, Providence, April.

Genette, G. (1980). *Narrative discourse*. Ithaca: Cornell University Press.

Goffman, E. (1972). *Encounters: Two studies in the Sociology of Interaction*. London: Penguin.

Jensen, J. F. (1988). Adventures i computerville: Games, inter-action & high tech paranoia i Arkadia. *Kultur & Klasse 63*. Copenhagen: Medusa, pp. 81–120.

Juul, J. (1999). *A clash between game and narrative*. M.A. Thesis, University of Copenhagen. www.jesperjuul.dk/thesis.

Juul, J. (2000). *What computer games can and can't do*. Paper presented at the Digital Arts and Culture conference, Bergen, August. www.jesperjuul.dk/text/WCGCACD.html.

Juul, J. (2004). Introduction to game time. In Noah Wardrip-Fruin and Pat Harrigan (Eds.), *First person: New media as story, performance, and game*. Cambridge, MA: MIT Press.

Murray, J. H. (1997). *Hamlet on the holodeck: The future of narrative in cyberspace*. New York: The Free Press.

Ryan, M.-L. (2001). *Beyond myth and metaphor: The case of narrative in digital media*. Keynote speech at the Computer Games and Digital Textualities conference, Copenhagen, March.

15

NARRATIVITY IN COMPUTER GAMES

Britta Neitzel

Marcel becomes a plumber.
—Gérard Genette, 1988, p. 19

Game or Narrative

Research work on computer games cannot avail itself of a long tradition—popular computer games are just thirty-five years old, after all. Narratives, on the contrary, are a large and influential part of our culture. Stories have long served as structures to give order and a sense of meaning to the world. And it is not only literature that tells stories. History can be seen as a certain type of storytelling as well; films tell stories, drama, comic strips and even painting contain narrative features. Thus it seems reasonable to assume that computer games tell stories as well.

The issue of narrativity in computer games has, in fact, gained a certain prominence, with opinions covering a spectrum ranging from general negation to euphoric affirmation. Out of studies of hypertext in the 1980s and 1990s arose questions about the possibilities of "interactive storytelling" as a new form of narrative in digital media (cf. e.g., Bolter, 1991; Landow, 1992, 1994). These studies have expanded to include verbally based computer games, the so-called text adventures.

In this tradition, computer games are seen in connection with other texts based on computer technology. The text and the changes it undergoes remain in the foreground (e.g., in Ryan, 1999). Murray (1997) includes computer games in her study of narrative in cyberspace by observing them, along with chatterbots, MUDs, 3D movies, and finally the holodeck, in relation to their narrativity. In *Computers as theatre*, Laurel (1991) examines computer applications and interfaces using the metaphor of the theatre and Aristotelian dramatic theory. In her study as well, computer games represent only one application among several. Finally, Aarseth's (1997) focus is on verbal media and, apart from his insightful analysis of the text adventure, he does not consider computer games.[1]

In the last years, focused and decisive scientific analysis of the popular computer game has grown, with various conferences held. Since 2001, academic game research has its first platform with the online journal *Game Studies* (www.gamestudies.org).

But studies in computer games still fall far short of forming different schools. Nevertheless, a vehement and often polemic body of criticism has emerged directed at studies that see the computer game as one possible form of future storytelling, or simply treat the computer game as a narrative medium at all.

This criticism is mainly borne by the fear that methods developed for the study of literature are insufficient to deal with the specifics of computer games, and would, on the contrary, simply incorporate them into its own territory, treating computer games as a derivative of literature. This position argues that computer games are games after all, and that because games are something completely different from narratives, they couldn't possibly be studied according to narrative criteria.[2]

A position that simply treats the computer game as narrative, or one that negates any relation between narratives and games, are both too narrow in scope. In the first case, there is a danger of overlooking differences between games and narratives; computer games are, in fact, more than "interactive narratives." The second position, on the other hand, risks disregarding similarities between computer games and narratives just because not every game has the same structure and computer games are structured differently than, for example, ball games. Common to both positions is that they are based on exclusivity and are aimed at fundamental principles, an approach that fails to acknowledge the specifics of the computer: the computer is a hybrid medium that integrates various forms and other media and in so doing dissolves distinctions between them (cf. Thomsen, 1994). Digital memory and processing mechanisms allow the computer to adapt almost unlimited surfaces for equally innumerable functions, as well

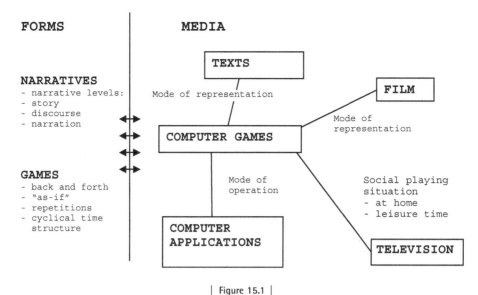

| Figure 15.1 |
Relationships between computer games and other media

as to integrate and change the structures of other media. The computer as toy, and thus the computer game, must be described specifically in reference to this dissolution of boundaries and integration of various elements. The fact that computer games are games by no means excludes them from having narrative qualities. Thus, in this chapter I take a third viewpoint, based on the assumption that there are commonalities and overlapping elements in computer games and narratives, as well as a transitional zone between nonnarrative and narrative computer games.[3]

Figure 15.1 shows some broad relations between computer games and other media. These involve similarities in the modes of operation, representation, as well as more social and cultural similarities, for example media use in certain locations and times.

Not every computer game, however, has relationships to each of the media mentioned here. Especially the manner of presentation divides the computer games into two categories. The text adventures, of course, have something in common with written texts, whereas the presentational style of all other computer games can be described in comparison to other visual media, especially film. But this is not the only difference among computer games. Arcade games, for example, are played in a different environment than those played on a console or computer. *Pong* (Atari, 1972), for instance, differs fundamentally from *Tomb Raider* (Core, Eidos, 1996)—in regard to narrativity, for one thing.

For the case of the narrativity of computer games, the differentiation between medium and form in figure 15.1 taken from Niklas Luhmann (cf. Luhmann, 1995,

pp. 165–214) is crucial. According to Luhmann, media represent a loose coupling of elements consolidated through form. Each form depends on a certain medium for its realization, while simultaneously introducing, as form, a certain structure into these media. Because the narrative as well as the game only ever appear in a certain medium, they will be understood here as forms that can be combined with various media.[4] Thus a certain computer game can take over narrative as well as ludic forms—and also forms that are not mentioned here in detail. By no means are either narrative or game fully described forms yet—nor will they ever be—but some defining features as the narrative levels in case of the narrative and the "as-if," the repetitions, and the back and forth movement in case of the game appear in most of the definitions.

Computer games not only have varying relationships to other media, but there are also differences among the computer games themselves. Due to this variety of computer games, it is necessary to narrow my focus of attention in this chapter. What I will discuss on the following pages is the single-player computer game based on a graphic surface. I will neither consider multiplayer games, because they are played in a different "narrative" situation, nor text adventures, 3D environments such as the CAVE or "holodecks," because they have a different mode of presentation.

Because the debate over narrativity in computer games is rooted in the differentiation between game and narrative, I will focus on some definitions of the game, the computer game, and the narrative to provide a frame for the following in-depth analysis of the narrativity of computer games. This analysis will orient itself to the narrative levels developed in narratology: story and plot as levels describing the events told as well as their order will be discussed, followed by the levels of discourse and narration, dealing with the modes of representation and questions of authorship. When necessary, I will consider relationships to other media—as figure 15.1 shows—as well.

Play and Games

In theories of play and games concerned with the cultural meaning of their subject, play is seen mainly as a fundamental human activity that finds expression in various forms of games.[5] A consistent pattern appearing in these theories is the differentiation between play and game, which can be characterized by the opposition of freedom and regulation or of determination and indetermination. The German pedagogue Hans Scheuerl describes this as follows:

Play, playing is a series of movements which can be differentiated through moments of freedom, ambivalence, relative unity, a special time structure and relationship to reality, from other series of movements.

Games are improvised or established agreement and rule structures in the framework of, or according to the norm of which, one uses play activities to produce and give form to such series of movement. (1975, pp. 347–348.)

In this definition, play is a particular action, whereas a game provides the structural boundaries for the play activities. It is not only Scheuerl who defines the relation of play and game in this way. Johan Huizinga describes play as "a free act that takes place ... within a specially designated time in a specially designated place, according to specific rules which are strictly adhered to" (Huizinga, 1994, p. 22).

Roger Caillois (1958) also considers freedom and regulation as the two defining elements of games. He makes the distinction between *paidia* and *ludus*, *paidia* referring to the type of unrestricted casual play that develops in all directions—the urge to play itself— whereas *ludus* is defined by the use of practice and rules. It is only when both tendencies combine that individual games develop.

Both the freedom of play and the determination through the game belong together. Every game is dependent on this determinate indetermination.

An extremely insightful and simple structural explanation for the necessity of limits in games comes from F. J. J. Buytendijk (1933). In his opinion, a defin-

ing feature of games is a back and forth motion that might go on among the players, as well as between a player and an object. A back and forth among the players means that choices are made in turn. A back and forth between player and play object develops when, for example, a ball is repeatedly thrown against a wall, repeatedly caught, and then thrown against the wall again. Such an oscillating movement naturally needs fixed points between which it can commute: "If one were to throw a ball and it didn't come back, then no game would develop.... Without a playing field the player's activity would be lost" (p. 118).

In addition to the spatial limitations, the time limits and the rules—that is to say, instructions for play—there are also boundaries created by fiction (cf. Caillois, 1958). These arise when a world of "as if" comes into play, for example in the theatre. Theatre is also a good example of how various forms of limitation can be implemented at once.

The fact that limitations exist, and the various forms they take lead to the establishment of certain structural patterns within the game. In the simplest case, this is the constant repetition of a back and forth movement between the boundaries; a movement that can also be varied slightly, but that essentially has no end and lapses back into itself. This, for its part, leads to a cyclical time structure within games. According to their inner structures, games are not laid out along chronological lines. Although a game lasts a certain amount of time and is imbedded in a chronology, it can, on basis of its inner temporality, be observed as a unified whole with no relationship to a past or future existing outside of itself. Thus the game is taken out of a temporal continuum, as is the present in some time models, where it represents not something that elapses, but rather an intermediate point, devoid of any expansion, where the future turns into the past.

According to Luhmann (1980), this turning point is heavily dependent on the effects of actions. He assumes that the past sets in only from the point at which the changes resulting from a chain of actions are no longer reversible. Before that occurs, there is an expanded present in which certain tendencies for the future, though already introduced, could still possibly be steered in another direction. One could remain in this present, and possibly negotiate what should be. The future, then, would be open. In other words, a state of being is maintained, the result is not yet decided, and one is still in the process of fixing an outcome. In this sense, we can describe games as a process of expanding the present, in which certain defining tendencies for the future are laid down by the rules, but not the exact chain of events or the result.

According to these conceptualizations, play is first and foremost an activity carried out in line with the various rules and limitations that make up individual games. What all games have in common, however, is that they must be played. Without the process of play, there would remain only rigid rule constructions. When studying computer games, then, it's important to first clearly define the object of study. Is it the structures, the rules and the play object—the hardware—or the game itself, which proceeds under the constraints of all these things? The answer is simple. Games cannot be adequately described without considering the process of play.

In so doing, it is important to differentiate between two aspects indicated by Espen Aarseth (1997). He warns against confusing the object with the experience one has with the object. He defines the object as a "material entity that determines it [the work] in a way the individual readings do not" (p. 46). But in the case of the computer game, we must bear in mind that the object is not only a material entity, but also a procedural one.

The Playing Field of the Computer Game

Because games are defined by certain boundaries (be they temporal, spatial, or rules that define the actions), I like to describe the specifics of computer games by referring to their spatial boundaries that lead to further characteristics.

Every computer game separates the actual space in which the player is situated, and the virtual space of the fictional game activity. The player can manipulate the virtual space with the help of various input devices— for example, a keyboard, a mouse, a joystick, or console controllers—and the effects of these manipulations can simultaneously be viewed on a monitor as the output device. Herein lie, of course, the similarities between computer games and other computer applications that figure 15.1 addresses. The input and output devices regulate the ways the player gains access to the game. The input device defines which actions the player can carry out in the game—for example, in combination with the *Tomb Raider* program, pressing the (x)-button on the PSX and PS II controller results in a shot by Lara Croft; the output device, that is, the monitor in combination with the *Tomb Raider* software, defines how the player sees these actions and the world of the

game. This distancing and mediation through the use of technical equipment is specific to the computer game. In other games, for example ball games, the player can manipulate real objects, with or without accessory equipment, or the play can take place in the imagination, with objects and environments that exist entirely in the fantasy of the players.[6] The indirect manner in which computer games manipulate objects of play—here a key is pressed and somewhere else an object moves—requires technical mediation. In computer games, graphic elements can move about on a monitor and, depending on the game, create entire worlds of their own. This quality of visualization is relevant for playing computer games. Just as the condition of the ball makes a difference to a ball game, it is the quality of the images and the laws under which they operate that make a difference in computer games.

By this we can separate text-based computer games from image-based ones. There is also a further subdivision amongst the image-based games, between those in which one appears to be playing with the objects on the monitor and those in which one seems to enter and manipulate a world that is pictured on the monitor screen. Commenting on the first category, which applies to the early arcade and console games, Bolter and Grusin (2000, p. 91) refer to *opaque* interfaces, whereas in the second category the interface is *transparent*. I will return to this distinction.

Specific to the computer game is that seeing and acting are separated through the *apparatus* (Baudry, 1986), and are continuously brought back together again in the course of play. The player acts. The computer takes the effects of the actions out of the spatial-material reality of the player and distributes them in the virtual space of the monitor. This virtual space, including the effects of the actions, is observed and interpreted, which then influences the subsequent actions.

Thus we can define computer games as a process of self-observation with continuous feedback. In this process, the position of the player is doubled. In addition to the position as an agent that the player has in every game, he or she is also assigned the position of an observer, which in turn determines her position as an agent in the visual space. In this way the player takes on a position divided into active and observational functions, which are integrated during the process of play. The activities unite the player with the game, propelling it forward. The position of observation, which relates to the presentation of the objects or the world on the monitor, connects the player with the game in another way: as with the camera position in film, this position organizes the point of view, in a purely spatial sense, from which the activity can be observed. The perspective also has the effect of regulating the player's level of involvement in, or distance to, the game. To prevent a growth of terminology, I will use the term *point of action* for the active position and *point of view* for the position of observation.

One might be tempted to define the perspective of observation as a perspective of perception. The term "observation" though, goes farther than "perception." Perception happens all the time, and it only happens where one's own body is (Luhmann, 1955, pp. 275ff). The player's body, however, is not in the virtual playing field. The term "observing" takes this difference into account: "All observation is the introduction of a differentiation within a space which remains unmarked, out of which the observer executes the act of making a distinction" (Luhmann, 1995, p. 92). In the case of computer games, the observer is the player who, from a position in front of the monitor, makes the distinction between his or her own world and the world of the game. This distinction also enables the player to observe him or herself as another—as the avatar, for example. This self-observation alone allows a player, in the function of an avatar, to take action within the world of the game: the player attributes the actions of the avatar to her or himself as another.

Playing computer games distinguishes itself from other forms of play and also from activities with non-computer-supported textual and pictorial media, through the interaction with an imaginary world. This world can—not only, but also—be seen, and one can enter into it, though only indirectly, through the use of technical equipment. It was this penetration into a "world behind the monitor" that was the primary scene for computer games, as we know them today. Before that, the world behind the monitor had always been closed. Television had an audience that could only watch. Now one could play with this world. Out of an imaginary visual space emerged a virtual space for activity. But this space for activity, which is the playing field of the computer game, also remains a space for representation. Or as Brenda Laurel (1991, p. 1) puts it, the potential of the computer lay "in its capacity to *represent action in which humans could participate*."

The connectedness of the level of action and the level of representation with the simultaneous distinction between these two levels links computer games to narrative, because the distinction between representation and what is represented forms the basis of every narrative. A narrative is the "*representation* of a real or fictional chain of *actions*" (Metzler, 1984, p. 132).

This structural equivalent provides the prerequisite for examining computer games according to narrative criteria, subject of the next section.

Narrative Structure

In his open definition, Christian Metz describes the narrative as a "doubly temporal sequence ... there is the time of the thing told and the time of the telling (the time of the significate and the time of the signifier)" (Metz, 1974, p. 18). He thus distinguishes between two levels, each with its own temporal quality. On the basis of this he distinguishes between forms of media. To explain the differences he uses the example of film footage of a caravan traveling through the desert:

- The narrative invents one time scheme in terms of another: several successive shots show the caravan on its way through the desert.
- The description transports a space into a time: several successive shots show the desert.
- Finally, the image transports a space into another space: a single shot shows the desert.

Metz doesn't discuss the possibility of transporting time into a space, in the case of the film: a single shot of the caravan in motion. However, this isn't relevant for the film, because in film, aside from rare experimental situations, there are always multiple shots. But this case is significant for the early computer games. They show movements on an image. One plays with the objects shown on the surface of this image—be they lines and dots (a bat and ball) in *Pong*, tanks and "Space Invaders" in *Space Invaders* (Midway, Taito, 1978), or a spaceship and asteroids (*Asteroids*, Atari, 1979). In *Tetris* (1987) as well, there is no temporal level of representation. Bolter and Grusin (2000, p. 91), as stated above, describe this sort of representation as *opaque*: "There is nothing behind or beyond the interface, as there appears to be with a perspective painting or photograph." And, we can now add, a temporal quality is missing. The portrayal is thus not recognized as portrayal, as independent from that, which is portrayed. The players, then, play with the interface.

It was the *Mario Brothers* games from Nintendo that first incorporated the representation of various rooms, and later horizontal scrolling screens,[7] so that

Britta Neitzel

Table 15.1
Levels of narrative

	Presented Parts	Story	Level of Arrangement of Action	Level of Representation (Abstract)	Media Components of Representation	Object of Study
Aristotle	Events	Fabula	Mythos (plot)			Action (abstract)
Russian formalism	Motives	Fabula	Suyzhet/action			Suyzhet (abstract)
Todorov	Actions, personnage	Histoire	Discourse			Narrative (abstract)
Genette	Événéments	Histoire	Narration			Récit verbal (concrete)
Chatman	Events, existents	Story	(Plot)	Discourse		Narrative (abstract)
Bordwell	Events	Fabula	Suyzhet		Style	Film (concrete)
			Narration			

the portrayal also took on identifiable characteristics. These games mark the transition from presentation to representation and establish the possibility for narrativity: the two temporal sequences.

Narrative theory generally maintains that narrative consists of at least these two levels. With regard to the represented—the story—there is general agreement, but when dealing with the level of representation, there is divergent thought. Table 15.1, which gives an overview of narrative levels as conceptualized in literary and cinematic theories of narrative, shows this. It may also help to clarify the relations of the terms used in the different languages.

Presented Parts
Most scholars describe the elements a story consists of as events and actions.[8] Todorov (1977) and Chatman (1978) alter this action-centered conception. Todorov also includes people, whereas Chatman speaks of events and existents. Furthermore, he distinguishes the events in respect to their importance for the narrative: "Events are either logically essential or not (kernels versus satellites)." The satellites can be left out, whereas the kernels cannot (cf. Chatman, 1978, p. 32).[9]

Story
The story consists of the presented parts or as Bordwell (1985, p. 49) puts it, "the fabula embodies the action as a chronological, cause-and-effect chain of events occurring within a given duration and a spatial field."

It is now also an accepted principle that the story is not an independent precursor to the storytelling; rather, it is put together or summarized by the recipient, based on information contained in the text. These informations are given through the arrangement of actions in the discourse.

Arrangement of Actions
The level of the arrangement of actions (plot/mythos) relates to the order of the events in the text. Through this arrangement, which results in the actual order of events given in the text (Tomashevsky, 1965, p. 67), the recipient is led in a certain direction, so that he or she can construct the story—or be obstructed in doing so.

A precise relation between the events and the plot is already laid out in the Aristotelian concept. In his conception of tragedy, Aristotle differentiates between the individual parts that are portrayed, which he calls events, and the unifying force, the mythos, which brings them together. In his conception, the mythos[10] leads the action forward and should create plots that "should be constructed dramatically, that is around a single, whole, and complete action, with beginning, middle, and end" (1995, p. 115). So Aristotle does not see the events that occur in the tragedy as being independent of their given order, but as subject to the laws of composition. It is not the separate parts that lead to the conclusion; on the contrary, the whole and complete action determines the individual parts, which are brought together by the mythos in order to fulfill their duty in leading to the conclusion.[11]

Discourse and Narration

The term *discourse* as used by Todorov and Chatman is far wider reaching than the term suyzhet or plot. It includes not only the arrangement of the actions, but also the narrative situation, including the role of the narrator, the focalization of the events and the mode of narration—concepts I will refer to later.

Genette (1980) and Bordwell (1985) highlight the procedural element of this level, as well as its dependency on the medium in which the narrative is realized.[12] They both choose the term *narration*. Although the plot represents the result of the arrangement of action, it is in itself part of the process of narration. Questions of authorship also relate to the level of narration.

The Form of the Story in Computer Games

Beginning—middle—end, the three fundamental elements of the story according to Aristotle have a long-standing tradition. This structure appears in an elaborated form in Lotman 1977 and in Campbell 1965. As set out in the last paragraph, especially the ending—the point everything leads to—where meaning is given to everything that came before, is an important component of this model.[13]

The first game that clearly used this canonic story structure was *Donkey Kong* (Nintendo, 1981). The monkey Donkey Kong has abducted the princess and brought her back to his country. The task of the game's protagonist (a carpenter who later became Mario the plumber) is to save the princess. In order to achieve his goal he has to overcome various obstacles. When he manages to conquer all the obstacles, the princess is saved.

A story like this is given to the player as a horizon of meaning at the beginning of the game and it is also calculated as an option in the program. The story doesn't need to be fully realized in order to be recognizable as according with the narrative canon. Missing segments are expanded upon, as shown by cognitive research dealing with processes related to order and the development of meaning in narratives.

In this vein, Mandler and Johnson (1978) conclude that in the course of a lifetime, every human being learns certain schemata for recognition of narratives. Two influences are mainly responsible for creating these schemata: "One is the frequent hearing of stories, and consists of knowledge of the pattern of events in stories, including their typical beginning and end. The other has to do with experience of the world and

Table 15.2
The story schema of *Tomb Raider*

(1) *Setting* Introduction of the protagonist; can contain information about physical, social, or temporal context in which the remainder of the story occurs	Lara Croft sits in a hotel lobby. A messenger from Jacqueline Nadla comes, realizes that Lara is an adventuress.
(2) *Introductory event* An action, an internal event, or a natural occurrence which serves to initiate or to cause a response in the protagonist	Lara gets the contract from Jacqueline Nadla to search for the "Scion" in the Andes.
(3) *Protagonist's reaction* An emotion, cognition, or goal of the protagonist	Lara is in the Andes and makes her way to the caves of Qualopek.
(4) *Attempt* An overt action to obtain the protagonist's goal	Lara runs through the caves.
(4a) *Complicating actions*	Various opponents and obstacles need to be overcome in the search for the "Scion."
(5) *Result* An event, action, or endstate which marks the attainment or nonattainment of the protagonist's goal	Lara has found all the parts of the "Scion."
(6) *Reactions to the result*	She declines to hand over the pieces of the "Scion" to her employer, who could use them to do evil. Lara sails off into the sunset on Nadla's yacht.

Note: The schema is taken from Stein (1978, 235). Branigan (1992, 14f.) refers to Stein as well, but replaces her point (4) "attempt" with (4a) "complicating actions." Example: *Tomb Raider* (Eidos, 1996).

includes knowledge of causal relationships and various sorts of effects of actions" (p. 338).

Schema theory studies the relationship of memory performance and narrative text structures in particular, starting with the assumption that a story will be better remembered when it is based on the schema (cf. Mandler & Johnson, 1978, p. 339; Stein, 1978, p. 234). The schemata that have been developed resemble the complete, classic structure of a story (cf. Todorov 1971; Branigan 1992). In nonformalized form, it looks like table 15.2.

These schemata represent a macrostructure of stories. They serve to expand on the narrative when some parts don't appear in the story. For example, we can then speak of a story with an open end when (5) and (6) are omitted. It is these elements that terminate the present tense of the game. When (4a) is left out, one is possibly forced to speculate on what happened in the meantime, and can fill the empty space from memory with suitable events. (cf. Mandler & Johnson, 1978)

Alongside the schematic concept, which is mainly used to describe memories, there is the concept of the script. The script is a dynamic model applied to formulate expectations in a certain sequence (Herman, 1997, p. 104). If, as in the case of *Tomb Raider*, the points (1) Lara in the hotel lobby, (2) Jacqueline Nadla's offer, (3) Lara in the Andes, and a preview of (5) the "Scion" is found are already given, then the player can activate the script "complete, whole story." During the course of the game the player can compare the events of the game with the schema for the story, to determine if it is in fact complete. On the other hand the player can realize that there is no story in the game. One could say that, in this respect, the story is told before the game is played.

Just as this story is set up by the player to be completed, it is also programmed in the computer as a possible narrative, which can be actualized. In the process of actualization, Lara Croft fights her way, in various environments, through "complicating events," finds all the parts of the "Scion" and finally, after the death of Jacqueline Nadla, uses Nadla's yacht to leave the scene of the action, taking off for the open seas. The condition for arriving at this conclusion is the actualization of all *kernels*, that is to say, the actualization all necessary events that, taken together, are also sufficient for reaching the end. This story can be called the *minimal story* of the game. In contrast to the minimal story is one that depicts an ideal path, the so-called *complete solution* or the *walk-through*. The walk-through describes the possibility of mastering the game completely, showing the way one needs to go in order to collect all the objects, find all the "secrets," and kill all one's opponents, events that then appear in the score table.

The difference between the minimal story and the ideal story is that in the minimal story only the *kernels* are taken into account. In contrast, the ideal story takes the *satellites* into account as well.

The walk-through is not a story that is told in order to say "what has happened" (cf. Todorov, 1977, p. 20). It is, in fact, more of a recipe for creating the ideal story, in other words, an instruction for actions. The following example, part of a walk-through for *Tomb Raider*, shows this:

Now. Max out your health if it isn't 100% and save your game, then walk cautiously into the valley until you can see a broken rope bridge above you and a massive bloody great T-Rex thundering toward you. Scream judiciously and start *firing and jumping backward nonstop. Keep on the run, and don't let this bugger get close! unless you really like the idea of becoming a coprolith. Keep an eye on your health bar and remember that you can heal yourself mid-fight if you have to. To do this, press Escape to bring up the inventory and freeze the action, use a medipack, and return to the fight with a sigh of contentment from Lara.*" (Lynn Hendricks, 1996–2000)

This recipe for mastering the "Lost Valley" level in *Tomb Raider* differs from a story in its use of the imperative. Another conspicuous feature is that the player is addressed in reference to various functions. "Save your game" and especially "press Escape" refer not to the diegesis[14] but explicitly to what the player does—pressing buttons. "Walk cautiously into the valley" and also "a sigh of contentment from Lara" on the other hand, refer to an action in the diegesis. These two statements also mark an indecision in respect to who the active character is, as shown by the switch from the second to the third person. In other words, the first quote addresses the player (though it is obviously not the player who actually walks into the valley), and the second describes an action by the avatar. Finally, "until you can see" refers to observation. Thus three fields of action for the player are addressed here: the player's actions as player, the player's actions as avatar in the diegesis, and the observational actions of the player.

For a nonplayer, the walk-through seems incomplete; the world in which the avatar moves is not fully defined. One cannot read a walk-through as a story but has to be fully engaged in the game to understand what it's about.

Walk-throughs, as the name suggests, are mainly signposts or route maps consisting of static and dynamic elements, just like a story. But the imperative mode doesn't change until the moment the player begins to pursue a path, at which point there is a transition from possibility to actuality. And it is precisely this following of a path executed in the game.

The story is actualized by the avatar's walking, running, and jumping, which then creates a plot and can be compared with the act of narration, according to de Certeau: "The act of walking is for the urban system what the utterance (the speech-act) is for language or for formulated statements" (De Certeau, 1988, p. 189).

There are two main things that lend credence to this comparison: (1) These actions differ from one another in every round that's played. This means they relate not to the story but the plot. Play itself, with its continuous repetition, writes itself into the game through the modes of movement. (2) The locomotive actions are not listed in the score tables of the game; they influence only the time it takes to absolve a level. What is being measured here is performance; this result doesn't represent the story time, but the narrative time.

Story Models

In action games or action-adventure games the player can be certain that there exists already one fixed ending in the program in the mode of possibility. Each round and all plots can be seen as attempts to reach this ending.

Todorov (1971) defines narratives built on this kind of forward-moving and for the most part action-based stories as *mythological narratives*. They work with the change of a positive state into a negative one and the subsequent restoration of the original state.[15]

Yet he proposes two more categories of narratives:[16] the *gnoseological* and the *ideological* narratives.

The *gnoseological narratives* are build on a transition from ignorance to knowledge. These narratives are concerned with the realization of meaning. In *The quest for the Holy Grail*, one of his examples, it is not so much about finding the Grail as about understanding what the Grail means, and the reinterpretation of actions in light of subsequent developments. In principle, this search for knowledge is infinite. Such narratives tend to be retrogressive, which becomes even clearer in Todorov's second example, the detective story, the point of which is to find out what happened before. These stories have an ending, but it is uncertain.

In adventure games we find a gnoseological story structure. Here the player as avatar is thrown into a situation in which she doesn't know right away what to do, where she is exactly, what the environment is like or what events have occurred, and "the player of an adventure game ... is not guaranteed that the events thus far are at all relevant to the solution of the game" (Aarseth, 1997, p. 112).[17] The player is given no concrete indications about the end or the way to get there, so she can't imagine a story and then try to play it out. More important is to get a basic sense of orientation and gain knowledge about the world and the situation. According to Aarseth, an adventure "effectively disintegrates any notion of story by forcing the player's attention on the elusive 'plot.' ... Instead of a narrated plot, cybertext produces a sequence of oscillating activities effectuated (but certainly not controlled) by the user."[18]

In fact, the more or less successful attempts of a player to navigate through a game differ greatly from the careful, deliberate plot construction of a novel or film. The player's actions are movements in search of meaning. Here, in contrast to the action-adventures, the player is given no meaningful story as a means of orientation. Aarseth calls this intentional withholding of information, an intrigue that the player voluntarily submits to.

Regardless of the grade of difficulty a player can, depending on the individual game, construct a story retrospectively, because adventure games also work with a program that connects certain routes and events with one another, leading, in the end, to one or to multiple endings. Here a model is calculated for the territory a player can cover during the course of the game, and for the actions that she can carry out at certain locations. The origin of the adventures, the cartography of caves, is still evident in even the most advanced graphic adventures. Specific activities are linked to individual locations and have to be performed sequentially, because the access to the individual locations or situations is controlled, allowing not only a network but also a sequence of events to arise.[19]

The third of Todorov's categories is mentioned here only in passing, the category of the *ideological narratives*, denoted by consistently unchanging, virtually regulated patterns of relationships between people. This regulated behavior becomes clear in *Les liaisons dangereuses*, where rules such as "When person A loves person B, then person B doesn't love person A" are laid down. The ideological stories differ from the mythological and gnoseological ones mainly in that they don't propel the story in a certain direction, but function more like rules for play that enable the same situation to be played out again and again with a different cast. A large ideological portion is naturally present in all games. This is particularly clear in simulations (e.g., *SimCity*, Maxis, 1994, *The Sims*, Maxis, EA, 2000) and strategy games (e.g., *Age of Empires*, but also large parts of *Command and Conquer*, Westwood, Virgin, 1996), in which the goal of the game is the establishment of functional cycles, which operate according to unchanging rules. The cyclical time structure and the repetitions found in games are present here. In this case, though, it's not a story that's being written but history, so if we want to work with narratological vocabulary in case of the simulations and strategy games—though in my opinion it is not very fruitful—we must change the narrative genre.

The categories of mythological, gnoseological, and ideological narratives are very useful for the categorization of computer games because they correspond to the categories of action, adventure, and strategy games. Mixtures are, in any case, possible.

Story and Plot in Computer Games

To describe the relationship between story and plot, I would like to return to the example *Tomb Raider*.

The story ends sooner or later, depending on how close Lara comes to achieving the goal. The prescribed goal, however, allows for only two fundamentally different conclusions: the pleyer either reaches the goal or not. Through a common beginning and the prescription of identical goals, the virtual story, which achieves the goal, always establishes the background for the played stories in which it is not achieved. The middle, that is, carrying out the task, will vary in the various rounds. For the ending, however, in respect to the theory there are only two possibilities, because failure to reach the goal can only be seen as negation of achieving the goal. This possibility can only be understood in connection with the first. The achievement of the goal will also be taken into consideration in the case of failure to achieve the goal. Meaning is established through choice and the reduction of complexity (cf. Luhmann, 1971). Thus if a story creates meaning by leading to a certain end, the negation of this end also constructs meaning (because the negation always considers the object that is negated, cf. Luhmann, 1975). It is not the meaning that is being negated, but the choice.

With this in mind, the continuous repetitions in the process of playing can be counted as part of the logic of the interaction of story and plot. Janet Murray (1997, p. 30) defines a story told through repetitions of single sequences or of the entire piece as a *multiform story*.[20] She uses various films as examples: *It's a Wonderful Life* (Frank Capra, 1946), *Rashomon* (Akira Kurosawa, 1950) and finally *Groundhog Day* (Harold Ramis, 1993),[21] in which a weatherman relives the same day as many times as he needs to reach his goal, winning the love of a coworker. "Because of his (*sic*) simulation structure, *Groundhog Day*, though it has none of the shoot-'em-up content of videogames, is as much like a videogame as a linear film can be" (Murray, 1997, p. 36). But what Murray overlooks is that this film differs from the two others, and above all bears a resemblance to computer games through presence of a prescribed goal. Each day is a new attempt to win the colleague's love, and when it fails, the day begins anew.[22]

Murray attributes the similarity of film and video games mainly to their simulation structure. She rates the failed attempts as simulation, so things only really come to a head when an attempt is successful or the game ends, that is to say, the goal is reached. Thus in her argument the concluded story is also seen as a horizon of meaning. It would be more precise then, in the case of *Groundhog Day* and also of the computer games, not, like Murray, to speak of a *multiform story*, but of a *multiform plot*, because the story has only one form. This form, however, is shown in text in several forms on the level of the plot. The story with its intrinsic meaning holds together the repetitions of almost always the same, which are played out on the level of the plot.

In a computer game the player can start over again from the beginning until all obstacles have been overcome and the goal is achieved. The difference between the weatherman Phil and a computer game player is that Phil is a character of the story and can't escape repeating the same day as long as he hasn't reached the goal, whereas a computer game player has the option of avoiding repetitions by breaking off the game. Thus, whereas the repetitions of Phil's day are laid down in the story that result in a fixed plot, the repetitions in a computer game can be assigned to the actual playing of it, which results in a different plot in every single round.

Story Time and Narrative Time

The process of playing a computer game thus corresponds to the process of narration. This process leaves behind traces on the level of the discourse, which makes up certain relationships with the level of the story, for example, in respect to temporality.

In verbal narration, the two temporal sequences—story and narration—always make up a specific temporal relationship. According to Genette (1980), there is a *subsequent narration*—the story time comes before the time of the narration—*prior narration* (e.g., predictions), *simultaneous narration*, and *interpolated narration*. The most frequent form is the subsequent narration: first something happens, and afterwards the events are narrated.[23]

The explicit temporal relationship cannot, however, be found in nonverbal narrative forms such as film or theatre, which has ignited a protracted discussion over whether film in fact narrates or rather, *shows* or presents something in the here and now. This is a discussion that I can't take up here.[24] There is, however, an established opinion that film does have narrative qualities and gives the impression that the story has happened earlier, in any case not *now* (cf. Juul, 2001, p. 13).

But in computer games, the story events arise during play, developing simultaneously with the discourse. The events occur only when they are triggered by the discourse. Before that, they only exist in the mode of possibility in the program. Their realization is dependent on the act of playing or narration, respectively. Thus it is not a matter of simple simultaneous narration, as with a live broadcast on television, but of an interpolated narration in which "the story and the narrating can become entangled in such a way that the latter has an effect on the former" as Genette (1980, p. 155) writes.[25] This is precisely the case in computer games: the actions on the level of the discourse influence the actions of the story. Computer games and a novel with interpolated narration differ, however, in the fact that the real actions, which produce a computer game and leave their traces in the discourse, also occur simultaneously with the discourse and the story. There is simultaneity between the real actions, the narrative actions, and the story actions. This reinforces the relevance of the question of whether playing computer games can be compared with storytelling, or if it's better understood as actions carried out under certain regulations, as in other types of games. The difference between computer games and other games, however, is that if the line of actions can be interpreted as a story, it is one that happens *now*, but *not here*, because the events occur somewhere else, namely in the virtual world.[26] Moreover, the player knows that the possible routes through the game as well as the end have already been programmed; in the course of the game, it only has to be found and attained.

The Role and Perspective for the Player—Narrative Discourse

The temporal relationship described in the last paragraph is not the only relation between story and discourse; there are also different *narrative situations* (cf. Stanzel, 1969). A narrative situation describes the relationship between the narrator and the story events and existents in the text. A narrator tells the story from a certain standpoint and is in itself part of the discourse.

Terms such as *first-person narrative* or *third-person narrative* indicate different narrative situations. In analogy to these terms genre descriptions such as *first-person shooter* or *third-person shooter* are used to label computer games.

Because the locomotive actions are the narrative actions in the computer game, then the narrative situation is to be determined on the basis of the location from which these actions are carried out, and the man-

ner in which they are carried out. This means the point of action has to be further elaborated upon. Additionally, the point of view, or the given perspective on the game-world, has to be taken into consideration.

Aarseth (1997) and Ryan (2001) define the role of the player according to a personal or impersonal perspective, or an internal or external mode, respectively.

When a personal perspective is present, according to Aarseth (1997, p. 63), "the text requires the user to play a strategic role as a character in the world described by the text." The impersonal perspective, which he uses as an opposition, means simply that the reader reads. Non computer-supported narratives, but also hypertexts such as Michael Joyce's *Afternoon*, belong to this category. This categorization is too inexact for computer games because too many of them employ a personal perspective. The differentiation Ryan makes is helpful here, because it applies to the relationship between the player and the virtual world:

In the internal mode, the user projects himself as a member of the fictional world, either by identifying with an avatar, or by apprehending the virtual world from a first person perspective. In the external mode, the reader situates himself outside the virtual world. He either plays the role of a god who controls the fictional world from above, or he conceptualizes his activity as navigating a database. (Ryan, 2001, p. 12)

According to this, action adventures (e.g., *Tomb Raider*) and the so called first-person shooters such as *Doom* and *Quake* (ID Software, 1996) work with the internal mode, whereas simulations and strategy games apply the external mode. Here too, we can make further distinctions to help clarify the mingling of categories that arises in Ryan when she speaks of identification with an avatar but also of adopting a particular perspective. The blurred term *identification* can better be understood here according to George Herbert Mead's (1962, pp. 152 ff) definition as the adoption of a specific attitude and position of action. The perspective, on the other hand, clearly applies to perception, the view of the goings on, and thus to the point of view earlier developed. Both of these methods for the player to access and bond with the game need to be reflected upon.

Hence I'd like to use a distinction made by Gérard Genette (1980) in his discussion of narrative mood. He finds fault with blending the categories *perspective* and *voice*. *Voice* applies to the narrator and his or her relationship to the story, thus answering the question

"Who speaks?"[27] To adopt this for the analysis of computer games the question must be reformulated as "Who acts?" because no one speaks in computer games,[28] but the plot is created through actions. The question relates to the point of action.

The point of view, on the other hand, describes the visual angle on the story allowed by the discourse, and so answers the question "Who sees?" I will discuss this question in the first place and after that refer to the point of action.

The point of view, the perspective or the focalization, as Genette calls these aspects of the mood, apply to the extent of knowledge that the discourse will reveal about the narrated world.

He defines three types of focalization consisting of:

- *zero focalization* or the *non-focalized* story, i.e., a story that employs an omniscient narrative;
- *internal focalization*, in which one or more people in turn narrate from their own viewpoints; and
- *external focalization*, in which the viewpoint concentrates on the actions of one person, although nothing about the feelings of this person is revealed, as in the novels of Dashiell Hammett.

Apart from the still rare situations in which characters of the computer game speak, players gain all knowledge in computer games through the things they can see, the perspective in a spatial sense. This perspective in the computer game influences the distance of the player to the virtual world. The different points of view on the virtual world correspond approximately to Genette's standardizations.

The first variant is the *subjective perspective* (internal focalization), dominant in the first-person shooters, where no avatar is visualized; there is merely a hand or a weapon at the bottom edge of the screen. The spot at which the body belonging to the hand, as well as the eyes belonging to the body should be situated, remains empty. The screen image represents the field of vision of an avatar that the player must imagine and to whom, as part of this imagining, the player lends body and eyes. Thus the diegesis is not closed, but extends itself beyond the monitor to the player.

Action adventures (e.g., *Tomb Raider*) visualize an avatar capable of seeing. Before Lara Croft enters the caves of Qualopek, she looks inside. In the game, the avatar can be seen from behind most of the time, followed by a virtual "camera." From this follow-mode, one can switch to the view-mode, in which the avatar can look in various directions. This point of view is connected to the movements of the avatar; it is not a substitute for the viewpoint, rather a *viewing-with*. It is *semisubjective*, in reference to Mitry (1998, p. 218).[29] In Genette's terms, this would be external focalization.

The third perspective in the computer game, the *objective* point of view (zero focalization), is the oldest and most diversified. The objective point of view presents a space-for-action from outside. Within the virtual world there is no point from which to view this world. Until the arrival of the first-person shooters at the beginning of the 1990s, all computer games employed the objective perspective. The first games showed a frontal or aerial view. Later, the objective co-view was created by horizontal scrolling screens in the Jump'n Runs (e.g., *Sonic the Hedgehog*, Sega, 1990). Even though the sophisticated avatar here could already carry out various actions, there was one thing it couldn't do: see. What was pictured was the environment for the avatar's actions.

Graphic adventures, too, employ the objective perspective. They present an avatar in its space-for-action. The avatar has no viewpoint. An especially clear indication that this is the representation of a space-for-action, is the use of "takes," which sizes correspond exactly with the sector of the virtual world that can be manipulated. Simulations and strategy games likewise employ an objective perspective that shows the space-for-action from above.

In recent times the possibility of changing the perspective during the game has become more and more frequent.

The *point of action* describes the position from which action can be taken, and how it will be taken. This position can reside either within or without the diegesis, so that one can speak of an intradiegetic and an extradiegetic point of action. This distinction basically corresponds to the distinctions by Ryan and Aarseth.

An intradiegetic point of action is clearly present when a game pictures an avatar, which is found in the diegesis and is initiator of the action. An intradiegetic point of action is also present, however, when the player is assigned a role in the diegesis that is not visualized through an avatar. This is the case in *Civilization* (Microprose, Activision, 1996), for example, where the player chooses a ruler character who then guides the fortunes of his subjects. An extradiegetic point of action is present when the player doesn't take on such a role, as is the case in *Myst* and *Tetris*.

If instead of focusing on the point of departure of the actions we look at their point of destination, or goal, then we can make the distinction between a *concentric* and *ex-centric* point of action. The *ex-centric* point of action enables the action to be initiated at multiple locations in the virtual world, as in, for example, simulations and strategy games. Team sport games as well operate on this principle. Centered actions can only be executed from one location. Through this addition, strategy games and action games can be differentiated in relation to the point of action: where the point of action is intradiegetic in both genres, the centering provides a category for further subdivision.

A third division within the point of action is the one between *direct* and *indirect* actions. Depending on how the commands of the implied author are carried out, a structure of command can or cannot be recognized on the monitor. Whereas in the case of *Tomb Raider*, for example, every press of a button instantly results in an action from Lara, the player in graphic adventures clicks on certain objects or characters, which the avatar then approaches to examine or address. Some adventures, such as *Grim Fandango* (Funsoft, Lucas Arts, 1998) or *Silent Hill* (Konami, 2000), combine indirect and direct points of action. Simulations and strategy games also use the indirect position of action, which, in some games, *Command and Conquer* for example, is included in the diegesis in that the troops, when chosen, confirm the command with a "Yes Sir!"

If one wants to be exact, then we can understand the difference between the direct/indirect point of action as a modality of action, because it describes primarily the relative distance between the story (when present) and the discourse. An indirect point of action increases the distance and facilitates the process of distinguishing between story and discourse.

The narrative situations can be described according to the point of view and the point of action. The *Tomb Raider* series, for example, employs a semisubjective point of view and a direct, intradiegetic, and centered point of action. But with the constant developments of the ways computer games picture action, these concepts have to be developed and specified as well.

The Function of the Player—Questions of Authorship and Narration

One of the biggest differences between games and narratives lies in the way the recipient and player, respectively, take part in the narrative or game. This touches the level of narration, which incorporates the issue of the author of the narrative or the game. To discuss this question I will use Aarseth's (1997, pp. 62–65) and Ryan's (2001, pp. 11–23) models of the tasks a player has in

course of playing a computer game and further specify them. Based on the tasks of the player, I will then propose a model for authorship in computer games.

The recipient reads or sees (in the case of film) a narrative produced by someone else, interprets it, and then constructs a story on the basis of this interpretation. The recipient's task is primarily an interpretative one. In the computer game, the player establishes a concrete order of events in the course of playing the game. The player is responsible for creating the plot, in addition to the interpretative task. The interpretive function, as Ryan emphasizes, is also inherent in every computer game, because events have to be interpreted in order to proceed with the game. The time that remains for this interpretation varies from genre to genre, whereas in real-time based action games there is hardly any time left for consideration or interpretation, games played in rounds do provide the option to consider how things should progress.[30] These considerations apply mostly to forming the plot.

Apart from the interpretative function—which, as Ryan remarks, comes into play in every intelligent handling of text—Aarseth defines another three user functions: the *explorative*, the *configurative*, and the *textonic* function. The explorative function comes to bear when the user chooses to take certain routes and explores the virtual world. This function is primarily offered by hypertext novels.

The configurative and the textonic functions differ in regard to the level of the game they influence. If the player performs a textonic function, the game is permanently altered as the textons, i.e., the strings of "signs as they exist in the text" (Aarseth, 1997, p. 62) are changed or supplemented. That means the player intervenes in the program. This rarely occurs in computer games. An exception are the "level editors" in *Doom* and its successors, where it is possible to change the surface texture of the game so that it no longer takes place at a military base, but in a school or a gallery, for instance. Aarseth relates the configurative function to the alteration of the scriptons, the strings of "signs as they appear to the player" (p. 62). These changes effect the surface level of the game and can manifest as, for example, killing opponents, instigating certain events or in narrative terms, creating a certain plot.[31]

Ryan brings the textonic and configurative functions together under the term *ontological* function, because she is primarily interested in the player's relationship to the virtual world, and both functions contribute to creating or altering parts of the virtual world. Inevitably, her approach has to neglect the fact that textonic changes apply to the game, whereas configurative changes apply to the round in question. In the most extreme instance, textonic alterations mean that a new game is programmed.[32]

I don't want to pursue these questions further here. Instead, I'd like to take a closer look at the possibilities and restrictions of the explorative and configurative function, because this aspect is decisive in exploring the question of narrativity in computer games.

The explorative and configurative functions are necessary for every game and their effects are restricted to the plot. The player chooses from possibilities given by the program and transfers them to the process of play, and so places a text-space in a time. This process of temporalization is also found in narratives; in literature it is the process of reading, and in film the projector fulfills this function. By constantly inputting information throughout the game, the player prompts the computer to process the sequence of events.

It is only in the course of play that possible plots are actualized, individual objects combined with one another, actions produced and brought into chronological order. The program itself does not contain a chronology of events; rather, it organizes possible sequential and causal relationships in algorithms, object definitions, and databases. A potential narrative portrayal first arises during the game, only then are chains of actions formed.

Hence, by carrying out the explorative and configurative functions the player could be described as a *co-author* in narratological terms, as it is the player who ultimately determines what comes to pass. However, this would overrate the role of the player, who is not an equal co-author. I would much prefer to adopt the term *implied author* from literary theory to define the player's function as an author implied by the game. Narratology designs the instance of the implied author from the content of the text based on the model of a real author. According to this conception, the implied author is the authority that creates the text on the one hand, and on the other hand is dependent on the text.

We find precisely this functionality in the implied author of the computer game, who is appointed by the game and takes part in creating it. He or she initiates certain sequences but not the entire text in the sense of a real author, because the chain of events is dependent on the virtual world with its possibilities and restrictions, which are not brought forth by the implied author, but dictated by the program and the hardware.[33]

But the term *implied author* takes into account the feeling that many players apparently get from the game: the stories they tell about their game experience indicate that they actually do see themselves as the originators of the events and as decisive participants in a story.

Thus the elaboration on the user functions leads us to call the authority taken over by the player the *implied author*. But the implied author isn't the only authority responsible for production of the game. Another narrative instance, which I'd like to call the *implied creator*, has superiority. The implied creator is responsible for forming the virtual world, that is, for the setting, the characters, and the happenings in this world. Among the elements laid down by the implied creator are also the characteristics of the avatars, for example, their looks and modes of taking action, as well as hindrances and restrictions to action. Thus the authority of the *intrigant*, coined by Aarseth (1997), also belongs, in my opinion, to the creator. Aarseth's *intrigant* is a kind of *Diabolus in machina* in text adventures who spins the web of intrigue from which the player as *intriguee* has to wriggle out.[34]

The implied creator makes the initial selection out of all the possibilities imaginable by first presenting them as options in the program. From these the implied author, in a second stage of selection, can choose. In this second stage, all of the events relevant to the plot, and the links between them, are produced by the implied author during play, while the creator remains humbly in the background as setting. The creator doesn't show itself directly during the course of the game, but through its work, that is, the world that it has created.[35]

This world provides a pool of possible events from which the *arrangement of action* can choose in order to integrate some of them into a plot. The events not chosen for the plot remain as non-actualized possibilities in the background. Without these non-actualized possibilities everything would be determined and no story could emerge, just a logical sequence. To make sense, a story needs these non-actualized possibilities, the events that could have happened but didn't (cf. Luhmann, 1971, pp. 26 ff).

Both authorities, the implied author and the implied creator, are necessary for the computer game. Without the implied author, no process of playing would emerge and thus no plot would be created. The game would just be a set of rules. Without the implied creator, there would be no world in which to play and create plots.

The implied creator is, in a less metaphorical manner, responsible for everything except the plot construction. This means the composition of the virtual world, but also the way the virtual world is pictured, the perspective it appears in, and also for the temporal relationship between story and discourse.

In computer games we can speak of four different levels of representation:

1. The world design—rules of the virtual world (implied creator).
2. The visual design—presentation of the virtual world (implied creator).
3. The arrangement of action (implied author).
4. The temporal design—temporal relationship between story and discourse (implied creator).

Facing these levels of representation it seems not feasible to simply adopt the established model of narrative authorities used to study literature. The four levels presented here relate much more closely to the levels of cinematic discourse Tom Gunning (1994, pp. 10–28) developed.

Conclusion

The narrativity of computer games can be described according to the levels of the narrative developed in narratology.

First and foremost, regarding the level structure of narratives leads to the insight that computer games contain a structural equivalent to narratives: a level of actions presented and a level of representation. The level of representation distinguishes computer games from other games and is the prerequisite for a narrative analysis.

In reference to the level of the story, narratology may help to describe the models used to make sense of a game by adding a story structure to it. But not every computer game incorporates a story.

When it comes to the level of plot, things get more complicated. The arrangement of the actions on the plot level is done by the instance of the implied author who represents the player of the game. The plot changes in every round, which means that in case of the computer game there is a *multiform plot*.

The active involvement of the player separates computer games from noninteractive narrative media. In regard to the question of authorship one has to assume a model of shared but incongruent authorship. Whereas the implied author sets up the plot, the instance of an *implied creator* is responsible for creating a world where the actions can take place, as well as for the presentation of this world.

In respect to the level of the discourse that describes the modes of the presentation of the story one can adopt terminology and methods from literary and filmic narrative theory, but these terms have to be altered and reshaped to be useful for the analysis of computer games. Especially when the clear distinction of story and discourse is in question, narratology comes to its limits. Because in computer games there are no words that tell about the actions of the story, neither are there pictures that show these actions, but acting itself propels the discourse and is simultaneous pictured. This means that the clear distinctions between acting (in a game) and sympathetic experience (of a story) are dissolved and overlapped.

Thus examining computer games in regard to their narrativity provides insights in the structure of the games and also contributes to the description of this dissolution and shifting of boundaries. And it opens a perspective on the qualities of computer games that cannot be described by the means of narratology.

Notes

1. Readings on adventure games as narratives he names are: Niesz & Holland, 1984; Buckles, 1987; Randall, 1988; Ziegfield, 1989.
2. Marku Eskelinen (2001) is an especially staunch proponent of this viewpoint: "Outside academic theory people are usually excellent at making distinctions between narrative, drama and games. If I throw a ball at you I don't expect you to drop it and wait until it starts telling stories. On the other hand, if and when games and especially computer games are studied and theorized they are almost without exception colonised from the fields of literary, theatre, drama and film studies. Games are seen as interactive narratives, procedural stories or remediated cinema. On top of everything else, such definitions, despite being successful in terms of influence or funding, are conceptually weak and ill-grounded, as they are usually derived from a very limited knowledge of mere mainstream drama or outdated literary theory, or both." (p. 1)

   As justified as this criticism might be in certain instances where an overly generalized approach is taken to computer games, it clearly highlights the political battle surrounding computer games that has flamed up within the scientific community.
3. This position is held not only by myself, but is also found in Juul 2001, and Ryan 2001. In his

work on text adventures, Espen Aarseth (1997) takes narratological terms and reshapes them (pp. 97–128). My dissertation (Neitzel, 2000) is based on the same procedure.

4. Additional forms that could be mentioned here are enumeration and description.

5. Kolb (1990, pp. 13–20) calls these theories anthropologic-phenomenological theories of games. They examine the relationships of people to play from a phenomenological standpoint. In these theories, the phenomenon play is often looked at as a fundamental pattern for explaining cultural or social processes (cf. Huizinga, 1994; Caillois, 1958).

   In contrast, the mathematically based theory of games describes games as rule-constructions in which strategic decisions lead, as efficiently as possible, to the best possible result.

6. Card games and Chess, for example, constitute a mixed form; the players manipulate objects, which represent certain values and functions. In role playing, or *mimicry*, however, the part played by the imagination is obvious: one acts as if one were someone else.

7. These bear resemblance to parallel tracking shots.

8. These actions are considered to be connected with the nonfictional world—Aristotle (1995) uses the term *mimicry*; Todorov (1977) speaks of the evocation of reality.

9. This distinction is first established in Tomashevsky (1965, p. 68), who distinguishes between *bound motifs*, which cannot be omitted without disturbing the story and *free motifs*, which may be omitted. Roland Barthes (1966, p. 9) introduces a difference between *cardinal functions* and *catalysts*. The former denote an alternative with repercussions for the progression of the story, whereas the later simply complete the narrative space between the cardinal functions.

10. The term *mythos* is only found in the German translation of the *Poetics*. But the mythos is not a reference to historical record, which Fuhrmann (1992, p. 26) elaborates on: "With mythos, Aristotle usually means none other than the fabula, the subjet, the plot and the action of a drama." Apart from the fact that this doesn't lessen the confusion of terminology, Fuhrmann does not consider the active element contained in the term mythos. The mythos means the act of assembling, what arises is a plot with a certain form.

11. The task of the mythos and the form of the plot determine not only the tragedy, with which Aristotle is mainly concerned in his *Poetics*, but narrative poetry, the epos, as well. On the representational level, i.e., the events, and the level on which these events are joined together, i.e., the mythos or the plot, epos and tragedy are the same, both should portray a self-contained line of action (Aristotle, 1995, p. 115).

    For Aristotle, the difference between the epos and the tragedy mainly lies in the manner of portrayal. Whereas the epos reports, using the first- or third-person narrative form, the tragedy represents "by direct enactment of all roles." (p. 35).

12. Bordwell's category of *style* definitely indicates this.

13. Culler (1980) analyzes this explicitly. He suggests a double reading of narratives. The first should look at the chain of events starting with the beginning; the second reading should consider the event only in connection with the narrative conclusion, which is what leads to stories being told at all. Thus the story of Oedipus, the abandoned shepard's son, for example, doesn't meet Aristotle's rigorous requirements until it meets up with the prophecy. Not until then does Oedipus' full identity become known and his actions seem unavoidable—it *had* to happen like this. Freud's methods also have a similar basis, the aim being to explain certain traumata and give meaning to a behavior. Even everyday stories aim at resolution, as Labov (1972) shows.

14. The term *diegesis* is borrowed from film theory, where it designates the filmic world (cf. Souriau, 1948).

15. This structure can be seen quite clearly in Greimas' analysis, where these stories are described as the transfer of an object of value. Put very simply, his elaborate work can be paraphrased: the princess is here, the princess is somewhere else, the princess is here again (cf. Greimas, 1971).

16. Todorov positions this categorization on a middle level, which is located between the analysis of an individual work and a genre (e.g., narrative or drama). He talks for this reason of "middle categories."

17. This structure is applicable to text adventures as well as graphic adventures.

18. Aarseth's use of the term plot complicates this statement. It also complicates his general description of the relationship between the story and the plot in adventure games.

    In one case he uses *plot* in the sense of the *suyhzet* coined by the Russian Formalists—that is, the actual given order of the various parts of the story in the text—and there's no problem with that because when the text appears, then it appears, however intentional it might be.

    In another instance, he also uses plot in the sense of a narrative model. A plot-model refers to the laws of composition of the action (cf. Sklovskij, 1966). It represents a model for the arrangement of action. One doesn't find a model like this while playing the adventure game. It is eclipsed by the unsuccessful attempts and repetitions carried out by the player to get through the game, and it is just these actions that constitute the *suyzhet*.

19. Regarding the difference between "controlled access" and "random access" (cf. Aarseth, 1997, p. 63).

20. Unfortunately, Murray is not precise in her terminology. Although she starts by defining the *multiform story* on page, in her next sentence she ascribes *It's a Wonderful Life* a *multiform plot*, returns to *multiform story*, and finally uses the term *multiform narrative*.

21. Another interesting example in this respect is *Dial "M" for Murder* (Alfred Hitchcock, 1954). Here the story is told in various modes and time structures. First, the plan for the murder night is introduced (future, conjunctive), then the reconstruction of the events after the plan has been carried out is imagined (future II, conjunctive), after that, the actual evening takes place (present indicative), and after that, the events and the plan that lead to them are reconstructed in three different versions until the right one, as the viewer knows, is arrived at.

22. Let it be duly noted that Phil the weatherman does in fact change his goal during the course of the film. At first he just wants sex with his colleague, and it isn't until about two-thirds of the way into the film that he redefines his goal and determines to win her love—the general structure of the film, however, remains unchanged.

23. As with any activity, every game can, of course, be retold in this sense, but this is not what we are dealing with here.

24. The difference between *showing* and *telling* can be traced back to Plato's distinction between mimesis and diegesis. In depths: Plato, 1979; Genette, 1980, pp. 162–185; Branigan, 1984; Metz, 1997, esp. pp. 152–189; or in summary, Neitzel, 2000, 110–117.

25. His examples for the interpolated narration are diaries and also epistolary novels, in which the letter is simultaneously a medium of narration and an element of the story.

26. In regard to the cinematic narrative it may also be asked if the distance between story, discourse, and observation is established through spatial differences instead of temporal ones.

27. The perspective is one of the chief modalities in the narrative, the other is distance. Both contribute to the regulation of narrative information (cf. Genette, 1980, p. 162).

28. Again, the exception here is the text adventure, about which I won't elaborate.

29. Mitry, 1998, p. 218 describes the semisubjective image as follows: "Retaining all the attributes of the describing image [the camera remains as impersonal as possible], the associated image adopts the viewpoint of a particular character who, objectively described, occupies a special position in the frame (close shot, mid-shot, or right in the foreground). The camera follows him wherever he goes, acts like him, sees with him and at the same time."

30. The success of *Myst* (Cyan, Broderbund, 1993) and its successors may even lie in the possibility of contemplation.

31. Aarseth's model clearly relates to the structuralistic model of deep-structure and surface-structure with the possibility of transformation between the two levels—for this transformation he uses the term "traversal function" (1997, p. 64).

32. A distinction could be made as well between necessary and optional textonic changes—*Quake* can be played straight away in the given environment, whereas certain MUDs require the addition of textons for play.

33. The implied author corresponds to the *interactor* or *derivative author* in Murray, 1997, p. 153: "We could perhaps say that the interactor is the author of a particular performance within

an electronic story system, or the architect of a particular part of the virtual world, but we must distinguish this derivative authorship from the origination authorship of the system itself." Aarseth, 1997, p. 127, uses the term *implied user*: "The implied user, on the other hand, is both responsible for the action and the game's outcome and does not have the implied *reader's* privileges of tmesis and distancing."

34. Aarseth also introduces a creator but does not specify its function.

35. The similarity of this creator-authority with God, who creates a world and allows people to move about in it is, of course, deliberate. This is particularly evident in computer games that deal with a visually represented world.

References

Aarseth, E. J. (1997). *Cybertext. Perspectives on ergodic literature*. Baltimore: Johns Hopkins University Press.

Aristotle. (1995). *Poetics*. Cambridge, MA: Harvard University Press.

Barthes, R. (1966). Introduction à l'analyse structurale des récits. *Communications, 8*, 1–27.

Baudry, J.-L. (1986). Ideological effects of the basic cinematographic apparatus. In P. Rosen (Ed.), *Narrative, apparatus, ideology: A film theory reader* (pp. 286–298). New York: Columbia University Press.

Bolter, J. D. (1991). *Writing space. The computer, hypertext, and the history of writing*. Hillsdale, NJ: Lawrence Erlbaum Associates.

Bolter, J. D., & Grusin, R. (2000). *Remediation: Understanding new media*. Cambridge, MA: MIT Press.

Bordwell, D. (1985). *Narration in the fiction film*. London: Routledge.

Branigan, E. (1984). *Point of view in the cinema. A theory of narration and subjectivity in classical film*. Berlin: Mouton.

Branigan, E. (1992). *Narrative comprehension and film*. London: Routledge.

Buckles, M. A. (1987). Interactive fiction as literature: Adventure games have a literary lineage. *Byte*, May, 135–142.

Buytendijk, F. J. J. (1933). *Wesen und Sinn des Spiels. Das Spielen des Menschen und der Tiere als Erscheinungsform der Lebenstriebe*. Berlin: Kurt Wolff/Der neue Geist Verlag.

Caillois, R. (1958). *Les jeux et les hommes. Le masque et le vertige*. Paris: Gallimard.

Campbell, J. (1965). *The hero with a thousand faces*. New York: Pantheon Books.

Chatman, S. (1978). *Story and discourse: Narrative structure in fiction and film*. Ithaca: Cornell University Press.

Culler, J. (1980). Fabula and syuzhet in the analysis of narrative: Some American discussions. *Poetics Today, 1*(3), 27–37.

de Certeau, M. (1988). *Kunst des Handelns*. Berlin: Merve.

Eskelinen, M. (2001). The gaming situation. www.gamestudies.org/0101/eskelinen.

Fuhrmann, M. (1992). *Dichtungstheorie der Antike. Aristoteles—Horaz—"Longin,"* Darmstadt: Wissenschaftliche Buchgesellschaft.

Genette, G. (1980). *Narrative discourse*. Oxford: Basil Blackwell.

Genette, G. (1988). *Narrative discourse revisited*. Ithaca, NY: Connell University Press.

Greimas, A. J. (1971). Narrative grammar: Units and levels. *Modern Language Notes, 86*, 793–806.

Gunning, T. (1994). *D.W. Griffith and the origins of American narrative film: The early years at Biograph*. Urbana: University of Illinois.

Hendricks, L. (1996–2000). avault.com/cheats/getcheat.asp?game=tombwalk.

Herman, D. (1997). Scripts, sequences, and stories: Elements of a postclassical narratology. *PMLA Publications of the Modern Language Association of America, 112*(5), 1046–1059.

Huizinga, J. (1994). *Homo ludens. Vom Ursprung der Kultur im Spiel*. Reinbek: Rowohlt.

Juul, J. (2001). Games telling stories? A brief note on games and narratives. www.gamestudies.org/0101/juul-gts/.

Kolb, M. (1990). *Spiel als Phänomen—Das Phänomen Spiel. Studien zu phänomenologisch anthropologischen Spieltheorien*. Sankt Augustin: Academia Verlag Richarz.

Labov, W. (1972). *Language in the inner city: Studies in the black English venacular*. Philadelphia: Philadelphia University Press.

Landow, G. P. (1992). *Hypertext. The convergence of contemporary critical theory and technology.* Baltimore: Johns Hopkins University Press.

Landow, G. P. (Ed.). (1994). *Hyper/Text/Theory.* Baltimore: Johns Hopkins University Press.

Laurel, B. (1991). *Computers as theatre.* Reading, MA: Addison-Wesley.

Lotman, J. M. (1977). *Probleme der Kinoästhetik. Einführung in die Semiotik des Films.* Frankfurt/Main: Syndikat.

Luhmann, N. (1995). *Die Kunst der Gesellschaft.* Frankfurt/Main: Suhrkamp.

Luhmann, N. (1980). Temporalstrukturen des Handlungssystems. Zum Zusammenhang von Handlungs- und Systemtheorie. N. Luhmann (Ed.), *Soziologische Aufklärung 3,* (pp. 126–150). Opladen: Westdeutscher Verlag.

Luhmann, N. (1971). Sinn als Grundbegriff der Soziologie. In J. Habermas, & N. Luhmann, (Eds.), *Theorie der Gesellschaft oder Sozialtechnologie—Was leistet die Systemforschung* (pp. 25–100). Frankfurt/Main: Suhrkamp.

Mandler, J. M., & Johnson, S. (1978). Erzählstruktur und Erinnerungsleistung. Eine Grammatik einfacher Geschichten. In W. Haubrichs (Ed.), *Erzählforschung. Theorien, Modelle und Methoden der Narrativik,* vol. II, (pp. 337–379). Götlingen: Vandenhoeche Ruprecht.

Mead, G. H. (1962). *Mind, self, and society from the standpoint of a social behaviorist.* Chicago: University of Chicago Press.

Metz, C. (1974). *Film language. A semiotics of the cinema.* New York: Oxford University Press.

Metz, C. (1997). *Die unpersönliche Enunziation oder der Ort des Films.* Münster: Nodus.

Metzler Literaturlexikon. Stichwörter zur Weltliteratur. (1984). Ed. by Günther and Irmgard Scheikle, Stuttgart: Metzler.

Mitry, J. (1998). *The aesthetics and psychology of the cinema.* London: Athlone Press.

Murray, J. H. (1997). *Hamlet on the holodeck. The future of narrative in cyberspace*: Cambridge, MA: MIT Press.

Neitzel, B. (2000). *Gespielte Geschichten. Struktur- und prozessanalytische Untersuchungen der Narrativität von Videospielen,* www.dbthueringen.de/servlets/Derivate Servlet/Derivate-2063/Dissertation.de

Niesz, A. J., & Holland, N. N. (1984). Interactive Fiction. *Critical Inquiry 11,* 110–129.

Plato. (1979). *The republic.* Cambridge: Cambridge University Press.

Randall, N. (1988). Determining literariness in interactive fiction. *Computers and the Humanities, 22,* 182–191.

Ryan, M.-L. (Ed.). (1999). *Cyberspace textuality. Computer technology and literary theory.* Bloomington: Indiana University Press.

Ryan, M.-L. (2001). Beyond myth and metaphor—The case of narrative in digital media. www.gamestudies.org/0101/ryan/.

Scheuerl, H. (1975). Zur Begriffsbestimmung von "Spiel" und "Spielen." *Zeitschrift für Pädagogik 21,* 341–349.

Sklovskij, V. (1966). *Theorie der Prosa.* Frankfurt/Main: Fischer.

Souriau, E. (1948). La structure de l'univers filmique et le vocabulaire de la filmologie. *Revue Internationale de la Filmologie,* 7–8, 231–240.

Stanzel, F. K. (1969). *Die typischen Erzählsituationen im Roman: dargestellt an Tom Jones, Moby-Dick, The Ambassadors, Ulysses u.a.* Wien: Braumüller.

Stein, N. L. (1978). The comprehension and appreciation of stories: A developmental analysis. In S. S. Madeja (Ed.), *The arts, cognition, and basic skills* (pp. 231–249). St. Louis, M.: Cemrel.

Thomsen, C. W. (Ed.). (1994). *Hybridkultur. Bildschirmmedien und Evolutionsformen der Künste.* Arbeitshefte Bildschirmmedien 46, Siegen: DGF Sonderforschungsbereich.

Todorov, T. (1977). Categories of the literary narrative. *Film Reader 2,* 19–37.

Todorov, T. (1971). The two principles of narrative. *Diacritics 1,* 37–44.

Tomashevsky, B. (1965). Thematics. In L. T. Lemon & M. J. Reis (Eds.), *Russian formalist criticism: Four essays* (pp. 61–95). Lincoln: University of Nebraska.

Ziegfield, R. (1989). Interactive fiction: A new literary genre? *New Literary History 20,* 341–372.

Part V

Games as a Cultural Phenomenon

Identity

THE GAME OF LIFE: NARRATIVE AND LUDIC IDENTITY FORMATION IN COMPUTER GAMES

Jos de Mul

Human identity is not a self-contained entity, hidden in the depths of our inner self, but is actively constructed in a social world with the aid of various expressions, such as social roles, rituals, clothes, music, and (life) stories. These expressions not only mediate between us and our world (*referentiality*) and between us and our fellow man (*communicability*), but also between us and ourselves (*self-understanding*). Consequently, changes in these mediating structures reflect changes in the relationship between us and our world, in our social relationships, and in our self-conception.

In recent decades the domain of expressions has been (massively[1]) extended by computer games and, as a result, we witness the emergence of a new tool for identity formation. In this chapter I shall examine the way computer games construct our identity in comparison with traditional narrative media, such as novels and movies. My investigation is primarily philosophical: it aims at a *conceptual* clarification of the relationship between (playing) computer games and human identity. However, though this study is not empirical, one of its aims is to contribute to the theoretical framework for empirical research in this field. The theoretical starting point of my investigation is Ricoeur's theory of narrative identity. I will argue that this theory provides a fruitful conceptual framework for understanding the way playing computer games construct personal identity. However, because his theory exclusively focuses on standard linguistic narratives, we will have to amend this theory in order to apply it within the domain of computer games.

I will develop the argument in three sections, starting with a short analysis of the concept of identity. Against this background, I explain Ricoeur's theory of narrative identity and discuss some constraints that prevent its application to computer games. In the next section, after a short analysis of the concepts of play, game, and computer game, I discuss the narrative dimension of computer games and the interactive dimension that distinguish computer games fundamentally from narratives. Then I present an outline of a theory of ludic identity, and discuss the transformation in our present culture from narrative to ludic identity construction. Finally, I formulate some aspects of this transformation that are crucial for its evaluation.

Narrative Identity and Its Discontents
Human Identity
Like so many words in everyday language, "identity" has no unequivocal meaning, but a number of connotations. This is connected to the long history of the concept, during which the phenomenon identity has taken on various interpretations. The word has its etymological roots in the Latin concept *identitas*, which in turn is derived from the concept *idem*—the same. In the context of our discussion of human identity it is useful to distinguish among logical, anthropological, and reflective identity.

As *logical* concept, "identity" refers predominantly to *numerical unity* (x = x). Adapted to human persons, the concept identity indicates the unique relation that every person has with him or herself. This logical principle of identity means that a person is identical to the self and to no one else. Concerning this *personal identity*, it is possible to distinguish between physical identity and psychic identity, as a person has both a unique body and—narrowly intertwined with it—a unique mind. In a less strict sense, the concept "identity" is often also used to designate extreme similarity, for example when we refer to "identical twins." Though identical twins are not numerically identical, they share the same genetic characteristics.

However, in common language, the concept "identity" generally not only refers to this rather formal logical notion of identity, but also to the "sameness of essential or generic character in different instances" (Merriam-Webster Dictionary). In this *anthropological* meaning, the concept refers to the *spatial* and *temporal* continuity of the personality.

Spatial continuity lies in the fact that the elements from which the physical and psychic identity are constructed do not form a loose conglomerate, but an internal nexus, in which part and whole are closely connected.[2] This is already clear on the physical level, where the different body parts are integrated into the unity of the body. Thoughts, actions, and desires are linked together in a meaningful way, too. For example, the way an ambitious person visualizes the future is internally connected with bodily and psychic desires and the actions undertaken aim at the realization of these desires. In a healthy person, all aspects of the personality are more or less integrated. Of course, this integration is never complete—human life is characterized by all kinds of dissociative states, such as (day)-dreaming, religious or sexual ecstasy, immersion in a movie or a (computer) game, highway hypnosis, intoxication by alcohol and other drugs, and so on. However, when the meaningful nexus is largely or completely lost—for example in the case of dissociative identity disorders—the result is a disintegration, or even a total loss, of the person's identity in this spatial sense.

Temporal continuity lies in the fact that in the course of our life we remain more or less the same person (that is, the same spatial unity of bodily and psychic elements). To a certain extent we keep the same body during our lives, and thanks to memory and expectation our (conscious) mind also occupies a certain *permanence in time*.[3] However, this continuity is never complete. Our psychological continuity is characterized by interruptions (sleep) and gaps (forgetting). Moreover, our bodily and psychological continuity is not static: it develops over time from birth to death under influence of biological growth and renewal (almost all of the cells in our body are gradually replaced by new ones), learning processes, new experiences and, finally, decay. Also with regard to the temporal nexus, sometimes we see that radical discontinuities—for example, by a complete loss of memory or the loss of a part of the body, a transgender operation, the development of an disruptive addiction, dementia, or a religious or political conversion—may result in fundamental changes or even total disintegration of the temporal (bodily and psychic) identity.[4]

A third and crucial aspect of the human identity concerns the *reflective* dimension of identity. We encounter this dimension when we pose the question for whom the spatial and temporal continuity characteristic of personal and cultural identity arises. Although other people can ascribe a personal or cultural identity to us (which can have a great influence on the way in which we experience our selves), finally *we ourselves* are the ones who experience our personal (and cultural) identity—that is to say, the meaningful spatial and temporal nexus. Reflectivity denotes self-awareness, self-reflection, having a self-image. We express ourselves and recognize ourselves in self-(re)presentations. Whether someone possesses a female, Islam, or fan identity (or possibly integrates all three) is not only always somewhat arbitrary, determined by physical characteristics, actions, habits, or thoughts, but is also dependent on whether this person regards and recognizes herself as such. A phenomenon such as transsexuality shows that the objective and the experienced reality do not necessarily correspond.

Narrative Identity

In the history of modern philosophy there has been much discussion about the *ontological* status of human identity, about its specific mode of being. We can distinguish two extreme positions. On the one hand, the rationalist tradition starting with Descartes, defined the I or self as *a substance with consciousness*, "a thing that thinks" (Descartes, 1968, p. 106). Following the Christian notion of the eternal human soul, this tradition, conceives of this thinking substance as an isolated, timeless, noncorporeal entity. On the other hand, the more skeptical movement within the empirical tradition, at least starting with Hume, denied the I or self any real substance. According to Hume, consciousness is nothing else than the continuous stream of perceptions and ideas: "I always stumble on some particular perception or other, of heat or cold, light or shade, love or hatred, pain or pleasure. I never can catch myself at any time without a perception, and never can observe anything but the perception.... The identity which we ascribe to the mind of man is only a fictitious one" (Hume, 1956, pp. 252, 259). Or, in the words of Daniel Dennett, a temporary humean skeptic, it is "a theorist's fiction" comparable with an abstractum such as "the center of gravity" of an object in physics, that does not refer to any characteristic of the object (Dennett, 1992).

Though the skepticism against the Cartesian conception of the self as a timeless substance is justified, Hume and Dennett seem to throw away the baby with the bathwater. Unlike the case of an entity, which does not have a subjective experience of its center of gravity, a person consciously does experience him- or herself. In the passage quoted from Hume, even he turns out to be *someone* who claims to be unable to find himself behind the flow of consciousness (Ricoeur, 1992,

p. 128)! The problem seems to be that both Descartes and Hume seem to agree that the self, if it exists, must be a substance. With the phenomenologist Heidegger, however, I want to argue that human *existence* is fundamentally distinguished from the ontological status of objects such as stones because human beings *exist in time and space* (Heidegger, 1996). Existing does not simply mean that we are situated in time (after all, this is also true for a stone), but that our being has a fundamentally temporal character. Although we always live in the present, unlike the stone, in our acting we are always oriented toward our future *possibilities* and we are also always determined by the possibilities we realized in the past. In *Oneself as another*, Paul Ricoeur denotes the distinction between the identity of mere occurent entities such as a stone and the identity of human beings by the concepts *même* (*idem*) and *soi-même* (*ipse*), or, in other words, *same*-identity and *self*-identity, respectively (Ricoeur, 1992, pp. 1–3, 116f.). This concerns the difference between identity as sheer *permanence in time* and identity as *selfness*, the personal involvement in, and the reflective consciousness of, our own existence.

According to Ricoeur, the problems flowing from Descartes's concept of identity arise from the very fact that he unfoundedly conceives human identity as a substance. In fact, we are concerned here with a metaphorical transfer—intangible human identity is presented as if it were a mere entity like a stone. This metaphorical transfer (and the conceptual confusion that goes with it) is seductive, because the self also has a certain permanence in time because of its bodily and psychological continuity. Therefore there is a certain *overlap* of the *same* and the *self*. But in these two cases the permanence in time is of a fundamentally different order. As opposed to the stone, the self remaining the same in the time—Heidegger calls this self-constancy (*Selbstständigkeit*) (Heidegger, 1996, p. 281)—is not simply continuing to be the same in time, but the contingent realization of a possibility. Ricoeur clarifies this self-preservation of the self with the example of an illocutionary act such as making a promise. If we keep a promise, it is not because we simply remain the same person, but rather it is a result of a volitional effort. Our identity is not a simple fact, but a continuous task, only ending with our death. In our everyday existence we are always, as we like to say about our websites, "under construction."

The confusion surrounding the notion of personal identity is further increased by the fact that we have a tendency to identify ourselves with opportunities realized in the past and therefore seclude ourselves from future opportunities. What at first was simply possibility takes on the form of an aggregate of character traits and ingrained habits. A "second nature" emerges that contributes to the continuity of our personal identity. This fundamental passivity that ensures that much remains the same in us, makes us identifiable to ourselves and to others. In this case there appears to be not so much a question of an overlap, but rather of a transformation of the *self* into the *same*. Although this tendency is a natural part of human existence, the degree to which it appears is culturally and historically variable. Although personal (and cultural) identity in traditional societies is generally quite stable, in modern culture our identity is characterized by a high level of flexibility and changeability. As Sherry Turkle notes,

Not so long ago, stability was socially valued and culturally reinforced. Rigid gender roles, repetitive labor, the expectation of being in one kind of job or remaining in one town over a lifetime, all of these made consistency central to definitions of health. But these stable social worlds have broken down. In our time, health is described in terms of fluidity rather than stability. What matters most now is the ability to adapt and change—to new jobs, new career directions, new gender roles, new technologies. (Turkle, 1995, p. 255; cf. Gergen, 1991)

It is against the background of the discussion about the ontological status and the flexabilization of human identity that Ricoeur presents his theory of narrative identity (Ricoeur, 1985, 1991a,b, 1992) . Ricoeur takes Heidegger's notion of the existential self as his starting point, but he implicitly criticizes Heidegger for sticking to Descartes' immediate positing of the "I." Unlike Descartes and Heidegger, Ricoeur does not believe that we have an immediate access to the self in introspection or phenomenological intuition. Self-knowledge is in almost all cases mediated. We know ourselves mainly via the indirect route of the cultural expression of ourselves in actions, utterances, images, music, nutrition, fashion, housing, institutions, religion, and so on.

Narratives are especially important in this respect. "The narratives of the world are numberless.... Narrative is present in every age, in every place, in every society; it begins with the very history of mankind and there nowhere is or has been a people without narrative.... Narrative is international, transhistorical, transcultural: it is simply there, like life itself" (Barthes,

1982, p. 79). Or, as Hayden White writes, "To raise the question of the nature of narrative is to invite reflection on the very nature of culture and, possibly, even on the nature of humanity itself" (White, 1980, p. 1).

This is also the starting point for Ricoeur: "Answering the question 'Who?'... implies the narration of a life story" (Ricoeur, 1985, p. 335).[5] It is only in the stories we tell others and ourselves about our lives and about (real or fictious) other lives that we articulate our own selves, and only by identifying ourselves with these stories our identity comes into being. Thus, for Ricoeur narrative is not only a suitable *metaphor* for human identity, but is also preeminently the *medium* with whose help we give our identity form. Our identity is contained in our life story. That story is not pregiven and static, but attains form in our actions and our narrative reflection on them. According to Ricoeur, in this process we can distinguish a threefold mimesis.

The first level, referred to as *mimesis₁*, is connected with the narrative prefiguration of our daily life. In Ricoeur's view this lies in the practical knowledge that guides our actions. We experience our dealings with our fellow human beings in terms of meaning: we distinguish motives and interests, we set standards and ascribe values, we attempt to realize certain ideals in life. Therefore in a certain sense our actions already contain an implicit narrative. Our life is an unremitting "Quest of Narrative" (Ricoeur, 1991a).

Ricoeur designates the expression of the experienced prenarrative coherence in explicit narratives (varying from the everyday narratives we tell about ourselves to autobiography and—more general—in the art of novel) as *mimesis₂*. This stage is described in dramaturgical terms, derived from Aristotle's analysis of tragedy in his *Poetics*. Central in Aristotle's argument is the notion of the plot (*mythos*), the expression of a series of mutually connected and motivated actions. According to Ricoeur, the plot (*mise en intrigue*) can be understood as "a synthesis of the heterogeneous" (Ricoeur, 1992, p. 141). The plot brings the heterogeneous elements of which a story consists—events, such as actions and happenings, and existents, such as settings and characters (cf. Chatman, 1978)—to a unity. The Aristotelian plot can be regarded as a complete whole. It is a *whole* because all the elements within the plot are linked and there are no elements unrelated to the plot. In the plot every element has meaning in the light of the whole. It is *complete* because together the elements give the narrative closure. In a nutshell, the plot has a beginning, a middle, and an end (Aristotle, 1984, vol. 2, p. 2321).

Ricoeur calls this the meaningful configuration created by the plot *concordance*. However, this concordance is no static state, but is continuously jeopardized by *discordances*, such as reversals of fortune that threaten the meaningful closure of the narrative. A story is the representation of an act that is continuously frustrated by more or less unforeseen settings and happenings. This makes the story a *dynamic* whole. For that reason Ricoeur calls the story a discordant concordance (Ricoeur, 1992, p. 141).

The third step in the construction of narrative identity, *mimesis₃*, consists of the reflective application of the narrative configuration on the self, resulting in an identification with the *characters* of the story. The unity of the story—the plot—is closely connected to the *characters* figuring in it. Telling a story is telling who does what and why. In the story we witness how the character develops. Just like the plot, characters show a dialectic of concordance and discordance. In the character, contingent events get a narrative coherence. From a psychoanalytical point of view, we could say that the identification that characterizes mimesis₃, consists in the internalization of the object of desire— the state of concordance obtained by the characters in the story. This is not a simple imitation, but an appropriation or assimilation that results in a change in the identity of the identifying person (cf. Freud, 1953, vol. IV, p. 156).

However, just as in the case of the plot the stability obtained by this internalization is rather shaky, as it is continuously confronted by the return of the heterogeneous, which threatens the concordance of our identity. A sublime love, a personal vendetta, a crisis or addiction, illness and death—these are all happenings that give our life story unexpected turns, that keep challenging the concordance of the character and ultimately may destroy it. Until its very end the (life) story it is characterized by this dialectic between concordance and discordance.

The theory of narrative identity helps us to better understand the above mentioned relationship between the same and the self on the one hand, and between the self and the other on the other hand. The tension between the *same* and the *self* turns out to be no other than that between concordance and discordance in our life stories. Every story can be located somewhere between the extremes of stories in which the character simply remains the same (such as is often the case in fairy tales with its stable roles) and stories in which the character completely disintegrates in its confrontation with the heterogeneous. Ricoeur mentions Robert

Musil's *The man without qualities* as a novel in which the self completely loses its identifiable characteristics. Because of the close connection between plot and character, it does not surprise that the crisis of the character in this novel correspond with a crisis of closure of the story. For that reason, *The Man Without Qualities* perhaps represents the crisis of Western culture in which the grand narratives have lost their persuasiveness (Lyotard, 1984; cf. De Mul, 1999).

The narrative model of identity also throws an elucidating light on the social dimension of human identity. By telling our life story we are always already entangled in the dialectics between the *self* and the *other* (Ricoeur, 1992, p. 141). The other is present in different roles in the stories we identify our selves with. In the first place, we identify ourselves with the others that appear in the stories that are being told in our (sub)culture. In the second place, the other is constitutive for our identity because it is always part of our life story, as relative, lover, neighbor, colleague, employer, stranger, enemy, and so on. In the third place, are we always actors in the stories of others. All these dialectical relationships mean that we are continuously entangled in a multiplicity of stories and that our identity, as a result, is a "tissue of stories" (Ricoeur, 1985, p. 356). Just as in the case of Mead's account of the self and Turkle's investigation of our identity in the age of the Internet, in Ricoeur's theory of narrative identity, the self is a multiple self.

Ricoeur emphasizes the constructive role of literary narratives. But doesn't this mean that he neglects the difference between life and story? After all, "stories are not lived but told" (Mink, 1970, p. 557). Ricoeur argues that it is just because our life is not a story, because it is unarticulated, poly-interpretable and without closure, that we need the concordance of stories to control the continuous threat of the heterogeneous. This confirms that narrative identity is no sheer representation of an already given entity, but a construction. As this construction is foremost a creation of our imagination we can agree with Hume and Dennett that our narrative identity is a (literary) fiction, but we should immediately add that it is no theoretical abstract, but a meaningful nexus that we experience and live. Our identity might be called virtual, in the sense that it is a fiction that creates real effects in our daily lives (cf. Heim, 1993, pp. 109–110).

Broadening Ricoeur's Theory of Narrative Identity

Later, I will try to demonstrate that Ricoeur's theory of narrative identity offers a fruitful conceptual framework for an investigation of identity formation that takes place in playing computer games. However, first I have to discuss some problems that stand in the way of a successful application of Ricoeur's theory in the domain of computer games. The first one, which I will now address, has to do with Ricoeur's rather restricted conception of narrativity. The second problem, which I will discuss in the next section, is more fundamental and concerns the question whether we can approach computer games from a narrative perspective at all.

In the books and articles in which Ricoeur has developed his theory of narrative, he refers to various narratives in order to develop and illustrate his theory. However, it is striking that he takes hardly any other narratives into account but linguistic ones. It has to be admitted he is not completely alone in this. Some narratologists hold that narratives only exist in language. Mieke Bal, for example, in the first edition of her *Narratology: Introduction to the theory of narrative*, restricts narratives to narrative texts, and defines a text as "a finite, structured whole composed of language signs" (Bal, 1985, p. 5). She further defines a story as "a fabula that is presented in a certain manner" and a fabula as "a series of logically and chronologically related events that are caused or experienced by actors" (Bal, 1985, p. 5). Moreover, she adds as defining characteristics that in narrative texts there are always two types of speakers, one that has no specific function in the history narrated, and one that does have such a function (though the narrator and actor can be united in one person) and that with regard to narratives three levels should always be distinguished: text, story (which—following Aristotle and Ricoeur—have been called plot in the foregoing), and fabula (history).

However, given this definition of narrative the restriction of the analysis to linguistic texts is not evident and even not very convincing. It is not clear why a stage play, a dance, or a movie could not count as a narrative. As Barthes notes, narrative is a code or form that can be expressed in various media or substances:

Narrative is first and foremost a prodigious variety of genres, themselves distributed amongst different substances—as though any material were fit to receive man's stories. Able to carried by articulated language, spoken or written, fixed or moving images, gestures, and the ordered mixture of all these substances: narrative is present in myth, legend, fable, tale, novella, epic, history, tragedy, drama, comedy, mime, painting (think of Carpaccio's Saint Ursulla), *stained glass windows, cinema, comics, news items, conversation.* (Barthes, 1982, p. 79)

For that reason it is not that strange that Bal in the second edition of her book broadens the spectrum of her theoretical model to include discussions of visualization and visual narrative, and gives various examples from art and film (Bal, 1997). In this broad conception of narrative, computer games are not in principle excluded from having a narrative dimension and as such play a similar role in identity construction as novels, stage plays, films, and comics. And, as we will see in the next section, many computer games in fact do have a narrative dimension.

Ricoeur's theory of narrative identity is not only constrained by his exclusive focus on linguistic narratives, but also by the fact that even within this already restricted domain he hardly takes any other narratives into account than novels belonging to the modern, Western tradition. This is surprising in the light of the fact that, as we have noted, with Barthes, narratives are international, transhistorical, and transcultural. In the globalized and multicultural societies that characterize present Western culture, we not only are increasingly in contact with narrative traditions from other cultures, but immigrants also import and assimilate these traditions in our own culture.

This constraint in Ricoeur's theory should be mentioned, because Ricoeur's preference for the classical, Western canon is connected with a preference for a specific cultural and historical determined type of narrative, that has, as we will see, less in common with the structure of computer games than some of the transcultural narratives that presently are developing in multicultural cultures. Though Ricoeur talks about discordant concordance, it is clear that the emphasis is mainly on concordance. In "Life in quest of narrative," he frankly speaks about "the primacy of concordance over discordance" (Ricoeur, 1991a, p. 22). This primacy also comes to the fore in the interpretations Ricoeur gives in *Time and narrative* of the modern novels of Woolf, Mann, and Proust. In his interpretation of Woolf's *Mrs. Dalloway*, for example, we see that he does not recoil from some interpretative violence. Though the two protagonists in the novel, Clarissa and Septimus, because of insoluble conflicts between their personal and public life, respectively, end up in an existential crisis and in suicide, Ricoeur does manage to present the story as a story about authentic self-realization in which concordance finally has the last word. Examples such as this show that Ricoeur remains chained to the classical, Aristotelian tradition, which is characterized by a desire for closure.

Ajit Maan has argued that Ricoeur seems to presuppose that this Western type of narrative is the universal model for human identity (Maan, 1999, p. 84). Everything that does not fit in this model would be considered disassociative at best (p. 57). Maan argues that specific spatial and temporal continuities are no intrinsic characteristics of personal, sexual, ethnic, or cultural identity, but social and political constructions instead. In her view "assuming that narratives structure affects action and identity, narrative choice should include not only alternative plots in terms of content but also alternative formal structures" (p. 16). In this context she discusses the "internarrative" novel *Fault lines*, by Meena Alexander. In this novel, Alexander—born in India, raised in Egypt, and now living and working in the United States—gives an account of her life, offering the different aspects of her multiple identity equal rights. The organizational principle of this novel is not so much temporal continuity but rather spatial discontinuity. The result is a heterogeneous fabric with multiple beginnings recurring repeatedly throughout the narrative. "Even the final chapter contains a re-telling of a beginning. These beginnings do not lead to a middle. There is no middle that leads to a resolved ending" (Maan, 1999, p. 45).

This structure, which reminds of the organizational principle of computer games and other hypermedia, prevents that certain aspects of her identity are being suppressed or sacrificed to other aspects. Although Alexander describes herself as "homeless, shelterless, with no fixed place to belong, and a blabber of multiple tongues" (Alexander, 1993, p. 177), her narrative is no expression of sheer chaos, but rather an impressive attempt to reconfigure this chaos in a liveable nexus (Maan, 1999, p. 37).

This experience of contingency and heterogeneity of the migrant could be extended to life in our present postmodern culture, which is being characterized by multiphrenia, "the splitting of the individual into a multiplicity of self-investments" (Gergen, 1991, pp. 73–74). The concordant unifying narrative Ricoeur is talking about is no longer able to express the fragmented identity of the postmodern citizen, to which Turkle referred. As Maan argues, new narrative structures might be better capable to express and to make livable the new forms of identity. And perhaps computer games are expressions of these new forms of identity too.

Computer Games: Narrativity and Beyond

By broadening Ricoeur's theory of narrative identity to include nonlinguistic and nonstandard Western narratives, I hope to make this theory more suitable for the analysis of identity construction in the playing of computer games. However, according to many theorists in the field of computer games, narratives and computer games are so fundamentally different in their "grammar" that their study requires an essentially different conceptual apparatus (Juul, 1998; for a more nuanced account see his contribution in this volume). In order to be able to judge this critique, we have to compare the ontologies of narratives and computer games.

Play, Games and Computer Games

It doesn't seem to be a sheer coincidence that Wittgenstein illustrated his notion "family resemblance" with the help of the concept of "game." Just as in the cases of "identity" and "narrative," the concept of "game" does not refer to one essential characteristic, but to a series of similarities and relationships. Card games have some things in common with board games, which in turn have some things in common with ball games. Not all games are amusing, and not all involve winning and losing. What counts as skill and luck varies among them. Even when we restrict ourselves to computer games, we can distinguish various types and genres. However, this does not mean we can give no description of games and computer games.

Games can be regarded as a subclass of play, that is, (mostly) joyful activities that are often temporally and spatially set apart from everyday life. What is merely play is not serious; it has no goal other than itself. However, as Gadamer notices in his phenomenological analysis of play in *Truth and method*, play has its own, even sacred, seriousness (Gadamer, 1989, p. 102). It fulfils its purpose only if the player loses himself in play. "The movement of playing has no goal that would bring it to an end; rather, it renews itself in constant repetition" (p. 102). Most games present the playing person with a task. Moreover, play has its own type of intentionality: we are always playing *something* (p. 107). However, play is not a so much a re-presentation of that something but rather a presentation: "Its mode of being is self-presentation" (p. 108).

When play transforms into structure, it can become either drama (a stage play) or game. In both cases it gets a *specific structure* that makes the play into something independent from the player(s). However, in order to be, they have to be played. The game can

therefore—following Huizinga's famous definition—be defined as "a free act that takes place within a specially designated time in a specially designated place, according to specific rules which are strictly adhered to" (Huizinga, 1970, p. 13). Like play, games present the players with a specific task, often in a competition. The outcome of the game depends on the actions of the player(s).

Often in plays and games we use attributes such as balls or cards. Computer games distinguish themselves from other games by their technological mediation (see the contribution of Britta Neitzel in this volume). In the case of computer games, the distinctive game space is a *virtual space*, which can be manipulated with the help of various input devices (mouse, joystick, and so on) of which the effects can be viewed on an output device (monitor). The monitoring process gives the computer player the possibility of continuously observing the results of the action. It is, as Neitzl defines it, "a process of self-observation with continuous feedback." This distinction between the *point of action* and the *point of view* enables the player to reflect upon the self as another, that is, as an avatar. Another aspect Neitzl points at is that computer games as we know them represent action in which humans could participate. Although this is often not true for puzzles (*Tetris*) and simulations (*SimLife*), it is for most action and fighting games (*Tomb Raider*), adventures (*McGee's Alice*), role playing games (*Final Fantasy Mystic Quest*), sports games (*Formula 1*), and strategy games (*Civilization*). As Neitzl justly notes, it is this connectedness of the level of action to the level of representation that links computer games to narratives, as these are as well representations of a real or fictional chain of actions.

The Narrative Dimension of Computer Games

We can formulate the following minimal definition of a narrative. It is the representation of a series of logically and chronologically related events in a specific setting, with a beginning, a middle, and an end, and caused or undertaken by actors. The closure that characterizes most stories is connected with the fact, first described by Tzvetan Todorov, that they represent a transformation in which (1) a state of equilibrium at the outset is (2) disrupted by some event (action or happening), (3) the recognition of this disruption by the (main) character, followed by (4) an attempt to repair the disruption, and finally (5) the reinstatement of the initial equilibrium (Branigan, 1992, p. 4). In this narrative scheme we recognize Ricoeur's dialectics between concordance and disconcordance. At first glance this description is also applicable to many computer games. Most of these games have this kind of quest structure—designated by Frye as the master genre of the romance (Frye, 1957)—in which the protagonists undergo a series of trials in order to achieve their goal. Moreover, in many games we also find existents (characters and settings) and events (happenings and actions).

Let us take as representative example of a standard third-person action game *Enter the Matrix* (2003). As in the movie *The Matrix Reloaded* (2003), on which the game is based, the initial state of equilibrium—man ruling the world—is disturbed by machines taking control and attempting to destroy the human population. The task of the characters—Niobe and Ghost, two side characters in the movie, acting against the setting of the locations of *Matrix* the movie—is to reinstate the initial equilibrium. It opens with the character or avatar of your choice—Niobe and Ghost have different skills and subtasks—in a post office, trying to get a specific PO box to retrieve some information. As you make your way through the game, you have to chase airplanes, rescue captured rebels, navigate through a sewer system, destroy a nuclear power plant, and fight off a sentinel attack from aboard your hovercraft, the Logos.

As Juul has argued, in these kinds of narrative games the story is in a sense external to the playing of the game itself—provided in advance or in breaks between the playing, written on the package, in the manual or in introduction and transition movie-sequences—and as the ideal story the player has to realize (Juul, this volume). But the actual playing is not narrative. In fact computer games such as *Enter the Matrix*—and as said before, this game seems to be representative of the mainstream of action and fighting games, adventures, role playing games, sports games, and strategy games—show that these games in fact are a hybrid *combination*, and not so much an integration of game and narrative.[6] It is true that a narrative unfolds, but this does not occur in the game itself. Of course, this is not to to say that these kinds of hybrids are a failure. What the great success many of these games demonstrates is that you can add narrative elements to a game in a creative manner without spoiling the game. The narrative framework in which the game elements are presented even enhance the pleasure of playing the game. For fans of the *Matrix* movie triology, the narrative context will enhance the pleasure of playing the game,[7] also offering the modes of identification by the reflective application of the narrative configuration on the self, as discussed earlier.

However, this does not elucidate yet the distinctive contribution of the game elements of the computer game to identity construction. In order to analyze this contribution, we have to focus on the aspects of the computer game that do not overlap with narrative. This is where we are not concerned with the point of view of the player, but with his point of (inter)action.

Computer Games versus Narratives: Interaction versus Interpretation

If there is one single characteristic that distinguishes (computer) games from narratives it must be (inter)-action. Whereas the reader (or viewer) of a narrative is presented with a chain of events imagined by the author (or director) of the story, in the computer game the chain of events is the result of the player's action. This is not to say that the reader is a passive consumer of the story; with regard to the reading of narratives the reader plays a double role, occupying at the same time a *passive point of view* and an *active point of interpretation*. As has become a standard presupposition in narratology, a story only comes into being when the reader actively constructs it by interpreting the narrative elements by linking them to each other. In this sense, readers have a certain freedom of interpretation and different readers can read different stories, depending on their foreknowledge. However, with the exception of certain avant-garde texts such as Julio Cortázar's *Hopscotch* (Cortázar, 1987; cf. De Mul, 2000), in the case of narratives the order of the narrative elements or *lexia* is determined by the author and not by the reader. In computer games, on the other hand, the player is (inter)active in the sense that he or she determines the sequence of the elements that appear on the monitor.

A narrative is *linear* and the elements of the narrative are linked together by a narrative *causality*. Narrative speaks the language of fate, every action and event is caused by the preceding actions and motives. It is thanks to this specific chain of actions and events that a narrative in a book can be translated into a film. Both media share the same narrative grammar. Conversely in a game a player has relatively great *freedom* to determine the sequence of actions himself. The game, therefore, is necessarily *multilinear*; if the player cannot choose between various options there is no game at all.

Of course the freedom of the player is not absolute. Like every game, there is a set of rules that determine which actions can be undertaken and which not. In this context the distinction Joyce makes between exploratory and constructive hypertexts can be applied to games (Joyce, 1995, p. 42). Explorative games are games in which the nature and the number of lexia is fixed and the freedom of the player is restricted to the sequence in which they are presented during the game. In the case of constructive games, however, the player is able to change the nature and number of lexia. We can think of *Doom*, for example, where players are able to construct their own settings, or of the *Tomb Raider* game, which was hacked by players in order to subvert gender roles (Schleiner, 1998). These games are versions of what they are becoming, a structure for what does not yet exist. In these cases there is what Andy Cameron calls *real interactivity*, "the ability to intervene in a meaningful way within the representation itself, not to read it differently" (Cameron, 1995). Cameron elucidates his point by stating that interactivity in music would mean the ability to change the sound, interactivity in painting to change colors, or make marks, interactivity in film the immersion of the spectator in the scene and the ability to change the way the movie ends. Real activity in computer games is the ability to change the representation and/or rules of the game.

The multilinearity of the game that is connected with its interactivity has important consequences for the temporal and spatial organization of games, compared to that of narratives (Juul, 1998; cf. his contribution in this volume). The narrative has three temporal levels: that of the plot (the signifier), that of the related narrative (the signified), and that of the reader or viewer. A sequence of shots in a film, lasting only a few minutes, can cover many years of the narrative. When watching a film, both temporal layers are interpreted together by the viewer. Because the times of the plot and the narrative are different, the narrator also shows the three dimensions of time. It does not only take place at the time of the reading, but by means of flashbacks and flash forwards, the plot also presents the past and the future.

Computer games such as *Enter the Matrix* lack this temporal stratification. Where the reader or the person watching a film undergoes great temporal mobility by means of flashbacks and flash forwards, the computer game player is inevitably confined to the present. Because he finds himself in an eternal present, he is able to carry out the same actions over and over again. Other than the protagonist of a narrative, who sooner or later inevitably dies, the player is immortal. In *Enter the Matrix*, every time you are shot dead, you can begin the game again.

With regard to spatial organization, the narrative and the game also differ significantly. The situation here, however, is the other way round. In contrast to film, the game has a spatial stratification. It has three spatial dimensions. Interactivity means that you can go in various directions—to the left or right, forwards or backwards, up or down. Just as in the narrative there is a difference between the time of the plot (the signifier) and the time of the narrative (the signified), in the game there is a difference between the space of the game interface (the signifier) and the virtual space disclosed up by the game (the signified). And also in the game there is a third dimension in which both these spaces are interpreted together—that of the player. In contrast, in the narrative, the three spatial dimensions implode into a one-dimensional, that is to say sequential, path that the protagonists tread through the narrative space. Their fate is that they are doomed to wander this single path. From the notion of the spatial dimension, the game and the narrative are as chess and a game of chess. The rules of chess enclose a space within which an unlimited number of different games of chess can be played.

We can also illuminate the difference between narrative and game by looking at the relationship between plot and action. In the narrative, the plot determines the action. Whereas in the narrative the action is motivated by the plot, in the computer game the plot is dependent on the action. When at the right moment the player of *Enter the Matrix* pulls the trigger of his gun and shoots the sentinel, he can enter the next room where another challenge awaits him. When he shoots too late and is himself shot dead, he changes the plot. The discursive causality here seems to be reversed—the action determines the plot, or seeks for it in vain (Aarseth, 1994).

When, finally, we look at the "pleasure bonus" that the narrative and computer game respectively offer the reader, viewer, and the player, again we see an important difference. In the classic narrative the pleasure lies in the satisfaction it gives to know how the narrative ends. From a psychoanalytical point of view, we should call it an end-pleasure (Freud, 1953, vol. VII, p. 209; cf. De Mul, 1999, pp. 180–182). When, understood in Aristotelian terms, there is no ending, the reader is frustrated. The game, however, does not have an end. Without doubt one can stop *Enter the Matrix* after having gone through all levels, but then in fact we stop because of the closure of the accompanying narrative. Games that have no or hardly any narrative context, such as *Tetris*, invite us to play again in order to beat our personal record. Of course, after some time we will stop playing the game, for example, because we are exhausted or bored, but only to continue our playing after a while. The lust provided by the computer game is never an end-pleasure but necessarily always remain a fore-pleasure. This is one of the reasons that playing computer games easily leads to addiction. This fore-pleasure is connected with phantoming the rules of the game and improving one's skills in order to improve the personal record.

Ludic Identity

Now that I have described the main difference between narrative and computer games, I am able to analyze the implications of this difference for the formation of identity and give a tentative answer to the question how computer games affect our personal identity.

Ludic Identity Formation

In the previous section, we noticed that narratives and games have a number of characteristics in common. The same can be said for the formation of narrative and ludic identity. Just as narratives, computer games are expressions that, among other things, play a function in the formation of our identity. They are able to do this because both give expression to important aspects of human life that structure our lived experiences and by doing that enable the reflective identification with this structure. With regard to the construction of ludic identity we can discern three stages, which I will call, following Ricoeur's notion of threefold mimesis, $play_1$, $play_2$, and $play_3$.

Play$_1$ refers to the ludic prefiguration of our daily life. We experience nature and the human world as playful, for example, when we notice the play of light or waves, when we see the play of animals and children, or experience the play of sexual seduction. Everywhere in our world we experience movements backwards and forward that renew themselves in constant repetition. Varying the words of Friedrich Schlegel, we could say that the (computer) games we play are nothing but a remote imitation of the infinite play of the world (cf. Gadamer, 1989, p. 105).

The expression of this experienced pre-ludic coherence in (computer) *games* forms the level of play$_2$. Central here is the *set of rules* that determine the possible movements backwards and forwards that determine a specific play. The result is not so much, as in narrative, a causal chain of events, but a playing field (*Spielraum*), that is a *space of possible action*. This playing field can be regarded as an *infinite whole*. The game of *Tetris*

for example, consists of a finite set of existents and constitutive rules that disclose an infinite number of different game sessions. It does not have a closure, but is always fundamentally *open* to further (renewal of) action. We always want to beat the present high score. Unlike the narrative, of which the end is always already determined (every narrative refers to a story that already took place, even when the story is situated in the present), the outcome of a game is fundamentally indeterminate.

In the third stage of the formation of the ludic identity, play$_3$, the player identifies with the space of possibilities disclosed by the game. The field of possible action is reflectively applied to the self. The infinity of possible outcomes, connected with the constitutive rules, is internalized. As in the case of the reflective application of the narrative to the self, in the case of ludic identity there is no simple imitation of these rules, but they are being appropriated or assimilated and as a result change the identity of the player.

As in the case of narrative identity in the construction of ludic identity there is a constant dialectic between concordance and discordance. Every game can be located somewhere between games in which with every single action the number of possibilities increase and those in which they decrease. Whereas in many action games and aventures that are designed according a "tree of death" with every choice the number of possible outcomes is reduced (the initial choice for Niobe or Ghost in *Enter the Matrix* restricts the number of possible actions, as each of the characters have a distinct set of tasks and skills), simulation games often do increase the number of possible outcomes with every choice made. However, when we compare narratives with games in regard to the balance of concordance and discordance, the dominance seems to be opposite. Whereas in the case of narrative identity the predominant tendency is toward an increase of closure and thus concordance (novels such as Robert Musil's *Man without qualities* remain an exception), in the case of ludic identity the predominant tendency is toward an increase of openness. In every situation the ludic self is in search for new possibilities in order to increase the field of possible action. In this sense the temporal dimension of narrative and games is opposite. Whereas narration, although taking place in the present, aims at an understanding of what have happened in the past, playing, which also takes place in the present, is directed at future possibilities.

In the case of ludic identity there is an additional dialectic between the self and the other. The other is always present, not only as a player we want to identify ourselves with, but also as opponent or teammate, as enemy or lover, the other present possibilities for reciprocal and/or collective action.

A possible objection could be that life is no game, but we could formulate an analogue answer as Ricoeur did in reply to the critique that life is no story. Just because our life is no game, not always joyful and full of possibilities, we need games to oppose the continuous threat of closure. And just as in the case of narrative identity, ludic identity is a creation of our imagination that creates real effects in our daily lives.

Growing Dominance of Ludic Identity?

Narrative and ludic identity do not represent alternatives that mutually exclude each other, but are two identity formations that co-exist and are entangled in many ways, in the same manner as stories and games. We could perhaps clarify their relationship a bit further by returning for a moment to Heidegger's analytics of human existence. Earlier I noted that according to Heidegger, existing in time means that living in the present, we are always oriented toward our future possibilities, and at the same time we are always constrained by the possibilities we have realized in the past. In a concise formula, Heidegger calls man a thrown possibility (*geworfene Möglichkeit*) (Heidegger, 1996, p. 135). However, our attitude toward our past and our future possibilities is not the same. We interpret and narrate our past and we play with and act upon, our future projects. Of course these dimensions are not completely separate. Our past is not simply behind us, but continuously effective in our present acting, and in our interpretations we continuously revise our past. The choices we make in our actions are always grounded in our past. It is for that reason that narratives and games are often narrowly entangled. Though situated in the past, stories can inspire new future possibilities. Though oriented toward the future, games often repeat possibilities from the past. As we already noticed, human beings tend to identify themselves with the choices made in the past and for that reason become less playful as they grow older. However, oriented toward past and future, they are the expressions of two fundamentally different dimensions of human life.

This does not mean, however, that they are always in balance. In Western culture, since the age of modernity there seems to be a growing dominance of the projective dimension of our existence above our thrownness. In the modern era, man understands himself predominantly as an autonomous, free acting subject. The modern subject can be conceived of as a *Homo volens*, that shapes life autonomously. Modern technology has given this autonomous subject powerful means to increase the power to choose and act. The computer game can be regarded as a popular derivate of this modern ideology. In this light it is no coincidence that interactivity became the buzz word in amusement industry. No less in the computer game than in the "game of life," the modern subject continuously has to make choices. Whereas in the premodern culture most choices—your life partner, occupation, religion—usually were made for you, as a modern subject, you continuously have to choose. Whether it concerns the simple choice between the left or right door in a computer game or the choice for a certain lifestyle, every time the emphasis is on the volitional dimension of our personality. As we already noticed with Turkle, this necessitates a flexibility of our selves.

Of course, computer games do not cause this change in identity. This transformation of the modern self is a complex process in which, among many other things, social, political, economic, and technological developments play a role.[8] However, the massive dissemination of computer games in Western and westernized cultures without doubt is also part of this complex process. It demonstrates that in our culture on the level of the existents there has been a major shift from settings to character and on the level of the events from happenings to actions. Reflection gradually has shifted from interpretation of meaning to reflective feedback on action.

Without doubt this transformation partly has been on the ideological level only. That modern subjects, following Descartes, regard themselves as autonomous entities does not mean that they really *are* autonomous. Modern history is characterized by a stream of happenings that has demonstrated that many things are still not yet or—in the age of increasing autonomic technologies (Kelly, 1994)—no longer under our control. Even in our computer games we constantly face the possibility that the game will be over. However, they also promise us that we always can start all over again.

Connected with the shift from narrative and interpretation to game and action we can discern a shift from temporally organized identity to spatially organized identity. Earlier, we saw that human identity has these two dimensions. But also in this case there is no eternal—ahistorical or acultural—balance between these dimensions. In an age where the number of different roles increases so much that some sociologists even talk about a "saturation of the self" (Gergen, 1991), the number of activities we are engaged in at the same time increases no less, and, moreover, these roles and activities keep changing all the time over time, the spatial organization of the many changing aspects of our selves becomes more and more important. The personal computer with its many windows open all the time is a moving metaphor for the way we try to deal with this change in our selves, and at the same time seems to be a device that stimulates this change and at the same time enables us to cope with it. The same counts for the remote control, that increasingly is primarily used not to determine the sequence of the images on the screen, but rather to follow different channels at the same time. Computer games, with their spatial rather than temporal organization, play a no less important role in this transformation of our selves toward and of our world view. The world itself is no longer conceived of from a sheer historical perspective, but rather as a database, a playing field that enables us to (re)configure all kinds of different worlds. The evolution of life on earth is no longer a narrative in the sense that it is a causal chain of events, but rather a database full of genes that can be recombined in an infinite number of possible worlds. Spielberg's *Jurrasic Park* offers a still fictive but far from implausible view on this brave new world. Likewise, genetic manipulation, aesthetic surgery, and the like make our bodily and psychic characteristics less and less to our narrative fates and increasingly objects of choice. Again, this view has a strong ideological dimension, so we may expect that stories about what went wrong will also continue to be told. Our future selves probably will remain a more or less hybrid mix of narrative and ludic identities. But as we have seen in the discussion of Alexander's internarrative novel, even these narratives are gradually becoming more spatial in their organization and structure. The historical consciousness that emerged in the last centuries and from which the art of the novel also sprouted, will at least be contrasted with a spatial consciousness that does not think in terms of past decisions but rather in terms of parallel possibilities.

Three Pedagogical Afterthoughts
In the previous sections I have mainly restricted myself to a neutral exposition of the (partial) transformation of narrative identity into ludic identity that, in my view, can be discerned in our present culture and in which computer games play—already for quantative reasons—an increasingly important role. As I believe it is impor-

tant to understand before one judges, I have tried to postpone an evaluation of this transformation. Though it is not my intention to give a comprehensive evaluation in this last subsection (it is for the reader to judge), I do want to provide three pedagogical afterthoughts about some aspects of the process described that, at least in my view, may be important for further evaluation.

First, it is important to keep in mind that computer games are not "just games" but play a constitutive role in our cognitive development and in the construction of our identity. This role may even be more fundamental than in the case of narratives, because the emotional involvement in computer games is very strong. Some decades ago Sherry Turkle explained that this is connected to the fact that computer games are about action: "When you play a video game you enter into the world of the programmers who made it. You have to do more than identify with a character on the screen. You must act for it. Identification through action has a special kind of hold. Like playing a sport, it puts people into a highly focused, and highly charged state of mind. For many people, what is being pursued in the video game is not just a score, but an altered state" (Turkle, 1984, p. 83). For that reason the exposure to possible undesirable contents of computer games (such as violence, sexism, or racism, see Herz, 1997, p. 183), might be more intense than in the case of narratives. However, this does not already have implications for the effect, because in case playing violent games has a positive effect of catharsis, this may be for that very reason stronger than in the case of reading violent novels or watching violent movies. Anyway, we should not forget that computer games are ontological machines in the sense that they, just like narratives, not only structure our (concept of the) world, but also (our concept of) ourselves.

Next, connected with the strong involvement in computer games is the danger of addiction. This danger is reinforced by the fact that because of the predominantly fore-pleasure oriented satisfaction of computer games they already have an inherent stimulus to repetition. More in general, computer games are part of a technological world that has a strong addictive character as a whole. The modern ideology of makability results in a heavy dependence on technological means, independent of their success. However, as serious as an addiction may be, we should not exaggerate this danger in the case of computer games. In my opinion, an addiction to computer games is closer to a passion for reading novels or watching movies than an addiction to alcohol or crack. Reading stories, watching movies, and playing games are activities that are not instrumental but rather have their goal in themselves. They share this feature with an addiction to alcohol and other drugs. However, as these kinds of addiction can ruin your life, in the case of a passion for narratives and games, the opposite is the case. That narratives and games take place in a time and space beyond the seriousness of everyday life does not mean that they have no value. In so far as they are ontological tools that sharpen our imagination and enable us to construct new images of ourselves and the world, their value for our lives cannot easy be exaggerated! Because of its long history and respectable status not many people are inclined to designate a passion for literature as an addiction, and movies have emancipated themselves in a relatively short time from a fairground attraction to an art form comparable to literature. We value novels and movies, although we know that many trivial novels and cheap movies do not fulfil the ontological promise of great art. I would not be surprised if computer games follow the same path, so that in the future, in the midst of an ocean of game pulp, we will encounter wonderful games that will disclose new worlds and new modes of self-realization for its players.

Finally, if there is a danger connected to computer games, it will not so much lie in the depiction of violence or other undesired behavior or in the addictive qualities of these games, as in the impact they might have on human world openness. In the previous section I referred to Heidegger's definition of human existence as thrown possibility. Having possibilities require the more fundamental possibility to disclose a world. By "world" Heidegger means the all-governing expanse of an *open* relational context (Heidegger, 1975, p. 42). That means that even within a strict finite world, an infinite number of relations can be disclosed. As human beings we not only exist in time, but also in space. This means that we are not simply in space (as the stone is in space), but that we continuously discover and found space: geographical space, but also room to move and to imagine (Heidegger, 1996, p. 96 ff.).

However, in many—perhaps most—computer games today, especially those that are sheer exploratory instead of constructive, the freedom to move is rather restricted, as the field of possibilities itself is preprogrammed and finite. When we identify our selves with the help of these impoverished expressions, we impoverish ourselves. Although written more than ten years ago—a long time, given the short history of computer games—the following warning of Provenzo is still topical:

Bettelheim has pointed to the fact that children, as well as adults, need "plenty of what in German is called Spielraum. Now Spielraum is not primarily 'a room to play in.' While the word also means that, its primarily meaning is 'free scope, plenty of room' to move not only one's elbows but also one's mind, to experiment with things and ideas at one's leisure, or, to put it colloquially, to toy with ideas." Video games such as Nintendo, with their preprogrammed characters and their media-saturated images, present almost no opportunity to experiment or toy with ideas.... Compared to the worlds of imagination provided by play with dolls and blocks, games such as reviewed in this chapter [meant are a series of Nintento games] ultimately represent impoverished cultural and sensory environments for the child. (Provenzo, 1991, pp. 93, 95)

In *The Republic*, Plato banned narrative because in his view the artists have a bad influence on their audiences. If he had lived now, he might have made the same conclusion for computer games. In both cases the argument overlooks that we derive our very identity from these expressions. Our humanity is closely linked to the gift of narration and play. Being in principle programmable by the player, computer games can help and even inspire us to disclose new worlds and dimensions of the self. Therefore it would be precarious to condemn them as such. However, it is wise to keep distinguishing the ones that enrich our world and ourselves from those that threaten to impoverish it.

Notes

1. See Introduction on the impressive rise of the computer game since the eighties.
2. This idea is especially developed in the hermeneutical and structuralist tradition in philosophy and psychology. The German founder of the human sciences (*Geisteswissenschaften*), Wilhelm Dilthey, introduced the notion of a "nexus of life" (*Zusammenhang des Lebens*) in which the intellectual, volitional, and emotional dimensions are structurally integrated. For a more detailed exposition of Dilthey's hermeneutics, see my *The tragedy of finitude: Wilhelm Dilthey's hermeneutics of life* (De Mul, 2003). For an exposition of the structuralist theory of cognitive structure and development and its relationship to the hermeneutical conception, see Van Haaften et al., *Philosophy of development. Reconstructing the foundations of human development and education* (Van Haaften, Korthals & Wren, 1997).

3. In the Anglo-Saxon tradition since Locke, this temporal continuity, and the implied role of memory, is central in the theory of personal identity. In his *An essay concerning human understanding* (1690), Locke states that memory is determinate for our identity: "For, since consciousness always accompanies thinking, and it is that, which makes every one to be what he calls self, and thereby distinguishes himself from all other thinking things, in this alone consists personal identity, i.e. the sameness of rational being: and as far as consciousness can be extended backwards to any past action or thought, so far reaches the identity of that person" (Locke & Nidditch, 1975, p. 335).

4. Although the emphasis in this chapter is on *personal* identity, we can also distinguish these spatial and a temporal dimensions (as well as the types of discontinuity mentioned) with regard to the identity of groups or cultures. A culture is not a loose conglomerate of elements, but shows a certain nexus. A specific subculture, such as that of fans, has a more or less coherent set of language, history, patterns of behavior, and institutions shared by members of this culture. Because this unity of traditions and habits demonstrates a historical tenacity, here, too, it can be said that there is a temporal continuity. Personal identity never can be isolated from belonging to a certain group or culture. A fan derives identity at least partly from belonging to the subculture of fans. Moreover, personal identity for an important part appears in social intercourse and communication: "We carry on a whole series of different relationships to different people. We are one thing to one man and another thing to another. There are parts of the self which exist only for the self in relationship to itself. We divide up in all sorts of different selves with reference to our acquaintances. We discuss politics with one and religion with another. There are all sorts of different selves answering to all sorts of different social reactions. It is the social process itself that is responsible for the appearance of the self; it is not there as self apart from this type of experience" (Mead & Morris, 1934, p. 142). In the discussion of the theories of narrative and ludic identity in the following sections we will notice again that personal identity cannot be isolated from this social dimension.

5. Kevin J. Vanhoozer calls this Ricoeur's "narrative correction of the description of Dasein's temporality" (Vanhoozer, 1991, p. 45). In this respect, Ricoeur rather takes Hegel's metaphysics of mediation as his source of inspiration, as well as the hermeneutical transformation of this metaphysics by Wilhelm Dilthey. In his work Ricoeur repeatedly refers to Dilthey's aforementioned notion of the "nexus of life" (*Zusammenhang des Lebens*) and the idea, connected with this notion, that the understanding (*Verstehen*) of the nexus of our lived experiences (*Erlebnisse*) is only possible via the detour of the expressions (*Ausdrücke*) of these lived experiences (see De Mul, 2004, pp. 225–263).

6. That we are confronted here with a fundamental difference becomes clear when we think about the fact that it is impossible to translate narratives in games, whereas it is possible to translate the story of a book into a movie or a play (Brooks, 1984, pp. 3–4). Games will only be recognized as being based on a book or movie if additional narrative context is provided. The fighting scenes in *Enter the Matrix* are only recognizable as a translation of a part of the story of *The Matrix Reloaded* because of the narrative setting and charter derived from the movie, not because of the game action as such.

7. It should be added, however, that the narrative element reduces the games repeatability. Unlike puzzle games such as *Tetris*, if you know the end of the story of the adventure game, then repeatably playing the game again loses its appeal (Juul, 1998).

8. "Technology does not determine society: it embodies it. But neither does society determine technological innovation: it uses it" (Castells, 1996, p. 5; cf. Hughes, 1994).

References

Aarsteth, E. (1994). Nonlinearity and literary theory. In G. P. Landow (Ed.), *Hyper/Text/Theory* (pp. 51–86). Baltimore/London: John Hopkins University Press.

Alexander, M. (1993). *Fault lines: A memoir*. New York: Feminist Press at the City University of New York.

Aristotle (1984). *The complete works of Aristotle: The revised Oxford translation*. Princeton, NJ: Princeton University Press.

Bal, M. (1985). *Narratology: Introduction to the theory of narrative*. Toronto: University of Toronto Press.

Bal, M. (1997). *Narratology: Introduction to the theory of narrative* (2nd ed.). Toronto: University of Toronto Press.

Barthes, R. (1982). Introduction to the structural analysis of narratives. *Image, music, text* (pp. 79–124). London: Fontana Paperbacks.

Branigan, E. (1992). *Narrative comprehension and film*. London: Routledge.

Brooks, P. (1984). *Reading for the plot: Design and intention in narrative*. New York: Knopf.

Cameron, A. (1995). *The future of an illusion: Interactive cinema*. http://www.mfj-online.org/journalPages/MFJ28/Dissimulations.html.

Castells, M. (1996). *The information age: Economy, society and culture. Volume I: The rise of the network society*. Oxford: Blackwell Publishers.

Chatman, S. B. (1978). *Story and discourse: Narrative structure in fiction and film*. Ithaca, NY: Cornell University Press.

Cortázar, J. (1987). *Hopscotch*. New York: Panthenon Books.

De Mul, J. (1999). *Romantic desire in (post)modern art and philosophy*. Albany: State University of New York Press.

De Mul, J. (2000). The work of art in the age of digital reproduction. Some remarks on the transformation of the avant-garde. In B.-N. Oh (Ed.), *Art, life and culture* (pp. 59–80). Seoul: Seoul National University.

De Mul, J. (2004). *The tragedy of finitude. Dilthey's hermeneutics of life*. New Haven: Yale University Press.

Dennett, D. C. (1992). The self as a center of narrative gravity. In F. Kessel, P. Cole, & D. Johnson (Eds.), *Self and consciousness* (pp. 275–288). Hillsdale, NJ: Erlbaum.

Descartes, R. (1968). *Discourse on method and the meditations*. Harmondsworth: Penguin.

Freud, S. (1953). *The standard edition of the complete psychological works of Sigmund Freud*. London: Hogarth Press.

Frye, N. (1957). *Anatomy of criticism: Four essays*. Princeton: Princeton University Press.

Gadamer, H. G. (1989). *Truth and method* (2nd, rev. ed.). New York: Crossroads.

Gergen, K. (1991). *The saturated self: Dilemmas of identity in contemporary life*. New York: Basic Books.

Heidegger, M. (1975). *Poetry, language, thought*. New York: Harper & Row.

Heidegger, M. (1996). *Being and time*. Albany: State University of New York Press.

Heim, M. (1993). *The metaphysics of virtual reality*. New York: Oxford University Press.

Herz, J. C. (1997). *Joystick nation: How videogames ate our quarters, won our hearts, and rewired our minds*. Boston: Little Brown and Co.

Hughes, T. P. (1994). Technological momentum. In M. R. Smith & L. Marx (Eds.), *Does technology drive history? The dilemma of technological determinism* (pp. 101–113). Cambridge, MA: MIT Press.

Huizinga, J. (1970). *Homo ludens: A study of the play element in culture*. New York: J. & J. Harper Editions.

Hume, D. (1956). *A treatise of human nature*. London: Everyman's Library.

Joyce, M. (1995). *Of two minds: Hypertext pedagogy and poetics*. Ann Arbor: University of Michigan Press.

Juul, J. (1998). *A clash between game and narrative*. M.A. Thesis, University of Copenhagen. www.jesperjuul.dk. thesis.

Kelly, K. (1994). *Out of control*. Reading: Addison-Wesley.

Locke, J. (1975). *An essay concerning human understanding*. Oxford: Clarendon Press.

Lyotard, J. F. (1984). *The postmodern condition: A report on knowledge*. Minneapolis: University of Minnesota Press.

Maan, A. K. (1999). *Internarrative identity*. Lanham, MD: University Press of America.

Mead, G. H., & Morris, C. W. (1934). *Mind, self & society from the standpoint of a social behaviorist*. Chicago: The University of Chicago Press.

Mink, L. O. (1970). History and fiction as modes of comprehension. *New Literary History, 1*(1), 541–558.

Provenzo, E. (1991). *Video kids: Making sense of Nintendo*. Cambridge, MA: Harvard University Press.

Ricoeur, P. (1985). *Temps et récit III: Le temps raconté* (Vol. III). Paris: Éditions du Seuil.

Ricoeur, P. (1991a). Life in the quest of narrative. In D. Wood (Ed.), *On Paul Ricoeur: Narrative and interpretation* (pp. 20–33). London: Routledge.

Ricoeur, P. (1991b). Narrative identity. In D. Wood (Ed.), *On Paul Ricoeur: Narrative and interpretation* (pp. 188–199). London: Routledge.

Ricoeur, P. (1992). *Oneself as another*. Chicago: University of Chicago Press.

Schleiner, A. M. (1998). Does Lara Cloft wear fake polygons? www.opensorcery.net/lara2.html.

Turkle, S. (1984). *The second self: Computers and the human spirit*. New York: Simon and Schuster.

Turkle, S. (1995). *Life on the screen: Identity in the age of the internet*. New York: Simon and Schuster.

Van Haaften, A. W., Korthals, M., & Wren, T. (Eds.). (1997). *Philosophy of development. Reconstructing the foundations of human development and education* (Vol. 8). Dordrecht: Kluwer Academic Publishers.

Vanhoozer, K. J. (1991). Philosophical antecedents to Ricoeur's *Time and Narrative*. In D. Wood (Ed.), *On Paul Ricoeur: Narrative and interpretation* (pp. 34–54). London/New York: Routledge.

White, H. (1980). The value of narrativity in the representation of reality. In W.J.T. Mitchell (Ed.), *On narrative* (pp. 1–33). Chicago: University of Chicago Press.

Jos de Mul

COMPUTER GAMES AS EVOCATIVE OBJECTS: FROM PROJECTIVE SCREENS TO RELATIONAL ARTIFACTS

Sherry Turkle

Computers offer themselves as models of mind and as evocative objects, "objects to think with," for thinking about a range of philosophical and psychological questions, including questions about knowing, selfhood, and what we mean when we say something is "alive." They do this through the field of artificial intelligence, in which some researchers explicitly endeavor to use computers to model the human mind. And they do this in a far more concrete way: we are continually shaped by our hands-on engagement with computational objects, among these the objects of the computer "games" culture that have come to include the landscapes of online role-playing and simulation worlds as well as robotic pets and digital creatures. We relate to such objects as psychological machines, not only because so many of these new objects might be said to have primitive psychologies, but because they cause us to reflect upon our own.

Claude Lévi-Strauss (1966) described a process of theoretical tinkering, or "bricolage," through which individuals and cultures may use the objects around them to develop and assimilate ideas. Computational toys and games are key elements in today's cultural bricolage: What are we thinking about when we are thinking about computational toys and games? What does their "holding power" suggest about our emerging sensibilities?

In this chapter I draw on arguments and language from my writing (1984, 1995, 1997, 2005) to illustrate how computational toys and games have served as both a reflection of and emissary for computation in the wider culture. Here I have chosen three themes that make clear the central role of games in the development of computer culture: the shift from transparency to opacity in interface design, the growing use of the Internet as a landscape for identity play, and our evolving relationships with artificial creatures.

Thinking about Thinking by Thinking about Interfaces

What are we thinking about when we are thinking about computer game interfaces? For one thing, we are thinking about ways of knowing (Turkle, 1995). The earliest computer games were written for the interfaces of the early personal computers that supported them. Indeed, many of the children and teenagers who played the early games soon wanted to write games of their own on these same machines. The personal computers of the 1970s and the first generations of the IBM PC presented themselves as open, "transparent" objects, potentially reducible to their underlying mechanisms. These systems invited users to imagine they could understand the machines' "gears" as they turned, even if very few people ever tried to reach that level of understanding. In the spirit of traditional modernist ways of knowing, the technology encouraged users to think of understanding as reaching beyond the magic to the mechanism. In contrast, the 1984 introduction of the Macintosh's iconic style presented the public with simulations (the icons of file folders, a trashcan, and a desktop) that did nothing to suggest how their underlying structure could be known. As one user said, "The Mac looked perfect, finished. To install a program on my DOS machine, I had to fiddle with things. It clearly wasn't perfect. With the Mac, the system told me to stay on the surface." This is the kind of involvement with computers that has come to dominate the field; no longer associated only with the Macintosh, it is nearly universal in personal computing.

We have become accustomed to opaque technology; we have learned to take things at interface value. If the transparent early IBM PC modeled a modernist technological aesthetic, the Macintosh-style interface was consistent with a postmodern one whose theorists have suggested the search for depth and mechanism is futile, and that it is more realistic to explore the world of shifting surfaces than to embark on a search for origins and structure. It would not be an exaggeration to say that, to date, the Macintosh style of simulated desktop has been our most widely disseminated cultural introduction to the epistemology of simulation and virtuality. It has served as what Bruno Latour (1988) called "foot soldier" for new ideas. Culturally, the new computer interfaces have served as such foot soldiers or idea-emissaries. We are increasingly accustomed to navigating screen simulations and have grown less likely to ask of the computers around us, "What makes you work?"

In the 1980s, most computer users who spoke of transparency were referring to a transparency analogous to that of traditional machines, an ability to "open the hood" and poke around. But when, in the mid 1980s, Macintosh computer users began to talk about transparency, they were talking about seeing their documents and programs represented by attractive and easy-to-interpret icons. They were referring to an ability to make things work without needing to go below the screen surface. This was, somewhat paradoxically, a kind of transparency enabled by complexity and opacity. Today, the word "transparency" has taken on its Macintosh meaning in both computer talk and colloquial language. In a culture of simulation, when people say that something is transparent, they mean that they can easily see how to make it work. They don't mean that they know why it is working by reference to an underlying process. This is true of the interfaces of computer operating systems and it is true of the simulation games we play.

"Your orgot is being eaten up," flashes the message on the screen. It is a rainy Sunday afternoon and I am with Tim, age thirteen (Turkle, 1995). We are playing *SimLife*, Tim's favorite computer game, which sets its users to the task of creating a functioning ecosystem. "What's an orgot?" I ask Tim. He doesn't know. "I just ignore that," he says confidently. "You don't need to know that kind of stuff to play." I suppose I look unhappy, haunted by a lifetime habit of not proceeding to step two before I understand step one, because Tim tries to appease me by coming up with a working definition of orgot. "I think it is sort of like an organism. I never read that, but just from playing, I would say that's what it is."

The orgot issue will not die. A few minutes later the game informs us: "Your fig orgot moved to another species." I say nothing, but Tim reads my mind and shows compassion: "Don't let it bother you if you don't understand. I just say to myself that I probably won't be able to understand the whole game any time soon. So I just play." I begin to look through dictionaries in which orgot is not listed and finally find a reference to it embedded in the game itself, in a file called READ ME. The text apologizes for the fact that orgot has been given several and in some ways contradictory meanings in this version of *SimLife*, but one of them is close to organism. Tim was right—enough.

Tim's approach to *SimLife* is highly functional. He says he learned his style of play from video games: "Even though *SimLife*'s not a video game, the user can play it like one." By this he means that in *SimLife*, as in video games, one learns from the process of play. You do not first read a rulebook or get your terms straight. Tim is able to act on an intuitive sense of what will work without understanding the rules that underlie the game's behavior. At one point in the game he says, "My trilobytes went extinct. They must have run out of algae. I didn't give them algae. I forgot. I think I'll do that now." Tim can keep playing even when he has no very clear idea what is driving events. When his sea urchins become extinct, I ask him why.

Tim: I don't know, it's just something that happens.

ST: Do you know how to find out why it happened?

Tim: No.

ST: Do you mind that you can't tell why?

Tim: No. I don't let things like that bother me. It's not what's important.

Fifty years ago, a child's world was full of things that could be understood in simple, mechanical ways. A bicycle could be understood in terms of its pedals and gears, and a wind-up car in terms of its clockwork springs. Many of the people who built or bought the first generation of personal computers understood them down to the bits and bytes. The operating systems that followed were far more complex, but invited that "old-time" reductive understanding. Today, computer users such as Tim can completely ignore such understandings. Tim can stay on the surface, taking things at (inter)face value.

Another aspect of this aesthetic is clear when I interviewed a tenth-grader named Marcia about another of the "Sim" games, *SimCity*, which asks the game player to act as the mayor of a virtual town, with its own economy, politics, social life, and problems with energy and pollution (Turkle, 1997). Marcia boasts of her prowess as mayor and reels off her "Top ten most useful rules of Sim." Among these, number six grabs my attention: "Raising taxes always leads to riots."

Marcia seems to have no language for discriminating between this rule of the game and the rules that operate in a "real" city. She has never programmed a computer. She has never constructed a simulation. She has no language for asking how one might write the game so that increased taxes lead to increased productivity and social harmony. And she certainly does not see herself as someone who could change the rules. Like Tim confronted with the orgot, she does not know how to "read" a simulation; she does not know how to measure, criticize, or judge what she is learning. Marcia's situation—she is a fluent "user" of simulations but not a fluent thinker about them—confronts us with the problematic nature of our current moment. Marcia may not need to see the registers on her computer or the changing charges on a computer chip, but she needs to see something. She needs to be working with simulations that teach her about the nature of simulation itself.

Thinking about Identity by Thinking about Virtuality

When I write on a computer, I shuffle the text on my computer screen. Once I would literally have had to cut and paste. Now I call it cut and paste. Once I would have thought of it as editing. Now with computer software, moving sentences and paragraphs around is just part of writing. This is one reason I now remain much longer at my computer than I used to with a pen in hand or at my typewriter. When I want to write and don't have a computer around, I tend to wait until I do. In fact, I feel that I must wait until I do.

Why is it so hard for me to turn away from the screen? The windows on my computer desktop offer me layers of material to which I have simultaneous access: fieldnotes, previous drafts of this chapter, a list of ideas not yet elaborated but which I want to include, transcripts of interviews with computer users and game players. When I write at the computer, all these are present and my thinking space seems somehow enlarged. The dynamic, layered display gives me the comforting sense that I write in conversation with my computer. After years of such encounters, a blank piece of paper can make me feel strangely alone.

There is something else that keeps me at the screen. I feel pressure from a machine that seems itself to be perfect and leaves no one and no other thing but me to blame. It is hard for me to walk away from a not-yet-proofread text on the computer screen. In the electronic writing environment in which making a correction is as simple as striking a delete key, I experience a typographical error not as a mere slip of attention, but as a moral carelessness, for who could be so slovenly as not to take the one or two seconds to make it right? The computer tantalizes me with its holding power—in my case, the promise that if I do it right, it will do it right, and right away.

I am held by the possibilities of "conversation" among the multiple windows on my screen and the way an instantly responsive machine allays my anxieties about perfection. But other people are drawn by other sirens. Some are captured by virtual worlds that appear to be unsullied by the messiness of the real. Some are enthralled by the sense of mind building mind or merging with the mind of the computer. If one is afraid of intimacy yet afraid of being alone, even a stand-alone computer offers an apparent solution. Interactive and reactive, the computer offers the illusion of companionship without the demands of friendship. One can be a loner yet never be alone (Turkle, 1984).

Just as musical instruments can be extensions of the mind's construction of sound, computers can be extensions of the mind's construction of thought. A novelist refers to "my ESP with the machine. The words float out. I share the screen with my words." An architect who uses the computer to design goes further: "I don't see the building in my mind until I start to play with shapes and forms on the machine. It comes to life in the space between my eyes and the screen." Musicians often hear the music in their minds before they play it, experiencing the music from within before they experience it from without. The computer can be similarly experienced as an object on the border between self and not-self. Or, in a new variant on the story of Narcissus, people are able to fall in love with the artificial worlds that they have created or that have been built for them by others. People are able to see themselves in the computer. The machine can seem a second self, a metaphor first suggested to me by a thirteen-year-old girl who said, "When you program a computer there is a little piece of your mind, and now it's a little piece of the computer's mind." An investment counselor in her mid-forties echoes the child's sentiment when she says of her laptop computer: "I love the way it has my whole life on it."

The computer, of course, is not unique as a compelling extension of self. At each point in our lives, we seek to project ourselves into the world. The youngest child will eagerly pick up crayons and modeling clay. We paint, we work, we keep journals, we start companies, we build things that express the diversity of our personal and intellectual sensibilities. Yet the computer

Sherry Turkle

offers us new opportunities as a medium that embodies our ideas and expresses our diversity.

In the early years of the computer culture, the most dramatic instances of such projections of self onto computers occurred in the esoteric domain of programming. Now, as in the case of the novelist and architect, it is quite common for people to project themselves into the simulations that play on their screens, into screen images and actions. Computer holding power, once closely tied to the seductions of programming, today is tied to the seductions of the interface. When video games were very new, I found that the holding power of their screens often went along with a fantasy of a meeting of minds between the player and the program behind the game. In Internet gaming, the program no longer has this presence; one enters the screen world as Alice stepped through the looking glass.

To take an example that began in the early 1990s, networked game software known as MUDs (short for MultiUser Domains), enabled people from all over the world to join online virtual communities that existed only through and in the computer. The key element of "MUDding," the creation and projection of a "persona" into virtual space, also characterizes more recent online gaming communities (sometimes known as Massively Multiplayer Online Role Playing Games) such as *Everquest*, *Ultima Online*, and *Sims Online*. Thus, my description of life in MUD environments illustrates psychological aspects of online role-playing games in general.

When you join a MUD, you create a character or several characters, you specify each one's gender and other physical and psychological attributes. Other players in the MUD can see its description. It becomes your character's self-presentation. Created characters need not be human and there may be more than two genders. In the course of play, characters have casual and romantic sex, hold jobs, attend rituals and celebrations, fall in love and get married. To say the least, such goings-on are gripping: "This is more real than my real life," says a character who turns out to be a man playing a woman who is pretending to be a man. As players participate in MUDs, they become authors not only of text, but also of themselves, constructing selves through social interaction.

In traditional role-playing games in which one's physical body is present, one steps in and out of character; MUDs, in contrast, offer a parallel life. The boundaries of the game are fuzzy; the routine of playing them becomes part of their players' everyday lives.

MUDs blur the boundaries between self and game, self and role, self and simulation. One player says: "You are what you pretend to be … you are what you play." Players sometimes talk about their "real" selves as a composite of their characters and sometimes talk about their MUD characters as means for working on their "real" lives. Some of the most active participants in online gaming work with computers all day. It is common practice for them to periodically put their virtual personae to "sleep" and remain logged on to one or several games while pursuing other activities, returning to the games from time to time. In this way, they experience their lives as a "cycling through" between the "real world" and a series of games, each in its own "window." Their identity on the computer is the sum of their distributed presence.

This certainly is the case for Doug, a Dartmouth College junior who when I met him was playing four characters distributed across three different MUDs (Turkle, 1995). One is a seductive woman. One is a macho, cowboy type whose self-description stresses that he is a "Marlboros rolled in the tee shirt sleeve kind of guy." Then there is "Carrot," a rabbit of unspecified gender who wanders through its MUD introducing people to each other. Doug says, "Carrot is so low-key that people let it be around while they are having private conversations. So I think of Carrot as my passive, voyeuristic character." Doug's fourth character is one that he plays on a FurryMUD (MUDs on which all the characters are furry animals). "I'd rather not even talk about that character because its anonymity there is very important to me," Doug says. "Let's just say that on FurryMUDs I feel like a sexual tourist." Doug talks about playing his characters in windows that have enhanced his ability to "turn pieces of my mind on and off."

I split my mind. I'm getting better at it. I can see myself as being two or three or more. And I just turn on one part of my mind and then another when I go from window to window. I'm in some kind of argument in one window and trying to come on to a girl in a MUD in another, and another window might be running a spreadsheet program or some other technical thing for school.... And then I'll get a real-time message [that flashes on the screen as soon as it is sent from another system user], and I guess that's RL [real life]. It's just one more window.

The development of the windows metaphor for computer interfaces was a technical innovation motivated by the desire to get people working more efficiently by "cycling through" different applications, much as time-sharing computers cycle through the computing needs of different people. But, in practice, windows have become a potent metaphor for thinking about the self as a multiple, distributed, "time-sharing" system. The self is no longer simply playing different roles in different settings, something that people experience when, for example, one wakes up as a lover, makes breakfast as a mother, and drives to work as a lawyer. The life practice of windows is of a distributed self that exists in many worlds and plays many roles at the same time. MUDs extend the metaphor. Now, in Doug's words, "RL" can be just "one more window." Today's game worlds blur distinctions between the real and the artificial. Vandals "really" do damage in the virtual world of *Sims Online*; political protest about real world globalization takes place on its virtual streetcorners. Infidelities committed in virtual relationships with online partners feel transgressive, causing stress to the physical bodies that lie beyond the game.

When people adopt online personae they cross a boundary into highly charged territory. Some feel an uncomfortable sense of fragmentation, some a sense of relief. Some sense the possibilities for self-discovery, even self-transformation. A twenty-six-year-old history graduate student says, "When I log on to a new MUD and I create a character and know I have to start typing my description, I always feel a sense of panic. Like I could find out something I don't want to know" (Turkle, 1995). A twenty-year-old undergraduate says, "I am always very self-conscious when I create a new character. Usually, I end up creating someone I wouldn't want my parents to know about. It takes me, like, three hours." Online personae are objects-to-think-with for thinking about identity as multiple and decentered rather than unitary.

In the 1990s, online experiences with "parallel lives" were part of the cultural context for social scientists theorizing healthy, "flexible" selves (Gergen, 1991; Lifton, 1993; Martin, 1994) that cycle through multiple states of being. The philosopher Daniel Dennett (1991) spoke of the flexible self in his "multiple drafts" theory of consciousness. Dennett's notion of multiple drafts is analogous to the experience of several versions of a document open on a computer screen with the user able to move among them at will. Knowledge of these drafts encourages a respect for the many different versions, while it imposes a certain distance from them. The historian and social theorist Donna Haraway (1991a) equated a "split and contradictory self" with a "knowing self," and was optimistic about its possibilities:

"The knowing self is partial in all its guises, never finished, whole, simply there and original; it is always constructed and stitched together imperfectly and is therefore able to join with another, to see together without claiming to be another." Ian Hacking (1995) wrote about an increase in cases of Multiple Personality Disorder (MPD), characterized by aspects of self split off from each other. What most characterizes the Dennett and Haraway models of the self is that the lines of communication between its various aspects are always open. In their work, this open communication is presented as encouraging an attitude of respect for the many within us and the many within others.

A similar attitude animates the work of the psychoanalyst Philip Bromberg (1994), who insisted that our ways of describing "good parenting" must shift away from an emphasis on confirming a child in a "core self" and onto helping a child develop the capacity to negotiate fluid transitions between self states. The healthy individual knows how to be many, but smoothes out the moments of transition between self states. Bromberg wrote, "Health is when you are multiple but feel a unity. Health is when different aspects of self can get to know each other and reflect upon each other. Health is being one while being many." Here, within the American psychoanalytic tradition, is a model of multiplicity without dissociation, that is, multiplicity as a conscious, highly articulated cycling-through. Its contours are illuminated by a case study of a man deeply involved with computer gaming. I refer to him as Case, a thirty-four-year-old industrial designer (Turkle, 1995).

Case reports that he likes participating in online virtual communities as a female because (some would think paradoxically) it makes it easier for him to be aggressive and confrontational. Case's several online female personae—strong, dynamic, "out there" women—remind him of his mother, whom he describes as a "Katherine Hepburn type." His father was a mild-mannered man, a "Jimmy Stewart type." Case says that in "real life" he has always been more like his father, but he came to feel that he paid a price for his low-key ways. When he discovered MUDs, he recognized a chance to experiment:

For virtual reality to be interesting, it has to emulate the real. But you have to be able to do something in the virtual that you couldn't in the real. For me, my female characters are interesting because I can say and do the sorts of things that I mentally want to do, but if I did them as a man, they would be obnoxious. I see a strong woman as admirable. I see a strong man as a problem. Potentially a bully.

For Case, if you are assertive as a man, it is coded as "being a bastard." If you are assertive as a woman, it is coded as "modern and together."

My wife and I both design logos for small businesses. But if I say "I will design this logo for $3,000, take it or leave it," I'm just a typical pushy businessman. If she says it, I think it sounds like she's a "together" woman. There is too much male power-wielding in society, and so if you use power as a man, that turns you into a stereotypical man. Women can do it more easily.

Case's gender-swapping gives him permission to be more assertive within his virtual community and more assertive outside of it as well: "I've never been good at bureaucratic things, but I'm much better from practicing [in the online world] and playing a woman in charge. I am able to do things—in the real, that is—that I couldn't have before because I have played Katherine Hepburn characters."

Case says his Katherine Hepburn personae are "externalizations of a part of myself." In one interview with him, I use the expression "aspects of the self," and he picks it up eagerly, for his online life reminds him of how Hindu gods could have different aspects or subpersonalities, all the while being a whole self. In response to my question, "Do you feel that you call upon your personae in real life?" Case responds:

Yes, an aspect sort of clears its throat and says, "I can do this. You are being so amazingly conflicted over this and I know exactly what to do. Why don't you just let me do it?" MUDs give me balance. In real life, I tend to be extremely diplomatic, nonconfrontational. I don't like to ram my ideas down anyone's throat. On the MUD, I can be, "Take it or leave it." All of my Hepburn characters are that way. That's probably why I play them. Because they are smart-mouthed, they will not sugarcoat their words.

In some ways, Case's description of his inner world of actors who address him and are capable of taking over negotiations is reminiscent of the language of people with MPD. But the contrast is significant: Case's inner actors are not split off from each other or his sense of "himself." He experiences himself very much as a collective self, not feeling that he must goad or repress this or that aspect of himself into conformity. He is at ease, cycling through from Katherine Hepburn to Jimmy Stewart. To use Bromberg's language, online life has helped Case learn how to "stand in the spaces between selves and still feel one, to see the multiplicity and still feel a unity." To use the computer scientist Marvin Minsky's (1987) phrase, Case feels at ease cycling through his "society of mind," a notion of identity as distributed and heterogeneous that undermines traditional notions of identity. Identity, after all, from the Latin *idem*, has been habitually used to refer to the sameness between two qualities. On the Internet, however, one can be many and usually is.

An experience with online role-playing can begin very simply—with assuming a new name. Yet it may lead to exploring previously unexamined aspects of one's sexuality or to challenging the idea of a unitary self. Such experiences can be compelling, so compelling that they are widely feared as "addictive" and discussed in the popular media in terms usually reserved for the discussion of drugs.

In my own studies of Internet social experience, I have found that the people who make the most of their "lives on the screen" are those who approach online life in a spirit of self-reflection. They look at what they are doing with their virtual selves and ask what these actions say about their desires, perhaps unmet, as well as their need for social connection, perhaps unfilled. If we stigmatize the computational medium as "addictive" (and try to strictly control it as if it were a drug), we will not learn how to more widely nurture this discipline of self-reflection.

For some people, cyberspace is a place to act out unresolved conflicts, to play and replay personal difficulties on a new and exotic stage. For others, it provides an opportunity to work through significant problems, to use the new materials of "cybersociality" to reach for new resolutions. These more positive identity effects follow from the fact that for some, cyberspace provides what Erik Erikson would have called a "psychosocial moratorium," a central element in how Erikson thought about identity development in adolescence. Today, the idea of the college years as a consequence-free time-out seems of another era. But if our culture no longer offers an adolescent time-out, virtual communities often do. It is part of what makes them seem so attractive. Time in cyberspace reworks the notion of the moratorium because it may now exist on an always available window.

Online games thus created new landscapes for personal growth; they were also philosophically rich environments. In 1995, in *Life on the screen*, I told how in the late 1960s and early 1970s, I was first exposed to notions of identity and multiplicity of self. My introduction to these ideas, most notably that there is no such thing as "the ego"—that each of us is a multiplicity of parts, fragments, and desiring connections—took place in the intellectual hothouse of Paris; they presented the world according to such authors as Jacques Lacan, Gilles Deleuze, and Félix Guattari. But despite such ideal conditions for absorbing theory, my "French lessons" remained merely abstract exercises. These theorists of poststructuralism, and what would come to be called postmodernism, spoke words that addressed the relationship between mind and body, but from my point of view had little to do with my own.

In my lack of personal connection with these ideas, I was not alone. To take one example, for many people it is hard to accept any challenge to the idea of an autonomous ego. Although in recent years many psychologists, social theorists, psychoanalysts, and philosophers have argued that the self should be thought of as essentially decentered, the normal requirements of everyday life exert strong pressure on people to take responsibility for their actions and to see themselves as unitary actors. This disjuncture between theory (the unitary self is an illusion) and lived experience (the unitary self is the most basic reality) is one of the main reasons why multiple and decentered theories have been slow to catch on—or when they do, why we tend to settle back quickly into older, centralized ways of looking at things.

By the early 1990s, I was using my personal computer and modem to join online communities. In this new context, I experienced my French lessons in action. What had been theoretical, was brought almost shockingly down to earth. Online, my textual actions were my actions—my words made things happen. In different communities I had different routines, different friends, different names. Different personae explored different aspects of self. In this context, the notion of a decentered identity was concretized by experiences on a computer screen.

One day on a MUD, I came across a reference to a character named "Dr. Sherry," a cyber-psychotherapist who had an office in the rambling house that constituted this MUD's virtual geography. There, I was informed, Dr. Sherry administered questionnaires and conducted interviews about the psychology of MUD-ding. I had every reason to believe that the name "Dr. Sherry" referred to my own career as a student of the psychological impact of technology. But I did not create this character. Dr. Sherry was me but she was not mine. On the MUD, my character had another name—and did not give out questionnaires or conduct interviews. Dr. Sherry was a character name someone else created as an economical way to communicate an interest in a certain set of questions about technology and the self. I

experienced Dr. Sherry as a little piece of my history spinning out of control. I tried to quiet my mind—I told myself that surely one's books, one's public intellectual persona, are pieces of oneself in the world for others to use as they please. Surely this virtual appropriation was flattering. But my disquiet continued. Dr. Sherry, after all, was not an inanimate book, an object placed in the world. Dr. Sherry was a person, or at least a person behind a character who was meeting with others in the world. Well, in the MUD world at least.

I talked my disquiet over with a friend who posed the conversation-stopping question: 'Well, would you prefer if Dr. Sherry were a 'bot' [an intelligent computer program that roams cyberspace] trained to interview people about life on the MUD?" This had not occurred to me, but in a flash I realized that this, too, was possible. It was even likely to be the case. Many bots or "puppets" roamed this MUD. They appeared in the game as though they were human characters. Players create these programs for many reasons: bots help with navigation, pass messages, and provide background animation in a MUD. When you enter a virtual café, you are usually not alone. A waiter bot approaches who asks you if you want a drink and delivers it with a smile.

Characters played by people are sometimes mistaken for these little artificial intelligences. I myself have made this mistake several times when a character's responses seemed too automatic. And sometimes bots are mistaken for people. I have made this mistake too, fooled by a bot that offered me directions or flattered me by remembering our last interaction. Dr. Sherry could indeed have been one of these. I was confronted with a double that could be a person or a program.

As things turned out, Dr. Sherry was neither: it was a composite character created by several college students who wished to write a paper on the psychology of MUDs and who were using my name as a kind of trademark or generic descriptor for the idea of cyber-shrink. So not only are MUDs places where the self is multiple and constructed by language, they are places where people and machines are in a new relation to each other, indeed can be mistaken for each other.

Thinking about Aliveness by Thinking about Computational Companions

Children have always used the objects of their play to create models for understanding their world. The genius of Jean Piaget (1960) showed that it is the business of childhood to take objects and use how they "work" to construct theories of space, time, number, causality, life, and mind. When Piaget was formulating his theories through the mid-twentieth century, a child's world was full of things that could be understood in simple, mechanical ways. A bicycle could be understood in terms of its pedals and gears, a windup car in terms of its clockwork springs. Children were able to take electronic devices such as basic radios and (with some difficulty) bring them into this "mechanical" system of understanding.

Since the end of the 1970s, however, with the introduction of electronic toys and games, the nature of objects and how children understand them has changed. When children today remove the back of their computer toys to "see" how they work, they find a chip, a battery, and some wires. Children sense that trying to understand these objects "physically" will lead to a dead end and try to use a "psychological" kind of understanding (Turkle, 1984). Children ask themselves if the games are conscious, if the games know, if they have feelings, and even if they "cheat." Earlier objects encouraged children to think in terms of a distinction between the world of psychology and the world of machines, but the computer does not. Its "opacity" encourages children to see computational objects as psychological machines.

Over the last thirty years, I have observed and interviewed hundreds of children as they have interacted with a wide range of computational objects, from computer programs on the screen to robots off the screen (Turkle, 1984, 1995, 2005). My methods are ethnographic and clinical. In the late 1970s and early 1980s, I began by observing children playing with the first generation of electronic toys and games. Since the mid 1990s, I have worked with children using new generations of computer games and software, including virtual and robotic "pets," and with children experimenting with online life.

Among the first generation of computational objects was Merlin, which challenged children to games of tic-tac-toe. For children who had only played games with human opponents, reaction to this object was intense. For example, although Merlin followed an optimal strategy for winning tic-tac-toe most of the time, it was programmed to make a slip every once in a while. So when children discovered strategies that allowed them to win, when they tried these strategies a second time, they usually would not work. The machine gave the impression of not being "dumb enough" to let down its defenses twice. Robert, seven, playing with his friends on the beach, watched his friend Craig perform the "winning trick," but when he tried it, Merlin

did not make its slip and the game ended in a draw. Robert, confused and frustrated, accused Merlin of being a "cheating machine" (Turkle, 1984). Children were used to machines being predictable. But this machine held surprises.

Robert threw Merlin into the sand in anger and frustration. "Cheater. I hope your brains break." He was overheard by Craig and Greg, aged six and eight, who salvaged the by now very sandy toy and took it upon themselves to set Robert straight. Craig offered the opinion that "Merlin doesn't know if it cheats. It won't know if it breaks. It doesn't know if you break it, Robert. It's not alive." Greg adds: "It's smart enough to make the right kinds of noises. But it doesn't really know if it loses. That's how you can cheat it. It doesn't know you are cheating. And when it cheats it doesn't even know it's cheating." Jenny, six, interrupted with disdain: "Greg, to cheat you have to know you are cheating. Knowing is part of cheating."

In the early 1980s, such scenes were not unusual. Confronted with objects that spoke, strategized, and "won," children were led to argue the moral and metaphysical status of machines on the basis of their psychologies: Did the machines know what they were doing? Did they have intentions, consciousness, and feelings? These first computers that entered children's lives were evocative objects: they became the occasion for new formulations about the human and the mechanical. For despite Jenny's objections that "knowing is part of cheating," children did come to see computational objects as exhibiting a kind of knowing. Children's discussions about the computer's aliveness came to center on what the children perceived as the computer's psychological rather than physical properties. To put it simply, physics gave way to psychology as the criteria for aliveness. Jenny was part of the first generation of children who were willing to invest machines with qualities of consciousness as they rethought the question of what is alive in the context of "machines that think."

Over the past decades, the objects of children's lives have come to include machines of even greater intelligence, toys and games and programs that make these first computer toys seem primitive in their ambitions. The answers to the classical Piagetian question of how children think about life are being renegotiated as they are posed in the context of computational objects (simulation games, robots, virtual pets) that explicitly present themselves as exemplars of "artificial life."

Although the presence of the first generation of computational objects (the games such as Merlin,

Simon, and Speak and Spell) disrupted the classical Piagetian story for talking about aliveness, the story children were telling about such objects in the early 1980s had its own coherency. Faced with intelligent toys, children took a new world of objects and imposed a new world order in which psychology had given way to physics as the discourse children used for talking about aliveness.

By the 1990s, computational objects that evoked evolution and "artificial life" (for example computer programs such as the games of the *Sim* series, which stress decentralized and "emergent" processes) strained that order to the breaking point (Turkle, 1995). Children still try to impose strategies and categories, but they do so in the manner of theoretical bricoleurs or tinkerers, making do with whatever materials are at hand, making do with whatever theory can fit a prevailing circumstance. When children confront these new objects and try to construct a theory about what is alive, we see them cycling through theories of "aliveness." We have met Tim, who at thirteen says of *SimLife*: "The animals that grow in the computer could be alive because anything that grows has a chance to be alive." Laurence, fifteen, agrees. "The whole point of this game," he tells me, "is to show that you could get things that are alive in the computer. We get energy from the sun. The organisms in a computer get energy from the plug in the wall. I know that more people will agree with me when they make a *SimLife* where the creatures are smart enough to communicate. You are not going to feel comfortable if a creature that can talk to you goes extinct."

An eleven-year-old named Holly watches a group of robots with "onboard" computational intelligence navigate a maze. The robots use different strategies to reach their goal, and Holly is moved to comment on their "personalities" and their "cuteness." She finally comes to speculate on the robots' "aliveness" and blurts out an unexpected formulation: "It's like Pinocchio. First Pinocchio was just a puppet. He was not alive at all. Then he was an alive puppet. Then he was an alive boy. A real boy. But he was alive even before he was a real boy. So I think the robots are like that. They are alive like Pinocchio (the puppet), but not 'real boys.'"

She clears her throat and sums up her thought: "They [the robots] are sort of alive."

Robbie, a ten-year-old who has been given a modem for her birthday, uses her experience of the game to develop some insight into those computer processes that led adults to use the term "virus" for programs that "traveled." She puts the emphasis on mobility instead of communication when she considers whether the creatures she has evolved on *SimLife* are alive.

I think they are a little alive in the game, but you can turn it off and you cannot "save" your game, so that all the creatures you have evolved go away. But if they could figure out how to get rid of that part of the program so that you would have to save the game and if your modem were on, then they could get out of your computer and go to America Online.

Children cycle through evolution and psychology in their new discourse of aliveness. In children's talk about digital "travel" via circulating disks or over modems, in their talk of viruses and networks, biology and motion are resurfacing in a new guise, now bound up in the ideas of communication and evolution. Significantly, the resurfacing of motion (Piaget's classical criteria for how a child decides whether a "traditional" object is alive) is now bound up with notions of a presumed psychology: children were likely to assume that the creatures on *Sim* games have a desire to "get out" of the system and evolve in a wider computational world.

Comments about life by children who have played with the popular artifacts of artificial life (small mobile robots, the games of the *Sim* series, and *Tierra*, a program that simulates evolutionary selection through survival of the fittest) includes the following notions: the robots are in control but not alive, would be alive if they had bodies, are alive because they have bodies, would be alive if they had feelings, are alive the way insects are alive but not the way people are alive; the Tierrans are not alive because they are just in the computer, could be alive if they got out of the computer and got onto America Online, are alive until you turn off the computer and then they're dead, are not alive because nothing in the computer is real; the *Sim* creatures are not alive but almost-alive, they would be alive if they spoke, they would be alive if they traveled, they're alive but not "real," they're not alive because they don't have bodies, they are alive because they can have babies, and finally, for an eleven-year-old who is relatively new to *SimLife*, they're not alive because these babies don't have parents. She says, "They show the creatures and the game tells you that they have mothers and fathers, but I don't believe it. It's just numbers, it's not really a mother and a father." There is a striking heterogeneity of theory here. Different children hold different theories and individual children are able to hold different theories at the same time.

In the short history of how the computer has changed the way we think, it has often been children who have led the way. For example, in the early 1980s, children, prompted by computer toys that spoke, did math, and played Tic-Tac-Toe, disassociated ideas about consciousness from ideas about life. These children were able to contemplate sentient computers that were not alive, a position that grownups are only now beginning to find comfortable. By the 1990s children were pointing the way toward multiple theories of aliveness in the presence of computational artifacts that are designed to seem like creatures.

Sara, a fifth-grader, jumped back and forth from a psychological to a mechanistic language when she talked about a small robotic creature she had built out of Lego blocks and programmed with the Logo computer language. Sometimes she called it a machine, sometimes a creature. When Sara considered whether her machine would sound a signal when its "touch sensor" was pushed, she said, "It depends on whether the machine wants to tell ... if we want the machine to tell us ... if we tell the machine to tell us" (Resnick, 1989, p. 402). In other words, within a few seconds, Sara "cycled through" three perspectives on her creature (as a psychological being, as an intentional self, and as an instrument of its programmer's intentions). These perspectives are equally present for her; for different purposes, she finds one or another of them more useful.

In his history of artificial life, Steven Levy (1992, pp. 6–7) suggested that one way to look at where artificial life can "fit in" to our way of thinking about life is to envisage a continuum in which *Tierra*, for example, would be more alive than a car, but less alive than a bacterium. My observations suggest that children are not constructing hierarchies but are heading toward parallel, alternating definitions of life, which they "alternate" through rapid cycling. Multiple and alternating definitions, like thinking comfortably about one's identity in terms of multiple and alternating aspects of self, become a habit of mind.

Today's adults grew up in a psychological culture that equated the idea of a unitary self with psychological health, and in a scientific culture that taught that when a discipline achieves maturity, it has a unifying theory. When adults find themselves cycling through varying perspectives on themselves (as when they cycle through a sequence such as "I am my chemicals" to "I am my history" to "I am my genes"), they usually become uncomfortable (Kramer, 1993). But such alternations may strike the generation of children who are growing up today as "just the way things are."

Children speak easily about factors that encourage them to see the "stuff" of computers as the same "stuff" of which life is made. For example, the seemingly ubiquitous "transformer toys" shift from being machines to being robots to being animals (and sometimes people). Children play with these plastic and metal objects and, in the process, they learn about the fluid boundaries between mechanism and flesh.

I observe a group of seven-year-olds playing with a set of plastic transformer toys that can take the shape of armored tanks, robots, or people (Turkle, 1995). The transformers can also be put into intermediate states so that a "robot" arm can protrude from a human form or a human leg from a mechanical tank. Two of the children are playing with the toys in these intermediate states (that is, in their intermediate states somewhere between being people, machines, and robots). A third child insists that this is not right. The toys, he says, should not be placed in hybrid states. "You should play them as all tank or all people." He is getting upset because the other two children are making a point of ignoring him. An eight-year-old girl comforts the upset child. "It's okay to play them when they are in-between. It's all the same stuff," she said, "just yucky computer 'cy-dough-plasm.'" This comment is the expression of a cyborg consciousness as it expresses itself among children: a tendency to see computer systems as "sort of" alive, and to fluidly "cycle through" various explanatory concepts (Haraway, 1991b).

When my daughter was seven years old, I took her on a vacation in Italy. We took a boat ride in the postcard-blue Mediterranean. She saw a creature in the water, pointed to it excitedly, and said, "Look Mommy, a jellyfish. It looks so realistic." When I told this story to a research scientist at Walt Disney, he responded by describing the reaction of visitors to Animal Kingdom, Disney's newest theme park in Orlando, populated by "real," that is, biological, animals. He told me that the first visitors to the park expressed disappointment that the biological animals were not realistic enough. They did not exhibit the lifelike behavior of the more active robotic animals at Disney World, only a few miles away. What is the gold standard here? Have we given up the notion of such standards to make boundary transgression the norm?

A recent *New Yorker* cartoon summed up recent anxieties about such transgressions: Two grown-ups face a child in a wall of solidarity, explaining, "We're neither software nor hardware. We're your parents." It reminded me of a young woman I once interviewed whose position on simulation and authenticity was:

"Simulated thinking can be thinking, but simulated feeling can never be feeling. Simulated love is never love." The more our artifacts seek pride of place beside us as social and psychological equals, the more we are confronted and challenged by the issue of authenticity. Authenticity is becoming to us what sex was to the Victorians—an object of threat and obsession, taboo and fascination.

Looking toward the future, children's willingness to transgress traditional boundaries may increasingly involve relationships with "virtual pets" and robots (Turkle, 2005). The first of these on the American market were the tiny virtual pet Tamagotchis, which asked their owners to feed them, play games with them, inquire about their health and mood, and, when they are still babies, clean up their virtual "poop." Good parenting of a Tamagotchi produced a healthy offspring; bad parenting led to illness, deformity, and finally, to the pet's virtual death. The Tamagotchis were only the first in a series of computational objects designed for children that ask children for nurturance. And each demands that children assess its (the object's) "state of mind" in order to play with it. For example, in order to grow and be healthy, Tamagotchis need to be fed, cleaned, and amused. The Furbies simulate learning and loving. They are cuddly, they speak and play games with the child. Furbies add the dimensions of humanlike conversation and tender companionship to the mix of what children can anticipate from computational objects. In my research on children and Furbies, I found that when children play with these new objects they want to know their "state," not to get something "right," but to make the Furbies happy. Children want to understand Furby language, not to "win" in a game over the Furbies, but to have a feeling of mutual recognition. They do not ask how the Furbies "work," but take the affectively charged toys "at interface value."

In the case of the toys, the culture is being presented with computational objects that elicit emotional response and that evoke a sense of relationship. As the culture apprehends these objects, call them "relational artifacts," there is less a concern with whether these objects "really" know or feel and an increasing sense of connection with them. In sum, we are creating objects that push our evolutionary buttons to respond to interactivity by experiencing ourselves as with a kindred "other."

In my previous research on children and computer toys, children described the lifelike status of machines in terms of their cognitive capacities (the toys could "know" things, "solve" puzzles). In my studies on children and relational artifacts, among these Furbies, I have found that children describe these new toys as "sort of alive" because of the quality of their emotional attachments to them and because of their fantasies about the idea that the toys might be emotionally attached to them. So, for example, when I ask the question, "Do you think the Furby is alive?" children answer not in terms of what the Furby can do, but how they feel about the Furby and how the Furby might feel about them.

Ron (age six): Well, the Furby is alive for a Furby. And you know, something this smart should have arms. It might want to pick up something or to hug me.

Katherine (age five): Is it alive? Well, I love it. It's more alive than a Tamagotchi because it sleeps with me. It likes to sleep with me.

Jen (age nine): I really like to take care of it. So, I guess it is alive, but it doesn't need to really eat, so it is as alive as you can be if you don't eat. A Furby is like an owl. But it is more alive than an owl because it knows more and you can talk to it. But it needs batteries so it is not an animal. It's not like an animal kind of alive.

Today's children are learning to distinguish between an "animal kind of alive" and a "Furby [or robot] kind of alive." The category of "sort of alive" becomes used more and more. Will they also talk about a "people kind of love" and a "computer kind of love"?

With relational artifacts we are in a different world from the old "AI debates" of the 1960s to 1980s in which researchers argued about whether machines could be "really" intelligent. The old debate was essentialist; the new objects sidestep such arguments about what is inherent in them and play instead on what they evoke in us: When we are asked to care for an object, when the cared-for object thrives and offers us its attention and concern, we experience that object as intelligent, but more important, we feel a connection to it. The old AI debates were about the technical abilities of machines. It appears that the new AI debates, with roots in children's relationships with toys, games, and robotic creatures, may be more about the emotional vulnerabilities of people.

Coda: Artificial Worlds and the Psychology of Scary/Safe

The pioneers of computing, and those who referred to themselves as computer "hackers" (when this term connoted virtuosity, not criminality) had a style of computer mastery that played with risk and with a style of virtuosity that was characterized as "flying by the seat of one's pants." For hackers the holding power of computing was that it was a superb medium for playing with issues of control. Playing with control means constantly walking the narrow line between having it and losing it. This has been termed the psychology of "scary/safe." Life is danger and triumph, screen to screen of it, a constantly shifting drama that can provide strong defenses against anxiety.

First, scary/safe helps to deny vulnerability. It is reassuring to have a medium that offers reassurance through a promise of total mastery. It is reassuring to play in safe microworlds where the rules are clear. This makes computer worlds powerful. You go from one block of intransigent code to another. You debug one part of the program; you debug another. This emotional aesthetic translated into the classic computer games culture. Each screen, each level of a computer game, presents a new danger. Each screen is mastered in its turn, yet you always return to danger again. Life is exhausting, but the repetition of microworld triumphs is reassuring

When I first began studying the computer culture, hackers were commonly called "computer people." No more. In a certain sense, if we take the computer to be a carrier of a way of knowing, of a way of seeing the world and what is important, we are all computer people now. We live much of our lives in artificial worlds. They tend to be complex, multilayered, and self-referential. However, we are at a moment in history when playing in closed systems of our own devising may reinforce dangerous habits of mind. The real world is messy and painted in shades of gray. In that world we need to be comfortable with ambivalence and contradiction. We need to be able to put ourselves in the place of others in order to understand their motivation.

Immersion in programmed worlds and relationships with digital creatures and robotic pets puts us in reassuring microworlds where the rules are clear. When we think about artificial worlds we are too often not thinking about ambivalence, complex human relationships, about moral dilemmas that aren't battles between good and evil. To cultivate these things requires the discipline to resist all binary formulations. This is not a discipline well practiced in the company of any computer toy, virtual game world, or robotic creature we have ever experienced. It is a discipline well practiced in the socially situated, physically embodied, always complex, and often irrational presence of other people. To acknowledge that computational relationships do not provide us with all that we need does not devalue their contributions. It does, however, put them in their place.

Acknowledgments

This material is partially based upon work supported by the National Science Foundation under Grant No. 0115668. Any opinions, findings, conclusions or recommendations expressed in this material are those of the author and do not necessarily reflect the view of the National Science Foundation.

References

Bromberg, P. (1994). Speak that I may see you: Some reflections on dissociation, reality, and psychoanalytic listening. *Psychoanalytic Dialogues 4*(4): 517–547.

Dennett, D. C. (1991). *Consciousness explained*. Boston: Little, Brown.

Gergen, K. (1991). *The saturated self: Dilemmas of identity in contemporary life*. New York: Basic Books.

Hacking, I. (1995). *Rewriting the soul: Multiple personality and the sciences of memory*. Princeton, NJ: Princeton University Press.

Haraway, D. (1991a). The actors are cyborg, nature is Coyote, and the geography is elsewhere: Postscript to "Cyborgs at large." In C. Penley & A. Ross (Eds.) *Technoculture*. Minneapolis: University of Minnesota Press.

Haraway, D. (1991b). A cyborg manifesto: Science, technology, and socialist-feminism in the late twentieth century. In D. Haraway (Ed.), *Simians, Cyborgs, and Women: The Reinvention of Nature*. New York: Routledge.

Kramer, P. (1993). *Listening to Prozac: A psychiatrist explores antidepressant drugs and the remaking of the self*. New York: Viking.

Latour, B. (1988). *The pasteurization of France*. (Alan Sheridan & John Law, trans.). Cambridge, MA: Harvard University Press.

Levi-Strauss, C. (1966). *The savage mind*. Chicago: University of Chicago Press.

Levy, S. (1992). *Artificial life: The quest for a new frontier*. New York: Pantheon.

Sherry Turkle

Lifton, R. J. (1993). *The protean self: Human resilience in an age of fragmentation*. New York: Basic Books.

Martin, E. (1994). *Flexible bodies*. Boston: Beacon.

Minsky, M. (1987). *The society of mind*. New York: Simon and Schuster.

Piaget, J. (1960). *The child's conception of the world*. (Joan & Andrew Tomlinson, trans.). Totowa, NJ: Littlefield, Adams.

Resnick, M. (1989). "LEGO, logo, and life." In C. G. Langton (Ed.), *Artificial life: The proceedings of an interdisciplinary workshop on the synthesis and simulation of living systems*. Santa Fe Institute Studies in the Science of Complexity, vol. 6. Redwood City, CA: Addison-Wesley.

Turkle, S. (1984). *The second self: Computers and the human spirit*. New York: Simon and Schuster.

Turkle, S. (1995). *Life on the screen: Identity in the age of the internet*. New York: Simon and Schuster.

Turkle, S. (1997). "Seeing through computers: Education in a culture of simulation." In *The American prospect* Vol. 8, No. 31, March 1, 1997–April 1, 1997.

Turkle, S. (2005). New introduction and epilogue. In *The second self: Computers and the human spirit* (revised 2nd Ed.). Cambridge, MA: MIT Press.

Representation of Identity: Gender, Ethnicity, and History

GAMING WITH GRRLS: LOOKING FOR SHEROES IN COMPUTER GAMES

Birgit Richard and Jutta Zaremba

Kickin' Off with the Prototype: Lara Croft

Even those who have never played the computer game *Tomb Raider* will know its protagonist Lara Croft (figure 18.1). She was the star in promotion-clips for cars such as the French Seat, was seen on huge posters promoting the German financial magazine *Die Welt*, made it on the cover of the British magazine *The Face*, acted in an animated commercial for the American sports company Nike, was the heroine in an ad campaign for the American cable-TV SciFi Channel, acted in a clip for the British energy drink Lucozade or in a music video of the German pop band Die Ärzte. The virtual heroine is a popular example of the female figures in the 1990s, which form a connection of gender discourses and digital technology, and are a part of our cultural practice. However, the reception of Lara Croft causes highly various reactions and classifications, especially among the female audience: ranging from "female enemy number one," in radical old-school feminist polemic, up to "postfeminist icon" in a stylized postmodern jubilation.

This obvious discrepancy is comparable to the paradigm shift that feminists see in fashion (see Graw, 1997 for an overview), as it is no longer regarded as a manipulative instrument for the realization of male power fantasies but as the main medium of (bodily) performance (Graw, 1997; Richard, 1998). A rather unquestioned enthusiasm is reflected in the celebration of the idea of masquerade in the context of sexual identity construction (Doane, 1985). The female object of fashion turns into the offensive subject of fashion. However, as Isabelle Graw points out, fashion does not unreservedly provide its instruments for visual self-realization and the free play with masquerade. Especially regarding an artificial idol such as Lara Croft, the economic context is of particular significance because the figure originates directly from the entertainment industry. Some virtual characters are modest and can be instrumentalized for commercial interests; they do not have an autonomous potential that could be developed by the users. The increasing number of virtual hosts and search agents in the Internet show this, as well as the first virtual porno stars, made available via 0190-numbers (these are specific numbers in Germany; they mainly offer telephone sex).

Lara Croft is an idol whose reception is in its ambivalence similar to that of pop-icon Madonna. She presents a posthuman idol with split, multiple, and artificially created identities and body images (Deitch, 1992). In the posthuman world there are no essential differences between bodily existence and computer simulation, cybernetic mechanism and biological organism, robot teleology and human goals (Hayles, 1999). In the cases of Croft and Madonna, these are no longer only a product of one industry, but instead the star constructs his or her image or the users create and modify the pictorial supply in other media forms, corresponding to the wishes and needs of users and fans.

Both characters, Madonna and Lara, are comparable on the level that they represent different levels on the scale of virtual models of femininity, although they are presented and represent themselves in different media. In computer games, only the female heroines are exposed to these shifts between diverse levels of virtuality. In the case of Lara Croft, the virtual model is the predecessor, followed by her duplicate in flesh, embodied by the human lookalike and then again by the remedialization in the movie. Cate Archer (*No One Lives Forever*) is the duplicate of photo-model Mitzi Martin, who was singled out in a game casting. Julie Strain, however, protagonist of *Heavy Metal F.A.K.K.*, already shows numerous degrees of virtuality and medial shifts. The computer game and the animated movie are based on the adult cartoon *Heavy Metal*, whose real protagonist is the B-movie queen Julie Strain. The animated and drawn figures are modeled after her. The real Julie Strain, though, performs avatar roles, poses in a game-like style, and wears the same outfit like the game figure. The potential return to female

| Figure 18.1 |
Prototype with beard

representations in flesh is actually a promise transported by the games. This is constitutive to the meaning of the female figures and suggests always a transformation from reality to virtuality and back again. This is paralleled at the same time by the impossibility of a level change. However, to concentrate medial figure-transformations on Lara as the virtual original, which are not achievable for her duplicate in reality, is in fact not appropriate to the process of the medial shift (Deuber-Mankowsky, 2001, p. 69). In her terminology, original—copy—duplicate, Deuber-Mankowsky does not consider that the female body is continuously adapted to artificial originals, to reality models of femaleness. So the differences between the computer animated figure Lara and the medially propagated body models are only gradual.

In the sense of Umberto Eco (1973, 1990), some artificial figures are double coded. The users or spectators can either simply adore and idolize them or admire them for the artistry of their ambiguous performances.

This chapter intends to trace the characteristics, contradictions, and potentials of the virtual idols in computer games such as Lara Croft. Actually, Lara Croft is not only the most popular but also one of the prime female heroines in the genre of computer games: in 1996, two years after the appearance of Sony PlayStation, game producer Eidos/London put *Tomb Raider* on the market. Similar to television series, this action game was followed by annual sequels.

The Narrative Context of the Game, Remediation, and Body-Sampling

Like most of the games heroines, Lara owns a vague fictional biography to initiate the illusion of a real personality and an outrageous lifestyle. As it is also done in

the case of famous models and actresses, the fictional biography should suggest an exclusively individual star, guaranteeing a high potential for identification processes of female users.

Lara Croft is put into a loose biographical frame: She is a descendant of a British noble family, although after a dispute with them she got disinherited. After the death of her parents, she works as an author and travel writer. She becomes a renowned archaeologist who searches for treasures and adventures—as the title *Tomb Raider* indicates. The saga of *Tomb Raider* makes Lara travel across the world. Via the game levels, the players are brought from China to Venice, from the ice-desert to India, from London to Arizona, up to Egypt.

Lara is the top-fit and full-bosomed heroine who shoots and punches her antagonists, climbs and swims courageously through dark unknown spaces, constructed in multiperspective. Quite exceptional for the construction of a female protagonist is the fact that Lara at no point has any orientation toward domesticity. This is in contrast to many novel protagonists in nineteenth century, who, after their excursions in the world, either return to become domestic and familiar or (if their way does not open up this option) have to pay for their escapades and die (as exemplified in the movie *Thelma and Louise* from 1990, director Ridley Scott). As we can see in Lara's country house, a home does exist, but it has only scanty equipment and is in the spaces of traditional femininity not functional (the kitchen has no cooking utensils, the shower is defective, etc.). For this reason, Lara exchanges private against public space. She throws herself quickly into new adventures and thereby strongly resembles a western hero, the "lonesome cowboy," or Odysseus with his numerous tasks, who restlessly moves on to new challenges:

The figure of Lara Croft unites all the essential qualities of an action hero. She has no ties, no family obligations and no need to earn her living.... Her getting ahead in the game involves overcoming obstacles and fighting enemies, taking the initiative without hesitation and staying right on target; the game is so structured that short-cuts, detours and evasive actions are impossible. This kind of independence and self-assertion corresponds to the stereotype of the male hero. (Schmidt, 1999, p. 36)

Analogous to this, social contacts play no role in Lara's world. There are no deeper human relations or a potential partner, which, for the presentation of a female cosmos, is quite unusual. Instead, Lara Croft is absolutely autonomous. Neither a man nor a family support her or take any responsibility; she is an independent individual, like a lone wolf, self-conscious, strong, and clever. In the elimination of danger and hindrances, Lara is throughout confronted with opponents who are inferior to her, bodily as well as mentally, and who are part of a ritualized primitive, yet highly technologized universe: monsters, demons, wild animals, and knaves, who in their malevolence are unmistakably connoted, so that the barrier against shooting them down is reduced. In opposition to classical horror movies such as *The Beauty and the Beast* (Jean Cocteau, 1946), in which the woman often develops a kind of affinity to the monster because both share the status as outsiders (Williams, 1990), Lara's aim is not to save the world or to save any subjects at all. Instead, Lara stubbornly fights her way through the universe like *The Terminator* (James Cameron, 1984) or Ripley in *Alien 3* (David Fincher, 1992), doing their own single-fighter thing, although based on a messianic plot (Creed, 1989). Medialized female protagonists can be found very early: It starts with the cheeky and frivolous cartoon character Betty Boop in 1932 and the erotic movie amazon Wonder Woman in 1941, followed by sexy heroine Barbarella (Roger Vadim, 1968) embodied by Jane Fonda and the cool sex-appeal of Emma Peel, "girl with a gun" in the television serial *The Avengers* (1961–1969 in its native England and debuting on American TV in 1966). However, since the end of the 1980s, the active heroines became more tough and dangerous, as for example the policewomen in the thriller *Blue Steel* (Kathryn Bigelow, 1990) or the woman duo in the buddy-movie *Thelma and Louise*. Then, during the 1990s, this tendency calmed down by more calculable TV-detectives and superintendents or by erotic fantasy series such as *Xena* (a serial started in 1995 in the United States, which has also been transformed into a computer game). What all of them have in common is their status as an artificial figure, which in an artificial synthesis melts diverse and in fact often ambiguous ideas and projections, as evident in the bodily performance of the *Tomb Raider* heroine:

As a real body-sampling, Lara Croft merges different projections and fictions: Her arms and knees are slim, while her thighs have a muscular shape, yet her lengthened extremities and small waist correspond to digitally retouched images of photo-models and the extreme curves of bottom and breasts are reminiscent of fetishist images of women in comics. This kind of fetishism is also in accordance with Lara Croft's clothes, which are obviously less adapted to the requirements of the surrounding area of her adventures, but instead an aesthetic which is a performance of her naked body—her legs, arms and the cleavage of course. (Schmidt, 1999, p. 46)

Lara's individualized and cool manner in asserting herself corresponds with a new definition of femininity in 1990s girl-culture. "Images of self-confident, cheeky and ambitious girls in Doc Marten's boots jump out of every magazine. Far away from giving up femininity to get equality, these girls have insisted on their rights and keep their femininity unrestricted and even excessively" (McRobbie, 1999, p. 10).

Lara Croft, though, is not specifically an aggressive riot grrl, in the sense of Courtney Love. Courtney Love, the widow of Kurt Cobain from Nirvana, represents a rebellious female with her all-female band Hole and was the incarnation of wild autonomous girl. She combined girl's dresses with female lipstick and played loud punk music and set herself in scene as an aggressive dirty "slut." Lara's exaggerated maintenance of femininity is expressed in fantasy-like body proportions (huge bosom, extreme waist, ultra-long legs) and in exclusively designed sexy clothes (hot pants, tight shirts, etc.). By the over-fulfillment of female proportions that are designed for the male gaze, the sexual aggressive component of Lara Croft's "masculine" power and thirst for action is undermined. There are also strategies to bring Lara back to her female roots and cut the aggressive and uncontrollable components in her visual appearance. In 1999, the huge billboards advertising *Tomb Raider 3* showed her framed by red roses, in a long slashed evening gown. This indicates an endeavor for a romantic embedding, intended to balance the potential threat of this character. Also in the video of the song "Männer sind Schweine" (Men are Pigs) by Die Ärtze, Lara, who desperately punches, fights, and shows off her bare teeth to the members of the band, is in her helplessness and with a humorous twinkle tied in again. Truly, Lara is not intended as a threatening terror for men, but as a courageous and top-fit though harmless dream-woman, whose physical attractions can be looked at with impunity, lust, and joy.

Computer games, as Georg Seesslen rightly notes, belong to representational systems and can only be understood in relation to other representational systems (Seesslen, 1984). According to Bolter and Grusin, the dialectics between immediacy and hypermediacy cause an ongoing differentiation of new media like computer games. The term "remediation" (Bolter & Grusin, 1999) means the representation of one medium in another, which in the case of the computergame leads to an adaptation and absorption of other media like film, TV, and so on. "In addition to remediating the computer itself, computer games also remediate television and film. Video games are played on a repurposed television set, one in which an attached control unit transforms the screen into a different medium" (Bolter & Grusin, 1999, p. 91).

Therefore, *Tomb Raider* must be examined in the context of television, movies, and cartoons, because an isolated consideration of a single medium would only be able to catch just a partial meaning. So we must take into account the principle of "transcodability" between games and the parallel media of film and cartoons.

The most obvious connection between games and films are the prefabricated video sequences in computer games called "cut scenes," which are movie-like animations serving as an intro into the actual game play. Although cut scenes suggest a high aesthetic and narrative level, the quality of a digital animation is by far higher in a film than in a game, because the capacity of computer graphics is low compared to the resolution of movie pictures (King & Krzywinska, 2002). Lev Manovich also describes the presentation-mode of games in technical parameters by using the term "cinematic interface":

The camera is ... controlled by the user and is in fact identical with her own sight. Yet it is crucial that ... one sees the virtual world through a rectangular frame, and that this frame always presents only part of a larger whole. This frame creates a distinct subjective experience that is much closer to cinematic perception than it is to unmediated sight.... In the beginning of the 1990s, many games ... used digital video of actors superimposed over 2-D or 3-D backgrounds; by the decade's end, they had switched to fully synthetic characters rendered in real-time. (Manovich, 2001, p. 83)

This technical evolution described by Manovich was giving way to a dynamical point of view in games, leaving the choice about the perspective (first person or third person) up to the user. So the point of view is a unique difference between games and films: most games use the first-person perspective, which is only rarely found in films. Also, the "persecuting camera" with a third-person perspective combined with the

bird's-eye-view used in games such as *Tomb Raider* just appear in very specific cinematic contexts only (King & Krzywinska, 2002).

Another important aspect is the games' production of space that differs from cinematic representation. Because interactivity and navigation elements are dominant in computer games, space is far more experienced than perceived. The result is a difference in spatial quality that is not bound to real world and thereby offers creative opportunities:

In a video game, not only the representation of space, but even its implication, depend on being programmed and actively created.... Through combinations of the spatial structures discussed above, video game space goes beyond cinematic space and shows the various possibilities for organising space within adiegetic world, as well as broadening our sense of what a diegetic world can be through added elements like navigation and interaction. (Wolf, 2002, p. 74)

The huge aesthetical influence between cartoons and games derives from their common use of stereotypes. Because especially cartoons with male and female superheroes come along with stereotypes in characters and action, computer games share the combination of iconic figures with fragmented narrations. In addition, cartoons and games use "reincarnated animation characters" (Manovich, 2001), and thereby employ the structure of an immediate and endless re-animation of the central character shortly after his or her death. The most important point about the character construction in cartoons as well as in games lies in the "universal" appeal of the hero/ine. The appeal of a character does not need to be very realistic, because the faces and bodies function as iconographical instead of representational codes (McCloud, 2002). Where a movie always puts an actress on the place of the female protagonist, cartoons and games offer a universal and therefore a structurally more open character to the reception of their audience.

Within the context of film and cartoons, medial transpositions can be found concerning the character of Lara Croft, who stands in the tradition of the attractive action heroine—in preceding as well as in paralleling media. Just as the announcement of the comic figure Wonder Woman evokes the mythic goddess Aphrodite: "As lovely as Aphrodite—as wise as Athena—with the speed of Mercury and the strength of Hercules—she is known only as Wonder Woman" (Horn, 1980, p. 130), there are also for game heroines iconological quotations of former beautiful women.

With regard to Lara Croft, Gunzenhäuser locates them in the type of the fetishist femme fatale (Gunzenhäuser, 2000, p. 215). By fetishizing the strong superheroine, she loses her terror and is put back to the state of a desirable object.

Fetish Aesthetics?

The over-sexualized comic-superwoman finds her parallel in the game-woman, which is also fetishized by oversexuality. Regarding the wide range of fetishizing, a number of questions come up: What does it look like in the case of the games and their heroines, and are there repetitive patterns of sexualizing? Where can we find special characteristics, typical only for virtual characters? How can this be theoretically related to gender? Is there an analogous fetishizing of femininity in society, which can be discovered in games, too?

The interesting thing about Lara Croft's artificial body, which displays quite mannerist exaggerations, is an overlapping of the religious, sexual, and fashionable aspects of fetishism.

Fetishism, in its original religious sense, signifies a ritual object that gives its worshipper safety and security. That is precisely what the virtual avatar Lara Croft supplies, who, in a recurring ritual, exposes herself anew to all kinds of dangers and builds a protective shield for the users, who feel secure behind her.

In psychoanalysis, the sexual aspect of fetish can be seen in the substitute object the fetishist uses to achieve sexual excitement. Such potential objects and instruments can be the entire body, a part of the body, or a piece of dress. The overeroticizing of some particular parts of Lara's body—especially her breasts, but also her legs, her waist, and her pouting lips—represent a promising, ultrafeminine sexuality, providing the fetishist with the illusion of control over the desired or "over the unruly, gender- and race-marked, essentially mortal body" (Balsamo, 1997, p. 127). And here also fashion takes up its part. But fetishism in fashion differs from sexual fetishism, as it only refers to the erotic code, whereas the sexual element is only subtly involved (Steele, 1996). Lara's tight, fashionable dress covers the objects of sexual desire, so that they can be erotically charged at any given time but without the intention of a direct sexual invitation or pornographic display. The staging of mutual covering and revealing of Lara's naked skin gives signals of fetishistic structures that Linda Williams subsumes under the visual process of "the implantation of perversion" (Williams, 1991, p. 47).

On a closer examination, the figure of Lara can be regarded as an icon. According to Gottfried Kerscher,

| Figure 18.2 |
Lara's outfit on an auction for UNICEF

an icon must be seen in contrast to an image. Whereas the art-based image gives shape to an idea tied to a sociopolitical background, the icon is a pure visualization of certain contents, as it can be seen, for example, in advertising (Kerscher, 1999, p. 111). So by analyzing Lara's outfit, we regard her as a visual icon connected with codes of gender and design.

Lara's outfit is designed out of a subtle and ambiguous mixture of male and female clothing (figure 18.2). It refers to everyday contemporary clothing that men and woman wear in material reality. Her plain and rather sporty dress is tight fitting, and the size XXS shows off her female curves. The "male" pieces of clothing are functional and erotic at the same time. Lara's spatial independence and mobility are symbolized by the backpack, which enables her to wear everything on her body. Then again, the functional straps and slings for guns and other equipment have an erotic meaning, too, as, for example, the straps on her thighs, which erotically separate her long legs and look like stocking suspenders. The turquoise, tight muscle-shirt, leaving her shoulders bare, is usually worn by men. In female fashion this shirt would have had shoulder straps, like the skinny shirts that are currently worn by young women. However, for combat, a shirt like this would have been too fragile, running counter to Lara's robustness.

The shorts are also an element of 1990s fashion, in reference to the girlie-outfit worn in the rave scene, playing with similar ambiguities: the hyper-proportions of an adult woman are contradicted by infantile forms such as ponytail, pigtails, and shorts. The black hot-pants she wears enable her to stand in a stable straddle-legged posture, without running the danger of losing her dignity or looking "disreputable," which would surely be the case if this woman of combat wore a skirt. But despite this, shorts are of course not functional for fighting or for crossing pathless and difficult terrain. The clothes indicate Lara Croft's potential vulnerability. The change of covered and bare skin and the calculated interruptions and subdivisions through dress are important for the representation. Lara Croft in long trousers or leggings is hardly imaginable. The black gloves resemble those worn by men, usually for driving or by free-climbers and other actors of adventure and extreme sports. They underline Lara's activity and athleticism. Further accessories are a belt with an oversized rectangular metal buckle, and red sunglasses, which testify to her youthful coolness, experience, and fearlessness.

Thus the dress ensemble shows throughout a mixture of opulent femininity together with "male" pieces of clothing. Precisely these body discourses, as well as the multiply coded language of dress, mark Lara Croft's ambivalence as a heroine and model of identification. The same body, which guarantees safety, power, and self-confidence, turns—in its over-perfection—any endeavor toward its imitation into an inaccessible attempt. This forms the background on which we also have to see the numerous Lara Croft lookalike contests, in which young women compete as body doubles and try to perform as the most perfect embodiment of Lara Croft. But the pressure of a perfect body, which an ideal artificial body causes, did not begin with the idols of computer games. The desperate physical endeavors to achieve the perfect body started increasingly with the hype of aerobics in the 1980s (interestingly initiated by ex-Barbarella Jane Fonda).

In general, Lara is a model of identification that unites all the perpetual promises of beauty, success, and adventure. Compared to stars in the real world, as a virtual character Lara does not age—she gets even younger in *Tomb Raider 5*—as this option is limited technically by the digital graphics. For the identification process, a core design of the figure is requested. Like all the other digital avatars, she also has endless new lives after death. Female as well as male users learn by repetition the successful and courageous navigation of dark and claustrophobic spaces and the purposeful confrontation with evil powers, thus rehearsing their own power fantasies with positive feedback. Flexibility and accuracy of aim guarantee superiority and security,

strategic thinking and employment of strength lead to the pleasures of power. An interactive computer game suggests an illusion of the control of events, which in *Tomb Raider* are caused by the heroine. The archeologist Lara Croft takes the users into hidden worlds, so they navigate between different time levels, without losing their orientation:

As a body, Lara is very present, she is fast, flexible and superior. In her posture of attack—standing with legs apart, very space taking often focused in close-up and therefore huge on the screen—she seems almighty. She is familiar with the spaces in which she moves and we have to adapt to her tempo and walking pace.... On the one side there is Lara as an archeologist who moves between past and present, on the other side are the players—teenagers who have to orientate themselves between the worlds of children and adults, between ignorance and new knowledge, between masculinity and femininity. They are challenged to find a definite sexual identity: And in this situation Lara takes the players by their hand and guides them through a plain and not very complex world in which she is versed and very powerful. (Gunzenhäuser, 2000, p. 101)

Obviously, here lies the key to the access and reception of Lara Croft: In *Tomb Raider*, not only an effortless change of space and time takes place, but also an oscillation between genders. Lara Croft unites a tough killer instinct with pin-up style, aggression with fragility. This is paralleled by a definite bodily (over) femininity, which in its inaccessibility of an computer-animated ideal has to end in a disorientation for those female users who try to imitate her. This disorientation is technically preconditioned and therefore accompanied by an apparent ironical gesture on the side of the game industry. The figure of Lara acts in many pictorial forms in diverse media networks, thus causing loops. As formerly Tamagotchi and Kyoko Date, Lara's world is supplemented by the virtual world of the web and by media such as television (music videos), but moreover—as the lookalike contests testify—also by reality. By the transfer to interactive media, the Lara character experiences an extension of her construction options. Her binary coding allows an autonomous extension of the fantastic worlds and a configuration of the player's personal projections.

Lara's character remains indefinite; as an artificial figure she has only a poor or limited character construction, she shows no specific personality, which therefore opens her up to all kind of projections. For this reason, a marketable usage of her image for video

| Figure 18.3 |
Cover of the comic: Xena from the TV serial

clips and advertisements is as possible as individual receptions, which see in her for instance a playful digital excess of femininity or an ironic icon of a heroine. This double-coded (Eco, 1973) heroine—designed for satisfying the male gaze and at the same time giving empowerment to female users—causes on the one hand an illusion of her controllability, whereas on the other—by giving interviews and thereby mediating an autonomous character—her virtual character suggests a possibility of potential communication.

Other Characters: Xena, the Autonomous Warrior Princess

Another heroine that leads exclusively through the computer game as a single fighting woman is the figure of the Amazon Xena (figure 18.3). Like Lara Croft, Xena is the only choosable character to play the game with and therefore owns an absolute autonomous status within the gameplay. With the game *Xena—the Warrior Princess*, the principle of remediation can be stated very clearly, comprising the media of cartoon, TV, and game.

The cartoon Xena is completely modeled on the earlier television serial from 1995 with the same name. Interestingly, the cover of the cartoon is not drawn but instead taken from the successful television serial. The cartoon also contains a guide, background information on the actresses, and a quiz game. The fantasy figure of the serial is highly popular, shown in the United States since 1995 and in Germany since 1996. The serial, filmed in New Zealand, deals with the ancient warrior princess Xena and her fellow Gabrielle on their adventurous paths fighting for the good. Yet the brunette Xena has a dark past as a brutal and murderous war-commander; this is the cause of many dangerous, magical, and gloomy situations, which the blonde and virtuous Gabrielle comes to aid. To pay off debts from the past, Xena wants to help others through a combination of charisma, mastery of acrobatics and armory (especially the deadly chakram), and the knowledge of deadly acupressure. Her companion Gabrielle has formerly been a fair Amazon queen, who then began to travel around with her idol Xena. Gabrielle is an exquisite female poet, peaceful, innocent, and optimistic. Both women are connected in deep friendship, courage, intelligence, strength, and skill. They also have both had bad experiences with men. Xena gave birth to a son, whom she sorrowfully gave away; Gabrielle was also forced to sacrifice her daughter. So both women are experienced, independent, and at the same time take responsibility. As ideal heroines they complete each other. There is the tall and dark Xena as the aggressive, powerful, and courageous warrior, and the blonde, gentle Gabrielle as harmonic and truthful companion. Eventually the series was not only followed by the cartoon, but also by the computer game *Xena*.

The PlayStation game, dating from 1999, advertises the popular TV heroine on the package. Her face in close-up looks directly at the viewer, her dark hair with a wild fringe fall on her provocative eyes, and her resolutely pouting lips signal eroticism. A component of danger is indicated by Xena's sword and a licking fire in the background. In the game, the player starts directly with the figure Xena, who—at that point—does not wear the sword. In the animated intro, Xena wanders with her companion on an idyllic mountain path and both communicate as friends on the prevention of dangers. The player has the option to pass with Xena through twenty-seven game levels. On a training level, the user can test Xena's moving capability and potential armory. The game vaguely adopts the framework of the TV serial, in which Xena is a courageous warrior princess who wants to help other human beings and who subsequently has to defeat numerous lurking enemies. Like her television aspect, Xena is strong, acrobatic, and trained in combat. To kill increasingly stronger enemies (a giant Cyclops, for instance), she is also capable of throwing her chakram (a metal disc functioning as a missile) at any time, with no loss of energy (figure 18.4). Occasionally, in close combat,

| Figure 18.4 |
Xena the Warrior Princess and the Cyclops

she rages triumphantly and spins around several times impressively.

Gabrielle exists as a game figure on the level of the Amazon's village. The level cannot freely be chosen, but to get there requires a certain degree of game experience. Analogous to the TV serial, Gabrielle's competencies are her quickness of repartee and action, whereby she is just as able to defend herself with her staff.

Leeloo, the Weakened Female Protagonist from The Fifth Element

Another unusual and already cloned protagonist is presented by the figure Leeloo from the science fiction movie *The Fifth Element*, produced in 1997 and directed by Luc Besson. Here the principle of remediation is connecting film and game, but this time the successful cult movie has had a strong esthetical and structural influence on the game. Therefore the game is merely adapting cinematic elements, whereas the film is still absolutely absorbing most of the game elements. Correspondingly, the cinematic dominance comes along with a weakening of the female protagonist in the game.

The story is as follows: At the end of the nineteenth century, scientists discover an ancient inscription, describing a weapon for the destruction of evil on earth. Activating the weapon requires the fifth element. When an extraterrestrial spaceship lands in the Egyptian temple, the aliens remove four stones, which present the four elements. Three hundred years later, New York is threatened by a huge fireball, but at the moment when the aliens want to come to the government's aid, they are destroyed, apart from a few intact

cells. On the basis of the cells, scientists clone the alien Leeloo (Milla Jovovich), who, due to her superhuman powers, can flee from the laboratory to search for the fifth element. She meets the taxi driver Korben Dallas (Bruce Willis), who decides to help her while police, government, and industrials are on the hunt for her. Together, they fight their way through corrupt and chaotic New York to save the world.

Despite its positioning in the science fiction genre, the movie is more like an action-fantasy comedy and achieves its success mainly because of its bombastic equipment, brilliant special effects, and a number of well-known stars and amusing gags, which are in fact self-ironic.

The production of a computer game reveals the endeavor toward the marketing of a successful movie and its hero or heroine. In 1998, after the big success of the movie *The Fifth Element*, the companies Ubi Soft, Kalisto, and Gaumont published the action and adventure game with the same name. The package of the game advertises only the female game figure Leeloo, who highly resembles the actress Milla Jovovich. On the front cover, Leeloo poses against a background of a futuristic city. She looks provocatively at the viewer, her arms akimbo; she expresses coolness, confidence, and strength, although altogether she bears more resemblance to a model than to an aggressive warrior.

The diagonal side view presents her body up to knee height. Posing with arched back, her body is dressed in a tight white top, nylons with a seam along her thighs, and a kind of plastic belt with big holes. The belt is a mixture of holster, braces, and corset with panty, which in its disfunctionality at the same time covers and accentuates genitals and bosom. On the back of the package, three screenshots show Leeloo in action; only the fourth screenshot represents the male hero. This is in contrast to the movie ads, which primarily showed the male actor Bruce Willis, the movie's star and main publicity figure. However, the computer game is nearly exclusively intended for male users, focusing entirely on Leeloo's eroticism—although neither in the movie nor in the game are her outfits as sexy as on the package of the computer game.

Diverse movie sequences serve as cut scenes for the structure of the game. For example, the game has the same intro as the movie, and also each new game level starts with a spectacular film sequence. In contrast to the movie, the computer version starts with the male figure of Korben Dallas, who breaks into the nuclear laboratory to activate Leeloo with a gene-card. Only

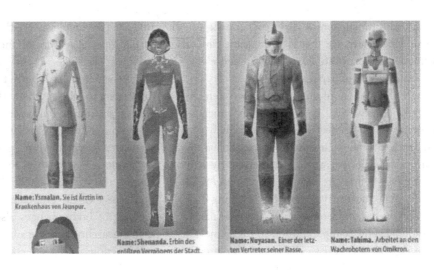

Name: Ysmalan. Sie ist Ärztin im Krankenhaus von Jaunpur.

Name: Shenanda. Erbin des größten Vermögens der Stadt.

Name: Nuyasan. Einer der letzten Vertreter seiner Rasse.

Name: Tahima. Arbeitet an den Wachrobotern von Omikron.

| Figure 18.5 |
The Nomad Soul: Characters

then, male and female users have the option to move on via Leeloo, who wears the special movie outfit (a fire-red bob and a scanty, white bondage suit, designed by Jean Paul Gaultier). Although Leeloo is equipped with superhuman take-off powers and easily practices huge leaps, acrobatic climbs, and quick punches, the combat strengths and strategies of the virtual Leeloo remain far behind the movie character. In particular, the computer-animated Leeloo is presented as very vulnerable and weak; one-armed, flying robots literally knock out her energy. In total, this simple realization and the missing of new digital extras in the game shows its complete dependence on the movie and makes no use of its interactive potential. Here, the opportunity of games in creating a genuine kind of space—especially in regard to the spatial skills acted out by the superhuman Leeloo—has not been used.

The Exception: The Nomad Soul and its "Body-Switcher"
The package of the computer game *The Nomad Soul* shows no picture of its twenty-six game figures. Instead, there is a slim harlequin-like figure with white make-up, vaguely reminiscent of David Bowie, who is singing a song in the game, portrayed in a screenshot on the back of the package. The mysterious character on the package gives us a hint of the forthcoming masquerade, which is taking place in the plot of the game, because the users constantly have to change their game figures.

The game, produced in 1999 by Eidos/Quantic Dream, is a mixture of an adventure, action, and fantasy game. In the game, gloomy demons from damnation are looking for fresh human souls, of whom they can take possession to maintain and secure their power.

Those bodies that are possessed by the demons are merely empty frames. *The Nomad Soul* is situated in a futuristic science fiction setting, with a corrupt state system made up of a number of towns, resembling a mixture of Orwell's 1984 and Ridley Scott's *Blade Runner*. In *The Nomad Soul*, it is not possible to direct only one fixed figure; instead, the game contains a number of characters, which must be adopted and interchanged by the players in the scope of the game. So because of the wandering souls, The Nomad Soul has not one protagonist but twenty-six figures, and nearly the half of them (twelve figures) are female characters (figure 18.5).

A brief description of the female figures is present in the game. In addition to a short profile of the character, introducing her competencies, preferences, and dislikes, the descriptions give information on the body measure, eye color, size, weight, and blood-group of each woman. This is complemented by a list of their programmed capabilities, such as quickness, strength of attack, flexibility, resistance, and combat experience. The short biographies, introducing twelve fictive women figures, suggest a wide cultural range of female stereotypes: the journalist Betsy loves truth, nature, and sport; Tahim'a masters difficult languages and artificial intelligence; literature-student Eva likes short skirts, sports, boys, and partying; Samyaz'n has a third eye, is able to speak with death, and feels attracted to solitude or body guard; Iman stands out by fighting techniques and extreme beauty, prefers fashion and modern painting. Two women, Telis and Jenna, are quite central in the game, because they are the only figures who have a modified look: Jenna exists in a characterizing pilot overall as well as in the shape of an animal-like demon, who looks like a futuristic female Taurus. Telis is a demon of a similar appearance that is at the same time a young woman in a short white dress who gets more vulnerable in scanty white underwear.

Through the option of interchange between all characters, *The Nomad Soul* is an exception concerning the exchange of gender positions by which the constructedness of the characters becomes obvious. This is primarily reflected in the fact that nearly half of the twenty-six figures are female. *The Nomad Soul* contains not only the usual option for selecting figures, but, moreover, game sequences, explicitly visualize gender-swapping. For example, in one of the scenes, a male figure approaches the Eva character, who lasciviously leans against a wall while her body is panned in detail. Simultaneously, in the lower side of the picture, the man's thoughts are faded in: "Great body, I'd like to take it over." Shortly afterwards, an energy crown emerges from Eva's brain. She touches her head and looks astonished at her strengthened body parts, while a tone comes up sounding like the loading of energy. Then we read the sentence: "The reincarnation magic was effective. Now I got a new body." The figure of the man is now motionless and transparent, and a view from above shows the young and self-confident Eva in a light pink dress, disappearing with shaking hips toward new challenges.

The common male perspective of panning or judging the female body is joined by a modification of desire: "Great body, I'd like to posses it" turns into "Great body, I'd like to take it over." The male taking possession of the other sex turns into a playful trying out of the other sex. Her power boosts to the same extent as the conqueror's powers shrink and his body fades away. Besides its magic aspect, the term "reincarnation magic" indicates that the players of *The Nomad Soul* can experience not only one transformation, but a chain of transformations, which depend on their selections, from male to female, female to male, male to male, and female and female. All body meetings start with a panning and estimation of the respective figure, whereby female and male bodies are differentiated by the comments. The virtual take-over of the male body is announced by the phrase "I'd like to possess it," whereas the female body is addressed with "I'd like to take it over." Therefore the "incorporation" of the female body turns into a playful experiment with transsexual connotations. These body changes present an endless journey within male and female bodies, a nomadic body-serial; therefore, *The Nomad Soul* could as well be named "The Nomad

Body." The emphasis on the body is intensified by a further special feature of the game: there is a "body-switcher" available for the game on the Internet. The "body-switcher" is a tool that enables male and female users to take any body they want from *The Nomad Soul* at any time. This switch option, which is offered after optional pre-information about a figure, can be seen as a free-flourishing gender shift for both sexes. Even more clearly than the options in all the other games, the "body-switcher" visualizes the construction aspect of the embodiments. In addition, the high number of body changes also emphasizes the relative exchangeability and the obvious fictionality of gender constructions.

The dynamic of the body-switcher is closely connected to the phenomenon of the "shapechanger" that is embedded in Donna Haraway's technique-fetishist discourse of the "female cyborg" (Haraway, 1990). As a possible feminine identity construction in post-industrial society, Haraway establishes the term "female cyborg" as a symbolic metaphor for the artificiality of female body conceptions. According to this, all women are cyborgs, organic robots heading toward a "post-gender world," a society of self-constructed hybrid organisms and apparatuses. In Haraway's view, the blurring of gender boundaries caused by female cyborgs is ambivalent, as they could change their form as "shapechanger," but without the option of a voluntary shift between human being and machine: "Maybe she is not so much bad as she is shapechanger, whose dislocations are never free" (Haraway, 1991, p. 20). Among the game-protagonists of *The Nomad Soul*, the "shapechanger" phenomenon can be found in the diverse outfits and in the high capability of bodily adaptation on the diverse levels of a game (figure 18.6). However, as indicated by Haraway, there is no autonomous

| **Figure 18.6** |
The Nomad Soul: Bodyswitcher

boundary between human and machine. Even the easy shape changing of the "body-switcher" option is a programmed pattern, and presumably the main attraction lies less in a boundary than in the merged practicability of shape changes.

The question regarding the maintenance of gender stereotypes arises despite all the shape shiftings. Given the oversexualizing of the virtual heroines, gender differentiation seems to be highly popular as an orientation within the virtual world. One reason for this lies in the rating of femininity within 1990s girl culture, which combined an individualized, cool manner in asserting oneself with an exaggerated maintenance of femininity (McRobbie, 1999, p. 7).

An aspired, cultural readability of gender conceptions is difficult to deal with. This could explain why such a remarkable, gender-nomadic game such as *The Nomad Soul* did not achieve a bigger success and does not have a fan community in the Internet. Angerer also regards the orientation-function of definite bodily assignments as a fixed point within a world of increasingly dissolving cultural norms. Therefore an excessive gender expression among the cyber-bodies of the virtual protagonists functions within existing gender boundaries (Angerer, 1996, p. 4).

Media-Bodies and Body Weapons

As Marie-Luise Angerer points out, body perception alters with the new media of communication. The new social factors of digital networks and transformed ways of communication in everyday life, transform pure institutional body inscriptions into a play of representation. Angerer points to the multiplication of identity constructions, which emanate from media, moving continuously between virtual and real life. Angerer comments on the effect of the developing media technology on the female body: "No doubt—realities, identities, perceptions are going to reproduce themselves. The creation of virtual realities has introduced a new order of difference into the actual reality" (Angerer, 1996, p. 2).

With current changes in bio- and communication technology, it is no longer possible to understand identity as fixed to the physical body. The overlapping of electronic media and human body demonstrate the instability of bodily boundaries. This specific moment of instability produces fluctuating references with regard to existing gender constructions, so that Judith Halberstam is paying attention to the artificiality of all gender concepts: "Gender is an automatic construct, an electronic text that shifts and changes in dialogue with users

and programs" (Halberstam, 1991, p. 446). According to Halberstam, cybernetics reveal gender and its representations as technological productions and relate the postmodern subject to feminist debates about technology and gender.

The multiplication and construction of identity raise the following question with regard to computer games: Do computer games represent a shift in the portrayal of gender, or is this simply an option of selecting between diverse male and female characters? For the construction of identity in cyberspace, the terms "virtual cross-dressing" or "gender swapping" signify a playful entry and take-over to the other sex.

Only a few games start directly with a female figure, as in *Xena*. In a lot of games, female figures appear late on the scene, on higher levels. In the beginning of *Virtua Fighter*, there are options for a selection among all figures, even though only two out of ten are female. It is quite common for a game to start with a male hero and then continue with females, as in *The Fifth Element*, when the player has to start with Korben to get access to Leeloo. All this shows that the user can only rarely choose from a quantitatively equal number of the sexes; instead, regarding the figure's relevance and strategy, the game is fixed and determined. Therefore, the flourishing gender-shift would be limited in its variety and importance of female figures, although the experience of a virtual gender-shift is possible in principal.

Xena and Gabrielle are models of female game figures. They are the Amazons from the middle ages, fighting for peace, but wearing a rather scarce armor; Leeloo from *The Fifth Element* is the wild, cloned, half-naked hybrid woman; or Anezka from *Vampire* is the young virtuous nun, who is also shown in the common fetishist side perspective, which emphasize the contours of breast, waist, and bottom. However, in case of Anezka, another point becomes evident: because the nun prefers the romantic love of a handsome knight to the religious commands, an animation sequence is made possible, showing Anezka running upset through the dark forest searching for the beloved knight, thereby getting bitten by a male vampire. This shows the importance of a standardized fictive narration, already contained in the historic myths of femininity and which on demand can simply get actualized. Here it is the narration of the young devoted nun, whose virtue succumbs to a dangerous, romantic love. Precisely in this context of narration and discourse of the body, Judith Butler speaks of "bodily intelligibility" (Butler, 1993, p. 17). It means understanding a body via aesthetic elements and narrative conventions. So in the postmodern practice of pastiche, the digital beauties refer to historic art and body constructions, by combining and juxtaposing diverse cultures of image and text.

The overmodeling of bodily features means a high degree of selection as well as stylization. Nearly all virtual protagonists display huge breasts, extreme wasp waists, and ultra-long legs. This applies to all of the quite diverse figures, including the Amazon Xena, the alien Leeloo, the lady of the castle Millenia, the young nun, and of course Lara Croft, whose appeal is further completed by big, pouting lips. Actually, Lara Croft has particularly outsized breasts; this is why she is the prime virtual sex symbol.

Additionally, there are further discourses of femininity. The corrupt world in *The Nomad Soul* is also expressed through the numerous sex shops and bars as well as by the uncountable prostitutes in the streets. Dressed in a different color in each city, wearing miniskirts and stockings, they pass energetically through the streets or are engaged as table-dancers and strippers. The animating fetish-character of these women forms the constant background of the other figures' actions, producing an atmosphere of subculture and sex.

The sexualizing of the game protagonists' bodies is increased in their fetishist character by an additional weapon potential. For the performance of the heroine's dangerousness, they often have an arsenal of weapons available. Xena has from the beginning a deadly throwing chakram made of metal, and she also fights with a sword. With the figure Millenia, the user can activate a number of deadly traps, such as bombs, javelins, rocks, and electric chairs. In *Tomb Raider*, Lara Croft uses a selection of machine guns, grenades, harpoons, or rapid-fire guns (figure 18.7).

Randi Gunzenhäuser claims that weapons can be found among all female protagonists, and that the

reason for Lara's particular popularity is her extreme corporal engagement (Gunzenhäuser, 2000). However, it must be said that, first of all, not all of the female protagonists have fire weapons at hand: Leeloo, compared to her male companion, has no weapons, Pai Chan and Sarah Bryant in *Virtua Fighter 2* have none, nor does the ruler Ekatharina or the nun Anezka in *Vampire*. However, Gunzenhäuser's more important claim, that Lara Croft's bodily engagement is exceptional, must be opposed. Not only because a comparable engagement can also be found in Xena, but moreover, female figures without any weapons bring their bodies even more extremely into action. The kick-boxers Pai and Sarah fight exclusively and very artfully with their bodies; Leeloo also has to practice impressive acrobatic leaps to survive. The twelve female characters of *The Nomad Soul* do not directly fight with weapons, because they appear via 3D first-person mode (therefore figure-unspecified), but they carry out numerous physical fights in kickboxing sequences. For this reason, we can modify Gunzenhäuser's argument: The strongest weapon of the game heroines is their body, in the sense of a multifunctional digital body-weapon. They are superhuman virtual figures, perfectly adapted to their surroundings, who search for the best possible way through danger. It has to be stated here that in case of the stylized figures of digital computer heroines, body, weapon, and technique are turned into desire. They represent definite virtual fetishes of technology, thereby connecting technology and desire. Thomas Foster interprets this connection of technology and female body as a synthesis of imaginary controllability in the sense of a male repulse against fear (Foster, 1996, pp. 289 ff).

The Denial of Age and the Monstrous Metamorphosis as Empowerment of the Female Body

The discourse of female beauty is related to the denial of aging. Kathleen Westward regards aging in contemporary society as at least as important as the category of gender: "Technological culture is a youth culture" (Westward, 1994, p. 63). This technically practicable youth can be seen in the fact that female virtual characters do not age. Lara Croft and her colleagues have a concrete date of birth, but this is elegantly dated back each year. Also, in the progress of the game the protagonists do not visibly age. Production costs would rise immensely if all aging processes were shown. Despite all the repetitive small virtual deaths of the figures—which is also a phenomenon of many cartoons, film,

| Figure 18.7 |
Body-Weapons

and TV series—their characteristics remain unaltered, undiminished, guaranteeing "timeless" entertainment.

Older women exist only sporadically in the games. Apart from the stereotypical marginal figure of a warty, cunning witch in *Vampire*, there is the central, fully animated figure Ekatharina as the wise woman, who is mistress, savant, and adviser. She is not a warrior but a mighty ruler. Her power is tied to the discourse of motherhood. In a modification of the ancient she-wolf of Rome, Ekatharina gives her blood as a tonic to her male inferiors or as bribery to the enemies. An erotic loading of her otherwise strict and reserved mien occurs only when a demon takes her shape. Dressed exactly like Ekatharina, but obviously younger and with flashing eyes, the demon approaches Prince Christian to seduce him. She winds around the confused hero and suddenly tears her veil away to show off her charred skin and big fangs. The scene ends with an audible wolfish breath. The sequence expresses the psychological male fear of aging and decay of the desirous and promising female body.

A similar though even more monstrous scene appears in *The Nomad Soul*, when the components, beauty, age, and death, come together, here in the case of a younger woman. The child-woman Tels kneels injured and distressed with bowed head on the ground while the camera circles around her bloody body. She is dressed only in white underwear. When her husband runs up to her, she exclaims, "Take me in your arms, darling," then bursts into a loud and witchlike laughter and is the demon Tels. Her body winds under pain and in the following shot her extremities appear absurdly lengthened. After a sudden cut, the upper part of her body is shown as a burned torso, and her breasts and face appear black like those of a mummy. But she is still moving, and eventually she turns into a snorting and fighting beast. This is followed by a kickboxing sequence with a man, whom she attacks in a quick, unerring, and brutal manner. In the side-view, her pointed breasts are clearly recognizable, but at the same time the demon Tels resembles an artistic combat machine that can kick, punch, and perform leaps. When her husband falls screaming to the ground, she pulls him up and inhales his energy, his soul, out of him, and throws him away. In the meantime, this is contrasted with the human agent Kay'a, who watches the whole scene with horror from a hidden position. She is the beautiful, young, emotional, and seductive opposite, and in the end tries to rush to the man's aid.

The Nomad Soul also visualizes the man's fear of his lover's corporal aging. Actually, the performance resembles a sequence of the movie *The Shining*, when during a kissing scene in a bathroom, the body of the desired woman suddenly ages right in front of the hero while the woman bursts out into a toothless, mocking laughter. In *The Nomad Soul*, however, the fear of the moldering and decaying body of the beloved extends the discourse of aging, by distorting the nightmare of the evil, obscene but at the same time powerful partner into monstrosity. Apparently she has only waited for the chance of a deadly fight and cooperates with evil powers. The woman's overemphasized sexual attraction turns into a monstrous activity; woman and beast merge in raw brutishness. The appearance of a new, young and beautiful woman signals the female care for the injured man, as well as the maintenance and storage of the good in desirable beauty. So aging and aggressive femininity are rejected, when in the end youth and beauty restore feminine harmlessness.

Successful protagonists can be recognized by their combat strength. They always have to prove themselves physically. At the same time, they are allowed to express weaknesses and corporal efforts, too, as for example, when Lara or Alice groan under the strain of difficult leaps. However, these weaknesses must be distinguished from the basically weak female body, which is exemplified by April Ryan (*The Longest Journey*). In her case, femaleness is connoted by bodily deficiency, and therefore only a man's hand can open up the decisive move in the game. Other games rely upon the transformation of the corporal appearance to express strength and the willingness to engage in deadly aggression. Only in the form of the devilish is the female body capable of facing men successfully. Often the marking of the female body as aggressive can only be achieved through artifice. The woman's body passes through a metamorphosis into the devilish. The sudden change is experienced as painful, as expressed by gesture, body posture, and screaming. Actually, an associative connection to the process of birth is easy to assume. The mystery of the female life-giving nature once again reverses into images of the birth of evil. The fusion of female body and weapon is realized by taking on the appearance of the demon, which is reminiscent of the female figure Tels in *The Nomad Soul*. Alice changes as well from a girl into a diabolic horned creature.

The oversexualized representation of the figures can be perceived as another, though less obvious strategy toward the weakening of female strength. The potential threat of the fighting female body is neutralized by an overemphasis on the feminine body parts. The female hyperbody, created in a sense of double-drag

(Anne-Marie Schleiner, 1999), conceals its strength. In combat, it is hindering, and in its bareness it shows off its vulnerability. As a biological signal of gender, the breasts are deliberately in the foreground. However, to evoke no frightening images of "Vagina Dentata," the genitals are less accentuated. This shows the ambivalence of perceiving the female body simultaneously as seduction and as inscrutable threatening weapon.

Autonomous Waiting Gestures and the Female Avatar as a Virtual Shield of Protection

Animated intermediate sequences in the game produce an important free space to articulate the personality of the digital, female art figures. The sequences have no influence on the course of the game. So-called waiting gestures emerge during game interruptions and are initiated as a direct appeal to the gamers. They are independent from the users' actions and offer an opportunity to work out individual features. April Ryan's (*The Longest Journey*) waiting gestures are a sign of insecurity. She looks carefully and searchingly around, makes gestures of embarrassment, like the arrangement of her hairdo. The gestures signal her waiting for support as well as the concentration on her own look.

In the case of Alice (*American McGee's Alice*) these gestures look different. The camera perspective changes whenever the game is interrupted. Alice stands in front of the player and expresses her annoyance at the interruption. Her waiting gestures consist of looking at her hands and fingernails, scraping her feet, picking cool and demonstratively with a knife, cleaning her nails, or casual throwing games with the knife. On the game's website, these gestures are particularly striking: Alice addresses the gamers directly and via pressing a special button, a spider emerges from behind a mushroom. Alice crushes the spider in a casual manner and kicks it out of the picture. Falling out of the line of the stereotypical image of the arachnophobic girl, this is an expression of Alice's autonomous subject status. Clichés of femininity cannot be found here; she tramples the spider, whereas other female figures would need the support of a man for its elimination.

The animated sequences suggest autonomous actions on the side of the protagonist, even though they are preprogrammed. This shows that the personality of the "sheroes" emerge on the audiovisual level only in the form of actions, gestures, and aesthetic expression. The specific personality is given a shape.

In general, the handling of the game requires on the user side a lot of skill and good reaction time. So

when Lara Croft and, with her, Xena, Millenia, and Leeloo, embody the respective interface, and definite separations between the world of users and the universe of the game no longer exist, then users can less clearly disconnect from the plot of the game, and the virtual heroine supports the immersive character of the computer game. The action is not viewed from Lara's perspective, but from the perspective of a third person. For a direct orientation the user, by pressing a key, can use the survey function, but this autonomous look around is time consuming and because of close-ups often confusing. Therefore, as the game figure always partly obstructs the view of the surrounding and approaching enemies, most of the time the users, despite their skills, have no absolute control over the events, which come off with help of the figures. This raises a question regarding the impression of the user: does he or she play with the figure, or is it the other way around? From the perspective of perception theory, both might be the case, because the player actively moves a figure, which via the game program again challenges his or her reactions.

The intermediary function of the virtual heroine therefore exists on a number of levels. Each protagonist is a protecting avatar of the user in a dangerous game. She embodies the interface and involves the users increasingly in the game, and she is also the image of the motherly matrix. Lara Croft is, in addition to this, also the almighty guide through a sexually ambiguous world and mediates between the diverse time levels, which could explain the success of Lara Croft. The intermediating, digital protagonist invites the users to conquer the heroines and the games by the means of body and media technology. Precisely the digitality of the artificial female bodies, which do not have a specific personality and are therefore open to projections of all kinds, enables, in the case of Lara Croft, a marketable image for video clips and advertising. The cybergoddess Lara Croft signals a postmodern identity, which is marked by fragmenting, artificial, and flowing experimental components. The high degree of Lara's artificiality, her multimedia aspect, multifunctionality and the patchwork construction of her body sampling, lead to a whole range of identity options. But at the same time modern discourse, in the sense of a stable, essential, and homogenous identity, can be found: Lara's course of life is constructed toward stringency and the fulfillment of her true mission. Her behavior is predictable and repetitive, and her over-sexualizing underlines an essential, existing femininity.

In that sense it is not a postmodern strategy that rules, but body representation functions again as a locality of power. The ideal of the commodity "woman" gets continued and the hypersexualizing reinforces the idea of a biological difference in the guise of zeitgeist. Indeed, the ostensible unequivocal is again and again sabotaged by a vague irony.

However, in general, Marie Luise Angerer points to the discursive inconvertibility also of the virtual subject-conception and reminds us of the original subject separation in the context of digital surroundings. So in the understanding of Lacan's mirror state that characterizes the process of identification ex negativo as a misunderstanding, superficial appearance, and fictive vision, the psychoanalytical constitution of the subject manifests itself in virtual three-dimensional process of identification. Referring to Katherine Hayles, the additional occurrence of the cyberspace multiplies the problems of the identification process: "Moving into cyberspace binds subject and object positions together in a reflexive dynamic that makes their identification problematic" (Hayles, 1993, p. 187). The developing "terminal identity" (Bukatman, 1990, p. 203) is therefore tied to body reactions as well as being extremely disorientated, because precisely the body, its representation, and with that the ego and the other, oscillate continuously.

Elisabeth Grosz's interpretation of a general gender instability is interesting with respect to the ambivalence of the heroine's body discourses. Grosz thinks that the instability of gender exists as instability of sex, namely, in a sense of a potential bodily capability, which becomes culturally unacceptable (Grosz, 1994, p. 140). This means that decided bodily deviations in respect of the virtual female figures have a dangerous effect precisely because of their practicability. One must not necessarily see these potentials of threatening artificiality as pure models of resistance. But what Gunzenhäuser notices for Lara Croft can be referred to other protagonists: the reception of virtual female game figures is dependent on the player/viewer/interpreter.

Virtual Models of Femininity and the Connection Between Genre and Openness

For the gamers, the offered identifications depend on the genre of the game, which structurally conditions interactions and the degree of immersion. Allowing either the mechanical selection of a female figure as design-respective skin option (Konoko in *Oni*) in a pure combat game, or an active shaping of the character by experiencing and projecting into the figure. The genre of the game plays an important role in the potential development of a female character. In the point and click adventure *The Longest Journey*, April Ryan is bereaved of her game decision. The protagonist cannot be changed by the gamer, and by her design she does not open up any projections toward further adoptions. This can be traced back to the nonviolent game structure, which does not demand a break with female role conceptions.

Therefore the active, strong, and fighting side of the female protagonist can be experienced in the shooter genre. In the beat 'em up game *Oni*, protagonist Konoko is characterized by her direct combative bodily engagement, resulting in functional and complete clothing. Her sex is not emphasized; femaleness remains an option of design. The naturalistic body representation, simulated movements, wide standing positions, the return of energy for special throws, are products of the genre. As a basic modification from the model in literature, the heroine in *American McGee's Alice* appears always bodily active in combat during threatening situations, thus following no naturalistic principle.

The interesting heroines are "open characters," not to be misunderstood in the sense of "anything goes." Rather, the characters are created in a multi-layered way and in Umberto Eco's understanding of double-coding, they are open to diverse levels of reception. The figure of Lara Croft achieves a maximum openness. However, in the case of April Ryan, this is reversed into meaninglessness. The double-coding of significant "sheroes" also allows the appropriation of specific groups of recipients such as youth cultures. Alice is particularly suitable to the fantasy world of the goths (see Richard, 1998). *Xena—the Warrior Princess* comes from the imagery universe of heavy metal music, though serving lesbian fantasies at the same time. Julie Strain can be classified along a continuum ranging from heavy metal to rockers. Additionally she serves the specific field of heterosexual, sadomasochistic fantasies. Her fantasy outfits, which are an eclectic mixture of costumes from various periods, enable a self-confident and combative exhibition of her sexualized body.

It is striking that the games without a direct relation to the present show the phenomenon of female body identity as cultural construct. And in reverse, the more current or modern a protagonist appears, the less actually accepted social gender images are called into question. The veiling of femininity as a construction is particularly evident in *The Longest Journey*. The frightened April Ryan wears contemporary fashion, such as short T-shirts showing off her belly. Shopping, the concentration on her own appearance, and the look in the mirror are important parallel actions. Her lack of self-confidence excludes an offensive presentation of her body or even an aggressive sexuality. The adoption of a young female fashion produces the reality effect in the case of April Ryan. However, as the end of the game shows, this is the blind alley of adaptation and subordination. Therefore we can state that in the investigated games a strengthening of the female characters' position happens through the leaving of contemporary culture on a visual level. The chronological recourse and anticipation form the conditions for the users to recede from their biographic reality and contemporary time. This process is constitutive for the subjective appropriation of the figure because it creates a difference to the everyday culture of the users. A contemporary setting and outfit of a female character immediately re-integrate it back into common gender role play. Within that frame there is no freedom in experimenting with the character without constantly recalling stereotypes. Only in fantastic worlds and costume are "unlimited" gender projections possible. They inspire the fantasies of the users and loosen the grip of dual gender construction.

Positioning a figure in the intermediate stage between girl and woman achieves the same effect of distance. A historized infantilism (see the tendencies toward infantilism in youth cultures, such as girlie in tech culture) represents a subversive option to break out of the heterosexual gender play. Alice is female yet not really a women, and therefore deliberately distinguished from Lolita-figures. The shape of her body as well as her dress (a blue girllike dress with puffed sleeves) resist fetishizing. A glance under the skirt of the protagonist—in many games a quite popular perspective—is disappointing for a stereotypical male. The more obvious figure and contexts are fed from the pictorial reservoir of the fantastic, futuristic, or historic, the better a difference to the heterosexual metaphysics of gender can be constructed. In the design of objects and spaces, the game *Alice*, with its "medieval" somber atmosphere, borrows directly from artists Hieronymous Bosch and Pieter Brueghel (figure 18.8).

We can highlight the elements that relate to the symbols of goth and punk culture. Alice wears a white apron embroidered with an alpha sign and a necklace with the Greek omega. These adopted Christian symbols stand for the beginning and the end. The big white bow that ties the apron in the back, is decorated with a skull. Using these creepy gothic elements frees the her-

| Figure 18.8 |
Gothic Alice

oine Alice from contemporary constraints. This is also certified by the fan websites, which serve as a further indicator for the esteem of the protagonist's offered identification. Only the evident characters have their own universe in the web and animate to further image productions (Alice, Lara, Julie).

The range of ambivalently designed protagonists in the market of PC and PlayStation games has increased between 1999 and 2001. The offered typologies range from the "clean" Lara Croft, B-movie and porno queen Julie Strain, "goth" Alice, tough Konoko, up to the loser April Ryan.

Conclusion

Who of these heroines are particularly suitable for identifications and what kind of features are supportive of the process of an individual autonomy? The heroines perform virtuously medial shifts among the game, the movie, and virtual levels. Materialization and dematerialization in both directions are their flexible features. Further qualities of the powerful heroines are their capacity for visual transformation. To equip their female hypersexualized (*Nomad Soul*) or childlike bodies (*American McGee's Alice*) with power and strength, they have to experience temporal metamorphosis.

The qualities of the female figures emerge from a comparative analysis of waiting gestures: April Ryan shows gestures of embarrassment. In contrast, Alice's gestures are impatient and crude, breaking with the image of the girllike protagonist in the nice dress. Alice is the "gothic" articulation of an emancipatory designed

| Figure 18.9 |
Alice fanart

girlie-type. This is also confirmed by the package, showing Alice simultaneously as girllike and reserved, feminine-seductive, and psychopathically aggressive (figure 18.9). Different from Lara Croft, the protagonist can be experienced more as an acting subject than as a sexual object.

The distance from the present, pictorially shown in the surreal and gothic elements, produces a creative free space, which is independent from contemporary conceptions and designs of femaleness and extend the stereotypical heterosexual metaphysics of gender.

In the commercial game world, the embodiment of "Zeitgeist" leads to a concealed reconstitution of traditional images of femininity. Emancipatory offers are only possible in those games, which depart from contemporary design in setting and female figure, either into historical, futuristic contexts, or into surreal worlds. Body samples, patchwork identities from different times and aesthetic worlds, as well as the openness to projections are the characteristics of the "sheroes" that enable a successful identification.

Acknowledgments

Special thanks to Astrid Baxmeier, Harald Hillgärtner, Verena Kuni, Sebastian Richter, Arndt Röttgers, and Heike Jenss (translation), who have worked as scientific assistants on the research project of the Ministry of Culture and Science in Hessia (HMWK) in Germany "Frauenbewegungen-kultureller und sozialer Wandel—Forschungsfeld III Kulturelle Konstruktionen von Geschlechtern." The title of the project is: "Die Repräsentation der Konstruktion von Weiblichkeit in Computerspielen." The results of the research will be available through a website and a CD (Graphics Tina Öcal and Harald Hillgärntner) See www.birgitrichard.de.

References

Angerer, M.-L. (1996). alt. feminism/alt. sex/alt. identity/alt. theory/alt. art. See gewi.kfunigraz.ac.at/jauk/d_jauk-hinz/6000volt/springer.html.

Balsamo, A. (1997). *Technologies of the gendered body: Reading cyborg women*. Durham: Duke University Press.

Barth, M. (1999). *LaraCroftism*. München: Kunstraum München.

Bolter, J. D., & Grusin, R. (1999). *Remediation. Understanding new media*. Cambridge, MA: MIT Press.

Bukatman, S. (1990). Who programms you? The science fiction of the spectacle. In A. Kuhn (Ed.), *Alien Zone*. London: Verso Books.

Butler, J. (1993). *Bodies that matter. On the discursive limits of "Sex."* New York: Routledge.

Creed, B. (1989). Horror and the monstrous-feminine: An imaginary abjection. In J. Donald (Ed.), *Fantasy and the cinema* (pp. 63–90). London: British Film Institute.

Deitch, J. (1992). *Posthuman*. Ausstellungskatalog: Feldkirchen.

Deuber-Mankowsky, A. (2001). *Lara Croft—Modell, Medium, Cyberheldin*. Frankfurt/Main: Suhrhamp.

Doane, M. A. (1985). Film und Maskerade, Zur Theorie des Weiblichen Zuschauers. In *Frauen und Film*, Magazine, Berlin, no. 38.

Eco, U. (1973). *Das offene Kunstwerk*. Frankfurt/Main: Suhrhamp.

Birgit Richard and Jutta Zaremba

Eco, U. (1990). Die Innovation im Seriellen. In U. Eco, *Über Spiegel und andere Phänomene*, (2d Ed.). München: Suhrhamp.

Foster, T. (1996). The sex appeal of the inorganic: Posthuman narratives and the construction of desire. In R. Newman (Ed.), *Centuries ends, narrative means*. Stanford, CA: Stanford University Press, pp. 276–301.

Graw, I. (1997). Modenschau. Über feministische Modekritiken. *Texte zur Kunst*. Berlin. März, Nr. 25, 73–81.

Grosz, E. (1994). *Volatile bodies. Toward a corporal feminism*. Indianapolis: Indiana University Press.

Gunzenhäuser, R. (2000). Darf ich mitspielen? Literaturwissenschaften und Computerspiele. In G. Braungart, K. Eibl, & F. Jannidis (Eds.), *Jahrbuch für Computerphilologie 2*, (pp. 87–120), Paderborn.

Halberstam, J. (1991). Automating gender: Postmodern feminism in the age of the intelligent machine. My computer, my self. *Feminist Studies* 17/3, Herbst, pp. 439–459.

Haraway, D. (1990). A manifesto for cyborgs: Science, technology and socialist feminism in the 80s. In L. J. Nicholson (Ed.), *Feminism, Postmodernism*. New York: Routledge, pp. 190–233.

Haraway, D. (1991). Interview with Constance Penley and Andrew Ross. In C. Penley & A. Ross (Eds.), *Technoculture*. Minneapolis: University of Minnesota Press, pp. 1–20.

Hayles, N. K. (1993). The seductions of cyberspace. In V. A. Conley (Ed.), *Rethinking technologies*. Minneapolis: University of Minnesota Press, pp. 173–190.

Hayles, N. K. (1999). How we became posthuman: Virtual bodies in cybernetics, literature, and informatics. Chicago: The University of Chicago Press.

Horn, M. (1980). Women in the comics. New York: Chepsea House Publishers.

Jones, C. Female enemy number one? http://www.compactiongames.miningco.com/library/blara.htm.

Kerscher, G. (1999). Bild, Icon, Eyecatcher. Zur Bildstrategie im Internet. In Institut für moderne Kunst Nürnberg (Ed.), netz.kunst. Nürnberg: Institut für moderne Kunst netz.kunst, p. 110–117.

King, G., & Krzywinska, T. (2002). Computer games/Cinema/Interfaces. In F. Mäyrä (Ed.), *CGDC conference proceedings* (pp. 141–153). Tampere: Tampere University Press.

Manovich, L. (2001). *The language of new media*. Cambridge, MA: MIT Press.

McCloud, S. (2002). Abstract reasoning: *Computer Gaming World 6*, 39.

McRobbie, A. (1999). Coding the feminine in the 1990s. In M. Barth (Ed.), *LaraCroftism* (pp. 6–11). München: Kunstraum München.

Richard, B. (Ed.). (1998). Die oberflächlichen Hüllen des Selbst. Mode als ästhetisch-medialer Komplex, Kunstforum International Band 141, June–September.

Schleiner, A.-M. (1999). Female-bobs arrive at dusk. www.opensorcery.net/Female.bob.html.

Schmidt, B. U. (1999). Lara Croft—A "good girl" going everywhere. In M. Barth (Ed.), *LaraCroftism* (pp. 36–47). München: Kunstraum München.

Seesslen, G. (1984). Pacman & Co. In *Die Welt der Computerspiele*. Hamburg: Rowohlt.

Steele, V. (1996). Fetisch, mode, sex und macht. Hamburg: Rowohlt.

Williams, L. (1991). Film body. An implanatation of perversions. In R. Burnett (Ed.), *Explorations in film theory. Selected essays from ciné-tracts* (pp. 46–71). Bloomington: Indiana University Press.

Williams, L. (1990). Wenn sie hinschaut. In *Frauen und Film, 49*, 3–20.

Wolf, M.J.P. (Ed.). (2002). *The medium of the video game*. Austin: University of Texas Press.

19

GENDERED GAMING IN GENDERED SPACE

Jo Bryce and Jason Rutter

Digital gaming, like other leisure and consumption practices, inhabits human, social, and interactive space. Rule sets, programming code, and digital designs only become a game when they are played. Textual exegesis is not the main motivation for playing games; rather it is the experience, enjoyment, challenge, and competition derived from playing that is important. Placing digital games within such a social perspective raises questions not only about representation, but access, use, and the position of gaming within other social phenomena. One area where such a positioning is evidently important is when approaching gender and gaming.

This chapter unpacks the central issues that surround the gendering of gaming and highlights differences in approaches and questions that one might ask. It examines the paradox presented between quantitative reports and estimates suggesting comparatively high levels of female participation in digital gaming and ethnographic, or real world, observations of gaming events and cultures that continue to show a large inequality in gender participation.

Over the past twenty years, there have been frequent debates concerning the lack of female participation and representation in gaming, presenting it as one of the problematic aspects of this leisure activity. Some have claimed that the representation of females within digital games is consistently sexualized and stereotypical, potentially reinforcing societal objectification of women and use of sexual violence. Although not taking issue with such findings, this chapter broadens out some of these arguments, suggesting that issues relating to the gendering of computer gaming have often been oversimplified, ignoring the range of game genres and gaming spaces, and the complexity of the leisure activity in relation to broader gender dynamics.

Through this chapter we suggest that the gendering of computer gaming is consistent with the reinforcement and reproduction of established gender roles, and the gendering of particular leisure activities.

Our arguments aim to challenge the self-perpetuating myth of gaming as a male only activity and argue that female gamers do exist but are often rendered "invisible" by male-dominated gaming communities, the games industry, and academic research.

This we do through examining computer gaming in three key respects: *game content*, *gaming spaces*, and *gaming activities*.

The Central Paradox

Although boys and male adolescents appear as regular gamers in self-report investigations of the frequency of gaming in schoolchildren, even studies from the early and mid 1990s suggest that a large percentage of females report playing computer games for approximately one to two hours a week. For example, Funk (1993) found that 75 percent of females, compared with 90 percent of males, played computer games in the home, and Colwell and Payne (2000) showed that 88 percent of the twelve to fourteen-year-old females surveyed played computer games on a regular basis. Similarly, contemporary research reported by Interactive Digital Software Association (IDSA) suggests that approximately 42 percent of U.S. computer gamers are female (Interactive Digital Software Association, 2003).

Although we may question the methodologies of commercial research and its market agenda, such figures point toward a growing representation of women in computer gaming activities. Given such figures, why is there a continued alignment in both popular and academic discourses of digital gaming as a leisure pastime with boys, violence, and a masculine culture? Why are females assumed not to play with the "boys' toys"? Why is female participation in, and consumption of, gaming marginalized? Why are female gamers underrepresented in gaming competitions and events? Why, given the recent developments in digital game research and market analysis, are we still having problems locating the *invisible* female gamer?

A Research Context

Both academic and popular discourse have marginalized computer gaming as a leisure activity restricted to male children and adolescents, strongly associated with media effects discourse. This recurring discourse suggests that the consumption practices associated with computer gaming are solitary and male, that gaming is domestic and part of a transitional phase of leisure interest—something boys will grow out of. Research has consistently taken a media effects or text-based research perspective that fails to interrogate the everyday practices of being "a computer gamer" or being excluded from being so.

Commercial research has demonstrated the significance of computer gaming consumption by suggesting a far larger and more diverse consumer community for leisure software and gaming hardware. For example, ScreenDigest & the European Leisure Software Publishers Association[1] (ELSPA) have estimated that the global market for games and edutainment software will reach $18.5 billion in 2003. Additionally, they record that in the eight years between 1995 and 2003, almost nine software titles for each household were sold in the U.K., with over 900 million units in Europe, and nearly 3 billion globally being sold during that time (Screen-Digest and ELSPA, 2003).

However, this growing popularity of computer gaming and its strong association exclusively with children and adolescents has been frequently been constructed as problematic by parents, politicians, teachers, and the media. Relatives of a teacher killed in the shooting at Columbine High School in the United States recently named twenty-five companies in a lawsuit claiming $5 billion worth of damages from the games industry. Although the case was unsuccessful, it is notable that is was rejected not because of any perceived failure to link gaming and violence but because the court decided that producers of games could not have foreseen the future events that occurred in the "Columbine Massacre." This demonstrates the complex cultural and legal attitudes toward children, masculinity, and violence that form the media effects discourse.

In more mundane terms, a number of negative consequences are regularly offered as indications of the unhealthiness of gaming. These include suggestions that gaming precipitates aggressive behavior in real life, reduces involvement in social and educational activities, and reinforces gender stereotypes (Dill & Dill, 1998). Research concerns have also focused on the physical effects of the use of gaming technologies and the effects of lack of physical exercise and addiction in those spending significant amounts of leisure time playing computer games (Greenfield, 1994; Maeda et al., 1990; Spence, 1993). Further, some have raised concerns over the educational consequences of excessive computer gaming, although the claim that children and young adults who spend a significant amount of their leisure time playing computer games may be truant, neglect homework, and generally be less interested in their education is largely unsubstantiated (Creasey & Myers, 1986; Fromme, 2003; Griffiths, 1991). Similarly, existing literature that claims to support the hypothesized negative consequences of child and adolescent computer gaming is conflicting, lacking cohesion, and far from conclusive (Griffiths, 1999; Harris, 2001).

Defining Gender

At this stage it is necessary to present the working definition of "gender" that underpins the work included in this chapter.

Although the experience of gender is often linked to biological sex, the two terms are not interchangeable. Leplae provides a useful illustration of the difference between sex and gender when she points out that "women are biologically determined to have children [sex], but not to look after them [gender]" (Leplae, 2002). Gender is a social and cultural identity—conventionally associated with biological sex—that influences the way individuals present themselves to the world and the ways in which others act toward them. It also determines the norms, expectations, and roles regarded as acceptable, and the nature of interactions between and within the sexes.

This perspective claims that there is no "natural," unchangeable, or essential core to gender, or to what it means to be masculine and feminine. Gender is a way of labelling practices and individuals. It is culturally and historically specific such that gender identities and roles vary between and within cultures over time as the social frameworks that create and maintain gender differences change. Indeed, by dissociating gender from sex it becomes apparent that differences between males and females are socially constructed within our everyday social experiences. Thus, as Haraway points out:

Gender is always a relationship, not a preformed category of being or a possession that one can have. Gender does not pertain more to women than to men. Gender is the relation between variously constituted categories of men and women (and variously arrayed tropes), differentiated by nation, gen-

eration, class, lineage, color, and much else. (Haraway, 1997, p. 28)

This is useful in demonstrating that gender is not a politically neutral series of categorizations and that the enactment of gender roles has significant social consequences. Although it is beyond the remit of this chapter to explore fully different conceptualisations of sex and gender, in this chapter we will show how gender produces and maintains the power asymmetries, exclusions, and constraints that produce significantly different experiences of digital gaming for males and females.

Gendered Game Content

Analysis of the relationship between gender and computer gaming generally focuses on two issues: *representation of females within games* and the *dominance of masculine game themes*. The first of these issues takes a textual approach to the analysis of game content as embodying gendered, patriarchal, and stereotypical representations of females. Content analysis has highlighted a general lack of female game characters, and the sexualized and stereotypical representations of those female characters included within games (Bryce & Rutter, 2002; Dietz, 1998; Greenfield, 1994; Kafai, 1996; Kinder, 1996). This contributes to the perception that digital games embody masculine interests and activities, as part of a masculine culture that is at best unappealing, or at worst offensive, to females.

This research has demonstrated that female game characters are routinely represented in a narrowly stereotypical manner; for example, as princesses or wise old women in fantasy games, as objects waiting on male rescue, or as fetishized subjects of male gaze, which "has the power to see and not be seen" (Haraway, 1988) in first-person shooters (Bryce & Rutter, 2002; Dietz, 1998). Female characters in computer games fulfil roles linked to stereotypes of "feminine" skills and characteristics (Gailey, 1993). Such roles emphasize gendered passivity of the female characters against male action, and investigations into gaming texts often parallel work done on gender roles in children's books (Ernst, 1995; Fox, 1993; Temple, 1993). Similarly there has been a highlighting of the dominance of "masculine" game themes (e.g., war, competition, sports, acquisition, etc.), as well as high levels of game violence (Dietz, 1998; Greenfield, 1994; Kafai, 1996; Kinder, 1996). This further contributes to the perception that computer games embody masculine interests and activities.

The determinist view of gaming texts and the associated perceptions of gender differences in the popularity of computer gaming led to debates of whether games producers might encourage female gaming by producing games with a recognizably "feminine" theme. This brought about the release in 1991 of the pink version of Nintendo's GameBoy—predictably enough labelled the GameGirl—and a series of attempts to cash in on the "new" girl gamer market after the success of Mattel's *Barbie Fashion Designer*. As one might imagine, the majority of attempts to exploit the female gamer market by the larger publishers represents a discourse that works within and reproduces contemporary gendered stereotypes of what may be "appropriate" for female gamers.

However, there is a danger in extrapolating research on specific games that are not representative of the current range gaming texts, genres, and formats. Individual games, characters and violent representations must be considered in relation to the diverse variety of game genres and representations of violence in the contemporary games market. Within Europe and elsewhere a range of both mandatory and voluntary systems of game certification regulate game content and themes by offering guidelines on the appropriateness (or otherwise) of content ranging from innuendo to sexual violence; derogatory ethnic characterizations to portrayal of tobacco and alcohol use. These, largely industry developed, guidelines go some way to officially regulating sexualized representations of female game characters and depictions of violence toward women (see, for example, the Pan Europe Game Information scheme—www.pesi.info.).

Given the regulation of contemporary game content, some have claimed that levels of game violence have been overestimated. Academic literature on the prevalence of game violence suffers from a lack of conceptual clarity in defining game violence and its measurement, with studies using vague and varying definitions of violence and its prevalence in computer game content. Recent figures provided by ELSPA (ScreenDigest and ELSPA, 2000) suggest that over 90 percent of all the games rated by the U.K.'s Video Standards Council in the year 2000 were suitable for anyone up to the age of fifteen, and a large proportion of games published in the U.K. (69 percent) are suitable for the age range three to eleven.

Such contention highlights the need to consider the complexity of gendered representations in contemporary computer games and their reception. The noted stereotypical representations of female game characters takes a passive view of the meanings constructed in relation to representations of masculinity and femininity in games.

The linking of text or authorial intention and audience reading is problematic. Poststructuralist reading/audience theory and work influenced by the Birmingham Centre for Contemporary Cultural Studies has since the mid 1980s demonstrated the manner in which people take oppositional or even self-contradictory stances to texts while still enjoying them. In the context of gender and gaming it is overly deterministic to assume that there is a causal relationship between female representation in a text, and the nature of consumption of that text by female gamers.

This debate is highlighted by differences in the opinions between "girl gamers" and "grrrl gamers," as examined by Cassell and Jenkins (1998). Grrrl gamers claim that a significant amount of female gamers have similar game preferences, interests, and aptitudes in regard to "masculine" game themes as male gamers. They also disagree with the production of computer games that specifically target females (Cassell & Jenkins, 1998). Although this does not directly engage with the literature from leisure studies, such a viewpoint is consistent with the decreasing differentiation between male and female leisure activities. (We discuss this in greater detail in the next section.)

Claims about the gender appropriateness of texts, although structurally verifiable, can fall into a similar trap as approaches to representations of game violence: namely that they generalize from an unverified sample. With games based on licenses such as *Who Wants to Be a Millionaire*, *Pokémon* and *Weakest Link*, along with strategy games such as *The Sims* outselling first-person shooters and football games across gaming platforms, exclusionary arguments become somewhat difficult to maintain.

Recent research examining constructions of the meaning of media content has illustrated gender differences in the productive consumption of texts (Abercrombie & Longhurst, 1998; Jenkins, 1992; Radway, 1987). It is possible that females construct different meanings in relation to the themes of computer games (Bryce & Rutter, 2001), may play computer games in a masculine fashion, and/or may construct their own oppositional reading of game texts. This is consistent with research conducted by Gailey (1993) suggesting the active interpretation of cultural messages within games by children in relation to both class and gender.

Yates and Littleton (1999) also provide evidence of the productive consumption of game texts by male

and female gamers, suggesting that female gamers construct nonvoyeuristic perspectives on Lara Croft. They argued that female gamers distinguish "between structural elements (e.g., problem solving, strategy) and the representational elements (e.g., characters and graphics)" (p. 576), the effect of which was (among players of both genders) a diverse set of readings. Their research also highlights the importance of examining the social construction of computer gaming in the context of everyday life and leisure practices which can itself provide further understanding of the gender dynamics of computer gaming. Such an approach moves from textual exegesis and places gaming within a real world context in which gaming practices are negotiated in real time and space.

Gendered Spaces

Michel Foucault has described our age as "above all the epoch of space." He argues, "We are in the epoch of simultaneity: we are in the epoch of juxtaposition, the epoch of the near and far, of the side-by-side, of the dispersed" (Foucault, 1986, p. 22). For Foucault, as inhabitants in the modern world, we divide up and name the spaces we use. We appropriate them, move between them, and define the relationships between them. As such we have domestic space, private space, office space, leisure space, family space, religious space, and so forth.

The fact that computer and video games are situated and experienced within specific and local spaces is often overlooked in writing on gaming. In much of the utopian perspectives on online gaming the local and everyday world crumbles away in the clamor to explore the brave new digital frontier. The utopian or spectacular visions of digital gaming and online gaming communities neglect the more mundane, real world context and social environment within which gaming takes place. Drawing broadly on the sociology of interaction, we are able to move away from spectacular examples of gender work in digital gaming (e.g., Kennedy, 2002) to examine more representative experiences, as well as areas in which females are marginalized or excluded.

Through such a perspective, many of the routine and taken for granted modes of social interaction become apparent through a process described by Garfinkel as "making commonplace scenes visible" (Garfinkel, 1967, p. 36). This allows us to recognize that many of the "properties of social life that seem objective, factual, and transsituational, are actually managed accomplishments or achievements of local processes" (West &

Fenstermaker, 1993, p. 152). Although it is not our intention to explore it here, one may regard such a position as having parallels with situated knowledge (Haraway, 1988) or feminist standpoint theory (Harding, 1986; Harding & Hintikka, 1983; Smith, 1990). However, the interactionist perspective is not inherently political and has not been "constructed in opposition to the all-powerful dictates of rationalist/empiricist epistemologies" (Harding, 1997).

Both these perspectives make it apparent that the real world context and social environment within which gaming takes place is overlooked in textual content and media effects research. Computer gaming has most regularly been associated with "bedroom culture" (McRobbie, 1991; McRobbie & Garber, 1976). Originally conceived as female use of domestic space, bedroom culture highlights the manner in which girls are restricted from full access to many social spaces, and are instead left on the periphery of public social spaces (such as playgrounds). This concept contrasts with notions of the lack of female youth subcultures when compared with the male youth subcultures Hebdige describes (1979). It also permits the examination of the presence of female youth subcultures within the domestic rather than highly visual, public environments. With the increasing encroachment of public and masculine spaces into domestic environments (such as through the domestication of ICTs and consumption practices) and the growing privatization of childhood, the idea of bedroom culture has become less gender specific while still pointing toward a useful concept for understanding the space allocated young people for expression, leisure, and gaming practice (Livingstone & Bovill, 2001).

However, this is only one strand of the development of computer gaming and, as we have argued, gaming has a much broader demographic than its positioning as solely a children's toy. In mainframe computer labs, arcades, and bars, public computer gaming has predated domestic gaming in both chronology and technology. Although lab-based and textual research has all too often assumed an individual asocial space for gaming, it is impossible to neglect the fact that much gaming is social and played with friends in the playground and arcades, or with family in front of the TV. This suggests the concurrent existence of domestic gaming with developments and changes in leisure-related and competitive public gaming.

We maintain that many public gaming spaces are male-dominated and this gender asymmetry works toward excluding female gamers at a stage prior to the gendering of gaming texts. Our view is consistent with the gendering of public leisure spaces and their association with masculinity as places in which women are granted limited access and assume particular roles (Hey, 1984).

Public gaming spaces such as gaming competitions or LAN parties follow similar patterns and can therefore easily be considered to be masculine—that is, male dominated—spaces. This perception contributes to constraints on female access and participation in public gaming activities. Such exclusion may be reinforced by the stereotypical and offensive behavior of males toward females in public game spaces ranging from belittlement as "only girls," to patronizing female competitors through the well-meaning provision of prize giving, or objectification via the display of pornography at the event.

The gendering of public game spaces is consistent with ethnographic research conducted by the authors at the U.K. Console Championships (UKCC) and various U.K. LAN parties. The UKCC was undeniably a male event in both organization and competitor membership. The majority of females who did attend appeared to fit into acceptable nongamer roles. They were mothers who brought their sons to the competition (sometimes across a large part of the country) and who sat in the hotel foyers looking bored but offering support, encouragement, or sympathy when necessary. They played the role of girlfriends who, like mothers, were there to provide support and a listening ear but were displayed to enhance the cultural capital of the gamer. Even female competitors appeared marginalized regardless of the gaming aptitude. As with the playground proxemics alluded to above, at the UKCC female competitors were all too often relegated to the periphery of the events and often stood side-on to the consoles while watching others play, rather than the face-on stance of the male gamers intent on watching play.

Given the level of female gaming outlined above, it would seem reasonable to hypothesize that the invisibility of female gaming is a product of the general gender dynamics of public gaming rather than a verifiable lack of interest by females in computer games. Of course, to extrapolate from the invisibility of females at public gaming events to making assumptions about female domestic participation in computer gaming is problematic.

Indeed, there is growing evidence that many females prefer to participate in gaming within domestic contexts with friends, families, and partners (Buchanan & Funk, 1996; Griffiths & Hunt, 1995). This suggests that computer gaming may form part of joint leisure activities within existing social networks. Given the claimed importance of the social aspect of leisure for females, developments in multiplayer gaming may also encourage female participation, and this is borne out by IDSA's (IDSA, 2000) research that suggests that female gamers actually make up the majority of online gamers (53 percent). However, the issue remains one of understanding why this majority of gamers is effectively invisible from casual observation.

The idea that female activities are rendered invisible by patriarchal systems and behavior is not new. Just as in leisure activites such as digital gaming, it has been pointed out that women's contribution to work environments is marginalized and rendered invisible. For example, Stepulavage discusses the manner which in the workplace women's labor and achievements are framed as lacking in the need for knowledge and skilfulness (such as in the case of gendered roles such as administration or hairdressing). However, she successfully illustrates that this conception is a product of class, gender, and race relations, and where work is concerned "nothing is as simple as it seems." Indeed, our behavior and work practice has to be learned, tacit knowledge is required, and the relevance of potential solutions to a problem needs to be evaluated (Stepulevage, 1999). Such knowledge is often not put into words, written down in manuals, or taught through courses. It is know how—as Wajcman suggests often visual or tactile (Wajcman, 1991)—that intertwines with the actions that make technologies work.

Indeed, public game spaces are only one of many contemporary game spaces. Gaming now occurs in spaces that are multiple and provide simultaneous immersion in public and private leisure spaces (Bryce & Rutter, 2001). One profound aspect of the increasing merging of gaming platforms and network technologies is the manner in which online gaming offers the potential to extend social networks and allow public gaming in a domestic context. As networked gaming increasingly allows competitive leisure activity in domestic spaces, there are implications for the spatial organization of leisure and the blurring of geographical and game space. In these situations gaming is neither entirely domestic nor entirely public, occurring in virtual, social, and technologically mediated space (Bryce & Rutter, 2002).

Online gaming provides the opportunity to compete without the limitations of geographical location but, generally, within the limitations of temporal location (the obvious exception here are games such as email chess). This allows the formation of online communities around game skills and competencies. For female gamers, the anonymity of virtual game spaces provides the opportunity to compete against male opponents free from the markers of gender, reducing stereotypical behavior toward female gamers (Bryce & Rutter, 2002). Participation in these spaces may consequently lead to greater female participation in public competitive game spaces by building confidence in gaming skills and abilities that enable females to feel they can compete on a socially equal basis with male gamers.

Gendered Activities

Given that computer gaming is routinely claimed to be more popular and more frequently engaged in by males (Buchanan & Funk, 1996; Colwell, Grady, & Rhaiti, 1995; Dietz, 1998; Greenfield, 1994; Griffiths & Hunt, 1995; Kafai, 1996), it is seems a reasonable extrapolation that the activities and practices that constitute computer gaming are also gendered. Indeed, these are the activities that define computer gaming as a social practice. It is the negotiated experiences of everyday gaming that give a reality to game texts and realize the socially situated nature of gaming activities.

The gendering of gaming experiences is, in part, related to perceptions of gendered game content and notions of gender roles and appropriate leisure activities. Some have suggested that females are more affiliative and nurturing, preferring leisure activities that have a stronger social aspect (Grusec & Lytton, 1988). This, when linked to a general (but largely empirically unsupported) perception that gaming is not a social activity but a solitary activity for male "nerds" or "geeks," seems quite neatly to offer a model for understanding gendered gaming. However, such an argument is essentialist and circular in nature, ignoring the actual negotiation and resistance that occurs within gaming strategies.

This raises two issues that relate to the gendering of computer gaming: first, access and participation in gaming activity is restricted and exclusion is experienced at a local level. Second, that exclusion creates expectations of rejection that, together with the identification of gaming as a male activity, discourages women from attempting to enter into gaming practices or associating themselves with being "a gamer." Indeed, comparative studies of the frequency of gaming in males and females may also reflect a lack of self-identification as a gamer by females who may perceive themselves as infrequent gamers who have a more casual commitment to the activity (Bryce & Rutter, 2002).

Although neither of these propositions is inaccurate, the circular relationship of reinforcement that exists between them does not offer a position to examine the origins, or a means to break out, of the cycle. Indeed, as previously argued, gaming developments demonstrate that computer gaming is an increasingly social, public and multigendered leisure activity.

It is apparent that gaming practices are undergoing rapid social and technical changes, and at the same time it is noticeable that gendered perceptions of gaming are changing. This is demonstrated by groups such as grrl gamers—female online gaming clans and web communities. This is not a phenomenon unique to gaming, and is consistent with the increased participation of females in other leisure activities that have been previously perceived to be "male" (e.g., football/soccer, rugby, and extreme sports) (Bryce & Rutter, 2002). In such activities female players and gamers are not only seeking parity with male counterparts, but are adopting and enacting oppositional stances to categorizations of gender appropriateness, access to leisure activities, and consumption. Although we do not wish to argue in a Fiskian sense (Fiske, 1989) that all gaming is an act of political challenge, it is possible to understand female gaming within a context of resistance to the constraints placed upon female leisure in contemporary society. This is most clear in areas where visible female participation in "masculine" leisure activities challenges dominant gender stereotypes (Wearing, 1998).[2]

Crucially, however, it is not necessary to look toward spectacular acts of opposition or web-based presentations of the self to see evidence of the gendering of gaming activities and the routine exclusion of female gamers. Schott and Horrell (2000) successfully begin to unravel the routine and everyday manner in which gaming is negotiated in domestic settings. They demonstrate how, even in homes in which the gaming machine belongs to a female member of the family, it is fathers, brothers, or male cousins who take control of the technology as part of what they claim to be "support or collaborative play" (p. 41). Access to the technology and gaming is controlled by the male player who assumes the role of expert by interpolating the female gamer into a subordinate role. This creates an environment in which girl gamers are reproduced as not having the skills or technological competence to compete with the boys.

Such behavior reproduces the perception of computer gaming as a masculine and technological activity. Indeed, some have effectively argued that technology incorporates masculine culture and as such excludes

females through the promotion of the idea of female technological inferiority and the gendering of technological artefacts (Cockburn, 1985; Wajcman, 1991). Given that such technologies are central to computer gaming practices and activities, their perception as masculine is a vital, but often ignored, aspect of the gendering of gaming. Like the experience of gendered spaces, it is a form of gendered exclusion that is experienced, negotiated and reproduced at a routine and everyday level. This further contributes to the lack of visibility of the female gamer.

Conclusion

In the enthusiasm for digital gaming that has recently re-emerged within academic circles and its emphasis on technological progress, consumer choices, and digital texts, it is easy to forget that gaming technologies are commercial technologies. They are designed to maximize a place within a market and are located within an existing system of capital and power inequalities. The increased presence of gaming technologies within our homes, leisure areas, and other parts of our everyday lives obscures the fact that woman have had extremely limited involvement in the development of these technologies (and continue to do so).

Given that such technologies are central to digital gaming practices and activities, their perception as masculine is a vital, but often ignored, aspect of the gendering of gaming. Like the experience of gendered spaces, it is a form of exclusion that is experienced, negotiated, and reproduced at a routine and everyday level, further contributing to the lack of visibility of the female gamer.

There is a social turn that converts the technical aspects of digital gaming—the hardware and software—the things of "science," into the technologies that have a place within everyday routines and experiences. They become objects and agents that have use, meaning, visibility, and value within our homes and active lives. We negotiate the properties of these technologies through the things we do with and around them. As such, these properties are not permanently written (although it may be difficult to rewrite some of the more deeply scored meanings) but properties whose meaning is changeable, contextual, and, often, specific.

In this chapter we have argued that is it important to see gendered gaming situated beyond the game text, and that an overly deterministic approach to the construction and influence of gender is restrictive. Instead, we put forward the need to recognize that gendered

Jo Bryce and Jason Rutter

terms such as "masculinity" and "femininity" are not themselves unitary and static concepts but are given form and meaning through gendered interaction. We have argued for exploring the central importance of the local management and negotiation of gaming situations as well as the possibility of resistance to dominant concepts of masculinity and femininity within this local interaction.

Throughout this chapter we have argued against the fetishization of gaming texts or technologies. In exploring a form of leisure consumption such as computer gaming it is all too easy to give priority to the technology over the people who use it and to view technology as an autonomous agent acting upon the gendering of gaming. Like gaming texts, technologies are created within and incorporate specific cultural values, but these values are open to resistance, negotiation, rereading, and reproduction only through their use. This use is, we have argued, always situated and specific.

Acknowledgments

The authors would like to thank Judy Wajcman and Dale Southerton for support and helpful comments during the writing of this chapter.

Notes

1. Now the Entertainment and Leisure Software Publishers' Association.
2. Of course, the challenge of gender role is not necessarily unidirectional. It is also possible to consider the resistance of dominant conceptualizations of masculinity by male gamers. It is also possible that male gamers may construct an alternative masculine role that challenges the traditional masculine emphasis on physical strength and competition.

References

Abercrombie, N., & Longhurst, B. (1998). *Audiences.* London: Sage.

Bryce, J., & Rutter, J. (2001). In the game—in the flow: Presence in public computer gaming. www.digiplay.org.uk/Game.php.

Bryce, J., & Rutter, J. (2002). Spectacle of the death-match: Producing character and narrative in first-person shooters. In G. King & T. Krzywinska (Eds.), *Screenplay: Cinema-videogames-interfaces* (pp. 66–80). London: Wallflower Press.

Buchanan, D. D., & Funk, J. B. (1996). Video and computer games in the 90's: Children's time commitment and game preference. *Children Today, 24,* 12–15.

Cassell, J., & Jenkins, H. (1998). *From Barbie to Mortal Kombat: Gender and computer games.* London: MIT Press.

Cockburn, C. (1985). The material of male power. In: D. MacKenzie & J. Wajcman (Eds.), *The social shaping of technology,* Milton Keynes, Open University Press. pp. 125–146.

Colwell, J., Grady, C., & Rhaiti, S. (1995). Computer games, self-esteem and gratification of needs in adolescents. *Journal of Community and Applied Social Psychology, 5,* 195–206.

Colwell, J., & Payne, J. (2000). Negative correlates of computer game play in adolescents. *British Journal of Psychology, 91,* 295–310.

Creasey, G. L., & Myers, B. J. (1986). Video games and children—Effects on leisure activities, schoolwork, and peer involvement. *Merrill-Palmer Quarterly Journal of Developmental Psychology, 32,* 251–262.

Dietz, T. L. (1998). An Examination of violence and gender role portrayals in video games: Implications for gender socialization and aggressive behavior. *Sex Roles, 38,* 425–442.

Dill, K. E., & Dill, J. C. (1998). Video game violence: A review of the empirical literature. *Aggression and Violent Behavior, 3,* 407–428.

Ernst, S. B. (1995). Gender issues in books for children and young adults. In S. Lehr (Ed.), *Battling dragons: Issues and controversy in children's literature* (pp. 66–78). Portsmouth, NH: Heinemann.

Fiske, J. (1989). *Understanding popular culture.* London: Routledge.

Foucault, M. (1986). Of other spaces. *Diacritics, 16,* 22–27.

Fox, M. (1993). Men who weep, boys who dance: The gender agenda between the lines in children's literature. *Language Arts, 70,* 84–88.

Fromme, J. (2003). Computer games as a part of children's culture. *Game Studies, 3,* www.gamestudies.org/0301/fromme/.

Funk, J. B. (1993). Reevaluating the impact of computer games. *Clinical Paediatrics, 32,* 86–90.

Gailey, C. W. (1993). Mediated messages—Gender, class, and cosmos in home video games. *Journal of Popular Culture, 27*, 81–97.

Garfinkel, H. (1967). *Studies in ethnomethodology*. Englewood Cliffs, NJ: Prentice-Hall.

Greenfield, P. M. (1994). Video games as cultural artefacts. *Journal of Applied Developmental Psychology, 15*, 3–12.

Griffiths, M. (1991). Amusement machine playing in childhood and adolescence: A comparative analysis of video games and fruit machines. *Journal of Adolescence, 14*, 53–73.

Griffiths, M. (1999). Violent video games and aggression: A review of the literature. *Aggression and Violent Behavior, 4*, 203–212.

Griffiths, M., & Hunt, N. (1995). Computer game playing in adolescence—Prevalence and demographic indicators. *Journal of Community and Applied Social Psychology, 5*, 189–193.

Grusec, J. E., & Lytton, H. (1988). *Social development: History, theory, and research*. New York: Springer-Verlag.

Haraway, D. (1988). Situated knowledges: The science question in feminism and the privilege of partial perspective. *Feminist Studies, 14*, 575–599.

Haraway, D. (1997). *Modest witness @ second millennium femaleman meets Onco Mouse: Feminism and technoscience*. London: Routledge.

Harding, S. (1986). *The science question in feminism*, Ithaca, NY: Cornell University Press.

Harding, S. (1997). Comment on Hekman's "Truth and method: Feminist standpoint theory revisited": Whose standpoint needs the regimes of truth and reality? *Signs, 22*, 382–391.

Harding, S., & Hintikka, M. (Eds.). (1983). *Discovering reality: Feminist perspectives on epistemology, metaphysics, methodology, and the philosophy of science*. Dordrecht: Reidel.

Harris, J. (2001). *The effects of computer games on young children—A review of the research*. London: The Home Office.

Hebdige, D. (1979). *Subculture: The meaning of style*. London: Routledge.

Hey, V. (1984). *Pubs and patriarchy*. London: Tavistock.

IDSA. (2000). State of the industry report 2000–2001. Washington, DC: Interactive Digital Software Association.

Interactive Digital Software Association. (2003). Essential facts about the computer and video game industry: 2003 sales, demographics and usage data.

Jenkins, H. (1992). *Textual poachers: Television fans and participatory culture*. London: Routledge.

Kafai, Y. B. (1996). Electronic play worlds: Gender differences in children's construction of video games. In Y. B. Resnick (Ed.), *Constructionism in practice: Designing, thinking, and learning in a digital world* (pp. 25–38). Mahwah, NJ: Ablex.

Kennedy, H. (2002). Lara Croft: Feminist icon or cyberbimbo? On the limits of textual analysis. *Game Studies*, http://www.gamestudies.org/0202/kennedy/.

Kinder, M. (1996). Contextualising video game violence: From Teenage Mutant Ninja Turtles 1 to Mortal Kombat 2. In P. M. Greenfield & R. R. Cocking (Eds.), *Interacting with video* (pp. 28–35). Norwood, NJ: Ablex.

Leplae, J. (2002). Gender terminology, RoSa. http://www.rosadoc.be/site/maineng/pdf/17.pdf.

Livingstone, S., & Bovill, M. (Eds.). (2001). *Children and their changing media environment: A European comparative study*. Mahwah, NJ: Lawrence Erlbaum Associates.

Maeda, Y., Kitokawa, T., Sakamoto, K., & Kitamoto, I. (1990). Electroclinical study of video-game epilepsy. *Developmental Medicine and Child Neurology, 32*, 493–500.

McRobbie, A. (1991). *Feminism and youth culture: From Jackie to Just Seventeen*. London: Macmillan.

McRobbie, A., & Garber, J. (1976). Girls and subcultures. In S. Hall & T. Jefferson (Eds.), *Resistance through rituals: Youth subcultures in post-war Britain* (pp. 209–222). London: Hutchinson.

Radway, J. A. (1987). *Reading the romance: Women, patriarchy, and popular literature*. London: Verso.

Schott, G. R., & Horrel, K. R. (2000). Girl gamers and their relationship with the gaming culture. *Convergence, 6*, 36–53.

ScreenDigest, & ELSPA. (2000). Interactive leisure software: New platforms, new opportunities. London: Screen Digest.

ScreenDigest, & ELSPA. (2003). Interactive leisure software: Global market assessment and forecast to 2006. London: Screen Digest.

Smith, D. (1990). *The conceptual practices of power: A feminist sociology of knowledge*. Boston: Northeastern University Press.

Spence, S. A. (1993). Nintendo hallucinations: A new phenomenological entity. *Irish Journal of Psychological Medicine, 10*, 98–99.

Stepulevage, L. (1999). Becoming a technologist: Days in a girl's life. *Information, Communication & Society, 2*, 399–418.

Temple, C. (1993). If "Beauty" had been ugly? Reading against the grain of gender bias in children's books. *Language Arts, 70*, 89–93.

Wajcman, J. (1991). *Feminism confronts technology*. Cambridge: Polity.

Wearing, B. (1998). *Leisure and feminist theory*. London: Sage.

West, C., & Fenstermaker, S. (1993). Power, inequality, and the accomplishment of gender: An ethnomethodological view. In P. England (Ed.), *Theory on gender/feminism on theory* (pp. 151–174). New York: Aldine.

Yates, S. J., & Littleton, K. (1999). Understanding computer game cultures: A situated approach. *Information, Communication and Society, 2*, 566–583.

20

SERIOUS PLAY: PLAYING WITH RACE IN CONTEMPORARY GAMING CULTURE

Anna Everett

[W]ho would have predicted that young black and Latino males would spend enough time in Times Square video arcades during the late seventies to make those games the million-dollar industry that they are?
—Greg Tate

In the 80s and 90s you never saw black characters. If there were any black ones, they would get beat up, really whumped so fast, before they had time to get into character.
—Orpheus Hanley

I hacked another game and created a game called Blacklash.... I was fed up with companies making black games that have got no relation to black people whatsoever. You'll have someone make a game, and one of their characters got dreadlocks—and it's like someone put a mop on his head.[1]
—Richard-Pierre Davis

Machines have the morality of their inventors.
—Amiri Baraka

When my preteen niece challenged me to a game of *Super Mario Brothers* during a family Christmas gathering a decade ago, it was my reintroduction to video game play since my casual initiation during the *Pac-Man* and *Ms. Pac-Man* computer game craze of the mid 1980s. I was unprepared for the seductive and addicting qualities of this second generation of video games due, in part, to the striking evolution of gaming hardware and software packages, narrativity, and character designs from blocky, one-dimensional geometric renderings to the more technically accomplished Disneyesque animation standards featuring fully individuated cartoon character types. I am thinking here of Mario and Luigi, popular characters of the *Super Mario Brothers* game franchise, which has been described as "one of the best selling games ever."[2] At the time, I found the hand-eye coordination demands of interactive play (predicated on mastering the action keys of

Nintendo's control pads) a welcome distraction from and counterbalance to the cerebral demands of my graduate school course of study. From that moment on, I became a fan of video game entertainment, unaware of how this seemingly innocuous diversionary play would become an important part of my later scholarship and research interests.

Exhilarated by my easy mastery of relatively complex controller key commands and minimal "story" advancement demands, using intuition instead of manual instruction (although my niece talked me through the basics), I rushed out and bought my own Nintendo console and *Super Mario Brothers* game. Looking back on that pleasurably fateful Christmas break, I suspect the lure of video game play for me (an African American woman graduate student) was only differentiated from that of more traditional players to the extent that my pleasure inhered in a displacment of the high-stakes, immersive intellectual work of graduate study, temporarily, onto the no-stakes "immersive play" of the game. Of course this is not to suggest that traditional players are not highly educated. My point is to stress the suprising fetish object gameplay had become for me as my weekends increasingly became structured around this alternative mode of intellectual engagement and interactivity. The work/play dialectic of intellectual growth at school and digital dexterity (fingers in this case) at home effected a balanced scale of my "transmedia"[3] mastery during the ensuing decade, which happened to coincide with the gaming industry's own development of interactive play designs.[4]

However, as the current research progressed, my efforts to dissociate my objective study of race in video games from my subjective experiences with and frustrations about enjoying gaming, despite its encrusted discourses of racial difference and otherness, seemed less crucial. After all, Hayden White reminds us that hoary, or "outmoded conceptions of objectivity" do little to conceal the subjective nature of evidence and facts "constructed by the kinds of questions which the investigator asks of the phenomena before him"[5] (White, 1978, p. 43). Moreover, I am convinced that White's observations about objectivity in discourse production in the field of history remain pertinent. About writing histories of History, White argues, "It is difficult to get an objective history of a scholarly discipline, because if the historian is himself a practitioner of it, he is likely to be a devotee of one or another of its sects and hence biased; and if he is not a practitioner, he is unlikely to have the expertise necessary to distinguish between the significant and the insignificant events of the field's development" (p. 81). As a practitioner and historian of popular culture, and a longstanding fan and foe of video game texts, I share White's estimation, and easily recognize its applicability to my concern with examining race matters in the short history of video games.

Until late 1999, most public concern about video games focused on presumed dangerous behavioral consequences for minors and impressionable teens due to excessively violent content[6] and, to a lesser extent, on gender bias.[7] Race was the structured absence in this latest iteration of generation-gap politics between parent and youth cultures. The present discussion addresses this all-too-familiar lacuna by interpolating race matters into the fracas. I situate my critique of gaming culture within a discursive ambit that includes select game titles, video game journalism, personal interviews, and formal and informal survey data that specifically engage matters of race in video and computer games. Finally, I reference methodological approaches and precedents from influential and emerging scholarship on cultural theory, gaming, and other modes of contemporary popular culture as hermeneutic touchstones, or useful conceptual models in this interrogation.

Game Boys Remaster Orientalist and High-Tech Blackface Metanarratives

Because the video game industry privileges "boys in their pre- and early teen" years (Bolter & Grusin, 2000, p. 91), I am acutely aware that my mature, black, and female body is marked and thus marginalized as a shadow consumer in the gaming industry's multibillion dollar marketplace. Moreover, my informal surveys of video game cover art and game descriptions, print and online game reviews, manufacturer strategy guides, and popular media coverage of expert gamers uncover not only an essential and privileged male gaming subject, but one who is "universalized" under the sign of whiteness. For me, this distinct racial discourse in gaming culture's dramatic movement from its second- to third-

generation of sophisticated 3D character designs, with various racial types in tow, begged the question, "When and where does the racial problematic enter in contemporary culture's moral panics about gaming's potential dangers?"

Society's vocal moral outrage over gaming culture's gender troubles (to borrow Judith Butler's fecund phrase), especially its sexist and mysogynistic constructs of women and girls, did not find a parallel in terms of race. Nonetheless, racially offensive depictions of minority groups, namely blacks, Asians, and Jews, appear to demand similar scrutiny and just concern. To be sure, I am not suggesting returns to outmoded logics of behavioral and media effects determinism because we know the communication process is more complex and nuanced than that. And, Stuart Hall reminds us that dominant discourses, such as Orientalism, do not constitute a closed system of meaning in the sender–message–receiver feedback loop, because audience-receivers' interpretive processes are subject to distortions (Hall, 1986, pp. 134–135). Yet we must not underestimate the lure and "textual erotics" that certain representational possibilities promise over others. In other words, although it certainly is the case that readers/audiences and, of course, gamers can and do actively resist and often misread dominant plot structures, Peter Brooks's assertion that "the reading of plot [is] a form of desire that carries us forward, onward, and through the text" (Brooks, 1984, p. 37) is instructive. Thus we see that part of the pleasure *is* reading the plot "correctly" and as intended, which Brooks's notion of "textual erotics" illuminates. In this way, gaming plot structures that posit an occidental *self* in conflict with an oriental *other* structure in a narrative pleasure principle predicated upon Orientalism's binary logics.

After all, as Marsha Kinder warns in *Playing with power*, the danger in gaming's "cultural reinscriptions" is that "within particular social and economic contexts, the recognition of specific allusions makes certain intertextual relations payoff—especially at the point of purchase" (Kinder, 1991, p. 45). The payoff in these games' intertextual relations is their reinforcement of dominant culture's racist hegemony, and their redeployment and reification of specious racial difference for new generations and their new media culture industries. In his study of Asian American representations in American televisual discourses, Darrell Hamamoto stresses the fact that we must recognize how race is a fundamental organizing principle of America's pluralist society, and that we cannot afford to ignore the real consequences of this reality for nonwhite Americans

(Hamamoto, 1994, p. x). We know that popular culture texts are effective conduits for the transmission, if not preferred reception, of privileged socio-cultural-political messages and ideas. However, we should not presume some *a priori* value neutrality when narratives find novel expressive appratuses, such as with computer games.

Clearly, encryption message senders presume decryption message receivers, otherwise the attempted communication exchange process is futile, and more importantly, cost-ineffective. Given the importance of the profit motive in the gaming industry, we likewise can presume a correlative if not a cause-effect dynamic at work here. Even taking into account contemporary media theories of the polysemous nature of signs and signification, privileged cultural ideologies (i.e., race and gender differences) remain "transcendent signifiers" or primary cultural reference points. It is in such racialized and orientalizing discourses that Roland Barthes's assertion that there is no "zero degree of meaning" gains some material force. As Barthes cogently puts it, "discourse scrupulously keeps within a circle of solidarities … in which 'everything holds together'" (Barthes, 1974, p. 156), for gaming's readerly participants. In other words, we are confronted with the resilience and tenacity of ideology and its stranglehold on a particular circuit of cultural meaning. Terry Eagleton further clarifies the solidarities of how ideology holds together: "It is one of the functions of ideology to 'naturalize' social reality, to make it seem as innocent and unchangeable as Nature itself. Ideology seeks to convert culture into Nature, and the 'natural' sign is one of its weapons" (Eagleton, 1983, p. 117). These analyses remind us that resistance to what Wolfgang Iser calls an "ideal meaning" and its corollary the "ideal reader" are predicated upon, in this case, an understanding of encrypted (or encoded) meanings that represent desirable gaming heroes naturally as predominantly white, and victims and antagonists naturally as nonwhite "others."

What, then, are the means by which we can effectively explore this racialized meaning-encryption-decryption feedback loop in popular and alternative computer games? To the extent that gaming's readerly and writerly narrative structures draw upon and are imbricated in such traditional meaning-making media as print, theater, film, and television, insights gained from influential and emerging work on ideologies and theories of race become especially productive. Indeed, poststructuralist, postcolonial, and critical race theories, whiteness studies, and cultural studies provide effective epistemological lenses for critiquing the racial discourse in gaming's parallel and support industries: the computer magazines and specific game tie-ins—the strategy guides.

"Reading Race" in Video Game User Manuals and Strategy Guide Texts

Because videogame magazines and strategy guides increasingly constitute a significant element of gaming culture's specific narrative dispositions and logics of mastery, how they engage the racial problematic becomes a key concern in this study. Any excursion into computer superstores, or perusals of retail store magazine aisles and magazine stands conveys well the sophisticated nature of these specialized texts' visual appeal. To compete in an oversaturated marketplace, gaming magazines, like the others, attract their readers with splashy and visually sumptuous cover art, usually featuring recognizable game characters in striking and vibrant photorealistic renderings. Other visceral lures in cover art feature celebrity images and interviews, film or TV show tie-ins to games, samples of "free games," scantily clad, buxom young women, and most important, text promising "cheat" keys to mastering gameplay such as "the latest tricks, tips, and game shark codes,"[8] or "how to unlock each character."[9]

Although the gaming magazine and strategy guides' cover art warrant detailed analyses of their own, we are most concerned with the textual discourses and meaning assumptions between the covers. To investigate the racial discourse of these specialized texts, I have selected as exemplars *Next Generation* (October 1996), *Computer Player* (October 1996), *Playstation Magazine* (October 1999), *Incite* (2000, both Video and PC Gaming editions), and *Prima's Official Strategy Guide* (2000, both their *Ready 2 Rumble Boxing: Round Two*, and *Tekken Tag Tournament* editions) (figures 20.1, 20.2).

That there are specific generic, ideological, and representational coherences unifying these different texts is granted and thus not at issue. However, it is the photographic confirmation of an unbearable whiteness of being underpinning the editorial hierarchies and advertising copy of these magazines that suggested this particular line of inquiry. For instance, the investigative journalism in Michael Marriott's *New York Times* article "Blood, gore, sex and now race: Are game makers creating convincing new characters or 'high-tech blackface'?" and Anthima Chansanchai's *Village Voice* article "Yellow perils: Online 'coolies' rile Asian Americans" foregrounds the dominance of white males in video

| Figure 20.1 |
Prima's Official Strategy Guide for Midway's game sequel *Ready 2 Rumble Boxing: Round 2* (© Prima Games)

game design and production. But it was the above mentioned gaming magazines' own practices of including photos or drawings of their editorial teams, ad copy featuring young white males as ideal consumers, and the strategy guides' rhetorical privileging of white game characters that struck me. And although *Incite*'s "PC Gaming" magazine features photos of its lone black and two Asian males, and one white woman, among its nine-member editorial team, I would argue that this racial inclusiveness, though important, does little to balance the magazine's overriding narrative ecology of whiteness.

Another ideological touchstone informing our concern with the intersections of race, representation, and gaming interactivity is the matter of new media commercialization. Along this critical axis, the editors of one *Next Generation* (*NG*) article sum up the limitations of the gaming industry's ability to break out of dominant culture's discursive formations because of their commercial imperatives. In its special feature article "Money Makes the Games Go Round," the *NG* editors admit that:

From Silicon Graphics to 3DO, the world of gaming comes with strings attached, held in the hands of a coterie of venture capitalists.... You might think that the game business is driven by creativity, which it is to a greater degree, but the barriers to entry get higher every day.... The cost of distribution, marketing, and of course, development for games are reaching Hollywood proportions.... You end up paying the stores all kinds of marketing money to get them to put your product on the shelf. On top of all this, you have to

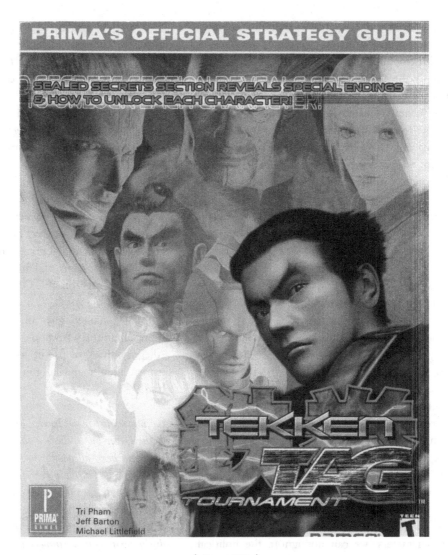

PRIMA'S OFFICIAL STRATEGY GUIDE

SEALED SECRETS SECTION REVEALS SPECIAL ENDINGS
& HOW TO UNLOCK EACH CHARACTER!

Tri Pham
Jeff Barton
Michael Littlefield

| Figure 20.2 |
Nameco's *Tekken Tag Tournament* (© Prima Games)

make sure that people know your software is out there. Now, what developer can afford to do all that?[10]

The answer, of course, is that gaming magazines are tapped to share the financial burden of marketing games to this very lucrative target market. Unquestionably, then, our analysis must encompass this commodification of gaming narrativity and iconographical representations, which we know from other media texts are difficult to disaggregate from dominant cultures' institutional racism, or what Aldon Lynn Nielsen discusses as the "frozen metaphors within American speech" (Nielsen, 1988, p. 3).

In Nielsen's analysis of how poetic language often constructs representational blackness within a "white discourse as a set of self-confirming propositions," we find a useful approach for avoiding essentializing positions in this look at gaming discourse. As he correctly points out:

Through the power of white hegemony, the signifiers of that system have been placed into circulation within society such that they are distributed fairly evenly across the population. It is thus not necessary that the full discourse appear each time that its operations are to be manifested. It is required, as [Hans Robert] Jauss has pointed out, only that one element of the system be presented. . . . Only one small portion of the imaging system, only a suggestion of blackness need appear for the entire structure to be articulated. (p. 6)

This is an important point because it reminds us that rarely is language as transparent or clear-cut as once imagined. Instead, as part of a cultural as well as linguistic syntax and structure, words are often sedimented with troubling ideologies of race. For example, in designing the game *Daikatana*, John Romero of *Doom* and *Quake* fame created "a well muscled African American [character named] Superfly Johnson." As imagined by Romero, this character was crafted to be a "large menacing character" (quoted in Chansanchai, 1997, p. 25) who achieves his narrative and gameplay impact through an intertextual reference to American society's reified imagery of the criminalized black male brute icon of historic films and television news. This is in addition to the character's easily understood Blaxploitation film moniker *Superfly*. If we have learned anything from semiotics, structuralism, and poststructuralism's influential critical demystifications of linguistic and imagistic signifying functions, as Nielsen illustrates, it is that cultural inscriptions acquire meaning only as part of intact language systems that more or less rely on readers' varying fluency in diverse media literacies.

To reiterate a previous point, this presumptive media literacy thesis does not foreclose what cultural studies' proponents advocate as readers' negotiated and oppositional reading practices against such ideal meaning—reception structures. So, despite the fact that gamers might read against, say *Prima's Official Strategy Guide*'s penchant for privileging *Ready 2 Rumble Boxing: Round 2*'s white characters against the game's nonwhite characters in the mode of address and descriptions of racialized characters, we can not ignore the political economy served by the games' and game magazine editors' abilities to draw upon only a small portion of racial difference signifiers to naturalize their strategic positioning of white characters to maximize game points.

The focus here on some rhetorical contours of gaming magazines' and strategy guides' racial discourses reveals a binary address to ideal players according to a racialized "You" versus "Them" conflict structure that is rapidly becoming a standard and understood functional motif. The problem is that such standardization practices increasingly reify or naturalize nonwhite characters as objectified third-person Others whose alterity[11] is so irremediably different that ideal players would have little to no incentive to adopt them as avatars or skins. Indeed, the welcome diversification of game characters is significantly delegitimated when minority characters function primarily as objects of oppression, derision, or as narrative obstacles to be overcome or mastered.

Another structured form of gameplay based on racialized characters is crafted by designers of the role play game *Imperialism: The Fine Art of Conquering the World*. This particular game conveys explicitly gaming's colonialist remythologizing aspects along the lines of what Abdul R. JanMohamed terms "the economy of the Manichean Allegory." *Imperialism* is a neo-colonialist strategy-sim game that bears out the racist logic of colonialist power relations that postcolonial theorist Abdul R. JanMohamed describes: "The colonialist's military superiority ensures a complete projection of his self on the Other: exercising his assumed superiority, he destroys without any significant qualms the effectiveness of indigenous economic, social, political, legal moral systems and imposes his own versions of these structures on the Other" (JanMohamed, 1995, p. 20).

JanMohamed goes on to highlight colonialism's representational economies in terms of an Manichean Allegory that are useful for us when thinking about games, their manuals, guides, and iconographies. For him,

the imperialist is not fixated on specific images or stereotypes of the Other but rather on the affective benefits proffered by the manichean allegory, which generates the various stereotypes.... The fetishizing strategy and the allegorical mechanism not only permit a rapid exchange of denigrating images which can be used to maintain a sense of moral difference; they also allow the writer to transform social and historical dissimilarities into universal, metaphysical differences.... African natives can be collapsed into African Animals and mystified still further as some magical essence of the continent. (pp. 21–22)

In the game manual's section called "Imperialism Basics," the countries in *Imperialism* articulate not only how certain racialized characters are programmed at a strategic disadvantage, but how the game structures-in biased advantages. As if a complete confirmation of JanMohamed's charge, the manual states:

In Imperialism *there are two types of countries. The first type, Great Powers, are actors in the game, each ruled by a human or by a wily computer foe. The second type,* Minor Nations, serve as regions for exploitation and battle by the Great Powers. *A Minor Nation in* Imperialism cannot *develop into a Great Power*, nor can it win the game.... *In* Imperialism, *colonization refers to a "peaceful" takeover.* (*Imperialism* manual, 1997, p. 13 [emphases added])

| Figure 20.3 |
Imperialism's game box cover design (© Strategic Simulations)

It is telling enough that *Imperialism* programs a nineteenth-century colonialist military ethos into contemporary gameplay, as it states, "modeled on the real world of the nineteenth century" (p. 1), yet recasting colonialism as "peaceful." But coupled with the game's striking cover art displaying an illuminated white-skin hand grasping a globe (figure 20.3), such representational economies advance a worrisome, yet unrepentant ideology of neo-colonialist Eurocentrism that posits imperialism as spreading the necessary light of western civilization. And given this game's obvious Eurocentrism, it might be reasonable to presume its relative lack of appeal for nonwhite gamers interested in mastering strategy-sim games.

However, one gamer informed me that this particular genre does not necessarily foreclose participation, pleasure, and mastery from those gamers other than the ideal or targeted end user. In his article "Black spectatorship: Problems of identification and resistance," Manthia Diawara problematizes what he calls the "impossible position" of black spectators, which bears similarly on black gamers. Following feminist filmmaker and theorist Laura Mulvey's ideas of gendered spectatorship, Diawara notes that black film spectators' pleasure in film and TV texts are obtained via transgender and transracial identification with white male characters as heroic ideals (Diawara, 1993, pp. 211–214) or by resisting this narrative hegemony altogether through "active criticism" and oppositional filmmaking (p. 219). I have argued elsewhere and in a related context that black spectators attenuate their visual displeasure by deliberately misreading "explicit antiblack character types so as to recode and reinvest such images with transcendent meanings to suit their own visual imaginings" (Everett, 2001, p. 309). Such approaches certainly seem pertinent to and applicable strategies for black gamers.

Civilize This! Or in Geek-Speak: RTFM!

Despite game designs' restraint on users according to what Jean Francois Lyotard suggests is the tyranny of the computer bit (the basic unit of information regulated and circumscribed by the programmer) (Lyotard, 1991, p. 34), one black geek lets us in on some subversive tactics and strategies to avoid such gaming circumscription and frustration. This geek, University of California, Santa Cruz doctoral candidate Rebecca Hall, informed me that the first rule of geekness is to RTFM (*read the freaking manual*), and for gamers it is essential for circumventing the game's prescriptions, understanding its Byzantine rules, and mastering the gameplay of any genre. Hall finds it important to read closely and thoroughly any game's manual before attempting to play because she hates having an information deficit when her goal is to overcome some games' discursive tyranny. Hall became a video game fan in the mid 1980s. A favorite game was Avalon Hill's *Civilization*, a precursor to such strategy-sims as *Imperalism*. What is interesting about Hall's approach to *Civilization* and what makes it pertinent to our study is her example of how people actually play these games. In addition, her deployment of a stealth essentialism strategy that allows her to win games by playing against the norm speaks volumes about gamers' willingness to refuse and reject games' privileged narratives while still finding hours of challenging and pleasurable play. Hall's own description of her gameplay makes the point convincingly. It is important, however, to note that *Civilization* is not a wargame (wargames do not generally appeal to female gamers), but according to one website, FunagainGames, "The object of the game is to gain a level of overall advancement to which cultural, economic, and politial factors are important. The winner is the player who maintains the best balance between activities of nomads, farmers, citizens, merchants and adventurers."[12]

Hall's gameplay is a novel enactment of this ideal scenario, and how she describes her stealth essentialism approach is revealing. The game begins with the dawning of civilizations somewhere between 4000–8000 B.C. to 250 B.C. What Hall appreciates most about the game is that game players set the condition for winning, whether it is through world conquest, being the first to launch a successful spaceship from earth, spiritual transcendence, or heading a world-class government. Where some of her acquaintances who play the game opt for traditional European civilizations as game avatars, she also notes that the game presents other options as well.[13] As she puts it:

There are ten-fifteen different peoples that you can pick, and they have different characteristics, like the Zulu, who are militaristic and expansionistic. This means you go into the game with certain technologies and advantages (military). And in this way it is coded. The Egyptians are spiritual and commercial, the Americans (I don't know why there

are Americans and Abe Lincoln in 4000 B.C., right?) ... And there's the Sioux and the Chinese.... They all have strengths and weaknesses, and anyone of them can win.[14]

As for Hall, it is important to play and win as an African civilization, which the game essentializes as Chaka Zulu (although sometimes she renames the character after an actually existing seventeenth-century African queen of Angola, named Nzenga). Hall continues:

When I play the Zulu ... [with rules establishing that] you know how to build stone walls and you have the wheel. And then you've got to dedicate certain of your resources to research. So over time you learn more and more technology. If you pick a culture that is scientific you start ahead of the game. But the Zulu are not scientific. So what I do (and this is where the resistance part comes in) is, I take the military advantage that is there, but then I focus more of the resources on the scientific. By the time I get to 1000 B.C. they are both the strongest militarily and the strongest scientifically, which positions them in a way that is stronger than the other groups.... There is also a telos.... After you've done enough research you go into different ages, like the Barbarian Age, the Premodern, the Enlightenment, whatever. And by the time you get to the 1800s, and the way I play it, the Zulus have the railroad by 1000 A.D. You see Chaka in a suit, with the bone piercing in the ear—you know. So, its got the Western telos—right, but, it's a little bit subversive, and it is racially coded [according to white norms].... I wonder how much I am deluding myself, but this game is different.[15]

Hall is not alone in her appreciation of *Civilization*'s various interactive modes wherein militarism is merely one of its many strategic foci. Other gamers, some hailing from Germany, England, and so on, who reviewed the game *Civilization* for the website FunagainGames, also find its nonwargame emphasis particularly appealing. As Lane Taylor from London writes to the website, "*Civilization* is NOT a war game ... or is it? The great thing about this game is that it can be different things to different people. If you want to play it as a war game, you can; if you want to play as a trading game, you can; if you want to play as a building game, you can." For Hall, it was finally a chance to "pick the Zulu and kick everybodies' asses" both militarily and scientifically in a popular videogame not designed for that purpose. And no matter how opaque, incomplete, and generally incompetent the technical writing of the manuals, Hall's example reminds us of the necessity to

RTFM before one can effectively resist or transgress programmers' tyranny of the bit!

Playing the "Skin" Game

Where the strategy-sims marginalize the Other, both qualitatively and quantitatively, gaming's sports and fighting genres, by contrast, foreground the Other in their interactive fictions. Still, first-person games such as Nameco's *Tekken Tag Tournament* and Midway's *Ready 2 Rumble Boxing: Round 2*, for example, are in little danger of contributing to what Uma Narayan and Sandra Harding call "decentering the center." It is difficult to discern any progress between sports and fighting games' overrepresentation of racial minorities and strategy-sims' underrepresentation of these groups when white male characters (especially Americans) are continually privileged. For example, as in real life (RL) sports, all of the characters in *Ready 2 Rumble Boxing: Round 2* (R2R-2) bear colorful names and nicknames that enliven and amplify their stereotypical "personalities," and delimited skills (figure 20.4). The problem is that such charged enunciations appearing in strategy guides and manuals either fire or dull users' imaginations as they "select" or choose to play as these highly racialized game "skins." Writing for *Prima's Official Strategy Guide to R2R-2*, Keith Kolmos and his team reinforce heroic and sympathetic stereotypes of white game characters, while redeploying ridiculous and pernicious ones for black and other Others.

Afro Thunder and his cousin G. C. Thunder as "arch rivals" not only evoke the discourse of black-on-black violence, but because the former "went Hollywood for a while" (Kolmos, 2000, p. 22) and the latter uses "boxing as a vehicle for opening a chain of hair facilities" (p. 62), and because each is "more of a performer than a boxer," these black skins are silly, malevolent, and trivialized dissimulations of black boxers' RL dominance of the sport. Furthermore, black skin Butcher Brown's King Kong look, "much-needed mental stability" and "banned ... deadly knock-out punch" complete the familiar rhetoric of black male criminality and brawn over brains image. (Interestingly, these characters "special moves," and "combo moves" were programmed with too many skill deficits to be purely coincidental or insignificant.)

Again, high-tech blackface and black "skins" are not the only representational casualties of the "joystick nation," to borrow J. C. Herz's terminology. As surprised as I was to discover Maori, Brazilian, Hawaiian, Taiwanese, Mexican, and Thailand "skins" also among

Midway's *R2R-2* pugilistic ensemble, I was less surprised by the rhetoric and rendering that constructed them. Like the black American "skins," these other racialized Others also were marked by such rhetorical differences as "Beast from the East," "Maori fighting ways are savage," "400-pounder ... short on ring experience but long in the tooth," "lacking confidence," and so on. These are not exactly the skill levels that lure most users. These avatars are even more undesirable when white, ethnic "skins" representing Italy, Croatia, England, Canada, and America are described sympathetically, powerfully, and affirmatively: "high tolerance for pain," "dedicated to boxing," "story is enough to bring a tear to your eye," "out to prove to the world that he'll be able to beat the best with just one hand," "although he's laid back, Brock gets pretty serious when he hits the canvas," "improved on his formerly rudimentary boxing skills," "refined skills and superior knowledge of the sweet science" (Kolmos, 2000, p. 34–73). With such visual and narrative inducements, and at costs ranging from five to more than fourteen dollars an issue, these texts and their alluring codifications of whiteness should not be underestimated. After all, stories of the comic book's strong influence on directors of films, music videos, and television shows are legion and legendary. To some extent, these guides seem more potent as imagistic ideals for the computer literate Internet generation. And their discourses of racial difference can be subtle and disarming.

Conclusion: *Ethnic Cleansing*—The Game

[Ethnic Cleansing is] the most politically incorrect video game made. Run through the ghetto blasting away various blacks and spics in an attempt to gain entrance to the subway system, where the jews have hidden to avoid the carnage. Then, if YOU'RE lucky ... you can blow away jews as they scream "Oy Vey!," on your way to their command center. The Race war has begun. Your skin is your uniform in this battle for the survival of your kind.—Ethnic Cleansing[16]

In February 2002, analysts of the U.S. videogame industry announced record shattering retail sales of interactive game units in 2001 that topped out at $9.4 billion.[17] That same month, cybersleuth H.A. alerted our virtual community on the Afrofuturism listserv to the existence of an alarming, tour de force racist computer game called *Ethnic Cleansing* by simply posting its URL, or web address, under the subject "Ethnic

(a)

(b)

(c)

(d)

(e)

| Figure 20.4 |

(a) Butcher Brown, (b) Selene Strike, (c) Jet "Iron" Chin, (d) Ma Ma Tua, (e) Wild "Stubby" Corley (© Prima Games)

Cleansing: The Game!" Despite H.A.'s uncharacteristic lack of commentary in that initial post, the following few days were abuzz in thoughtfully passionate, detached, enraged, and engaged responses. For some, the question concerned whether or not black people should use the same "powerful open source game engine, Genesis 3D," used to create the racist *Ethnic Cleansing* game, to create games of retaliation or overdue reparations for centuries of oppression and legalized injustice against African Americans. Others, especially L.d.J., were unconvinced that the Internet could be "the great equalizer," given troubling developments in gaming culture as reported by the Anti Defamation League (ADL). L.d. J. posted information from the ADL on hate groups' "manipulation of available technology to create violently racist and anti-Semitic versions of popular video games ... with titles such as *Ethnic Cleansing* and *Shoot the Blacks*."[18]

Clearly such use of the Internet for recruiting youths to the ideology of hate does not exactly embody the progressive revolutionary imperative of the temporary autonomous zone (TAZ) that Hakim Bey imagined when he spoke of data-piracy and other forms of leeching off the Internet itself for "reality hacking" and "the free flow of ideas" (Bey, 1991, p. 108). But the fact remains that manipulated games began proliferating on the Internet to be "previewed, purchased or downloaded on the websites of the nation's most dangerous hate groups" including "neo-Nazis, white supremacist and Holocaust deniers."[19] The ADL reports that "In 'Ethnic Cleansing,' the player kills Blacks and Hispanics (the game uses pejorative terms) before entering a subway ... sound effects, described as 'Realistic Negro Sounds,' turn out to be 'monkey and ape sounds' that play when dark-skinned characters are killed in the game's first level."[20] What struck me about this particular egregiousness was its eerie resonance with Lester A. Walton's 1909 essay about "The degeneracy of the moving picture theater," where Walton describes his encounter with the early cinema's profiteering on black pain and suffering. Walton writes incredulously: "Several days ago, the writer was surprised to see a sign prominently displayed in front of the place bearing the following large print 'JOHN SMITH OF PARIS, TEXAS, BURNED AT THE STAKE. HEAR HIS MOANS AND GROANS. PRICE ONE CENT!'" (Walton, 1909, p. 6). Most salient here is Walton's admonition that our failure to protest vigorously against such racist commodification of black victimhood would engender worse images in the future. As Walton put it, "If we do not start now to put an end to this insult to

the race, expect to see more shocking pictures with the Negro as subject in the near future" (p. 6). Certainly there has been a steady historical progression of pernicious representations of blackness in many film and television texts that bear out Walton's prescience. Unfortunately, video games such as *Ethnic Cleansing* only exacerbate the situation.

Exactly one month after H.A. posted *Ethnic Cleansing*'s URL to the Afrofuturism list, ABC's *World News Tonight* ran a segment on the game and its intergenerational group of hatemongerers, revealing that the game's January 20, 2002 launch was planned to coincide with the nation's official Martin Luther King, Jr. holiday.

This is not the only time television has addressed gaming issues. On July 10, 2002, ABC's news show *Nightline* aired a program entitled "Just a Game: Playing *Grand Theft Auto 3*" (*GTA3*) that interrogates this game's excessive violence, incredible photorealism, amazing popularity, and staggering financial success. Certainly, I am interested in *Nightline*'s disclosure that *GTA3* has sold three and a half million copies at $50 each, and concerns about the game's "stunning realism" taking interactive gaming to a new level.[21] However, I am more interested in how the discourse of race and gaming gets played out in *Nightline*'s latest moral panic and traditional versus new media rivalry episode couched as news. *Nightline* points out the fact that the games' graphic violence has attracted both detractors and loyal consumers, that the U.S. congress has denounced the game, and that *GTA3* has been outlawed in Australia, with other countries considering bans. The program also highlights the debate about whether or not *GTA3*'s high-tech make-believe and ferocity might be considered cathartic, whereas others ask if *GTA3* and others of its ilk should be called games at all.[22]

Obviously this timely show has a general relevance for this essay because it concerns video games and social values. However, certain aspects are especially pertinent as these issues intersect with race matters. First of all, *Nightline*'s in-studio panel of four, including host Ted Koppel, consists only of white males. And despite the show's packaged introductory piece featuring African American reporter Michele Martin, the all-white male panel assembled to discuss the issue displays the still unbearable whiteness of being in mainstream media's future vision and current conceptualizations of new media technologies and gaming cultures' increasing cultural power and much-lamented societal influences. Secondly, I was struck by the fact that the only representations of "minority" (particularly black) characters in *Nightline*'s select video clips of *GTA3* were victims of the game's narrative violence meted out quite gratuitously by the game's white male protagonist. At this point it is important to state that *Nightline*'s all-white and all-male panel is not the biggest problem here. The biggest problem is that *Nightline* anchor Ted Koppel and his fellow white male guests, D.C. police officer Sergeant Gerald Neill, seventeen-year-old *GTA3* player Steve Crenshaw, and Cornel University instructor James Garbarino, find a way to evoke black criminality despite the obvious absence of blacks as gamers or participant agents in this story. Moreover, this panel constructs a narrative of normative suburban whiteness capable of neutralizing and policing video games' violent influences that, noticeably, hinges on conflating real life street-level violence in urban areas with the game's virtual urban violence.

Now, what angered me about this hyperbolic discussion of video game violence and the show in general was the fact that the show began with exculpatory rhetoric surrounding a white, seemingly middle- to upper-class female parent who purchased *GTA3* for her underaged, thirteen-year-old son and two of his same-aged white friends to enjoy and master, despite the game's clearly labeled warning of unsuitability for children. *Nightline* continued in this vein by using seventeen-year-old Steve Crenshaw as a privileged *GTA3* native informant who could serve double duty. First, he signified an older, more age appropriate and mature white teenaged boy fan of *GTA3* (obviously one experienced with earlier iterations of the *Grand Theft Auto* game). And second, Crenshaw's apparent normalcy and reiteration of the thirteen-year-old's statement that gamers understood the difference between real life and video game fantasy functioned to absolve the thirteen-year-old *GTA3* player, his irresponsible mother, and his two friends of blame. And, as I have been arguing throughout this chapter, a significant transposition is effected around race, but in this instance *Nightline*'s Koppel, the police officer, and the elite university instructor effectively displace *GTA3*'s social menace onto urban—read black—communities. Even though *Nightline*'s television viewers are shown powerful images of *GTA3*'s white male protagonist's unprovoked shootings of police officers and prostitutes (with graphic displays of blood spurting from their wounded digital bodies), and his hit and run vehicular massacres of black and other characters for extra game points, still Koppel, Sergeant Neill, and instructor Garbarino unproblematically inculpate blackness, or more accurately urban people, as the problem.

The consensus of the panelists is that *GTA3*'s narrative fantasy becomes a dangerous step toward reality for those who desire to act out the game's violent scenarios. *Nightline*'s experts do concede that most kids won't go out and kill. However, when Koppel, asks Sergeant Neill to use his twenty-plus years of police experience to ascertain where *GTA3* might rank in comparison to "poverty, drugs, gang warfare," as a societal threat, he betrays a racist assumption about which groups are susceptible to gaming's putative corruptions, especially with such racially charged signifiers of urban decay and blight. Sergeant Neill's reponse is equally telling. He states: "This is a game. But it is a violent game. There is a thing called *urban terror*. There are some parts that are controlled by *armed youths who are urban terrorists*, and this game isn't a part of that for the average person. But for someone who lives in *that* neighborhood, *his reality is different from Steve*'s"[23] [emphasis added]. Again, the implicit racial opposition being constructed here cannot be denied. For young Steve Crenshaw not only functions in this rhetoric as the responsible, white face of *GTA3* fandom, but the sergeant is clearly positioning him as an average person in opposition to youthful urban terrorists that most *Nightline* viewers would presume to be poor black and other minority youths. Once again, the hegemony of white supremacy is interpolated here and it only undermines sober and fair discussion about gaming culture and its uses and abuses.

Returning briefly to the Afrofuturism list's engagement with the racist videogame *Ethnic Cleansing*, a few points should be made. Significantly, responses to the game were varied, cogent, passionate, thoughtful, and quite provocative. The discussion thread ranged from ideas about the creation of black owned and operated video game businesses, including the establishment of manufacturing factories in Africa;[24] the development of black games and game consoles with the goal of replicating a movement much like "what the black comic book industry did in the early 90's."[25] Still others saw the issue in much broader global terms, and within a post-September 11 ideological context. For example, regarding historical racism in gaming, g-tech writes:

In fact, if you really want to be technical about it games like this have existed for, oh ... maybe fifteen years or so since the first iteration of DOOM to be exact. Nothing new here. What has changed is the ability of propaganda pieces like this to garner attention, thus giving them a bit of legitimacy and free press.... In essence, we are doing the work for them.... The gaming community isn't dumb, they aren't mindless drones who are being brainwashed or hypnotized. They are people like you, me, the guy across the street, etc. who are probably getting a bigger kick out of the competition of winning rather than the look of the toons (toons are the characters for you non-gamers). In fact, the subject of cheating is much more of a problem than racism.[26]

For g-tech it is important not to buy into the alarmist hype surrounding *Ethnic Cleansing*, especially when the game is decontextualized and removed from larger geopolitical factors. G-tech continues:

In fact the most popular shooters are the patriotic ones. Take a look at the sales of Soldier of Fortune, Rainbow Six, Counterstrike, Operation Flashpoint, Delta Force Land Warrior, Return to Castle Wolfenstein, Medal of Honor *and others if you want to see some really scary stuff. Teaching kids that it's OK for America to send covert operatives into foreign countries and assassinating or killing [leaders of] other cultures and getting points or rewards for it is probably the biggest problem we may face in the future. On their own the games are harmless, but coupled with a real war where you can mimic the actions of the real soldiers in a virtual environment, a President who supports these shadow wars and a patriotic state of mind in the country and you have a recipe for trouble. I can't begin to count how many "Get Bin Laden" scenarios are popping up all over the net.*[27]

Although I selected this particular post to highlight, some Afrofuturists participating in the *Ethnic Cleansing* discussion thread were not convinced by the arguments presented here, and presented convincing counter-arguments that I cannot elaborate in this space. However, one is particularly pertinent and makes a great concluding point because it addresses several issues at the heart of this essay. One of Mr. B's numerous responses to g-tech's commentary that is pertinent for us is his respectful yet counter response to g-tech's remark that "on their own the games are harmless." Mr. B. replies: "I would never consider anything that structures the way people spend their time among a wide variety of options 'harmless.' They [games] might not be causal or deterministic, they are definitely not neutral, and as a result, not harmless in my opinion.... Let's keep this discussion going. I don't think we're at odds here, but we do need to refine exactly what we are talking about."[28]

We have been talking about the need to pay attention to how video and computer games, like other forms of popular entertainment, might be considered in relation to issues of identity politics, reproduction of racist ideologies and hegemonies despite gaming's novel expressive hardware apparatuses. At issue here has been the concern over the politics of representation regarding race, and the question about gaming culture's ability to replicate or challenge existing portrayals of specific groups in films, TV shows, and print media. We are talking about the ascendancy of a very powerful and technically evolving medium, and we want be sure that race does not remain the structured absence or specious virtual presence in our concern about where the future of gaming is headed.

Acknowledgment

This article is excerpted from Anna Everett's forthcoming book, *Digital diaspora: A race for cyberspace* (in press).

Notes

1. Richard Pierre Davis is a UK-based community activist and technology worker who teaches information technology to disadvantaged groups around the globe. (Interview by author, tape recording, London, England, July 9, 2001.)
2. For almost everything you ever wanted to know about the *Super Mario Brothers* games, go to the online *Super Mario Brothers* Headquarters at www.smbhq.com\who.htm.
3. I follow Marsha Kinder's usage of this term in her important book *Playing with power in movies, television and video games*, p. 3.
4. Henry Jenkins treats the subject of immersive play and interactivity in computer games more thoroughly in "'Complete freedom of movement': Video games as gendered play spaces," in *From Barbie to Mortal Kombat: Gender and computer games*.
5. Hayden White has been very influential in advancing the critical project of writing revisionist historiographies. See his essay "The burden of history," in *Tropics of discourse: Essays in cultural criticism*.
6. See for example, Carey Goldberg's article "Children and violent video games: A warning," *New York Times*, December 15, 1998, A14, which begins "It's almost Christmas. Do you know what your children are playing? Might they perhaps be ripping out the spines of their enemies, perpetrating massacres of marching bands and splatting their screens with sprays and spurts of pixelated blood?"; see also, John

Anna Everett

M. Glionna, "Computer culture breeds ambivalence," *Los Angeles Times* November 19, 2000, A30; a Reuters wire story on video game violence picked up by the *Philadelphia Enquirer* newspaper. The story was entitled "Study questions video-game ratings," *Philadelphia Enquirer* August 1, 2001, A3; and for a less-condemnatory perspective see, Steve Lohr's "The virtues of addictive games: Computer pastimes no longer viewed as brain poison," *New York Times*, December 22, 1997, C1+; Austin Bunn's article "Video games are good for you: Blood, guts, and leadership skills?" *Village Voice*, September 21, 1999, 31; and Ted C. Fishman's "The play's the thing: The video-game industry, already a juggernaut, plans to swallow even more of children's time. So who's complaining," *New York Times Magazine*, June 10, 2001, 27.

7. For important scholarly discussions of gender bias in video gaming that address the subject of girl's problematic positionings within gaming culture, see Marsha Kinder, *Playing with power in movies, television, and video games*, Yasmin B. Kafai, "Video game designs by girls and boys: Variability and consistency of gender differences," *Kid's media culture*, ed. Marsha Kinder (Durham: Duke University Press; 1999), and in the same anthology, Heather Gilmour, "What girls want: The intersections of leisure and power in female computer gameplay."

8. See the March 2000 cover of *Incite* magazine's "Video gaming." *Incite* also published a "PC Gaming" magazine version.

9. *Prima's official strategy guide* made this boast on the cover of its special 2000 *Tekken Tag Tournament* issue.

10. "Money makes the games go round," *Next Generation*, October 1996, 59–63.

11. I borrow this phrasing from Abdul R. Jan-Mohamed, "The economy of the Manichean allegory," p. 18.

12. See a game description and several reviews of *Civilization* at the website called Funagain-Games, at www.funagain.com.

13. I conducted this interview on gaming culture with former lawyer, now Ph.D. candidate, Hall on May 5, 2002, in Santa Barbara, California.

14. Hall interview.

15. Hall interview.

16. The game *Ethnic Cleansing* could be found during the first months of 2002 at www.resistance.com/ethniccleansing/catalog.htm.

17. The NPD Group, who conducted the study, noted that video game accessories also posted record-breaking sales. The top selling PC games were *The Sims* by Electronic Arts. See the full online report, "NPD reports annual 2001 U.S. interactive entertainment sales shatter industry record," 7 February 2002, www.npd.com/corp/content/news/releases/press_020207. htm.

18. These quotes are excerpted from H. Allen, "*Ethnic Cleansing*: The Game!" AfroFuturism, Feburary 20, 2002, and L. Johnson, "Racist video games target youth," February 25, 2002, both at http://afrofuturism.net.

19. L. Johnson, "Racist video games target youth," February 25, 2002.

20. Ibid.

21. Michele Norris and Ted Koppel, "Just a Game," ABC's *Nightline*, June 10, 2002. This show explores the popularity of the first-person sim game *Grand Theft Auto 3*.

22. "Just a Game," *Nightline*, June 10, 2002.

23. Sergeant Gerald Neill, comments made on *Nightline*, June 10, 2002.

24. Mr. B, "Re: —Racist video games target youth—," Internet, Afrofuturism list, February 26, 2002.

25. C_splash, "Re: —Racist video games target youth—," Internet, Afrofuturism list, February 26, 2002.

26. G-tech, "Re: —Racist video games target youth—," Internet, Afrofuturism list, February 26, 2002.

27. Ibid.

28. Mr. B. "Re: —Racist video games target youth—," Internet, Afrofuturism list, February 26, 2002.

References

Baraka, A. (1971). Technology & ethos: Vol. 2, book of life. In *Raise race rays raze: Essays since 1965*. New York: Random House.

Barthes, R. (1974). *S/Z: An essay*, translated by Richard Miller. New York: Hill and Wang.

Bey, H. (1991). *The temporary autonomous zone: Ontological anarchy, poetic terrorism*. Brooklyn: Autonomedia.

Bolter, J. D., & Grusin, R. (2001). *Remediation: Understanding new media*. Cambridge, MA: MIT Press.

Brooks, P. (1984). *Reading for the plot*. Cambridge, MA: Harvard University Press.

Butler, J. (1999). *Gender trouble: Feminism and the subversion of identity*. New York: Routledge.

C_splash. (2002). Re: —Racist video games target youth—. Internet, Afrofuturism list, February 26.

Chansanchai, A. (1997). Yellow perils: Online "Coolies" Rile Asian Americans. *Village Voice*. 7 October, p. 25.

Diawara, M. (1993). "Black spectatorship: Problems of identification and resistance." In M. Diawara, *Black American cinema*. New York: Routledge, pp. 211–220.

Eagleton, T. (1983). *Literary theory: An introduction*. Minneapolis: University of Minnesota Press.

Everett, A. (2001). *Returning the gaze: A genealogy of black film criticism, 1909–1949*. Durham: Duke University Press.

G-tech. (2002). Re: —Racist video games target youth—. Internet, Afrofuturism list, February 26.

Gilmour, H. (1999). What girls want: The intersections of leisure and power in female computer gameplay. In M. Kinder (Ed.), *Kid's media culture*. Durham: Duke University Press.

Goldberg, C. (1998). Children and violent video games: A warning. In *New York Times* December 15, A14.

Hall, S. (1986). Encoding/decoding. In *Culture, media language: Working papers in cultural studies, 1972–1979*. London: Hutchinson, pp. 128–138.

Hamamoto, D. Y. (1994). *Monitored peril: Asian Americans and the politics of TV representation*. Minneapolis: University of Minnesota Press.

Herz, J. C. (1997). *Joystick nation: How videogames ate our quarters, won our hearts, and rewired our minds*. Boston: Little, Brown and Company.

Imperialism: The fine art of conquering the world: A user manual. (1997). Sunnyvale, California: Strategic Simulations.

JanMohamed, A. R. (1995). The economy of the Manichean allegory. In B. Ashcroft, G. Griffiths, & H. Tiffin (Eds.), *The post-colonial studies reader*. New York: Routledge, pp. 18–23.

Jenkins, H. (1999). Complete freedom of movement: Video games as gendered play spaces. In J. Cassell & H. Jenkins (Eds.), *From Barbie to Mortal Kombat: Gender and computer games* (pp. 262–297). Cambridge, MA: MIT Press.

Kafai, Y. B. (1999). Video game designs by girls and boys: Variability and consistency of gender differences. In Ed. M. Kinder, *Kid's media culture*. Durham: Duke University Press.

Kinder, M. (1991). *Playing with power in movies, television and video games*. Berkeley: University of California Press.

Kolmos, K. (2000). *Prima's official strategy guide: Ready 2 rumble boxing, round 2*. Roseville, CA: Prima Communications; Inc.

Lyotard, J. F. (1991). *The inhuman: Reflections on time*. Stanford: Stanford University Press.

Marriott, M. (1999). Blood, gore, sex and now: Race: Are game makers creating convincing new characters or "high-tech blackface"? *New York Times* October 21, D7.

Mr. B. (2002). Re: —Racist video games target youth—. Internet, Afrofuturism list, February 26.

Narayan, U., & Harding, S. (2000). *Decentering the center: Philosophy for a multicultural, postcolonial, and feminist world*. Bloomington: Indiana University Press.

Nielsen, A. L. (1988). *Reading race: White American poets and the racial discourse in the twentieth century*. Athens: University of Georgia Press.

Taylor, L. Not a war game? Funagain Games. www.kumquat.com/cig-kumquat/funagain/04253.

White, H. (1978). *Tropics of discourse: Essays in cultural criticism*. Baltimore: Johns Hopkins University Press.

Walton, L. A. (1909). The degeneracy of the moving picture. *New York Age*, August 5, p. 6.

21

SIMULATION, HISTORY, AND COMPUTER GAMES

William Uricchio

The year is 1967. The cars are monstrously powerful, extremely light, and the tires are so hard that a single set will often last three race weekends! Brakes are terrible. Forty gallons of volatile gasoline surround the driver—contained by nothing more than a thin skin of fragile aluminium—and there are no seatbelts. The circuits are breathtakingly beautiful, supremely challenging, and brutally, lethally, dangerous. Almost forty percent of the drivers on the grid today will eventually die at the wheel of a racing car. It is the golden age of motor racing, and you are at the wheel.

Over two years after its release, Grand Prix Legends *stands alone among all racing simulations and games as the most uncompromisingly realistic simulator of race car dynamics—and arguably the most rewarding consumer racing software product—ever published.*
—Eagle Woman

Thrills, speed, and a high likelihood of explosive accidents all enhanced by refined controls and state-of-the-art replication of the driving experience, and is it any wonder that *Grand Prix Legends* has all the makings of a great game? Judging by the comments in various online discussion groups, Sierra Sports has amply satisfied the demands for historical accuracy made by most of its fans. With customers clamoring for more historical simulations—from the 1965 season (the last of the gentlemanly races) to the season just finished—we might inquire into the historical claims and implications of such games. The details of the cars and conditions of the track seem historically accurate, and many of the players come to the game with detailed knowledge of the 1967 race, the drivers' tactics, and so on. Indeed, this wealth of information and historically correct detail seems to be a source of player pleasure, allowing gamers to enter the simulated world of 1967 and relive it in their own terms. But if we take interac-

tivity to be one of the distinguishing characteristics of computer games,[1] the interaction between a present-day player and the representation of a historically specific world would seem to challenge any notion of a unique configuration of historical "fact" and "fixity," giving way instead to the historically inconsistent and ludic. Such an interaction provokes fundamental questions regarding the place of computer games in systems of historical representation, questions that this chapter will address.

One might be tempted to conclude that computer games, in sharp contrast to media such as print, photography, film, audio recording, and television, are somehow incapable of being deployed for purposes of historical accuracy, documentation, and thus representation. Although they can integrate all of these earlier media, computer games might seem closest to historical documentation only when emulating them, in the process suppressing games' defining interactive relationship with the gamer. Of course, one might imagine a fixed progression of events (as in a film or television program) visually or acoustically accessible from different points of view, but this would be closer to computer modeling than ludic experience. Is the computer game thus an inappropriate platform for the representation of history? Perhaps (and the 1967 *Grand Prix Legends* may well be a limiting case were we to pursue this argument). But in this chapter, I want to complicate the relationship of computer games to history, suggesting a fuller set of interactions with the process of historical inscription, that is, with the ways in which human subjects encounter textualizations of the past and are "written into" the past. I would also like to explore the relationship of computer games to the larger cultural processes of understanding history, specifically, with disciplinary debates within the historical profession. In this latter case, I am struck by the happy coincidence of the roughly parallel development of poststructuralist historiography (charged by its critics with upsetting the applecart of the historical trade by challenging notions of facticity, explanatory hierarchies, master narratives, and indeed, the interpretive authority of the historian) and computer-facilitated hypertext and games (empowering the user—and in the wake of the author's over-celebrated demise—enabling one to organize one's own text). Together, these two practices coincide within what might broadly be considered the postmodern *Zeitgeist*, giving both theory and form to a new way of organizing historical experience, developments that I will briefly sketch later in the chapter.

In the pages that follow, I would like to consider the outer ends of a spectrum of historical computer games as sites to tease out the possibilities and implications of historical representation and simulation. These two extremes have different historiographic appeals. One sort, such as the 1967 *Grand Prix Legends* game or the *Battle of the Bulge*, is specific in the sense that it deals with a particular historical event—a race, a battle—allowing the player to engage in a speculative or "what if" encounter with a particular past. In these games, efforts are usually taken to maximize the accuracy of historical detail, allowing the setting and conditions to constrain and shape game play. At the other extreme are games that deal with historical process in a somewhat abstracted or structural manner. *Civilization III* and *The Oregon Trail* typify these historically situated games in which a godlike player makes strategic decisions and learns to cope with the consequences, freed from the constraints of historically specific conditions. Although games of this sort also elicit speculative engagement with the past, they tend to be built upon particular visions or theories of long-term historical development. That is, in place of the constraining role of historical specificity of the former games (a historical specificity inculcated through encrusted layers of historical scholarship, training, and popular memory), these less specifically situated games tend to be more evidently structured by unspoken historical principle (or better, ideology), rendering them closer to structuralist notions of history. In both cases, history in the Rankean sense of "*wie es eigentlich gewesen ist*" is subverted by an insistence on history as a multivalent process subject to many different possibilities, interpretations, and outcomes.[2] Not surprisingly, some historians and educators have attacked the game industry for its inadequate engagement with the facts and its inappropriate irreverence for the past. And not surprisingly, the industry has responded by limiting its claims ("it's only entertainment") and pointing to its positive effects ("players are rendered so enthusiastic about history that they actually read about it").

Were one to inscribe these critical reactions and responses historically, one would have good grounds to see them as now familiar reenactments of the fears that have accompanied the early years of previous media, such as the motion picture. For example, when used for purposes of historical representation, the once new medium of film was loudly attacked by a historical establishment more familiar with the abstraction of print, and was defended in terms nearly identical to those deployed by the gaming industry.[3] But although these continuities are important to keep in mind, there are also some important distinctions. Unlike film, computer game remakes are seen as improving with each iteration, pointing among other things to the very different relationship of each medium to its underlying technology (film's relatively stable relationship to technology in contrast to the dynamic state of computing technology). Perhaps more fundamentally for the argument at hand, film and the subset of computer games that this paper will consider also differ in terms of their relationship to history. Films, like books, are primarily bound up in a relationship of historical representation, in fixing, for good or ill, a particular rendering of the past. The computer games that I will be discussing, by contrast, are bound up in a process of historical simulation, offering some fixed elements and underlying principles, but thriving upon the creative interaction of the user. The difference, I will suggest in the course of my argument, is crucial.

Homo Ludens—Playing and Prototypes

Although deconstruction, as a conscious, systematic philosophy, has been most prominent among intellectual historians, the mode of thought it represents, even its distinct vocabulary, is permeating all aspects of the new constructivist history. Historians now freely use such words as "invent," "imagine," "create" (not "re-create"), and "construct" (not "reconstruct") to describe the process of historical interpretation, and then proceed to support some novel interpretation by a series of "possibles," "might have beens," and "could have beens."—Gertrude Himmelfarb

The development that Gertrude Himmelfarb describes relates to the poststructural historical turn that is roughly coincident with the emergence of hypertext and games. I invoke her words here because they so clearly characterize the historical endeavor as play.

Think of them as imperatives: invent! imagine! create! Consider them as modes of engagement: the subjunctive, the speculative, the "what if." This notion of play, if I may so characterize Himmelfarb's descriptors before defining the term, also seems to share something very basic with historical computer games, something more than the destabilized hierarchies and subverted master narratives that are held in common between games and poststructuralist history. Indeed, one could easily imagine these imperatives and modes of engagement as promotional descriptors for historical computer games.[4] Although Himmelfarb along with many other respected historians lament this ludic turn in the writing of history, she has articulated the problem in ways that point to the conjuncture of the new history with games.

Play, the *sine qua non* of games generally, has many forms and flavors. Within the community of historians, perhaps the most important intervention on the topic remains Johan Huizinga's, whose now classic *Homo ludens* asserted that civilization "arises *in* and *as* play, and never leaves it" (Huizinga, 1955, p. 173). Huizinga traces this expansive notion of play across various cultural sectors, and although he offers a number of compelling (and at times contradictory) definitions of the term, his most succinct is worth recalling. "Play is a voluntary activity or occupation executed within certain fixed limits of time and place, according to rules freely accepted but absolutely binding, having its aim in itself and accompanied by a feeling of tension, joy, and the consciousness that it is 'different' from 'ordinary life'" (p. 28).

Huizinga's definition covers many possibilities, which is a good thing considering the rich genealogy that historical computer games draw upon. Board games, role playing games, re-enactments, and simulations have all contributed to the formation of historical computer games generally, with a number of more specific references informing the development of particular titles. Wargames (regardless of platform) have arguably had the most influence on historical computer games, particularly because they tend to be event-oriented and historically specific in their references.[5] In the words of the *Wargames handbook*:

A wargame is an attempt to get a jump on the future by obtaining a better understanding of the past. A wargame is a combination of "game," history and science. It is a paper time-machine.... A wargame usually combines a map, playing pieces representing historical personages or military units

and a set of rules telling you what you can or cannot do with them. Many are now available on personal computers. The object of any wargame (historical or otherwise) is to enable the player to recreate a specific event and, more importantly, to be able to explore what might have been if the player decides to do things differently. (Dunnigan, 2003)

Using the past as a way to understand the future, a time-machine, a rule-bound set of possibilities ... these terms resonate with various definitions of history. As with *Grand Prix Legends*, the tension between the specific and the speculative gives this genre its power, and speaks directly to Huizinga's notion of play even within the oxymoronic context of war. Indeed, the richer the specific historical detail, the more profound and pleasurable the play with the speculative.[6] A good example of the importance of specific detail (and detailed knowledge) as the basic stuff of history and gaming play can be found in Ciril Rozic's description of the Battle of the Bulge as a site for gaming:

The Battle of the Bulge is everything but novel to wargaming. This period of the war in the West has been well documented and there are a great number of publications circulating in the military history realm, which is paralleled by a host of board and computer games, as well as scenarios for generic game systems. Whatever other reasons for the omnipresence of Bulge-related titles, the battle surely doesn't lack in appeal from a historian's and gamer's point of view. On the high operational level, it begins with an overwhelming surprise attack, followed by some intense fighting to contain it, and ends with a steady counterattack to push the Germans back. Meanwhile, the balance of resources changes drastically, as the German pool of supply and replacements diminishes and the Americans inject forces from other regions to help ease the pressure. Historically, the few weeks' clash of arms saw a diversity of tactically and technically interesting situations: fast-paced mechanized thrusts, huge offensive and defensive artillery barrages, river crossings, frantic bridge building and blowing, encirclements which ended in surrender and those that did not, air attacks, German deception unit action, parachute troop and supply drops, assaults on fortified positions, supply depot captures, and sticky traffic jams (this list is not final!). The task before any ambitious game maker is, therefore, quite serious. (Rozic, 2003, p. 1)

The possibilities are countless and the opportunities for obsessively detailed gaming scenarios *and* speculative intervention endless. Historical re-enactors, or role playing gamers, or historians proper would each approach this battle with similarly detailed bodies of knowledge. What each constituency would make of the encounter, how they would frame and deploy their knowledge, and just how much "lift" the ludic would offer their arrangements of the details would, however, differ. The attention to detail within the gaming world can be daunting, and one way to gauge it is through the clustering of games around particular historical moments. The Battle of the Bulge has spawned many, but so too have figures such as Napoleon and events such as the American Revolution. The *Napoleonic computer games anthology* lists forty-four different simulation games and modifications (many more are out there), including titles on particular campaigns (*Napoleon's Campaigns: 1813, 1815*), and the battles of Quatre Bras, Jena, Ligny, and of course Waterloo (Vitous, 2003). In addition, specific titles unpack into further detail. The American Revolution-based *Campaign 1776*, for example, contains some forty-seven distinct scenarios, including four on the battle of Brandywine (September 11, 1777), eight on the first and second battles of Saratoga (September 19 and October 7, 1777), and so on, written from both historical and what-if vantage points (Campaign, 1776).

A quick look at the many reviews of these games and scenarios circulating on gamer websites offers insight into the parameters of play that are highly regarded (or abhorred). "Graphically attractive as an educational tool, its utility as an entertainment device ranked right up there with kidney stones" (*War Collage* by Game Tek, 1996); "Historically accurate and enhanced game play place it first among the Napoleonic simulations of the Battle of Borodino" (*Napoleon in Russia, Battleground 6* by TalonSoft, 1997); "the game was commendable for ease of play, but marred by ahistorical tactics necessary for achieving victory" (*Napoleon at Waterloo* by Krentek, 1984). "It was a failure: there was little of the ambience of the Napoleonic Era, and tactical combat seemed to yield artillery with ranges of 20 miles" (*L'Empereur* by Koei, 1991) (Vitous, 2003). Generally, as already suggested, those reviewers who look beyond issues of technology and interface (themselves important factors in historical simulation) tend to value both historical accuracy and opportunities for creative intervention. Play emerges in the space between the constraint of detail and the exhilaration of improvisation.

At the other end of the historical gaming spectrum, a very different approach to play appears in those games structured around historical eras rather than particular historical moments. Games such as Sid Meier's *Civili-*

zation series, *Age of Empires*, *The Oregon Trail*, and *Europa Universalis*, although responsive to certain historically relevant parameters, make no claims to historical specificity. Simulation games along the same lines as *SimCity*, *Civilization*, and so forth require strategic management of resources, investments, and populations in order for the player to progress to the next stage of gameplay. One might argue that these games differ from the historically specific games just discussed only in terms of the amount of detail they contain, but detail makes all of the difference in terms of the historical claims involved. Historically specific simulation games address a particular event; and even though the nature of that address can differ—although it generally centers on correct period detail—the game's claims offer a framework for play, meaning, and critique. By contrast, nonspecific simulations of the *Civilization* type are abstracted from the particularity of historical event, allowing the impact of decisions to be played and tested out in various worlds, but without bearing the burden of any specific referent. Although the principles and details may seem just as fine grained as in a specifically specific simulation, the referential claims are absent. Rather than a what if simulation with a known case study as the referent, nonspecific simulations provoke a wider range of interrogations, encouraging a more abstract, theoretical engagement of historical process.

Small wonder that games of this genre such as *Hidden Agenda* would be used for the training of CIA agents or that *SimCity* would be used at the 1994 Mayors Conference in Portland for planning purposes. Sid Meier, a key developer of historically oriented games, put it best: "We're not trying to duplicate history. We're trying to provide you with the tools, the elements of history and let you see how it would work if you took over." A *New York Times* interview with Meier revealed the crux of the extremely successful *Civilization* strategy: to achieve the greatest effect, developers of historical strategy games try to inject just the right dose of reality. Often this is achieved not so much by deciding what to include in the game, but by deciding what not to include. David Kushner, author of the *Times* story, concluded "Too much information can make the game too arcane or controversial for its own good. For that reason, the historical data used to construct *Civilization*-like simulations seldom run deeper than the content of an illustrated history book for children" (Kushner, 2001).

Kushner's comments partially miss the point. It is certainly true that historical detail tends to be limited to the broad markers of time and place, and to stay clear of specific events. In the *Oregon Trail*, for example, the date selected for the start of the game has implications for how it unfolds, because the earlier you start, the fewer cities there are to start from, and fewer destinations:

If you start in 1840, you can only start from Independence, Missouri, and your destinations are either the Willamette Valley or Southern Oregon. If you start in 1860, there are several starting points (St. Louis, Independence, St. Joseph, etc.) and you have more destinations that are actually named (Sacramento, Oregon City, Jacksonville, Or. etc.).... A nice feature of this section is that it is representative of the time you are travelling, i.e., 1846 itinerary contains only that information that was available in 1846. A nice touch of realism. (Cunningham, 2003)

But the complexity of the game appears in the process of historical simulation rather than in the representation of the historical moment. That is, players are called upon to make difficult choices about what they will bring with them on a westward journey constrained by limits of money and space—farming implements, food, weapons, medicine, spare wheels, and so on. Depending upon what route is chosen, what climactic factors they encounter (flooding, drought), and what sort of trading occurs along the way, users gain first hand knowledge of the struggles to cross the wilderness and the strategies to survive. *Civilization, Age of Empires,* and so on use basically the same structure, focusing more on the epochal development of broadly historical cultures, requiring strategic decisions about allocations of limited resources, and confronting the player with the consequences of their actions.

But how historical is it? In an opinion no doubt shared by many traditionalists within his profession, Martin Ryle, professor of history, found the emphasis on process rather than event problematic:

I find that historical simulations that are based upon manipulation of quantities of things like economic production, religious intensity, foreign trade, bureaucratic development, and literacy indeed fall more into the realm of sociology or anthropology than history. Certainly, these simulations may be quite interesting and enlightening to the historian, but they are, I think, fundamentally unhistorical. The discipline of history focuses on the particular, on a given time and place and on the particular evidence that remains from that time and place. (Ryle, 1989)

But such a view may reflect a fundamental critique of the efforts of the *Annaliste* histories of Fernand Braudel, Roger Chartier, Emmanuel Le Roy Ladurie, and others with their focus on the broad structures of history such as economics, anthropology, linguistics, and so on. This is not to suggest that games such as the *Oregon Trail* (which lacks hostile Native Americans), or *Colonization* (which lacks slaves), or *Civilization* (which lacks a Hitler in twentieth-century Germany) are historically unproblematic. Rather, it is to say that, at a moment of shifting historical paradigms, the games' thin ("childlike") historical detail and their focus on process as play are not necessarily the main source of their problems.

Rethinking History

History is the most powerful construction of realistic conventions as we have known them since about 1400.—Elizabeth Ermarth

If Elizabeth Ermarth is right,[7] then a great deal is at stake in tampering with the contours of historical representation. The successively linguistic, interpretive, and rhetorical turns in the writing of history have created a quiet panic in some quarters, a panic amplified in the wake of the wars that have played out over the definition of common culture. History has been particularly vulnerable in these conflicts, cursed as it is with a double identity. On the one hand, history refers to the past as a set of lived occurrences. In this sense it has the status of event, of a now gone but infinitely complex reality. On the other hand, the term "history" refers to the *representation* of the past, a snapshot of that vast and multidimensional complexity. In this sense, history is inherently partial, deforming, delimiting, and grounded in a "presentist" point of view. No imaginable set of "historical" representations can do justice to the fullness of "history" as past. Although tacitly acknowledged by most historical practitioners, the limits and inherent subjectivity of history as written tend to be bracketed off from discussion, allowing historians to get on with their jobs. But the poststructuralists made their mark by embracing (and indeed, celebrating) precisely this long-suppressed representational uncertainty.[8] In a double move, they challenged the established explanatory master narratives that dominated the field, and at the same time asserted the need for boldly and articulately partial histories, histories embedded in a clearly defined point of view. Poststructuralism, consistent with the broader cultural turn of which it was a part, also posed the challenging question of who speaks for whom in the writing of history? In an era where issues of multiculturalism, gender, class, and generation emerged in the forefront of social policy and academic debate, it was but a small step to connect the dots between the partiality of representation and the issue of who was doing the representation. Robert Berkhofer neatly summed up these twin critiques: "If the first crisis of representation questioned whether and how historical actuality could ever be re-presented, the second crisis of representation undermined both the authority and the objectivity of traditional history. The first crisis of representation is encapsulated in the slogan, 'Question Reality,' and the second in another, 'Resist Authority' (Berkhofer, 1995, p. 3). The result, at least for some within the historical profession, was described by Lyotard as a posture of "incredulity towards meta-narratives." Focus shifted instead to such issues as the exploration of narrative convention and implication, or ways of enabling the subject to construct personal histories, or even the creation of speculative histories.

I am struck by the broad coincidence between these developments within the historical profession (and, as mentioned, parts of the larger culture) and the emergence of a new set of representational possibilities centered on the computer. Over the long haul, we will no doubt see the connection, but for the moment it remains coincidence (though a mutually reinforcing one), devoid, as far as I can tell, of specifically shared causality. That said, digital technologies have found a ready market among historians, facilitating a quiet transformation in the writing and conception of history. Cleometrics, digitally enhanced access to archival documents, and Internet–facilitated discussion groups typify relatively noncontroversial applications that have had an accelerating effect on the flow of ideas. Other technologies, by contrast, have found more restricted embrace and engendered more controversy. For example, hypertext-based historical essays have permitted rich multimedia linkages of data and analysis, yet have implicitly subverted the authority of the historian and master narrative, instead ceding the creation of coherence and meaning to the reader. Simulation technologies have engendered similar problems, emerging as they do from programming intensive efforts that assume a high degree of historical speculation and give rise to wide-ranging user structured meanings.

Digital technologies have not only offered historians new ways to pursue their research, communicate with one another, and give form to their ideas; they have also opened access to wider publics. This can be seen both in the relatively easy access that lay audiences have to online data and debates, and particularly to the newly empowered position that ordinary readers have when encountering hypertextual historical documents. The turn to the reader common to both of these extensions parallels developments that may be found in very different ways on the gaming boards of dedicated historical "players" or in the reenactments staged by members of (usually war-related) historical societies or even participants in living historical museums (Williamburg, Skansen, etc.). These sites attest to an engagement of the popular historical imagination, and to their participants' active construction of historical meaning. Gabrielle Spiegel has argued that

If one of the major moves in post-structuralist thought has been to displace the controlling metaphor of historical evidence from one of reflection to one of mediation (that is, a shift from the notion that texts and documents transparently reflect past realities, as positivism believed, to one in which the past is captured in the mediated form preserved for us in language), then we need to think carefully about how we understand mediation and how that understanding affects our practice. (Spiegel, 1992, pp. 197–198)

What happens if we push the notion of mediation beyond language, to the domain of game, enactment, or simulation? Does this allow us to slip out of the well-critiqued trap of representation? And if so, where does it land us?

Representation and Simulation

Historical sims recreate a past event or time period as accurately as possible. Many of the games are also included in other genres with simulation game, like combat or flight. This is a great genre for history buffs.—C. Marchelletta

Representation has emerged as a central term in the critical appraisal of history (as text), and the concept has served as the grounds upon which contestations over accuracy, adequacy, and notions such as objectivity and consistency have been waged. These precarious but well-charted shoals need not be revisited here, for literature on the topic is rich (Iggers, 1997). The previous section simplified the current debate over historical representation in terms of two opposed positions. One position assumes that responsible research efforts have the potential to provide an accruing and ever-more accurate understanding of the past, and that somehow, with enough effort, the space between history as past and history as text can be minimized. The other position assumes an unbridgeable gap between the events of the past and the ever-shifting representational efforts of an ever-changing present, an assumption that instead reflects upon the contours of the present (and the position of the subject within it) and their relationship with the process of constructing an understanding of the past. The implications for computer games seem evident enough. As previously suggested, games' capacities for historical articulation turn on the relationship between a set of possible resemblances familiar from other media (image, the word, sound) and the notion of interactivity (and thus, representational variation or instability) at the core of the game form. Games by definition subvert the project of consolidation and certainty associated with the former brand of history. Instead, predicated as they are upon a reflexive awareness of the construction of history, they seem relevant to the notion of history as time-bound meaning situated in an ever-changing present.

"Representation" is not a term one often sees in the description of historical games. Genres such as wargames are sometimes invoked, but even here there seems to be a preferred level of abstraction occupied by descriptors such as simulations and role playing games. Kevin Robert Burns of The Historical Simulation Boardgamers Society of Japan offers at least one pragmatic reason:

To attract more people to the hobby, I suggest we use the term "historical simulation games," rather than wargames. Historical simulation is really what they are about after all. History involves many things, only one of which is war.... Admittedly, the subject matter of the games "Third Reich" and "War and Peace" amongst others, are the Second World War and the Napoleonic Wars respectively.... (but) they are historical games, and that is what I hope to learn about, when I sit opposite you, and roll the dice. (Burns, 2003)

The use of the terms "simulations" and "sims" is widespread within the gaming community—whether role playing, board gaming or computer gaming—particularly that portion of it that is concerned with history. Some within the theoretical community, the *ludologists* in particular, have subsequently embraced this term, extracting games from a discursive framing as narrative or a conceptual framing derived from film or television studies.[9]

Simulation is a curious word in the English language. From the mid fourteenth century until the mid twentieth century, it was associated with meanings ranging from "false pretense" and "deception" to "the tendency to assume a form resembling that of something else." After World War II, the term finally gave way to the more familiar "technique of imitating the behavior of some situation or process by means of a suitably analogous situation or apparatus, especially for the purpose of study or personnel training."[10] This rather dramatic shift in meaning, located by the *Oxford English dictionary* in 1947, indicates a move away from simulation both as willful *misrepresentation* and something akin to *representation*, to a modeling of behavior that is dynamic in nature, analogous in relationship, and pedagogical in goal. Unlike a representation, which tends to be fixed in nature, a simulation is a process guided by certain principles. Simulation is capable of generating countless encounters that may subsequently be fixed as representations, fixed, that is, as narrative or image or data set summations of a particular simulated encounter; whereas representation does not necessarily generate or include within it simulation. The difference is a crucial one, and speaks to just how radically the term transformed over the past half decade. A simulation is a machine for producing speculative or conditional representations.

Simulations have a history older than the recent change in the term's meaning (and older than the computer). Flight simulators, for example, can be dated to within a decade of the Wright Brother's first airplane flight, and economics, physics, and engineering have far deeper histories of relying upon carefully scaled models (whether physical or mathematical). But the simulations most relevant to the study of history played out in the arena of cold war politics (both political and wargames), or were imagined as a possible future for historical pedagogy (Clemens, 1976, pp. 109–126; Corbeil, 1988, pp. 15–20; Shafer, 1977, pp. 9–10). What qualities should be accentuated in a historical simulation? Professor Cary's "Formats and tips of effective historical simulations," although pertaining to role-playing simulation games, offers several indications relevant to computer games.

First, it is important to be historically accurate—to be true to what the people of those times, whose roles you are playing, would have said. You should not take your present-day attitudes into the presentation. Rather, you should become *the person whose role you are playing. Give that person's views, not your present-day critique of those views. For example, if you are debating the peace treaty to end World War I, you should be Wilson. Be Lloyd George. Be Clemenceau. Be Lenin, or Keynes, or Churchill (critics of the treaty at the time).* (Cary, 2003)

Simulation through the alignment of subjectivities (knowledge, motives, perceptual horizons) has a proven track record, predicated as it is upon a compelling mode of address. But Cary's dictate about historical accuracy can also be deployed more fundamentally. The *Wargames handbook* reminds us that computer wargames are more difficult to learn than other computer games because "wargames are, at heart, simulations of real life events. A simulation is, by its nature, a potentially very complex device. This is especially true of historical simulations, which must be capable of recreating the historical event they cover. Recreating history imposes a heavy burden on the designer, and the player who must cope with the additional detail incorporated to achieve the needed realism" (Dunnigan, 2003). The burden of history weighs heavily upon both the construction of the subject-player and the environment that defines and constrains the player's possibilities.

These twin considerations find clear articulation in the discourse surrounding historical simulation games. Consider *Versailles, 1685.*

The game is set in the late Seventeenth Century with French nobility at its zenith in power and prestige. The player assumes the role of Lalande, a valet of the King's inner chambers. Monsieur Bontemps, sort of a chief-of-staff has discovered a plot to destroy Versailles. Limited by his high visibility, Bontemps entrusts Lalande with gathering information to foil the coup. In his position as valet, Lalande is able to discreetly access the most private areas of the grand palace. Lalande has exactly one day to complete his task.

Versailles is a learning opportunity as much as an entertainment product. Beatrix Saule, Chief Curator of Versailles for over twenty years had strong input into accurately translating the Palace to the computer screen. The Chateau has been reconstructed as it was in 1685, down to the very paintings and wall hangings present at the time. Not only will the player be able to access rooms of the Palace which have been closed to the public for decades, but even areas that no longer exist such as the Ambassadors' Staircase are brought back to life.

Also faithfully recreated is a day in the life of the King. Almost every moment of the King's day was ritualized into a ceremony that the player will experience as his valet. These are cleverly divided into the game as "Acts." Here player

will have a multitude of tasks to accomplish and leads to explore. (Klimushyn, 1997)

Point of view, domains of knowledge and access, and motivation all speak to the construction of the role playing subject, just as the text situates that construction within the possibilities and constraints of "authorized" period detail (spatial and visual regimes, temporal cycles). Together with events (and thus the progression of play) structured around royal ritual, these elements combine to produce to the twin appeals of entertainment and education that the game addresses. *Versailles 1685* provides near endless possibilities, and thus outcomes for the king and his minions within the confines of the palace, allowing the player to experience various scenarios and to use those experiences for purposes of understanding, entertainment, and for re-telling in the form of narrative representation.

A more explicitly event-centered example may be found in *The Civil War Online.* This military, economic, and political simulation of the American Civil War combines both role playing and third-person wargaming for its impact. Beginning in 1861 and lasting until the end of 1863, when, in the eyes of the game developers, the military fortunes of the Confederacy had doomed it to extinction, *CWOL* is built upon on "historical facts." The game uses the years of 1861, 1862, and 1863 for historical background of the majority of the game, arguing that after the triple Union victories at Gettysburg, Vicksburg, and Chattanooga, the Confederacy had little hope of achieving a military solution. In the words of the developers, "players are challenged to try to alter the outcome, but the challenges each country faced in the 1860's are evident and will remain if the national team does not address the strategic, diplomatic, economic, and political obstacles in their path to victory" (The Distance Simulations Group, 2003). This is simulation in the spirit of the post-1947 turn of the word, enabling a testing and modeling through an analogous situation with the purpose of learning. The game is inspired by various historical representations, yet as a simulation, offers its users the opportunity to play with variations and speculate what would have happened if.

Virtual Histories, Real Constraints

Narrative history, they [White, La Capra, Mink, etc.] argue, is always written with the advantage of hindsight. The historian's explanations of events are not like scientific hypotheses, subject to disconfirmation by subsequent events but are constructed in accordance with preconceived literary forms.... Sometimes an imaginative or rigorous historian introduces counter factuals ... but we are generally short of methodologies for modeling such scenarios. One of the advantages of the computer, and the hypertext, it seems to me, is that it offers the potential for thinking about historical relationships in new configurations. We can think of multiple beginnings and endings, and exploit the labyrinthine linkages of the hypertext to represent them.—Graeme Davison

Graeme Davison speaks to a notion of history termed by Niall Ferguson, *virtual history*, that is, what-if or speculative history. Davidson's remarks pertain to written histories, where poststructuralist historians challenged the notion of where familiar histories begin and end, and explored the implications of narrative form for the telling of these histories. Although games are built around radically hypertextual principles, many of the more historically specific games (*The Battle of Jena*, etc.) in fact operate with fixed starting points, in this sense sharing one of the key assumptions of traditional linear histories. True, much of what follows in the games is up for grabs, but it still falls within the terms of the critique posed by White et al. regarding the problem of where a particular historical episode begins. The more process-oriented games (*Civilization*, etc.) are more interesting in this regard, because they permit a radical reframing of familiar events and extend the user's intervention to such things as the control over the genesis of an episode. I mention this as a proviso of sorts, because the radicalization of hypertextual form evident in most games doesn't always map onto the critique offered by the community of poststructuralist historiographers. That said, hypertextual form, with its shift in narrative determination from the author to the reader, is certainly capable of calling into question beginnings, endings, and everything in between. The new and improved *Europa Universalis* (version II) for example, supports the following claim: "One of the results of all the additional options is that *Europa Universalis* isn't as straight jacketed by history as it used to be. You'll see more fantastic outcomes like France getting swallowed by her neighbors, Byzantium beating back the Turks, England knocked out of the seas, or Poland biting off swathes of Russia. *Europa Universalis* goes to new places it couldn't reach before" (Chick, 2003).

As I have already suggested, for the purposes of this chapter we can discern a spectrum of historical engagement in games, defined by two poles. One pole is marked by particular historical events. Efforts are taken to maximize historical accuracy, allowing the setting, conditions, and period details to constrain and shape game play. For all of their efforts to provide an array of ludic possibilities, such efforts also tend to bring with them certain structuring assumptions, such as the starting point for a historical experience. The other pole is marked by historical process, albeit in a somewhat abstracted or structured manner. Although games of this sort also elicit speculative engagement with the past, they tend to be built upon particular visions of long-term historical development. Much as with structuralist histories, games such as *Civilization* are built upon notions such as societal coherence, progression, and increasing complexity as a sign of advance. Indeed, *Civilization* boils down to several ideologically positioned maxims such as the more efficient production, the more advanced the civilization; and the more democracy, the better. There has, as of this writing, been little analysis of the tendencies latent in the structuring logic of the process games.[11] Kacper Poblocki, in an important departure from this trend, offers a detailed analysis of *Civilization* and comes to the following conclusion: "This history is not contingent in any way, but it is the history of the west." "The United States is made the inheritor of all the human advancement and elevated to the position of the most perfect and most 'civilized' state of all" (Poblocki, 2002, pp. 163–177). These tendencies can be found embedded in the basic cause-effect logic of the game, where they are at their most insidious, but they are also remarkably explicit, there in the texture of surface detail.

Virtual history, even if simulated in the ludic space constituted by historical computer games, seems to have a complicated relationship to the poststructuralist critique. On the one hand, whether historically specific or process oriented, the hypertextual foundation of games seems closely to correlate to the demands for historical possibility. Their embeddedness in play and the controlling agency that they cede to the user seems to fulfill the claims for reflexivity and subjectivity so central to the new history. And yet, it seems as though there are contradictions, sites of stubborn adherence to the historiographic status quo. Historically specific games are sometimes constrained by the sheer detail that gives them specificity, such as having defined and unalterable starting points and falling into the trap discussed by White and his colleagues. And process oriented games, for all their seeming lack of constraint, can be built around organizing principles that reveal a structuralist understanding of historical process. These organizing strategies might be embedded in the logic

William Uricchio

of the game's progression, or they might be evident in the terms of play, but in either case they work against the apparent freedom celebrated by the games themselves.

But some might respond that this seeming paradox between the radical possibilities of virtual history and the constraints and structuring agencies of traditional history is beside the point. "The historical aspect of these games is just the icing on the cake," said Graham Somers, a twenty-two-year-old college student in Vancouver who runs an *Age of Empires* fan site called *HeavenGames*. "I have a definite love of history, and certainly sending an army of knights and battering rams into an enemy town has a historical basis, but the main thing is it's a lot of fun. They are games, after all" (Kushner, 2001, p. 6). Indeed, they are games. And the extent to which, as both games and simulations, they offer a new means of reflecting upon the past, working through its possibilities, its alternatives, its "might-have-beens," it would seem that they succeed where other forms of history fail.

Where might we look for future developments? Greater investment on the part of the historical community may well hold benefits for the game industry. This is not to suggest (as some historians have), that greater attention to correct period detail or more pedagogical pop-ups will improve the games. Rather, we might think of the rule systems that characterize various brands of history as constituting the potential rule systems for game play. By embedding various historiographic epistemologies as structuring agencies rather than relying implicitly on narratives of truth, progress, and the American way, a new dimension could be added to play, more coherently addressing history's rich complexity and relevance. At the same time, historians would benefit by being more attentive both to the possibilities that simulation—as distinct from representation—holds as a way of coming to terms with the poststructuralist turn in historiography. Moreover, games have spawned communities of interest, debate, and creative investment that have much to offer the interested historian. Particularly because of their participation in historical simulation, players' retrospective process of representation would seem to shed light on the larger uses of history that have proven to be so evasive in other media.

"History has never been so addictive" declared *Time* magazine (Chris Taylor, "New From E3," *Time*, 20 May 2001), speaking of the computer game revolution and *Civilization* in particular. Perhaps. But considering the pace of ongoing changes in computing and transmission technologies, considering how recent the development of computer games, and considering the generational demographic of the heaviest computer game users, the future of things past has never been more promising.

Notes

1. For the purposes of this chapter, I use the term "computer games" broadly and do not distinguish among the various available platforms.
2. Ranke's notion of "what really happened" has been the battle cry of those historians who see their profession as objective, accretive, and teleologically governed as each generation of scholarship refines the truth and contributes additional data. One counter-critique is that such a historical notion leads inevitably towards the idea of reconstruction.
3. For a detailed case study based on the early U.S. film industry, see William Uricchio and Roberta E. Pearson, *Reframing culture: The case of the Vitagraph quality films* (Princeton: Princeton University Press, 1993), chapter 4.
4. For a developed discussion of play in terms of computer games, see Gonzalo Frasca, *Videogames of the oppressed*, MA Thesis, Georgia Institute of Technology (2001).
5. Indeed, their relevance is implicit in the very definition of the wargames genre. See Rex Martin, *Cardboard warriors: The rise and fall of an American wargaming subculture, 1958–1998* (Ph.D. dissertation, 2001, Pennsylvania State University).
6. Although differently mediated, the historical novel also derives its power from a mix of rich period detail and narrative invention.
7. Although there is reason to challenge her: consider such discourses as physics and sociology, not to mention conventions in visual representation such as perspective, as "realist" alternatives to history's interpretive strategies.
8. The literature on poststructuralist historiography is extensive. See among others, Hayden White, *The content of the form: Narrative discourse and historical representation* (Baltimore: Johns Hopkins University Press, 1990); Michel de Certeau, *The writing of history* (New York: Columbia University Press, 1992); Keith Jenkins, ed., *The post-modern history reader* (New York:

Routledge, 1997); Keith Jenkins, *Rethinking history* (New York: Routledge, 2003).

9. One of the central debates in computer game theory regards the epistemological framing of the game encounter: as narrative (a mode of representation familiar from film or television studies or literature or art history) or as something distinctive. Some advocates of the latter have seized upon "simulation" as the nonrepresentational alternative. For more, see Espen Aarseth, *Cybertext. Perspectives on ergodic literature* (Baltimore: Johns Hopkins University Press, 1997); Marie-Laure Ryan, *Narrative as virtual reality. Immersion and interactivity in literature and electronic media* (Baltimore: Johns Hopkins University Press, 2001). The Ludologists have at least two clearly demarcated camps, one interested in the study of games-as-such (Jesper Juul), and the other interested in the study of games as systems (Gonzalo Frasca). See Frasca's site www.ludology.org.

10. Oxford English Dictionary Online (2002).

11. Kurt Squire's dissertation, *Replaying history: Learning world history through playing* (Ph.D. dissertation, Indiana University, January 2004), is an important exception; unfortunately, it was not consulted for this chapter.

References

Aarseth, E. (1997). *Cybertext: Perspectives on ergodic literature*. Baltimore: Johns Hopkins University Press.

Berkhofer, R. (1995). *Beyond the great story: History as text and discourse*. Cambridge: Harvard University Press.

Burns, K. (2003). The historical simulation boardgamers society of Japan. www07.u-page.so-net.ne.jp/tg7/kevin/articlesabouthistoricalgaming.htm.

Cary, P. (2003). Formats and tips for effective historical simulations. www.holycross.edu/departments/history/ncary/HistSimTips.htm.

Certeau, M. de. (1992). *The writing of history*. New York: Columbia University Press.

Chick, T. (2003). Back to the past. http://www.cgonline.com/reviews/europauniv-02-r1.html.

Clemens, W. (1976). Simulation in Soviet studies, *Soviet Union* 3:1, pp. 109–126.

Corbeil, P. (1988). Rethinking history with simulations, *History Microcomputer Review* 4:1, 15–20.

Cunningham, R. (2003). How the West was won … again. A review of the Oregon Trail II. www.worldvillage.com/wv/school/html/reviews/oregon2.htm.

Davison, G. (1997). History and hypertext. *The Electronic Journal of Australian and New Zealand History*. www.jcu.edu.au/aff/history/articles/davison.htm.

The Distance Simulations Group. (2003). *Civil War OnLine* www.distance-simulations.com.

Dunnigan, J. (2003). *The complete wargames handbook*. www.hyw.com/Books/WargamesHandbook/1-what_i.htm.

Eagle Woman Grand Prix Legends. www.eaglewoman.racesincentral.com/gpl.

Ermarth, E. (1997). Sequel to history. In K. Jenkins (Ed.), *The postmodern history reader*. London: Routledge.

Ferguson, N. (1998). *Virtual history*. London: Papermac Books.

Frasca, G. (2001). *Videogames of the oppressed*. MA Thesis, Georgia Institute of Technology. www.ludology.org/articles/thesis.

Himmelfarb, G. (1980). The new history. *New York Review of Books*, 17.

Huizinga, J. (1955). *Homo ludens: A study of the play element in culture*. Boston: Beacon Press.

Iggers, G. (1997). *Historiography in the twentieth century: From scientific objectivity to the post-modern challenge*. Middletown: Wesleyan University Press.

Jenkins, K. (1997). *The post-modern history reader*. New York: Routledge.

Jenkins, K. (2003). *Rethinking history*. New York: Routledge.

Klimushyn, C. (1997). An educational day in the king's court: Versailles 1685. www.cdmag.com/articles/002/168/versailles_review.html.

Kushner, D. (2001). In historical games, truth gives way to entertainment. *New York Times*, September 6, p. 6.

Marchelletta, C. (2003). Top 4 historical sims. *Computer Simulation Games*. www.compsimgames.about.com/cs/historicalsims/tp/historical.htm.

Martin, R. (2001). *Cardboard warriors: The rise and fall of an American wargaming subculture, 1958–1998*. Ph.D. dissertation, Pennsylvania State University.

Poblocki, K. (2002). Becoming-state: The bio-cultural imperialism of Sid Meier's Civilization. *Focaal—European Journal of Anthropology 39*, 163–177.

Rozic, C. (2003). *The wargamer: Computer war and strategy gaming.* www.wargamer.com/reviews/bulge_44/page1.asp.

Ryan, M.-L. (2001). *Narrative as virtual reality. Immersion and interactivity in literature and electronic media.* Baltimore: Johns Hopkins University Press.

Ryle, M. (1989). *Humanist mailing list*, vol. 2, no. 592. lists.village.virginia.edu/lists_archive/Humanist/v02/0117.html.

Shafer, R. (1977). Computer in the (history) classroom. *American Historical Association Newsletter, 15*:7, 9–10.

Spiegel, G. (1992). History and post-modernism. *Past and Present*, Volume 1992, issue 135.

Uricchio, W. & Pearson, R. E. (1993). *Reframing culture: The case of the Vitagraph quality films.* Princeton: Princeton University Press.

Vitous, J. (2003). Napoleonic computer games anthology. austerlitz.wargamer.com/articles/computer_game_anthology/default.html.

White, H. (1990). *The content of the form: Narrative discourse and historical representation.* Baltimore: Johns Hopkins University Press.

Part VI

Games as a Social Phenomenon

22

VIOLENT VIDEO GAMES

Jeffrey Goldstein

It is traditional to begin pieces like this with an example of horrendous violence committed by adolescents and to note that the criminals were fond of video games with violent themes. Research is then cited to demonstrate that a relationship exists between violent video games and aggressive behavior (e.g., Anderson & Dill, 2000; Bartholow & Anderson, 2002; Fleming & Rickwood, 2001; Grossman, 1999). The goal of this chapter is to look critically at definitions and empirical studies bearing on the video game violence issue. We will also consider why and how people play violent video games, and include perspectives that go beyond traditional social psychology.

Discussions of violent video games are clouded by ambiguous definitions, poorly designed research, and the continued confusion of correlation with causality. What is a violent video game, and how does its violence differ from violence in other media, and from violence as we know it in reality? How do the consumers of violent video games perceive the violence before them?

Meanings of Violence in Video Games

There is violence and there is "violence." The violence in video games can be categorized along different dimensions: whether it involves fantasy characters or representations of humans; whether the perspective of the player's character is first-person or over the shoulder, whether the motivation for violence is clear or justified. The context of violent stories also vary along dimensions of realism, involvement, excitement, how violence/conflict begin and end, whether they are presented in an erotic or a humorous context. Variations in the nature of video game "violence" have rarely been studied.

Media researchers often speak of the amount of violence in the media, but they do not typically consider the meaning or interpretation of that violence by its audience (Gauntlett, 2001). Discussing television violence, Heather Hendershot (1998, p. 34) writes in *Saturday*

Morning Censors that "violent images on TV were often simply referred to as 'television violence,' as if television representations *were* violence in the same way that, say, a kick in the head is violence. This is wishful thinking.... Unfortunately, excising bad images will not necessarily fix problems outside the world of television." Regardless of the degree of violence in a video game, players tend to focus on the game's mechanics and its objective, rather than its violence (Karlsen, 2001; Green & Bavelier, 2003).

Violence American Style?

Symbolic or mock violence seems always to have been a part of play and entertainment. Sports such as football, in which opponents "attack" and "defend" territory, are clearly military metaphors (Guttmann, 1983, 1998; Goldstein, 1994, 1995; Regan, 1994; Twitchell, 1989), but even games regarded as innocent—chess, card games, and the Japanese board game Go—have their origins in military conflict and strategy (Fraser, 1966). In this respect, video games continue a long history of incorporating conflict and fantasy aggression into play.

According to *PC Data*, in 1999, 6 percent of PC and video games sold in the United States contained violent content. Of 338 computer games published in Denmark in 1998, seventeen games (5 percent) could be judged to contain "a considerable amount of violence" (Schierbeck & Carstens, 2000, p. 130). Of the top-selling games in the U.S. in 2002, 11.5 percent were shooters (www.theesa.com/pressroom.html).

The exaggerated, punctuated use of violence in films and video games may be a particularly American product, according to Marsha Kinder (2001). Acts of violence are used in a comic way to further a story about guilt and punishment. The serial and comic use of a rhythmic violent spectacle is similar to dance numbers in a musical film, "until it is no longer certain whether the narrative is orchestrating the violence or whether the violent events are orchestrating the narrative." On-line games such as Anarchy, Ultima, and EverQuest grant "more agency to their thousands of players who come from all over the world. Perhaps these are the sites where players will invent new modes of representing violence and generate peaceful alternatives" (Kinder, 2001).

To investigate children's engagement with violent video games, Holm Sorensen and Jessen (2000) interviewed and observed thirty-one Danish boys and girls, age five to seventeen years, while the children played video games. The researchers note that competition, challenge, and achievement are crucially important, particularly for boys. It is especially significant for the children that computer games offer them influence over the course of the game.

The social aspect of playing computer games is another essential reason for the children's interest.... Computer games generate friendship and social events, and computer games can be cultivated as a common interest.... Children's fascination with violent computer games cannot be understood without considering the above-mentioned [i.e., social] aspects. The violent elements fascinate some children, but this fascination should not be mistaken for a fascination with violence in the real world. On the contrary, all children in the investigation repudiated real-life violence. The violent elements in computer games are attractive as spectacular effects, but also because they prompt excitement and thrill. Computer games are, thus, in line with genres known from the film industry: action movies, animation, thrillers and horror movies. Computer games have inherited the content of violence from a cultural tradition within fiction, as well as genre features, such that spectacular effects are emphasized. Generally, these effects contain an element of exaggeration, which is fully recognized by children. In relation to this, the act of playing violent computer games can be seen as a parallel to the violent and "rough" play traditionally found among boys. (p. 120)

Television Violence and Video Game Violence
Research on the effects of televised violence is often applied willy-nilly to video games.

For instance, Dill and Dill (1998) argue that video games with violent themes should have the same negative effects as television violence, namely, "priming of aggressive thoughts, weakening of inhibitions against antisocial behavior, modeling, reinforcement, decreased empathy for others, and the creation of a more violent world view." (p. 409)

Anderson and Dill (2000), in a section titled "Unique Dangers of Violent Video Games," write that video games may have greater effects than violent television or violent movies for at least three reasons: first, identification with the aggressor, especially in first-person shooter games; second, the active participation and involvement in video games; third, the "addictive nature" of video games. Anderson and Dill claim that violent video games are the ideal means by which to learn aggression, with exposure to aggressive models, reinforcement, and behavior rehearsal.

Of course, as a unique medium, video games differ from television and film not only in their interactivity, but in the nature of their stories, in their open-endedness, and in their ability to satisfy different needs of their users. According to Holm Sorensen and Jessen (2000), involvement with characters in a video game differs from involvement with fictitious characters in other media. In games, the characters do not act or react as they do on film, thus weakening identification with them. "Identification with computer games is not as strong as with movies.... Playing computer games does not lead to a sort of intensified movie experience. It is a question of another type of excitement and experience that is more closely related to game and play experiences than to fiction genres, such as film or, for that matter, literature" (p. 121). The Danish children in the Holm Sorensen and Jessen study judge violence on TV, film, and video to be much worse, more violent and realistic than violence in computer games. (For other attempts to understand how viewers interpret media violence see Buckingham, 1993; Coelho, 1998; and Messenger Davies, 1997.)

Tobin (2000) says there are unstated assumptions in the media violence debate:

Researchers, teachers, and other adults can understand media effects on children solely by analyzing texts because children are naïve, ignorant, and vulnerable media consumers who unthinkingly soak up the meanings of the noxious media texts to which they are exposed. I disagree with these assumptions about the power media texts hold over children. I am not suggesting that children's readings are always insightful and resistant. Rather, my position is that we cannot know in advance of doing research how particular children will make sense of particular media texts.... Children can watch a movie full of ideological messages we find repugnant, and emerge unscathed, just as they can go through a lesson full of educational messages we find uplifting and come out having learned little or nothing. (pp. 147–148)

Third-Person Effects in Media Research

Those least familiar with video games are most likely to believe that they are harmful (Casas, 2000; Ferreira & Pais-Ribeiro, 2001; Sneed & Runco, 1992). The belief that the media affect others, but not oneself, is known as the "third-person effect" in media research (Perloff, 1999). Criticism of youth culture reflects the belief that the media are capable of turning good children bad. Even young people demonstrate the third-person effect. In studies by Aisbet (1997), Cumberbatch, Maguire, and Woods (1993), and Kline (2000), older children expressed concern for the potential impact of violent video games on younger children.

Critics of media violence claim that harmful material influences us by making us the same. "So horrible things will make us horrible, not horrified. Terrifying things will make us terrifying, not terrified. To see something aggressive makes us feel aggressive, not aggressed against. And the nastier it is, the nastier it is likely to make us. This idea is so odd, it is hard to know where to begin in challenging it," writes Barker (2001, p. 38).

Theoretical Mechanisms

Social and cognitive learning and imitation are the most often cited mechanisms that transform media violence into real violence (Fleming & Rickwood, 2001; Schutte et al., 1988; Silvern & Williamson, 1987). Dill and Dill (1998) write, "Repeated exposure to aggressive video games could make aggressive cognitions and affect chronically available, thus increasing the likelihood of aggressive responses. In the long term, this would mean that chronic exposure to violent video games would lead to increases in the tendency of an individual to act aggressively and that this effect would be pervasive."

According to Anderson (2001),

Only the cognitive route is specifically tied to the violent content of video games. Even nonviolent games can increase aggressive affect, perhaps by producing high levels of frustration. Similarly, exciting nonviolent games can increase arousal. But only violent games should directly prime aggressive thoughts and stimulate the long-term development of aggressive knowledge structures.... The real crux of the violent video game debate lies in their unique ability to directly increase aggressive cognitions.

One obvious interpretation of any media effect is that it is due to arousal. Exposure to violent video games increases physiological arousal. According to Jonathan Freedman (2001),

If the violent video game is more arousing than the non-violent comparison program, one would expect more aggression in the condition with higher arousal. If so, there is no reason to attribute the effect to the violence—it might be just the arousal.... Because of this problem, one must be extremely cautious in interpreting the results of this research and especially cautious in deciding that the effects are due to the amount of violence in the games.

In speculating on the long-term effects of violent video games, Anderson and Dill (2000) write,

Each time people play violent video games, they rehearse aggressive scripts which teach and reinforce vigilance for enemies, aggressive action against others, expectations that others will behave aggressively, positive attitudes towards use of violence, and beliefs that violent solutions are effective and appropriate. Furthermore, repeated exposure to graphic scenes of violence is likely to be desensitizing.... Long-term video game players can become more aggressive in outlook, perceptual biases, attitudes, beliefs, and behavior than they were before the repeated exposure. (p. 774)

The mechanisms through which these presumed effects arise are thought to be social learning and imitation, the physically arousing effects of violent imagery, and the development of cognitive structures supporting aggression.

Three research strategies have been used to study the effects of violent video games: correlational studies, including field studies, experiments, and meta-analyses. Each approach has its strengths and weaknesses, but none of this research can tell us whether or when violent video games cause aggressive behavior in whom.

Correlates of Playing Video Games with Violent Themes

The majority of consumers of video games are male, and those who prefer violent video games are likely to be above average in aggression, and to show other characteristics of aggressive males: namely, poorer school performance, more delinquency, and so on (Anderson & Dill, 2000; Funk et al., 2002; Wiegman & van Schie, 1998). These correlations do not imply causality, although some researchers interpret their correlations in causal terms (e.g., Wang & He, 2000).

Correlational studies do not necessarily indicate that violent video games cause these problems. On the contrary, aggressive children may be drawn to violent video games. Or a third factor, such as hyperactivity, need for arousal, or low educational attainment, could be a cause of both aggressive behavior and the desire for violent entertainment. In some studies, either no such effects were found (Gibb et al., 1983; Winkel, 1987), or were found only for arcade games (Lin & Lepper, 1987), or only for one sex. For instance, in a sample of Portuguese twelve- to seventeen-year-olds, Ferreira and Pais-Ribeiro (2001) found that playing violent video games was predictive of physical aggression, but *only in the female subsample*. The frequency of boys playing video games *in video arcades* was predictive of total, physical, and verbal aggression.

Rather than assuming that video games are responsible for these correlates, Roe and Muijs (1998) suggest that some youngsters use video games as a means of displaying competence and gaining status that they are unable to obtain through other means, such as performance in school. In other words, poor grades may give rise to an interest in playing video games, rather than the other way around.

Wiegman and van Schie (1998) examined the relationship between amount of time children spent playing video games and aggressive as well as prosocial behavior. No significant relationship was found between video game use in general and aggressive behavior, but a significant negative correlation with prosocial behavior was found. Children who prefer aggressive video games were less prosocial than those with other game preferences. Children who preferred playing aggressive video games tended to be less intelligent than those with other game preferences.

Colwell and Payne (2000) studied the relationships among questionnaire measures of social isolation, self-esteem, and aggression among 204 twelve- to fourteen-year-old students in North London. "Analysis of a scale to assess needs fulfilled by game play provided some support for the notion of 'electronic friendship' among boys, but there was no evidence that game play leads to social isolation." (p. 295) Play was *not* linked to self-esteem in girls, but a negative relationship was obtained between self-esteem and frequency of play in boys. Self-esteem was not related to the number of games with aggressive content named among three favorite games, but was positively correlated with total exposure to game play.

Funk and colleagues (2002) examined relations between a preference for violent electronic games and adolescents' self-perceptions of problem behaviors and emotions. Thirty-two boys and girls aged eleven to fifteen completed the Youth Self-Report (YSR), a standardized self-report measure of adolescent problem behaviors, and listed their favorite electronic games. The predicted relationships with externalizing behaviors, including aggression, were not found. However, across all YSR subscales, children with higher preference for violent games had more clinically significant elevations than those with low preference for violent games.

A recent review of correlational studies concluded that they were ambiguous (Subrahmanyam et al., 2001).

Does Playing Violent Video Games Cause Aggressive Behavior?

Correlational studies are inherently unable to establish cause-and-effect, so psychologists resort to laboratory experiments in which some factors are manipulated, whereas others are controlled. In the typical laboratory experiment, university students are randomly assigned to play a violent video game or a nonviolent video game, for anywhere from four to seventy-five minutes, typically around fifteen minutes. Following play, some measure of "aggression" is made. We will examine each component of this situation, and ask whether subjects *play* a video game, whether the video game can be regarded as *violent*, and whether the experiment measures *aggressive behavior*.

Playing *Violent Video Games?*

Play is a voluntary, self-directed activity (Garvey, 1991), an experience that probably cannot be captured in a laboratory experiment. In video game research, the duration of play is too short for anything like the play experience to be replicated. Being required to play a violent video game on demand for ten or fifteen minutes is not "playing."

Few studies have considered how and why people play violent video games, or why people play at all. Experimental research does not recognize the fact that video game players freely engage in play, and are always free to stop. They enter an imaginary world with a playful frame of mind, something entirely missing from laboratory studies of violent video games. One of the pleasures of play is this very suspension of reality. Laboratory experiments cannot tell us what the effects of playing video games are, because there is no sense in which participants in these studies play.

Playing Violent *Video Games?*

There is much confusion about the definition of "aggression" and terms such as "media violence" and "violent video games." Psychologists define violence and aggression as "the intentional injury of another person." However, there is neither intent to injure nor a living victim in a video game. Players do not engage in aggressive behavior when playing a video game, but participate in a fantasy involving mock violence. They push buttons or manipulate a joystick that has consequences for digital characters on a two-dimensional screen. During play they display none of the facial expressions and experience none of the emotions normally associated with real life aggression, but instead reflect those of concentration and play (Holmes & Pellegrini, this volume; Holm Sorensen & Jessen, 2000).

Distinguishing Fantasy from Reality   Some educators have expressed concern that children below a certain age cannot distinguish real violence from fantasy aggression and therefore are at greater risk of learning and imitating violent behaviors. Whether this is so is an empirical question that has not very often been studied. However, researchers themselves sometimes fail to distinguish real from fantasy violence. For example, Dill and Dill (1998) write,

In violent video games, aggression is often the main goal, and killing adversaries means winning the game and reaping the benefits. While in real life, murder is a crime, in a violent video game, murder is the most reinforced behavior.... The violent video game player is an active aggressor ... the players' behavioral repertoire is expanded to include new and varied aggressive alternatives. (p. 412)

Of course, in a video game there is no literal killing, murder, or aggressive behavior.

Does the interactive nature of video games make them more influential than the more passive activities of television or film viewing? On the contrary, according to a study by Holm Sorensen and Jessen (2000). They assessed how capable Danish children were of distinguishing between fiction and reality and to establish whether they are able to account for this distinction:

The children in the investigation, including the youngest who were five years old, are fully aware and can account for the difference between computer games as fiction and computer games as reality.... It is also important that this exact feature [interactivity], which is usually described as a problem in relation to violent computer games—the fact that the player himself must conduct violent deeds—actually makes children aware that their actions take place in a fictitious universe. For children, computer games are in fact "games" with their own rules. From an early age, they are aware that these rules do not apply outside the realm of the game, with the exception that children can include elements and rules from the games in their play. (pp. 120–121)

Causes Aggressive Behavior?

Reviews of video game research are as variable in their conclusions as the individual studies that comprise them. The same two dozen or so studies of violent video games are said to support different conclusions. Some reviews conclude that violent video games cause aggressive behavior (Anderson & Dill, 2000; Ask, 1999; Dill & Dill, 1998; Unsworth & Ward, 2001), whereas others find the evidence is inadequate to reach any conclusion (Bensley & Vaneenway, 2001; Cumberbatch, 2001; Durkin, 1995; Durkin & Low, 1998; Federal Trade Commission, 2001; Gunter, 1998; Griffiths, 2000; van Feilitzen, 2000).

Sakamoto (2000) reports that the same controversies surround violent video games in Japan as in western countries. "The arguments concerning the harmfulness of video games have become heated every fifth year (p. 66)." Sakamoto notes that early research found no relationship between video games and violence, but recent Japanese research has occasionally reported such a relationship. Sakamoto concludes, as have many others who have reviewed the research, that it is insufficient to draw conclusions about a causal connection between video games and violence. The clear consensus is that there is no consensus.

Inconsistent Results   It is difficult to know what to make of complex and inconsistent results between and within video game studies. For example, Kirsh (1998) had boys and girls aged eight to eleven play either a "very violent" video game (*Mortal Kombat II*) or an "action-oriented, non-violent video game" (*NBA Jam*). Immediately following video game play, children interpreted a series of ambiguous stories in which a same-sex peer caused a negative event to happen, but where the intent of the peer was unclear—for example, a child is hit in the back with a ball. After each story, children were asked six questions about the harmdoer's intent and emotional state, and potential retaliation and punishment. Responses were coded in terms of amount of "negative and violent content."

According to Kirsh, children exposed to the violent video game "responded more negatively" to the ambiguous provocation stories than children exposed to the relatively nonviolent *NBA Jam* on three of the six questions. There was no significant difference between those who played *Mortal Kombat* or *NBA Jam* in whether they regarded the other's behavior as intentional or accidental. Kirsh hypothesized that children who played the violent video game would retaliate more and expect more punishment than children who played the nonviolent video game. This hypothesis was partially supported. When asked, "What would you do next?" children playing the violent video game responded "significantly more negatively" than children playing the nonviolent video game. However, the question about prospective punishment for the harmdoer, "Do you think the kid should be punished a lot, a little, or not at all?" was not significant. Do these data support any conclusion whatsoever about the effects of violent video games?

Two meta-analyses (Anderson & Bushman, 2001; Sherry, 2001) report small effect sizes ($r = .19$ and $.15$, respectively). In the Sherry meta-analysis, playing time emerged as a *negative* predictor of aggression ($r = -.19$). That is, the more one played violent video games, the weaker the relation to aggressive behavior.

In a study by Anderson and Ford (1986), university students who played a "highly aggressive" video game (*Zaxxon*) for twenty minutes were not more hostile than a group that played a less aggressive game (*Centipede*). Likewise, in studies by Ballard and Lineberger (1999), Scott (1995), and Winkel et al. (1987), the level of aggressive content in video games bore no relation to subjects' aggressive behavior.

In an experiment by Ballard and Lineberger (1999), 119 male university students played either a nonviolent video game (*NBA Jam*) or one of three levels of a violent video game (*Mortal Kombat*). After playing the video game for fifteen minutes, participants rewarded and punished a male or female confederate in a teacher/learner situation. Participants rewarded male (but not female) confederates with significantly more jellybeans after playing *NBA Jam* than under any of the *Mortal Kombat* conditions. Participants punished confederates significantly more after playing *Mortal Kombat II* than after playing *NBA Jam*. However, those who played the more violent *Mortal Kombat II* were not more punitive than those who played a less violent version of *Mortal Kombat*.

In a study of elementary school children, Graybill, Strawniak, Hunter, and O'Leary (1987) found no

effects of video games on aggressive behavior, which was measured by pushing buttons that could reward or punish another child.

Scott (1995) measured the aggressiveness of university students with the Buss-Durkee Hostility Inventory and the Eysenck Personality Questionnaire. No signficant differences in aggressiveness were found between students after playing a nonaggressive, a moderately or a highly aggressive video game. Scott concludes that there is a "general lack of support for the commonly held view that playing aggressive computer games causes an individual to feel more aggressive."

Cooper and Mackie (1986) randomly assigned eighty-four boys and girls, ten to eleven years old, to play or to observe a violent video game (*Missile Command*), a nonviolent video game (*Pac-Man*), or a pen-and-paper game for eight minutes. They were then observed during a free play period, where they could choose from a variety of toys, including an aggressive toy (a spring-release fist that fires darts), an active toy (basketball), a skill game (pinball), and a quiet toy (building logs). Children were then given an opportunity to punish or reward another child for various actions. Children who played or observed the aggressive video game spent more time playing with the aggressive toy than did other children. This was particularly so for girls. Boys' play with the aggressive toy was not affected by the type of video game played. Cooper and Mackie also found that children who played the violent video game were more active afterwards, changing often from one activity to another. Although video games clearly influenced the children's postgame *play*, the video games had no effect on *interpersonal aggression*. Children who played *Missile Command* did not differ from those who played *Pac-Man* in how much punishment or reward they administered.

Perhaps the best-known experiment of video games with violent themes was conducted by Craig Anderson and Karen Dill (2000). They selected video games as similar as possible on enjoyment, frustration, and physiological arousal, but which differed in whether they contained violent themes. They chose *Castle Wolfenstein 3D* as the violent game and *Myst* as the nonviolent game.[1]

In the main experiment, more than two hundred university students participated in two sessions, during which they played the assigned video game three times for fifteen minutes each. In the first session, participants played the game for fifteen minutes and completed measures of affect and world view, and played the game again for fifteen minutes before completing a cognitive measure, namely, the *reaction time* to recognize aggressive words (e.g., "murder"). Anderson and Dill claimed people with quicker reactions have relatively greater access to aggressive thoughts. During the second session, participants played the game for fifteen minutes and completed a behavioral measure—twenty-five trials in a "competitive reaction time task" in which the participant is told to push a button faster than his or her opponent. If participants lose this race, they receive a noise blast at a level supposedly set by their opponent. Aggressive behavior was operationally defined as the intensity and duration of retaliatory noise blasts the participant delivered to the unseen opponent.

The predicted effect of the violent video game on aggression was found only for the *duration* of noise, but not for the *intensity* of noise blasts. That is, participants pressed the noise button longer, but did not deliver louder (i.e., more "aggressive") noise blasts. There were no statistically significant effects of any of the independent variables—sex, trait irritability, video game type—on the noise intensity settings. On the other hand, Bartholow and Anderson (2002) report effects with noise *intensity* but *not duration*.

The type of video game played had no effect on state hostility or on measures of crime perception or feelings of safety.

Those who played the violent video game recognized aggression-related words more quickly than those who played the nonviolent game. Anderson and Dill conclude that "playing the violent video game increased accessibility of aggressive thoughts and aggressive behavior, but did not reliably increase state hostility. These findings suggest that violent video games takes a cognitive and not an affective path to increasing aggressive behavior in short-term settings" (p. 786). Thus, according to Anderson and Dill, the danger in exposure to violent video games seems to be in the ideas they teach and not primarily in the emotions they incite in the player. However, the validity of their dependent measure as an indication of aggressive cognition is unknown. Word recognition is typically used to reflect perceptual or semantic salience (Grainger & Dijkstra, 1996), a phenomenon that has no clear connection to aggressive behavior.

Brown (2000) finds Anderson and Dill's conclusions "disturbing." Of the behavioral measure of aggression (blasts of noise), Brown (2000) writes,

For whatever reason, the intensity of the noise didn't vary with any of the factors tested: gender, irritability score, and game type had no effect on the intensity of the *sound chosen by the participant. The duration of the sound did vary, however. As one might predict, participants tended to be more aggressive in general when setting the duration of the noise immediately following trials where they "lost" (i.e., were subjected to a burst of noise). Following a "win" trial, the only pattern was that females tended to be more aggressive than males, delivering longer noise blasts.*

In an Australian sample of eight- to twelve-year-olds, Fleming and Rickwood (2001) found no differences between violent and nonviolent video game play on a paper-and-pencil test of aggressive mood (though play was limited to four minutes!).

Dill and Dill (1998) review video game research as it relates to violence. "Precious few true experiments have been done to assess the effects of playing violent video games on aggression-related outcomes; there is no real 'programmatic' line of research yet in this area. Much of what has been done has focused on very young children and has examined aggressive free play as the main behavioral dependent measure" (p. 419). "All experiments that measured aggressive affect, in contrast, have used undergraduate participants. Two of these studies showed increases in aggressive affect after violent video game play, one found no differences between violent and nonviolent video game play, and two found no differences." (p. 419)

Among the unsettled issues surrounding violent video games is whether repeated play has more intense or qualitatively different effects than short-term play; whether it is boys or girls who are most influenced by violent games; whether it is affect, behavior, or cognition that is influenced by the violent content of games. What cognitions (besides reaction time) does video game content affect? How do players use their experience with violent video games in their relationships with others? It has been said that violent video games are apt to promote violent solutions to problems, but I know of no research on this issue.

Measures of Aggression   It is not possible to observe real aggression in the laboratory, so researchers must improvise indirect indicators of potential aggression. For example:

· Hitting a bobo doll (Schutte et al., 1988).
· Coding children's interpretations of ambiguous stories (Kirsh, 1998).
· Listing aggressive thoughts and feelings (Calvert & Tan, 1994).

- Administering blasts of white noise to an unseen person, in the "teacher-learner" paradigm, in which errors on a "learning task" are "punished" (Anderson & Dill, 2000; Bartholow & Anderson, 2002; Wiegman, van Schie, & Modde, 1997).
- Withholding money from another (Winkel, Novak, & Hopson, 1987).
- "Killing" characters in a video game (Anderson & Morrow, 1995; Ask, 1999; Ask, Autoustinos, & Winefield, 2000).
- Time elapsed to recognize aggressive words (Anderson & Dill, 2000).

Ask, Autoustinos, and Winefield (2000) studied experienced video game players, who competed in a *Mortal Kombat 3* (*MK3*) tournament. In *MK3* the winning player has the opportunity either "to kill or not kill" the opponent's fighter at the end of each round. This was used as the measure of aggressive behavior. Ask and colleagues had two teachers rate each player for aggression toward peers and toward teachers. They report that "the competitor's tendency to kill their opponent's videogame character upon winning was associated with their aggressive behavior at school" (p. 91). Players who used more "kill" responses in *MK3* were also students who teachers saw as more aggressive.

In experiment 1, sixteen males competed in a *MK3*_tournament with cash prizes for the winners. The final playoff took place before an audience of about forty other students. Six of the sixteen players never used the "kill" option and were thus excluded from the analysis (!), leaving ten competitors in the sample. In the pre-tournament trials, the ten players used the kill option 67 percent of the time, whereas in the competitive tournament, they used the kill option 84 percent of the time. This is a statistically significant increase. Ask et al. note that the results could have been due to (a) the reward offered to winners, or (b) the presence of an audience, and did not necessarily have anything to do with the violent images in *MK3*.

Experiments 2 and 3 eliminated the audience and rewards for winners and instead offered each participant $5. In experiment 2, there was no support for the hypothesis that competition would increase the use of the "kill" option, whereas in experiment 3, there were more "kill" responses under competitive than under noncompetitive conditions. This research shows a tendency for experienced game players to choose the "kill" option in *Mortal Kombat 3* more when they are in competition against others than when playing individually. Perhaps there is greater reliance on the "kill"

option during competition because it is a strategic response within the game—for example, it could demoralize the opponent. Ask and colleagues do not report the relationship between use of the "kill" option and success in the tournament, so we do not know whether it was a winning strategy or not.

Almost all of the research involved analogues of aggression rather than the real thing. One can and I believe should question whether these analogues have anything to do with aggression.... There is not the slightest evidence that playing violent video games causes any long-term or lasting increase in aggressiveness or violence.... There is no scientific reason to believe that violent video games have bad effects on children or on adults, and certainly none to indicate that such games constitute a public health risk. (Freedman, 2001)

Aggressive Play and Aggressive Behavior Studies of violent video games do not always distinguish *aggressive play* from *aggressive behavior* (for example, Schutte et al., 1988; Silvern & Williamson, 1987). Observations of children on the playground may confuse mock aggression (pretending to engage in martial arts) with real aggression (attempting to injure someone). What appears to an observer to be aggressive behavior may instead be aggressive *play*, where there is no intent to harm anyone. In the rare study that measures both aggressive *play* and aggressive *behavior* (e.g., Cooper & Mackie, 1986), violent video games affect the former and not the latter.

According to Griffiths (1999), "the majority of studies on very young children tend to show that children become more aggressive after playing or watching a violent video game, but *these were all based on the observation of free play.*" (pp. 209–210) Grififths questions whether this is a valid measure of aggression.

The objective of a study by Robinson and colleagues (2001) was to assess the effects of reducing television, video tape, and video game use on aggressive behavior and perceptions of a mean and scary world. Third- and fourth-grade children (mean age 8.9 years) in an elementary school in California received a six-month classroom curriculum to reduce television, video tape, and video game use (the children were encouraged to limit media use to 7 hours a week). A second, control school, did not receive such instruction. In September (pre-intervention) and April (post-intervention), children rated their peers' aggressive behavior and reported their perceptions of the world as a mean and scary place. A random sample of children was observed for physical and verbal aggression on the playground.

Parents (more than 80 percent of them mothers) were interviewed by telephone and reported aggressive and delinquent behaviors on a behavior checklist.

Compared to controls, children who had received instruction in reducing media use showed statistically significant decreases in peer ratings of aggression and verbal aggression. Differences in observed physical aggression, parent reports of aggressive behavior, and perceptions of a mean and scary world were *not* statistically significant between the two groups.[2] The authors note that the intervention was targeted at all television, video tape, and video game use, instead of violent media. They did not assess specific exposure to violent media, so they do not know whether violent media exposure was reduced. Nevertheless, the authors conclude, "These findings support the causal influences of these media on aggression and the potential benefits of reducing children's media use."

Poole (2001) has criticized the methods and conclusions of Robinson et al. (2001). Children's "aggression" was measured in five different ways:

1. peer ratings of aggression (classmates answered questions such as "Who says 'Give me that' a lot?")
2. observed verbal aggression (observers stood in the playground and counted instances of "verbally aggressive" acts per minute)
3. observed physical aggression (playground observation)
4. parent reports of aggressive behavior
5. the children's perceptions of the world as a "mean and scary" place.

In fact, the psychologists found statistically significant decreases in what they called "aggression" in the study group only on the first 2 measurements above. That is, actual physical aggression did not decrease after 6 months of limited exposure to television, video tapes and video games. That ought to be surprising if you buy the idea that media actually affect behavior. Nor did parents report any decrease in their children's aggression; nor did children say that they found the world less mean and scary.

It would be a step forward if researchers differentiated levels and types of media violence, distinguished real from dramatic from fantastic violence, and considered aggressive play something other than aggressive behavior.

Meta-Analysis of Video Game Research
Meta-analysis combines the results of many different studies into a single statistical analysis. It is a correla-

tional technique that estimates the average effect size among variables over a number of independent studies that used different measurements and participant samples. Like a correlation coefficient, effect size is represented by a figure ranging between 0 and 1.0. An effect size is considered "small" if it is .30 or less, "moderate" if it is between .30 and .60, and "large" if it exceeds .60. Meta-analysis is about the *quantity*, not the *quality* of data. For example, if aggression is not clearly defined and measured in individual studies, combining studies will not improve their reliability or validity.

Two meta-analyses of violent video games have been published, Anderson and Bushman (2001) and Sherry (2001). Anderson and Bushman analyzed thirty-five research reports, with a total of 4,262 participants. They included a study if it examined the effects of playing violent video games on aggressive cognition, affect, aggressive behavior, physiological arousal, or prosocial behavior.

The average effect size of thirty-three tests of the relation between video game violence and aggressive behavior was $r = .19$, and with aggressive affect, $r = .18$, small effects. Effects were greater if the target in the games was an inanimate object rather than an image of a person. This finding may have a bearing on discussions of game realism, where it has been suggested that increasing realism necessarily strengthens the association between aggressive behavior and games with violent images. These data suggest that it is unrealistic images that are associated with the most aggressive behavior. Interviews with gamers by Holm Sorensen and Jessen (2000) corroborate this.

Prosocial behavior, which was measured in eight studies, was negatively correlated with violent video games ($r = -.18$), suggesting that those who play violent video games tend to be less prosocial. Violent video games are positively correlated with physiological arousal.

Video game violence was related to aggressive cognition ($r = .27$). Anderson and Bushman conclude, "Therefore, violent video games may increase aggression in the short term by increasing aggressive thoughts." However, "aggressive thoughts" have not been measured directly, but through such measures as reaction time to selected words. Whether this bears any connection to aggressive behavior remains to be seen.

It is difficult to draw firm conclusions from the existing research because different, incompatible measures of aggression are used, and this threatens the validity of the research. Measures range from actual behavior (aggression during free play, willingness to help or harm another) to paper-and-pencil measures of aggressive feelings. Sherry (2001) asks, "Do video games cause people to *act* aggressively or to *feel* aggressive or both?" He also observes that "the literature on video game effects is littered with mixed findings from studies that use a wide range of games, treatment exposure times, and subject pools, obscuring clear conclusions."

Sherry gathered thirty-two independent studies in which violent video game play was the independent variable and some measure of aggression was the dependent variable. This compares with thirty-three studies in Anderson and Bushman's sample (2001).

The overall correlation between video game play and aggression in this meta-analysis, based on a sample of 2,722 individuals, is $r = .15$, a small effect size. This is far lower than the effect of television violence on aggression. According to Sherry, "Overall, this analysis suggests that there is a correlation between video game play and aggression, but that relationship is smaller than that found for television.... Researchers in this area will need to develop new theories that acknowledge experiential and social differences between video game use and television viewing."

Conclusion: Video Games and Aggressive Behavior
Nearly everyone who reviews the existing research on violence and electronic games arrives at the same conclusion: the research is too inconsistent and insubstantial to allow any conclusions to be drawn. Bensley and Van Eenwyk (2001) review all available studies and find flaws in each of them. They summarize: "In conclusion, current research evidence is not supportive of a major concern that violent video games lead to real-life violence." Van Feilitzen (2000), in her introduction to a UNESCO volume on children and media violence, notes:

Several authors in this book emphasize precisely the fact that inquiries on influences of the violence in electronic games are very few and have employed a limited number of methods. According to some studies, young children become more aggressive in their subsequent play, *but these studies have used only one type of method. Among the very few studies that have included the newer, more violent electronic games, there are some ... indicating that the games can contribute to aggression also among older children and young people. At the same time, however, other studies have provided conflicting or inconclusive findings.* (p. 19)

Mark Griffiths (2000), writing in the same UNESCO volume, summarized the published research on video game violence:

All the studies that have examined the effects of video games on aggression have only involved measures of possible short-term aggressive consequences. The majority of the studies on very young children—as opposed to those in their teens upwards—tend to show that children do become more aggressive after either playing or watching a violent video game but all these studies were based on the observation of a child's free play after playing a violent video game [emphasis added].... There is much speculation as to whether the procedures to measure aggression levels are methodologically valid and reliable. (p. 32)

Nevertheless, some researchers reason that "because so many people are exposed to violent media, the effect to society can be immense even if only a small percentage of viewers are affected by it.... It might be that only 1 in 1,000 viewers will behave more aggressively immediately after viewing a particular program, but the cumulative effects may well increase the aggressiveness of most (if not all) of the 1,000 viewers" (Bushman & Anderson, 2001, p. 482). Of course, there may also be one in a thousand viewers who benefit, for example, using entertainment as distraction from emotional distress.

Of course the media affect emotions and behavior. That is why people use them. However, there is no evidence that media shape behavior in ways that override a person's own desires and motivations. Can a violent video game make a person violent? It can if he wants it to. Why don't violent video games increase aggression among the researchers who study them? Because they have a higher purpose—understanding violent video games—that transcends the contents of the game. The focus is on something other than the mock aggression taking place on the screen. Young people may also have other goals in mind when they play violent video games, including trying to improve their score, distraction, emotional and physiological self-regulation, and to have common experiences to share with friends. The media may affect some people, but not necessarily in ways that media violence researchers typically fear. Media effects may vary from relaxation and distraction to emotional and physical reactions. There is no evidence that media influence people in ways that go against their grain.

Dissenting Views of Media Violence
Some psychologists have made strong claims about the causal link between media violence and violence in society. The American Medical Association, American Psychological Association, and the American Academy of

Pediatrics have issued public health warnings about violent video games. Bushman and Anderson (2001) state that the scientific community speaks with one voice about media violence, with only the entertainment industry and news media failing to accept the conclusion that portrayals of violence in film, television, and video games cause aggressive behavior. However, there are three types of dissenting view. First, there are disagreements within the scientific community itself. Not all researchers agree that the existing research supports the conclusion that media violence is a causal factor in interpersonal violence. Second, although social psychologists have appropriated the topic of media violence as their own, other scholars engaged in media studies have come to different conclusions about the role of media violence in society. European media scholars are especially critical of the American "effects model." Third, there are commentators from various quarters who remain unconvinced by the scientific evidence produced by psychologists. We describe these dissenting strands of literature further below.

Variance among Researchers

Not every study finds evidence of a causal link between media violence and real violence. For example, field studies by Charlton, Gunter, and Hannan (2002), Feshbach and Singer (1971), and Milgram and Shotland (1973) found no effects of media violence on aggressive behavior. Nor did research by Doob and MacDonald (1979), Hennigan et al. (1982), Messner (1986), Wiegman, Kuttschreuter, & Baarda (1992), or Winkel, Novak, and Hopson (1987). Neither are all psychologists convinced that the evidence to date is sufficient to support a causal connection (Fowles, 1999; Freedman, 2001, 2002; Gadow & Sprafkin, 1989). British media researcher David Gauntlett (1995) has gone so far as to write, "The search for direct 'effects' of television on behavior is over: Every effort has been made, and they simply cannot be found" (p. 120).

In a re-examination of studies claiming to show harmful effects of media violence, Fowles (1999) and Freedman (2002) point to inconsistencies and misinterpretations of studies central to the debate. For instance, Fowles criticizes the often-cited research of Eron for its methods and ambiguous results. "It is difficult to believe that a study with such a weak single finding has been taken so seriously by so many thoughtful people" (p. 37). The multinational study by Eron and Huesmann obtained results that are uneven from country to country.

In the Polish study, although average violence viewing increased during the 3-year research period, aggression decreased.... For the Australian children studied, the result was null: "Present data did not indicate that a relation exists in Australia between children's early violence viewing and the level of their aggression three years later," wrote Eron and Huesmann (p. 192). Positive correlations were found for city children in Israel but not for rural children. Finally, the Dutch researchers [Wiegmann et al., 1992], like the Australian researchers, could discern no correlation.

It is often asserted that repeated exposure to media images of violence desensitizes people to the real thing. Fowles does not believe that the research supports this view. "Even George Comstock, normally sympathetic to the violent effects literature, concedes about desensitization studies that 'what the research does not demonstrate is any likelihood that media portrayals would affect the response to injury, suffering, or violent death experienced firsthand'" (p. 30).

Freedman (2001) addresses two problems with existing research on violent video games: the choice of games and demand characteristics. It is very difficult to do adequate experimental research on violent video games. One problem is the difficulty of finding two video games that are equal in all respects, except one of them contains violence and the other does not. Only then could we be sure, if they have different effects, that this is due to the violent content and not to some other feature of the games, such as their level of excitement, involvement, activity, or sound effects.

Medical research uses the "double-blind" technique to insure against unintentional bias. In a double-blind experiment, neither the recipient of a treatment, nor the person administering the treatment, knows whether it is the actual treatment or a placebo. Nothing approaching this standard is possible in media violence research.

When experimenters choose a violent game, they may be giving the message that they approve of such games and might therefore approve of or even expect the subjects to behave violently.... The possibility of demand causing the results is not unlikely or far-fetched. It is a well-known phenomenon in experimental research and a continual almost ubiquitous source of problems in interpretation.... This leaves almost all of the results open to the alternative and uninteresting interpretation that they are caused by demand factors rather than the variable of interest, namely the direct effect of violence in the video game." (Freedman, 2001)

Another problem with laboratory experiments of violent video games is how the participants perceive them, when they are often told nothing about why they are being asked to play a violent video game.

Media Studies

Social psychologists are not the only scholars interested in media violence. Media studies scholars trained in the European tradition of critical theory tend to dismiss the "media effects" research as irrelevant for understanding media violence, or as inadequate to the task (Carter & Weaver, 2003). Martin Barker and Julian Petley (2001) write, "It could be said that there is little point in trying to question the methodology of those people working within the effects model, because, by our own definition of that work, they are much more concerned with creating an illusion of empiricism to support their prejudged conclusions than in designing methodologically sound research. In other words, they're not going to stop." Savage (2004), a criminologist, finds no reason to conclude that media violence is a cause of criminal violence.

Gauntlett (2001, p. 5) believes the solution is "to raise awareness of the flaws in that research in the hope that this will make it more difficult for the press to report their findings uncritically and, perhaps more importantly, to produce new kinds of research which will tell us [something] more subtle and interesting about possible media influences than anything which the effects researchers can provide."

Other Critics

Child clinical psychologist and crime novelist Jonathan Kellerman (1999) calls media violence "the scapegoat we love to hate." Concerning juvenile crime he writes, "If increased public safety is our goal, efficiency also dictates that we cease pouring money into research and clinical activities that have little direct impact upon rates of child criminality. A prime example of such diminished returns is the flood of studies conducted on the factor most often blamed for childhood criminality: media violence" (p. 71).

Richard Rhodes (2000) asks,

Is there really a link between entertainment and violent behavior? The American Medical Association, the American Academy of Pediatrics, and the National Institute of Mental Health all say yes. They base their claims on social science research that has been sharply criticized and disputed within the social science profession, especially outside the United States. In fact, no direct, causal link between exposure to mock violence in the media and subsequent violent behavior has ever been demonstrated, and the few claims of modest correlation have been contradicted by other findings, sometimes in the same studies.... If we want to reduce (violence) even further, protecting children from real violence in their lives—not the pale shadow of mock violence—is the place to begin.

One study cited as establishing a causal relationship between media violence and real violence is the epidemiological research of Centerwall (1989), who found an increase in murder rates following the introduction of television in South Africa. Rhodes notes that homicide rates in France, Germany, Italy, Japan, and the United States failed to change with increasing television ownership in the same period, and in some cases actually declined. In the most recent such study, Charlton, Gunter, and Hannan (2002) failed to find any effect of the introduction of television to the south Atlantic island of St. Helena.

Among claims by researchers are that repeated exposure to media violence desensitizes children to witnessing aggression and raises the likelihood that they will use it, and that children learn from TV, film, and video games that violence is rewarded.

"Though some statistical support has been obtained for [these] suppositions, not a single causal link between media violence and criminality has ever been produced," writes Kellerman (1999, p. 72). He continues:

This is not to say media violence is harmless. To the extent that gory junk attracts high-risk youngsters, it's anything but. Is it possible that an already psychopathic boy with a head full of violent impulses that have festered since early childhood, sitting around the house sucking on a joint or sniffing glue while he watches Scream, *can be spurred to imitate what he sees on the screen? Absolutely. The same is true of printed violence—serial killers often collect violent pornography and true-crime magazines in order to heighten sexual arousal.... Given no bloody books, no Freddy Krueger on video, no thrash metal or gangsta rap, would Billy Rotten of bullying, cat-mutilating proclivities have picked up a knife and stabbed his mother anyway? No way to know for sure, but I'd bet yes. And the likelihood of Billy's engaging in serious violence somewhere along the line would remain extremely high no matter what he read or viewed, because the variables that strongly influence violent behavior are likely to be a lot more personal than those elicited by wielding the remote control.* (pp. 77–78)

What's Missing from Video Game Research?

The role of volition or choice is absent from video game research. What are the effects of voluntary (as opposed to enforced) exposure to violent entertainment? Missing from research is any acknowledgment that video game players freely engage in play, and are always free to leave, or pause. Except in laboratory experiments, no one is forced to play a violent video game.

The Attractions of Violent Video Games

Almost no studies of the presumed harmful effects of video games have considered how and why people play them. People play video games for many different reasons. Some play to experience excitement, some to become experts or to impress their friends, others because video games are challenging or educational. Some play widely vilified games in order to elicit predictable, if negative, reactions from teachers or parents. Immersion in a game can be highly pleasurable (Koepp et al., 1998). Men and women enjoy different kinds of games and enjoy play for different reasons (Goldstein 1994, 1998, 1999; Kline 2000; Malone, 1981).

When there are few cues to their unreality, bloody images lose their appeal (McCauley, 1998). In one study, boys who played video games with violent themes showed the same positive facial expressions, quality of peer interaction, and enjoyment as those who played "neutral" games (see Holmes & Pellegrini, this volume). Similarly, violence, if it is to be entertaining, must fulfill certain requirements: it must have a moral story, in which good triumphs over evil, and it must carry cues to its unreality—music, sound effects, a fantasy storyline, cartoonlike characters. People are highly selective in the violence they seek or tolerate (McCauley, 1998; Zillmann, 1998).

We play video games largely for the expected effects they will have on us. Youngsters are willing to expose themselves to unpleasant media images because the benefits of doing so outweigh the costs. Players, like researchers, have overriding reasons for engaging with violent themes, even if they find them repugnant.

It is surprising that social psychologists so rarely consider the social lives of gamers. A Danish study of five- to seventeen-year-olds did so, and concluded that violent computer games could not be understood without considering their social aspects (Holm Sorensen & Jessen, 2000).

Not all questions can be answered with the tools of social psychological research. To quote John Dewey, "An idea has no greater metaphysical stature than, say, a fork. When your fork proves inadequate to the task of eating soup, it makes little sense to argue about whether there is something inherent in the nature of forks or something inherent in the nature of soup that accounts for the failure. You just reach for a spoon."

Notes

1. According to Andy Brown (2000) in *The Tech Report*, the games studied by Anderson and Dill are not comparable: *Myst* is an adventure game with "brain teaser" puzzles, whereas *Wolfenstein* is a first-person shooter game.
2. Of Gerbner's notion that children who consume long hours of television are likely to see the world as a "mean and scary place," Burke and Burke (1999, p. 198) write, "Well, good for TV, because the world sure as hell is a mean, scary place—and has been for most of this (20th) century. Those heavy TV viewers are going into life with their eyes open" (p. 198).

References

Aisbett, K. (1997). How children view aggressive content in interactive games: Are they doomed? In T. Newlands & M. Roger (Eds.), *Children and interactive multimedia: A place to play?* Sydney: College Institute of New South Wales, Australia.

Anderson, C. A. (2001). Playing by the rules. University of Chicago, Public Policy Institute. http://cultural-policy.vchicago.edu.

Anderson, C. A., & Bushman, B. J. (2001). Effects of violent video games on aggressive behavior, aggressive cognition, aggressive affect, physiological arousal, and prosocial behavior: A meta-analytic review of the scientific literature. *Psychological Science, 12,* 353–359.

Anderson, C. A., & Dill, K. E. (2000). Video games and aggressive thoughts, feelings, and behavior in the laboratory and in life. *Journal of Personality and Social Psychology, 78,* 772–790.

Anderson, C. A., & Ford, C. M. (1986). Affect of the game player: Short-term effects of highly and mildly aggressive video games. *Personality and Social Psychology Bulletin, 12,* 390–402.

Anderson, C. A., & Morrow, M. (1995). Competitive aggression without interaction: Effects of competitive versus cooperative instructions on aggressive behavior in video games. *Personality and Social Psychology Bulletin, 21*, 1020–1030.

Ask, A. (1999). To kill or not to kill: Competitive aggression in adolescents Ph.D. dissertation, University of Adelaide, Australia.

Ask, A., Autoustinos, M., & Winefield, A. H. (2000). To kill or not to kill: Competitive aggression in Australian adolescent males during videogame play. In C. van Feilitzen & U. Carlsson (Eds.), *Children in the new media landscape* (pp. 83–92). Goteborg, Sweden: UNESCO International Clearinghouse on Children and Violence on the Screen.

Ballard, M. E., & Lineberger, R. (1999). Video game violence and confederate gender: Effects on reward and punishment given by college males. *Sex Roles, 41*, 541–558.

Barker, M. (2001). The Newson report. In M. Barker & J. Petley, *Ill effects: The media/violence debate* (2d ed.) (pp. 27–46). London: Routledge.

Barker, M., & Petley, J. (2001). *Ill effects: The media/violence debate* (2d ed.). London: Routledge.

Bartholow, B. D., & Anderson, C. A. (2002). Effects of violent video games on aggressive behavior: Poetntial sex differences. *Journal of Experimental Social Psychology, 38*, 283–290.

Bensley, L., & Van Eenwyk, J. (2001). Video games and real-life aggression: Review of the literature. *Journal of Adolescent Health, 29*, 244–257.

Buckingham, D. (1993). *Children talk television*. London: Routledge.

Burke, T., & Burke, K. (1999). *Saturday morning fever: Growing up with cartoon culture*. New York: St. Martin's.

Bushman, B. J., & Anderson, C. A. (2001). Media violence and the American public: Scientific facts versus media misinformation. *American Psychologist, 56*, 477–489.

Calvert, S. L., & Tan, S. (1994). Impact of virtual reality on young adults' physiological arousal and aggressive thoughts. *Journal of Applied Developmental Psychology, 15*, 125–139.

Carter, C., & Weaver, C. K. (2003). *Violence and the media*. Buckingham, UK: Open University Press.

Casas, F. (2000). Perception of video games among Spanish children and parents. In C. van Feilitzen & U. Carlsson (Eds.), *Children in the new media landscape* (pp. 123–126). Göteborg, Sweden: UNESCO.

Centerwall, B. S. (1989). Exposure to television as a cause of violence. In G. Comstock (Ed.), *Public communication and behavior* (vol. 2, pp. 1–59). San Diego, CA: Academic Press.

Charlton, T., Gunter, B., & Hannan, A. (2002). *Broadcast television effects in a remote community*. Mahwah, NJ: Lawrence Erlbaum Associates.

Coelho, K. A. (1998). *Deciphering violence: The cognitive structure of right and wrong*. New York: Routledge.

Colwell, J., & Payne, J. (2000). Negative correlates of computer game play in adolescents. *British Journal of Psychology, 91*, 295–310.

Cooper, J., & Mackie, D. (1986). Video games and aggression in children. *Journal of Applied Social Psychology, 16*, 726–744.

Cumberbatch, G. (2001). *Video violence: Villain or victim? A review of the research evidence concerning screen violence (video and computer games) and violence in the real world*. London: Video Standards Council. www.videostandards.org.uk.

Cumberbatch, G., Maguire, A., & Woods, S. (1993). Children and video games: An exploratory study. Birmingham: Communications Research, Aston University.

Dill, K., & Dill, J. (1998). Video game violence: A review of the empirical literature. *Aggression and Violent Behavior, 3*, 407–428.

Doob, A. N., & MacDonald, G. E. (1979). Television viewing and fear of victimization. *Journal of Personality and Social Psychology, 37*, 170–179.

Durkin, K. (1995). *Computer games, their effects on young people: A review*. Sydney: Office of Film & Literature Classification.

Durkin, K., & Low, J. (2000). Computer games and aggression research in Australia and New Zealand. In C. van Feilitzen & U. Carlsson (Eds.), *Children in the new media landscape* (pp. 79–82). Göteborg, Sweden: UNESCO.

Ferreira, P. A., & Pais-Ribeiro, J. L. (2001). The relationship between playing violent electronic games and aggression in adolescents. *Aggressive Behavior, 27,* 166–167.

Feshbach, S., & Singer, D. (1971). *Television and aggression: An experimental field study.* San Fancisco: Jossey Bass.

Fleming, M. J., & Rickwood, D. J. (2001). Effects of violent versus nonviolent video games on children's arousal, aggressive mood, and positive mood. *Journal of Applied Social Psychology, 31,* 2047–2071.

Fowles, J. (1999). *The case for television violence.* Thousand Oaks CA: Sage.

Fraser, A. (1966). *A history of toys.* London: Weidenfeld & Nicholson.

Freedman, J. (2001). Evaluating the research on violent video games. Cultural Policy Center, University of Chicago. http://culturalpolicy.uchicago.edu/.

Freedman, J. (2002). *Media violence and its effect on aggression.* Toronto: University of Toronto Press.

Funk, J. B. (2001). The violence debate. Cultural Policy Center, University of Chicago. http://culturalpolicy. uchicago.edu/.

Funk, J. B., Hagan, J., Schimming, J., Bullock, W. A., Buchman, D. D., & Myers, M. (2002). Aggression and psychopathology in adolescents with a preference for violent electronic games. *Aggressive Behavior, 28,* 134–144.

Garvey, C. (1991). *Play* (2d ed.). Cambridge, MA: Harvard University Press.

Gauntlett, D. (1995). *Moving experiences.* London: John Libbey.

Gauntlett, D. (2001). The worrying influence of "media effects" studies. In M. Barker & J. Petley, *Ill effects: The media/violence debate* (2d ed.). London: Routledge, pp. 47–62.

Gibb, G. D., Bailey, J. R., Lornbirth, T. T., & Wilson, W. P. (1983). Personality differences between high and low electronic video game users. *Journal of Psychology, 114,* 143–152.

Goldstein, J. (1999). The attractions of violent entertainment. *Media Psychology, 1,* 271–282.

Goldstein, J. (1998). Immortal Kombat: The attractions of video games with violent themes. In J. Goldstein (Ed.), *Why we watch: The attractions of violent entertainment* (pp. 53–68). New York: Oxford University Press.

Goldstein, J. (1995). Aggressive toy play. In A. D. Pellegrini (Ed.), *The future of play theory* (pp. 127–150). Albany: State University of New York Press.

Goldstein, J. (1994). Sex differences in toy play and use of video games. In J. Goldstein (Ed.), *Toys, play, and child development* (pp. 110–129). New York: Cambridge University Press.

Grainger, J., & Dijkstra, A.F.J. (1996). Visual word recognition: Models and experiments. In A.F.J. Dijkstra & K.J.M. de Smedt (Eds.), *Computational psycholinguistics.* London: Taylor & Francis.

Graybill, D., Strawniak, M., Hunter, T., & O'Leary, M. (1987). Effects of playing vs. observing violent vs. non-violent video games on children's aggression. *Psychology: A Quarterly Journal of Human Behavior, 24,* 1–8.

Green, C. S., & Bavelier, D. (2003). Action video game modifies visual selective attention. *Nature, 423,* 534–537.

Griffiths, M. (2000). Video game violence and aggression: A review of research. In C. van Feilitzen & U. Carlsson (Eds.), *Children in the new media landscape: Games, pornography, perceptions. Children and media violence, yearbook 2000* (pp. 31–34). Goteborg, Sweden: UNESCO International Clearinghouse on Children and Violence on the Screen.

Griffiths, M. (1999). Violent video games and aggression: A review of the literature. *Aggression & Violent Behavior, 4,* 203–212.

Griffiths, M. (1997). Video games and aggression. *The Psychologist,* Sept., 397–401.

Grodal, T. (2000). Video games and the pleasures of control. In D. Zillmann & P. Vorderer (Eds.), *Media Entertainment* (pp. 197–214). Mahwah, NJ: Erlbaum.

Grossman, D. (1995). *On killing: The psychological cost of learning to kill in war and society.* Boston: Little, Brown.

Grossman, D. (1999). *Stop teaching our kids to kill: A call to action against TV, movie and video game violence.* New York: Crown.

Gunter, B. (1998). *The effects of video games on children: The myth unmasked.* Sheffield, UK: Sheffield Academic Press.

Guttmann, A. (1983). Roman sports violence. In J. Goldstein (Ed.), *Sports violence* (pp. 7–20). New York: Springer Verlag.

Guttmann, A. (1998). The appeal of violent sports. In J. Goldstein (Ed.), *Why we watch: The attractions of violent entertainment* (pp. 7–26). New York: Oxford University Press.

Hendershot, H. (1998). *Saturday morning censors: Television regulation before the V-chip*. Durham: Duke University Press.

Hennigan, K. M., Del Rosario, M., Heath, L., Cook, T. D., Wharton, J. D., & Calder, B. J. (1982). Impact of the introduction of television on crime in the United States: Empirical findings and theoretical implications. *Journal of Personality and Social Psychology, 42*, 461–477.

Holm Sorensen, B., & Jessen, C. (2000). It isn't real: Children, computer games, violence and reality. In C. van Feilitzen & U. Carlsson (Eds.), *Children in the new media landscape: Games, pornography, perceptions. Children and media violence, yearbook 2000* (pp. 119–122). Goteborg, Sweden: UNESCO International Clearinghouse on Children and Violence on the Screen.

Holmes, R. M., & Pellegrini, A. D. (1999). Children's social behavior during video game play with aggressive and non-aggressive themes. Paper presented at International Toy Research conference. Halmstad, Sweden.

Karlsen, F. (2001). *Computer games and violence: A qualitative analysis of elements of violence in computer games*. OSLO, Norway, Norwegian Film Board.

Kellerman, J. (1999). *Savage spawn: Reflections on violent children*. New York: Ballantine.

Kinder, M. (2001). Violent ruptures. University of Chicago, Cultural Policy Center, Oct. 27. http://culturalpolicy.uchicago.edu/.

Kirsh, S. J. (1998). Seeing the world through Mortal Kombat-colored glasses: Violent video games and the development of a short-term hostile attribution bias. *Childhood, 5*, 177–184.

Kline, S. (2000). Killing time? A Canadian meditation on video game culture. In C. van Feilitzen & U. Carlsson (Eds.), *Children in the new media landscape: Games, pornography, perceptions. Children and media violence, yearbook 2000* (pp. 35–60). Goteborg, Sweden: UNESCO International Clearinghouse on Children and Violence on the Screen.

Koepp, M. J., Gunn, R. N., Lawrence, A. D., Cunningham, V. J., Dagher, A., Jones, T., Brooks, D. J., Bench, C. J., & Grasby, P. M. (1998). Evidence of striatal dopamine release during a video game. *Nature, 393*, 266–268.

Lin, S. & Lepper, M. R. (1987). Correlates of children's usage of video games and computers. *Journal of applied social psychology, 17*, 72–93.

Malone, T. (1981). Toward a theory of intrinsically motivating instruction. *Cognitive Science, 4*, 333–369.

McCauley, R. C. (1998). When violence is not attractive. In J. Goldstein (Ed.), *Why we watch: The attractions of violent entertainment* (pp. 144–162). New York: Oxford.

Messenger Davies, M. (1997). *Fake, fact, and fantasy: Children's interpretations of television reality*. Mahwah, NJ: Erlbaum.

Messner, S. F. (1986). Television violence and violent crime. *Social Problems, 32* (3), 218–235.

Milgram, S., & Shotland, L. (1973). *Television and antisocial behavior: Field experiments*. New York: Academic Press.

Perloff, R. M. (1999). The third person effect in mass media research. *Media Psychology, 1*, 353–378.

Poole, S. (2001). The latest report on media "aggression" analysed. www.joystick101.org.

Regan, P. M. (1994). War toys, war movies, and the militarization of the United States, 1900–1985. *Journal of Peace Research, 31*, 45–58.

Rhodes, R. (2000). Hollow claims about fantasy violence. *New York Times*, Sept., 17.

Robinson, T. N., Wilde, M. L., Navracruz, L. C., Farish Haydel, K., & Varady, A. (2001). Effects of reducing children's television and video game use on aggressive behavior. *Archives of Pediatrics & Adolescent Medicine, 155*.

Roe, K., & Muijs, D. (1998). Children and computer games: A profile of the heavy user. *European Journal of Communication, 13*, 181–200.

Sakamoto, A. (2000). Video games and violence: Controversy and research in Japan. In C. van Feilitzen & U. Carlsson (Eds.), *Children in the new media landscape: Games, pornography, perceptions. Children and media violence, yearbook 2000* (pp. 61–78). Goteborg, Sweden: UNESCO International Clearinghouse on Children and Violence on the Screen.

Savage, J. (2004). Does viewing violent media really cause criminal violence? A methodological review. *Aggression and violent behavior, 10*, 99–128.

Schierbeck, L., & Carstens, B. (2000). Violent elements in computer games: An analysis of games published in Denmark. In C. van Feilitzen & U. Carlsson (Eds.), *Children in the new media landscape: Games, pornography, perceptions. Children and media violence, yearbook 2000* (pp. 127–132). Goteborg, Sweden: UNESCO International Clearinghouse on Children and Violence on the Screen.

Schutte, N. S., Malouff, J. M., Post-Gorden, J. C., & Rodasta, A. L. (1988). Effects of playing video games on children's aggressive and other behaviors. *Journal of Applied Social Psychology, 18*, 454–460.

Scott, D. (1995). The effects of video games on feelings of aggression. *Journal of Psychology, 129*, 121–132.

Sherry, J. (2001). The effects of violent video games on aggression. *Human Communication Research, 27*, 409–431.

Silvern, S. B., & Williamson, P. A. (1987). The effects of video game play on young children's aggression, fantasy, and prosocial behavior. *Journal of Applied Developmental Psychology, 8*, 453–462.

Sneed, C., & Runco, M. A. (1992). The beliefs adults and children hold about television and video games. *Journal of Psychology, 126*, 273–284.

Subrahmanyam, K., Kraut, R., Greenfield, P., & Gross, E. (2001). New forms of electronic media. In D. G. Singer & J. L. Singer (Eds.), *Handbook of children and media* (pp. 73–99). Thousand Oaks, CA: Sage.

Tobin, J. (2000). *"Good guys don't wear hats" Children's talk about the media.* New York: Teacher's College Press, Columbia University.

Twitchell, J. (1989). *Preposterous violence.* New York: Oxford University Press.

Unsworth, G., & Ward, T. (2001). Video games and aggressive behavior. *Australian Psychologist, 36*, 184–192.

Van Feilitzen, C. (2000). Electronic games, pornography, perceptions. In C. van Feilitzen & U. Carlsson (Eds.), *Children in the new media landscape* (pp. 9–12). Goteborg, Sweden: UNESCO International Clearinghouse on Children and Violence on the Screen.

Van Schie, E.G.M., & Wiegman, O. (1997). Children and video games: Leisure activities, aggression, social integration, and school performance. *Journal of Applied Social Psychology, 27*, 1175–1194.

Wang, J., & He, M. (2000). Investigation of personality and mental health status of electronic game addicted adolescents and youth. *Chinese Mental Health Journal, 14*, 316.

Wiegman, O., & van Schie, E.G.M. (1998). Video game playing and its relations with aggressive and prosocial behaviour. *British Journal of Social Psychology, 37*, 367–378.

Wiegman, O., Kuttschreuter, M., & Baarda, B. (1992). A longitudinal study of the effects of television viewing on aggressive and prosocial behaviors. *British Journal of Social Psychology, 31*, 147–164.

Wiegman, O., van Schie, E.G.M., & Modde, J. M. (1997). Computerspelletjes en hun effecten. [Computer games and their effects.] *Justitie Verkenningen, 23*, 21–34.

Winkel, M., Novak, D. M., & Hopson, H. (1987). Personality factors, subject gender, and the effects of aggressive video games on aggression in adolescents. *Journal of Research in Personality, 21*, 211–223.

Zillmann, D. (1998). The psychology of the attraction of violent entertainment. In J. Goldstein (Ed.), *Why we watch: The attractions of violent entertainment* (pp. 179–211). New York: Oxford University Press.

23

DOES VIDEO GAME ADDICTION EXIST?

Mark Griffiths and Mark N. O. Davies

The rise and popularity of computer games as a leisure phenomenon has become an ever-increasing part of many young people's day-to-day lives. Coupled with the rise in popularity and usage, there have been a growing number of reports in the popular press about excessive use of the video games ("joystick junkies"). Although the concept of "video game addiction" appears to have its supporters in the popular press, there is a form of "knee-jerk skepticism" within the academic community—not least among those working in the field of addiction research.

It is not hard to understand the skepticism. For many people, the concept of video game addiction seems far-fetched, particularly if their concepts and definitions of addiction involve the taking of drugs. Despite the predominance of drug-based definitions of addiction, there is now a growing movement that views a number of behaviors as potentially addictive (e.g., gambling, computer game playing, exercise, sex, and now the Internet). Such diversity has led to new, all encompassing definitions of what constitutes addictive behavior.

Researchers have consistently argued that excessive gambling is no different from (say) alcoholism or heroin addiction in terms of the core components of addiction (i.e., salience, tolerance, withdrawal, mood modification, conflict, relapse). If one can show that a behavior such as pathological gambling can be a bona fide addiction, then there is a precedent that any behavior that can provide continuous rewards in the absence of a psychoactive substance can be potentially addictive (i.e., a behavioral as opposed to a chemical addiction). Such a precedent opens the floodgates for other excessive behaviors to be theoretically considered as potential addictions (such as video games).

In addition to press reports, researchers have alleged for over twenty years that social pathologies are beginning to surface among excessive video game players. For instance, Soper and Miller (1983) claimed "video game addiction" was like any other behavioral addiction and consisted of a compulsive behavioral involvement, a lack of interest in other activities, association mainly with other addicts, and physical and mental symptoms when attempting to stop the behavior (e.g., the shakes). More recently, such addictions (including addictions to the Internet and slot machines) have been termed "technological addictions" (Griffiths, 1995a, 1996a) and have been operationally defined as nonchemical (behavioral) addictions that involve excessive human-machine interaction. They can either be passive (e.g., television) or active (e.g., computer games), and usually contain inducing and reinforcing features that may contribute to the promotion of addictive tendencies (Griffiths, 1995a). Technological addictions can thus be viewed as a subset of behavioral addictions (Marks, 1990) and feature core components of addiction first outlined by Brown (1993) and modified by Griffiths (1996b), such as salience, mood modification, tolerance, withdrawal, conflict, and relapse.

Research into the area of video game addiction needs to be underpinned by three fundamental questions: (1) What is addiction? (2) Does video game addiction exist? (3) If video game addiction exists, what are people actually addicted to? The first question continues to be a much-debated question both among psychologists within the field of addiction research as well as those working in other disciplines. For many years, the first author has operationally defined addictive behavior as any behavior that features all the core components of addiction. It is the first author's contention that any behavior (e.g., video game playing) that fulfils these six criteria is therefore operationally defined as an addiction. In the case of video game addiction it would be:

Salience: This occurs when video game play becomes the most important activity in the person's life and dominates their thinking (preoccupations and cognitive distortions), feelings (cravings), and behavior (deterioration of socialized behavior). For instance, even if the person is not actually playing a video game, they will be thinking about the next time that they will be.

Mood modification: This refers to the subjective experiences that people report as a consequence of engaging in video game play and can be seen as a coping strategy (i.e., they experience an arousing "buzz" or a "high" or paradoxically tranquilizing feel of "escape" or "numbing").

Tolerance: This is the process whereby increasing amounts of video game play are required to achieve the former mood modificating effects. This basically means that for someone engaged in video game playing, they gradually build up the amount of the time they spend online engaged in the behavior.

Withdrawal symptoms: These are the unpleasant feeling states and/or physical effects which occur when video game play is discontinued or suddenly reduced, e.g., tremors, moodiness, irritability.

Conflict: This refers to the conflicts between the video game player and those around them (interpersonal conflict), conflicts with other activities (job, schoolwork, social life, hobbies and interests) or from within the individual themselves (intrapsychic conflict and/or subjective feelings of loss of control) that are concerned with spending too much time engaged in video game play.

Relapse: This is the tendency for repeated reversions to earlier patterns of video game play to recur and for even the most extreme patterns typical of the height of excessive video game play to be quickly restored after periods of abstinence or control.

Having operationally defined addiction, it is the first author's belief that video game addiction does indeed exist, but that it affects only a very small minority of players. There appear to be many people who use video games excessively but are not addicted as measured by these (or any other) criteria. The third question is perhaps the most interesting and the most important when it comes to researching in this field. What are people actually addicted to? Is it the interactive medium of playing? Aspects of its specific style (e.g., an anonymous and disinhibiting activity)? The specific types of games (aggressive games, strategy games, etc.)? This has led to much debate amongst those of us working in this field. Research being carried out into Internet addiction may lead to insights about video game addiction. For instance, Young (1999) claims Internet addiction is a broad term that covers a wide variety of behaviors and impulse control problems. This is categorized by five specific subtypes:

Cybersexual addiction: compulsive use of adult websites for cybersex and cyberporn.

Cyber-relationship addiction: over-involvement in online relationships.

Net compulsions: obsessive online gambling, shopping, or day-trading.

Information overload: compulsive web surfing or database searches.

Computer game addiction: obsessive computer game playing (e.g. *Doom, Myst, Solitaire,* etc.).

In reply to Young, Griffiths (1999, 2000a) argued that many of these excessive users are not "Internet addicts" but just use the Internet excessively as a medium to fuel other addictions. Put very simply, a gambling addict or a computer game addict who engages in their chosen behavior online is not addicted to the Internet. The Internet is just the place where they engage in the behavior. However, in contrast to this, there are case study reports of individuals who appear to be addicted to the Internet itself (e.g., Young, 1998; Griffiths, 1996a, 1998, 2000b). These are usually people who use Internet chat rooms or play fantasy role playing games—activities that they would not engage in except on the Internet itself. These individuals to some extent are engaged in text-based virtual realities and take on other social personas and social identities as a way of making themselves feel good about themselves. In these cases, the Internet may provide an alternative reality to the user and allow them feelings of immersion and anonymity that may lead to an altered state of consciousness. This in itself may be highly psychologically and/or physiologically rewarding. Obviously for those playing online computer games, these speculations may provide insights into the potentially addictive nature of computer games for those playing in this medium.

Other insights into the potentially addictive nature of video games has come from research into slot machines. Both video game machines and slot machines fall under the generic label of "amusement machines" (Griffiths, 1991a). The main difference between video game machines and slot machines are that video games are played to accumulate as many points as possible, whereas slot machines are played (i.e., gambled upon) to accumulate money. Griffiths (1991a) has suggested that playing a video game could be considered as a non-financial form of gambling. Both types of machine (in the case of arcade games) require inserting a coin to play, although the playing time on a slot machine is usually much less than on a video game machine. This is because on video games the outcome is almost solely due to skill, whereas on slot machines the outcome is a product of chance. However, the general playing philosophy of both slot machine players and video game players is to stay on the machine for as long as possible using the least amount of money (Griffiths, 1990a, 1990b). Griffiths has argued that regular slot machine players play *with* money rather than for it and that winning money is a means to an end (i.e., to stay on the machine as long as possible).

Besides the generic labelling, their geographical juxtaposition, and the philosophy for playing, it could be argued that on both a psychological and behavioral level, slot machine gambling and video game playing share many similarities (e.g., similar demographic differences such as age and gender breakdown, similar reinforcement schedules, similar potential for "near miss" opportunities, similar structural characteristics involving the use of light and sound effects, similarities in skill perception, similarities in the effects of excessive play, etc.). The most probable reason the two forms have rarely been seen as conceptually similar is because video game playing does not involve winning money (or something of financial value) and therefore cannot be classed as a form of gambling. However, the next generation of slot machines are starting to use video game graphics and technology. Although many of these relate to traditional gambling games (e.g. roulette, poker, blackjack), there are plans for developing video gambling games in which people would win money based on their game scores. This obviously gives an idea of the direction that slot machines and the gaming industry are heading.

Furthermore, there are a growing number of researchers who suggest that arcade video games share some common ground with slot (gambling) machines, including the potential for dependency (e.g., Brown & Robertson, 1992; Griffiths, 1991a, 1993, 1997a; Fisher, 1994; Gupta & Derevensky, 1997). As Fisher and Griffiths (1995) point out, arcade videogames and slot machines share some important structural characteristics, these being:

• The requirement of response to stimuli which are predictable and governed by the software loop.
• The requirement of total concentration and hand-eye coordination.
• Rapid span of play negotiable to some extent by the skill of the player (more marked in video games).
• The provision of aural and visual rewards for a winning move (e.g., flashing lights, electronic jingles).

• The provision of an incremental reward for a winning move (points or cash) that reinforces "correct" behavior.
• Digitally displayed scores of "correct behavior" (in the form of points or cash accumulated).
• The opportunity for peer group attention and approval through competition.

As with excessive slot machine playing, excessive video game playing partly comes about by the partial reinforcement effect (PRE) (Wanner, 1982). This is a critical psychological ingredient of video game addiction whereby the reinforcement is intermittent—people keep responding in the absence of reinforcement hoping that another reward is just around the corner. Knowledge about the PRE gives the video game designer an edge in designing appealing games. Magnitude of reinforcement is also important. Large rewards lead to fast responding and greater resistance to extinction—in short to more "addiction." Instant reinforcement is also satisfying.

Video games rely on multiple reinforcements (i.e., the "kitchen sink" approach), in that different features might be differently rewarding to different people. Success on video games comes from a variety of sources and the reinforcement might be intrinsic (e.g., improving your highest score, beating your friend's high score, getting your name on the "hall of fame," mastering the machine) or extrinsic (e.g., peer admiration). Malone (1981) reports that video game enjoyment is positively correlated to a presence or absence of goals, the availability of automatic computer scores, the presence of audio effects, the random quality of the games, and the degree to which rapid reaction times enhance game scores.

Empirical Research on Video Game Addiction

To date, there has been very little research directly investigating video game addiction. Furthermore, almost all of it has concentrated on adolescents only. Shotton (1989) carried out a study specifically on "computer addiction" using a sample of 127 people (half children, half adult; 96 percent male) who had been self-reportedly "hooked" on home video games for at least five years. Seventy-five of these were measured against two control groups, and Shotton reported that the computer dependent individuals were highly intelligent, motivated, and achieving people but often misunderstood. After a five-year followup, Shotton found that the younger cohort had done well educationally, gone on to university, and then into high ranking jobs.

However, Shotton's research was done with people who were familiar with the older generation of video games that were popular in the earlier part of the 1980s. The video games of the 1990s onwards may in some way be more psychologically rewarding than the games of a decade ago in that they require more complex skills, improved dexterity, and feature socially relevant topics and better graphics. Anecdotal accounts of greater psychological rewards could mean that the newer games are more "addiction inducing," although such an assertion needs empirical backing.

Griffiths and Hunt (1995, 1998) undertook a more recent questionnaire study with almost four hundred adolescents (twelve–sixteen years of age) to establish the level of "dependence" using a scale adapted from the DSM-III-R criteria for pathological gambling (American Psychiatric Association, 1987). Eight questions relating to the DSM-III-R criteria were adapted for computer game playing and examined a number of addiction components including:

1. salience ("Do you frequently play most days?")
2. tolerance ("Do you frequently play for longer periods of time?")
3. euphoria ("Do you play for excitement or a 'buzz'?")
4. chasing ("Do you play to beat your personal high score?")
5. relapse ("Do you make repeated efforts to stop or decrease playing?")
6. withdrawal ("Do you become restless if you cannot play?")
7. conflict ("Do you play instead of attending to school related activities?")
8. conflict ("Do you sacrifice social activities to play?")

A cut off point of four was assumed to indicate a participant was playing at dependent (i.e., addictive) levels at the time of the study. Scores on the adapted DSM-III-R scale indicated that sixty-two players (16 percent) were dependent on computer games (i.e., scored four or more on the scale). Furthermore, 7 percent of the sample claimed they played over thirty hours a week. The dependence score correlated with gender, as significantly more males than females were dependent. Dependence score also correlated with how often they played computer games, the mean session length playing time, and the longest single session playing time. Further analysis indicated that those dependent were significantly more likely to have started playing computer games to impress friends, because there was nothing else to do, for a challenge, and to

meet friends. Dependent players were also significantly more likely to report aggressive feelings as a direct result of their computer game playing. There are a number of problems with the findings of this study. Although the criteria for the scale were all based on the different components of dependence common to other addictive behaviors (e.g., salience, euphoria, tolerance, withdrawal, conflict, etc.) it could be that these are less relevant for excessive computer game playing. There was also an assumption made that computer game playing was similar to gambling in terms of the consequences of excessive behavior. Alternative explanations could be that excessive computer game playing cannot be conceptualized as an addiction at all or that the scale is more a measure of preoccupation rather than dependence. A replication study found very similar results (Griffiths, 1997b). It is also worth noting that 7 percent of the sample in Griffiths and Hunt's (1995, 1998) study claimed to play computer games for over thirty hours a week. Other studies have reported similar findings (Fisher, 1994; Parsons, 1995; Phillips et al., 1995; Griffiths, 1997b).

There is no doubt that for a minority of children and adolescents video games can take up considerable time. Whether these studies suggest video games may be addictive is perhaps not the most salient issue here. The question to ask is what the longitudinal effect of any activity (not just video game playing) that takes up thirty hours of leisure time a week has on the educational and social development of children and adolescents? At present we do not know the answer to such a question. However, it is our contention that any child who engaged in any activity excessively (whether defined as an addiction or not) every day over a number of years from a young age, would have their social and/or educational development negatively affected in some way.

There is also the question, "If video games are addictive, what is the addictive process?" One potential way of answering this question is to produce possible theoretical accounts of video game addiction and test the hypotheses empirically. McIlwraith (1990) proposed four theoretical models of television addiction in the popular and psychological literature that would seem good models to test the boundaries of video game addiction. Substituting "video game" for "television" in McIlwraith's account would leave the four explanations as thus:

1. Video game addiction is a function of the video game's effects on imagination and fantasy life, i.e.,

people who play video games to excess have poor imaginations.

2. Video game addiction is a function of the video game's effects on arousal level, i.e., people who play video games to excess either do so for its arousing or tranquillizing effects.

3. Video game addiction is a manifestation of oral, dependent, or addictive personality, i.e., people who play video games to excess do so due to their inner personality as opposed to the external source of the addiction.

4. Video game addiction is a distinct pattern of uses and gratifications associated with the video game medium, i.e., people who play video games to excess enjoy the physical act of playing or play only when they are bored, etc.

Few of these explanations for home video game playing have been empirically studied, although some empirical evidence by Griffiths and Dancaster (1995), and evidence from arcade video game addiction (Fisher, 1994) appear to support the second theoretical orientation, that video game addiction is a function of the video game's effects on arousal level. Recent research by Koepp et al. (1998) demonstrated dopaminergic neurotransmission during video game playing. This may have implications for understanding the underlying addictive process in playing video games. If it is accepted that video game playing can be addictive, then it is appropriate to look for the neural foundation of such behavior. Over recent years, the role of the mesotelencephalic (nucleus accumbens) dopaminergic system that is constructed as a circuit between the midbrain and the forebrain (within the medial forebrain bundle) has been widely accepted as the neural substrate of reinforcement (Julien, 1995). The work has until now focused on modeling the psychopharmacological process of drug-seeking behavior.

Koepp et al. (1998) have clearly demonstrated an increase in the release of dopamine within the ventral striatum (nucleus accumbens) as a function of video game playing. This parallels evidence of a similar activity with the mesotelencephalic dopaminergic system that is thought to underpin the addictive properties of drugs such as morphine (Glick et al., 1992), alcohol (Harris, Brodie, & Dunwiddie, 1995), and cocaine (Volkow, 1997)—although recent evidence has begun to illuminate the multifaceted nature the psychopharmacology of drug addiction (Rocha et al., 1998). It would therefore seem reasonable to propose that the mesotelencephalic dopaminergic system may well underlie what has been referred to as behavioral addiction

(Griffiths, 1996b), with video game playing being one example. Consequently, a way forward in studying behavioral addiction is to incorporate within a single model, psychological evidence on the behavioral repertoire of game addicts with the evidence concerning *in vivo* changes in the functional neurochemistry of the brain. Out of such collaboration a model similar to Stolerman's psychopharmacological model of drug addiction (Stolerman, 1992) may well be possible in the near future with respect to behavioral addiction.

In addition to neurochemical research, there are further reports of behavioral signs of video game dependency among adolescents. Dependency signs reported include stealing money to play arcade games or to buy new games cartridges (Klein, 1984; Keepers, 1990; Griffiths & Hunt, 1995, 1998), truancy from school to play (Keepers, 1990; Griffiths & Hunt, 1998), not doing homework/getting bad marks at school (Griffiths & Hunt, 1998; Phillips et al., 1995), sacrificing social activities to play (Egli & Meyers, 1984; Griffiths & Hunt, 1998), irritability and annoyance if unable to play (Griffiths & Hunt, 1998; Rutkowska & Carlton, 1994), playing longer than intended (Egli & Meyers, 1984; Griffiths & Hunt, 1998), and an increase in self reported levels of aggression (Griffiths & Hunt, 1995). There is no doubt that for a minority of people (particularly adolescents) that video games can take up considerable time and that to all intents and purposes they are "addicted" to them. However, the prevalence of such an addiction is still of great controversy, as is the mechanism by which people may become addicted. This is one area where research appears to be much needed. The need to establish the incidence and prevalence of clinically significant problems associated with video game addiction is of paramount importance. There is no doubt that clearer operational definitions are required if this is to be achieved.

As argued above, the only way of determining whether nonchemical (i.e., behavioral) addictions (such as video game addiction) are addictive in a nonmetaphorical sense is to compare them against clinical criteria for other established drug-ingested addictions. However, most researchers in the field have failed to do this, which has perpetuated the skepticism shown in many quarters of the addiction research community. The main problems with the addiction criteria suggested by most researchers is that the measures used a) have no measure of severity, b) have no temporal dimension, c) have a tendency to over-estimate the prevalence of problems, and d) take no account of the context of video game use. There are also concerns about the sampling methods used. As a consequence, none of the surveys to date conclusively show that video game addiction exists or is problematic to anyone but a small minority. At best, they indicate that video game addiction may be prevalent in a significant minority of individuals but that more research using validated survey instruments and other techniques (e.g., in-depth qualitative interviews) are required. Case studies of excessive video game players may provide better evidence of whether video game addiction exists by the fact that the data collected are much more detailed. Even if just one case study can be located, it indicates that video game addiction actually does exist—even if it is unrepresentative. There are case study accounts in the literature that appear to show that excessive video game players, including those that play online (e.g., Griffiths, 2000b), display many signs of addiction (e.g., Keepers, 1992). These case studies tend to show that the video games are used to counteract other deficiencies and underlying problems in the person's life (e.g., relationships, lack of friends, physical appearance, disability, coping, etc.). Again, further work of a more in-depth qualitative nature is needed to confirm the existence of video game addiction.

Excessive Video Game Play—Other Negative Consequences

Other indirect evidence of addictive and excessive play comes from the many health consequences reported in the literature. The risk of epileptic seizures while playing video games in photosensitive individuals with epilepsy is well established (e.g., Maeda et al., 1990; Graf et al., 1994; Harding & Jeavons, 1994; Quirk et al., 1995; Millett et al., 1997). Graf et al. (1994) report that seizures are most likely to occur during rapid scene changes, and high-intensity repetitive and flickering patterns. However, for many individuals, seizures during play will represent a chance occurrence without a causal link. Furthermore, there appears to be little direct link to excessive and/or addictive play as occasional players appear to be just as susceptible.

In addition to photo-sensitive epilepsy, the medical profession for over twenty years voiced a number of concerns about video game playing. As early as the 1980s, rheumatologists described cases of "Pac-Man's Elbow" and "Space Invaders' Revenge," in which players have suffered skin, joint, and muscle problems from repeated button hitting and joystick pushing on the game machines (Loftus & Loftus, 1983). Early research by Loftus and Loftus indicated that two-thirds of (arcade) video game players examined complained of blisters, calluses, sore tendons, and numbness of fingers, hands, and elbows directly as a result of their playing. There have been a whole host of case studies in the medical literature reporting some of the adverse effects of playing video games. These have included auditory hallucinations (Spence, 1993), enuresis (Schink, 1991), encoprisis (Corkery, 1990), wrist pain (McCowan, 1981), neck pain (Miller, 1991), elbow pain (Miller, 1991), tenosynovitis—also called "nintendinitis" (Reinstein, 1983; Brasington, 1990; Casanova & Casanova, 1991; Siegal, 1991), hand-arm vibration syndrome (Cleary, McKendrick, & Sills, 2002), repetitive strain injuries (Mirman & Bonian, 1992), and peripheral neuropathy (Friedland & St. John, 1984). Admittedly, some of these adverse effects are quite rare and "treatment" simply involved not playing the games in question. In fact, in the cases involving enuresis and encoprisis, the children were so engaged in the games that they did not want to go to the toilet. In these particular cases they were simply taught how to use the game's "pause" button!

There has also been some speculation that excessive play may have a negative effect on both heart rate and blood pressure, and one study (Gwinup, Haw, & Elias, 1983) suggested that some individuals with cardiovascular disease could experience adverse effects. More recent research has highlighted both gender and ethnic differences in cardiovascular activity during game play (Murphy et al., 1995). Although some authors (e.g., Segal & Dietz, 1991) have suggested that game playing may lead to increased energy expenditure when compared with activities such as watching television, the energy increase identified is not sufficient to improve cardiorespiratory fitness.

Other speculative (i.e., not empirically tested) negative aspects of video game playing that have been reported include the belief that video game play is socially isolating and prevents children from developing social skills (Zimbardo, 1982). For instance, Selnow (1984) reported that video game players use the machine as "electronic friends." However, this does not necessarily mean that players play the machines instead of forming human friendships and interacting with their peer groups. Further to this, Colwell, Grady, and Rhaiti (1995) reported that heavy video game players see friends more often outside school (and have a need for friends) more than nonheavy players. Rutkowska and Carlton (1994) reported there was no difference in "sociability" between high and low frequency players and reported that games foster friendship. This finding was echoed by Phillips, Rolls, Rouse, and Griffiths (1995), who found no difference in social interactions between players and nonplayers.

It has also been suggested that video game playing may prevent children and adolescents from participating in more educational or sporting pursuits (Egli & Meyers, 1984; Professional Association of Teachers, 1994). In this context, it is worth noting that childhood obesity has also been linked with video games. For instance, Shimai, Yamada, Masuda, and Tada (1993) found that obesity was correlated with long periods of video game playing in Japanese children. This has also been found in young French children (Deheger, Rolland-Cachera, & Fontvielle, 1997). In the UK, Johnson and Hackett (1997) reported that there was an inverse relationship between physical activity and playing video games in schoolgirls.

What is clear from the case studies displaying the more negative consequences of playing is that they all involved people who were excessive users of video games. From prevalence studies in this area, there is little evidence of serious acute adverse effects on health from moderate play. Adverse effects are likely to be relatively minor and temporary, resolving spontaneously with decreased frequency of play, or to affect only a small subgroup of players.

Excessive players are the most at-risk from developing health problems, although more research appears to be much needed. The need to establish the incidence and prevalence of clinically significant problems associated with video game play is of paramount importance. There is also no doubt that clearer operational definitions are required if this is to be achieved.

Taking all factors and variables into account and by considering the prevalence of play, the evidence of serious adverse effects on health is rare. An overview of the available literature appears to indicate that adverse effects are likely to affect only a very small subgroup of players and that frequent players are the most at-risk from developing health problems. Those that it does affect will experience subtle, relatively minor, and temporary effects that resolve spontaneously with decreased frequency of play. However, the possible long-term effects and its relationship to conditions such as obesity have not been fully examined and must remain speculative.

Conclusion

This chapter has demonstrated that research into video game addiction is a little studied phenomenon. Obviously more research is needed before the debate on whether video game addiction is a distinct clinical entity is decided. From the sparse research, it is evident that video games appear to be at least potentially addictive. There is also a need for a general taxonomy of video games, as it could be the case that particular types of games are more addictive than others. Another major problem is that video games can be played in many different ways, including on hand held consoles, on a personal computer, home video game consoles, on arcade machines, and on the Internet. It may be the case that some of these media for playing games (such as in an arcade or on the Internet) may be more addictive because of other factors salient to that medium (e.g., disinhibition on the Internet). Therefore, future research needs to distinguish between excessive play in different media.

Research also demonstrates that males are the most excessive users of video games (Kaplan, 1983; Griffiths, 1991b, 1993, 1997a), and this again mirrors many other youth addictions (Griffiths, 1995b). Reasons as to why males play video games significantly more than females have been generally lacking. Explanations may include:

1. the content of the games—most video games have traditionally contained masculine images (Braun et al., 1986) although this is changing with the introduction of strong female lead characters such as Lara Croft. Furthermore, video games are designed by males for males (Gutman, 1982) although there have been "female" forms of game hardware and software introduced, e.g., *Ms. Pac-Man*, Nintendo's *GameGirl*.
2. socialization—women are not encouraged to express aggression in public and feel uncomfortable with games of combat or war (Surrey, 1982). It could be that male domination of video games is due more to the arcade atmosphere, its social rules, and socialization factors than the games themselves.
3. sex differences—males on average perform better in visual and spatial skills (particularly depth perception) (Maccoby & Jacklin, 1974) that are essential to good game playing, e.g., hand-eye coordination (Keisler, Sproull, & Eccles, 1983). Therefore, the average male player would be more likely to score higher than the average female player and thus be more likely to persist in playing.

It is also apparent that there are gender differences between the types of game played. For example, Griffiths and Hunt (1995) reported that males preferred beat 'em ups and puzzlers and that females preferred platform games. Another study by Griffiths (1997b) reported that males play more beat 'em ups and sport

Mark Griffiths and Mark N. O. Davies

simulations, and that females play more puzzlers and platformers. Although there are some slight differences in these findings, they do seem to suggest that males prefer the more aggressive type of games. In fact, Griffiths (1997b) went on to report that 42 percent of boys' favorite games were violent, whereas only 9 percent of the girls' were. This was also echoed by Parsons (1995), who reported that females prefer less aggressive games than males, and that males prefer violence. More research is therefore needed into the relationship (if any) between violent video games and potential addictiveness. There is also the question of developmental effects—do video games have the same effect regardless of age? It could well be the case that video games have a more pronounced addictive effect in young children but less of an effect (if any) once they have reached their adult years. There is also the social context of playing: does playing in groups or individually, with or against each other, affect potential addictiveness of games in any way? These all need further empirical investigation.

It does appear that excessive video game playing can have potentially damaging effects upon a minority of individuals who display compulsive and addictive behavior, and who will do anything possible to feed their addiction. Such individuals need monitoring. Using these individuals in research would help identify the roots and causes of addictive playing and the impact of such behavior on family and school life. It would be clinically useful to illustrate problem cases, even following them longitudinally and recording developmental features of the adolescent video game addict. This would help determine the variables that are salient in the acquisition, development, and maintenance of video game addiction. It may be that video game addiction is age-related, like other more obviously "deviant" adolescent behaviors (e.g., glue sniffing) because there is little evidence to date of video game addiction in adults.

There is no doubt that video game play usage among the general population will continue to increase over the next few years and that if social pathologies (including video game addiction) do exist, then this is certainly an area for development that should be of interest and concern to all those involved in the addiction research field. Real life problems need applied solutions and alternatives, and until there is an established body of literature on the psychological, sociological, and physiological effects of video game playing and video-game addiction, directions for education, prevention, intervention, and treatment will remain limited in scope.

References

American Psychiatric Association. (1987). *Diagnostic and Statistical Manual for Mental Disorders (Third Edition)*. Washington, DC: American Psychiatric Association.

Brasington, R. (1990). Nintendinitis. *New England Journal of Medicine, 322*, 1473–1474.

Braun, C.M.J., Goupil, G., Giroux, J., & Chagnon, Y. (1986). Adolescents and microcomputers: Sex differences, proxemics, task and stimulus variables. *Journal of Psychology, 120*, 529–542.

Bright, D. A., & Bringhurst, D. C. (1992). Nintendo elbow. *Western Journal of Medicine, 156*, 667–668.

Brown, R.I.F. (1993). Some contributions of the study of gambling to the study of other addictions. In W. R. Eadington & J. A. Cornelius (Eds.), *Gambling Behavior and Problem Gambling* (pp. 241–272). Reno: University of Nevada Press.

Brown, R.I.F., & Robertson, S. (1993). Home computer and video game addictions in relation to adolescent gambling: Conceptual and developmental aspects. In W. R. Eadington & J. A. Cornelius (Eds.), *Gambling Behavior and Problem Gambling* (pp. 451–471). Reno: University of Nevada Press.

Casanova, J., & Casanova, J. (1991). Nintendinitis. *Journal of Hand Surgery, 16*, 181.

Cleary, A. G., Mckendrick, H., & Sills, J. A. (2002). Hand-arm vibration syndrome may be associated with prolonged use of vibrating computer games. *British Medical Journal, 324*, 301.

Colwell, J., Grady, C., & Rhaiti, S. (1995). Computer games, self-esteem, and gratification of needs in adolescents. *Journal of Community and Applied Social Psychology, 5*, 195–206.

Corkery, J. C. (1990). Nintendo power. *American Journal of Diseases in Children, 144*, 959.

Deheger, M., Rolland-Cachera, M. F., & Fontvielle, A. M. (1997). Physical activity and body composition in 10 year old French children: Linkages with nutritional intake? *International Journal of Obesity, 21*, 372–379.

Egli, E. A., & Meyers, L. S. (1984). The role of video game playing in adolescent life: Is there a reason to be concerned? *Bulletin of the Psychonomic Society, 22*, 309–312.

Fisher, S. E. (1994). Identifying video game addiction in children and adolescents. *Addictive Behaviors, 19*, 5, 545–553.

Friedland, R. P., & St. John, J. N. (1984). Video-game palsy: Distal ulnar neuropathy in a video game enthusiast. *New England Journal of Medicine, 311*, 58–59.

Glick, S. D., Merski, C., Steindorf, S., Wank, R., Keller, W., & Carlson, J. N. (1992). Neurochemical predisposition to self-administer morphine in rats. *Brain Research, 578*, 215–220.

Graf, W. D., Chatrian, G. E., Glass, S. T., & Knauss, T. A. (1994). Video-game related seizures: A report on 10 patients and a review of the literature. *Pediatrics, 3*, 551–556.

Griffiths, M. D. (1990a). The acquisition, development and maintenance of fruit machine gambling in adolescence. *Journal of Gambling Studies, 6*, 193–204.

Griffiths, M. D. (1990b). The cognitive psychology of gambling. *Journal of Gambling Studies, 6*, 31–42.

Griffiths, M. D. (1991a). The observational analysis of adolescent gambling in UK amusement arcades. *Journal of Community and Applied Social Psychology, 1*, 309–320.

Griffiths, M. D. (1991b). Amusement machine playing in childhood and adolescence: A comparative analysis of video games and fruit machines. *Journal of Adolescence, 14*, 53–73.

Griffiths, M. D. (1993). Are computer games bad for children? *The Psychologist: Bulletin of the British Psychological Society, 6*, 401–407.

Griffiths, M. D. (1995a). Technological addictions. *Clinical Psychology Forum, 76*, 14–19.

Griffiths, M. D. (1995b). *Adolescent gambling*. London: Routledge.

Griffiths, M. D. (1996a). Internet "addiction": An issue for clinical psychology? *Clinical Psychology Forum, 97*, 32–36.

Griffiths, M. D. (1996b). Behavioral addictions: An issue for everybody? *Journal of Workplace Learning, 8*(3), 19–25.

Griffiths, M. D. (1997a). Video games and children's behavior. In T. Charlton & K. David (Eds.), *Elusive links: Television, video games, cinema and children's behavior* (pp. 66–93). Gloucester: GCED/Park Publishers.

Griffiths, M. D. (1997b). Computer game playing in early adolescence. *Youth and Society, 29*, 223–237.

Griffiths, M. D. (1998). Internet addiction: Does it really exist? In J. Gackenbach (Ed.), *Psychology and the Internet: Intrapersonal, Interpersonal and Transpersonal Applications* (pp. 61–75). New York: Academic Press.

Griffiths, M. D. (1999). Internet addiction: Internet fuels other addictions. *Student British Medical Journal, 7*, 428–429.

Griffiths, M. D. (2000a). Internet addiction—Time to be taken seriously? *Addiction Research, 8*, 413–418.

Griffiths, M. D. (2000b). Does internet and computer "addiction" exist? Some case study evidence. *CyberPsychology and Behavior, 3*, 211–218.

Griffiths, M. D., & Dancaster, I. (1995). The effect of Type A personality on physiological arousal while playing computer games. *Addictive Behaviors, 20*, 543–548.

Griffiths, M. D., & Hunt, N. (1995). Computer game playing in adolescence: Prevalence and demographic indicators. *Journal of Community and Applied Social Psychology, 5*, 189–194.

Griffiths, M. D., & Hunt, N. (1998). Dependence on computer games by adolescents. *Psychological Reports, 82*, 475–480.

Gupta, R., & Derevensky, J. L. (1997). The relationship between gambling and video-game playing behavior in children and adolescents. *Journal of Gambling Studies, 12*, 375–394.

Gutman, D. (1982). Video games wars. *Video Game Player*, fall 1982.

Gwinup, G., Haw, T., & Elias, A. (1983). Cardiovascular changes in video game players: Cause for concern? *Postgraduate Medicine, 74*, 245.

Harding, G.F.A., & Jeavons, P. M. (1994). *Photosensitive Epilepsy*. London: Mac Keith Press.

Harris, R. A., Brodie, M. S., & Dunwiddie, T. V. (1995). Possible substrates of ethanol reinforcement: GABA and dopamine. *Annals for the New York Academy of Sciences, 654*, 61–69.

Hart, E. J. (1990). Nintendo epilepsy. *New England Journal of Medicine, 322*, 1473.

Johnson, B., & Hackett, A. F. (1997). Eating habits of 11–14-year-old schoolchildren living in less affluent areas of Liverpool, UK. *Journal of Human Nutrition and Dietetics, 10*, 135–144.

Julien, R. M. (1995). *A primer of drug action: A concise, nontechnical guide to the actions, uses and side effects of psychoactive drugs.* Oxford: Freeman.

Kaplan, S. J. (1983). The image of amusement arcades and differences in male and female video game playing. *Journal of Popular Culture, 16*, 93–98.

Keepers, G. A. (1990). Pathologicical preoccupation with video games. *Journal of the American Academy of Child and Adolescent Psychiatry, 29*, 49–50.

Keisler, S., Sproull, L., & Eccles, J. S. (1983). Second class citizens. *Psychology Today, 17*(3), 41–48.

Klein, M. H. (1984). The bite of Pac-Man. *Journal of Psychohistory, 11*, 395–401.

Koepp, M. J., Gunn, R. N., Lawrence, A. D., Cunningham, V. J., Dagher, A., Jones, T., Brooks, D. J., Bench, C. J., & Grasby, P. M. (1998). Evidence for striatal dopamine release during a video game. *Nature, 393*, 266–268.

Loftus, G. A., & Loftus, E. F. (1983). *Mind at play: The psychology of video games.* New York: Basic Books.

Maccoby, E. E., & Jacklin, C. N. (1974). *The psychology of sex differences.* Stanford, CA: Stanford University Press.

Maeda, Y., Kurokawa, T., Sakamoto, K., Kitamoto, I., Kohji, U., & Tashima, S. (1990). Electroclinical study of video-game epilepsy. *Developmental Medicine and Child Neurology, 32*, 493–500.

Malone, T. W. (1981). Toward a theory of intrinsically motivating instruction. *Cognitive Science, 4*, 333–369.

Marks, I. (1990). Non-chemical (behaviorial) addictions. *British Journal of Addiction, 85*, 1389–1394.

McCowan, T. C. (1981). Space Invaders wrist. *New England Journal of Medicine, 304*, 1368.

McIlwraith, R. (1990). Theories of television addiction. Paper presented at the American Psychological Association, Boston.

Miller, D.L.G. (1991). Nintendo neck. *Canadian Medical Association Journal, 145*, 1202.

Millett, C. J., Fish, D. R., & Thompson, P. J. (1997). A survey of epilepsy-patient perceptions of video-game material/electronic screens and other factors as seizure precipitants. *Seizure, 6*, 457–459.

Mirman, M. J., & Bonian, V. G. (1992). "Mouse elbow": A new repetitive stress injury. *Journal of the American Osteopath Association, 92*, 701.

Murphy, J. K., Stoney, C. M., Alpert, B. S., & Walker, S. S. (1995). Gender and ethnicity in children's cardiovascular reactivity: 7 years of study. *Health Psychology, 14*, 48–55.

Parsons, K. (1995). Educational places or terminal cases: Young people and the attraction of computer games. Paper presented at the British Sociological Association Annual Conference, University of Leicester.

Phillips, C. A., Rolls, S., Rouse, A., & Griffiths, M. (1995). Home video game playing in schoolchildren: A study of incidence and patterns of play. *Journal of Adolescence, 18*, 687–691.

Phillips, W. R. (1991). Video game therapy. *New England Journal of Medicine, 325*, 1056–1057.

Professional Association of Teachers. (1994). The street of the Pied Piper: A survey of teachers' perceptions of the effects on children of the new entertainment technologies. Derby: Author.

Quirk, J. A., Fish, D. R., Smith, S.J.M., Sander, J. W., Shorvon, S. D., & Allen, P. J. (1995). First seizures associated with playing electronic screen games: A community based study in Great Britain. *Annals of Neurology, 37*, 110–124.

Reinstein, L. (1983). De Quervain's stenosing tenosynovitis in a video games player. *Archives of Physical and Medical Rehabilitation, 64*, 434–435.

Rocha, B. A., Fumagalli, F., Gainetdinov, R. R., Jones, S. R., Ator, R., Giros, B., Miller, G. W., & Caron, M. G. (1998). Cocaine self-administration in dopamine-transporter knockout mice. *Nature Neuroscience, 1*, 132–137.

Rushton, D. N. (1981). "Space Invader" epilepsy. *The Lancet, 1*, 501.

Rutkowska, J. C., & Carlton, T. (1994). Computer games in 12–13 year olds' activities and social networks. Paper presented at the British Psychological Society Annual Conference, University of Sussex.

Schink, J. C. (1991). Nintendo enuresis. *American Journal of Diseases in Children, 145*, 1094.

Segal, K. R., & Dietz, W. H. (1991). Physiologic responses to playing a video game. *American Journal of Diseases of Children, 145*, 1034–1036.

Selnow, G. W. (1984). Playing video games: The electronic friend. *Journal of Communication*, *34*, 148–156.

Shimai, S., Yamada, F., Masuda, K., & Tada, M. (1993). TV game play and obesity in Japanese school children. *Perceptual and Motor Skills*, *76*, 1121–1122.

Shotton, M. (1989). *Computer addiction? A study of computer dependency*. London: Taylor and Francis.

Siegal, I. M. (1991). Nintendonitis. *Orthopedics*, *14*, 745.

Soper, W. B., & Miller, M. J. (1983). Junk time junkies: An emerging addiction among students. *School Counsellor*, *31*, 40–43.

Spence, S. A. (1993). Nintendo hallucinations: A new phenomenological entity. *Irish Journal of Psychological Medicine*, *10*, 98–99.

Stolerman, I. (1992). Drugs of abuse: Behavioral principles, methods and terms. *Trends in Pharmacological Sciences*, *13*, 171.

Surrey, D. (1982). "It's like good training for life." *Natural History*, *91*, 71–83.

Volkow, N. D. (1997). Relationship between subjective effects of cocaine and dopamine transporter occupancy. *Nature*, *386*, 827–830.

Wanner, E. (1982). The electronic bogeyman. *Psychology Today*, *16*(10), 8–11.

Young, K. (1998). *Caught in the net: How to recognize the signs of internet addiction and a winning strategy for recovery*. New York: Wiley.

Young, K. (1999). Internet addiction: Evaluation and treatment. *Student British Medical Journal*, *7*, 351–352.

Zimbardo, P. (1982). Understanding psychological man: A state of the science report. *Psychology Today*, *16*, 15.

Participation

.

24

COMPUTER GAMES AS PARTICIPATORY MEDIA CULTURE

Joost Raessens

As the reader can see in the other chapters of this book, many authors refer to concepts such as "interactivity" and "participation" to characterize the distinctiveness of computer games and the media culture that has developed around them. In this book, as well as elsewhere, these terms are used in various and sometimes contradictory ways, a situation that leads to confusion. When we look closely, there appear to be what I call three domains of participation: interpretation, reconfiguration, and construction. Therefore, in this chapter, I systematically discuss and challenge these concepts, and describe these three domains to characterize computer games as a form of participatory media culture.[1] Taking the theoretical framework of a young branch of philosophy, namely the philosophy of information and communication technology, as my starting point, I focus on the interpretation and evaluation of the ontological and political-ideological presuppositions and implications of computer games.[2] The ontological dimension refers to the specificity of computer games in relation to film and television, for example, and the political-ideological dimension refers to the tension between the dominant and the critical, social and cultural practices in the realm of computer games.

I start this chapter with a discussion of the specificity of computer games in order to determine in which way they, as opposed to film and television, are able to form a specific type of participatory media culture. Next I analyze the phenomenon of "interpretation." Even though the interpretation of computer games is not distinctly different from the interpretation of, say, films and television shows, this is nevertheless part of what I call participation. After this I focus on the phenomenon of "deconstruction" as a specific form of interpretation that seems characteristic for computer games. I continue by further defining the concept of participation as the active "reconfiguration" of existing game elements and the creative "construction" of new game elements. I finish this chapter with a discussion of participatory media culture from a political-ideological perspective.

Remediation and Specificity

Participatory media culture is not limited to cultural forms such as computer games (think for example of peer-to-peer technology based networks such as Napster, KaZaA and Gnutella; see Oram, 2001) nor to the digital so-called "new" media: computer games are remediating the participatory culture that has formed around media such as film and television. In this process of remediation computer games do "exactly what their predecessors have done: presenting themselves as refashioned and improved versions of other media. Digital visual media can best be understood through the ways in which they honor, rival, and revise linear-perspective painting, photography, film, television, and print" (Bolter & Grusin, 1999, pp. 14–15). One of the advantages of the concept of remediation is that it allows us to break with the modernistic novelty myth from which angle researchers often approach digital media in general, and computer games specifically. Computer games have to be defined based on specific combinations of technical, social, cultural and economic characteristics and not on exclusive, essential ones.[3] The view that participation is a new, exclusive, and essential characteristic of computer games ignores the fact that radio, film and television, for example, each have their own versions of this concept. As far back as 1932–1934, Bertolt Brecht and Walter Benjamin argued in favor of transforming radio from a distribution into a communication device that would make a listener not only a consumer but also a producer of information.[4] Also devices such as Xerox machines and audio/video recorders allow users not only to copy, but also to edit other people's material. We see such activities in participatory cultures that take shape in fan communities surrounding science fiction films and television shows such as *Star Trek* (see Jenkins, 1992; Jenkins & Tulloch, 1995).

Nevertheless, this approach has one pitfall. When studying ways computer games remediate the participatory effects of other media, you run the risk of being a victim of the "horseless carriage syndrome," the inclination to understand new techniques (the automobile) in terms of old techniques (horse-drawn wagons). The risk is that computer games' specific ability to shape participatory media culture will then be neglected. We should, therefore, not only focus on this remediation, but also on the distinguishing, specific characteristics or principles of computer games as a form of digital media: multimediality, virtuality, interactivity, and connectivity.

The particular thing about multimediality is not so much the combination of stationary and moving images, three kinds of sound elements (spoken word, music, and noises) and written text[5]—computer games share this with, for example, film and television—but the fact that these elements share one common digital code, a characteristic with all kinds of economic and legal implications. Think of the ease with which computer games can be (illegally) modified, copied, and distributed without the loss of quality.[6]

The second specific characteristic of computer games is virtuality, the possibility to simulate virtual worlds a gamer can explore. Michael Heim described VR as "an event or entity that is real in effect but not in fact" (Heim, 1993, p. 109); in other words, a digitally produced reality that can have effects which are comparable with effects of factual reality. This characteristic embodies the metamorphosis that computer games have undergone since the eighties: from an expression of "a modernist culture of calculation" in which a player enters a battle with the program behind the game, toward a "postmodernist culture of simulation" in which a players' activity is restricted to navigating the surface of the computer game (Turkle, 1996, p. 20).

Thanks to a third characteristic, interactivity, a gamer is able to control the game's proceedings and/or its conclusion. According to British film theoretician Andrew Cameron, interactivity means more than the interpretation of a computer game, it means "the ability to intervene in a meaningful way within the representation itself, not to read it differently" (Cameron, 1995, p. 33). In contrast with a "passive" film audience, an interactive game player is enabled, for example, to take up the role of narrator and influence the course of events and actions, possibly as a character in the plot. It is the purpose of this chapter to argue that participation is not only this (reconfiguration), but also "less"

(interpretation, in particular deconstruction), and "more" (construction).[7]

A game computer should after all not just be seen as a technology that can simulate multi-medial virtual worlds one can interact with; it is also increasingly being connected to other computers over the Internet. Whereas players of computer games on discs (CD-ROM, DVD-ROM) or cartridges can only navigate within the designated boundaries of the game, online gamers can jointly construct events and actions through the fourth characteristic, connectivity. For example, in massive multiplayer online role playing games (MMORPG's) such as *Ultima Online* (Electronic Arts, 1997), *Everquest* (Sony, 1998), and *Star Wars Galaxy* (Lucas, 2003), we see decentralized and self-organizing communities help shape the stories (Murray, 1997, p. 86; Murray & Jenkins, 1999, pp. 52–54). Furthermore, we see that this connectivity offers players the ability to exchange ideas, knowledge (like walkthroughs or cheat codes) and game-elements (like updates or patches) amongst each other via the Internet. We see these practices for example in the subcultures that have been formed around certain computer games and fans modifying these games.[8]

Interpretation

To place the concept of "interpretation" within participatory culture, I will use the conceptual framework developed in the British tradition of cultural studies.[9] The development of cultural studies meant a break with two principles that have long been dominant in the humanities and social sciences, and that are of importance with respect to this book on computer games. First of all, cultural studies broke with the traditional definition of culture that only allowed for the "higher," elitist art forms, such as literature, classical art and music. That is, cultural studies also focus on "lower," more popular art forms in which so-called "good taste" was sacrificed for commercial success and the demands of the general public.[10] In this context, think not only of pop music, soap operas, music videos on television, and Hollywood films, but also of computer games that enjoy great popularity, especially among a young mass audience. Cultural studies also focus on cultural practices that fall outside of the high culture/ low culture dichotomy by studying how we, as subjects, are constructed by the everyday and the ordinary— think of divergent social and cultural practices such as sports, shopping, design, and advertisement.

Secondly, the cultural studies movement resists the idea of an audience as a passive object at the mercy of the surrounding and influential top-down expressions of culture. Cultural texts, in contrast, are viewed as open texts that different groups of viewers interpret differently, depending on social, cultural, and other contexts: "Culture, as the site where meaning is generated and experienced, becomes a determining, productive field through which social realities are constructed, experienced and interpreted" (Turner, 1996, p. 14). Mainly in the area where these two principles converge, the influence of cultural studies is most pronounced.

It is important to note that cultural studies breaks both with the work of the Frankfurt School and the so-called media-effect theoreticians. Whereas the media-effect theoreticians focus mainly on the effects that the so-called powerful media as a form of one-way traffic exert on the audience, for Horkheimer and Adorno (1986), as they wrote in 1944, culture for the masses, such as film, is what reduces the audience to mindless slaves and thus to victims of capitalist consumer society.[11] In my opinion, there are still several arguments in favor of Horkheimer and Adorno's position. Despite the possibility to participate that computer games offer their users, and despite extensive participation by specific groups of users (think of fans, hobbyists, hackers), there is also an element of what Douglas Rushkoff calls "coercion" involved in computer games: manipulation encouraging users to buy products through different forms of marketing and the use of sophisticated, but sometimes rhetorical used notions such as "interactivity" and "participation." "It's not always easy to determine when we have surrendered our judgment to someone else. The better and more sophisticated the manipulation, the less aware of it we are" (Rushkoff, 1999, p. 3).

In the framework of this chapter on participation, I will limit myself to one of the two above-mentioned principles, namely the idea of "the active audience."[12] One of the starting points of cultural studies that is relevant with respect to this issue is Gramsci's concept of hegemony: Gramsci "acknowledges the power of the individual human agent within culture by analyzing not only the overdetermining structure that produces the individual, but also the range of possibilities produced for the individual" (Turner, 1996, pp. 29–30). Both the hegemony, sometimes called "domination," of certain forms of cultural expression, as well as the critical, political resistance of minorities against oppressive power relations, reveal that culture is in fact a constant struggle. According to Hall, "Gramsci's notion was that particular social groups struggle in many different ways, including ideologically, to win the consent of other groups and achieve a kind of ascendancy in both thought and practice over them. This form of power Gramsci called 'hegemony.' Hegemony is never permanent, and is not reducible to economic interests or to a simple class model of society" (Hall, 1997, p. 48; see Williams, 1988, pp. 144–146).

This struggle not only exists between different forms of culture—think of the struggle between television and computer games to get attention ("eyeball-hours")—but also within the individual expressions of popular culture. Different ideologically colored readings of computer games can be in disagreement, and, as it were, battle for hegemony. What lies at the foundation of this discussion is the idea of the active role of the audience in determining the meaning, or significance, of an expression of culture.

This active role of the audience is worded in an exemplary fashion by Stuart Hall in his article "Encoding/decoding" (1980). Hall shows that an expression of culture contains not only one opinion, but in the process of communication that stretches from design/production (encoding) to reception/consumption (decoding), the meaning of it is formed by a number of factors. Not only the design and production of a computer game, but also its reception and consumption has to be considered an active, interpretive, and social event. In other words, expressions of culture are "polysemic," that is, they are open to various readings by various (groups of) readers.

Hall distinguishes between three different reading strategies the "decoder-receiver" can use to interpret texts; the "dominant-hegemonic or preferred reading,"[13] the "negotiated reading," and the "oppositional reading." Respectively, these strategies point out the possibility to read a text according to the dominant ideology, the possibility to negotiate this dominant ideology and to varying degrees mix adaptive elements with oppositional elements, and the possibility to go against the dominant ideology and come up with a purely oppositional reading.[14]

The chapters by Birgit Richard and Jutta Zaremba, and Anna Everett further illustrate the fact that from a political-ideological viewpoint it is useful to allow for various readings of a single text.[15] Richard and Zaremba analyze different readings of the Lara Croft phenomenon, from 1996 on the protagonist of the *Tomb Raider* series. In the dominant reading, the male player enjoys Lara Croft in a harmless way (a "harmless dream woman, whose physical attractions can be looked at with impunity, lust and joy"). The negotiated reading brings to our attention that the portrayal of her self-conscious lifestyle could make it easier for young women to position themselves as such (a "postfeminist icon" who "at no point has any orientation toward domesticity"). The oppositional reading of Lara Croft condemns her as an object of lust, made by and for men, a stereotypical portrayal of femininity ("the over-fulfillment of female proportions that are designed for the male gaze" makes her "female enemy number one").[16] Everett demonstrates that in computer games, "blackness" is present, but almost always in stereotypical characters (as is the case with "whiteness") who are situated in a lower hierarchical position. Gamers who readily recognize themselves in such a position may consciously or unconsciously accept this dominant ideology, and, in Hall's terms, give a dominant reading of such computer games. Other groups will take up a more negotiated reading and search for nonracist role models they can identify with. In oppositional readings, finally, the dominant ideology (the "unbearable whiteness of being," as Everett calls it) will be unmasked as racist. In any case, these authors make clear that the meaning of the representation of, for example, gender and ethnicity in computer games—as well as the co-construction between them and other axes of signification, such as class and nationality—is under continuous discussion. Representations are thus not only reflections of society; they also play an active role in shaping it.

Deconstruction

Following the terminology of British cultural studies, authors like Ted Friedman and Sherry Turkle emphasize the political-ideological importance of computer games: "Computer programs, like all texts, will always be ideological constructions ... learning and winning ... a computer game is a process of demystification: One succeeds by discovering how the software is put together. The player molds his or her strategy through trial-and-error experimentation to see 'what works'— which actions are rewarded and which are punished" (Friedman, 1995, pp. 81–82).

Friedman's position is special in that he believes that the process of playing computer games as such reveals this ideological construction. Whereas other kinds of texts mask their ideologically colored constructedness, Friedman believes that "computer games reveal their own constructedness to a much greater extent than more traditional texts" (Friedman, 1995, p. 82): for *Sim City* this is "the political and economic premises it rests on" (Friedman, 1999, p. 133), and for *Civilization II* "the familiar ground of nationalism and

imperialism" (p. 134). Therefore, he does not agree with the critics who claim that these simulations give players the illusion that "they have encountered not just one version of the way the world works, but the one and only 'objective' version" (p. 143). The "baseline ideological assumptions that determine which strategies will win and which will lose" (p. 144) will become apparent while actually playing the game. That is why Friedman claims that "to win ... you have to figure out what will work within the rules of the game" (p. 136). The reason for this is for a large part found in the fact that a computer game, as opposed to, for example, a film, is played over and over again until the moment that all the game's secrets have been discovered.

In my view, we can describe this process of demystification as "deconstruction," the translation of the French word *déconstruction* (detachment, dissolution). This term, a central notion in the work of the French philosopher Jacques Derrida, refers to the method of interpretation that aims to bring to the foreground those elements that operate under the surface, but break through cracks in the text to disrupt its superficial functioning.

Not only Friedman, but also Turkle refers to this practice I describe as deconstruction. However, thanks to the development of computer games, this deconstruction is no longer self-evident, as Friedman seems to suggest. That is, Turkle notices a shift from "calculation and rules" to "simulation, navigation, and interaction" (1996, p. 19): "When video games were very new, I found that the holding power of their screens often went along with a fantasy of a meeting of minds between the player and the program behind the game. Today, the program has disappeared; one enters the screen world as Alice stepped through the looking glass" (p. 31).[17] Brenda Laurel notices this transition and accordingly refers to the specificity of computers by describing them as "machine[s] naturally suited for representing things that you could see, control, and play with. Its interesting potential lays not in its ability to perform calculations but in its capacity to *represent action in which humans could participate*" (1997, p. 1).

Let us take a closer look at Turkle's argument. She discusses this transition in the section "The Games People Play: Simulation and Its Discontents" (pp. 66–73). According to Turkle, the development of the computer game lead to the "socialization into the culture of simulation" (p. 67). Because in the early days of computer games (she refers to games such as *Space Invaders*, 1978, *Asteroids*, 1980 and *Pac-Man*, 1981) the rules were simpler and more easy to grasp, this meant that for the players "getting to know a game required you to decipher its logic, understand the intent of its designer, and achieve a meeting of the minds with the program behind the game" (p. 67).

Even though today computer games are still "recognizably rule-based," the rules have become much more complicated and less accessible. The reaction to this development was twofold: among certain groups of gamers (think of hobbyists and hackers), fan cultures developed in which knowledge of the rules was shared. Turkle also notices, however, an opposing development. Because the rules were getting more complex and because the games were characterized more and more by "realistic simulation through graphics, animation, sound, and interactivity" (p. 68), a large group of "average" users became interested only in the surface of the simulation, and not (or no longer) in the to-be-deconstructed depth of the game.

In the framework of this chapter on participatory media culture it is relevant that Turkle describes three possible answers to what she calls "the seduction of simulation" (p. 71), three answers that strongly resemble what I referred to earlier as dominant, oppositional, and negotiated readings. We can either surrender to the seduction ("simulation resignation"), we can reject it ("simulation denial"), or we can—and this is the option Turkle seems to favor—"take the cultural pervasiveness of simulation as a challenge to develop a more sophisticated social criticism." This social criticism would rest on an analysis of the assumptions that are built into the simulation: "Understanding the assumptions that underlie simulation is a key element of political power" (p. 71).

What makes Turkle's approach worth noting is that she not only adds a historical dimension to this form of participation, but she also manages to systematically distinguish between the ways different subcultures deal with it: "Although I have introduced the terms hacker, hobbyist and user to refer to specific people, they are best understood as different modes of relationship that one can have with a computer" (pp. 32–33). According to Turkle, a user is "involved with the machine in a hands-on way, but is not interested in the technology except as it enables an application. Hackers are the antithesis of users. They are passionately involved in mastery of the machine itself. The hobbyists in their own way were equally enthralled" (p. 32).[18]

In order to realize the distinctiveness of this process of deconstructing computer games, it is useful to draw a comparison with the pretensions of the so-called

"deconstruction" films of the 1960s (De Mul, 2002a, pp. 85–102; Raessens, 2002, pp. 149–150). French New Wave-films such as *Last Year at Marienbad* (Resnais, 1961) tried to tempt viewers to deconstruct the film, to make them aware of the ideological presuppositions of the classical Hollywood style: "Marienbad offers what we, using a term of Derrida, could refer to as the deconstruction of the *découpage classique* as it was developed in Hollywood Cinema" (De Mul, 2002a, p. 89). The goal of the *découpage classique* or "continuity editing" was "to control the potentially disunifying force of editing by establishing a smooth flow from shot to shot" (Bordwell & Thompson, 1986, p. 210). This method of editing concealed this underlying constructive process in order to have the often ideologically charged message come across as natural or transparent as possible.[19] The criticism Resnais and his contemporaries expressed aimed at making this naturalizing process visible and, wherever possible, expose it as such by including in their film contradictions that were spatially, temporally, or causally unsolvable. Attempts to mentally construct the causal and chronological story are doomed to fail using the available, ambiguous chunks of plot: "*Marienbad*'s story is impossible to determine. The film has only a plot, with no single consistent story for us to infer" (p. 304). The desired result intended was that the audience would become aware of the constructedness of film stories.

This analysis concurs with Hall's analysis of ideology, which claims that messages continually try to erase their own ideological presuppositions in order to come across as spontaneous presentations of so-called "reality." Hall calls this process of naturalization "the reality effect": "certain codes may ... be so widely distributed in a specific language community or culture, and be learned at so early an age, that they appear not to be constructed ... but to be 'naturally' given ... This has the (ideological) effect of concealing the practices of coding which are present. But we must not be fooled by appearances" (Hall, 1980, p. 132).

There are two explanations for Resnais' failed attempt; one is an overload, the other a shortage. It was an overload because it expected too much of the audience, which only wanted, in a more or less passive way, to enjoy an easily reconstructable story. The audience did not want to do the desired deconstructive labor. The reason for this is found in the enjoyment that an audience derives from fiction. Christian Metz, a French semiotician, has extensively studied this enjoyment, or lack of it, particularly in relation to such deconstruction films. According to Metz, viewers are not willing to give up the "lust premium" that is attached to a fictional film, and they do not enjoy the "intellectual-sadism" related to "deconstruction mechanisms," "disassembly," and "intellectual self-control": "The joy of a toy has to be converted into the enjoyment of tearing that toy apart" (Metz, 1980a, p. 19).

The second reason why the film failed was that it fell short of Resnais' ambitions to make the viewers actual co-creators of the film. Because *Marienbad* is a film, the plot is fixed and the enjoyment that can be derived from playing computer games is out of reach. This despite the gamelike structure of *Marienbad*: "The whole structure of *Marienbad* is a play with logic, space, and time which does not offer us a single, complete story as a prize for winning this 'game'" (Bordwell & Thompson, 1986, p. 308).

To me, computer games are possibly more able than avant garde films to make this deconstruction happen, and thereby more able to realize the emancipating functioning that is connected to it in an aesthetic and political sense. In the light of the foregoing description of British cultural studies, one could consider this the ultimate revenge of low culture computer games against high culture avant garde films. Looking through and exposing the hidden, naturalized, ideologically presupposed rules of the medium is in my opinion a form of participatory media culture. This does not imply, however, that we do not need to distinguish between different readings and genres of computer games. This kind of deconstruction is possible and commonplace in readings of computer games that are aimed at acquiring knowledge (for example, by hackers and hobbyists), and in specific genres (such as simulation games). Therefore it is probably no coincidence that both Friedman and Turkle focus on a rather specific group and genre for their studies. In everyday practice, however, such deconstruction will regularly be overshadowed by the different forms of enjoyment that users may experience while playing computer games. Not only film viewers, but also computer game players, seem to me, more superficial than Friedman and Turkle maintain, at least if we define superficiality as staying at the surface of the fiction, the story and the game, as opposed to the previous in-depth deconstruction.

Reconfiguration and Construction

The concept of "participation" is often considered another term for what some call "interactivity." In order to establish the relationship between both terms more clearly, I will first describe the concept of "interactivity" and a criticism of it after which I will discuss the

transition from interactivity to participation and finish with a further elaboration of the concepts of participation and "participatory media culture."

Interactivity

Interactivity refers to "a distinctive mode of *relating* to audiovisual representations or fictions. The player is provided with a way of directly taking a leading role in what occurs, given the means to control—at least in part—what will unfold within the scene on the screen" (Darley, 2000, p. 156).

This somewhat abstract relation of the player to the game, can be concretized as the possibility for the player to take up the role of narrator and influence the course of events and actions, possibly as a character in the plot.[20] In this way computer gamers can make Lara Croft (*Tomb Raider: The Last Revelation*, Eidos, 1999), Mario (*Super Mario 64*, Nintendo, 1996), Indiana Jones (*Indiana Jones and the Infernal Machine*, Activision, 1999), Link (*The Legend of Zelda*), and Niobe and Ghost (*Enter the Matrix*, 2002) move and carry out certain actions using keyboard, mouse, controller, or joystick. Even more specific are the games in which the player can play the role of an actual character, think of games such as *Doom*, *Quake*, *Half-Life*, *Soldier of Fortune*, and *No One Lives Forever*.

Along the lines of Metz' research on the specificity of film, we can consider this role as typical for the computer game. According to Metz, film viewers can be characterized by a perceptive, affective, and cognitive participation, but with bodily activation absent or limited to physically commenting on the film.[21] The immobile and predominantly silent film viewer behaves "like a viewer, not like an actor. The actors have their designated spot, which is elsewhere: at the other side of the film" (Metz, 1975, p. 118). If we, on the other hand, look at the history of computer games, it is remarkable that with increasing frequency we find ourselves in three-dimensional virtual worlds in which we not only stay close to the POV of the main character, but in which we are able to fulfill the role of main character due to this POV structure (see Rushkoff, 1997, pp. 177–178).

In making the player a character in the plot, computer games accomplish what has only been themed or tried in vain in film or other media. Both in the music video *Take On Me* (A-ha, 1985) and the film *The Purple Rose of Cairo* (Allen, 1985) a female character respectively walks into a comic book and a film to experience all kinds of adventures, while the film *Lady in the Lake* (Montgomery, 1946) goes even a step further by maneuvering its own audience into the position of being a character in the film. In the opening sequence, detective Philip Marlowe addresses the viewer talking about a case he has recently cracked. He announces that the viewer will take his place and see the same things he saw, after which he challenges the audience to solve the case like he did. The rest of the film merely consists of a series of POV-shots aimed at giving the audience a sense of being the character in the film. This failed for a number of reasons (Sobchack, 1992, pp. 230–248). In this context, the most important reason for this failure is that, after having been invited to play this part, the audience also wants to influence the actions and the course of events. Because this is impossible—it is after all, a film (cf. *Marienbad*)—the viewer is constantly confronted with the presence and limitations of this medium. The pleasure normally experienced while watching a fictional film is at best replaced by an intellectual appreciation for Robert Montgomery's experiment.

In Bolter and Grusin's terms we can describe this failure as an unsuccessful attempt at achieving transparent immediacy and an undesired realization of a consciousness of the construction of the film. We found comparable results in attempts to realize interactivity in the collectiveness of a cinema, for example, by occasionally giving the audience a choice over how the film will continue. The explanation for the failure of such experiments seems to lie in the fact that the influence exerted by the audience cannot be considered a direct result of the individual viewer's choice. In this sense interactive cinema seems to be an oxymoron, because cinema seems to need an audience, and interactivity an individual relation with, for example, a television or computer screen. Even computer games that are played with several people over a local network or the Internet are based on this starting point.

Criticism on the concept of "interactivity" is probably just as diverse as the attempts to define it. In *Cybertext* (1997), Aarseth qualifies interactivity as a form of "industrial rhetoric" (p. 48), which calls to mind all kinds of vague connotations to improve the selling potential of products, such as newspapers, video, and television. Aarseth demonstrates how this "commercial rhetoric is accepted uncritically by academics with little concern for precise definitions or implicit ideologies" (p. 48; see Manovich, 2001, pp. 55–61). One of Aarseth's justifiable pieces of criticism is that the promised ideological implications of "freedom for the user" and "equality of man and machine" are said to be caused by the mere technical ability of computers to respond to human input. Ascribing magical ability to a piece of technology in such a way is in conflict with the technological interactionism I adhere to: social processes are not only influenced by technological developments (as in technological determinism), nor are they solely controlled by human negotiations (social constructivism), but by both (De Mul, 2002b, pp. 29–39).

Using a number of examples, Aarseth demonstrates there is "a growing discontent with the dubiousness of the term" (1997, p. 48) and that the issue described using this terminology can better be described using the terms "participation, play, or even use" (p. 49). Consequently, he ends with the ravaging criticism that interactivity "is a purely ideological term, projecting an unfocused fantasy rather than a concept of any analytical substance. This should be sufficient reason for theorists not to use it" (p. 51). Also Laurel criticizes the term: "The search for a definition of interactivity diverts our attention from the real issue: How can people participate as agents within representational contexts" (1997, p. 21).

From Interactivity to Participation

I agree only partly with Aarseth's criticism of the ideological significance of the term "interactivity." I agree with his criticism of the authors who use it as a purely ideological term, i.e. those who do not define how it actually takes shape within a game and what the effects of it are outside the game. But to reject any ideological meaning is to flush away the political child with the purely ideological bath water. And, as I demonstrated above, interactivity is not necessarily a vague concept, but can be defined as the possibility for the player to take up the role of narrator and influence the course of events and actions, possibly as a character in the plot.

In my opinion this lack of precision in the term "interactivity" has, among other things, a historical background. In comparison with other forms of media like television and the PC, people seemed easily content with the vague term interactivity to determine the uniqueness of computer games. In chapter 27 of this book, Rushkoff shows that interactivity, as the specific characteristic of a computer game, was often mentioned by comparing it with the working of a TV-remote control (that deconstructed the content of television media) and the PC-computer's mouse and keyboard (with which we could create [construct] and disseminate our own content). Interactivity in the early is described by Rushkoff as moving around the pixels years on the screen, something I define as a form of reconfiguration. Hence Rushkoff describes the game *Pong* (1972): "You

Table 24.1
From interactivity to participation in computer games

Television: remote control	Deconstruction	**Computer game**	Deconstruction
Computer game: joystick	Move the pixels		Reconfiguration
PC: mouse and keyboard	Creation		Construction

▨ = interactivity in games
▨ = participation in games

were celebrating the simple ability to be able to move the pixels on the screen for the first time. It was a moment of revolution!" (p. 417) From a historical perspective he was of course correct, because that is about as far as the development was in those days.

If we look at today's computer games as a form of participatory media culture, we need to come to the conclusion that computer games are not only characterized by reconfiguration, but also, more or less, by deconstruction and by construction. We encounter this development in the scheme shown in table 24.1.

Participation

Thus, in my opinion, a more precise alternative for interactivity to characterize not only the specificity of computer games but also the media culture that has formed around them, is the concept of "participation." As already stated in the introduction, I consider participation to consist of three domains: that of interpretation (deconstruction is understood as a specific form of interpretation), the domain of the reconfiguration of existing game elements, and the domain of the construction of new game elements. In this section I will mainly focus on a short explanation of the latter two.

Espen Aarseth also noted that interpretation should be considered part of participation. In his analy-

sis of "user functions" (1997, pp. 64–65), he observes that the interpretive function is important for all texts (and thus, I would claim, also for computer games): "If all the decisions a reader makes about a text concern its meaning, then there is only one user function involved, here called interpretation" (p. 64). And only because an author such as Marie-Laure Ryan (2001) is exploring different forms of interactivity, she claims on the other hand that she sees "no point in regarding 'interpretive' as a distinctive user function, since interpretation is involved in all intelligent text handling." In this section, I will give an explanation of the domains of 'reconfiguration' and 'construction' against the background of the ideas of Aarseth and Ryan on this point (see table 24.2).

Reconfiguration First, reconfiguration exists in the exploration of the unknown, in the computer game represented worlds. In this "explorative function," the gamer is "making strategic choices about alternative paths and, in the case of adventure games, alternative actions" (Aarseth, 1997, p. 64). Characteristic of the "exploratory mode" is that "the user is free to move around the database, but this activity does not make history nor does it alter the plot; the user has no impact on the destiny of the virtual world" (Ryan, 2001). It is this exploration and attempt to control worlds that are unknown to the player, that is often mentioned as a specific characteristic of computer games (see Fuller & Jenkins, 1995; Johnson, 1997, pp. 72–75; Manovich, 2001, pp. 244–285).

Second, we speak of reconfiguration when a player in this process of exploration is invited to give form to these worlds in an active way by selecting one of the many preprogrammed possibilities in a computer game (this is what Aarseth calls the "configurative function," Aarseth, 1997, p. 64). Here, a player is "building the virtual world by selecting objects and actions from a fixed set of system-internal possibilities" (Ryan, 2001; see also Manovich, 2001, pp. 218–243).

Table 24.2
Domains of participation

Hall	Friedman	Turkle	Aarseth	Ryan	Domains of participation
Dominant Negotiated Oppositional	Demystification	Simulation resignation Simulation understanding Simulation denial	Interpretation		Interpretation
			Exploration Configuration	Exploration Selection	Reconfiguration
			Addition	Addition	Construction

Thus, reconfiguration enables the player "to control the transformation of a body of information to meet its needs and interests. This transformation should include a capability to create, change, and recover particular encounters with the body of knowledge, maintaining these encounters as versions of the material" (Joyce, 1995, p. 41). It is the actualization of something that is virtually, in the sense of potentially, already available as one of the options, created by the developer of the computer game.

Construction Construction, understood as the addition of new game elements, can exist in the making of new games or—and this is much more common—the modification of existing games, described as "to deconstruct and alter an existing system for the joy of it" (Diniz-Sanches, 2003, 67). By modification, "the users can extend or change the text by adding their own writing or programming" (Aarseth, 1997, p. 64) in which "the ability to add permanent components to the text presupposes the demiurgic power to co-create the virtual world" (Ryan, 2001).

Construction is an activity that can take a multitude of forms. It is suggested that, partly out of commercial consideration, you can find one of these forms in the preprogrammed hacker system that we encounter in *Enter the Matrix* (Atari, 2003): "The game also features a unique 'hacking system' that allows the player to hack into the game, or his/her character, exploring and unlocking secrets." However, these activities are better described as a form of reconfiguration. You can really speak of construction when players work with game-mods or game patches, editing tools and source codes. These mods or patches can be described as follows: "A patch (or a skin, a wad, a mod, a map or a shape) is an add-on to an existing game engine that alters the original code or state of a computer game. A patch can range from a simple repair of an error in the original game to elaborate manipulation and customization of graphics, sound, game play, architecture or other attributes of the original computer game." (Schleiner, [1])

Despite the fact that some of these practices of game modification have been accepted, encouraged and commercially exploited by developers and publishers, when "pirating, cracking, and repackaging games" (Rushkoff, 1994, p. 185) the gamer can still be considered as a point of resistance against the gaming industry. The act of copying, modifying and hacking of computer games, is a specific form of the piracy and parasitism that Gilles Deleuze and Hakim Bey

referred to in relation to digital culture: "the hacker culture and contingent 'open source'-methods are alive and kicking in the online gamer circuits" (Schleiner, [2]).[22]

It is important, finally, to notice that only a minority of gamers will engage in these more "radical" forms of participation. Compared to reconfiguration, construction seems to me a much less familiar use. More than with exploratory computer games, constructive ones "require a capability to act: to create, change, and recover particular encounters within the developing body of knowledge. These encounters … are versions of what they are becoming, a structure for what does not yet exist" (Joyce, 1995, p. 42).

The domains of reconfiguration and construction make clear that the relation between player and game is much more complex than the different forms of interpretation I described above as part of cultural studies: "The cultural studies' embrace of the model of resistant reading … only describes one axis of a more complex relationship between readers and texts" (Jenkins & Tulloch, 1995, pp. 262–263). Although you can give both negotiating and oppositional readings of a single character as Lara Croft (interpretation), we have to turn to a computer game such as *The Nomad Soul* (1999) to be able to play with a diversity of preprogrammed characters and their gender-identities (reconfiguratie). And it is the use of independently produced game patches (construction)—think of Lara Croft as female Frankenstein, as drag queen et cetera (see Schleiner [3])—that further increase the possibility of the player to really arrive at a diversity of "sheroes."

Participation in Political-Ideological Perspective

The political dimension resurfaces, publicly articulated or not, in the ideological criticism that is contained in many reflections on participatory media culture. Hence, considering the specific characteristics of computer games, I wonder in what way and to what extent computer games can contribute to the development of new, or the remediation of existing practices of participatory media culture in which the autonomy of users is as great as possible. You could call this a form of "intervention analysis": "Intervention analysis seeks not only to describe and explain existing dispositions of knowledge, but also to change them" (Jenkins & Tulloch, 1995, p. 238). At a time when the Western world is facing the transformation from "industrial capitalism" into "the new age of cultural capitalism" (Rifkin, 2000)—that characterizes itself as an "entertainment economy"

(Wolf, 1999) or "experience economy" (Pine & Gilmore, 1999), which is characterized by the sheer economic importance of cultural expression—it is becoming increasingly important also to give a political-ideological reading of computer games as participatory media culture.

It seems to me that this reading should consist of at least four elements, which I want to deal with in this final section. First of all, the question of who will have or get access to the media culture, the influence of which reaches all of us (top-down versus bottom-up). Second, a question concerning the results of this access to the practices of the media culture (homogenization versus heterogenization). Third, the matter of the status of the different forms of media culture that we should relate to (the real versus the possible). Fourth, these three elements combine to make it possible to distinguish between different levels of participation: culture participation versus participatory culture.

Top-Down versus Bottom-Up
The question of who can participate in our culture can be further elaborated on by asking whether we face or will face a top-down culture in which a small number of computer game developers and publishers run the show all by themselves (Microsoft, Electronic Arts, Atari, Eidos and others), or whether we face or will face a multitude of bottom-up cultures, in which computer gamers can (continue to) participate, one way or another. What is at stake here is the possibility for players to exert their fair-use rights on copyrighted material. As I described above, even in cases in which users have no control over the production of culture, they can still control its "consumption," described as "the art of using those imposed on it": "characterized by its ruses, its fragmentation ... its poaching, its clandestine nature, its tireless but quiet activity" (De Certeau, 1988, p. 31).

In line with Henry Jenkins' criticism of Mark Dery (1993), I would rather plead for an open, negotiating relation with producers from the computer game industry than for an attitude of refusal, or, as Jenkins formulates it, for the development "from jammers to bloggers":

Culture jammers want to opt out of media consumption and promote a purely negative and reactive conception of popular culture. Fans, on the other hand, see unrealized potentials in popular culture and want to broaden audience participation. Fan culture is dialogic rather than disruptive, affective more than ideological, and collaborative rather than confron-tational. Culture jammers want to "jam" the dominant media, while poachers want to appropriate their content, imagining a more democratic, responsive, and diverse style of popular culture. Jammers want to destroy media power, while poachers want a share of it. (Jenkins, 2002, p. 167).[23]

We see these bottom-up cultures both where independent games are being developed and spread—like *Waco Resurrection* (2003) and *Under Ash* (2003)—and where existing game-elements and game-engines are modified and used for own, for example, political purposes, like *Velvet-Strike* (2002), *Diplomatic Arena* (2003) and *Civilization IV—Age of Empire* (2003). These games could be played during the "Exploding Cinema: Power: Play" program of the International Film Festival Rotterdam 2004:

A new genre of critical games ... is emerging. People can be informed about economic exploitation or political migration via games ... Why remain a passive consumer when there is just as much fun to be had in adopting games to our own sets of rules ... One thing all the selected games ... within Power: Play have in common is the notion of empowerment, speaking out, looking critically, taking the initiative ourselves (Carels, 2004).

As the reader can see in Anne-Marie Schleiner's chapter of this book, we encounter these bottom-up cultures where gamers use sharing and open-source techniques to recycle existing products of the mainstream practices of the cultural industries.

Homogenization versus Heterogenization
In spite of the fact that within mass media processes of homogenization seem to prevail at first sight, there are still possibilities for processes of heterogenization (see Raessens, 1998, pp. 109–111; 2001; 2002, pp. 129–131). Relevant here is the critique of the Italian philosopher Gianni Vattimo on the work of Horkheimer and Adorno. According to Vattimo, Horkheimer and Adorno (1951, 1986) are of the opinion that the mass media would produce "a general homogenization of society" in which "the diffusion of slogans, propaganda (commercial as well as political) and stereotypical worldviews" would dominate (Vattimo, 1992, p. 5).

Vattimo, on the other hand, is much more optimistic about the role of the mass media. According to him, they have played a crucial role in "a general explosion and proliferation of 'Weltanschauungen,' of worldviews" (Vattimo, 1992, p. 5). All kinds of minorities and subcultures have seized the opportunity to express their views in the relative chaos of today's media. According to Vattimo, this is a development that has contributed to the rise of the postmodern society characterized by relativity, contingency, heterogeneity and diversity.

If we apply this analysis to computer games, we have to state that they, as a form of popular culture, contribute to the representation and reproduction of ideologically charged values. I would call for theoretical and practical resistance to homogenizing tendencies of the media, aiming to realize variety of expression rather than uniformity. This is how homogenization can be replaced by diversity, inequality, and singularity (Raessens, 1998, pp. 109–111).

Living in a period in which processes of globalization of economies and cultures put pressure on this cultural diversity (see Smiers, 2003)—as we live for example in "A world of Gameboys and Walkmen" (Rushkoff, 2001, p. 75) where toys are mainly made by and for white boys—the processes of heterogenization become of great importance, as I mentioned above in regard to gender and ethnic identities.

But also on quite another field, we see the necessity of these processes. Computer games are usually based on the sensor-motor model related to classical cinema, a model which is almost exclusively oriented toward the actuality and causality of action (Raessens & Kattenbelt, 2003). To do justice to the complexity of human experience, this dominance should be broken through with games that are also based on the intensity of feeling and the reflexivity of thought. An example of this dominance is the computer game *Metal Gear Solid* (1999). Although at specific moments, this game comes up with intensity and reflexivity, both domains of human experience are overruled by the dramatic mode. On the other hand, in the so-called "serious" or "non-entertainment" computer games we see the diversity of experience. In these games, it is not the entertainment value that is central, but an external purpose: receiving a certain experience, the communication of a message, the acquisition of knowledge, understanding and/or certain skills or the realization of a certain change of behavior (see Prensky, 2000 and chapter 6 of this book).

The Real versus the Possible
In the turbulence of the media Rushkoff sees, like Vattimo, the development of a proliferation of world-views that today's young people will have to relate to. Although this new world comes across to many older people as inconceivable and therefore frightening, the children of chaos are able to deal with it, and they picked up the necessary cognitive skills to survive in today's world partly while playing computer games.[24]

As Rushkoff demonstrates in his chapter in this book, gamers are the ones (as long as they are not only "gaming," but also become game programmers and thereby move from game to metagame) who realize that our reality is open source: "gamers know that the reality they are engineering isn't real" (p. 420) they have "the ability to rethink and redesign our world using entirely new rule sets" (p. 421). This analysis shows strong agreement with Vattimo's analysis of the postmodern: "If the proliferation of images of the world entails that we will lose our 'sense of reality' [psychologists warn us that this is the case with gamers,] as the saying goes, perhaps it's not such a great loss after all." (1992, p. 8). Although the reality of the world cannot be denied (see Zizek, 2002), there is an emancipating and liberating significance of this plurality and loss of reality. This can be found in the recognition of the plurality of perspectives that can no longer be suppressed or silenced in the name of a superior story. An allegedly comforting myth that wants to undo this plurality, and trade it in for a solid, singular, and authoritative reality then becomes unacceptable.[25] Gamers are well aware of the fact that the reality they find themselves in is but an actualized form of the many possibilities they have at their disposal, it is just one version of the way the world works, never the one and only objective vision. This could lead to a "potentialization of reality ... reality submerge into a multitude of possibilities" (Vuyk, 1992; Raessens, 2001, p. 228).[26]

Culture Participation versus Participatory Culture

To conclude I want to distinguish between "culture participation" and "participatory culture." Culture participation is a broad concept that refers generally to the fact that we participate in the surrounding culture be that in a passive and consumptive, or a more active and productive way. I consider participatory culture the latter, more active attitude that, as we have seen, makes special demands concerning the interpretation, the reconfiguration, and the construction of computer games.[27] Negotiated, oppositional, and deconstructive readings (more so than dominant ones), configuration and selection (more so than exploration), and construction (more so than reconfiguration) are all, in their own specific way, part of what I call participatory media culture. Computer games are not just a game, never just a business strategy for maximizing profit, but always also a battlefield where the possibility to realize specific, bottom-up, heterogeneous forms of participatory media culture is at stake.

Acknowledgments

I thank Chiel Kattenbelt, Jos de Mul and Mirko Schäfer for their comments on an earlier version of this chapter, and Joep Damen for help with the translation.

Notes

1. Whereas the French philosopher Gilles Deleuze defines philosophy as the creation of concepts (Deleuze & Guattari, 1991, pp. 8, 11), the philosophical method I will use in this chapter also involves analyzing and criticizing existing concepts.

2. Deleuze formulates this method as follows: "introducing the concepts of 'meaning' and 'value' to philosophy" (1962, p. 1). This allows us to interpret the forces that are articulated in computer games, for example, as homogeneous or heterogeneous, and to evaluate them, for example, as desirable or undesirable.

3. The view that the development of interactive technologies as such is sufficient for the realization of a new participatory culture has to be rejected as a form of radical "technological determinism." Also the social-constructivist view, which claims that mainly nontechnological factors matter, has to be considered: "Rather than talking about interactive technologies, we should document the interactions that occur among media consumers, between media consumers and media texts and between media consumers and media producers" (Jenkins, 2002, p. 157).

4. See Brecht, 1932–1933, p. 553: "den Zuhörer nicht nur hören, sondern auch sprechen zu machen"; and Benjamin, 1934, p. 110: "Und zwar ist dieser Apparat um so besser, je mehr er Konsumenten der Produktion zuführt, kurz aus Lesern oder aus Zuschauern Mitwirkende zu machen imstande ist."

5. The term "multimediality" refers to the multitude of means of expression ("matières de l'expression") see Metz, 1977, pp. 10, 17–18, 25, and 130–131.

6. Both the Dutch Association of Producers and Importers of Audio-visual Materials (NVPI) and the Entertainment Software Association (ESA) refer to the problem of piracy: "World-wide piracy is estimated to have cost the US entertainment software industry over $3.0 billion in 2001, robbing game developers and the game industry of revenue that could be used to underwrite the creation and marketing of an even wider array of game titles." See: www.theesa.com/piracy.html.

7. Janet Murray describes interactivity as the merger of agency ("the satisfying power to take meaningful action and see the results of our decisions and choices") and transformation ("Computers offer us countless ways of shapeshifting"), see Murray, 1997, pp. 126 and 154. A film viewer is passive in the sense that while watching a film there is no such thing as reconfiguration or construction, in my sense of the word. For an analysis of "The Viewer's Activity" while watching a film, see Bordwell, 1985, pp. 29–47.

8. These Internet-constructed collaborative fan communities are typical for participatory media culture; think also of peer-to-peer networks, collaborative and reader edited news networks (e.g., Slashdot, News for Nerds, Stuff that Matters), open-source based activities of programmers and users to develop software for general use, nonprofit activities (Linux) and the activities of bloggers. For further elaboration on these examples, especially concerning their implications on the practice of citizenship, see Uricchio, 2003.

9. British cultural studies for the most part came into existence in the 1970s at the Birmingham Centre for Contemporary Cultural Studies (CCCS, established in 1964) under the supervision of director Stuart Hall (see Turner, 1996).

10. The introduction of new, audiovisual technologies is often linked to the fear that the ever so tempting images and sounds will impair the reflexivity of the printing culture (Birkerts, 1996). Think of the novels by Aldous Huxley (*Brave new world*, 1932) and Ray Bradbury (*Fahrenheit 451*, 1953), in which, respectively, the film theatre from the 1930s and the rise of television in the 1950s is characterized as misleading. Since the 1970s, this fear is formulated with respect to computer games, which, by combining moving images, sound, and interactivity, supposedly only provide immediate satisfaction through stimulation of the senses.

11. A more current version of this position is visible in a discussion of *The Matrix Reloaded* (Wachowski, 2003): "We are not just plugged into their matrix to be sold movies and other entertainment products. These companies [the media giants], can also plug the nation into news narratives as ubiquitous and lightweight as *The Matrix Reloaded*, but with more damaging side effects.... One way or the other, we all inhibit the Matrix now" (Rich, 2003).

12. For a discussion of high versus low art, see Jenkins' chapter in this book. Using Gilbert Seldes' model of analysis (1957), he places computer games on the side of the so-called "living" art forms.

13. "We say *dominant*, not 'determined,' because it is always possible to order, classify, assign and decode an event within more than one 'mapping,'" Hall, 1980, p. 134. For a description of these three positions, see Hall, 1980, pp. 136–138.

14. One of the limitations of this model is formulated by Fiske: "Hall ... had overemphasized the role of class in producing different readings and had underestimated the variety of determinants of readings" (1987, p. 63). In Fiske's critique, the role of the text is dethroned and the importance of extratextual determinants of textual meaning are stressed. Think for example of the different readings of a text respectively by regular users, hobbyists, and hackers. See also Bryce and Rutter's approach in this book that "moves from textual exegesis and places gaming within a real world context in which gaming practices are negotiated in real time and space (p. 304)."

15. Turner (1996) discusses these issues in the sections "Women Take Issue" and "There Ain't No Black ..." in which the central argument revolves around the production of gender and ethnic subjectivity.

16. Richard and Zaremba are aware of the fact that a critical discussion of the Lara Croft phenomenon is in general limited to the negotiated or oppositional readings you can give of her. In a game such as *The Nomad Soul*, on the other hand, players can choose from a number of characters (reconfiguration), while using patches and the like (construction) can further increase the possibilities of creating your own "sheroes."

17. Turkle relates this transition to the rise of "The Macintosh Mystique": "With the Macintosh, personal computers began to present themselves as opposed and even hostile to the traditional modernist expectation that one could take a technology, open the hood, and see inside. The distinctiveness of the Macintosh was precisely that it did not encourage such fantasies; it made the computer screen a world unto itself. It encouraged play and tinkering. Mastering the Macintosh meant getting the lay of the land rather than figuring out the hierarchy of underlying structure and rules" (1996, p. 35).

18. Compare to Nissen, 1998, which describes hackers as the "masters of modernity and modern technology."

19. Christian Metz described this process as an attempt to disguise the "discours" as a "histoire," i.e., instead of having someone with an ideological motive tell the story, it is a story that transparently tells itself: "But characteristic for this 'discours,' and especially its editing principles, is that, in fact, it erases the traces of the 'énunciation' and disguises itself as an 'histoire'" (Metz, 1980b, p. 77).

20. See also Friedman, 1995, pp. 77–78: "The game player takes on the role of the protagonist.... The idea of computer 'role-playing' emphasizes the opportunity to identify with the character on the screen—the fantasy is that rather than just watching the hero, you can actually be the hero, or at least make all the hero's decisions yourself." Despite the fact that a simulation game such as *SimCity* (1987) "makes you Mayor and City Planner, and dares you to design and build the city of your dreams" (p. 80), something else happens, too: "'Losing yourself' in a computer game means, in a sense, identifying with the simulation itself" (p. 85).

21. See Metz, 1983, pp. 14, 16, and 21; and Metz, 1975, pp. 108, 112, and 118–119.

22. See Deleuze, 1990, p. 244: "piracy or the introduction of viruses" and Bey, 1994, p. 20: Internet-related forms of resistance, respectively those of the Web ("the marginal zine-netwerk, the BBS-networks, cracked software, 'hacking,' telephone-'phreaking'") and those of the "contra-Net" ("the clandestine, illegal and rebellious use of the Web, including data-piracy and other forms of parasitism").

23. In an earlier online version of "Interactive Audiences," Jenkins describes Dery's culture jammers as classic avant gardists who, in line

with the Frankfurt School, "celebrate their own freedom from media control even as they see the 'masses' as still subjected to manipulation … media consumers are largely blinded to their own interests, distracted by 'bread and circuses' entertainment." According to me, participatory media culture is more widespread than avant gardist criticism (Dery) and less widespread than the focus on fan cultures promoting do-it-yourself media production suggests.

24. *Children of chaos: Surviving the end of the world as we know it*, was published in 1996 under the more descriptive title of *Playing the future: How kids' culture can teach us to thrive in an age of chaos* (HarperCollins).

25. For example, George Bush's appropriation of the American myth of the Western to legitimize the war on terror. See Faludi (2003) and Raessens (2003).

26. Deleuze and Vattimo call this process "fabulization," referring to Nietzsche's text "Wie die «wahre Welt» endlich zur Fabel wurde" (1989, pp. 80–81): "It may be that in the world of the mass media a 'prophecy' of Nietzsche's is fulfilled: in the end the true world becomes a fable" (Vattimo, 1992, p. 7). For an extensive discussion of this process in relation to the films *eXistenZ* (Cronenberg, 1999) and *The Matrix* (Wachowski, 1999), see Raessens, 2001, pp. 252–262.

27. When we consider participation from the perspective of the rules of the game, we can define it as "re/de/construction": in the reconstructive mode, the player plays according to the rules of the game; in the deconstructive mode, he or she penetrates the rules; and in the constructive mode, he or she plays a kind of meta-game in which the rules themselves are played with and adapted.

References

Aarseth, E. (1997). *Cybertext. Perspectives on ergodic literature*. Baltimore: Johns Hopkins University Press.

Adorno, T. (1951). *Minima moralia*. Frankfurt am Main: Suhrkamp Verlag.

Benjamin, W. (1966). Der Autor als Produzent (1934). In W. Benjamin, *Versuche über Brecht*. Frankfurt am Main: Suhrkamp Verlag.

Bey, H. (1994). *De tijdelijke autonome zone. Immediatistische essays*. Amsterdam: Arsenaal.

Birkerts, S. (1996). *The Gutenberg elegies: The fate of reading in an electronic Age*. London: Ballantine Books.

Bolter, J., & Grusin, R. (1999). *Remediation: Understanding new media*. Cambridge, MA: MIT Press.

Bordwell, D. (1985). *Narration in the fiction film*. Madison: University of Wisconsin Press.

Bordwell, D., & Thompson, K. (1986). *Film art: An introduction*. New York: Alfred A. Knopf.

Brecht, B. (1992). Der Rundfunk als Kommunikationsapparat. Rede über die Funktion des Rundfunks (1932–1933). In *Bertolt Brecht*. Werke, Schriften 1. Frankfurt am Main: Suhrkamp Verlag.

Cameron, A. (1995). Dissimulations. The Illusion of Interactivity. *Millennium Film Journal*, *28*, 32–47. See: mfj-online.org/journalpages/MFJ28/Dissimulations.html.

Carels, E. (2004). The state of play. In E. Houtenbrink (Ed.), *Catalogue 33rd International Film Festival Rotterdam*. Amsterdam: Publish Amsterdam.

Certeau, M. de. (1988). *The practice of everyday life*. Berkeley: University of California Press.

Darley, A. (2000). *Visual digital culture: Surface play and spectacle in new media genres*. London and New York: Routledge.

Deleuze, G. (1962). *Nietzsche et la philosophie*. Paris: Presses Universitaires de France.

Deleuze, G. (1990). Post-scriptum sur les sociétés de contrôle. In *Pourparlers*. Paris: Les Editions de Minuit, pp. 240–247.

Deleuze, G., & Guattari, F. (1991). *Qu'est-ce que la philosophie?* Paris: Minuit.

Dery, M. (1993). Culture jamming: Hacking, slashing and sniping in the empire of signs. See: www.levity.com/markdeny/jam.html.

Diniz-Sanches, J. (2003). The modern Age. In: *Edge*, issue 126, pp. 58–67. See: www.edge-online.com.

Faludi, S. (2003). An American myth rides into the sunset. *The New York Times*, March 30, 2003. See www.nytimes.com/2003/03/30/opinion/30falu.html.

Fiske, J. (1999). *Television culture*. London: Routledge.

Friedman, T. (1995). Making sense of software: Computer games and interactive textuality. In S. Jones (Ed.), *Cybersociety: Computer-mediated-communication and community*, pp. 73–89. London: Sage Publications. See also www.duke.edu/~tlove/simcity.htm.

Friedman, T. (1999). Civilization and its discontents: Simulation, subjectivity, and space. In G. Smith (Ed.), *On a silver platter. CD-ROMs and the promises of a new technology*. New York: New York University Press.

Fuller, M., & Jenkins, H. (1995). Nintendo and new world travel writing: A dialogue. In: S. Jones (Ed.), *Cybersociety. Computer-mediated communication and community*. London: Sage Publications.

Hall, S. (1996). Encoding/decoding. In S. Hall, D. Hobson, A. Lowe, & P. Willis (Eds.), *Culture, media, language. Working papers in cultural studies*, 1972–79 (pp. 128–138). London: Hutchinson.

Hall, S. (Ed.). (1997). *Representation. Cultural representations and signifying practices*. London: Sage Publications.

Heim, M. (1993). *The metaphysics of virtual reality*. New York: Oxford University Press.

Horkheimer, M., & Adorno, T. (1986). Kulturindustrie, Aufklärung als Massenbetrug. In S. Fischer Verlag. Dialektik der Aufklärung (pp. 128–176). Frankfurt am Main: Fischer Verlag.

Jenkins, H. (1992). *Textual poachers: Television fans & participatory culture*. New York: Routledge.

Jenkins, H. (2002). Interactive audiences? In D. Harries (Ed.), *The new media book* (pp. 157–170). London: BFI Publishing.

Jenkins, H., & Tulloch, J. (1995). *Science fiction audiences. Watching Doctor Who and Star Trek*. London: Routledge.

Johnson, S. (1997). *Interface culture: How new technology transforms the way we create and communicate*. San Francisco: Harper.

Joyce, M. (1995). Siren shapes: Exploratory and constructive hypertexts. In *Of two minds. Hypertext pedagogy and poetics*, (pp. 38–59). Ann Arbor: The University of Michigan Press.

Laurel, B. (1997). *Computers as theatre*. New York: Addison-Wesley Publishing Company.

Manovich, L. (2001). *The language of new media*. Cambridge, MA: MIT Press.

Metz, C. (1983). A propos de l'impression de réalité au cinéma. In *Essais sur la signification au cinéma, tome I*. Paris: Editions Klincksieck.

Metz, C. (1980a). Over mijn werk. Interview met Marc Vernet en Daniel Percheron. In *Seminar semiotiek van de film. Over Christian Metz*, (pp. 11–58). Nijmegen: SUN.

Metz, C. (1980b). Histoire/Discours (aantekening over twee voyeurismen). In *Seminar semiotiek van de film. Over Christian Metz* (pp. 77–84). Nijmegen: SUN.

Metz, C. (1975). Le film de fiction et son spectateur. In *Communications 23*.

Metz, C. (1977). L'enchevêtrement des spécificité: spécificité multiple, degré de spécificité, modes de spécificité. In C. Metz, *Langage et cinéma* (pp. 169–176). Paris: Editions Albatros.

Mul, J. de. (2002a). *Cyberspace odyssee*. Kampen, Klement.

Mul, J. de. (2002b). *Filosofie in cyberspace. Reflecties op de informatie- en communicatietechnologie*. Kampen: Klement.

Murray, J. (1997). *Hamlet on the holodeck. The future of narrative in cyberspace*. New York: The Free Press.

Murray, J., & Jenkins, H. (1999). Before the holodeck: Translating Star Trek into digital media. In G. Smith (Ed.), *On a silver platter. CD-ROMs and the promises of a new technology*. New York: New York University Press.

Nietzsche, F. (1989). *Götzen-Dämmerung oder Wie man mit dem Hammer philosophirt*. München: Deutscher Taschenbuch Verlag.

Nissen, J. (1998). Hackers: Masters of modernity and modern technology. In J. Sefton-Green (Ed.), *Digital diversions: Youth culture in the age of multimedia*. London: UCL Press.

Oram, A. (Ed.). (2001). *Peer-to-peer. Harnessing the power of disruptive technologies*. Sabastopol: O'Reilly.

Pine, J., & Gilmore, J. (1999). *The experience economy: Work is theatre and every business a stage*. Boston: Harvard Business School Press.

Prensky, M. (2000). *Digital game-based learning*. New York: McGraw-Hill.

Raessens, J. (1998). Filmregisseurs als artsen van de cultuur. Guattari over film en de productie van subjectiviteit. In H. Oosterling & S. Thissen (Eds.), *Chaos ex machina. Het ecosofisch werk van Félix Guattari op de kaart gezet*. Rotterdam: Faculty of Philosophy, Erasmus University.

Raessens, J. (2002). *Filosofie & film. Viv®e la différence: Deleuze en de cinematografische moderniteit*. Damon: Budel.

Raessens, J. (2003). Bush en de mythe van het Wilde Westen. In *De Helling 2*. Amsterdam: Stichting Westenschaprelilk Bureau GroenLinks.

Raessens, J. Cinema and beyond. Film en het proces van digitalisering. In J. de Mul (Ed.), *Filosofie in cyberspace. Reflecties op de informatie- en communicatietechnologie* (pp. 119–154). Kampen, Klement.

Raessens, J. & Kattenbelt, C. (2003). Computer games and the complexity of experience. In: M. Copier and Raessens, J. (Eds.), *Level up: Digital games research conference 2003* (pp. 420–425). Utrecht: Utrecht University, Faculty of Arts.

Rich, F. (2003). There's no exit from the Matrix. *The New York Times*, May 25.

Rifkin, J. (2000). *The age of access: How the shift from ownership to access is transforming capitalism*. London: Penguin Books.

Rushkoff, D. (1994). *Media virus: Hidden agendas in popular culture*. New York: Ballantine Books.

Rushkoff, D. (1997). *Children of chaos: Surviving the end of the world as we know it*. London: Flamingo.

Rushkoff, D. (1999). *Coercion: Why we listen to what "they" say*. New York: Riverhead Books.

Rushkoff, D. (2001). *Bull: Dealing in futures just got more expensive*. London: Sceptre.

Ryan, M.-L. (2001). Beyond myth and metaphor: The case of narrative in digital media. *Game Studies. The International Journal of Computer Game Research*, *1*, 1. www.gamestudies.org/0101/ryan.

Schleiner, A. M. [1]. Parasitic interventions: Game patches and hacker Art. See: www.opensorcery.net/patchnew.html.

Schleiner, A. M. [2]. MUTATION.FEM. www.opensorcery.net/mutetext.html.

Schleiner, A. M. [3]. Does Lara Croft wear fake polygons? See: www.opensorcery.net.lara2.html.

Seldes, G. (1957). *The seven lively arts*. New York: Sagmore Press.

Smiers, J. (2003). *Arts under pressure. Promoting cultural diversity in the age of globalization*. London and New York: Zed Books.

Sobchack, V. (1992). *The address of the eye: A phenomenology of film experience*. Princeton: Princeton University Press.

Turner, G. (1996). *British cultural studies: An introduction*. London: Routledge.

Turkle, S. (1996). *Life on the screen: Identity in the age of the internet*. London: Weidenfeld & Nicolson.

Uricchio, W. (2003). Cultural citizenship in the age of P2P networks. See: www.hum.hu.dk/modinet/conference_aug/Uricchiofinal.pdf.

Vattimo, G. (1992). The Postmodern: A transparent society? In *The transparent society* (pp. 1–11). Cambridge: Polity Press.

Vuyk, K. (1992). *De esthetisering van het wereldbeeld*. Kampen: Kok Agora.

Williams, R. (1988). *Keywords. A vocabulary of culture and society*. London: Fontana Press.

Wolf, M. (1999). *The entertainment economy. How megamedia forces are transforming our lives*. London: Penguin Books.

Zizek, S. (2002). *Welcome to the desert of the real! Five essays on September 11 and related dates*. London: Verso Books.

25

I AM WHAT I PLAY: PARTICIPATION AND REALITY AS CONTENT

Jan-Willem Huisman and Hanne Marckmann

Most computer game manufacturers have been doing the same thing for years—producing CD-ROM games whose visual design is conceived to reflect reality as accurately as possible. Within this realistic world, you can then do a host of unrealistic things. *Grand Theft Auto: Vice City* (Rock Star Games, 2003) offer you the chance to run down your fellow man at 200 miles an hour. In *Unreal Tournament 2003* (Epic Atari, 2003) you can shoot everybody dead without embarrassment, whereas in *Black and White* (Lionhead Studios, 2001) you can even be God of your own world. But however exciting these games may be to play—and however much money they continue to generate—in no sense are they innovative.

At IJsfontein we try to develop games that have something new to offer. We proceed from two important elements: participation and reality as content. By participation we mean offering the user more than merely a choice between existing possibilities. We want to let him or her participate in building the game. If we look at *Quake* or *Carmageddon*, we see a clearly preprogrammed world in which all we can do is pick out a route. The interaction consists of choosing from the various possibilities on offer. Interactive this may be, but it is not participation. We will discuss our vision on participation later.

When we talk of reality as content, we are distancing ourselves from the quest for realism in visual design. In our view, an even more realistic replication of everyday reality has no added value for the gameplay. So what if we have achieved total realism? The closer we get to this "hyperrealistic virtuality," the more it will disappoint us, simply because it will never be real. Instead of giving reality its place in the visual design, IJsfontein is investigating other roles for reality in games, by giving real elements a place in the content of the game or by exploring how we can take games out of the virtual world and give them a place in our daily reality. Later we will describe the search for a new relationship between virtuality and reality.

First, we introduce IJsfontein as a business, discuss our vision of the (technological) future, and introduce a number of IJsfontein projects that we will use later to illustrate the arguments.

IJsfontein

IJsfontein makes interactive products, primarily for a young target group. The company was set up in 1996 by three enthusiastic friends and now employs twenty-five people from various disciplines. It is based in Amsterdam, in The Netherlands, and its name translates as Ice Fountain.

In what follows we will outline our vision of the role of computers in human life and draw the implications for those making products for a young target group. We then present a number of concrete examples of IJsfontein products that embody the kinds of development that we would like to see in the game industry.

Vision

IJsfontein foresees a future in which computers will occupy an increasingly central role in daily life, as an extension of human capacity and as a component in various forms of communication. The boundaries between people and computers are becoming blurred. The computer will begin to support, reinforce, and replace certain aspects of human thinking, feeling, and interaction. In the context of such a future, IJsfontein believes in developing products linked to and supporting these, hitherto exclusively human, processes.

Playing, Learning, Discovering This vision of the future affects IJsfontein products in two important ways. First, it influences the content of the products themselves. IJsfontein makes products that support or reinforce the development of the child's mental processes. There is of course plenty of educational software available to teach children spelling or arithmetic, but computers can also play a role in less obvious processes. Interactivity helps children create things via the

Jan-Willem Huisman and Hanne Marckmann

computer and thereby aids in the development of creativity itself. The enormous connecting power of email and the Internet (chatrooms, MUDs, etc.) can encourage children to work together and teach them to communicate clearly, and the infinite potential of the virtual world directly engages the imagination. No longer restricted to daily reality, children can build and experience each other's imaginary worlds. Bearing all these possibilities in mind, IJsfontein defines three basic activities—"playing, learning, and discovering"—and builds magical worlds that invite children's participation.

Technology-Independent Products The decision to develop software on a human scale has an effect on the stance we as a company take in the marketplace. IJsfontein is, above all, determined to make technology-independent products. For us, games are about making good content. That sounds logical enough, but it means that our games must not only work on the newest computers, but also on slightly older models. The choice for technology-independent products proceeds from the desire to move the content of interactive media, such as games, on to the following step. Far too much emphasis is laid on the development of new technologies, with the development of content for current technologies getting squeezed out in the process. Prophets predict mountains of gold for each new technology. If these predictions are not met in a very short time, the desperate search moves on to another technology. This mode of investment ensures that there is never money available to develop *content* for *existing* technologies. Each time a medium does not rapidly realize its potential, the tap is turned off. At least half the money then plunged into new technologies would be much better employed making something innovative for the existing technology, which would allow the user to go straight to work.

Take the Internet, a medium that has touched our lives in numerous ways. Email has changed the way we communicate in both professional and private spheres. Chat programs (MSN and ICQ) play a major role in the social lives of the young. Developments such as these were immediately predicted when the Internet arrived, but when they failed to be profitable within the first two years, investment stopped and numerous companies went bankrupt. In the end, the prophets turned out to be right. The Internet simply needed more time to prove itself. But now, when the medium's potential has crystallized, a company can afford to develop interesting projects which marry the form of the medium to the desires of the public.

IJsfontein's technology-independent policy has helped keep our heads above water in turbulent times for the new media industry. We have never been caught by the latest technological fads, which repeatedly failed to justify the hype.

Development

CD-ROM IJsfontein first gained recognition with the CD-ROM game *Masters of the Elements* (1997), which has since been marketed worldwide and won two important prizes, La Fleche d'Or 1998 (Paris) and the Bafta Award (category Learning) 1999 (London). *Masters of the Elements* is a magical world full of secrets, puzzles, and games (figure 25.1). The game tells the story of a faraway land, in which live the Masters of the Elements. From the rooms of their castle they control Time, Gravity, Light, Electricity, and Heat. One day, the cat belonging to the Master of Fate disappears and the Forces of Nature threaten to fall out of balance. The children have to help find the cat, and in the process they learn the laws of nature.

IJsfontein replaced the basic mouse arrow with a hand that can turn pages, pick up, and point. The game is described as a "reality game in a fairy tale setting." The reality element is not in the visual design of the game, but in the learning experience it provides. The children actually learn the laws of physics. The advantage of *Masters of the Elements*' digital learning environment over a real environment (such as a classroom) is that the lessons learned can be immediately applied, without any danger to the child. A physics experiment in the real world could be actually dangerous.

ITV/Cross-Media IJsfontein has also received a lot of attention for its interactive television series *Typotoons* (figure 25.2; www.vpro.nl/typotoons), which won an Emma award in 2000. The series was first screened in 1999 by VPRO (a leading Dutch public TV company) and gave children the opportunity to create a story together that was then shown on TV. The story was put together with the help of a children's author with whom the children were in contact via the Internet. He could then develop the plot on the spot. The children could also read the story on the *Typotoons* website (the Typobox). At certain moments a "dead" point would arise in the narrative. It was then up to the children to suggest a word (existing or invented) that would take the story forward. Because the children each had one letter of the alphabet as an avatar, they had to work together to arrive at a word. An example: In episode 5, Billy, the main character in the story, goes to

| Figure 25.1 |
Masters of the Elements

| Figure 25.2 |
Typotoons

Jan-Willem Huisman and Hanne Marckmann

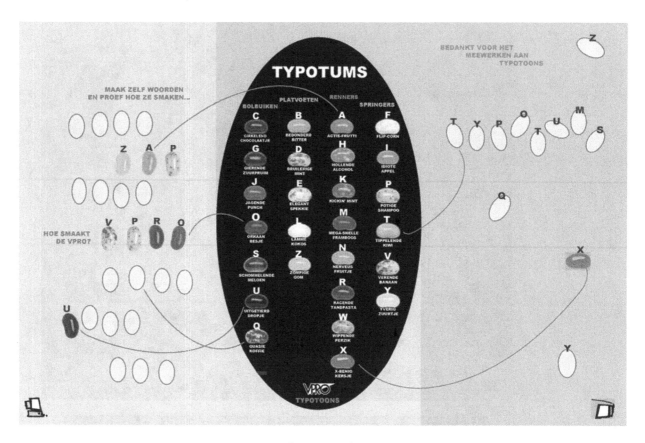

| Figure 25.3 |
Typotums

visit his grandfather at the North Pole. The online author writes in the Typobox: "Billy is collected by a sleigh pulled by huskies, but on the way he falls asleep. Then suddenly ..." The author stops writing and asks the children to think of a word. The children with the letters T,I,M, and P as avatars come up with the word "TIMPT." This is not an existing word, so the children are allowed to give it a meaning. They decide that a timpt is a mountain monster. The author now proceeds. "Then suddenly the sleigh hits a timpt. A timpt is a hairy monster that lives at the North Pole. Billy tumbles from the sleigh and lands at the feet of his grandpa, who has climbed onto a table to look over the timpt's shoulder. Wow, thinks Billy, isn't he big! That must be because ..." And now the children have to think of another word. And so on, until the story comes to a natural end. Meanwhile, at home, the children would draw the story they had made up and send the drawings in to the producer. These were animated for the next TV episode (*TypoTV*), after which the Typobox reopened on Internet and the next part of the story was written.

The children who sent in drawings received a bag of Typotums in the post that same week (figure 25.3).

These are sweets in the form of letters, which have different tastes. The T, for example, tasted of licorice, and the M tasted of Brussels sprouts. So as well as making the words in the Typobox, the children could now "taste" the words at home via the sweets. They could also share their experiences of the taste of specific words. This "timpt" tastes of licorice and Brussels sprouts ... uurrgh! The children were thus involved in the *Typotoons* format, even outside the virtual worlds of the Internet and television.

Typotoons combines various important features of new media in a format that allows children to jointly play the leading role. First, there is interactivity on two levels, content and visual design: the children contribute to writing the story and can send in drawings for animation. Each episode emerges from a dialogue between the makers and the watchers of the program. Instead of discovering a preprogrammed digital story, they make up the story themselves. They can then watch the result of their efforts on television each week. It provides their fifteen minutes of fame.

Second, *Typotoons* makes use of the Internet's connecting potential via the Typobox. The children as letters always have to work together. A letter on its own says nothing, but if you can all make a word you have something to say. They help each other think up good words and meanings by "chatting."

Thirdly, a significant role in the success of *Typotoons* was played by cross-mediality—specific advantages of different media were all used to create one total experience. Television allowed us to reach a broad public, the Internet created a peer-to-peer community, and the sweets made the game sensible.

Enhanced Reality   In searching for a new approach for the games industry, IJsfontein projects explore the relationship between the virtual and real worlds. Game designers no longer need to limit themselves to preconceived worlds and virtual facts. Modern mobile communication techniques and interactive technologies make it possible to extract input for a game from everyday reality. A game featuring a banker can take real stock exchange data from the Internet. An adventure game can download real weather predictions from the local meteorological website. *Road Quiz Show* (working title), an IJsfontein project that is still at the development stage, does precisely this.

The *Road Quiz Show* uses the real geographical environment as the driving force for the game. Every summer hundreds of thousands of people drive to the south of Europe with their children on holiday, heading for the sun. The position of each car can be quite cheaply and accurately determined by the basic cellphone system. At gas stations along the holiday routes, you buy a digital set of questions. These cover the area through which you are travelling. At the moment the cellphone registers your car passing a specific key point, it poses a question via the mobile phone. The question might refer to the length of a tunnel or the height of a mountain. Each correct answer gains the children a number of points. When enough points have been gained, they can pick up a prize at the next gas station. A new set of digital questions can then be bought. Thus the long journey becomes a game and the time flies past. Nor are you being forced into buying new technological equipment. You are playing on your mobile phone.

In Conclusion

The products described above all express part of IJsfontein's vision of the future of games. IJsfontein is seeking innovation via the concept of participation and by exploring the relationship between the virtual and real worlds. The multiplicity of channels now available

makes it possible to build these elements into games. But the game industry too often begins with the medium—the CD-ROM—for which it then develops a game. This sequence of working will never deliver genuinely new content for games and entertainment. The CD-ROM medium has specific characteristics that will influence, and in our view limit, the potential content of the game. Instead of letting "the medium be the message," a phrase that refers to the McLuhan idea that consequences of any medium result from the new possibilities that are introduced by a new technology (McLuhan, 1997, p. 7), IJsfontein prefers the thought that "the message is the medium": "That is, the characteristics of the message will shape the characteristics of the medium" (Castells, 1996, p. 340). IJsfontein begins with the content and only then asks which media are appropriate. In *Typotoons* we decided to deploy several media because Internet alone, or television alone, did not offer the level of participation that we were looking for. The potential for interaction in the virtual world of the CD-ROM is so limited, that it is time for committed participation in cross-media projects. A next step would then be to finally give reality a place as a game content element (*Road Quiz Show*).

Next we discuss the concept of participation, followed by an examination of the ways in which reality can be used as a game content element. We will use *Masters of the Elements, Typotoons, Road Quiz Show*, and other IJsfontein projects as examples.

Games and Participation

Participation is a buzzword in the game world. It literally means "taking part in." From now on, their interactive potential is supposed to make the user a participator in new media. But although interaction makes participation possible, they are not the same thing at all. Clicking on a website does not mean that you are participating in it.

We will now discuss the concepts of interaction and participation, followed by the pitfalls of introducing participation to games. IJsfontein has also developed a number of guidelines that make participation attractive. We end by discussing participation specifically in relation to our young target group.

Interaction and Participation

In most games, you are only busy discovering and mastering the rules that the makers have thought up for you. The dialogue between user and designer is closed. The designer has to have an answer to every possible question the user may have. There is a set of tools, enabling one to master preprogrammed situations. However big the world around which Lara Croft wanders may be, that world has been entirely thought up in advance. The user can add nothing to it nor change it in any way. Such interactivity as there is consists of being able to determine the sequence and length of the game. Because the complete product is already fixed, you are consuming the game rather than participating in it. This type of interactive environment is called an exploratory interactive environment (Joyce, 1995 p. 41).

Participation requires the creation of an open dialogue between user and designer. The designer lays down the framework and the form of communication in advance, but within them the user is free to introduce his or her own imagination. In *Typotoons*, the principle of "playful participation" is applied. The final product—the story—is not fixed in advance. The children can bring in their own ideas. They are not even limited to existing words. Within the world of *Typotoons*, everything is possible. A "timpt" becomes tangible and gets a meaning. A timpt is born on the spot. Environments that apply the principle of participation are called constuctive interactive environments (Joyce, 1995 p. 42).

For IJsfontein, projects that feature participation are important and—above all—fun. They always develop far beyond the original idea. Things happen that we could never have thought up by ourselves. In fact, participation is not only interesting to the user. For the designer too, the sum of the users' ideas is many times greater than his own imagination.

Pitfalls There are various ways to approach building an interactive environment that allows and invites participation. Such an environment turns out to be interesting only when the number of users is limited. The smaller the number of users, the greater the influence each one can have. In a game with thousands of participants, the player will never see his or her individual choices reflected in the final outcome. In this sort of game, major decisions are taken in a democratic manner: the majority determines what happens and the involvement of the individual is minimal.

On way to limit the number of participants is to think about the game's target group, but the choice of a target group automatically excludes other groups. In itself, this does not have to be a problem. A game might work very well for all the children in one hospital or one classroom. But the basis on which exclusion occurs is not always fair. In the case of *Typotoons*, a frequent complaint was that children were being excluded on technical grounds. To be able to join in writing the *Typotoons* story, the children had to log on to the Typobox after the television program. Thanks to the great success of the series, the box was full (150 participants) every time. Children with slow Internet connections were always too late. The ideal of participation was in this case undermined by technical factors. Because IJsfontein specifically aims to make technology-independent products, it will be important for us in the future to ensure that children with slow Internet connections can also join in.

Another way to limit the participants is to use a funnel model, which was used in *Tattletoons*. This means you provide several rounds in which many players can participate. Within every round a democratic mechanism selects a contribution of one of these many participants. The next round builds upon this selected contribution of the previous round. Again many players are allowed to contribute to this round of the game, and once again one of these contributions is selected. This mechanism ensures that every round each participant has the opportunity individually to contribute to the final result of the game (figure 25.4).

Second, the main attraction of an open dialogue between designer and user can also be the deepest trap into which you, the designer, can fall. Participation is based on the involvement and creative commitment of the participants. But it is equally possible that a game will be sabotaged by less committed players, and in the anonymous world of the Internet, the saboteur can often get away with his deed unpunished.

One recent IJsfontein project was a game that could be used as an interactive screensaver at work. The game divided all the employees into teams, which were then allocated a daily task. They had, for example, jointly to track down a number of game clues either within the company or on the Internet. The team members were in contact with each other over the company network. The fear that work would suffer was removed by setting a time limit of fifteen minutes for the daily task.

Everybody played anonymously, so you did not know whether you were playing against your boss or against someone in the mailroom. The intention here was to bypass the normal power structures within the company. However, it meant that no social bonds arose between the team members. This lack of bonds made it tempting to sabotage your own group. In an anonymous, virtual environment there are no real conse-

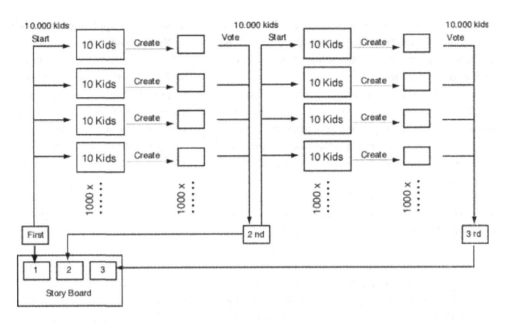

| Figure 25.4 |
Funnel

quences for your "real" self: nothing can ever be attributed to you.

This problem was finally solved by giving up anonymity within teams. You now knew who your teammates were. The normal power structures were still by-passed—you could still be better than your boss in another team—but social control did develop within the teams.

So sabotage can be limited. But this need take nothing away from the fact that participation is always based on collaboration between the user and the designer. As a designer, you never know what the input of the user will be nor how this will influence your original story. Telling a story complete with head, rump, tail, and motives is therefore impossible. This is what makes the game format so attractive as a vehicle for participation. Games provide the opportunity, within a number of restrictions (rules), to enter into an open dialogue with the user.

Finally, it is important to stress that an open dialogue does need some *guidance*. A game designer can be tempted by the idea of "open dialogue" into building a world in which nothing is fixed and everything is determined by the user. But virtual worlds in games are not a license to work without any bench marks. Certainly not when you're working for children. If all reference to daily reality is abandoned in a game, the player's attention is soon lost and nothing more can be learned. In this respect the principle of participation can be compared with a scientific experiment. If all

parts of the experiment are variable, it is never clear what has actually happened. You get the same feeling of being lost in a game that provides no link with what you have learned in the real world. These are terrible games to play. Their interactivity mainly resides in changing and influencing arbitrary objects, not in the flexible use of global laws.

Making Participation Attractive

At the moment, a player is usually seduced into playing a game by dramatic but realistic visual design. Yet although the beauty of the virtual world might well clinch the seduction, it is not the key to making the game environment satisfying. Three other factors are more important: first, the clear formulation of an end goal and of the contribution that the player must make toward its achievement; secondly, the successful division of complex interaction into digestible bites—levels; and finally, a well thought-out balance of power in the virtual world.

Goals A game must have a clear *goal*. If this goal is clearly formulated and the player's part in achieving this goal is similarly clear, taking part in the game becomes attractive. In the end people lose interest in an endless mission. You see this in many online chat communities where no end-goal is formulated. Intense discussions take place for a while on a given subject, to which all active chatters contribute. There is certainly real participation here, but the lack of a goal ensures that the community eventually loses its attractiveness and falls out of use. How many abandoned chat rooms are there on the Internet? In such a discussion it is never clear what your contribution was: you are never rewarded for your efforts.

By making visible the individual ideas of the participants, it is important to remember the need to limit their numbers. It is not satisfying for a player if his contribution is swallowed up in a large democratic process. It is only interesting if individual ideas remain visible as such in the end result. In *Typotoons*, the TV program used the meaning of a word thought up by a child. The drawings too are a good example of individual contributions to the whole.

The duration and viability of a game community are also linked to existence of a *solid core*. This core provides enough content to fuel the community motor. In *Typotoons*, the role was fulfilled by the children's author who took the children with him into the story and asked them for input at set times.

Levels of Participation To make participation in a game/community attractive, it is also important to introduce levels of participation—the more involved a player becomes in the game, the more influence he or she will want to exercise on the end outcome.

Internet Evolver, an IJsfontein project still in development, exemplifies this use of levels. In this community builder, the levels pair four phases of use with four types of activity: looking, feeling, applying (tweening), and developing. In an object-orientated,[1] open source environment, players can add and change objects. On his first acquaintance with the community, the player is only a visitor, "looking." He is allowed to look around the environment but has no further influence on it. There is no dialogue between the player and the designer. A visitor can thus not destroy anything in the environment, either by incompetence or ill will. The goal of the first activity, looking, is to create interest in the environment, to create a feeling of involvement.

If the player is interested by the first visit, he can go through to the second phase, where the activity is "feeling." He is now offered tools with which he can try small experiments. The dialogue between player and designer is still a closed dialogue; there is a measure of interaction, but not yet participation. The player can, for example, arrange small video images in order or listen to sound fragments. The aim is to give a feel of the environment, again with the intention of building involvement.

When all the tools have been mastered, there is nothing more to challenge the player at this level. He wants to start applying the tools for his own needs. In the third phase, an open dialogue begins between the designer and the player, although most of the power still lies with the designer, who has chosen the tools to be applied. The goal at this level is to retain the player's interest in the environment, now that he can apply everything on his own volition.

In the final phase, the player is not only free to apply existing objects, he is also allowed to add objects of his own. He can thus make contributions to the environment that the designer did not anticipate. He and his level-four colleagues can now build a world that interests them.

This phased plan is important for the game itself, but especially for the player. We help him develop and retain interest in this virtual world. The phased introduction of the required skills is essential for this. Suppose that the player was invited to build a tool of his own, for which a lot of technical knowledge is needed, at the first visit. The resulting frustration would prevent most players developing any sympathy for the environment. This frustration can be prevented by cutting the learning of skills into bits. Thus at each of the four levels, the player is reminded of what he can already do, rather than of what he can't do. The learning curve then looks like figure 25.5.

As far as the game itself is concerned, the effect of the levels is to minimize sabotage. The more deeply the player is involved in the game, the greater his will to make something of it. By the time he enters the final phase, he has simply invested far too much time in the game to want to destroy it.

Power Structures The problem with levels is that someone has to decide when the player is allowed to

| Figure 25.5 |
Graph—Skills by level

proceed to the next level. The designer can build in simple computer generated tests—if you possess the required skills, you can go through to the next level without the other participants being involved. But the disadvantage of this method is that no effective social bonds will develop. Nobody will know who is allowed in and who has to drop out. We have found that this decision is best left in the hands of the senior players, who have already achieved level four. A sort of committee determines who can move on. This is especially important when considering candidates for the final level, from which real influence can be exercised on the environment. The admission of an individual will effect all the participants in the community.

The decision to allow participation thus lies in the hands of a small, relatively powerful group, who have to make responsible decisions. Power structures play an important role in participation. When designing an environment that allows participation, close attention must be paid to how these structures are to be introduced. This can differ between environments.

Children and Participation

IJsfontein primarily develops game concepts for children up to the age of fourteen. In his book *Children of chaos: Surviving the end of the world as we know it*, Rushkoff describes this group as "screenagers," which he defines as children "born into a culture mediated by the television and computer" (Rushkoff, 1997 p. 3). These are children who have grown up with the computer and who are used to taking control of media. The process that began with the TV remote control has simply developed to cover the other forms of media. This familiarity with interactivity and with life in an environment where technological change is the only constant, means that this generation has no fear or inhibition toward new possibilities—such as participation.

At IJsfontein we call them "the undo generation." The "trial and error" learning process that takes place on the computer enables a child to experiment with everything. The undo function allows you to travel back in digital time after every choice and undo it if you want. This is also a feature of computer games. "Game over" actually means "start again," make different choices, and see what these choices produce.

The undo generation is therefore not afraid to make choices. Their just-do-it culture and attitude toward learning are enormous assets when it comes to designing participation environments. Ideas such as *Typotoons* are entirely based on the will and involvement of the players. After all, without the children nothing

happens, and the game stands still. Participating means making choices. Because making choices has become a natural process for the new generation, who have no fear of making the "wrong" choice, the threshold to participation is lower than ever before.

Participation with children has an additional dynamic. It stimulates the imagination. By leaving space for the child's imagination you make the game larger than the preconceived world of the designer. Children take the designer's ideas into their own world and then think up objects and events that are interesting and relevant for them. These they put back into the game. The open dialogue of participation between user and designer becomes even more interesting in today's network culture. A multiuser environment makes dialogue possible for a greater number of users, through which the game can expand far beyond the capacities of each participating individual. Rushkoff says, "So the dream our kids want to dream is a collective one. Through technology, they gain the ability to create what William Gibson called, in his book *Neuromancer*, a 'consensual hallucination'—a group exercise in world creation where reality is no longer ordained from above, but generated by its participants" (Rushkoff, 1997 p. 180).

Earlier we saw the importance of introducing a goal to a participation concept. In designing an environment for children it is especially important that participation is not the goal in itself. This emerged clearly in the interactive television series *Tattletoons* (figure 25.6), the successor of *Typotoons*. Here children could log onto the *Tattletoons* site, where they could follow and influence the lives of the virtual characters. Groups of children could write a storyboard for these characters and the best storyboard was then chosen, animated, and broadcast on television. It turned out that children did not find participating in making a storyboard interesting in itself. The goal "storyboard" did not give enough satisfaction. But when we turned writing a storyboard into a game, the motivation to take part in the writing increased. Each child could propose a part of the story and the children could jointly decide if this part was used or not. The power to approve a proposal varied from child to child, because nobody could vote for his or her own proposal. The competitive element stimulated the children's interest in participation.

Conclusion

Participation begins where interaction often ends—at the moment of choice between possible moves within

| Figure 25.6 |
Tattletoons

the game. Participation then involves the player in constructing the game world or the game story. This creates specific difficulties, but also opens a number of stimulating doors for both user and designer. In our view, much more use should be made of the participation concept, especially in games aimed at a young target group. This group is used to making choices, has a rich imagination, and enjoys collaboration.

Games and Reality

In this final section, we discuss the relationship between the virtual and real worlds. IJsfontein wants to dissent from the traditional striving for realism in the visual design of our media. In fact, realism has not only dominated games, all our media have been under its spell for centuries: from the camera obscura to film, we have constantly tried to mirror the reality that surrounds us. But as has already been said, we think that the route of (hyper-)realism is a dead end for the game industry. Realism means that computer images, movements, shapes, and sounds have nothing new to offer, nothing to add to the world of our daily experience. It was Manovich who first compared the use of digital image processing techniques to the development of painting (Manovich, 1995). Painters strove for realism right up

to the discovery of photography in 1839 by Daguerre. They were then released from the obligation to pursue reality, and discovered that paint had the potential to express their personal interpretations of the world. The art of painting expanded into a medium in which realism made room for imagination. The same argument can apply to games. Programs such as Photoshop and Flash make it possible to create worlds in which our imagination can have full play. For children with their rich imagination, this digital painting can be a real journey of self-discovery, a wonderful learning process. The future of games must surely lie in the area where all play begins: in the imagination.

Daily reality can now take on a different role in games. It can become a source of inspiration in terms of *gameplay* and *content*. Reality as content means that we enrich the virtual world with real elements, such as the unpredictable whims of the weather or the stock market. Real elements thus become virtual facts. But you can also turn the process around. You can give virtual elements a reference point in reality. With the aid of the mobile technology already in use (cellphone, GPS, laptops and notebooks, etc.), games do not have to be tied to a predetermined (virtual) place. We can finally go out to play again.

Realism in the Gameplay

In all media, IJsfontein is trying to achieve a *tactility* that corresponds to the experience of reality.[2] Realism then serves as an inspiration for the functional aspect of the game. In other words, we try to get the objects in the game to react as they would in everyday reality. A ball bounces, a feather floats, a chair has a weight that offers resistance when you try to move it. That sounds obvious enough, but in most games the same activity and energy are required to move a huge rock or to open a door.

Functional elements inspired by reality can create *tactile delusion* or *tactility*. No special controller is needed. The drag and drop principle, which every mouse can execute, is enough. What happens is that "weight" is introduced by adjusting the distance that the mouse must travel (or the number of mouse movements required) to move the object on the screen. If you have to move the mouse more than expected before the object reacts, the brain automatically associates this with the feeling of weight. And if, by the same token, only a tiny movement of the mouse is required, then the object seems light. The weight of objects in the virtual world is thus translated into the distance (or number of movements) that the mouse has to move in the real world. You are turning hand-eye coordination on its head.

The effect of tactile delusion cannot be compared with force-feedback controllers. Tactile delusion intensifies the experience in the virtual world by addressing the brain (the illusion), and there is nothing more convincing than an experience that takes place in the brain. Force-feedback joysticks give the same real experience for quite different virtual experiences, which soon becomes flat and boring. Experiences rooted in the brain are richer and more intense than any controller can give you. Play in the virtual world thus goes beyond the experience of looking and hearing. By playing on the brain, we get the player feeling. A part of the game is thus filled out by a fantasy induced in the brain of the player.

IJsfontein first used tactile delusion in the *Masters of the Elements* game. In one of the rooms of the castle, the children had to catch bats that were trying to fly out of the windows. To do this they had to move the mouse back and forth very fast. While testing the game, the children became so engrossed in the virtual world that they broke the mouse in the real world.

The principle of tactile delusion only works when users are used to the mouse. If there is no feeling for normal mouse behavior (i.e., drag and drop takes the same effort for all objects on the screen), then you can't surprise the user with a different behavior. With children this is not usually a problem, but some of the adults who play *Masters of the Elements* cannot get used to the gameplay that features tactile delusion.

This sort of adaptation, which is relatively easy to apply, brings modern technology ever closer to human dimensions. The brain is a perfect aid that we can deploy to induce feeling and fantasy in a virtual environment. But such adaptations can only be made after a close study of the technology and of society's habituation to it. Habituation only occurs (and can only be studied) when the technology has had time to mature. The search for new and better technologies will not, in the end, lead to better media. Precisely the opposite in fact, because the quality of the medium can only be improved through *deepening* its potential. An example is tactile delusion. That is why IJsfontein is appealing for more investment in existing technologies, rather than endlessly pumping money into developing new ones.

Reality as Content: The Real Becomes Virtual

In the search for a new relationship between the virtual and real worlds, one possibility would be to enrich pre-programmed worlds with unpredictable data from reality: the weather, the stock market, numbers of rail travelers, animal populations, and so on. These data could be complemented by personal aspects of the player, real time, and more. The result would be a game that is both dynamic and personal.

Biotoons is a cross-media game project (TV/web/CD-ROM) from IJsfontein that uses data such as these. The game is played each week in a different geographical location. The virtual world in which the game happens is dependent upon this real place. Teams of participants, each with an avatar—a biotoon—challenge each other to a race in the virtual world. Each biotoon has a specific quality (such as the ability to move over water) and requires a certain amount of energy. The race between the biotoons takes them through a virtual landscape that incorporates a number of variables taken from reality: a lake, a forest, the weather conditions, and so on. This creates a tension between the fixed, virtual qualities of the biotoon and the variable, real circumstances of the landscape and the weather. The participants have various choices available: for example, they can change the makeup of their team if they believe it is going to rain on the day

Jan-Willem Huisman and Hanne Marckmann

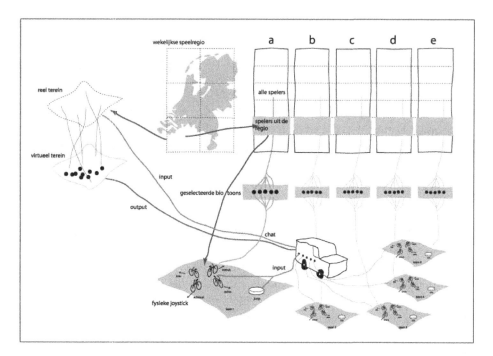

| Figure 25.7 |
Gamechart

of the race. If it does not rain, they are stuck with the team they have chosen, which may work against them. Additional details from the real world, such as the height of the river or a traffic diversion, create new challenges. They add an element of surprise that we would never have been able to program in advance. Nothing is more capricious than reality!

Besides these unpredictable factors, the game also incorporates one real factor that the players can influence themselves: the energy required for the biotoons. The team members are in contact with each other via the Internet. The player who lives closest to the scene of each week's race has to ensure that the entire team has enough energy to be able to play. To do this, he has to get out and about in search of an energy source in reality, a bicycle dynamo, for example. But to generate as much energy as possible, the player has to rope in family, friends, and neighbors to go cycling together. This is a rich source of live television. The real amount of energy generated by the bicycles then becomes the amount of energy available for the virtual race between the biotoons. *Biotoons* thus combines reality and virtuality in a variety of ways, and then adds the element of participation (figure 25.7).

The Body Another way of adding real data to the virtual world can be derived from new interactive techniques. Game actions are usually executed by the joystick, keyboard, or mouse. These objects involve only limited physical involvement. Game controllers may vibrate and react (force-feedback) these days, but feedback like this does not directly constitute a relationship between the body and what is happening on the screen. The feedback is always the same, whatever action is taking place. But above all, it is only a feed*back*, something you get back. You cannot direct (feed) the game with physical actions greater than those of your hands on the controller.

Earlier we discussed tactile delusion, which deceives the brain and makes the game experience more physical. IJsfontein has also experimented with practical ways to bring more of the body into the game. How, for example, could physical actions be made to direct the game? The installation *Emergency Stop*, made for Cinekid 2001 (the children's media festival in Amsterdam), offers two children the chance to compete against each other in a computer game. The children have to manipulate the events on the screen with real, physical actions (figure 25.8). The game's virtual characters move around by flying: they are suspended beneath a balloon (figure 25.9). To keep them in the air, the children have to keep the balloon inflated, which they do by blowing into a tube. The harder they blow, the higher their character rises. The aim is to collect various objects from the sky; to get hold of them, they have to pull on a large lever that

| Figure 25.9 |
Emergency Stop

| Figure 25.8 |
Emergency Stop

Jan-Willem Huisman and Hanne Marckmann

hangs next to the screen. The installation also has huge red buttons, which the children have to hit hard at the right moment to release the objects. *Emergency Stop* uses sensors to convert all these physical actions into virtual data for the game.

Interaction and Mobility: The Virtual Becomes the Real

In *Biotoons* and *Emergency Stop*, realistic data were fed into the virtual world, which gave rise to an exciting and attractive virtual world. The mingling of the virtual and the real can also take place the other way round, giving the virtual elements a place in the real world. These are called "enhanced reality" games.[3] The daily world is then the playing field, in which all sorts of game elements appear. It is more like playing outside, which kids used to do. "This car is my fort and that car is your fort and these berries are bullets which we're going to shoot at each other"... whatever the consequences. The world is a sandpit in which, with technology and imagination, you can build anything you want. Bonus points for a new game are out there on the street just waiting to be picked up!

IJsfontein's *Road Quiz Show* project is a step in this direction. The departure point for the game is the real environment, without which the game could not be played. *Road Quiz Show* adopts a simple question and answer format to address the environment, but you could extend the idea to projects where the key point brings much more into play than just a question on your mobile phone.

From this perspective, *The Game* (Fincher, 1997) is a highly futuristic film. Nicholas Van Orton, the chief character, is given a game for his birthday by his brother Conrad. The CRS (Consumer Recreation Services) has designed a number of physical and psychological tests to give him access to the game. Nicholas is then embroiled in a world of betrayal, pursuit, and finally murder. He loses millions of dollars and is left for dead in Mexico. Afterwards, it turns out that all these intrigues belong to the game. It was the perfect present for a rich, bored, arrogant businessman like Nicholas, who possessed everything but knew nothing of life's real pleasures—love and friendship.

In *The Game*, virtual elements were introduced by live actors, manipulated television pictures, and toys that provided keys to as yet unknown doors. The game elements in this film are therefore not just of a technological nature. To set up a game like this is would clearly be quite unaffordable, but technology might make it possible to play similar games at a realistic price.

Some years ago in Japan, it was popular to wear key rings with a little computerized transmitter, into which you could enter your personal preferences—for example, that you were fond of cats, hated noodles, and found a sense of humor an important quality in any future partner. All the key rings could communicate with each other, and as soon as your ring found someone else with a sense of humor, a fondness for cats, and a loathing for noodles, both key rings began to peep, which was the excuse to start talking. For those leading a busy life in a big city, this was an effective and amusing way of looking for kindred spirits.

The "find-your-perfect-match" key ring was specially developed for this mating game, but all around us there are thousands of tiny computers already in place that could be deployed in a mobile game: electric thermometers in cars, control panels in traffic lights, scanners at supermarkets, and more. If all these gadgets could communicate with each other, which is quite possible in theory as they all speak the same digital language, then the world would become a network of game related agents. The only thing the potential player would need to move through this network is a personal mobile computer—and this role seems perfectly conceived for the mobile telephone. The cellphone is not only a receiver of signals; it also gets the user to react, which adds an interactive element. Mobile interaction opens up a new world for participation projects. Just with existing cellphone technology and the small digital aids that already surround us, numerous games could be devised that would turn a simple trip to the shops into an exciting experience.

Botfighters (It's Alive, 2001) was a Swedish project in precisely this domain. The aim of the game was to track down and destroy other botfighters. The web was used to build and update your bot (robot). The mobile telephone was the tool via which the battle could be fought on the street. It warned you when another bot was in the neighborhood, and you could shoot at it by typing "shoot." Whether you won or not depended on the weapon you used, the distance between you and your rival, and the presence of protective "shields." As a botfighter you could always be involved in a game, wherever you were (see Sotamaa, 2002).

Conclusion

IJsfontein's believes that most computer game manufacturers have been doing the same thing for years now: producing CD-ROM games whose visual design is conceived to reflect reality as accurately as possible. Within this realistic world, you can then do a host of unrealistic things. In our vision, both the CD-ROM and the quest for realism in the visual design of virtual worlds are dead ends for the game industry. Instead, let's try something new. The key elements of this novelty for games can be found in participation and creating a new relationship between reality and virtual worlds. Participation offers the player a truly constructive interactive environment, what we call an open dialogue. This means that most of the time designers need to think beyond the CD-ROM, and start designing crossmedia concepts such as *Typotoons*, that use the charateristics of each medium to the fullest. Also, we argued that the relationship between the virtual and the real world should be reconsidered. Realism in visual design will not make gaming any more attractive. Realism in the gameplay, or realism in content might just do exactly that.

Acknowledgments

The authors wish to thank Hayo Wagenaar, and Rob Bland for the translation. For more information: www.ijsfontein.nl.

Notes

1. By "object orientated" we mean that the environment itself has fixed laws—e.g., gravity—but that the objects in it can be changed: a book always falls downwards, but in itself can be thick, thin, red, green, 10 cm or 10 meters high, etc. Here the objects were programmable (variable), but not the environment.

2. Jan-Willem Huisman's lecture at Doors of Perception 5 (1999) discusses the concept of tactility (see www.doorsofperception.com). The concept was also briefly discussed in Abrams, J. (Ed.) *If/then—Play* (Amsterdam, 1999, pp. 228–231).

3. For a fuller development of this concept, see, for example Ericsson (2003).

References

Abrams, J. (Ed.). (1999). *If/then—Play* Amsterdam: Bis Publishers.

Castells, M. (1996). *The rise of the network society*. Oxford: Blackwell Publishers.

Ericsson, M. (2003). Enchanting reality: A vision & big experiences on small platforms. In M. Copier & J. Raessens (Eds.) *Level up: Digital games research conference 2003*. Utrecht: Faculty of Arts, Utrecht University.

Joyce, M. (1995). *Of two minds. Hypertext pedagogy and poetics*. Ann Arbor: The university of Michigan Press.

McLuhan, M. (1997). *Understanding media. The extensions of man*. Cambridge, MA: MIT Press.

Manovich, L. (1995). What is digital cinema? www.manovich.net.

Rushkoff, D. (1997). *Children of chaos. Surviving the end of the world as we know it*. London: Flamingo.

Sotamaa, O. (2002). All the world's a botfighter stage: Notes on location-based multi-user gaming. In F. Mäyrä (Ed.), *Computer games and digital cultures: Conference proceedings*. Tampere, Finland: Tampere University Press.

26

GAME RECONSTRUCTION WORKSHOP: DEMOLISHING AND EVOLVING PC GAMES AND GAMER CULTURE

Anne-Marie Schleiner

Even at a higher level of design, it can be very valuable to have the thinking of lots of co-developers random-walking through the design space near your product.
—Eric Raymond[1]

What does the free software and open source software movement have to do with computer games? A search online for open source games will yield sparse results—Linux conversions of a few older classic PC games and even older arcade games, and some relatively low-tech role playing game engines such as the Japanese Hyperplay engine.[2] One interesting exception is the site alifegames.com, hosted on the vortex site of open source software development, "Source Forge." Alifegames is developing an action game called *bserene* where the player fights evolving A-life monsters in a colorful 3D "crystal world"[3] (figure 26.1). *bSerene's* graphics are not visually detailed, but photo-realistic visual detail in a futuristic crystal world is unnecessary, making the game a good candidate for open source Alife programmers to work on. (The effort required to build realistic 3D models, not a coding activity but a laborious digital sculpting process, is one of the impediments to developing thoroughly open source games.)

Although original Linux games developed through open source methods are still rare (as opposed to Linux remakes of popular games such as *Quake* and *Doom*), the very same factor that created an agreeable environment for open source software to flourish, the development of the Internet, has had a dramatic effect on PC gaming. In the early 1990s, when shooter game developers began to release the source code for their games on the Internet, gamers eagerly coded editors for inserting their own maps, visuals, and sounds, and distributed these to other gamers online. Now it is common for PC game developers to allow their game fans to insert their own custom "wads, mods, shapes, levels, add-ons, skins, tomes" into their games. Entire fan rings and Internet subcultures have formed around specific games and those who modify them. Even some of the smaller scale graphical multiplayer RPGs (role-playing games), such as *Vampire: The Masquerade* and *Neverwinter Nights*, allow players to create modifications.

In this chapter, I explore the phenomenon of game modification (also referred to as "game patching"), through analytical lenses culled from my research into gamer culture, gender representation in computer games, game mods as a hacker art form, and recent forays into the military-fetish boyland of the popular mod *Counter-Strike*. I begin with a general map of game engine structure, parts of which may be opened to players for modification, and locate the modifiable game within an ecosystem of modders, players, and network topologies.

Open and Closed Strata

There is a distinction between a purely open source game such as *bSerene* and a modifiable PC game. In a PC game, certain strata are open for modification and others are closed (and the original PC game developers retain proprietary ownership of all modifications made by others, no matter how much time a fan may invest). Although the particulars vary from game to game, the graphics, architecture, visuals, and sound tend to be open for modification, whereas the underlying software engine, "the code," remains closed and inaccessible to game fans and modders. Interestingly, in *The magic cauldron*, a text about games and open source, Eric Raymond suggests an alternate, and thus far to my knowledge untested, scenario in which the game software is open and the "artwork" is closed, proprietary, and unchanging.[4] In any event, the development process of computer games is not restricted to one flat plane of code (like an open source software app), but can be horizontally opened, distributed, and parallelized along multiple vertical strata. In the model of this multisorcery process shown in figure 26.2, a game is broken

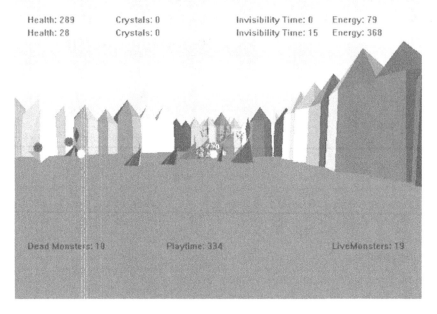

| Figure 26.1 |
bSerene crystal monsters

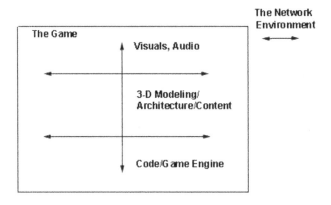

| Figure 26.2 |
PC games can open along multiple strata

into vertical strata such as code, 3D maps, and characters. At one or more of these levels the game may be opened along a horizontal axis (often facilitated through fan-made editing software and tutorials distributed on the Internet), and the development of, for example, characters or architecture may be altered, hacked, and "reauthored" by gamers other than the original game development house professionals.

Thus PC games are part of a modular ecosystem that can be both symbiotic and parasitic to the original host game engine. This ecosystem partakes of both the offline digital market economy and the online digital gift economy.

The results of this "multisorcery" or "opensorcery" processs, terms I use to evoke both open source characteristics and the magical power of multiple authors hacking and recreating, can be likened to a digital folk art movement, a profusion of amazing, fantastic, sometimes original, disturbing, pornographic, humorous, challenging, and beautiful game add-ons available for free download on the Internet. Although most of this artwork is at a stratum level above code, it shares some of the characteristics of software created in an open source environment. For example, skins, which are 2D texture maps for 3D game characters, are often created in an iterative "hackerish" fashion (the free software movement was based on the idea of multiple programmers being able to share and improve software among each other). Multiple authors may pass around a skin, making small changes and improvements on what was accomplished by previous authors. Similarly, a level may be altered and improved upon over time by various authors, such as the once popular "Aliens" *Doom* wad, which in a later iteration incorporated sound. My site, opensorcery.net, explores various aspects of these distributed open digital folk art forms, from early influential female gender hacks of shooter games, to artistic revisionings of 3D game space, to iterative digital art forms such as the DIY erotica of the international KiSS Community of electronic "paper doll" makers.[5]

Game Mod History

Let's meander even further back than mods in history to highlight some key moments when the desire to play games and hacking converged. As described in admittedly U.S.-centric chronicles of hacker history such as Steven Levy's *Hackers*, at MIT in the early 1960s a group of "hacker/programmer" undergraduate students would sneak access to monolithic mainframes to write "frivolous" programs such as "Expensive Calculator" and "Expensive Typewriter."[6] One of these playful hacks was *Spacewar*, a space opera inspired game programmed on the then new PDP-1, the first mainframe that used a keyboard rather than punch cards for input.[7] *Spacewar* is credited as the first computer game. *Spacewar* displayed player scores in octal and adapted an "expensive planetarium" program to simulate stars in space. Slug Russell's illicit *Spacewar* quickly spread to other mainframe research centers and mutated into other free computer games for privileged researchers and students. (Later computer games became big business when they moved from mainframe computers to console platforms such as Atari and pinball-like arcade machines such as *Pong*.)

Again a confluence of hacking and gaming surfaced in the late 1970s San Francisco Bay Area bootstrapping activities of the Homebrewer Computer Club. At the Homebrewers' Club, hardware hacking played an integral part in evolving the personal computer and the "hacker ethic," the creed that, among other things, advocates free distribution and access to knowledge. Hardware hackers, living in the Silicon Valley region of California, would gather at the Homebrewer's Club to share design plans and garage-made prototypes for personal computers (many of these hackers had day jobs at large computer firms such as IBM in the region who specialized in building expensive powerful business computers). In the Homebrewer Computer Club

Newsletter, the printing of a Steve Wozniak report of early plans for the Apple included the following wish for a game hack: "have TVT of my own design … have my own version of Pong, a videogame called breakthrough, a NRZI reader for cassettes very simple!"[8]

In the 1980s, when some high school students gained access to their own personal computers, hackers formally untrained as programmers developed strategies for decryption of Atari chips and created games that simulated popular arcade games, such as *Jawbreaker*, an adaptation of *Pac-Man* created for the Apple II. Some of these hackers then went on to work for PC game development companies such as Sierra Online, designing innovative yet graphically limited 1980s style games for PCs.

In the mid to late 1990s, the mutability of software on the PC platform (as opposed to the closed source code of concurrently popular games on consoles platforms such as Nintendo and PlayStation), allowed for game software engine hacks or patches or mods in the 3D shooter genre.[9] To recount a brief history of patching, in 1994 ID Software released the source code for *Doom*, a 3D tunnel networkable shooter game (one year after their release of the game commercially). Avid players of *Doom* got their hand on this source code and created editors for making custom *Doom* levels or what were referred to as "wads."[10] In 1996, Bungie Software bundled the *Marathon* series games with Forge and Anvil, game editing software for map making and inserting new textures, character (sprite) animations, sounds, and physical properties.

Also incorporating mods into their business plan, ID Software open sourced the files to the shooter *Quake* (*Quake* patches are known as "mods"), released a CD of patches for *Quake*, along with numerous "Mission Packs," new game scenario plug-ins that mimic the logic of patches (but are not free). For *Quake 3*, ID Software released a sophisticated editing software called Radiant, a tool for detailed construction of 3D levels for *Quake*. Another tool made outside of ID, called World Craft, is also popular among game modders and patchers of *Quake* and *Quake* engine derived games such as *Half-Life*. World Craft originated as a shareware editor coded independently by Canadian programmer Ben Morris (also the previous creator of a well-respected shareware *Doom* editor).[11] Game modification software or game SDKs (software development kits) have been developed for shooter games such as *Duke Nuke-Em*, *Unreal*, and *Tribes*.

A special tool set or SDK for modifying a game is not required if the original game files can be decompressed and the existing surface textures, characters, and sounds can be replaced with new customized files. If the file names remain the same, the software engine will not recognize the difference between the original files and the customized files. Or a player may even be able to access the game engine source code, alter it, and recompile it. But editing tools are helpful for building new 3D architectural spaces (maps and levels), and 3D characters (models). New versions of game modification tools for level building are becoming even more like the sophisticated software applications that 3D modelers use such as 3D Studio Max and Maya.

Contrary to what might be supposed, unsanctioned and sanctioned game patching and modification do not conflict with the commercial interests of the game software industry. In effect, game patching serves as inexpensive R & D for new trends in computer gaming that crystallize and evaporate in the accelerated, perpetually mutating laboratory of the Internet. Because it takes incredible programming effort to program a realistic game engine from scratch, many commercial game companies follow the logic of mods, licensing engines from other companies and repurposing these engines as new games. Also, in the near future, the ability to customize game worlds may be one of the strong attractions to playing (and buying) PC games, a competitive advantage over games on closed source (unmodifiable) console platforms such as PlayStation and X-Box.

Network Topologies

Every enemy is represented here in the zoo. Find the keys in succession. Be careful not to scare up too many of them at one time.
—Advice for the "Zoo" wad for *Doom* from a *Doom* fan home page

WELL Hey! My name is Kevin Conner, and I play Quake2, Half-life and any good game out there. I am an artist of many mediums; oils, acrylic, watercolor, pen and ink and of course ... QUAKE2SKINS!! Here on this page I shall have some links and some skins that I have made as well as an occasional sampling of my traditional art work.... I'm sure you'll find my skins very unique.... DOWNLOAD THEM! I'd love to see them on others while i am FRAGGING them ... eheh thank you and good night!
—Intro to a skinner page

The Internet has become the locus for computer gaming fans and hackers' exchange of patching, secrets, game guides, and "Easter eggs."[12] These hermeneutics of computer games, the distribution of guides to successful level completion, and of clues to finding secrets embedded in the game architecture, have encouraged the development of an information exchange infrastructure that also provides the necessary support venue for the distribution of game mods. Following the hacker ethics of shareware, freeware, and open source code, the mod artist will usually offer his work free of charge from his personal home page or gaming site. "His" work is usually the appropriate gender to describe a game patch artist, because the majority of game patchers are male, ranging from teenage boys to thirty-five-year-old men (although you never can be too certain of gender on the Internet). Traversing deeper into the Internet topology of the primarily male arena of game fan and hacking network culture reveals subsets of differentiated discourse domains.

"A ring is a circular collection of sites all focused on a related topic. Each member of the ring typically displays a graphic, called a ring fragment, that will allow visitors to move forward and backward through the ring," reads a definition of a ring from the Quake Engine Skin Artist ring site. Internet rings connect gamer websites one to the other along vectors of related topics through links that move sequentially from one site to the next, horizontal micronetworks that etch ordered pathways into the more haphazardly hyperlinked architecture of the web. It is also common to find a link on a ring member site to an overview index to all the sites belonging to that particular ring. One popular ring is the Quake Engine Skin Artist ring, including links to sites such as the "Skin Factory" and "Skins by DoodsEngel." Quake Skinners are boys mostly teenage to early twenties who design 2D monster and fighter outfits that are then mapped onto the prefabricated 3D-modeled figures in the network shooter games *Quake* and *Quake II*. Skinning constitutes a kind of monster high fashion workshop for boys, an imaginative play with various semantic units of monster fashion that are continually reinserted into the same syntagmatic chains: variations of head gear, human and animalian facial features, varieties of arm bands and arm muscle tone definition, varieties of fighter suits in various fabrics and colors, various weapon accessories. Skinning draws its monster fashion lexicon from the hybrid mythic and sci-fi sources of boys' fantasy culture, referencing both *Minotars* and *Star Wars* characters.

Many players of network *Quake* belong to clans that fight as collective units against other clans on numerous *Quake* servers. Sites dedicated to specific clans with their trademark clan skins form other strata of network game topology that overlap with the skinner rings. Interestingly, in contrast to the more testosterone laden atmosphere of the Quake Engine Skin Artist ring, a contingent of male and female skinners and their fem skin creations have achieved quite a web presence on the Quake Women's Forum site, where skins such as the custom female tattooed skins for the PMS (Psycho Men Slayer's) clan are freely distributed (also available for download from the PMS clan site).[13] The Quake Women's Forum also features daily news of female frag fests (network *Quake* games and tournaments), monthly in-depth profiles of women *Quake* players, email addresses of female *Quake* players, and shorter profiles of over three hundred *Quake* women players.

Some game patches offer more seditious mutations of computer game subject/avatar configurations. Patches such as the "Fighter Chicken" for *Doom* and the "Gumby Doll" patch for *Marathon Infinity* replace macho soldier characters with silly androgynous characters, undermining the male macho hero ideal common to many computer games. Early patches with female heroines, such as the "Female Cyborg Patch" and the "Tina-Bob" patch for *Marathon* were among the first patches to offer active female avatars (in place of trophy princesses) for game play in shooters, prefiguring the official release of *Tomb Raider* and other recent action adventure games with female heroines. Despite the sometimes problematic aspects of female avatar representation and implementation in both patches and official games as seen from the perspective of traditional feminist film theory and other feminist positions, the appearance of female avatars is a significant addition to the field of possible gender/subject avatar configurations between both female and male players and their avatars. (Who will deny me the abject pleasure, perhaps a queer one, in relishing in my avatar's ultra-fem proportions as she frags my male opponent into spattered bloody pixels or that my male opponent has not learned something by trying on a female skin?)

Nude Raider Patch versus Tomb Raider Fan Wars

A debate concerning female avatars was inscribed into the topology of online *Tomb Raider* fan culture in the late 1990s. Finally provided with prepackaged female heroine in the form of action adventure heroine Lara Croft, male gamers contested what sorts of female avatar representation were appropriate in 3D adventure gaming, and in the encompassing online fan culture. Many *Tomb Raider* fans belong to the Nude Raider web ring. The Nude Raider patch, an extremely international popular game patch circa 1997, hacked the Tomb Raider engine and replaced Lara Croft's shorts and halter top with nude textures (while retaining her ammunition belt). Nude Raider fan sites such as Naturally Lara often displayed screen shots of Lara in naked game play action. Some of these sites even featured "fake" nude Laras with smoother airbrushed surface polygons than the real Nude Raider patch allowed for. In response to the pornographization of their beloved Lara, more upstanding *Tomb Raider* fans, including many fans in the *Tomb Raider* Ring, began to post "Nude Raider free" banners on their sites (figure 26.3). These fans affected a more romantic stance toward Lara, regarding Nude Raider as disrespectful toward their beloved English lady. (Although I don't think they objected to her comic book heroine figure, judging by the choice of Lara pictures on their sites.)

Fan websites such as The Croft Times elevated Lara to celebrity status, spinning elaborate tales of Lara's personal and extra-curricular (outside the game) life. Fan fiction distributed through zines and club publications is common among fans of television series such as *Star Trek* and *Beauty and the Beast*. According to Henry Jenkins, this particular television fan culture is comprised mostly of women, and he reads the stereotype of brainwashed obsessive fans as a reification of mainstream culture's misogynist values.[14] On the other hand, but not too surprising considering the gender composition of the majority of gamers, computer game fan fiction is usually "penned" by male writers. Writers such as Michael L. Emery, author of *The flowers of God*, and Marc Farrimond, author of *Wedding bells*, post their romantic Lara Croft stories on The Croft Times and other fan fiction sites.[15]

Counter-Strike: A Professional and "Realistic" Mod

Before Counter-Strike, it [modding] seemed like a kind of folk art, of course the success of Counter-Strike (from underground mod, to over-the-counter retail success) has changed the online mod-community, now modding is a (possible) spring-board to a real job in the lucrative gaming industry.—Email response to *Velvet-Strike* from Michael

| Figure 26.3 |

A Lara Croft fan site with a "Nude Raider Free" banner displayed in the bottom left frame

There are very few academic or vocational programs that provide aspiring game industry workers with the skills and education necessary for designing or creating computer games (other than those who study computer science or IT to become programmers for games). It is common knowledge among gamers that if one wishes to acquire experience and material for some kind of portfolio for the game industry it can be beneficial to create a well-crafted mod. One case of a success story of a modder gone professional, written up in *Rolling Stone* magazine and other press, is Stevie Case, girlfriend of famous John Romero, the lead designer of *Doom* and *Quake*. Stevie Case was making mods before she worked at Ion Storm and then left to cofound Monkey Stone Games in 2001 with Romero.[16] Stevie "Killcreek" Case originally met John Romero by beating him at playing a deathmatch in one of his own games, *Quake*.

The well worshiped Gooseman, who is the primary creator behind the *Counter-Strike* mod based on the *Half-Life* engine, went a step beyond using a mod as an experience for getting into the game industry. Gooseman managed to distribute his mod as a commercial product (publisher Valve Software of the supporting engine *Half-Life* takes a cut). For the first time, a mod is inserted into the FPS (first-person shooter) chronology of most popular games whose sequence looks something like *Doom* + *Quake 1,2,3* + *Unreal* + *Counter-Strike*. (*Counter-Strike*'s popularity even eclipsed *Half-Life*, the game engine the mod was built on.)

Counter-Strike was the first online game or mod with a militaristic theme to achieve widespread popularity in the gaming community. Before *Counter-Strike*, military sims were more of a niche gaming genre, relegated to small columns in gamer zines. Prefiguring the post–September 11 wartime climate of the United States, *Counter-Strike* has become the playing ground for a generation of war hungry boys. There are, however, marked differences between American players and the rest of the world. The American players tend to approach online game space as an arena to express vengeful, militaristic aggression (especially post 9–11), whereas others, Brits, Europeans, and Asians, seem to maintain a firmer boundary between fantasy game world and personal world view.

Stepping back again along the FPS chronology that *Counter-Strike* belongs to, in the 1990s, within the shooter genre, characters evolved from white guy American soldiers into oversize funny male monsters of all shapes and stripes and pumped female fighting machines. It seemed to be about a kind of monster fantasy workshop, humorous macho role play, taking things to their frag queen extremes. Within online *Quake* and game hacker culture, gender restrictions and other boundaries opened up and female *Quake* clans such as PMS and Babes with an Attitude appeared.

Then, beginning with *Half-Life* and continuing with shooter games whose alleged appeal is "realism," a kind of regression took place. In terms of game play, games such as *Half-Life* are universally seen as advance-

| Figure 26.4 |
Velvet-Strike graffiti screenshot, by gamer Bobig

ments. Yet in *Half-Life* the player is only given one white everyman American geek guy to identify with. And all of the NPC (nonplayer character) researchers and scientists in the game are male. *Half-Life* remaps the original computer game target market back onto itself, excluding all others and reifying gamer culture as a male domain. In *Counter-Strike*, the player chooses to play on either the side of a band of terrorists or on the side of counterterrorist commandos, all male. The tactics of the terrorists and the counterterrorists are essentially indistinguishable from each other.

Disturbingly, one of the oft-cited appeals of *Counter-Strike* is its "realism." *Counter-Strike* is not about "silly" monsters bouncing around space ports like in the *Quake* series—in *Counter-Strike*, characters are realistically proportioned male terrorist fighters and commandos killing each other in stark bombed out bunkers. When a player is killed in *Counter-Strike*, their character really "dies" instead of immediately regenerating. (Although he or she gets to play again in a few minutes as soon as the next round begins.) So "realism" is not about faster game engines, graphics processing, and photorealism. It is about reproducing characters and gameplay environments that are considered closer to "reality" and farther from fantasy.[17]

Almost universally, with the exception of some German "lady squads," *Counter-Strike* (CS) is a male gendered arena. On CS servers visited, I have heard only male voices: male French voices, male Chinese voices, male Australian voices. Recently I co-authored an intervention "action" within *Counter-Strike* called *Velvet-Strike*[18] (figure 26.4). We created a website to propagate antiwar "sprays" for use inside *Counter-Strike* that take advantage of the ability to spray the graffiti-like logos that are a basic built-in feature of all *Half-Life* mods. Players can download these custom spray paints and use them in the game. We also listed a number of "intervention recipes," ways to intervene in gameplay as usual as a form of antiwar protest and commentary on game violence. We received a surprising barrage of varied hate mail, flames, and death threats in response, and trolls and spammers overran our discussion forum. A large portion of the hate mail was written by teenage American right-wing boys (if age can be inferred from spelling mistakes and spam styles, and nationality from email appendage). Hate mail from Europeans seemed more explicitly directed against the threat of women intruding on a boy's playground. One of the Spanish collaborators of *Velvet-Strike*'s female sounding first name, Joan, misled many gamer boys into directing their outrage at him. Here is one of my favorite hate mails telling us to leave CS alone and go play with our Barbies:

Hello,
What a stupid initiative!!! If you don't like the game just don't buy it, and don't piss off other people with your shit.
Just a woman could have think of making something like Velvet Strike....
if you don't realize that videogame is just a VIDEOGAME, an that its a fake world, well then, GO PLAY WITH YOUR BARBIE!
its the same kind of people as you that tell that violent movie influence people and make them commit murders. The facts is that most people are intelligent and can see THE difference
...
Anyway,

Although many of these flamers seem to have misunderstood our tongue-in-cheek intervention as a protest against all forms of game violence, the misogyny of emails originating from across continents is nevertheless striking. One may dismiss them as immature teenage boys who resent and fear women, but one should still question the implications of this pan-continental militaristic male playground. As one poster suggested on the *Velvet-Strike* forum, which was also overrun by misogynistic, homophobic, pro-American, right-wing hate mail and spam, comparisons can be drawn between the climate of prewar Nazi Germany and pre- (and post-Afghanistan) war America, as we build up to the next probable "campaign" against Iraq in the no-end-in-sight war on terrorism.

When violent simulations are clearly understood as fantasy playgrounds this is one matter (*Quake*, *Doom*, *Castle Wolfenstein*, etc.), but it is quite another when these simulations lay the groundwork for a particular direction of "reality." A few months ago, *Wired* reported on a skinhead web site distributing racist mods, including a revised version of *Castle Wolfenstein*, a game in which one supposedly fights against Nazis. The game house Nvidia will soon release *Delta Force: Black Hawk Down*, a game based on U.S. Army missions in Somalia. The U.S. Army itself recently released a free recruitment and blatant propaganda game, *America's Army*. *AA:O* is a very well designed and playable free network shooter built with the *Unreal Tournament* engine, an engine with superbly realistic lighting and particle effects. *AA:O* picks up the ball where *Counter-Strike* leaves off, capitalizing on the recent popularity of military shooters.

Mods Coming into Their Own as an Artists' Medium

In 1998, I invited artists to create game "patches, mods, and game add-ons" in an effort to bridge the worlds of gamers and artists. The exhibit was called "Cracking the Maze: Game Plug-ins and Patches as Hacker Art." One game company, Bungie, donated some games and game patching tools to the artists, and in some instances I fulfilled the dual roles of both tech support for the artists as well as art curator. The show went online a year later and featured some game mods by a variety of international artists and also some interesting mods from the deep pockets of gamer culture.[19] Since this time some game mod artists, many of whom grew up playing computer games and are entirely fluent in gameplay lexicons and grammars, have become more sophisticated and immersed themselves deeper within the possibilities of modifying various game engines. Some of the more recent artist-made mods have been assembled on the Australian website Select Parks.[20]

One artist whose work is featured on Select Parks and who also collaborated in the *Velvet-Strike* affront is Brody Condon. An avid American gamer as well as a formally trained artist, in his mods, Brody explores the violent dream logic of shooters, going to the unspoken places that most gamers prefer to ignore for a number of reasons. The illicit pleasure of simulated blood and death are among of the attractions of shooters and yet, due to the uneasy relationship between the game industry and censorship, a kind of tactical silence even regarding the pleasures of pixilated bloodletting has taken over the industry and players.

| **Figure 26.5** |

Adam Killer screenshot, by Brody Condon

Brody's "Adam Killer" (figure 26.5), a mod in which you face a field of identical game characters and shoot at them, brings the repetitive violent component of playing shooter games to the forefront of attention. His work employs a minimalist, elegant pixilated aesthetic of gore that has an altogether different quality than the messy excess of horror film. Brody has also applied a performance art Chris Burden-like interventionist approach to online shooters in the form of suicide missions in collaboration with John Brennan (aka BigBJ) in the shooter game *Tribes*.[21] For *Velvet-Strike*, Brody created a series of spray logos called "Love" of male soldiers touching each other in provocative ways. These sprays awakened strong currents of homophobia among male CS players.

Spanish-based Retroyou is another game mod artist thoroughly immersed in the mod medium. His "R/C" series of racing mods is stunning. Retroyou favors using mods created by one publisher whom he prefers to keep unknown (different mod artists tend to become "experts" of one or two engines or at least stick to a common publisher). In *"R/C [Paradise]"* small toy cars smoothly levitate off the race track and dissappear up into the sky. In *R/C FCK the Gravity Code*, Retroyou uses the dynamic physics movement algorithms already programmed into the racing game engine, reinserting entirely different graphics and drawings that zoom frenetically in and out at the player as he or she navigates

the game space. Retroyou's most recent mod, "Nostal-G" takes apart a flight simulator. Having only just begun this mod before the airplane attacks in New York, he put the project aside for a while but finished it in time for Read-me, an art show in Moscow in the summer of 2002.[22]

European net artist couple JODI (Joan Heemskerk and Dirk Paesmans) have immersed themselves in exploring game engines as art generating tools for the last four years. JODI have become intimately familiar with the file structure of *Quake 1*, its code structure and algorithms, and its loopholes and glitches. Time++ has been logged "playing" with the system, just as Nato addicts and V.J.s (video jockeys) spend hours tweaking sound and 3D/2D visuals, happening sometimes on interesting accidental effects. Unlike ID Software, the original designers of *Quake*, JODI search for beautiful bugs in the system, to make glitches happen that weren't supposed to, to tweak the game, even to demolish it. Their series "Untitled Game" is a collection of most of the *Quake* mods they have created in the last couple years. When the player pushes the spacebar to jump in E1M1AP, instead the world rotates uncontrollably. In G-R, the screen refreshes nonstop with bright RGB colors (no navigation at all). In Ctrl-9 and Ctrl-Space, navigation and looking about generate undulating black and white moiré patterns.[23]

Conclusion

In this chapter I have explored the phenomenon of game modification from some positions inspired by previous research and also my more recent investigations. I began by sketching a structural model of the different ways a game engine could be modified and then describing how this model departs from open source software development in that different strata or components of a game may be closed or open. I then journied a bit further back in history to explore interludes where computer games and hacking intersect. I described how the topography of the Internet has allowed present day game modding to flourish and I explored the culture of the gamers that has proliferated in this environment. I touched on gender avatar debates that surrounded the Nude Raider patch for *Tomb Raider* and I discussed the popularity of the military shooter *Counter-Strike* and some ominous implications as the shooter genre is co-opted as a male only military playground in the current American war climate. Finally I discussed game modding as an art medium that is being thoroughly adapted by artists who have grown up living and breathing computer games, artists whose mods push computer gaming in amazing, sometimes subversive, unexpected directions.

Notes

1. tuxedo.org/~esr/writings/cathedral-bazaar/cathedral-bazaar.html.
2. www.hypercore.co.jp/opensource.
3. www.alifegames.com/.
4. tuxedo.org/~esr/writings/l.
5. www.opensorcery.net.
6. Steven Levy, *Hackers: Heros of the computer revolution*, Dell Publishing, New York, 1994, p. 47.
7. Herz, J. C., *Joystick nation*, Little, Brown and Co., Boston, 1997, p. 5.
8. Levy, p. 247.
9. Although closed entertainment systems such as Nintendo, Sega, and Sony PlayStation, descendents of earlier entertainment systems such as Magnavox and Atari remain popular, especially in Japan, their closed architecture inhibits game hacking and patching.
10. David McCandless, "Legion of doom," *Wired Magazine*, March 1998.
11. www.gamegirlz.com/articles/wc_001.htm.
12. An Easter egg is secret personal data embedded by the programmers or designers of a software application or game, often photos of the workers or some kind of personal "in joke" not aimed at the general consumer.
13. www.planetquake.com/QWF/qwf.html.
14. Henry Jenkins, *Textual poachers*, Routledge, London, 1992, p. 19.
15. www.ctimes.net/fancorner/fanfic/index. Game fan fiction is also very common in the role playing game genre, where players publish extensive histories of the fantastic exploits of their guild or clan on their own guild or clan dedicated sites.
16. www.gignews.com/goddess_caseromero. htm.
17. A sucessor to *Counter-Strike*, *Urban Terror*, is another violent multiplayer *Half-Life* mod but the setting of urban terror is the city. (After the September 11 attack on the World Trade Center in New York, the *Urban Terror* simulation hit a little too close to home for some American gamers and they stopped playing it.)
18. www.opensorcery.net/velvet-strike. This project was a collaboration between myself, Brody Condon, and Joan Leandre, and also contains contributions by many others.
19. www.opensorcery.net/patchnew, switch.sjsu. edu/CrackingtheMaze/.
20. www.selectparks.net.
21. www.tmpspace.com.
22. www.retroyou.org.
23. www.untitled-game.org.

27

RENAISSANCE NOW! THE GAMERS' PERSPECTIVE

Douglas Rushkoff

The frightening news is that we are living in a story. The reassuring part is that it's a story we're writing ourselves. Alas, though, most of us don't even know it— or are afraid to accept it. Never before did we have so much access to the tools of storytelling—yet few of us are willing to participate in their creation. Gamers might be today's most likely candidates to helm what I hope will be a renaissance in our relationship to stories as well as the reality they mean to describe and influence.

We are living in a world of stories. We can't help but use narratives to understand the events that occur around us. The unpredictability of nature, emotions, social and power relationships led human beings, from prehistoric times, to develop narratives that described the patterns underlying the movements of these forces. Although we like to believe that primitive people actually believed the myths they created about everything from the weather to the afterlife, a growing camp of religious historians are coming to the conclusion that early religions were understood much more metaphorically than we understand religion today. They didn't believe that the wind or rain were gods; they invented characters whose personalities reflected the properties of these elements. The characters and their stories served more as way of remembering that it would be cold for four months before spring returns, than genuinely accepted explanations. The people were quite self-consciously and actively anthropomorphizing the forces of nature.

As different people and groups competed for authority, they used their narratives quite differently. They used their stories to gain advantage. Stories were no longer being used simply to predict the patterns of nature, but to describe and influence the courses of politics, economics, and power. In such a world, stories compete solely on the basis of their ability to win believers, to be understood as real. When the Pharaoh or King is treated *as if* he were a god, it means his subjects are still actively participating in the sham. He still needs to prove his potency, in real ways, at regular intervals. But if the ruler can somehow get his followers to accept the story of his divine authority as historical fact, then he need prove nothing. The story itself serves as a substitute for reality.

Since biblical times, we have been living in a world where the stories we use to describe and predict our reality have been presented as truth and mistaken for fact. These narratives, and their tellers, compete for believers in two ways: through the content of the stories, and through the medium or tools through which the stories are told. The content of a story might be considered the "what," where the technology through which the story is transmitted can be considered the "how." A story can vie for believers in both ways—through the narrative itself, or by changing the level of the playing field on which it is competing.

Exclusive access to the "how" of storytelling lets a storyteller monopolize the "what." In ancient times, people were captivated by the epic storyteller as much for his ability to remember thousands of lines of text as for the actual content of the *Iliad* or *Odyssey*. Likewise, a television program or commercial holds us in its spell as much through the magic of broadcasting technology as its teleplay. Whoever has power to get inside that magic box has the power to write the story we end up believing.

After all, we don't call the stuff on television "programming" for nothing. The people making television are not programming our TV sets or their evening schedules; they are programming *us*. We use the dial to select which program we are going to receive, and then we submit to it. This is not so dangerous in itself, but the less control we have over exactly what is fed to us through the tube, the more vulnerable we are to the whims of our programmers.

For most of us, what goes on in the television set is magic. Before the age of VCRs and camcorders, it was even more so. A television program is a magic act. Whoever has gotten his image in that box *must* be special. Back in the 1960s, Walter Cronkite used to end his newscast with the assertion, "and that's the way it is." It was his ability to appear in the magic box that gave him the tremendous authority necessary to lay claim to the absolute truth.

I have always recoiled when this rhetorical advantage is exploited by those who have the power to monopolize a medium. Back in college, I remember being incensed by a scene in the third *Star Wars* movie, *Return of the Jedi*. Luke and Han Solo have landed on an alien moon, and are taken prisoner by a tribe of little furry creatures called Ewoks. In an effort to win their liberation, Luke's two robots tell the Ewoks the story of their heroes' struggle against the dark forces of the Empire. C3PO, the golden android, relates the tale, while little R2D2 projects holographic images of battling spaceships. The Ewoks are dazzled by R2's special effects and engrossed in C3PO's tale. The "how" and the "what." They are so moved by the story that they not only release their prisoners, but fight a violent war on their behalf! I kept wondering, what if Darth Vader had gotten down to the alien moon first, and told *his* side of the story complete with his own special effects?

Similarly, television programming, like the many one-way media before it, communicates through stories, and it influences us through its seemingly magical capabilities. The programmer creates a character we like—with whom we can identify. As a series of plot developments bring that character into some kind of danger, we follow him, and a sense of tension rises within us.

This is what Aristotle, in his role as one of the first theater analysts, called the rising arc of dramatic action. The storyteller brings the character, and the audience, into as much danger as we can tolerate before inventing his solution—the rescue—allowing us all to let out a big sigh of relief. Back in Aristotle's day, this solution was called *Deus ex machina* (God from the machine) and one of the Greek gods would descend on a mechanism from the rafters and save the day. In an Arnold Schwarzenegger movie, that miraculous solution might take the form of a new, super-powered laser gun. In a commercial, well, it's the product being advertised. In any case, with a captive audience, the storyteller can pick whichever solution he wants and, if we've been following the story into increasing anxiety, we'll take it.

Television commercials honed this storytelling technique into the perfect thirty-second package. A man is at work. His wife calls to tell him she's crashed the car. The boss comes in to tell him he just lost a big account. His bank statement shows he's in the red. His secretary quits. Now his head hurts. We've followed the poor shlub all this way, and we feel his pain. What can he do? He opens the top desk drawer and finds his bottle of Brand A Pain Reliever! He swallows the pills as an awe-inspiring high-tech animation demonstrates to us the way the pill passes through his body, relieving his pain.

In a passive and mysterious medium, when we are brought into a state of vicarious tension, the storyteller can make swallow any pill he chooses. Only by accepting his solution can we be freed from our despair.

Interactive media changed this equation. Imagine if your grandfather were watching that aspirin commercial back in 1955 on his old console television. Even if he suspected that he were watching a commercial designed to put him in a state of anxiety, in order to change the channel and remove himself from the externally imposed tension, he would have to move the popcorn off his lap, pull up the lever on his recliner, walk up to the television set, and manually turn the dial. That's a somewhat rebellious action for a bleary-eyed television viewer. To sit through the rest of the commercial, however harrowing, might cost him only a tiny quantity of human energy until the pills come out of the drawer. The brain, being lazy, chooses the path of least resistance, and grandpa sits through the whole commercial.

Flash forward to 1990. A kid with a remote control in his hand makes the same mental calculation: an ounce of stress, or an infinitesimally small quantity of human effort to move his finger an eighth of an inch and he's free! The remote control gives viewers the power to remove themselves from the storyteller's spell, with almost no effort. Watch a kid—or yourself—the next time he channel surfs from program to program. He's not changing the channel because he's bored. He surfs away when he senses that he's being put into an imposed state of tension.

The remote control breaks down the "what." It allows a viewer to deconstruct the content of television media, and avoid falling into the programmer's spell. If he does get back around the dial to watch the end of a program, he no longer has the same captivated orientation. Kids with remotes aren't watching television— they are watching the television, *playing* television. Putting it through its paces.

Just as the remote control allowed a generation to deconstruct the content of television, the video game joystick demystified its technology. Remember back to the first time you ever saw a video game. It was probably *Pong*, that primitive black and white depiction of a ping-pong table, with a square on either side of the screen representing the paddle, and a tiny white dot representing the ball. Now, remember the exhilaration you felt at playing that game for the very first time. Was it because you had always wanted an effective simulation of ping-pong? Did you celebrate because you'd be able to practice without purchasing an entire table and installing it in the basement? Of course not. You were celebrating the simple ability to be able to move the pixels on the screen for the first time. It was a moment of revolution! The screen was no longer the exclusive turf of the television broadcasters. Thanks to the joystick, as well as the subsequent introduction of the VCR and camcorder, we were empowered to move the pixels ourselves. The TV was no longer magical. Its functioning had become transparent.

Finally, the computer mouse and keyboard transformed a receive-only monitor into a portal. Packaged programming was no longer any more valuable—or valid—than the words we could type ourselves. The addition of a modem turned the computer into a broadcast facility. We were no longer dependent on the content of Rupert Murdoch or CBS, but could create and disseminate our own. The Internet revolution was a "do-it-yourself" or DIY revolution. The people were now the content. New forms of community were being formed.

Of course this represented a tremendous threat to business as usual. Studies in the mid 1990s showed that families with Internet-capable computers were watching an average of nine hours less television per week. What's worse, Internet enthusiasts were sharing information, ideas, and even entire computer programs, for free! Software known as "freeware" and "shareware" gave rise to a gift economy based on community and mutual self-interest. People were turning to alternative news and entertainment sources for which they didn't have to pay—and, worse, they were watching fewer commercials. Something had to be done. And it was.

Through a series of both deliberate and utterly systemic responses to the threat of interactivity, the mainstream media sought to reverse the effects of the remote, the joystick, and the mouse. Borrowing a term from 1970s social science, media business advocates declared that we were now living in an "attention economy." True enough, the mediaspace might be infinite, but there are only so many hours in a day during which potential audience members might be viewing a program. These units of human time became known as "eyeball-hours," and pains were taken to create TV shows and web sites "sticky" enough to engage those eyeballs long enough to show them an advertisement. Perhaps coincidentally, the growth of the attention economy was accompanied by an increase of concern over the "attention spans" of young people. Channel surfing and similar behavior became equated with a very real but differently diagnosed childhood illness called Attention Deficit Disorder. Children who refused to pay attention were much too quickly drugged, before the real reasons for their adaptation to the onslaught of commercial messages were even considered.

The demystification of media enabled by the joystick and other tools was quickly reversed through the development of increasingly opaque computer interfaces. Whereas an early DOS computer user tended to understand a lot about how the computer stored information and launched programs, later operating systems such as Windows 95 put more barriers in place. Although these operating systems make computers easier to use in certain ways, they prevent users from gaining access or command over its more intricate processes. Now, to install a new program, users must consult "the wizard." What better metaphor do we need for the remystification of the computer? As a result, "computer literacy" no longer means being able to program a computer, but merely knowing how to use Microsoft Office.

Finally, the DIY ethic of the Internet community was replaced by the new value of commerce. The communications age was rebranded as an "information age," even though the Internet had never really been about downloading files or data, but, instead, about communicating with other people. The difference was that information, or "content," unlike real human interaction, could be bought and sold. It is a commodity. When selling information online didn't work, businesspeople turned to selling real products online. Thus, the e-commerce boom was ignited. Soon the Internet became the world wide web, whose opaque and image-heavy interfaces made it increasingly one-way and read-only—more conducive to commerce than communication.

Although very few e-commerce companies actually made any money selling goods, the *idea* that they could was all that mattered. News stories about online communities were soon overshadowed by those about daring young entrepreneurs launching multimillion-dollar IPOs (initial public offering of shares). Internet journalism moved from the culture section to the business pages, as the dot.com pyramid scheme became the dominant new media story.

And so a medium born out of the ability to break through packaged stories was now being used to promote a new, equally dangerous one: the great pyramid. A smart kid writes a business plan. He finds a few "angel investors" to back him up long enough for him to land some first-level investors. Below them on the pyramid are several more rounds of investors until the investment bank gets involved. Another few levels of investors buy in until the decision is made to "go public." This means that poor suckers like you and I can invest, too, by purchasing a newly issued stock on the NASDAQ exchange. Of course, by this point, the angels and other early investors are executing what's known as their "exit strategy." It used to be known as a carpet bag. In any case, they're gone, and we are left holding the soon-to-be-worthless shares.

Tragically, but perhaps luckily, the dot.com bubble burst, along with the story being used to keep it inflated. The entire cycle—the birth of a new medium, the battle to control it, and the downfall of the first victorious camp—taught us a lot about the relationship of stories to the technologies through which they are disseminated. And the whole ordeal may have given us another opportunity for renaissance.

Renaissance Now?

Many considered the birth of the Internet era a revolution. My best friends—particularly those in the counterculture—saw in the Internet an opportunity to topple the storytellers who had dominated our politics, economics, society, and religion, in short, our very reality, and to replace their stories with ones of our own. It was a beautiful and exciting sentiment, but one as based in a particular narrative as any other. Revolutions simply replace one story with another. The capitalist narrative is replaced by the communist; the religious fundamentalist's for the gnostic's. The means may be different, but the rewards are the same, as is the exclusivity of their distribution. That's why they're called revolutions; we're just going in a circle.

I prefer to think of the proliferation of interactive media as an opportunity for renaissance: a moment when we have the opportunity to step entirely out of the story. Renaissances are historical instances of widespread recontextualization. People in a variety of different arts, philosophies, and sciences have the ability to reframe their reality. Literally, renaissance means "rebirth." It is the rebirth of old ideas in a new context. A renaissance is a dimensional leap, when our perspective shifts so dramatically that our understanding of the oldest, most fundamental elements of existence changes. The stories we have been using no longer work.

Take a look back at what we think of as the original Renaissance—the one we were taught in school. What were the main leaps in perspective? Well, most obviously, perspective painting itself. Artists developed the technique of the "vanishing point" and with it the ability to paint three-dimensional representations on two-dimensional surfaces. The character of this innovation is subtle, but distinct. It is not a technique for working in three dimensions; it is not that artists moved from working on canvas to working with clay. Rather, perspective painting allows an artist to relate between dimensions. It is a way of representing three-dimensional objects on a two-dimensional plane.

Likewise, calculus—another key Renaissance invention—is a mathematical system that allows us to derive one dimension from another. It is a way of describing curves with the language of lines, and spheres with the language of curves. The leap from arithmetic to calculus was not just a leap in our ability to work with higher dimensional objects, but a leap in our ability to relate the objects of one dimension to the objects of another. It was a shift in perspective that allowed us to orient ourselves to mathematical objects from beyond the context of their own dimensionality.

The other main features of the Renaissance permitted similar shifts in perspective. Circumnavigation of the globe changed our relationship to the planet we live on and the maps we used to describe it. The maps still worked, of course—only they described a globe instead of a plane. Anyone hoping to navigate a course had to be able to relate a two-dimensional map to the new reality of a three-dimensional planet. Similarly, the invention of moveable type and the printing press changed the relationship of author and audience to text. The creation of a manuscript was no longer a one-pointed affair. Well, the creation of the first manuscript still was—but now it could be replicated and distributed to everyone. It was still one story, but now it was subject to a multiplicity of individual perspectives. This lattermost innovation alone changed the landscape of religion in the Western world. Individual interpretation of the Bible led to the collapse of Church authority and the unilateral nature of its decrees. Everyone demanded his or her own relationship to the story.

In all these cases, people experienced a very particular shift in their relationship to and understanding of dimensions. Understood this way, a renaissance is a moment of reframing. We step out of the frame as it is currently defined, and see the entire picture in a new context. We can then play by new rules.

It is akin to the experience of a gamer. At first, a gamer will play a video or computer game by the rules. He'll read the manual, if necessary, then move through the various levels of the game. Mastery of the game, at this stage, means getting to the end—making it to the last level, surviving, becoming the most powerful character or, in the case of a simulation game, designing and maintaining a thriving family, city, or civilization. And, for many gamers, this is as far as it goes.

Some gamers, though—usually after they've mastered this level of play—will venture out onto the Internet in search of other fans or user groups. There, they will gather "cheat codes" to acquire special abilities within the game, such as invisibility or an infinite supply of ammunition. When the gamer returns to the game with his new secret codes, is he still playing the game, or is he cheating? From a renaissance perspective, he is still playing the game—albeit, a different one. His playing field has grown from the CD on which was the game shipped, to the entire universe of computers where these secret codes and abilities can be discussed and shared. He is no longer playing the game, but a metagame; the inner game world is still fun, but it is distanced by the gamer's new perspective—much in the way we are distanced from the play-within-a-play in one of Shakespeare's comedies or dramas. And the meta-theatrical convention gives us new perspective on the greater story, as well. It is as if we are looking at a series of proscenium arches, and being invited, as an audience, to consider whether we are within a proscenium arch, ourselves.

Gaming—as a metaphor but also as a lived experience—invites a renaissance perspective on the world in which we live. Perhaps gamers and game culture have been as responsible as anyone for the rise in expressly self-similar forms of television, such as *Beavis and Butt-head*, *The Simpsons*, and *South Park*. The joy of such programs is not the relief of reaching the climax of the linear narrative, but rather the momentary thrill of making connections. The satisfaction is recognizing which bits of media are being satirized at any given moment. It is an entirely new perspective on television— where programs exist more in the form of Talmudic commentary—perspectives on perspectives on perspectives. We watch screens within screens—constantly reminded, almost as in a Brecht play—of the artifice of storytelling.

The great Renaissance was a simple leap in perspective. Instead of seeing everything in one dimension, we came to realize there was more than one dimension on which things were occurring. Even the Elizabethan world picture, with its concentric rings of authority— God, king, man, animals—reflects this newfound way of contending with the simultaneity of action of many dimensions at once. A gamer stepping out onto the Internet to find a cheat code certainly reaches this renaissance's level of awareness and skill.

But what of the gamer who then learns to program new games for himself? He, I would argue, has stepped out of yet another frame into our current renaissance. He has deconstructed the content of the game, demystified the technology of its interface, and now feels ready to open the codes and turn the game into a do-it-yourself activity. This is precisely the character and quality of the dimensional leap associated with today's renaissance, as well.

The evidence of today's renaissance is at least as profound as that of the one that went before. The sixteenth century saw the successful circumnavigation of the globe via the seas. The twentieth century saw the successful circumnavigation of the globe from space. The first pictures of earth from space changed our perspective on this sphere, forever. In the same century, our dominance over the planet was confirmed not just through our ability to travel around it, but to destroy it. The atomic bomb (itself the result of a rude dimensional interchange between submolecular particles) gave us the ability to destroy the globe. Now, instead of merely being able to circumnavigate "God's" creation, we could actively destroy it. This is a new perspective.

We also have our equivalent of perspective painting, in the invention of the holograph. The holograph allows us to represent not just three, but four dimensions on a two-dimensional plate. When the viewer walks past a holograph, he or she can observe the three-dimensional object over a course of time. A bird can flap its wings in a single picture. But, more importantly for our renaissance's purposes, the holographic plate itself embodies a new renaissance principle. When the plate is smashed into hundreds of pieces, we do not find that one piece contains the bird's wing, and another piece the bird's beak. No, each piece of the plate contains an image of the entire subject, albeit a faint one. When the pieces are put together, the image achieves greater resolution. But each piece contains a representation of the totality—a leap in dimensional understanding that is now informing disciplines as diverse as brain anatomy and computer programming.

Our analogue to calculus is the development of systems theory, chaos math, and the much-celebrated fractal. Confronting nonlinear equations on their own terms for the first time, mathematicians armed with computers are coming to new understandings of the way numbers can represent the complex relationships between dimensions. Accepting that the surfaces in our world, from coastlines to clouds, exhibit the properties of both two- and three-dimensional objects (just what *is* the surface area of a cloud?), they came up with ways of working with and representing objects with *fractional* dimensionality. Using fractals and their equations, we can now represent and work with objects from the natural world that defied Cartesian analysis. We also become able to develop mathematical models that reflect many more properties of nature's own systems—such as self-similarity and remote high leverage points. Again, we find this renaissance characterized by the ability of an individual to reflect, or even affect, the grand narrative. To write the game.

Finally, our renaissance's answer to the printing press is the computer and its ability to network. Just as the printing press gave everyone access to readership, the computer and Internet give everyone access to authorship. The first Renaissance took us from the position of passive recipient to active interpreter. Our current renaissance brings us from a position of active interpretation to one of authorship. We are the creators.

As game programmers instead of game players, we begin to become aware of just how much of our reality is, indeed, open source—up for discussion. So much of what seemed like impenetrable hardware is actually software, and ripe for reprogramming. The stories we use to understand the world seem less like explanations, and more like collaborations. They are rule sets—and only as good as their ability to explain the patterns of history or predict those of the future.

Consider the experience of a cartographer attempting to hold a conversation with a surfer. They both can claim intimate knowledge of the ocean, but from vastly different perspectives. Whereas the mapmaker understands the sea as a series of longitude and latitude lines, the surfer sees only a motion of waves that aren't even depicted on the cartographer's map. If the cartographer were to call out from the beach to the surfer and ask him whether he is above or below the forty-third parallel, the surfer would be unable to respond. The mapmaker would have no choice but to conclude that the surfer was hopelessly lost. If any of us were asked to choose which one we would rather rely on to get us back to shore, most of us would pick the surfer. He experiences the water as a system of moving waves and

stands a much better chance of navigating a safe course through them. Each surfer at each location and each moment of the day experiences an entirely different ocean. The cartographer experiences the same map, no matter what. He has a more permanent model, but his liability is his propensity to mistake his map for the actual territory.

The difference between the surfer and the cartographer's experience of the ocean is akin to pre- and postrenaissance relationships to story. The first relies on the most linear and static interpretations of the story in order to create a static and authoritative template through which to glean its meaning. The latter relies on the living, moment-to-moment perceptions of its many active interpreters to develop a way of relating to its many changing patterns. Ultimately, in a cognitive process not unlike that employed by a chaos mathematician, the surfer learns to recognize the order underlying what at first appears to be random turbulence. Likewise, the surfer understands each moment and event in his world—like a toss of the I-Ching coins were once understood—as a possible reflection on any other in the entire system.

The renaissance experience of moving from game to metagame allows everything old to look new again. We are liberated from the maps we have been using to navigate our world, and free to create new ones based on our own observations. This invariably leads to a whole new era of competition. Renaissance may be a rebirth of old ideas in a new context, but which ideas get to be reborn?

The first to recognize the new renaissance will compete to have their ideologies be the ones that are "rebirthed" in this new context. This is why, with the emergence of the Internet, we saw the attempted rebirth (and occasional stillbirth) of everything from paganism to libertarianism, and communism to psychedelia. Predictably, the financial markets and consumer capitalism—the dominant narratives of our era—were the first to successfully commandeer the renaissance. But they squandered their story on a pyramid scheme—indeed, the accelerating force of computers and networks tends to force any story to its logical conclusion—and now the interactive renaissance is once again up for grabs.

Were I in the futurism business, I'd predict that gamers will be the next to steer the direction of our renaissance, and that they may have entirely better results. For, unlike businessmen or even politicians, gamers know that the reality they are engineering isn't real. This is why cheating is not really cheating—

but merely playing from a new perspective. It's all play. Where gamers may have formerly been competing from within the game, now they meet and compete on an entirely new level—and, in comparison, they fight as gods. This is a powerful perspective from which to operate, and one that may grow in popularity as games become an even more central entertainment in mass culture.

Without even a convincing business-to-business strategy on which to hang their market hopes, increasing numbers of high-tech speculators are coming to the irrefutable conclusion that they just spent billions of their own and other people's money on a communications infrastructure that amounts, more than anything else, to a network gaming platform.

No, the Internet is not a content delivery system. It's not a way to download movies or even songs. It is a way of connecting gaming consoles. The only questions left are whether processing will be done on centralized servers or within the consoles, and how to cope with latency problems in transmission. The rest is a done deal. The gamers (remember who started this Internet craze, after all ...) managed to convince the world to build them the most expensive toy in the history of civilization. To some, this might seem like a sad turn of events. I don't think it is.

Renaissances afford us the ability to rethink and redesign our world using entirely new rule sets. The shift in perspective, itself, however, is probably more valuable than where it takes us. It is an open window—a moment when the very control panel of our world is up for grabs. For as surely as it opened up, this window will close again once a sufficient consensus has been reached. We will then go on, accepting some new, albeit more dimensionalized, picture of reality as the truth, and mistake yet another map as the territory.

Our present, mid-renaissance moment, however, is a window of opportunity. It is like the peak of a mystical experience or psychedelic trip—that moment when the journeyer thinks to himself, "how will I remember this when I am back to reality?" More often than not, the psychic traveler will scribble down some words ("I am one! It is one!") that appear nonsensical in the light of day—even though the insight they mean to communicate is quite penetrating.

So, assuming that we can even do it, what is it we want to embed in the civilization of the future? What would we want to remind ourselves of, once this little window has closed? I'd think, more than any ideology or narrative, the most important idea to associate with our renaissance is the notion that we are, as individuals and a collective, the writers of our own stories. And who or what might best accomplish this grand, transdimensional communication of autonomous, communitarian values?

I'd place my renaissance bet on the gamers' perspective: the very notion that our world is open source, and that reality itself is up for grabs. For, more than anyone else, a real gamer knows that we are the ones creating the rules.

About the Contributors

The Editors

Joost Raessens is Associate Professor of New Media Studies at Utrecht University, the Netherlands. He studied philosophy, film, and French, at the Radboud University (Nijmegen), the Sorbonne (Paris), and the Erasmus University (Rotterdam). Raessens is a member of the Research Institute Philosophy of Information and Communication Technology (ΦICT) at the Erasmus University. He has published on philosophy of art, cinematography, and computer games. In 2003 he was conference chair of the inaugural Digital Games Research Conference, "Level Up," organized by Utrecht University in collaboration with DiGRA. www.raessens.com

Jeffrey Goldstein is in the Department of Social and Organizational Psychology at Utrecht University, The Netherlands. He is the author or editor of fifteen books, including *The psychology of humor* (Academic Press), *Toys, play and child development* (Cambridge University Press), *Why we watch: The attractions of violent entertainment* (Oxford University Press), and *Sports, games and play* (Lawrence Erlbaum Associates). He is on the advisory board of the Interactive Software Federation of Europe, and the Netherlands Institute for the Classification of Audio Visual Media, and is chairman of the National Toy Council (London).

Contributors

Jo Bryce is a Lecturer in Psychology at the Department of Psychology, University of Central Lancashire, Preston, UK. Her research interests include technological development and changing leisure practices, gender and leisure, and the social and psychological aspects of digital gaming.

Together with Jason Rutter she represents the Digiplay Initiative—www.digiplay.org.uk—a broad-ranging investigation of digital gaming from the perspective of the individual, community and games industry.

Sandra L. Calvert, the Director of the Children's Digital Media Center, is a Professor of Psychology at Georgetown University. She is author of *Children's journeys through the information age* (McGraw Hill, 1999), and co-editor of *Children in the digital age: Influences of electronic media on development* (Praeger, 2002). Professor Calvert's research examines the role that interactivity and identity play in children's learning from entertainment media through studies conducted by the Children's Digital Media Center, which is funded by the National Science Foundation. She is also involved in media policy, recently completing research about children's learning from educational and informational television programs required by the Children's Television Act. Professor Calvert is a fellow of the American Psychological Association. She has consulted for Nickelodeon Online, Sesame Workplace, Blue's Clues, and Sega of America, to influence the development of children's television programs, Internet software, and video games.

Mark Davies completed his first degree in psychology and zoology at Nottingham University in 1983. For his Ph.D. he explored the application of Gibson's theory of visual perception to the control of flight behaviour in birds. In this chosen field Mark has published a range of peer-reviewed papers as well as an edited volume on the perceptuomotor control in birds. He has also published in the fields of statistical modeling, face-processing, trauma, and the psychology of online gaming. In relation to the latter Mark is particularly interested in the psychology of online multiplayer role-play gaming.

Gust de Meyer is a professor in the Department of Communication Sciences, Catholic University of Leuven, Belgium. He teaches about popular culture, video games, and the music industry, and has recently performed research on real life soaps, on brands and their role in the lifestyle of Flemish youngsters and elders, and on music television.

Jos de Mul is Professor in philosophy at the Department of Philosophy, Erasmus University Rotterdam and Scientific Director of the Research Institute Philosophy of Information and Communication Technology (ΦICT) in Rotterdam. He has published several books and many articles, mainly in the domain of the history of philosophy, aesthetics, and philosophy of technology. Some relevant publications are: *Romantic desire in (post)modern art and philosophy* (Albany, N. Y.: State University of New York Press, 1999) and *The tragedy of finitude: Dilthey's hermeneutics of life* (New Haven, Yale University Press, 2004). The English translation of his prize winning Dutch book, *Cyberspace odyssey* (2002), will appear in 2005. See www.demul.nl.

Anna Everett is an Associate Professor of Film, TV and New Media Studies, and she is the Director of the Center for Black Studies at the University of California at Santa Barbara. Her books and articles include *Returning the gaze: A genealogy of black film criticism, 1909–1949*; *The revolution will be digitized: Afrocentricity and the digital public sphere, New media: Theories and practices of digitextuality* (with John T. Caldwell), *Digital diaspora: A race for cyberspace* (in press), "The other pleasures: The narrative function of race in the cinema," "Lester Walton's ecriture noir: Transcoding cinematic excess" and "PC youth violence: What's the internet or video gaming got to do with it?" She founded and edits the newsletter *Screening Noir*.

Mark Griffiths is Professor of Gambling Studies at the Nottingham Trent University. He is internationally known for his work into gambling and gaming addictions and was the first recipient of the John Rosecrance Research Prize for "Outstanding scholarly contributions to the field of gambling research" in 1994 and the winner if the 1998 CELEJ Prize for best paper on gambling. He has published over one hundred and ten refereed research papers, two books, numerous book chapters and over two hundred and fifty other articles. His current interests are concerned with "technological addictions" particularly to computer games and the Internet.

Barrie Gunter is Professor of Mass Communication and Director of the Center for Mass Communication Research, University of Leicester. He was Head of Research at the Independent Television Commission. He has written forty-four books and more than two hundred journal papers, book chapters and technical reports on a range of media, marketing, management and psychology topics.

His recent books include *Media research methods* (Sage, 2000); *Broadcast television in a remote community* (Erlbaum, 2002, with T. Charlton & A. Hannan); *Media sex* (Erlbaum, 2002); *Violence on television: Distribution, form, context and themes* (Erlbaum, 2003, with J. Harrison & M. Wykes); and *News and the net* (Erlbaum, 2003). He is currently finishing books on *Children and television advertising* (Erlbaum, 2005, with C. Oates & M. Blades), *Media and body image: Looks could kill.* (Sage, 2005, with M. Wykes), and *Digital health: Meeting patient and professional needs online* (Erlbaum, 2005).

Over the past two years, he has been increasingly involved in research on e-government issues, especially in the field of e-health. He is also a partner in the British Life and Internet Project which is conducting rolling surveys of Internet users in the UK. This project will assess, among other things, the use of the Internet for health information and access to central and local government services.

Justin Hall is a writer with a personal website spanning ten years and five thousand pages (www.links.net). He contributes to a broad range of publications and conferences on issues of intimacy and stimulation in digital culture. Between 2001 and 2003, Hall lived in Japan, chronicling the emergence of mobile multiplayer media and the popular cameraphone. In the Fall of 2004, Hall enrolled as a graduate student in the Interactive Media MFA program at the University of Southern California School of Cinema-Television.

Robyn M. Holmes is Associate Professor of Psychology at Monmouth University. Her teaching and research interests are in children's play and toys, social cognition, and cross-cultural and qualitative approaches. She has published numerous articles and chapters on children's play and has authored two books, *How young children perceive race* and *Fieldwork with children*. Currently she is studying children's play during recess and cheating while playing board games.

Erkki Huhtamo is Associate Professor of Media History and Theory at UCLA, Department of Design, Media Arts. His main research fields are media archaeology and the history and aesthetics of media art. His writings have been published in 12 languages. His most recent book is an anthology (co-edited with Sonja Kangas) called *Mariosofia: Elektronisten pelien kulttuuri* (*Mariosophy: The culture of electronic games*), published in Finnish by the University Press of Finland in 2002.

Jan-Willem Huisman graduated cum laude as Interaction Designer from Utrecht School of the Arts in 1996, then graduated as Master of Arts in the field of multimedia design at the Royal College of Arts in London. As one of the founders of IJsfontein Interactive Media he is now CEO and responsible for conceptual quality of the company. Next to running IJsfontein he is also guest lecturer at different universities and design schools in the Netherlands. IJsfontein is a company based in Amsterdam that produces games and interactive media for children.

Henry Jenkins is the Director of the MIT Comparative Media Studies Program. He is the author or editor of nine books, including *From Barbie to Mortal Kombat: Gender and computer games, Rethinking media change: The aesthetics of transition, Hop on pop: The politics and pleasures of popular culture*, and *Democracy and new media*. He writes a monthly column, Applied Game Theory, for *Computer Games* magazine, has conducted Creative Leaders workshops at Electronic Arts, and heads a research unit which is exploring the educational uses of games.

Jesper Juul has a Ph.D. in video game theory from the Center for Games Research at the IT University of Copenhagen, where he is now Assistant Professor. He is an editor of the *Game Studies* academic journal on computer games. Co-organizer of the first (European) academic conference on computer games, "Computer Games and Digital Textualities" in March 2001, he has researched and published on the relation between games and narrative, on time in games, on emergent game play, and on game ontology. Jesper has also developed and programmed web-based multiplayer games and chat systems. www.jesperjuul.net.

John E. Laird is a Professor of Electrical Engineering and Computer Science at the University of Michigan and Associate Chair of the Computer Science and Engineering Division. He received his B.S. from the University of Michigan in 1975 and his Ph.D. in Computer Science from Carnegie Mellon University in 1983. His research interests spring from a desire to understand the nature of the architecture underlying artificial and natural intelligence. He is one of the original developers of the Soar architecture and leads its continued development and evolution. He is a Fellow of AAAI.

Steven Malliet is an Assistant Researcher in the Department of Communication Sciences, Catholic University of Leuven, Belgium. He is currently preparing a Ph.D. on the different learning mechanisms that can be associated with different types of video games.

Hanne Marckmann graduated cum laude as a commercial copywriter from Art School (Willem de Kooning Academy, Rotterdam). She graduated cum laude as a Master of Arts in the field of New Media and Digital Culture (University of Utrecht). She currently works as a concept developer/copywriter at Keesie, an advertising agency for children and youth. She also teaches media theory and computer games at the Willem de Kooning Academy, Rotterdam. Her interests lie in using the pleasures of gaming for education and advertising.

Britta Neitzel has conducted studies in theater-, film- and television studies, philosophy, and German linguistics in Erlangen, Munich, and Cologne. From 1993 to 2000 she was Assistant Professor for Media Culture at the Bauhaus-University, Weimar, in 2000/2001, was Visiting professor for Media Studies and Media Design at the Technical University Chemnitz, and from 2001 to 2003 was curator at the computer museum, Heinz Nixdorf MuseumsForum, Paderborn. Since March 2003, she has conducted a research project on play as a paradigm for computer usage. She is co-founder of an academic research network on computer games in German speaking countries, and a senior researcher at the University of Tampere, Finland.

Her selected bibliography includes Ph.D. Dissertation (2000) *Played stories: Inquiries on narrative structures and processes in videogames* (in German). *Aesthetik und Kommunikation: Computerspiele*, Berlin 2001; *Das Gesicht der Welt. Medien unserer Kultur*, München: Fink, 2004.

Anthony D. Pellegrini is Professor of Psychological Foundations of Education in the Department of Educational Psychology, University of Minnesota. His research is concerned with methodological issues in the general area of human development, with specific interests in direct observations of aggression, dominance, and social bases of cognitive processes.

Marc Prensky is an internationally acclaimed speaker, writer, consultant, futurist, designer and inventor in the critical areas of education and learning. Marc is the founder of Games2train, an e-learning company whose clients include IBM, American Express, Bank of America, and the U.S. Department of Defense. He is the author of *Digital game-based learning* (McGraw-Hill,

2001). Marc has created more than fifty software games, including the world's first fast-action videogame-based training tools and world-wide, multiplayer, multi-team on-line competitions. Marc has been featured in articles in *The New York Times* and *The Wall Street Journal*, has appeared on CNN, MSNBC and PBS, and was named as one of training's top ten "visionaries" by Training magazine. He holds a BA from Oberlin and graduate degrees from Middlebury, Harvard and Yale.

Isabelle Raynauld is a writer-director, professor and head of the Film Program and the History of Art and Film Studies at the University of Montreal. She earned her Ph.D. in 1990 at the University of Paris VII on the history, theory and practice of screenwriting. Her expertise and publications are about early cinema and multimedia. She is particularly interested in the relationship between technologies and screenwriting rules. She has been a Guest Professor on interactive narratives and on the history and practice of screenwriting at the Universities of Amsterdam (1996), Sorbonne Nouvelle (1998) and Utrecht (1999). In 2000 Raynauld was also a Visiting Scholar at the Comparative Media Studies Department at MIT, where she furthered her research on multimedia. She has directed five films, most recently *Blue Potatoes* (*Le Minot D'Or*), which received the Quebec Jutra Award for Best Documentry in 2002.

Birgit Richard is Professor for New Media at the Institute for Art Education at the Goethe University of Frankfurt. She works on topics like image culture, contemporary youth cultures and the aesthetics of everyday culture in general and she has edited volumes of the leading art magazine in the German language *Kunstforum International* on time, violence, genetic engineering, magic and art, fashion. She has just finished a research project on female characters in computer games and is currently working on a project on uniformity as a social phenomenon and on a project on medical images of the female body on the Internet.

Douglas Rushkoff is the author of ten books on media, culture, and values that have been translated into over twenty-five languages. They include *Nothing sacred, Media virus, Exit strategy, Cyberia, Ecstasy club,* and *Coercion,* which won the 2001 Marshall McLuhan Award. He is a regular commentator on National Public Radio, PBS Frontline, and CBS News Sunday Morning, as well as an essayist for *Time* magazine. Rushkoff is Professor of Communications at New York University's Interactive

Telecommunications Program, and on the boards of the Media Ecology Association and The Center for Cognitive Liberties and Ethics.

Jason Rutter is a Research Fellow at the ESRC Centre for Research on Innovation & Competition (CRIC) at The University of Manchester. A sociologist, his current research and publication interests center on social aspects of the use of information and communication technologies especially issues of consumption, trust, and interaction within domestic spaces. He has most recently published on digital gaming and mobile telecommunications.

Katie Salen is Director of Graduate Studies in Design and Digital Technology at Parsons School of Design, as well as a game designer and writer interested in the connections between game design, interactivity, and play. She has done design work for the XEN division of Microsoft (XBox Live), gameLab, the Design Institute, and Eyebeam Atelier. Katie writes a column on games for RES Magazine and recently completed *Rules of play*, a textbook on game design co-authored with Eric Zimmerman (MIT Press, 2003). She has curated several programs of game-related content for the Walker Museum of Art and the Lincoln Center in New York, and has taught game design at NYU, Parsons School of Design, and N.C. State University.

Anne-Marie Schleiner is engaged in gaming and net culture as a writer, critic, curator, and gaming artist/designer. Her work investigates avatar gender construction, computer gaming culture, and hacker art. She has curated online exhibits of game mods and add-ons including the exhibits "Cracking the maze: Game plug-ins and patches as hacker art," "Mutation.fem," and "Snow blossom house." She runs a site focused on game hacks and open source digital art forms called "opensorcery.net." She has taught digital art courses at various universities in the U.S. and Canada and worked as an independent artist in Germany and Spain.

Sherry Turkle is Abby Rockefeller Mauzé Professor in the Program in Science, Technology, and Society at MIT and the founder and current director of the MIT Initiative on Technology and Self. Dr. Turkle has written numerous articles on psychoanalysis and culture and on the "subjective side" of people's relationships with technology, especially computers. She is the author of *Psychoanalytic politics: Jacques Lacan and Freud's French revolution* (Basic Books, 1978; MIT Press paper, 1981; second revised edition, Guilford Press, 1992); *The* *second self: Computers and the human spirit* (Simon and Schuster, 1984; Touchstone paper, 1985; second revised edition, MIT Press, 2005); and *Life on the screen: Identity in the age of the internet* (Simon and Schuster, November 1995; Touchstone paperback, 1997). She is currently writing a book on the psychological impact of computational objects as they become increasingly "relational" artifacts.

William Uricchio is Professor of Comparative Media Studies at MIT and Professor of Comparative Media History at Utrecht University in the Netherlands. His research focuses on the emergence of new media forms (including old media when they were new) and in particular on the transition from technological possibility to cultural practice. A Guggenheim, Fulbright, and Alexander von Humboldt Fellow, Uricchio has published extensively on topics ranging from 19th century television, to the struggle over the nickelodeon as social space, to the construction of Batman as a popular cultural icon, to the role of P2P communities in (re)defining culture.

Michael van Lent is a Research Scientist at the University of Southern California's Institute for Creative Technologies. His research interests include artificial intelligence systems that explain their behavior and adapt their strategies to compete again and cooperate with humans especially in the context of commercial video games. Dr. van Lent received his Ph.D. from the University of Michigan under the direction of John Laird. He serves as the editor in chief of the *Journal of Game Development*.

Mark J. P. Wolf is an Associate Professor in the Communication Department at Concordia University, Wisconsin. He has a Ph.D. from the University of Southern California's School of Cinema/Television, and is the author of *Abstracting reality: Art, communication, and cognition in the digital age* (University Press of America, 2000), and editor of *The medium of the video game* (UT Press, 2001), *Virtual morality: Morals, ethics, and new media* (Peter Lang Publishers, 2003), and *The video game theory reader* (co-edited with Bernard Perron, Routledge, 2003). He lives in Wisconsin with his wife Diane and sons Michael and Christian.

Jutta Zaremba Since 1998 she has worked as an assistant for film and video in the Department of New Media at the Goethe University, Frankfurt and collaborated on the research-project "Die Konstruktion von weiblichen Repraesentationsbildern in Computer-spielen," which focuses on the representation of female icons in computer games. Specializing in media art, urban theory and gender studies, she currently is working on her Ph.D. about New York and Tokyo in the media arts.

Eric Zimmerman is a game designer and game design theorist. Eric is CEO of a game development company, gameLab, he founded in 2000 with Peter Lee that creates award-winning games in a variety of media on and off the computer. He has taught at New York University's Interactive Telecommunications Program, MIT's Comparative Media Studies Program, and the Digital Design Department at Parsons School of Design. He is co-author with Kate Salen of *Rules of play: Game design fundamentals* (MIT Press), and co-editor with Amy Schulman of *Re: Play–Game design and game culture.*

Games Index

A-10 Attack, 199, 203

ADAM Demo Cartridge, 198

Adventure, 30, 31, 196, 199, 200, 202

Aerobiz, 200

Afternoon, 94, 237

Age of Empire, 42, 119, 207, 235, 330, 331, 336

Age of Kings, 210

AI Fleet Commander, 201

AI wars, 201

Air-Sea Battle, 202

Alpha Beam with Ernie, 197, 199

Alpha Centauri, 111

America's Army, 412

American Football, 196, 202

American McGee's Alice, 257, 296, 297, 298, 299

Amidar, 195, 197

Anarchy, 340

Anvil of Dawn, 202

AquaZone, 196

Arcade Pinball, 200

Arkanoid, 49, 195

Armadillo Aerospace, 48

Asheron's Call, 206

Assassin, 51, 60

Asteroids, 30, 31, 72, 73, 74, 110, 178, 198, 202, 231

Astrocade Pinball, 200

Astro Fighter, 151

Astromash!, 50

Atari Baseball, 196, 202

Ataxx, 194, 195, 203

Atlantis, 202

Avengers, 199

Aviation Tycoon, 119

Babyz, 196

Baldur's Gate, 42, 111, 206

Barbie Fashion Designer, 125, 303

Basic Math, 199

Battle of the Bulge, 328, 330

Battle Ping Pong, 203

Battleship, 196

Battletech, 198

Battlezone, 30, 31, 32, 33, 41, 148, 198, 205

Beatmania, 202

Beginning Algebra, 204

Beginning Math, 203

Berserk, 200, 202

Beyond, 90, 94

Big Bird's Egg Catch, 197

Biotoons, xvii, 399, 400, 402

Black and White, 109, 175, 178, 207, 389

Black Out, 195

Blackjack, 71, 73, 197, 199

Blacklash, 311

Block Out, 201

Body Slam, 199

Boot Camp, 200

BotFighters, xiii, 50, 51, 402

Breakout, 16, 17, 195

Bronkie the Bronchiasaurus, 167

Bust-a-Groove, 202

Busted, 154

Caesar II, 200

Campaign 1776, 330

Carmageddon, 225, 389

Carnival, 202

CarWars, 48

Casino, 196, 197, 199

Castle Wolfenstein 3D, 40, 41, 48, 128, 346, 353, 412

Catz, 196

Centipede, 202, 346

Ceremony of Innocence, 89, 90, 94

Chopper Command, 194

Circus Atari, 197

Civilization, 37, 42, 200, 238, 257, 318, 324, 328, 330, 331, 335, 336 , 382

Civil War Online (CWOL), 334

Close Combat, 207

Clown Downtown, 200

Colonization, 331

Commanche 3, 203

Command-and-Conquer, 32, 109, 207, 235, 239

Commando Raid, 202

Computer Space, 16, 25, 26, 27, 30, 195

Conquest of the World, 196

Games Index

CoreWar, 201
Counter Strike, xvii, 43, 51, 405, 410, 411, 414
Crazy Climber, 201
Creatures, 196
Cremaster, 176
CRobots, 201
Civil War Online (CWOL), 334
Curse of Monkey Island, 206
Curse of Ra, 32
Cutthroats, 47

Dactyl Nightmare, 127, 198
Daggerfall, 196
Daikatana, 48, 315
Dance Dance Revolution, 9, 182, 202
Daytona U.S.A., 201
Dealer Demo, 198
Death Race, 27, 225
Death Star, 221
Defender, 31, 194
Delta Force, Black Hawk Down, 412
Delta Force Land Warrior, 323
Descent, 199, 200, 206
Deus X, 178, 180, 208
Devil Dice, 117
Diablo, 42, 54, 55, 202, 206
Dice Puzzle, 201
Dig Dug, 200
Diplomatic Arena, 382
Dodge 'Em, 198
Dogz, 196
Donkey Kong, 29, 30, 31, 33, 34, 35, 196, 201, 233
Donkey Kong Country, 39
Doom, 10, 31, 41, 48, 108, 116, 149, 200, 202, 206, 223, 237, 259, 316, 378, 405, 407, 408, 410, 412
Double Dragon, 38
Dragon Lore 2, 202
Dragon Quest, 39
Dragon's Lair, 196, 199
DrumMania, 202
Duckshot, 202
Duke Nuke-Em, 407
Dune II, 42
Dungeon Keeper, 205
Dungeons and Dragons, 24, 32, 42, 100, 200, 202

Effacer, Hangman from the 25th Century, 200
Einstein's Dreams, 90, 91, 94
Electronic Pinball, 200
Electronic Table Soccer!, 203
Emergency Break, 402
Emergency Stop, xvii, 402
Empire Strikes Back, 128, 148
Epyx Dunjonquest, 32
Eric's Ultimate Solitaire, 196, 197

Escape, 194
Ethnic Cleansing, 319, 321, 322, 323, 324
Europa Universalis, 330, 335
EverQuest, 43, 52, 54, 60, 94, 101, 117, 206, 223, 270, 340, 374
Evolution, 147
Extreme Pinball, 200

F/A-18 Hornet 3.0, 199, 203
Fallout, 202
Family Feud, 196
Fast ForWard, 103
Fax, 201
FIFA Soccer, 41
Fifth Element, xvi, 293
Final Fantasy, 39, 42, 175
Final Fantasy Mystic Quest, 257
Fishing Derby, 197, 202
Flight Unlimited, 199, 203
Flipper Game, 200
Formula 1, 257
Freeway, 198, 200
Frequency, 182, 183
Frogger, 30, 33, 197, 198, 200
Full Throttle, 207

Galactic Pinball, 200
Galaga, 49, 202
Galaxian, 31
Galaxy War, 16
Gamewheels, 162
Go, 25, 60, 71, 341
Golden Eye/007, 137
Gopher, 196, 197
Got'cha, 27
Gran Turismo, 41, 42, 207
Grand Prix Legends, 327, 328, 329
Grand Prix Monaco, 31
Grand Theft Auto 3 (GTA3), 178, 180, 321, 322, 324
Grand Theft Auto—Vice City, 389
Grand Track, 27
Great Wall Street Fortune Hunt, 196
Grim Fandango, 207, 239
Gross Out, 61
Guitar Freaks, 202
Gun Fight, 26, 31
G.U.R.P.S., 48

Half-Life, 43, 51, 206, 220, 222, 378, 407, 410, 411, 412, 414
Halo, 206
Haunted House, 196, 197, 199
Heavy Metal, 283
Hellfire Warrior, 32

Herzog Zwei, 42
Hidden Agenda, 330
High Velocity, 201
Hole Hunter, 197
Home Finance, 204
Home Pong, 26
Hot Shots Tennis, 196, 202
Human Cannonball, 202, 203
Hungry Hungry Hippos, 17
Hunt the Wumpus, 24
Hyperspace Delivery Boy, 49

Illuminati, 48
Immemory, 91, 94
Imperialism: The Fine Art of Conquering the World, 316, 317, 318
Indiana Jones and the Infernal Machine, 378
Indy 500, 198, 201
Infogenius French Language Translator, 204
Internet Evolver, 396
Interstate '76, 202
Ivory Tower, 202

Jawbreaker, 407
JediMUD, 202
Jeopardy!, 115, 196, 201
Jet Grind Radio, 184
Joint Force Deployment, 111
Joker's Wild, 196
Journey Escape, 198
Joust, 35
Jungle Hunt, 200

K. C. Munchkin, 200
Ken Uston Blackjack/Poker, 196, 197
Keystone Kapers, 196, 197
Killer, 64
King's Quest, 36, 37, 207
Kirby's Avalanche, 135
Kirby's Pinball Land, 200
Krull, 196

Leather Goddesses of Phobos, 203
Legend of Zelda, 37, 378
Leisure Suit Larry I–III, 37
L'Empereur, 330
Life and Death, 104
Liquidation, xiv, 88, 89, 93, 94
Little Computer People, 196
Lode Runner, 200
Longest Journey, 295, 296, 297
Lunar Lander, 30, 31

Madden Football 97, 202
Madden NFL 97, 207

Mageslayer, 202
Magic Cauldron, 405
Majestic, 178
Maniac Mansión, 37
Marathon, 149, 407, 409
Marathon Infinity, 409
Marble Madness, 129, 195
Mario Brothers, 35, 37, 127, 183, 221, 231
Mario Kart, 135, 201
Mario's Early Years, Fun with Numbers, 199
Mario Teaches Typing, 194, 199, 204
Marksman/Trapshooting, 203
Masters of the Elements, xvii, 390, 393, 399
Math Blaster, Episode 1, 199
Math Grand Prix, 199, 201
Maze Craze, 199, 200
Medal of Honor, 323
MegaMan, 135
Memory of Goblins, 165
Merlin, 274, 275
Metal Gear Solid, 383
Mickey Mania, 135
Midnight Magic, 200
Millennia, 296
Millipede, 202
Miniature Golf, 202
Minotars, 408
Miracle in Reverse, 94
Missile Command, 73, 77, 202, 223, 346
Missile Defence 3-D, 202
Mister Mouth, 17
Monkey Island, 207
Monkey Wrench Conspiracy, 111, 116, 120
Monopoly, 24, 77, 196, 200, 203
Montana, 197
Mortal Kombat, xi, 149, 199, 221, 346
Mortal Kombat II, 345
Mortal Kombat 3, 348
Mousetrap, 73, 197, 199, 200
Ms. Pac-Man, 199, 200, 311, 365
Multiple Use Labor Element (M.U.L.E.), 51, 52, 200, 202
Music Box Demo, 198, 204
Myst, xiv, 42, 85, 86, 88, 90, 92, 93, 94, 194, 196, 199, 200, 201, 203, 207, 238, 243, 346, 353

Napoleon at Waterloo, 330
Napoleon in Russia, Battleground 6, 330
Napoleon's Campaigns, 1813, 1815, 330
Naturally Lara, 209
NBA Basketball, 41
NBA Jam, 345, 346
Never Winter Nights, 405
NFL Football Trivia Challenge '94/'95, 201
NHL Hockey, 41, 202

Night Driver, 198
Night Stalker, 49
Nomad Soul, xvi, 291, 292, 294, 295, 298, 381, 385
No One Lives Forever, 378
Northern Lights, 202
Noughts and Crosses, 200
Nude Raider, 409, 409, 414

Objection!, 112, 120
Omega, 201
1000 Miles, 197, 201
Oni, 297
Operation Flashpoint, 323
Operation, 137
Oregon Trail, 328, 330, 331
Othello, 195, 196, 203
Outlaw, 194, 198
OutlawMOO, 202

Pachinko!, 200
Packy & Marlon, 167
Pac-Man, 27, 29, 31, 33, 35, 41, 49, 146, 151, 178, 194,
    195, 197, 199, 200, 311, 346, 364, 407
PaRappa the Rapper, 202
Parlour Games, 203
Password, 196
PernMUSH, 202
Phantasy Star (Online), 42, 52, 202
Pinball Challenge, 200
Pinball Dreams, 200
Pinball Fantasies, 200
Pinball Jam, 201
Pinball Quest, 201
Pinball Wizard, 201
Pipe Dream, 195
Pitfall!, 196, 197, 200
Pizza Tycoon, 119
Planetfall, 203
Playschool Math, 199
Pocket Billiards!, 203
Pokeball, 104
Pokémon, 53, 54, 105, 106, 304
Pole Position, 31, 91, 198, 201
Police Quest I–III, 37
Police Trainer, 203
Pong, 16, 25, 26, 27, 29, 31, 98, 110, 175, 196, 202, 203,
    228, 231, 379, 407, 416
Pop 'n' Music, 202
Populous, 37, 42
Portrait One, 87, 88, 94
Power Rangers Pinball, 201
Price is Right, 196
Progress Quest, 54
Proman, 88
Prop Cycle, 197, 199

Q-Bert, 50, 195
Qin, 120
Qix, 32, 195, 197
Quake, 10, 41, 48, 51, 109, 116, 149, 205, 206, 208, 237,
    243, 316, 378, 389, 405, 407, 408, 409, 410, 411, 412,
    413
Quantum, 197
Quest, 37
Quest for the Holy Grail, 235
Quest for the Rings, 196

Railroad Tycoon, 200
Rainbow Six, 323
Rampage, 225
R/C FCK the gravity Code, 413
Ready 2 Rumble Boxing, Round 2, 314, 316, 319
Real Pinball, 200
RealSports Tennis, 202
RealSports Volleyball, 202
Rebel Assault, 195, 199
Red Landscape, 94
Red Planet, 198, 201
Return to Castle Wolfenstein, 208, 323
Rex Ronan, 167
Rez, 178, 182, 183
RiftMUSH, 202
Riven, 85, 86, 201
Rivers of MUD, 202
Road Quiz Show, 393, 402
Robot Auto Racing Simulator (RARS), 201
Robot Battle, 201
Robotron, 127, 202
Rogue, 203
Roller Coaster Tycoon, 109, 111

Sacred Pools, 202
Safety Last, 185
Samba de Amigo, 202
Samurai Romanesque, 52, 53
Sea Battle, 49
Secret of Monkey Island, 37
7th Guest, 201
Sex Trivia, 201
Shenmue, 178
Shoot the Blacks, 321
Shooting Gallery, 203
Silent Hill, 239
SimAnt, 200
SimCity, 37, 106, 115, 119, 200, 207, 235, 268, 330, 385
SimFarm, 200
SimGolf, 202
SimLife, xvi, 257, 268, 275, 275
Simon, 33, 275
Sims, 54, 109, 111, 178, 187, 197, 207, 235, 304, 324
Sims Online, 270, 271

SimTower, 200
Skeet Shoot, 202, 203
Sky Diver, 202
Slot Racers, 201
Smack, 154
Snake, xiii, 47
Snood, 185
Soar Quakebot, 208
Sokoban, 201
Solaris, 199
Soldier of Fortune, 323, 378
Sonic, the Hedgehog, 38, 182, 238
Sonic Spinball, 201
Sorcery, xiii. 47, 48
Soul Edge, 199
Space Ace, 199
Space Channel 5, 54, 202
Space Commanders, 29
Space Invaders, 28, 29, 30, 31, 194, 198, 202, 219, 220, 231, 364
Space Panic, 29
Space Quest I–III, 37
Space Race, 27
Space Wars, 31, 100, 205
Spacewar, 4, 15, 16, 24, 25, 29, 31, 72, 407
Spaceward Ho!, 194, 200, 202
Speak and Spell, 275
Spinball, 201
Spy vs. Spy, 196, 197, 198, 200
Squirtle, 104
SSX, 180
Stampede, 197
Starcraft, 207, 222, 225
Starmaster, 199
Star Ship, 199
Star Trek, 24, 68, 100, 196, 199, 259, 409
Start Up, 119
Star Wars, 194, 196, 221, 222, 225, 374, 408, 416
Stellar Track, 202, 203
Straight Shooter!, 116
Stratego, 24, 196
Street Fighter, 38, 149, 176
Street Racer, 195, 197, 198, 201
Summer Games, 202
Sunflower, 202
Super Breakout, 195
Super GT, 201
Super Mario Bros., 35, 135, 201, 311, 323
Super Mario 64, 378
Super Mario Worlds, 39
Super Pinball—Behind the Mask, 201
Super Sushi Pinball, 201
Supercade, 16
Superfly, 316
Superman, 196, 197

Sure Shot Pool, 196, 203
Surround, 197, 199
Suspended Animation, 201, 203

Tank, 27
Targ, 148
Tattletoons, 394, 397
Teenage Mutant Ninja Turtles, 196
Tekken, 72, 149, 199, 315
Tekken Tag Tournament, 319
Tempest, 32, 195
Temple of Apshai, 32, 37
Tennis for Two, 23, 24
Tetris, 36, 54, 76, 104, 110, 117, 125, 128, 129, 164, 176, 185, 194, 195, 201, 223, 224, 226, 231, 238, 257, 259, 260, 264
Third Reich, 333
Thunderball!, 201
Tic-Tac-Dough, 196
Tic-Tac-Toe, 64, 75, 196, 200
Tierra, 275
Time Crisis, 71
Titus, 176
Toejam and Earl, 38
Tomb Raider, xvi, 41, 42, 149, 179, 185, 196, 206, 221, 222, 228, 230, 233, 234, 237, 238, 239, 257, 283, 284, 285, 286, 288, 294, 375, 378, 409, 414
Touch Typing, 204
Track & Field, 202
Tribes, 407, 413
Trivia, 165
Trivia Whiz, 201
Trivial Pursuit, 201
Triv-Quiz, 201
True Pinball, 201
Tsuppori Sumo Wrestling, 202
Tunnel Runner, 200
Tunnels of Doom, 200
Typotoons, xvii, 390, 391, 392, 393, 394, 396, 397, 403

UFO Invaders, 29
Ultima III—Exodus, 202
Ultima, 33, 37, 196, 202, 206, 340, 374
Ultima-Online, 42, 117, 206, 270
Um Jammer Lammy, 202
Under Ash, 382
Unreal Tournament, 206, 389, 412
Unreal, 51, 109, 116, 407
Unsafe Haven, 202
Urban Terror, 41, 414
Utopia, 49

Vampire—the Masquerade, 405
Vampire, 293, 294
Velvet-Strike, 382, 411, 412, 413

Venture, 32, 196
Versailles 1685, 334
Vib-Ribbon, 202
Video Checkers, 196
Video Chess, 196
Video Olympics, 202
Video Pinball, 194, 201
Video Poker, 197, 199
Video Trivia, 201
VikingMUD, 202
Virtua Fighter, 293, 294
Virtua Racing, 38
Virtual Boy, 40
Virtual Pool, 196, 203
Virtual Worlds, 111

Wabbit, 203
Waco Resurrection, 382
Wall Street Trader, 119
War & Peace, 333
War Collage, 330
Warcraft, 42, 207
Warioland, 210
Warlords, 198
Waverace, 138
Way Down East?, 185
Weakest Link, 304
We're Back, 135
Wheel of Fortune, 196
Who Wants to Be a Millionaire, 304
Wipeout, 91
Wizard of War, 32
Wizz Quiz, 201
Wolfenstein. *See* Castle Wolfenstein
World Cup Football, 27
World Series Baseball '98, 202
Wrestle War, 199
WWF, Mobile Madness, 49

Xena—the Warrior Princess, xvi, 289, 290, 293, 297
X-Men, 196

Yar's Revenge, 202
Yoshi's Island, 201
You Don't Know Jack, 101, 117, 199, 201

Zaxxon, 30, 37, 148, 202, 346
Zelda, 107
Zodiac, 202
Zork, 33, 65, 203, 206

Name Index

Aarseth, E. J., 220, 226, 227, 230, 235, 237, 238, 239, 240, 243, 244, 264, 337, 379, 380, 386
Abercrombie, N., 304, 308
Abrahamsson, J., 50
Abrams, J., 403
Ackerman, D., 97
Adorno, T., 375, 382, 386, 387
Adriaenssens, E. E., 163, 168
Agee, J., 184, 188
Agre, P. E., 205, 214
Ahlers, R., 112
Aisbett, K., 343, 353
Aldrich, C., 122
Alexander, M., 256, 264
Alioto, J., 149, 155
Allen, M., 121, 378
Allen, P. J., 364, 368
Alloi, E., 93
Alman, R. E., 149, 155
Alpert, B. S., 364, 368
Anderson, A. E., 147, 159, 221
Anderson, C. A., 134, 135, 142, 145, 149, 150, 155, 341, 342, 343, 345, 346, 347, 348, 349, 350, 351, 353, 354,
Angerer, M.-L., 293, 297, 299
Antoja, E., 43, 44
Apter, M. J., 75, 78
Aristotle, 94, 232, 242, 244, 254, 255, 259, 264, 416
Arneson, D., 24
Ascione, F. R., 149, 155
Ask, A., 345, 348, 354
Assanie, M., 214
Atkin, C., 149, 155
Atkin, M. S., 212, 214
Atkins, E., 156
Ator, R., 363, 368
Autoustinos, M., 354
Avedon, E., 59, 78

Baarda, B., 351, 357
Baer, R., 4, 16, 24, 25, 26, 27, 188
Bailey, J. R., 156, 344, 355
Bain, C., 187, 188
Bal, M., 255, 256, 265

Ball, H. G., 146, 155
Ballard, M. E., 149, 150, 155, 346, 354
Balsamo, A., 287, 299
Bandura, A., 134, 142, 149, 155
Bantock, N., 89
Baraka, A., 311, 324
Barker, A., 188
Barker, M., 343, 352, 354
Barkey, R., 122
Barney, M., 176, 187
Barrett, E., 95
Barth, M., 299
Barthes, R., 91, 94, 242, 244, 252, 255, 265, 313, 324
Bartholow, B. D., 341, 347, 348, 354
Bar-Yishay, E., 171
Barnum, P. T., 13
Barwood, H., 175, 177, 188
Bates, R., 169
Baudot, J. C., 19
Baudry, J.-L., 230, 244
Baxmeier, A., 299
Bebko, J. M., 147, 158
Bek, P., 69, 78
Bélanger, P. C., 94
Beloff, Z., 83, 90, 94
Bellour, R., 95
Bellows, M., 47
Bench, C. J., 353, 356, 363, 368
Benedict, J. O., 168
Benjamin, W., 5, 13, 373, 384, 386
Bensley, L., 345, 350, 354
Berger, A. A., xi
Bergeron, A., 88, 94
Berkhofer, R., 332, 337
Berkowitz, L., 149, 150, 155, 157
Berlo, D., 65, 78
Berlyne, D., 126, 130
Berry, B. D., 51, 98, 121
Besson, L., 290
Best, D., 135, 144
Bey, H., 321, 324, 386
Bickman, D., 131
Bigelow, K., 285

Name Index

Bilous, S., 95
Birdwell, K., 206, 214
Birkerts, S., 384, 386
Bittner, A. C, Jr., 147, 157
Bland, R., 403
Blechman, E. A., 168
Blunt, D., 163, 169
Boeckx, W., 168
Bolter, J. D., 227, 230, 231, 244, 285, 286, 299, 312, 325, 373, 386
Bonian, V. G., 364, 368
Bonime, A., 95
Boninger, M. L., 170
Bonnafont, E., 133, 142
Bordwell, D., 183, 184, 188, 222, 226, 232, 233, 242, 244, 377, 378, 384, 386
Bostem, F., 151, 156
Bosworth, K., 153, 155, 166, 169
Bottomore, S., 19
Bovill, M., 305, 309
Boyatzis, C., 134, 142
Bradbury, R., 384
Brand, S., 16, 19, 95
Branigan, E., 233, 243, 244, 257, 265
Brannon, C., 128, 130, 148, 156
Brasington, R., 151, 155, 364, 366
Braun, M., 17, 19, 147, 155
Brauel, F., 338
Braun, C. M. J., 365, 366
Breazeal, C., 214
Brecht, B., 373, 384, 386
Breen, C., 169
Brennan, J., 413
Bright, D. A., 151, 155, 366
Bringhurst, D. C., 151, 155, 366
Brodie, M., 131, 363, 367, 413
Bromberg, P., 271, 272, 278
Brooks, D. J., 353, 356, 363, 368
Brooks, P., 220, 226, 264, 265, 312, 325
Brooks, R. A., 210, 214
Brown, A., 353
Brown, D., 26, 27, 32, 33, 36, 44, 347
Brown, R. I. F., 361, 366
Brown, S. J., 167, 169
Browne, N., 204
Brunel, M., 5
Bruner, J., xiv, 126, 127, 130
Brunovska Karnick, K., 188
Brusa, J. A., 149, 155
Bryce, J., xiii, xvi, 303, 304, 306, 307, 308, 385, 423
Buchanan, D., 305, 306, 308
Buchman, D., 125, 126, 130, 133, 135, 136, 137, 141, 142, 143, 163, 169, 344, 355
Buchman, J., 214
Buckalew, L. W., 169

Buckalew, P. B., 169
Buckingham, D., 342, 354
Buckles, M. A., 241, 244
Bueschel, R. M., 5, 17, 18
Bukatman, S., 297, 299
Bullock, W. A., 344, 355
Burden, C., 413
Burish, T. G., 160, 171
Burke, K., 353, 354
Burke, T., 353, 354
Burnham, V., 4, 16, 188
Burns, K., 333, 337
Burroughs, W. S., 224, 226
Buscombe, E., 194, 204
Bushman, B. J., 346, 354, 350, 351, 353
Butler, C., 162, 169
Butler, J., 293, 299, 325
Bushnell, N., 4, 16, 24, 25, 26, 27, 33, 34
Buytendijk, F. J. J., 119, 244

Cahill, J. M., 154, 155, 167, 169, 171
Caillois, R., 119, 242, 244
Cain, J., 187, 188
Cajko, L., 169
Calder, B. J., 351, 356
Callahan, D., 170
Calvert, S., xi, xii, xiv, 125, 126, 127, 128, 130, 133, 134, 142, 149, 150, 155, 347, 354, 423
Camaioni, L., 130, 156
Cameron, A., 259, 265, 374, 386
Cameron, J., 183, 285
Campagnoni, D. P., 20
Campbell, J., 233, 244
Cantor, E., 181, 182, 188
Canty, D., 93
Caplovitz, A., 131
Capra, F., 236, 335
Carels, E., 382, 386
Carlton, T., 146, 151, 159, 363, 364, 368
Carlson, J. N., 363, 367
Carmack, J., 48, 49
Carnegie, D., 102, 122
Caron, M. G., 363, 368
Carse, J. P., 55
Carstens, B., 341, 357
Carter, C., 352, 354
Cary, P., 333, 334, 337
Casanova, J., 151, 155, 364, 366
Casas, F., 343, 354
Case, S., 410
Cassell, J., xi, 133, 136, 137, 142, 304, 308
Castle, L., 207, 209, 214
Castle, N., 14
Castells, M., 264, 265, 393, 403
Centerwall, B. S., 352, 354

Chagnon, Y., 155, 365, 366
Chaille, C., 148, 158
Chambers, J. H., 149, 155
Chandler, D., 64, 78
Chansanchai, A., 313, 325,
Charbon, P., 18, 20
Charlton, T., 351, 352, 354
Chartier, R., 331
Chaplin, C., 6, 184
Chapman, D., 205, 214
Chatman, S., 220, 221, 226, 232, 244, 254, 265
Chatrian, G. E., 364, 367
Chen, M., 121
Chick, T., 335, 337
Chin, E., 45
Chipman, S., 99, 121
Chisholm, A., 187
Church, D., 63, 72, 78, 214
Clarke, B., 164, 169
Clarke, D., 153, 155
Cleary, A. G., 364, 366
Clemens, W., 333, 337
Cliche, M., 94
Cockburn, C., 307, 308
Cocking, R, 133, 143, 159
Cocteau, J., 285
Coe, B., 18, 20
Coelho, K. A., 342, 354
Cohen, H., 157
Cohen, P. R., 212, 214
Colmer, M., 18, 20
Colwell, J., 151, 155, 301, 306, 308, 344, 354, 364, 366
Comstock, G., 134, 143, 351
Condon, B., 412, 414
Cook, T. D., 351, 356
Cooper, J., 134, 135, 138, 141, 142, 149, 150, 155, 346, 348, 354
Cooper, R. A., 170
Copier, M., xi
Corbeil, P., 333, 337
Corkery, J. C., 151, 155, 364, 366
Corno, L., 147, 155
Cortazar, J., 258, 265
Costa, N., 5, 10, 17, 18
Costello, M. J., 28, 42, 44
Costikyan, G., 50, 51
Cotton, B., 92, 94
Coulter, K., 214
Courchesne, L., 87, 94
Creasey, G. L., 302, 308
Creed, B., 285, 299
Crenshaw, S., 322
Crockford, D., 102
Cronkite, W., 416
Crawford, C., 102, 122, 193

Culler, J., 242, 244
Cumberbatch, G., 343, 345, 354
Cunningham, R., 331, 337
Cunningham, V. J., 353, 356, 363, 368

Dabney, T., 26
Dagher, A., 353, 356, 363, 368
Daguerre, L., 398
Dalquist, N. R., 151, 155
Damen, J., 384
Dancaster, I., 363, 367
Darby, C. E., 159
Darley, A., 378, 386
Davies, M., 423
Davies, N. O., xiii, xvii
Davis, R. P., 207, 214, 311, 323
Davison, G., 335, 337
De Certeau, M., 234, 244, 336, 382, 386
Deheger, M., 365, 366
Deitch, J., 293, 299
De Koven, B., 76, 78
Deleuze, G., 272, 384, 385, 386
Del Rosario, M., 351, 356
Demarest, K., 163, 169
DeMaria, R., 16
Dementij, G., 6, 17
De Meyer, G, xii, xiii, 6, 28, 29, 34, 39, 41, 42, 44, 423
De Mul, J., xiii, xv, 255, 258, 259, 263, 265, 377, 379, 384, 387, 424
Dennett, D. C., 252, 255, 265, 271, 278
Derevensky, J. L., 361, 367
Dermatis, H., 158, 170
Derrida, J., 376, 377
Dery, M., 325, 382, 386
Descartes, R., 252, 253, 265
Deuber-Mankowsky, A., 284, 299
Dewey, J., 353
De Winstanley, P., 127, 130, 156
Diawara, M., 317, 325
Dickson, W. K. L., 18
DieTrill, M., 158, 170
Dietz, T., 133, 137, 141, 142
Dietz, T. L., 303, 306, 308
Dietz, W. H., 364, 368
Di Gaetano, G., 122
Dijkstra, A. F. J., 347, 355
Dill, J., 133, 142, 149, 156, 302, 308, 342, 343, 345, 347, 354
Dill, K. E., 133, 134, 135, 142, 149, 155, 156, 302, 308, 341, 342, 343, 345, 346, 347, 348, 353, 354
Dilthey, W., 263, 264
Diniz-Sanches, J., 381, 386
Doane, M. A., 299
Dominick, J., 133, 142, 147, 149, 156
Donchin, E., 161, 169

Doob, A. N., 351, 354
Dorval, M., 148, 156, 158, 163, 169
Douglas, M., 278
Douglas, S. J., 16, 20
Doyle, M., 163, 171
Doyle, P., 210, 214
Drogin, E. B., 165, 171
Duncan, D. F., 168, 169
Dunningan, J., 329, 334, 337
Dunwiddie, T. V., 363, 367
Durkin, K., 345, 354
Dustman, R. E., 164, 169
Dustman, T. J., 164, 169
Dvorznak, M. J., 170

Eagleton, T., 313, 323, 325
Eccles, J. S., 365, 368
Eco, U., 88, 91, 94, 284, 289, 297, 299, 300
Edison, T., 8, 9, 18
Eggermont, E., 168
Egli, E. A., 146, 156, 363, 365
Einstein, A., 90, 91
Eisenstein, S., 181, 188
Elias, N., 364, 367
Elsaesser, T., 188
Emery, M. L., 409
Emmerson, R. Y., 164, 169
Ercolani, P., 130, 156
Erikson, E., 274
Ermarth, E., 331, 337
Ernst, S. B., 303, 308
Eron, L., 134, 137, 142, 143, 351
Eskelinen, M., 224, 226, 241, 244
Esselman, E., 135, 138, 143, 149, 150, 156, 157
Evans, B., 148, 157
Everett, A., xiii, xvi, 317, 325, 375, 376, 424

Fakazis, A., 122
Falstein, N., 121
Faludi, S., 386
Fan, Y. C., 169
Farish Haydel, K., 348, 349, 356
Farrimond, M., 409
Farris, M, 164, 165, 169
Fatsis, S., 64, 78
Favelle, G. K., 153, 156, 166, 169
Feinlieb, D., 95
Fenstermaker, S., 304, 310
Ferguson, N., 335, 337
Ferland, C., 170
Ferreira, P. A., 343, 344, 354
Feshback, S., 351, 355
Fey, M., 14, 17, 18, 20
Filipczak, B., 109
Fincher, D., 285, 402

Finkelstein, J., 131
Fiore, Q., 122
Fish, D. R., 364, 368
Fisher, S. E., 95, 163, 169, 361, 362, 363, 367
Fiske, J., 307, 308, 385, 386
Fitzgerald, S. G., 170
Fleming, M. J., 341, 343, 347, 355
Fling, S., 156
Flynn, J. R., 129, 130
Foehr, U. G., 131
Fontvielle, A. N., 365, 366
Ford, C. M., 145, 149, 155, 346, 353
Forsyth, A. S., 148, 156
Forty, A., 6, 20
Foster, T., 294, 300
Foucault, M., 304, 308
Fowles, J., 351, 355
Fox, M., 303, 308
Frank, I., 207, 213, 214
Frasca, G., 336, 337
Fraser, A., 341, 355
Freedman, J., 343, 348, 351, 352, 355
Frensch, P. A., 128, 130
Freud, A., 165, 169
Freud, S., 254, 259, 265
Friedland, R. P., 151, 156, 364, 367
Friedman, T., 376, 378, 385, 387
Friedrich-Cofer, L., 149, 156
Fromme, J., 302, 308
Frye, N., 258, 265
Fuhrmann, M., 242, 244
Fuller, M., 380, 387
Fumagalli, F., 363, 368
Funk, J., 125, 126, 130, 133, 134, 135, 136, 137, 138, 141, 142, 143, 156, 163, 169, 301, 305, 306, 308, 343, 355

Gadamer, H. G., 257, 265
Gagnon, D., 148, 156
Gagnon, S., 170
Gailey, C. W., 125, 130, 133, 141, 143, 303, 304, 309
Gainetdinov, R. R., 363, 368
Garbarino, J., 322
Garber, J., 305, 309
Gardner, J. E., 152, 156, 165, 166, 169
Garfinkel, H., 304, 309
Garrand, T., 95
Garris, R., 112
Garvey, C., 135, 138, 139, 143, 344, 355
Gastaut, H., 151, 156
Gates, P., 18, 20
Gauntlett, D., 149, 156, 341, 351, 355
Gaylord-Ross, R. J., 163, 169
Gelertner, D., 102, 121
Genette, G., 91, 222, 226, 227, 233, 236, 237, 243, 244
Gerbner, G., 353

Gergen, K., 252, 256, 262, 265, 271, 278
Germann, J., 125, 130, 133, 143, 163, 169
Germeny, B. A., 169
Geryck, B., 42, 44
Gibb, G. D., 146, 156, 344, 355
Gibson, W., 397
Giedion, S., 15, 17, 20
Gilles, B., 168
Gilmour, H., 325
Ginsberg, A., 224
Giros, B., 363, 368
Giroux, J., 155, 365, 366
Gitelman, L., 18, 20
Glass, L., 170
Glass, S. T., 364, 367
Glick, S. D., 363, 367
Glionne, J., 324
Godard, J.-L., 224
Godfrey, S., 171
Goffman, E., 222, 226
Gold, H., 17, 20
Gold, R. S., 168, 169
Goldberg, C., 323, 325
Goldstein, J., xiii, xvi, 133, 134, 137, 141, 143, 165, 169, 341, 347, 353, 355, 423
Goode, E., 122
Goupil, J., 155, 365, 366
Grady, C., 151, 155, 306, 308
Graf, W. D., 364, 367
Gramsci, A., 375
Grant, B. K., 204
Grasby, P. M., 353, 356, 363, 368
Graw, I., 283, 300
Graybill, D., 134, 135, 138, 143, 149, 150, 156, 157, 346, 355
Green, S., 130, 341, 355
Greenfield, P. M., 99, 100, 122, 126, 127, 128, 129, 130, 131, 133, 141, 143, 144, 145, 147, 148, 156, 159, 163, 170, 302, 303, 306, 309
Greimas, A. J., 242, 244
Griffith, D. W., 179, 184
Griffiths, M., xii, xiii, xiv, xvii, 133, 134, 137, 138, 141, 142, 143, 146, 149, 157, 158, 161, 169, 302, 305, 306, 309, 345, 346, 348, 350, 355, 356, 362, 363, 364, 364, 365, 366, 367, 368, 424
Grodal, T., 355
Gronowski, S., 5, 17, 18
Gross, E., 131, 134, 135, 140, 143, 149, 150, 157
Grossman, D., xi, 105, 122, 341, 355
Grosz, E., 297, 300
Grusec, J. E., 306, 309, 325
Grusin, R., 230, 231, 244, 285, 286, 299, 312, 325, 373, 386
Guattari, F., 272, 384, 386
Gulledge, J. P., 161, 171

Gunn, R. N., 353, 356, 363, 368
Gunning, T., 93, 94, 241, 244
Gunter, B., xii, xiv, 146, 157, 345, 351, 352, 355, 424
Gunzenhauser, R., 287, 288, 294, 297, 300
Gupta, R., 361, 367
Gutman, D., 365, 367
Guttmann, A., 341, 355
Gwinup, G., 364, 367
Gygax, G., 24

Hackett, A. F., 365, 367
Hacking, I., 271, 279
Hagan, J., 344, 355
Halberstam, J., 293, 300
Hall, E., 134, 139, 143
Hall, J., xii, xiii, 424
Hall, R., 318
Hall, S., 312, 325, 375, 376, 384, 385, 386, 387
Hallford, N., 66, 67, 79
Hamamoto, D. Y., 312, 313, 325
Hamlett, C., 153, 157, 163, 170
Hanley, O., 311
Hannan, A., 351, 352, 354
Haraway, D., 271, 279, 292, 300, 302, 303, 305, 309
Harawi, A., 91
Harding, C., 20
Harding, G. F. A., 364, 367
Harding, S., 305, 309, 325
Haring, T. G., 169
Harrigan, P., 187, 189
Harris, J., 302, 309
Harris, R. A., 363, 367
Hart, E. J., 151, 157, 367
Hartford, J., 214
Hastie, C., 163, 169
Haw, T., 364, 367
Hayes, B., 148, 157
Hayes-Roth, B., 210, 214
Hayles, N. K., 293, 297, 300
Hayward, J., 94
He, M., 344, 357
Heath, L., 351, 356
Hebdige, D., 309
Heidegger, M., 253, 261, 263, 265
Heim, M., 255, 265, 374, 387
Hendershot, H., 341, 456
Henderson, M., 93
Hendricks, G., 18, 20
Hendricks, L., 234, 244
Hennigan, K. M., 351, 356
Henningson, K. A., 168, 169
Herbert, A. P., 102, 122
Herman, D, 234, 244
Herman, L., 4, 16, 20
Hersant, Y., 10, 20

Name Index

Herz, J. C., xi, xiii, 15, 20, 29, 31, 44, 262, 265, 325, 414
Hey, V., 305, 309
Higinbotham, W., 23, 24
Hill, A., 325
Hillgartner, H., 299
Hillis, D., 102, 122
Himmelfarb, G., 328, 329, 337
Hintikka, M., 309
Hitchcock, A., 243
Hofferth, S., 131
Hoffman, J., 194
Hoffman, K., 149, 150, 157
Holland, J. C., 158, 170
Holland, N. N., 241, 245
Hollander, E. K., 165, 169
Hollingsworth, M., 164, 169
Holm Sorensen, B., 342, 345, 349, 353
Holmes, R. M., xii, xiv, 134, 136, 137, 140, 143, 345, 352,
    356, 424
Hopson, H., 149, 160, 344, 346, 348, 351, 357
Horkheimer, M., 375, 382, 387
Horn, E., 153, 157, 163, 170, 286, 300
Horrell, K. R., 307, 309
Horwitz, J., 35, 38, 39, 44
Houchard, B., 214
Houchard, S., 214
Huesmann, L R., 137, 143, 351
Hughes, T. P., 264, 265
Huhtamo, E., xii, xiii, 12, 18, 20, 424
Huisman, J. W., xiii, xvii, 304, 425
Huizinga, J., xiii, 59, 75, 76, 78, 79, 229, 242, 244, 257,
    265, 329, 337
Hume, D., 252, 255, 265
Hunt, N., 146, 157, 161, 169, 305, 306, 309, 359, 360, 361,
    362, 363, 365, 367
Hunter, B., 159
Hunter, T., 143, 156, 157
Hunter, W., 23, 24, 25, 26, 33, 34, 44
Huston, A. C., 125, 126, 130, 131
Huston, A. H., 149, 156
Huxley, A., 384
Hyun, O., 133, 143

Iggers, G., 333, 33
Ince, T., 179
Irwin, A., 134, 135, 143, 149, 150, 157
Izard, C., 134, 139, 143

Jacklin, C. N., 365, 368
Jackson, S., 48
Jacobi, S., 25, 29, 30, 36, 39, 40, 44
Jacobsen, P. B., 158, 170
JanMohamed, A. R., 316, 324, 325
Jarvis, E., 31
Jauss, H. R., 91, 94, 315

Jeavons, P. M., 364, 367
Jenkins, H., xi, xv, 94, 95, 133, 136, 137, 142, 184, 185,
    187, 188, 189, 304, 308, 309, 323, 325, 373, 374, 380,
    381, 382, 384, 385, 386, 387, 409, 414, 425
Jenkins, K., 336
Jenkins, R. A., 160, 171
Jenkins, W. M., 122
Jennings, H., 5, 20
Jensen, J. F., 220, 226
Jenss, H., 299
Jessen, C., 342, 345, 349, 353
Jo, E., 150, 157
Jobs, S., 16, 33
Johnson, B., 365, 367
Johnson, K., 187
Johnson, S., 234, 245, 380, 387
Johnston, P., 122
Jonas, W., 67
Jones, C., 300
Jones, H. A., 153, 157, 163, 170
Jones, M. B., 147, 157
Jones, S. R., 363, 368
Jones, T., 353, 356, 363, 368
Josephes, C., 86
Joyce, M., 237, 259, 265, 381, 387, 394, 403
Julien, R. M., 363, 368
Juul, J., xiii, xv, 73, 78, 220, 223, 225, 226, 236, 241, 244,
    257, 259, 264, 265, 337, 425

Kafai, Y. B., 129, 130, 133, 137, 143, 303, 306, 309, 324,
    325
Kammen, M. G., 187, 188
Kandinsky, W., 183
Kangas, S., 424
Kapel, D. E., 158
Kaplan, M., 86
Kaplan, S. J., 365, 368
Kappes, B. M., 164, 170
Karlsen, F., 341, 356
Kattenbelt, C., 383, 384, 388
Katz, J., 107, 122
Kay, J. P., 6, 20
Kaye, D., 127, 130, 156
Keaton, B., 184
Keepers, G. A., 146, 157, 363, 364, 368
Keighley, G., 206, 214
Keisler, S., 363, 368
Keller, S., 141, 143, 363, 367
Kellerman, J., 352, 352, 356
Kelly, K., 261, 265
Kennedy, H., 304, 309
Kennedy, R. S., 147, 157
Kent, S. L., xi, 4, 16, 17, 20
Kernan, J., 121
Kerscher, G., 287, 300

Kessler, F., 93
Kestenbaum, G. I., 150, 157
Kiesler, S., 152, 157
Kilpatrick, H., 127, 130, 156
Kinder, M., xi, 134, 143, 303, 309, 312, 323, 324, 325, 341, 342
King, G., xi, 286, 300
King, L., 187, 188
King, T. I., 162, 170
Kirsch, J., 135, 138, 143, 149, 150, 156, 157, 345, 346, 347, 356
Kitamoto, I., 309, 364, 368
Kitokawa, T., 309
Klass, D. W., 151, 155
Klein, M. H., 146, 157, 165, 170, 363, 368
Klemm, B., 134, 143
Klimushyn, C., 334, 337
Kline, S., 343, 353, 356
Knauss, T. A., 364, 367
Knirk, F. G., 147, 148, 158
Koblenz-Zulcov, C. J., 170
Koch, A., 17, 20
Kochman, W., 152, 159, 165, 170
Koepp, M. J., 353, 356, 363, 368
Kogan, M., 28
Kohji, U., 364, 368
Kokish, R., 166, 170
Kokush, R., 153, 157
Kolb, M., 242, 244
Kolko, D. J., 153, 157, 162, 170
Kolmos, K., 319, 325
Konoko, 297
Koop, E., 145
Koppel, T., 321, 322, 324
Korolenko, M., 95
Korthals, M., 263, 266
Kotler, J., 131
Kramer, P., 276, 279
Kraut, R., 131
Krichevets, A. N., 162, 170
Kroll, J., 175, 176, 179, 186, 188
Krueger, F., 353
Krzywinska, T., xi, 286, 300
Kubey, R., 133, 143
Kuni, V., 299
Kuo, H., 94
Kurokawa, S., 53, 364, 368
Kurosowa, A., 183, 236
Kurtz, B., 14, 20
Kushner, D., 330, 331, 336, 337
Kuttschreuter, M., 351, 357

Labov, W., 242, 244
Lacan, J., 272
Ladurie, E. L. R., 331

Laforest, M., 93
Lagerspetz, K., 137, 143
Lagny, F., 95
La Guardia, F., 14
Laird, J. E., xiii, xv, 208, 210, 214
Lambirth, T. T., 156
LaMorte, C., 24, 33, 36, 44
Lancy, D. F., 148, 156, 157
Landow, G. P., 95, 227, 245
Lang, F., 184
Lang, M. K., 159
Lantz, F., 88
Larose, S., 163, 170
Larson, R., 133, 143
Latour, B., 268, 279
Lauber, B. A., 130
Laurel, A., 164, 169
Laurel, B., 72, 82, 94, 227, 231, 245, 376, 379, 387
Lave, J., 145, 156, 159
Lawrence, A. D., 356, 363, 368
Lawrence, G. H., 161, 163, 165, 170
Leandre, J., 414
Le Diberder, A., xi, 14, 17, 20, 38, 44
Le Diberder, F., xi, 14, 17, 20, 38, 44
Lee, H., 133, 143
Lee, J., 131
Lee Hotz, R., 122
Lefebvre, M., 88, 93
Leplae, J., 302, 309
Lepper, M. R., 147, 157, 344, 356
Leuliette, E., 121
Levies, F., 20
Levine, N., 157
Levi-Strauss, C., 267, 279
Levy, S., 20, 146, 157, 276, 279, 407, 414
Lieberman, D. A., 103, 122, 167, 169, 170
Lifton, R. J., 271, 279
Lightman, A., 90, 93
Lilly, J., 24, 33, 36, 44
Lin, S., 157, 344, 356
Linden, L., 214
Lineberger, R., 346, 354
Linn, M. C., 148, 158
Lipson, A. S., 112, 122
Littlejohn, S. W., 67, 69, 79
Littleton, K., 304, 310
Livingstone, S., 305, 309
Lloyd, H., 185
Locke, J., 264, 265
Lockheed, M. E., 146, 157
Loftus, E. F., xi, 145, 146, 149, 151, 152, 158, 364, 368
Loftus, G. A., 145, 146, 149, 158, 364, 368
Lohman, D. F., 147, 158
Lohr, D., 128, 130, 148, 156
Longhurst, B., 304, 308

Name Index

Lornbirth, T. T., 344, 355
Lotman, B., 233, 244
Love, G., 152, 159
Low, J., 345, 354
Lowery, B. R., 147, 148, 158
Lucas, G., 221
Luhmann, N., 118, 229, 231, 236, 240, 245
Lund, K., 195
Lunenfeld, P., 95
Lupton, E., 11, 20
Lynch, W. J., 152, 158, 163, 170
Lyotard, J.-F., 255, 265, 317, 325
Lytell, R., 181, 188
Lytton, H., 306, 309

Maan, A. K., 156, 265
Maccoby, W., 135, 137, 143, 365, 368
MacDonald, G. E., 351, 354
Mackie, D., 134, 135, 138, 141, 142, 149, 150, 155, 346, 348, 354
Maeda, Y., 302, 309, 364, 368
Maguire, A., 354
Malliet, S., xii, xiii, 28, 29, 34, 39, 41, 42, 44, 425
Malone, T. W, 112, 115, 122, 126, 130, 353, 356, 368
Malouff, J., 144, 159, 343, 348, 357
Mandinach, E. B., 147, 155
Mandler, J. M., 234, 245
Manovich, L., 93, 94, 95, 286, 300, 380, 398, 403
Marchelletta, C., 332, 337
Marckmann, H., xvii, xviii, 425
Marey, R. J., 6, 17
Marintetti, F. T., 181, 188
Marjanovic, M., 214
Marker, C., 91, 94
Marks, I., 359, 368
Marlowe, P., 379
Marquis, J., 130
Marriott, M., 313, 325
Martin, E., 271, 279
Martin, J., 146, 158
Martin R., 336, 337
Masendorf, F., 164, 170
Masuda, K., 365, 369
Matillo, G., 134, 142
Matthews, T. J., 167, 170
Mayfield, M., 145, 158
McCarthy, J., 205, 214
McCauley, R. C., 353, 356
McCloud, S., 118, 122, 286, 300
McClure, R. F., 146, 158
McClurg, P. A., 147, 148, 158
McCowan, T. C., 151, 158, 364, 368
McEnroe, M. J., 168
McEvoy, M., 158, 170
McGrew, W., 139, 143

McGuire, F. A., 164, 170
McGuire, T. W., 152, 157
McIlwraith, R., 362, 368
Mckendles, D., 414
Mckendrick, H., 364, 366
McLuhan, M., 81, 93, 94, 97, 99, 107, 122, 127, 130, 393, 403
McRobbie, A., 285, 293, 300, 305, 309
Mead, G. H., 237, 245, 255, 264, 265
Mears, F. G., 146, 158
Meier, S., 37, 330
Méliès, G., 84
Mellinger, J. F., 151, 155
Merski, C., 363, 367
Mervau-Scheidel, D., 171
Merzenich, M. M., 121, 122
Messenger Davies, M., 342, 356
Messner, S. F., 351, 356
Metz, C., 91, 222, 223, 231, 243, 245, 377, 378, 384, 385, 387
Meyer, S., 171
Meyers, L. S., 146, 156
Michielsen, M., 169
Milgram, S., 351, 356
Miller, D. L. G., 151, 158, 364, 368
Miller, G. G., 148, 158
Miller, G. W., 363, 368
Miller, M. J., 145, 159, 359, 369
Miller, R., 95
Miller, S., 35, 38, 39, 44, 122
Millet, C. J., 364, 368
Mink, L. O., 255, 265, 335
Minsky, M, 272, 279
Mirman, M. J., 364, 368
Mitry, J., 238, 243, 245
Miyagawa, S., 178
Miyamoto, Shigeru, 30, 35, 175, 182, 188
Modde, J. M., 344, 348, 351, 357
Molyneux, P., 37
Mongeau, A., 93
Montgomery, R., 93, 378, 379
Moore, P., 99, 122
Morris, B., 407
Morris, C. W., 264, 252, 265
Morris, S., 41, 45
Morrow, M., 134, 142, 150, 155, 348, 354
Muijs, D., 344, 356
Mulder, R. M., 171
Mullet, M. B., 188
Mulvey, L., 317
Murdoch, R., 417
Murphy, J. K., 364, 368
Murray, J. H., xi, 82, 93, 94, 95, 220, 226, 227, 236, 243, 243, 245, 374, 384, 387
Musil, R., 255, 260

Musser, C., 20
Myers, B. J., 302, 308
Myers, M., 344, 355

Nairman, A., 147, 158
Narayan, U., 319, 325
Nasaw, D., 9, 10, 13, 20
Naveteur, J., 153, 158
Navracruz, L. C., 348, 349, 356
Neff, D., 214
Negroponte, N., 102, 122
Neill, G., 322, 324
Neitzel, B., xiii, xv, 242, 243, 245, 257, 425
Nelson, C., 20
Nelson, D. L., 171
Nesbitt, K., 134, 142
Nevin, M. L., 157
Newman, J., xi, 182, 188
Niesz, A. J., 241, 245
Nietzsche, F., 386, 387
Nissen, J., 385, 387
Nixon, K., 156
Norman, A. R. D., 146, 158
Norris, M., 321, 324
Novak, D., 149, 160, 344, 346, 348, 351, 357

O'Connor, T. J., 162, 163, 170
O'Keefe, B., 125, 131
O'Leary, M., 143, 156, 157
Oakley, C., 154, 158, 168, 170
Öcal, T., 299
Odin, R., 82, 91, 94, 95
Okagaki, L., 128, 130
Okolo, C., 164, 170
Oliver, R., 92, 95, 126, 130
Olsen-Rando, R. A., 166, 170
Oosterbroek, M, 169
Oram, A., 387
Orwell, G., 291
Oyen, A. S., 147, 158

Paik, H., 134, 143
Pais-Ribeiro, J. L., 343, 344, 354
Palsson, 164
Paperny, D. M., 168, 171
Park, A., 45
Parsons, K., 362, 366, 368
Pasta, D. J., 169
Patterson, J., 33, 44, 45
Pavlik, J., 152, 158
Payne, J., 301, 308, 344, 354
Pazhitnov, 223
Pearson, L. F., 7, 20
Pegelow, C. H., 163, 170
Peirce, C. S., 64, 79

Peiss, K., 11, 14, 20
Pellegrini, A., xii, xiv, 134, 136, 137, 140, 143, 345, 353, 356, 425
Pepin, M., 148, 156, 158, 163, 169, 170
Perez, R., 121
Perloff, R. M., 343, 356
Perron, B., xi
Perry, D., 181, 188
Perucchini, P., 130
Peterson, A. C., 148, 158
Petley, J., 352, 354
Phillips, C. A., 146, 151, 158, 362, 363, 364, 368
Phillips, W. R., 152, 158, 162, 170, 368
Piacenza, B., 95
Piaget, J., xiv, 115, 126, 127, 131, 144, 274, 275, 279
Pine, J., 382, 387
Pitts-Conway, V., 169
Plato, 107, 243, 245, 263
Plummer, H. R., 169
Poblocki, K., 335, 338
Pohlmann, K. C., 95
Polsson, K., 44
Poole, S., xi, 17, 29, 30, 31, 41, 42, 45, 179, 180, 188, 349, 356
Popple, S., 20
Porter, D. B., 170
Post-Gorden, J., 144, 159, 343, 348, 357
Prensky, M., xii, xiv, 121, 122, 383, 387, 425
Prince, G., 245
Provenzo, E., xi, 107, 122, 144, 263, 265
Pyck, K., 168

Quintas, E., 93
Quirk, J. A., 364, 368
Quittner, J., 152, 158

Rabin, C., 168
Rabinbach, A., 11, 17, 20
Rabinowitz, L., 11, 13, 21
Radway, J. A., 304, 309
Raessens, J., xi, xiii, xvii, 93, 377, 382, 383, 386, 387, 388, 398, 403, 423
Ramis, H., 236
Randall, N., 241, 245
Ray, J.-C., 153, 158
Raymond, E., 405
Raynauld, I., xii, xiv, 426
Redd, W. H., 153, 158, 161, 162, 163, 170
Redmond, M., 95
Regan, P. M., 341, 356
Regis, H., 151, 156
Reid, E., 152, 158
Reinstein, L., 151, 158, 364, 368
Resnais, A., 375, 377, 378
Resnick, H., 168, 169, 171

Name Index

Resnick, M., 276, 279
Rhaiti, S., 151, 155, 306, 308
Rheingold, H., 50, 51, 152, 157
Rhodes, R., 352, 356
Riccitelli, C., 171
Rice, R. E., 152, 159
Rich, F., 385, 388
Richard, B., xiii, xv, 283, 297, 300, 375, 385, 426
Richter, S., 299
Rickard-Figueroa, J. L., 153, 157, 162
Rickwood, D. J., 341, 343, 347, 355
Ricoeur, P., xv, 252, 253, 254, 255, 256, 257, 264, 266
Riddick, C. C., 165, 171
Rideout, V., 125, 131
Rifkin, J., 381, 388
Rigopulos, A.; 183, 188
Roberts, D., 125, 131
Robertson, S., 361, 366
Robinson, T. N., 348, 349, 356
Rocha, B. A., 363, 368
Rodasta, A., 144, 159, 343, 348, 357
Rodriguez, T., 156
Roe, K., 344, 347, 356
Rogers, K. H., 149, 155
Rogoff, B., 145, 158
Rolland-Cachera, M. F., 365, 366
Rolls, S., 158, 362, 363, 364, 368
Romero, J., 48, 49, 50, 325, 410
Roschin, O., 37, 45
Roth, L., 95
Rotten, B., 353
Rottgers, A., 299
Rouse, A., 158, 362, 363, 364, 368
Rouse, R. III, 61, 79
Rozic, C., 329, 338
Runco, M. A., 343, 357
Rushkoff, D, xi, xii, xiv, 375, 378, 379, 380, 381, 383, 388, 397, 403, 426
Rushton, B., 151, 159
Rushton, D. N., 368
Russell, S., 3, 4, 15, 16, 24, 31, 407
Rutkowska, J. C., 146, 151, 159, 363, 364, 368
Rutter, J., xiii, xvi, 303, 304, 306, 307, 308, 385, 423, 426
Ryan, E. B., 165, 171
Ryan, M.-L., 225, 226, 227, 237, 238, 239, 241, 245, 337, 338, 380, 381, 388
Ryle, M., 331, 338

Sakamoto, K., 309, 345, 356, 364, 368
Salen, K., xii, xiii, 424, 426, 427
Salend, S., 152, 159, 165, 171
Saltzman, M, 189
Salverda, F., 169
Samoilovich, S., 167, 171

Sander, J. W., 364, 368
Sanders, J. S., 147, 159
Santi, S. M., 170
Santilli, L., 167, 171
Santora, D., 152, 159, 165, 171
Sargent, E., 84, 95
Saum-Adelhoff, T., 300
Savage, J., 357
Scantlin, R., 125, 131
Scassellati, B., 214
Schäfer, M., 384
Schatz, T., 193, 204
Scheil, A., 171
Scheuerl, H., 229, 245
Schierbeck, L., 341, 357
Schiffer, M. B., 21
Schimming, J., 344, 355
Schink, J. C., 151, 159, 364, 368
Schlegel, F., 260
Schleiner, A.-M., xiii, xvii, 296, 381, 382, 388, 426
Schloss, P., 163, 171
Schmidt, B. U., 284, 285, 300
Schoech, D., 153, 155, 164, 169
Schott, G. R., 307, 309
Schreiner, C., 122
Schueren, B., 165, 171
Schutte, N. S., 134, 144, 149, 159, 343, 347, 357
Scott, D., 134, 135, 144, 149, 159, 346, 357
Scribner, S., 145, 159
Sedlak, R. A., 163, 171
Segal, K. R., 364, 368
Seidel, R. J., 147, 159
Seigel, J., 157
Seitz, L. K., 26, 45
Seldes, G., xv, 176, 177, 178, 179, 180, 181, 184, 185, 186, 187, 189, 385, 388
Sellers, J., 17, 21
Selnow, G. W., 35, 45, 151, 159, 364, 369
Seltzer, M., 6, 11, 21
Sennett, M., 178
Sesslen, G., 285, 300
Shafer, R., 333, 338
Shapira, Y., 171
Shearer, D., 164, 169
Sheff, D., 28, 29, 33, 35, 36, 45
Sherer, M., 154, 159, 167, 171
Sherry, J., 346, 349, 350
Sherry, L., 145, 149, 150, 159
Shimai, S., 365, 369
Shorvon, S. D., 364, 368
Shotton, M., 146, 159, 361, 362, 369
Siedi, A., 171
Siegal, I. M., 151, 159, 364, 369
Siegel, I. E., 152, 159
Sietsema, J. M., 162, 171

Sills, J. A., 364, 366
Silvern, S., 134, 140, 144, 149, 150, 159, 343, 348, 357
Singer, B., 187, 189
Singer, D., 351, 355
Singer, J. L., 357
Sirotkina, E. B., 170
Skillbeck, C., 163, 171
Skirrow, G., 21
Sklovskij, V., 243, 245
Slovin, R., 17, 21
Small, D., 148, 159
Small, S., 148, 159
Smiers, J., 383, 388
Smith, D., 310
Smith, L., 156
Smith, S. J. M., 364, 368
Sneed, C., 343, 357
Sniderman, S., 75, 79
Sobchack, V., 379, 388
Somers, G., 336
Soper, W. B., 145, 159, 359, 369
Souriau, E., 242, 245
Southerton, D., 308
Spector, S. G., 165, 171
Spector, W., 70, 175, 180, 185
Spence, J., 152, 159, 165, 166, 171
Spence, S. A., 151, 159, 302, 310, 364, 369
Spiegel, G., 332, 338
Spielberg, S., 262
Sproull, L., 152, 157, 365, 368
Squire, K., 175, 184, 185, 187, 189, 337
St. John, J. N., 151, 156
Stabler, N., 169
Stanzel, F. K., 237, 245
Starn, J., 168, 171
Steele, V., 287, 300
Stefansson, B., 151, 159
Stein, W., 152, 159, 233, 245
Steindorf, S., 363, 367
Steinkraus, K., 214
Stephens, P., 163, 169
Stepulevage, L., 306, 310
Stern, A., 214, 215
Stolerman, I., 363, 369
Stoll, C., 102, 122
Stone, M. K., 147, 158
Stoney, C. M., 364, 368
Strawniak, M., 143, 156, 157
Strein, W., 165, 171
Subrahmanyam, K., 125, 129, 131, 141, 144, 148, 159, 161, 163, 171, 344, 357
Sudnow, D., 3, 16, 17, 21
Suits, B., 77, 79
Surrey, D., 365, 369
Sutton-Smith, B., xiii, 78, 79, 134, 144

Swartz, S., 13
Szer, J., 152, 159, 162, 171

Tada, M., 365, 369
Takahashi, D., 214, 215
Takeuchi, M., 133, 144
Tallal, P., 121, 122
Tallalm, M., 122
Tan, S., 125, 127, 130, 134, 142, 149, 150, 155, 347, 354
Tan Boon, P., 187
Tannenbaum, P. H., 149, 159
Tapscott, D., 101, 122
Tashima, S., 364, 368
Tate, G., 311
Taves, B., 195
Taylor, C., 336
Taylor, L., 318, 325
Tedrake, R., 214
Temple, C., 303, 310
Thomas, D. L., 168, 171
Thomas, R., 167, 171
Thompson, D. L., 164, 170
Thompson, K., 377, 378, 384, 386
Thompson, P. J., 364, 368
Thomsen, C. W., 227, 245
Thorne, B., 141, 144
Thornton, D., 156
Tobin, J., 342, 357
Todorov, T., 232, 233, 234, 235, 241, 245, 257
Tomashevsky, B., 232, 242, 245
Tope, D. M., 160, 171
Traniel, Jack, 34
Tudor, A., 194, 204
Tulloch, J., 373, 381, 382, 387
Turkle, S., xi, xiii, xvii, 105, 122, 252, 255, 256, 262, 266, 274, 279, 374 376, 377, 378, 385, 426
Turner, G., 375, 384, 385, 388
Turner, V., 279
Turpin, B., 184
Twitchell, J., 341, 357
Tyson, J., 43, 45

Underwood, M., 64, 79
Unger, A., 214
Unsworth, G., 345, 357
Uraneff, V., 181, 189
Uricchio, W., xiii, xvi, 93, 336, 338, 384, 388, 427
Utvitch, M., 84, 93

Vadim, R., 285
Vandewater, E. A., 131
Van Eenwyk, J., 354
Van Evra, J., 134, 144
Van Feilitzen, C., 345, 350, 357
Van Haaften, A. W., 263, 266

Name Index

Vanhoozer, K. J., 264, 266
Van Houten, O., 169
Van Lent, M., xiii, xv, 208, 210, 214, 427
Van Schie, E. G., 134, 144, 343, 348, 351, 357
VanSickle, D. P., 170
Varady, A., 348, 349, 356
Varchol, D. J., 84, 86, 96
Vasterling, J., 153, 159, 162, 171
Vattimo, G., 382, 383, 386, 388
Verbruggen, D., 28, 29, 34, 39, 41,42, 44
Vilozni, D., 162, 171
Volkow, D., 363, 369
Vuyk, K., 383, 388
Vygotsky, L., 136, 144

Wachowski, 385, 386
Waddilove, K., 146, 160
Wagenaar, H., 403
Wajcman, J., 306, 307, 308, 310
Walker, S. S., 364, 368
Walton, L. A., 321, 325
Wang, J., 122, 344, 357
Wank, R., 363, 367
Wanner, E., 361, 369
Ward, T., 345, 357
Wardrip-Fruin, N., 187, 189
Wartella, E., 125, 131
Washburn, D. A., 161, 171
Watkins, B. A., 130
Wearing, B., 307, 310
Weaver, C. K., 352, 354
Wegener-Spöhring, G., 141, 144
Weinbren, G., 3, 16, 18, 21
Weinstein, L., 150, 157
Weisman, S., 165, 171
Weiss, L., 130, 156
Weizenbaum, J., 146, 160
Werden, J. I., 170
West, C., 304, 310
Westbrook, D. L., 212, 214
Westward, K., 294
Wharton, J. D., 351, 356
Whatley, D., 207, 215
White, B. E., 171
White, H., 252, 254, 266, 311, 312, 323, 325, 336, 337, 338
White, W. B. Jr., 147, 160
Wiegman, O., 134, 144, 343, 348, 351, 357
Wiest, J. R., 149, 150, 155
Wilde, M. L., 348, 349, 356
Wilkins, A. J., 159
Williams, J., 135, 137, 144
Williams, K., 36
Williams, L., 11, 21, 285, 287, 300
Williams, R., 36, 375, 388

Williamson, M., 214
Williamson, P., 134, 140, 144, 149, 150, 159, 343, 348, 357
Wilson, D. M., 169
Wilson, J. L., 16, 20
Wilson, W. P., 156, 344, 355
Winefield, A. H., 348, 354
Winkel, M., 149, 160, 344, 346, 348, 351, 357
Winn, W., 99
Wolf, M. J. P., xi, xiii, xv, 16, 17, 21, 286, 300, 382, 388, 427
Woo, J., 183
Wood, E., 99
Woodcook, S., 205, 215
Woods, S., 354
Woodward, J., 164, 169, 300
Wozniak, S., 16, 33, 407
Wren, T., 263, 266
Wright, J. C., 125, 126, 130, 131
Wright, K., 164, 171
Wright, W., 37

Yamada, F., 365, 369
Yates, S. J., 304, 310
Yevsevicheva, I. V., 170
Young, K., 360, 369

Zaremba, J., xiii, xv, 375, 385, 427
Zeldin, L. M., 170
Ziegfield, R., 241, 245
Zigrone, F., 93
Zillmann, D., 149, 159, 353, 357
Zimbardo, P., 151, 160, 364, 369
Zimmerman, E., xii, xiii, 179, 180, 187, 188, 189, 426, 427
Zizek, S., 383, 388

Subject Index

Abstract games, 195

Action games, 41–42, 205–206, 208, 210

Activision, 194, 238, 378

Adaptation games, 195–196

Addiction. *See* Video game addiction

Adventure games, 36–37, 153, 196, 206

Aesthetics, xiii, xv, 175–188, 193–202, 219–225, 227–241, 405–414

  fetish aesthetics, 287–289

Aggression, xvi, 345

  distinguished from aggressive play, 348–349

  measurement of, 348, 351

  while playing video games, 137–142

Aggressive play, 348–349

Aggressive video games. *See* Violent video games

American Academy of Pediatrics, 351, 352

American Medical Association, 351, 352

American Psychiatric Association, 362, 366

American Psychological Association, 351, 427

Animation, 118

Apple computer, 33, 36, 40, 407

Arcades, 4, 9, 12–15, 16n, 15–26, 38, 151

Archaeology of gaming, 4–15

Art, 176–188, 405–414

Artificial intelligence (AI), xv, 205–217, 278

  and character roles, 208–213

  and game genres, 205–208

Atari, xiii, 3, 16, 25–28, 30–36, 39, 40, 50, 51, 194–198, 201, 203, 221, 223, 224, 228, 231, 382, 389, 407, 414

Attention deficit hyperactivity disorder (ADHD), xiv, 164

Automata, 6–8

Automated spanking machine, 7

Biofeedback, 164

Board games, 196

Bots, 273

Buss-Durkee Hostility Inventory, 346

Capturing games, 196–197

Card games, 197

Catharsis, 150

CD-ROM, 393, 403

Channel F, 26–28, 32, 36

Children

  behavior during play, 135–142, 149–150

  and participation, 397

  and video games, 125–131, 146–149, 163, 389, 390

Cinema, 82, 178–180, 183, 184, 193, 314, 377

  and games, 184–185

  storytelling, 82

CNN, 426

Cognitive skills, 125–131, 146–149, 163, 262

Coleco, 32, 36

Collecting games, 197

Combat games, 197–198, 205–206. *See also* Violent video games

Commodore, 33, 34, 36, 40

Communication skills, 163

Computer games. *See also* Video games; Electronic games

  as aesthetic phenomena, xiii, xv, 175–188, 193–202, 219–225, 227–241, 405–414

  applications of, 97–121, 126, 152–154, 161–168, 198, 389–390, 396

  as contemporary art, 183

  as cultural phenomena, xiii, xv (*see also* Cultural studies; Gender; History; Race and ethnicity)

  and health, 150–153, 167–168

  history and development of, xii, 4–15, 23–44, 312, 327–336

  and identity, 251–263, 269–274

  narrativity in (*see* Narrative)

  and pain management, 162–163

  as participatory media (*see* Participation)

  and perception, 129

  reception of, xii, xiv, 4–15, 23–44, 321–322, 327–336

  representation and memory, 127

  as social phenomena, xiii, 251–256, 267–278, 305, 321, 341–353, 359–366

  terminology, xii

  and time, 223, 236–237

  and visual attention, 126, 129, 148–150

Computer game studies, 305

  classic texts, xi

Computer interface, 267–268

Cross-national research, 147

Cultural studies, 316, 374–376

Deconstruction, 376–378, 416
Diagnostic games, 198
Digital Games Research Association (DiGRA), xi
Dodging games, 198
Dopamine, 363
Driving games, 198
DSM-III (*Diagnostic and Statistical Manual of the American Psychiatric Association*), 362
Dutch Association of Producers and Importers of Audio-Visual Media (NVPI), 384

E-commerce, 417
Educational games, 104–109, 154, 198, 389–390, 396
Electronic Entertainment Expo (E3), 16n, 32, 187, 225
Electronic games and child development, 125–132, 274–277, 288
Entertainment Software Association (ESA), xii, 16, 187, 301, 306, 309, 384
Epileptic seizures, 151, 364–365
Escape games, 199
Ethnographic research, 305
European Leisure Software Publishers Association (ELSPA), 302, 303, 308, 309, 310
Eysenck Personality Inventory, 346

Fan culture, 409
Fantasy-reality distinction, 100–101, 345
Fantasy role-playing games, 153. *See also* Online games
Fighting games, 199
Film. *See* Cinema
Frankfurt School, 375, 386
French New Wave, 176
Furby, 277, 278

Gambling, 43, 361
  gambling games, 199
Game-based learning, xiv, 97–121. *See also* Educational games
  designing games for, 109–110
  effectiveness, 103–104
  the future of, 120–121
  justifications for, 97–101
  what players learn, 104–109
Game Boy. *See* Handheld games; Nintendo
Game design, xii, xiii, 62–78, 81–93, 109–115, 229–231, 314, 405, 410. *See also* Game development
  context, 65–67, 78
  and interactivity, 70–75
  structure, 65
  and systems, 67–69
Game developers, 34
Game development, 395–398
Game patches, xvii, 381, 405–414
Gender, xvi, 129, 148, 272, 301–308, 312–313, 365–366. *See also* Sex differences

definition, 302–303
gender depictions, stereotypes, 283–299
inconsistent research findings, 302
Genres, xv, 41–42, 193–203, 205–208, 317, 330. *See also* *specific genres*
  action games, 197–198, 205–206
  adaptation games, 195–196
  adventure games, 206
  capturing games, 196–197
  escape games, 199
  and femininity, 297–298
  fighting games, 199
  and gender differences, 365–366
  historical simulations, 331–336
  quiz games, 201
  racing games, 207, 212–213
  role-playing games, 42, 48, 114, 153, 201–202, 206, 213
  simulation, 207
  sports games, 207, 210, 211
  strategy games, 207, 210, 211, 212

Hacking, 278, 378–383, 406–407
Handheld games, 32, 36, 40. *See also* Mobile games
Health, 150–153, 162, 167–168
  adverse effects, 151, 364
  occupational therapy, 162
  pain management, 162–163
Historical simulations, 327–336
Historiography, 327
History of electronic gaming, xvi, 4–15, 23–44, 327–336

IBM, 33, 36, 40, 267, 407
Iconography, 194
Id Software, 48, 223
Ijsfontein, xvii, 389, 390, 393, 394, 396, 397, 399, 402, 425
IMAX, 183
Incite, 314, 324
Information processing, 126–129, 148–150
  perception, 126
  representation and memory, 127
  symbolic thought, 128
  visual attention, 126
Intel, 40
Intellivision Inc., 34, 36, 50
Interactive Digital Software Association. *See* Entertainment Software Association
Interactive fiction, 82–93, 219–223, 227–241. *See also* Narrative
  genres, 194–203
Interactive machines, 8–10
Interactive media, 11, 86–93, 390
  movies, 199
  writing for, 83–85
Interactive television, 390–393, 397

Interactive toys. *See* Electronic games
Interactivity, 4–5, 15, 70–75, 82, 86–89, 193–203, 225n, 314, 375, 377, 378–380, 384n, 416–418
 and learning, 389–390
 vs. iconography, 194
Internet, 40, 43, 98, 101, 120, 267, 272, 321, 359, 360, 374, 384, 390, 394, 405–408, 417, 418, 421, 424
Internet addiction, 360
Intrinsic vs. extrinsic games, 115–116

Japan, 28–31, 34, 178
Japanese Amusement Machine Manufacturer's Association (JAMMA), 38
Jumpstart, 122

Konami, 28, 30, 239

LAN (local area network) parties, 305
Lara Croft, 41, 179, 182, 185, 222, 230–239, 283–289, 294, 296–299, 304, 365, 375, 378, 381, 385, 394, 409
Learning, and video games, 97–121, 389–390, 396, 398
Lego, 276
Lightspan Partnership, 103, 121, 122
Linux, 405
Lionhead Studios, 48, 389
"Lively arts," 176–188
 definition, 176
Lucas Arts, 102, 207, 221, 239
Ludic identity, 260–262

"Magic circle." *See* Play
Magnavox, 26, 33, 34, 414
Management simulation, 199–200
Massachusetts Institute of Technology (MIT): 24, 105, 176, 187, 407
 Media Lab, 102, 115
Massive multiplayer online role playing games. *See* Multiplayer online role playing games
Mattell, 32–34, 36, 203
Maze games, 200
Meta-analysis, 150, 349
Metamorphosis, 294–296
Microsoft, 40, 42, 43, 175, 382, 426
 X-Box, 43, 175, 408
Midway, 26–32, 34, 221, 225, 231, 314, 319
Militarism in games, 121, 316–319, 412
Milton Bradley, 33, 34
Mobile games/gaming, 47–55, 214, 393
MSNBC, 426
MTV, 99, 101
MUDs (Multi User Domains) 152, 270–274
Multimedia, 13, 81–93, 98
 fiction, 82
Multiplayer online role playing games (MMORPGs), 10, 43, 50–54, 117, 213, 273, 374

Multiscope, 9
Multitasking, 99, 125

Narrative, xv, 82, 86–93, 118, 219–225, 227–241, 257–260, 415–416
 historical, 334, 335
 in different media, 221–222
 identity, 251–256
 levels of, 232–233
 nonlinear, 86, 91
 story and plot in computer games, 236
 structure, 231–237
 television and, 415–417
 temporal dimension, 222–223, 257
NASA, 175
Next Generation, 314, 324
Newsweek, 176, 179
New York Times, 48, 122, 176, 187, 313, 323, 324, 330
Nickelodeon Online, 427
Nightline (ABC News), 321, 322
Nintendo, xi, xii, xiii, 28–40, 43, 53, 107, 133, 135, 137, 151, 152, 162, 175, 231, 233, 263, 303, 365, 378, 407, 414
 Game Cube, 175
Nonverbal behavior, xiv, 134
 while playing video games, 136–142
NTT DoCoMo, 52, 53

Obstacle course games, 200
Occupational therapy, 162
Odyssey II, 33, 34
Odyssey, 26, 28
Online games, 37, 41, 43, 51, 271, 304, 306, 410. *See also* Internet; Multiplayer online role playing games; MUDs
Open source software, 405–414, 419
Oral storytelling, 220

Pain, 153
 pain management, 162
Parallel processing, 99
Participation, 3, 12, 50, 81, 91–93, 193, 306, 373, 377, 379–380, 390. *See also* Interactivity
 children and, 397
 games and, 393–398
 and gender, 306–307, 301–302
 levels of, 396
 political-ideological perspective, 381–383, 420
Participatory culture, xvii, 373–384, 389–403
Participatory media culture, 373–384
Patches. *See* Game patches
Pencil-and-paper games, 200
Penny arcade. *See* Arcades
Physiological arousal, 343
Physiotherapy, 161–162

Subject Index

Pinball machines, 200
  pinball games, 200
Platform games, 200–201
Play, 25–28, 110–115, 181–182, 257
  as distinguished from aggression, 348–349
  in the design of computer games, 229–231
  and learning, 274, 389–390
  "magic circle" of Huizinga, 75–78
  and meaning, 60–62
  theories of, 75–78, 229–230
  vs. work, 101
PlayStation, 39, 42, 54, 103, 119, 133, 164, 175, 284, 289, 407, 408, 414
Postmodernism, 48, 328, 374, 383
Poststructuralism, 327–329, 331–332, 335–336
Professional Association of Teachers, 146, 158, 365, 368
Programming games, 201
Prosocial behavior, 349
Proto-interactive machines, 8–10
Psychological effects of computer games, 145–154
  on children, 125–132, 135–142, 341–357
Psychotherapy, 165–166
Puzzle games, 201

Quiz games, 201

Race and ethnicity in videogames, 311–323, 383, 412
Racing games, 201, 207–208, 212–213
Realism of video games, 322, 399, 411
Remediation, 284–287, 373–374
Representation, historical, 327–336
Rhythm and dance games, 201
Ricoeur's theory of narrative identity, 253–256
Robots. See Automata
Role-playing games, 42, 48, 114, 153, 201–202, 206, 213.
  See also Online multiplayer role-playing games
Rubik's cube, 201

Science fiction, 373
Screenwriting, 83–85
  principles of, 84–85
Sega, xii, 28–31, 35–40, 52, 54, 238, 414, 423
  Dreamcast, 39, 40, 119
  Saturn, 39
Sex differences, xiv, 140–141
  in cognitive skills, 129
  inconsistent research findings, 302
  in playing computer games, 301–302
  in spatial orientation, 148
Shooting games, 199, 202. See also Violent video games
Sierra-On-Line, 36, 37, 407
Simulation, xvi, 37, 167, 203, 207, 268, 327–336
  games, 202, 330–331
  historical, 327–336
  and representation, 332–335

Slot machines, 10–14, 361
Social identity xv–xvi, 251–256, 260–262, 269–274, 321
Social isolation, 151
Social learning theory, 149, 343
Sony, 39, 42, 133, 164, 175, 284, 414. See also
  PlayStation
Spatial relations. See Visual and spatial skills
Sports games, 41, 207, 211, 213
Storytelling. See Narrative
Strategic opponents, 210–211
Strategy games, 37, 42, 202, 207, 211
Structuralism, 327, 332, 335–336

Table-top games, 202–203
Tactual delusion, 399, 400
Taito, 28, 31, 32, 49, 219, 220, 231
Tamagotchi, 288
Target games, 203
Television, 415
  compared to video games, 134, 342
  violence, 342
Text adventure games, 203
Theater, 181
Therapeutic applications of video games, xiv, 152–153, 161–168
Third-person effect, 343
3D games, 40–42, 48, 406–407
  and game genres, 41–42
Time, 330, 336, 424
Toys, electronic, 274–277
Training simulation, 203

Ubi Soft, 290
Universal Games, 28, 29
Uses and applications of video games, 141–142
  education, 104–109, 154, 198, 389–390, 396
  health and medicine, 150–153
  game-based learning, 97–121
  therapeutic settings, 152–153, 162, 164–165

Valve Software, 220, 410
Verbal interacting during play, 136, 141
Video game addiction xvi, xvii, 145–146, 359–367
  definition, 359–360
  empirical research on, 361–365
Video game consoles, 26–27, 32, 200–201. See also specific
  game devices
Video games. See also Computer games
  as art, 175–187, 405–414
  cognitive effects, 125–131, 146–149, 163, 262
  competition, 27–31, 34–41
  construction, 378–383
  deconstruction of, 376–378
  demographics, 125–126
  and education,153, 396

and the elderly, 164–165
genres, 193–203, 205–208, 317, 330
and health, 150–153, 162, 167–168, 364
industry crises, 27–32, 34–38
as interactive media (*see* Interactivity)
interpretation of, 374–376
and pain management, 162–163
and political ideology, 375–376, 379, 381–383
psychological effects, 145–154
in psychotherapy, 165–167
reconfiguration of, 378–383
and social behavior, 149–150
and social identity, xv–xvi, 251–256, 260–262, 269–274, 321
and storytelling, 219–225
temporal aspects of, 222–223
therapeutic uses of, 161–168
Video game magazines, 43, 313, 316–317, 426
Video game strategy guides, 313, 316–320
Video game addiction, 262–263, 359–370
definition, 359, 360
Video game arcades. *See* Arcades
Violent entertainment, attractions of, 353
Violent video games, xiv, 38, 133–134, 149–150, 197–198, 199, 202, 205–206, 303, 321–322, 341–357, 412, 413
and addiction, 359–366
attractions of, 353
as cause of aggressive behavior, 312, 344–353
correlates of playing, 343–344
definitions, 303, 341, 345
laboratory experiments, 344–349
and memory, 147
meta-analysis, 150, 349
and television violence, 134, 342
Virtual characters, 400
Virtual history, 335–336
Virtuality, 374, 400
Virtual reality, 43, 90–91, 125, 271–272, 393, 395, 398–403
involvement in, 91–92
Visual and spatial skills, xiv, 128, 129, 147–148
World Wrestling Federation (WWF), 49

X-box. *See* Microsoft X-Box
Xena, 289, 293, 294

Yesterdayland, 23, 26–29, 31, 37, 38, 45
Youth and media, 98–101, 107, 125–132, 146–149, 163, 274–277, 389, 390, 397

Printed in the United States
by Baker & Taylor Publisher Services